Gather up
the Fragments

A History of
the Diocese of London

By

Michael Power and Daniel J. Brock,

principal authors,

and other contributors

Published by the Diocese of London, Canada

2008

Dedicated to
the Catholic faithful,
living and dead,
of the Diocese of London

© Diocese of London 2008

Special thanks to the Jackman Foundation for generous assistance in bringing this publication to completion.

The Editorial Committee:
Father John Comiskey, chair, Jack and Louise Boyde, Sr. Rose-Marie Dufault, RHSJ, Pasquale Fiorino, Father Edward Jackman, OP, Joan Girvin Lenardon, Debra Majer, Sister Suzanne Malette, SNJM, Father Charles T. McManus, Ron Pickersgill and Lawrence Scully.

Editor for Parts One and Two: Krysia Lear, The Editorial Suite, Guelph, Ontario

Layout: Ron Pickersgill

Maps (pages vi-xiii) by Subhash Shanbhag

Front Cover: "A View of Detroit and the Straits Taken from the Huron Church," by Dr. Edward Walsh, 1804. Reproduced by permission of the William L. Clements Library, University of Michigan

Back cover: Armorial Bearings for the Roman Catholic Diocese of London in Ontario

A copy of the original manuscript of this book has been deposited with the Archives of the Diocese of London.

Published by the Diocese of London, 1070 Waterloo Street, London, Ontario, Canada N6A 3Y2.

Library and Archives Canada Cataloguing in Publication
Power, Michael, 1953-
    Gather up the fragments : a history of the Diocese of
London / Michael Power, Daniel J. Brock.
Includes bibliographical references and index.
ISBN 978-0-9784113-0-5
    1. Catholic Church. Diocese of London--History.
I. Brock, Daniel J., 1940- II. Catholic Church. Diocese of
London III. Title.
BX1423.L6P69 2008   282.71326   C2007-906831-6

CONTENTS

CONTENTS

CONTENTS

Preface

The 150th anniversary of the Diocese of London was a time of grace for us. The many different commemorative events that were organized at diocesan and parochial levels brought us together to celebrate our faith, to pray and to give thanks to God for the blessings he has poured out on our diocese since its founding in 1856.

For many of our people, these joyous celebrations have awakened an interest in learning more about the history of our diocese. For them and for the wider community interested in the origins of the Catholic Church in Southwestern Ontario and its expansion throughout the region, this book is a must.

The pastoral initiatives of the bishops of the diocese, the collaborative efforts of priests and laity in building up parishes and missions, and the founding of Catholic schools, universities, hospitals and organizations of social service by religious orders are all detailed here. It is fascinating to read the history of rapid growth, of decline and of rebirth.

We believe that the Son of God has taken on our human nature and radically transformed all of human history. In Christ, God offers us a share in his divine life and a unique role to play in his plan of salvation. The history of our diocese bears witness to this truth. It is the story of God's grace at work in the hearts of those faithful people — bishops, priests, women and men religious and lay faithful — who have gone before us. In the ordinary circumstances of their lives, they put their trust in God and responded to his call with justice, goodness, love, generosity and courage. This book is an eloquent testimony to their strong faith and their unfailing loyalty to the Church, surely an inspiration to all of us.

Many people were involved in the research and writing of this history. I am very grateful to all of them and congratulate them on their excellent work. In particular, I offer my thanks to Mr. Michael Power and Mr. Daniel Brock, principal authors, Ms Debra Majer, the assistant diocesan archivist, and Rev. John Comiskey and the other members of the history committee.

This book will be of great benefit to the London diocese and to the wider community. I highly recommend it, especially to all in our diocese. As we become more familiar with our history, we gain a broader perspective on the new challenges ahead of us. We grow in our appreciation of the accomplishments of our ancestors. The sacrifices that they made to build up our diocese encourage us to greater fidelity in living our Christian faith. As we look to the future, we draw strength from our past, confident that Jesus has been present throughout the history of our diocese and will be with us as its future unfolds.

Most Reverend Ronald P. Fabbro, CSB
Bishop of London

Introduction

Gather up the Fragments— A History of the Diocese of London was written as part of the celebration of the sesquicentennial of the diocese in 2006. It is a comprehensive, encyclopedia-style presentation of the diocese's rich and varied past, covering its pre-diocesan history and the episcopacies of its first ten bishops — from Bishop Pinsoneault, who arrived in 1856, the year the diocese was founded, to Bishop Fabbro, the current bishop, who presided over the 150th anniversary celebrations. Also included are the histories of religious communities, the cathedral, other parishes and missions and different institutions and organizations collectively called diocesan life. Every reader will find this account of the growth and development of the Church in Southwestern Ontario of interest.

This history incorporates a wide variety of topics. Woven throughout the narrative are numerous themes: the power and influence of bishops on the course of diocesan and local history; the ever-evolving relationship between priests and people; devotions, religious traditions and the regulation of liturgical practices and parochial life; language divisions; the gradual shift from a rural to an urban diocese; different periods of immigration; separate schools; the Second Vatican Council; and the rise of lay ministry, to name some of the more important ones. Readers will be treated to a wide range of personalities, historical eras and problems unique to the Catholic faithful as they built their diocese, parish by parish, in good times and in bad.

Gather up the Fragments rests upon a strong foundation prepared by earlier authors whose works are cited in the Select Bibliography. Among them can be counted Father Pierre Point, SJ (1860); Father John F. Coffey (1885); Father John R. Teefy, CSB (1892); Bishop Ralph H. Dignan (1919-1932); John K.A. Farrell/O'Farrell (1949); Ernest J. Lajeunesse, CSB (1960); Father Jerome T. Flynn (1966); John R. McMahon (1982); Michael W. Higgins and Douglas R. Letson (1990); Father John P. Comiskey (1997 and 1999); and Father Joseph P. Finn (1999).

Each of these historians has made a worthwhile contribution to our knowledge and understanding of London diocesan history. Without their work at hand, the endeavour to research and write this book would have been extremely difficult, and the result

of our labours a mere shadow of what it is. Father Point left us an invaluable and detailed picture of Jesuit ministry in Assumption parish, starting in 1843, and radiating outwards into the rest of Essex County and neighbouring Kent and Lambton counties. Father Coffey published his work on the history of the city and diocese of London on the occasion of the opening of the present St. Peter's cathedral in 1885. Father Teefy, an early Basilian scholar, celebrated the life of Archbishop Walsh and the history of the diocese of Toronto. Bishop Dignan, a native son of London, was the first to compose a general history of the diocese based on primary archival sources, but unfortunately he did not document his material. Father Finn made an heroic effort to update and correct Bishop Dignan's manuscript, and his work proved quite valuable in the matter of parish histories. Professor O'Farrell provided the first in-depth examination of Bishop Fallon, and Father Lajeunesse was a true pioneer in the documentation and interpretation of the history of the eighteenth-century French-Catholic settlement along the Detroit River. Both Father Flynn and Father Comiskey wrote on Bishop Walsh, perhaps the greatest bishop of London, and in an earlier work Father Comiskey examined the history of the local Church prior to 1856. John McMahon's thesis on Bishop Pinsoneault remains the fullest and frankest portrait of London's first bishop, a tragic figure. The biography of Cardinal Carter by Michael Higgins and Douglas Letson was a brave attempt to unravel this complicated personality who was bishop of London during and immediately after the Second Vatican Council.

We are indebted and grateful to these and other historians of different periods and events that make up the history of the diocese of London, but for all our dependence on the scholarship of others, *Gather up the Fragments* is a unique contribution to diocesan history. It is the result of much original research in the diocesan archives and the judicious and critical use of published and unpublished material. It has shored up and strengthened that historical foundation bequeathed to us, correcting inaccuracies and putting to rest certain misconceptions, and constructed a solid history that is both reliable and readable.

The first part of the title is taken from *John* 6:12. The setting is the miracle of the loaves and the fishes, precursor of the institution of the Eucharist. After the multitude had eaten, Jesus told his disciples, "Gather up the fragments, lest they be lost." The disciples gathered up enough fragments from the five barley loaves to fill twelve baskets, signifying the fulfillment of the Exodus Passover of the old dispensation and the anticipation of the Eucharistic Feast of the new dispensation.

The primary task of the Church historian is to write the history of the new dispensation, gathering up the fragments of facts of our long and storied past as a people united in faith, hope and charity, and to use our findings to write and publish new narratives, so that we may learn about the lives and good deeds of our ancestors in the faith and give to the rising generation of Catholics a testament to the past as well as to the future.

Gather up the Fragments —A History of the Diocese of London, a work more than three years in the making, is a modest contribution to a tradition that began at Pentecost, as recounted in the Acts of the Apostles, and continues to the present day, more now than ever. Catholic historians are busy documenting, recording and disseminating the history of their fellow believers wherever they have gathered to worship in community. Our baptism brings us together as one body, as we embrace the Gospel and the Eucharist and do good works done in the name of the Lord.

The Editorial Committee

Acknowledgments

Our sincere thanks go to the following: Ronald P. Fabbro, CSB, Bishop of London, for agreeing to support the project, for submitting to a lengthy interview and for writing the Preface; John Sherlock, emeritus Bishop of London, for giving four interviews; Father Edward Jackman, OP, of the Jackman Foundation of Toronto, for the foundation's generous financial support without which the project would never have materialized; Debra Majer, assistant archivist for the diocese; Father Len Desjardins, Jim De Zorzi, Mary Mousseau, Laurie McCormick and Mardie Lessard, for the loan of their photographs of the parishes and mission churches of the diocese; John McMahon, for his generous donation of photographs to the diocesan archives; Gillian Hearns, assistant archivist for the Archives of the Roman Catholic Archdiocese of Toronto; the parishes, religious communities and various diocesan offices, for their co-operation in providing much-needed information and illustrations; to the staff at the chancery; Guy Alden, for supplying a copy of Father Joseph Finn's updated version of Bishop Dignan's early history of the diocese; and John Burtniak, retired special collections librarian at Brock University, for copy editing.

Glossary

Ad limina apostolorum: translated, it means "to the threshold of the apostles" (e.g. the graves of Sts. Peter and Paul in Rome); an official visit of a bishop or group of bishops to Rome undertaken normally every five years

Apostolic Brief: a papal letter; a less formal and less weighty document than a papal bull (e.g. creation of a new diocese)

Apse: the semi-circular or polygonal termination to the chancel, aisles or transepts in a church; apsidal is the adjective

Baldacchino: a canopy that is suspended from the ceiling, attached to a wall or stands on pillars, so that it covers the altar

Benediction of the Blessed Sacrament: a short service consisting of the singing of Tantum Ergo with its prayer and a blessing given to the people by making the sign of the cross over them with the Blessed Sacrament in a monstrance or a ciborium

Border Cities: Sandwich, Windsor, Walkerville and East Windsor

Cathedraticum: annual contribution by parishes to support the diocesan bishop

Chancel: the space between the altar and the nave in a church, delimited by the communion rail, originally for the accommodation of the choir

Clerestory: the upper part of the nave, transepts and sanctuary of a church, perforated with a series of windows above the aisle roofs

Consecration: an ecclesiastical act by which a person or thing is set apart for some religious office, state or use and is superior to and more solemn than a blessing; examples of the consecration of a thing would be an altar or a debt-free parish church

Dean: a representative of a diocesan bishop in a particular area of the diocese; a senior priest with oversight of a collection of parishes; a dean's powers and responsibilities vary from diocese of diocese and have changed over the years

Dignissimus, dignior, dignus: translated, these words mean "most worthy," "very worthy" and "worthy"; the descending order of worthiness attached to three names in a *terna* for a new diocesan bishop

Dispensation: the relaxing of a law in special circumstances

Dowry: a one-time gift of money from an established parish to a newly erected parish; the new parish is usually contiguous to the donor parish and its territory carved out of the territory of the donor parish; occasionally, the bishop might direct more than one neighbouring parish to donate a dowry

Flèche: a slender spire rising from the junction of the nave and transepts of a church

Gothic architecture: a style popular in England and France from the twelfth century to the end of the sixteenth, which was not derived from classical forms and experienced a revival in England from the eighteenth century to the beginning of the twentieth; unique features include the pointed arch and stone vaulting; different styles include early English, decorated and perpendicular

Indult: a faculty granted by the Holy See to bishops and others to do something not permitted by the common law of the Church

Interdict: an ecclesiastical censure by which members of the Church, while remaining in the communion of the faithful, are excluded from participation in certain sacred offices, and from the reception or administration of certain sacraments; an interdict may be general or particular, local or personal

Melodeon: a small reed organ, a kind of accordion

Memorial: a written statement of acts, in the form of a petition, to a person or legislative body; in the case of the Church, to a bishop, the apostolic delegate or papal nuncio, or the pope himself

Monsignor: an honourary title given by the Holy See to priests, at the request of the local bishop; those with the title are Roman prelates: Chaplain to His Holiness (formerly Domestic Prelate), Prelate of Honour, Protonotary Apostolic (with the right to wear a mitre at Mass)

Narthex: the area of a church preceding the nave; sometimes the lower part of the church tower

Nave: that part of a church for the accommodation of the laity

Navvy: a British term for labourers on a canal, railway, road, etc.; the plural is navvies; short for navigator

Pallium: a circular band of white wool worn by the pope and archbishops; a symbol of the office of metropolitan archbishops

Peter's Pence: annual voluntary contribution of the Catholic faithful towards the expenses of the Holy See

Recusant: English Catholics who refused to attend services in a church of the Church of England; often convicted and fined according to the prevailing law and the attitude of law enforcement officials

Romanesque architecture: a style of architecture that was popular from the late tenth century to the thirteenth, in western and southern Europe; noted for its rich exterior outline (especially its towers), a clear organization of the interior, heavy walls, small windows, open timber roofs and barrel or rib vaults (ceiling)

Sacristy: a room in the church where is stored the sacred vessels, books, vestments and other accessories for divine worship and where the celebrant vests for the liturgy

Sanctuary: the area immediately around the altar

Seigneur: feudal lord

Tenebrae: translated, it means "darkness"; a name given to a special service of prayers, hymns, and readings during Holy Week.

Terna: a list of three names, usually those of priests, recommended to the Holy See to fill a vacant diocese

Transepts: arm-like divisions of a cruciform church; one on each side of the nave where it ends at the chancel

Ultramontanism: the doctrines and policies that upheld the full authority of the Holy See; a real or alleged exaggeration of papal prerogatives and those who supported them, often used in a derisive fashion; ultramontane is the adjective

Vespers ("Evening Prayer"): the evening hour of the divine office, or "Liturgy of the Hours"; evening service in churches of the Latin Rite

Vicar general: a deputy appointed by the bishop to assist him in the governance of the diocese

Sources consulted: Donald Attwater, ed., *A Catholic Dictionary.* 3rd ed. (New York: 1961); various dictionaries

Abbreviations used in End notes

ARCAT (archives of the Roman Catholic Archdiocese of Toronto)

ASV DAC (Archivio Secreto Vaticano Delegazione Apostolica Canadese)

CCHA (Canadian Catholic Historical Association)

CAR (*Canadian Annual Review*)

CR (*Catholic Record*)

DBB (*Dictionary of Basilian Biography*)

DCB (*Dictionary of Canadian Biography*)

DLA (Diocese of London Archives)

NCE (*New Catholic Encyclopedia*)

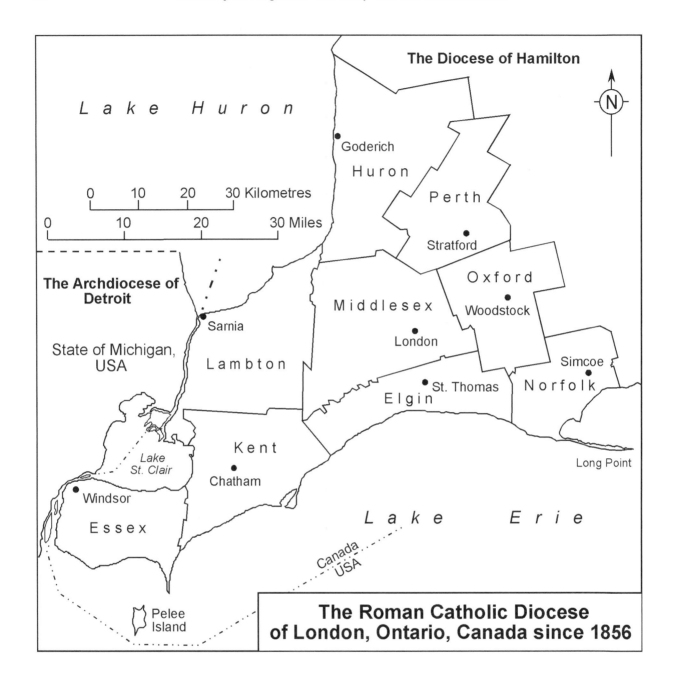

The Roman Catholic Diocese
of London, Ontario, Canada since 1856

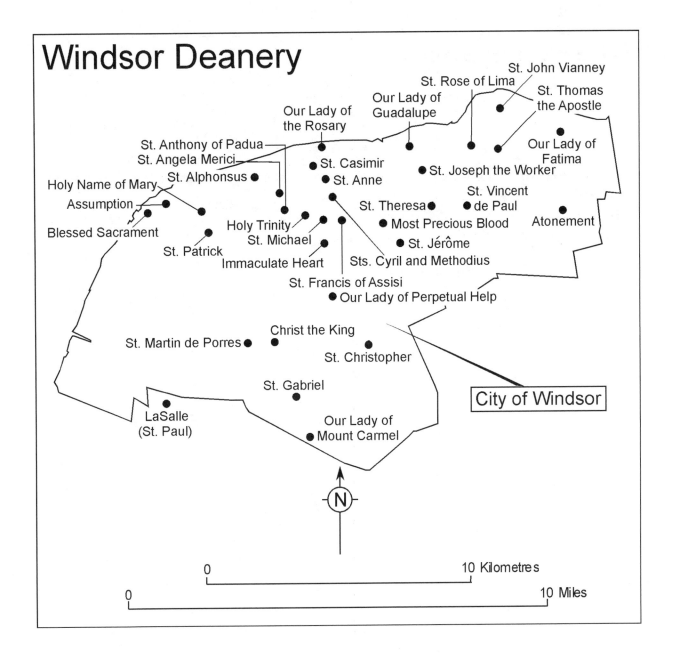

Windsor Deanery

St. John Vianney

St. Rose of Lima

St. Thomas
the Apostle

Our Lady of
Guadalupe

Our Lady of
the Rosary

Our Lady of
Fatima

St. Anthony of Padua

St. Angela Merici

St. Casimir

St. Alphonsus

St. Anne

St. Joseph the Worker

Holy Name of Mary

St. Vincent
de Paul

Assumption

St. Theresa

Blessed Sacrament

Most Precious Blood

Atonement

Holy Trinity

St. Michael

St. Jérôme

St. Patrick

Immaculate Heart

Sts. Cyril and Methodius

St. Francis of Assisi

Our Lady of Perpetual Help

Christ the King

City of Windsor

St. Martin de Porres

St. Christopher

St. Gabriel

LaSalle
(St. Paul)

Our Lady of
Mount Carmel

N

0   10 Kilometres

0   10 Miles

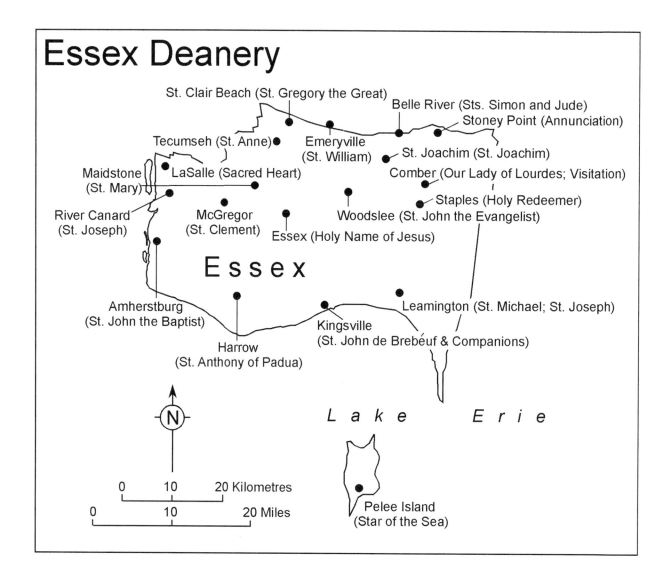

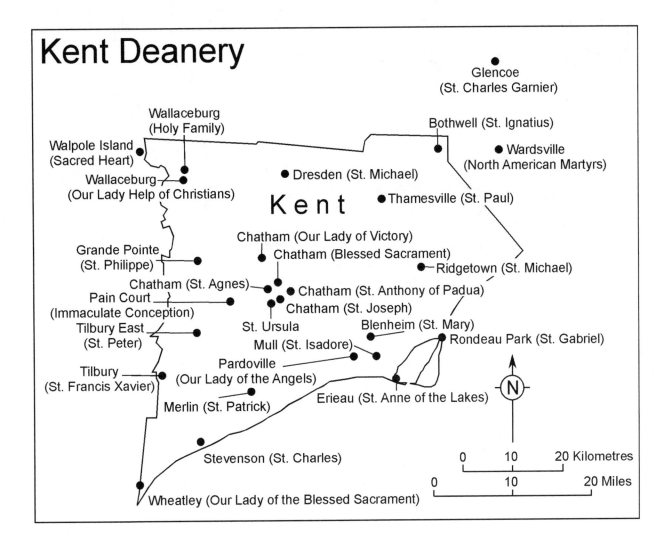

Kent Deanery

Glencoe (St. Charles Garnier)

Wallaceburg (Holy Family)

Bothwell (St. Ignatius)

Walpole Island (Sacred Heart)

Wardsville (North American Martyrs)

Wallaceburg (Our Lady Help of Christians)

Dresden (St. Michael)

K e n t

Thamesville (St. Paul)

Chatham (Our Lady of Victory)

Chatham (Blessed Sacrament)

Grande Pointe (St. Philippe)

Ridgetown (St. Michael)

Chatham (St. Agnes)

Chatham (St. Anthony of Padua)

Pain Court (Immaculate Conception)

Chatham (St. Joseph)

Tilbury East (St. Peter)

St. Ursula

Blenheim (St. Mary)

Mull (St. Isadore)

Rondeau Park (St. Gabriel)

Pardoville (Our Lady of the Angels)

Tilbury (St. Francis Xavier)

Merlin (St. Patrick)

Erieau (St. Anne of the Lakes)

N

Stevenson (St. Charles)

0   10   20 Kilometres

0   10   20 Miles

Wheatley (Our Lady of the Blessed Sacrament)

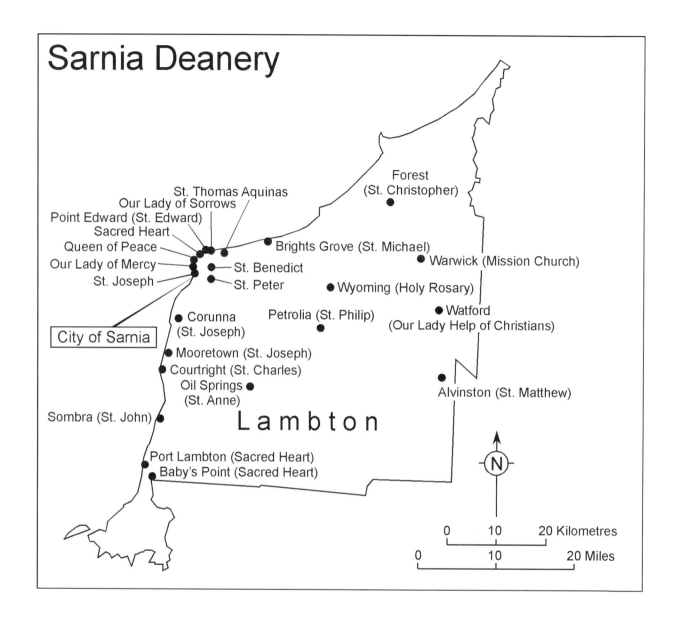

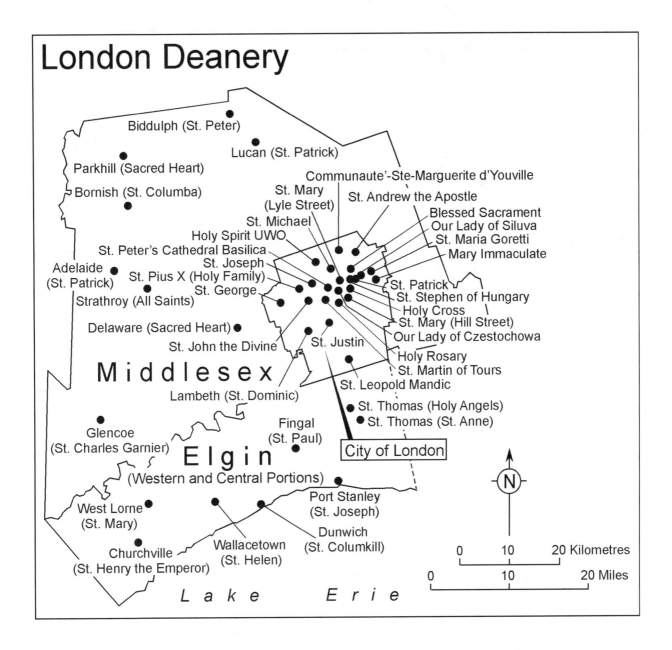

London Deanery

Biddulph (St. Peter)

Lucan (St. Patrick)

Parkhill (Sacred Heart)

Bornish (St. Columba)

Communaute'-Ste-Marguerite d'Youville

St. Mary (Lyle Street)

St. Andrew the Apostle

St. Michael

Blessed Sacrament

Our Lady of Siluva

Holy Spirit UWO

St. Maria Goretti

St. Peter's Cathedral Basilica

Mary Immaculate

St. Joseph

Adelaide (St. Patrick)

St. Pius X (Holy Family)

St. George

St. Patrick

St. Stephen of Hungary

Strathroy (All Saints)

Holy Cross

St. Mary (Hill Street)

Delaware (Sacred Heart)

Our Lady of Czestochowa

St. John the Divine

St. Justin

Holy Rosary

St. Martin of Tours

Middlesex

St. Leopold Mandic

Lambeth (St. Dominic)

St. Thomas (Holy Angels)

Fingal (St. Paul)

St. Thomas (St. Anne)

City of London

Glencoe (St. Charles Garnier)

Elgin (Western and Central Portions)

West Lorne (St. Mary)

Port Stanley (St. Joseph)

Dunwich (St. Columkill)

Churchville (St. Henry the Emperor)

Wallacetown (St. Helen)

0   10   20 Kilometres

0   10   20 Miles

N

L a k e   E r i e

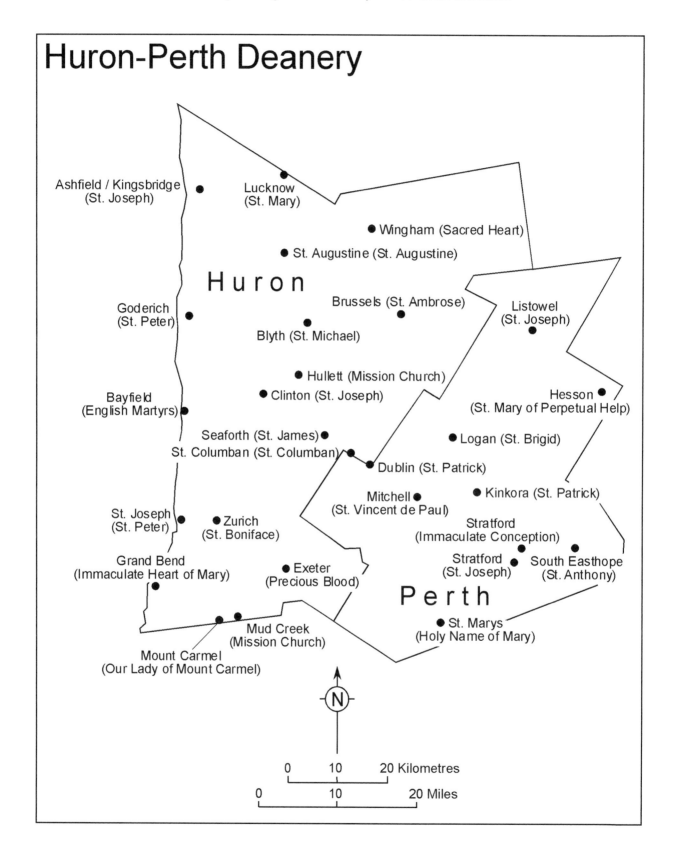

Huron-Perth Deanery

Ashfield / Kingsbridge (St. Joseph)

Lucknow (St. Mary)

Wingham (Sacred Heart)

St. Augustine (St. Augustine)

Huron

Brussels (St. Ambrose)

Listowel (St. Joseph)

Goderich (St. Peter)

Blyth (St. Michael)

Hullett (Mission Church)

Clinton (St. Joseph)

Hesson (St. Mary of Perpetual Help)

Bayfield (English Martyrs)

Seaforth (St. James)

Logan (St. Brigid)

St. Columban (St. Columban)

Dublin (St. Patrick)

Mitchell (St. Vincent de Paul)

Kinkora (St. Patrick)

St. Joseph (St. Peter)

Zurich (St. Boniface)

Stratford (Immaculate Conception)

Stratford (St. Joseph)

South Easthope (St. Anthony)

Grand Bend (Immaculate Heart of Mary)

Exeter (Precious Blood)

Perth

Mud Creek (Mission Church)

St. Marys (Holy Name of Mary)

Mount Carmel (Our Lady of Mount Carmel)

N

0   10   20 Kilometres

0   10   20 Miles

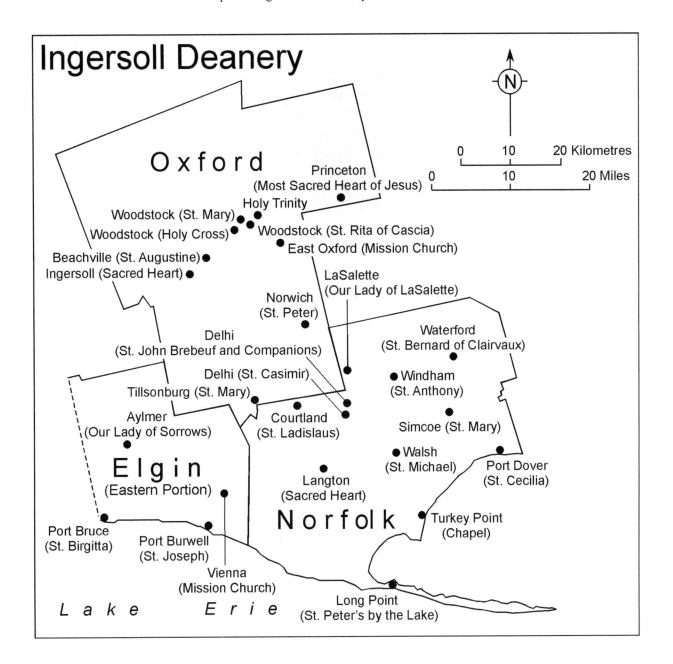

Ingersoll Deanery

N

0   10   20 Kilometres
0   10   20 Miles

O x f o r d

Princeton
(Most Sacred Heart of Jesus)

Holy Trinity

Woodstock (St. Mary)

Woodstock (Holy Cross)   Woodstock (St. Rita of Cascia)

Beachville (St. Augustine)   East Oxford (Mission Church)

Ingersoll (Sacred Heart)

LaSalette
(Our Lady of LaSalette)

Norwich
(St. Peter)

Delhi
(St. John Brebeuf and Companions)

Waterford
(St. Bernard of Clairvaux)

Delhi (St. Casimir)

Tillsonburg (St. Mary)   Windham
(St. Anthony)

Aylmer
(Our Lady of Sorrows)   Courtland
(St. Ladislaus)   Simcoe (St. Mary)

E l g i n
(Eastern Portion)   Walsh
(St. Michael)   Port Dover
(St. Cecilia)

Langton
(Sacred Heart)   N o r f o l k

Port Bruce
(St. Birgitta)   Turkey Point
(Chapel)

Port Burwell
(St. Joseph)

Vienna
(Mission Church)   Long Point
(St. Peter's by the Lake)

L a k e   E r i e

Armorial Bearings

for the

Roman Catholic Diocese of London in Ontario

As originally granted by Garter and his fellow Kings of Arms, 19 January 1968
Revision by Bruce Patterson, Saguenay Herald, 17 May 2004
Under the authority of Robert Douglas Watt, Chief Herald of Canada and
Her Excellency, Adrienne Clarkson, Governor-General of Canada

The shield, used since 1968, is divided vertically in two, black on the left side and gold on the right. On it are two keys. The one on the left has its bit, or ward, carved out in the shape of a shamrock. The keys are the opposite colour to their background. Around the shield is a border of two rows of alternating segments of black and gold.

The two keys allude to St. Peter, the patron of the cathedral and the seminary. This part of the design recalls the arms granted to the rector of the cathedral (1968), and this reflection of the one by the other is intended to emphasize the close relationship of a diocese and its episcopal seat. The ward of the left key has a fleur-de-lis in silhouette to recall the dedication of the diocese to the Blessed Virgin Mary under the title of the Immaculate Conception, while the ward of the right key has a shamrock in similar allusion to St. Patrick, the secondary patron of the diocese. These also recall the first Catholic settlers in the area, French and Irish.

The colours are black and gold to refer to the fact that the diocese must concern itself with both matter (black) and form (gold), the body and the spirit. The border is composed of a gold and black bricklike pattern to symbolize the fact that the life of a diocese must be built on spiritual and material elements; neither is to be despised but each is ordered and properly related one to the other.

The mitre, which ensigns the arms and was adopted in 2004, is white, and is in a traditional form with several features indicating its use by a Canadian diocese of the Roman Catholic Church. On the gold orphreys are three blue crosses with lily-like terminations; the number three indicates the Holy Trinity; blue is the colour of the Blessed Virgin Mary; and the lily is the symbol of St. Joseph, patron of the Church in Canada. On the lappets (white with gold lining) are red crosses with maple leaf terminations, representative of Canada.

Reverend John P. Comiskey
St. Peter's Seminary

Part I
From Mission to Diocese
in Southwestern Ontario

The Catholic faith took root in Southwestern Ontario, in 1748, when Father Armand de La Richardie, a Jesuit, moved the mission for the Huron people from the north to the south shore (the Windsor side) of the Detroit River. The small mission church grew within the evolving settlement of French pioneer families until, in 1767, it was large enough to become a parish. For the next sixty years, the history of the faith in Southwestern Ontario was the history of its development in Our Lady of the Assumption Parish.

Then in the early 1800s, an influx of Irish Catholic immigrants resulted in the faith taking root around St. Thomas and London and among a people who had brought a rich Catholic heritage with them. When Bishop Alexander Macdonell, whose diocese of Kingston extended to Windsor, visited in July and August 1827, he realized that the number of Catholic settlers warranted regular missionary visits. Soon, missions and parishes were established. The rapid growth in population and settlements meant more priests were needed, and by mid-century, the region needed its own bishop if the Church were to flourish. In 1856, the diocese of London was established and a bishop appointed.

The missionaries, priests and parishioners of the early Native, French and Irish missions and parishes laid a foundation on which the Catholic Church could thrive in Southwestern Ontario. From 1615 on, French missionaries persevered in planting the Church in spite of hardships they faced in the wilderness and their distance from support in Québec. Both the French and Irish were eager to celebrate the Eucharist regularly and as their communities grew they asked to build churches so they could have priests among them. They were loyal to the Church, giving generously and later would support institutions such as schools. Similarly, priests, brothers and sisters gave generously of their lives to found colleges, hospitals and other institutions to serve the poor. Devotion, generosity, loyalty, perseverance—these were some of the "enduring values" to which Bishop Ronald Fabbro, CSB, referred in his pastoral letter on the occasion of

the diocese's 150th anniversary.[1]

Also evident in the founding years were some of the challenges the diocese would face. While having two founding cultures would enrich the diocese, as would the cultures of later immigrants, it also challenged the diocese. Differing concerns over language and culture sometimes led to disagreements over the diocese's direction. As well, the Church faced the perennial challenge of responding to political, social and economic changes, while remaining faithful to its calling. For years, the number of pioneer communities exceeded the supply of priests and impoverished parishes had difficulty funding church buildings.

Until the diocese of London was erected, the Church in Southwestern Ontario also suffered from limited support and oversight because the ecclesiastical centres were so far away and travel was difficult. Until 1826, Upper Canada was a religious colony of Lower Canada. First it was under the jurisdiction of the vicariate apostolic of New France, which was established over the missionary region in 1658, and then under the diocese of Québec, which was erected in 1674. In 1819, the vicariate apostolic of Upper Canada was erected and in 1826, Upper Canada was transferred to the jurisdiction of the diocese of Kingston. In 1841, the Church in Southwestern Ontario came under the jurisdiction of the diocese of Toronto, which covered the western half of Upper Canada.

Native Peoples, Missionaries and Explorers, 1615–1748

Father La Richardie's decision to move the Huron mission can be seen as the culmination of Jesuit missionaries' efforts to maintain contact with the Hurons, an endeavour influenced by numerous factors. French missionaries travelled with the fur traders seeking to expand into lands west of the St. Lawrence. One expedition reached Georgian Bay, in Lake Huron, and the land of the Hurons, a beaver-hunting and agricultural people, who were intermediaries between the French and the Native peoples north of the Ottawa River. At the instigation of Samuel de Champlain, the Hurons became close trading allies of the French. Thus they were a prime objective for evangelization, first by the Recollets and then by the Jesuits. On 12 August 1615, Father Joseph Le Caron, a Franciscan Recollet, celebrated the first Mass in the country of the Hurons.

The Huron Confederacy or League, which was composed of four nations, had located their villages between the eastern shore of Nottawasaga Bay, in Georgian Bay, and Lake Simcoe. On the western shore of Nottawasaga Bay lived the Petuns, sometimes referred to as the Tobacco Nation. Father Charles Garnier, a Jesuit, evangelized them in the autumn of 1646, establishing a mission and bringing many into the faith. Both the Hurons and the Petuns had major trading routes extending to the Neutrals, who lived at the western end of Lake Ontario. The greatest concentration of Neutral villages was atop the Niagara escarpment within a twenty-mile (thirty-two km) radius of Hamilton.

To the east of the Niagara River was the Iroquoian Confederacy, the trading partners of the Dutch, in Albany, New York, and the sworn enemies of the Hurons and the French. Beginning in March 1649, the Iroquois Confederacy expanded northward nearly destroying the Hurons, Petuns and Neutrals. That forged a link between the Jesuits and Hurons that led to a mission church being established in Windsor nearly a century later. Some Hurons were adopted into the Iroquois Confederacy. Others fled to Gahoendoe (Christian Island) with the Jesuits, who, in 1650, brought about 300 of them to the Lorette mission, near Québec. A year later, another 300 Hurons made their way to Lorette.

In the meantime, a substantial number of Hurons joined the Petuns. When the Iroquois attacked them, they retreated northwestwards, finally settling at Chequemegon Bay, Lake Superior (Ashland, Wisconsin). It is estimated that only 500 survived the journey.[2]

In the spring of 1661, Father René Ménard, a Jesuit, met this remnant, but later he disappeared in the wilderness. In August 1665, Father Claude Allouez, another Jesuit, set up the Ottawa Mission, which was responsible for mission posts at Sault Ste. Marie in 1668 and St. Ignace at Michilimackinac in 1670. Father Jacques Marquette, a Jesuit, persuaded the Petun/Huron people of Chequemegon Bay to move to St. Ignace, where they lived for more than thirty years.

In 1701, the Petuns/Hurons heeded the call of Antoine Laumet, Sieur de Lamothe Cadillac, to settle at Fort Detroit on the north shore of the Detroit River. Joining them were a branch of the Ottawas, the Potawatomis and the Chippewas or Ojibways. The Jesuits of St. Ignace and Sault Ste. Marie did not follow them because they had differences with Cadillac over the liquor trade with the Natives, and the current French policy to indoctrinate the Natives into the French language and customs.[3] The Sulpicians were in charge of Ste. Anne's parish in Fort Detroit. By 1705, the Jesuits had returned to Québec.

On 4 June 1721, when Father Pierre-François-Xavier Charlevoix, a Jesuit emissary of the King of France, visited Fort Detroit, he noticed that the Hurons were the only Christians among the Native peoples living by the fort, but that they did not have any missionaries. "It is said," Charlevoix wrote in his *Journal of a Voyage to North America*, "that they [the Hurons] will admit of none, but [it] is only true of a few of their principal men who have not much religion, and who do not suffer the others to be heard, who have been a long time desirous of having missionaries sent them."[4]

In 1727, the Petuns/Hurons petitioned the governor general of New France for a Jesuit priest and in the following year, he sent them Father Armand de La Richardie, who headed a Native mission, grandly called The Mission of Our Lady of the Assumption among the Hurons of Detroit. By the time Father La Richardie arrived, most of the Christian Hurons had fallen away from their faith.[5] Within a dozen years, however, he had managed to convert the Huron chief, Hoosiens, whose example convinced about six hundred other Hurons to become Christians.

On 13 October 1742, La Richardie moved the mission to Bois Blanc Island (known locally as Bob-lo), to keep his flock from disintegrating in the face of threats from the Ottawa, Potawatomi and the Ojibway. In September 1744, Father Pierre Potier, another Jesuit, arrived at the mission. La Richardie left in 1746, after suffering a stroke, but returned in May 1747 with a grant of 5,000 *livres* to re-establish the Huron mission, this time at Pointe de Montréal on the south shore of the Detroit River.

The Hurons donated a parcel of land along the river to the Jesuits that was west of the present student centre at the University of Windsor. Father La Richardie and Father Potier oversaw the construction of a small mission church, and the first Mass was celebrated on 8 September 1749.

Father La Richardie returned to Québec in 1751. He left the care of the Huron mission in the capable hands of Father Potier, whose pastoral administration may be regarded as the more formal beginning of the development of the Catholic Church in Southwestern Ontario. Although Father La Richardie could not have imagined the long-term implications of transferring his mission to the south shore of the Detroit River, from our perspective his decision was momentous because it allowed the Catholic faith to settle and flourish in that region of Southwestern Ontario.

Development of Assumption Parish

For the remainder of the eighteenth century, the history of the Church in Southwestern Ontario is that of the gradual transformation of the Huron mission into Our Lady of the Assumption parish, the senior parish of the London diocese and the oldest continuous parish in Ontario. Economic changes made a profound impact on the development of the mission. The economic underpinnings of Fort Detroit and environs changed from a near total dependence on the fur trade to reliance on agriculture. From the farmsteads along the south shore of the Detroit River grew Windsor, the oldest continuous European settlement in Ontario. The French settlers attended Mass and other spiritual exercises at the Huron mission, rather than at Ste. Anne's across the river, but after a decade of this, they wanted their own church.

In 1765, sixty French Canadian families petitioned Bishop Briand of Québec for a parish. Briand granted their request, on 3 October 1767, but only after Father Simple Bocquet, the Sulpician pastor of Ste. Anne's convinced him that he was unable to meet their spiritual needs. Father Potier, the pastor at the mission church, understood the need for a new parish. He had opened a church register for the French Canadians, in July 1761, and approved of the construction of a new church in 1767. The mission became the parish of Our Lady of the Assumption with responsibility for the French and the Hurons. Eventually, the Hurons were displaced to a reserve in Anderdon Township, near Amherstburg, where their descendents, the Wyandots, lived into the 1880s. From Assumption parish, the faith slowly but steadily flowed into the crossroads, hamlets and villages of adjacent townships in Essex county, laying a foundation for the diocese of London.

Oddly enough, the political and ecclesiastical changes that caused upheavals on the wider stage during this period had little direct bearing on the spiritual and congregational life of Assumption's parishioners. These events included the collapse of New France in 1760, and the imposition of British (and Protestant) rule over a largely French Catholic population in 1763, with the Treaty of Paris, which ended the Seven Years' War between Great Britain and France. The British, however, promised the inhabitants of Canada the liberty of the "Catholick religion."[6] The division of the province of Québec into Upper Canada and Lower Canada in 1791 would be significant for the central area of Southwestern Ontario, but it had little impact on Assumption. In 1796, the British handover of Detroit to the Americans meant Ste. Anne's parish in Detroit was transferred to the diocese of Baltimore, leaving Assumption Parish an even more isolated outpost in the diocese of Québec.[7]

The uprising that the Ottawa chief Pontiac led in 1763 and his attack on Fort Detroit led only briefly to the loyalty of Father Potier and his parishioners being called into question. Not even Pope Clement XIV's disbandment of the Society of Jesus (Jesuits) in 1773, which had done so much in the area, had an impact on the parish. At the insistence of the government, Bishop Briand did not notify Father Potier of the decree to suppress the Jesuits, and the latter died in a household accident on 16 July 1781. The next three pastors were Father Jean-François

Hubert (1781–85), who was bishop of Québec from 1788 to 1797, Father Pierre Fréchette (1785–86), and Father François-Xavier Dufaux, a Sulpician (1786–96).

In 1794, Bishop Hubert appointed Father Edmund Burke vicar general of Upper Canada, the first attempt by a bishop of Québec to exert his authority over Upper Canadian Catholics in a more direct way. The Church in Lower Canada treated the Church in Upper Canada as little more than a colonial extension of itself. During his missionary work along the Detroit River frontier from 1794 to 1797, however, Burke seemed to be on the wrong side in every dispute, including several wild pew-throwing incidents. (his later career in Halifax, where he became the vicar apostolic of Nova Scotia, in 1818, was more successful.)

Harmony returned to Assumption with the appointment of Father Jean-Baptiste Marchand. He arrived on Christmas night 1796 and remained parish priest until his death on 16 April 1825, making his pastorate the longest in the parish. With his assistants, Father Félix Gatien (1801–06), and Father Joseph Crévier (1816–25), Father Marchand ushered in a new era for the parish. His first letter to Bishop Hubert, dated 31 January 1797, describes the parish at the time:

> The parish is made up of only 150 settlers including 12 at River Thames, 5 along the shore of Lake Erie and 4 at La Rivière aux Canards. As for the Hurons, there remain only four or five lodges with few occupants at La Rivière aux Canards. Fort Malden is an infant establishment where there are only two or three Catholics. Besides Niagara and Kingston, which can more easily be served from Montréal, the only mission that could be attended from this place is Sault Ste. Marie where there are only ten or twelve settlers.[8]

In 1801, Bishop Pierre Denaut was the first bishop of Québec to make a pastoral visit to Assumption parish.[9] In June, after confirming 580 candidates at Ste. Anne's in Detroit and another 295 at Rivière-aux-Raisins (Monroe, Michigan), Bishop Denaut confirmed 529 adults and children at Assumption parish. In addition, he noted in his official record of the visit that the parish had 600 communicants and 200 habitants (heads of households).[10] He also purchased property for a church in Amherstburg. Anxious to serve all the Catholics in his jurisdiction, in 1800, Father Marchand had persuaded Bishop Denaut to open two missions: St. John the Baptist in Amherstburg and St. Peter-on-the Thames, near Prairie Siding, Kent County. In 1802, he built churches in Amherstburg and Prairie Siding.

When the capable Father Crévier came to Assumption, in November 1816, he was placed in charge of both missions as well as the Huron Reserve in Anderdon Township. He was also given the responsibility for Sault Ste. Marie and Drummond Island, Michigan, in Lake Huron. A hard working priest, who succeeded Marchand as pastor in 1825, Crévier organized the construction of a second church in Amherstburg, in 1820, and of a replacement for St. Peter-on-the-Thames in Prairie Siding, in 1824. In that year he alerted the bishop of a settlement of thirty Irish Catholic families in the interior of Essex County (Maidstone Cross). In time, these people, would need a priest. In all probability, Father Crévier contributed, in 1826, to the erection of a chapel at Belle River, on the shore of Lake St. Clair.

In July 1816, Bishop Joseph-Octave Plessis, of Québec, paid an official pastoral visit to Assumption parish. He spent four days at Assumption, teaching catechism and giving sermons, exhortations and conferences to what he estimated were 1,000 communicants. Plessis thought that the parishioners were extremely lax in their morals and that they did not regularly participate in the sacraments. He confirmed 621 adults and children. At St. John the Baptist in Amherstburg (referred to as Malden), the bishop counted 150 communicants. Forty-four people came forward for confirmation. At St. Peter-on-the-Thames, Plessis was alarmed by the number of mixed marriages between Catholic men and Protestant women and by the presence of Moravians on neighbouring farms. There were 160 communicants in the mission and thirty-seven candidates for confirmation. The chapel, he remarked, was decorated and well supplied with linens and holy vessels, for which Father Marchand was responsible.[11]

Development of the Church in the Western District

In the eighteen hundreds, a new chapter began in the history of the Church in Southwestern Ontario, aided by two significant changes. The heavily forested Western District, which encompassed what is now Southwestern Ontario, was opened for settlement. The Church in Upper Canada gained jurisdiction over itself and was given a bishop who was a vigorous missionary.

In 1791, the division of Québec into Upper Canada and Lower Canada made settlement in largely undeveloped Upper Canada attractive, because British immigrants and Loyalists preferred to live under English laws and institutions. The driving force behind the settlement of much of southwestern Upper Canada was land agent Colonel Thomas Talbot. In 1803, he was given a land grant of 5,000 acres at Port Talbot, in Elgin County on the north shore of Lake Erie. In return for bringing in settlers, Talbot received land. Eventually, he had settlers in twenty-six townships, from east of London to Windsor; they cleared more than 500,000 acres in a short time.

In the 1820s, the Canada Company, led by businessman and adventurer, John Galt, opened another area, the Huron Tract. This one-million-acre tract of Crown Land was triangular in shape and extended from Goderich to Guelph, with its base being the shore of Lake Huron. It comprised nearly all of what are now Huron and Perth counties. The first settlers came from Ireland, Britain, Germany and Holland.

The Church in Upper Canada gained control over itself because Bishop Plessis wanted to divide his unwieldy diocese of Québec, which stretched from the Maritimes to the Red River in Manitoba. To his credit, the bishop also promoted the career of Father Alexander Macdonell, later to become the first bishop of Upper Canada. In 1804, soon after Macdonell's arrival in Lower Canada, he was appointed pastor of St. Raphael's in Glengarry County for a colony of Scottish Catholics. This formally opened a second front in the Catholic settlement of the province, which quickly extended to the tiny but growing communities of Kingston, York, (now Toronto) Niagara (Niagara-on-the-Lake) and Dundas, near Hamilton.

In 1807, Bishop Plessis made Macdonell the vicar general of Upper Canada, a rare example of his sharing power and authority. In 1819, Québec became an archdiocese and on 31 December 1820, Archbishop Plessis ordained Macdonell the titular bishop of Rhesaena and episcopal vicar of Upper Canada. On 27 January 1826, Macdonell became the bishop of Upper Canada.

The elevation of Bishop Macdonell ended Upper Canada's status as a religious colony of Lower Canada and allowed Macdonell freedom to conduct a more vigorous evangelization of Southwestern Ontario. He brought together priests and people in Upper Canada, as he established priest-led congregations throughout the province. He turned land grants for churches and government salaries for his clergy and teachers, and his place of honour among the political elite, to the Church's advantage. He did the same with the influx of Irish immigrants, who would do so much to enliven the Church in nineteenth-century Ontario. Thousands of Irish immigrants came to Canada in two waves, the first from 1825 to 1845 and the second from 1845 to 1849, during the Irish famine. The bishop founded missions and parishes in twenty-seven settlements, from which resident priests and their assistants served scattered Catholic flocks in more than a hundred townships and Native reserves. Macdonell was the mastermind behind this unprecedented expansion.[12] Aside from two lengthy overseas trips, the only interruption to Macdonell's missionary labours in Upper Canada was the War of 1812.

When Macdonell had arrived in Glengarry County in 1804 he estimated that the province had no more than 4,000 Catholics, three churches — St. Raphael and St. Andrew in the east and Assumption in the west, separated by 700 miles (1,120 kms.) — and two priests. Father Fitzsimmons, an Irish Franciscan, left in 1806, and Father Marchand at Assumption could not speak English.[13] By 1835, when Macdonell had relinquished the diocesan administration to his coadjutor, Bishop Rémi Gaulin, the diocese of Kingston boasted 59,752 Catholics, 32 missions and parishes, 22 pastors and 44 churches, "small and great, built and being built."[14]

A Mission in the District of London

The story of the Catholic Church in the London District (Middlesex, Oxford, Elgin and Norfolk counties), and by extension in the Huron Tract, began with the July–August 1827 episcopal tour of Bishop Macdonell, during which he also visited Assumption parish. Accompanying the bishop was Father James W. Campion, the missionary priest for Niagara and Dundas.

The two men travelled on horseback from Guelph to Port Talbot, on the invitation of Colonel Thomas Talbot, arriving at his home on Friday, 27 July. Bishop Macdonell performed a marriage at Port Talbot, and Father Campion baptized many children and even received one person into the Church in St. Thomas in Elgin County. From the Talbot settlement, they went to St. Thomas, Westminster Township and London Township. In the tiny town of London, which had become the district's administrative centre in 1826, they met Dennis O'Brien, one of the town's few Catholics. O'Brien became London's first general merchant and a staunch supporter of the Church.

So impressed was Macdonell by the faith of the people that he commissioned Father Campion to visit both settlements and the neighbouring townships at least twice a year. Campion returned on seven occasions, between January 1828 and May 1830.[15] On 19 July 1830, he was in Middleton Township, Norfolk County.

In September 1830, Hugh O'Beirne of Yarmouth, James Brady of Southwold Township and Michael McLaughlin, Patrick Smyth and Dennis O'Brien of London petitioned Bishop Macdonell for a resident priest. The self-constituted committee told the bishop that since 1827 the Catholic community had grown to 67 families or 200 souls, not counting single men. In his reply of 2 October 1830, the bishop said that he did not have the means to send them a pastor. Instead, he appointed Father John Cullen as the next missionary in the London District, who would visit them four times a year.[16] Between 19 January and 12 May 1831, Cullen was in Southwold, St. Thomas (twice), Talbot Street, London (twice) and Yarmouth.[17]

In September 1831, Bishop Macdonell separated St. Thomas and London from the mission at Dundas, combining the two settlements into a unified mission, and appointed Father Laurence Dempsey as the resident priest. Father Dempsey oversaw the construction of a small frame church in St. Thomas and named it in honour of St. George (later Holy Angels). It was enclosed, floored and glazed in time for Father Dempsey to celebrate the first Mass in

this church on Christmas Day 1831. Although many Protestants had generously subscribed to the church building fund, Father Dempsey's parishioners found it impossible to liquidate the debt, prompting the churchwardens to petition the bishop for assistance, on 4 April 1832. Father Dempsey supported the petition and added that "unless your purse assist us here, religion and church will fall to the ground."[18] To compound matters, he apparently had no chalice or missal and Father Cullen, his predecessor, had demanded the return of the vestments.

Matters must have been resolved because the mission did not lose its church or property, and Father Dempsey maintained his work as an "apostolic missionary." In addition to serving Catholics in St. Thomas, London and the immediate townships, he ministered to enclaves of Catholics in Goderich, Adelaide, Stratford and numerous crossroads in between, setting the stage for missionary activity in the Huron Tract. In Goderich, he purchased and cleared land for a church. In Adelaide, he met fifty recently arrived families. He wrote Bishop Macdonell that they were "the most depraved Crew I am told that ever came to America."[19]

In October 1833, Bishop Macdonell transferred Father Dempsey to the Penetanguishene mission, where he died on 9 November 1833, and he appointed Father (later Dean) Daniel Downie to St. Thomas and London. Father Downie built the first St. Lawrence the Martyr church, the forerunner of St. Peter's cathedral, in London, in 1834, in response to the growing population of Irish Catholics. Downie improved the cemetery in St. Thomas, bought vestments and began to register baptisms and marriages. He doubtlessly continued Father Dempsey's regular but infrequent visits to the Huron Tract. In 1834, Bishop Gaulin, conducted the first of three confirmation tours in Southwestern Ontario; he made his other tours in 1836 and 1838.

1835 Report on Church in Southwestern Ontario

Bishop Macdonell's 1835 report provides information on the state of the Church in Southwestern Ontario. He reported that Assumption had two priests — Father Angus Macdonell, the bishop's nephew, and Father George Hay — and 5,700 parishioners between Belle River and River

Canard. There were also nascent missions in Belle River and Maidstone Cross. The bishop thought that the "Catholics [of Sandwich and Essex County] were more numerous than in any other district west of Glengarry, and that their spiritual wants had been well looked after by a succession of zealous and devoted pastors."[20]

St. John the Baptist mission in Amherstburg had been elevated to a parish in 1828. Father Jean Lostrie had 2,130 parishioners in the townships of Malden, Colchester and Gosfield as well as on the Huron Reservation. Catholic soldiers stationed at Fort Malden were also parishioners. (Father Augustine Vervais, pastor from 1838 to 1843, estimated that there were 150 soldiers at the 8:30 a.m. Mass each Sunday.)

At St. Peter-on-the-Thames, at Prairie Siding in Raleigh Township, Father Jean-Baptiste Morin was the first pastor, starting in 1834. He took care of 2,350 Catholics in East and West Tilbury, Dover, Chatham, Harwich, Raleigh and Sombra, at the Dawn Native Reservation and at settlements along the Thames River and Lake St. Clair down to Belle River.

In his report, the bishop also noted that in the London District, Father Dempsey had founded the parish of St. George in St. Thomas and that Father Daniel Downie had built St. Lawrence the Martyr. In 1835, Father Downie was in charge of a congregation of 3,710 Catholics in twenty townships.

Growth in the Huron Tract

Responsibility for the Huron Tract was transferred from the St. Thomas/London mission to the Waterloo mission, when Bishop Macdonell was in St. Thomas, beginning 8 September 1834.[21]

Father Joseph Louis Wiriath, a native of Alsace, was the Waterloo missionary. From 1834 to 1837, he brought the sacraments to Catholics in Stratford, Irishtown (St. Columban), Goderich, Beachville (near Ingersoll) and crossroads communities in dozens of townships. In 1837, before his departure, Wiriath compiled a census of Catholics in his mission — a rare achievement for the time — which included those living in Perth, Huron, Oxford and Norfolk counties. Goderich had the largest concentration of Catholics, with 45 families or 143

souls.[22]

Father Wiriath's successor was Father Thomas Gibney, who, like Fathers Campion, Cullen, Dempsey and Downie, came from Ireland as part of Bishop Macdonell's plan to have Irish priests head Irish congregations in Upper Canada. Gibney is credited with building Catholic churches in Goderich (St. Isidore), Stratford (St. Simon) and Irishtown.

In 1838, Bishop Rémi Gaulin, Bishop Mac-donell's coadjutor, divided the Huron Tract mission into two parts. To Father Gibney went Guelph and Stratford (Stratford was given to Goderich in 1844), and to Father Peter Schneider went Waterloo, Wil-mot and Goderich.

Known as the Apostle of the Huron Tract, Father Schneider made Goderich his headquarters, from 1844 to 1852, when he was appointed to Brantford for a brief period, and from 1854 to 1869, when he returned to Europe.[23] He is likely the only priest to have served under Bishops Macdonell, Gaulin, Power, Charbonnel, Pinsoneault and Walsh.

Growth in the London District

While Father Gibney was ministering in the Huron Tract, Father Joseph Maria Burke, a European-educated Franciscan, took up duties as the missionary in the London District. Burke's mission served 3,536 Catholics in twenty townships.[24] He arrived in London on 23 September 1836 and was able to procure vestments and a chalice but had no missal.[25] Two months later, he registered the deed to the church and burial grounds.[26] It appears that he preferred London, a growing administrative centre, to St. Thomas as his residence. By 23 March 1837, he reported to Bishop Macdonell that he had erected an altar, twenty-four pews and a porch for St. Lawrence the Martyr in London, and, using $123 that he had collected in Toronto in February, had purchased lumber for an altar and a porch for the St. Thomas church.[27] In another letter to Bishop Macdonell, Father Burke wrote that he had acquired land for a church in Beachville on 16 July 1837 and celebrated the first Mass in the church on 20 September.[28]

Father Burke, who was in London during the Rebellion of Upper and Lower Canada in 1837, succeeded in keeping his congregation loyal to the government. Only five Catholics joined the rebels.

After Father Burke left the London District on

1 October 1838, [29] Father Michael Robert Mills succeeded him. In his report of 21 February 1839, he said that his mission had 750 Catholics scattered over 20 townships, with some 60 miles away from London. (Mill's number is lower than Burke's because he restricted his count to Catholics in London and St. Thomas, while Burke had included all those in the London Mission.) Total receipts in a calendar year amounted to $500, from which all expenses had to be paid. He complained that one sick call could cost him ten dollars in travel expenses.

The mission had three churches. The one in Beachville held 100 people but had no window frames or seats. St. George's church in St. Thomas was unfinished inside; average attendance was 120 people, exclusive of the military. St. Lawrence the Martyr church in London seated 180 people; average attendance, not counting the military, was 150 people. Mills told Bishop Macdonell,

> The state of education is almost at its lowest ebb. There is not even one decent school in the whole place. The few masters who may be, are usually ignorant and insolent and idlers. I hold a catechism class every Sunday evening in London when there, which continues for one hour, at least. About twenty children usually attend.[30]

Father Mills was transferred to Dundas on 6 June 1839. The next priest appointed to London was Father James O'Flyn (1839–40). When Bishop Gaulin recognized London as a parish in 1840, the year he became bishop of the diocese of Kingston, he appointed Father Constantine Lee as its pastor, where he was very popular with the Catholic soldiers of the 1st and 83rd Regiments.

A Bishop Closer to Home

On 17 December 1841, the Church in Southwestern Ontario became part of a new diocese, which Rome erected in the western half of Canada West. (In 1841, the colonies of Upper Canada and Lower Canada were joined to became the province of Canada, and "Canada West" was used to refer to the former Upper Canada.) The diocese's first bishop, the Halifax-born Michael Power, was consecrated on 8 May 1842, and he chose Toronto as his episcopal see. His territory extended from Oshawa to Manitoulin Island and to Windsor.

Bishop Power had many problems in Southwestern Ontario because that region's slowly evolving Church was still a part of the largely untamed Upper Canadian frontier. Circumscribed by geography, endemic poverty and the chance nature of provincial politics, Macdonell and Gaulin had done all in their power to build the foundations of a functioning Church administration. But it was time to leave the chaotic days of the late eighteenth and early nineteenth centuries behind. To grow and prosper in step with society, the local Church needed a disciplined clergy, a laity obedient to clerical leadership and a style of episcopal governance at once rigorous and personal.

Many factors, however, made it difficult for Bishop Power to give oversight to the distant southwestern region of the diocese. The Catholic population was steadily increasing, but there were never enough priests to satisfy the basic spiritual needs of the people on a regular basis. Moreover, the quality of the missionary clergy, with few exceptions, was middling to poor. The appointment of priests to parishes and missions took on the semblance of musical chairs, with few priests staying long enough in a location to establish a sense of stability. The priests needed a clear set of diocesan rules that would govern their public conduct. The lack of money led many missionary priests to complain about their "no-cash" congregations. Catholics were fairly good at acquiring property and constructing simple churches, but they struggled to maintain what they had and were often in arrears in their support of their pastors and in repaying moneylenders. Drunkenness was pervasive among the laity.

In 1842, the Catholic population in Southwestern Ontario was a modest 9,200. The region had five parishes, six missions with churches and numerous mission stations. The five parishes were Assumption in Sandwich, St. John the Baptist in Amherstburg, St. George/Holy Angels in St. Thomas, St. Peter-on-the-Thames in Raleigh, and St. Lawrence the Martyr in London. The missions included Goderich, Stratford, St. Columban, Beachville, Maidstone and Belle River. This amounted to a modest but functioning parochial structure.

At the helm of these parishes, missions, and mission stations were seven priests, among them

Father Patrick O'Dwyer, who was stationed in London from 1841 to 1844 and from 1846 to 1849. An uncompromising temperance preacher, he wrote Bishop Gaulin:

> Of all the congregations I yet met with, that of London surpasses all in calumny, detraction, luke-warmness, disrespect, disobedience to the church. I say Mass every morning, only a few women attend. It would take St. Paul to bring them to a sense of their duty …. London is a den of drunkards and tavern keepers.[31]

Father O'Dwyer convinced many of his parishioners to pledge to abstain from alcohol and became quite popular. When he was transferred to Ingersoll in 1849, he refused to leave and had to be forcibly removed from the high altar by the local constabulary.

Father Michael Robert Mills and Father James O'Flyn returned to London and St. Thomas. Mills was posted to St. Thomas, from 1843 to 1846. In 1843, he fulfilled a promise and visited Catholics in the Simcoe area.[32] O'Flyn, returned in 1850 to minister to the Catholics of Biddulph and McGillivray townships, and his name is associated with the early history of St. Patrick parish in Lucan.

Among the new priests who were stationed in Southwestern Ontario were Thadeus T. Kirwan, and Peter F. Crinnon. Dean Kirwan was pastor of St. Lawrence the Martyr, and built a second church on a larger lot diagonally opposite to the first. In 1855, he built a church in St. Marys. As dean of St. Gregory, which covered London and Brock districts, Kirwan wrote a frank and informative report on the state of the church under his charge, dated 17 August 1853. Father Crinnon built a church in Limerick, now Mount Carmel, and was pastor of St. Patrick's in Biddulph and St. Joseph's in Stratford before he became the second bishop of Hamilton (1874-82).

One of the first and best decisions that Bishop Power made in his short episcopate was to invite the Jesuits to return to Assumption parish in Sandwich. They arrived in July 1843, with Father Pierre Point at their head. This indomitable priest remained for seventeen years. He was superior of his community, parish priest, founder of Assumption College and, from 22 November 1846, dean of Sandwich and all French-speaking Catholics in the diocese. Among those who joined him were Father Jean-Pierre Choné, who later founded the Jesuit mission

on Manitoulin Island, and Father Dominique du Ranquet and Brother Joseph Jennesseaux, who worked together for six difficult years on Walpole Island and at Baby's Point (across from the island), Port Sarnia and Mooretown.

Father Point wrote a history of the Jesuit apostolate in Sandwich, Essex, Kent and Lambton counties. *Histoire du Sandwich* is the lengthiest and most informative report written by any priest during the episcopacies of Bishop Power and Bishop Charbonnel. Conscientious and hard working, the Jesuits never worried Bishop Power.

To regulate the conduct of diocesan clergy, the bishop sought to enact clerical (and lay) discipline through the Toronto diocesan synod of October 1842, and planned to enforce that discipline through twenty-two regulations. The primary object of the statutes was uniformity of behaviour and practice covering a range of matters: travel outside one's parish and clerical dress in public, private confession and confessional boxes, fees for the sacraments (strictly forbidden), baptism and baptismal fonts, marriage, sacramental registers, and the use of the Roman Missal and Breviary and *Butler's Catechism*.

Regulations were one thing, but convincing the clergy to abide by them proved to be another matter. There was no love lost between Bishop Power and a number of his priests. He rebuked Father Patrick O'Dwyer and even Father Angus Macdonell, one of his vicars general, for refusing to wear their cassocks in public. The bishop suspended Father Augustine Vervais from St. John the Baptist parish in Amherstburg, in October 1843, handing over the day-to-day administration of the parish to the lay churchwardens. And the bishop carried on a two-year battle with Father Michael Robert Mills, who was not shy about pointing out the bishop's weaknesses to the bishop.

Bishop Power was probably more successful, from a pastoral point of view, in his episcopal visitations. He was in Amherstburg, Sandwich and Raleigh in 1843; in Goderich, Stratford and Seaforth in 1844; and in Sandwich and Belle River, again, in 1845. He not only dispensed the sacrament of confirmation but also issued ordinances concerning the accounts of the churchwardens and the better management of church affairs.[33]

In January 1847, Bishop Power went to Europe to recruit much-needed priests and returned to a human tragedy. The thousands of Famine Irish flooding into Toronto were sick, hungry and destitute. While attending to their spiritual and physical needs, he contracted typhus and died on 1 October 1847, at forty-two years of age.

Need to Create the Diocese of London

The new bishop of the diocese of Toronto was Armand-François-Marie de Charbonnel, whom Pius IX consecrated in the Sistine chapel on 26 May 1850. He was bishop until he retired to France in 1860. A French aristocrat and a gifted man, Charbonnel was hobbled by a sense of personal inadequacy. He was overwhelmed by the enormous size of his diocese. The Catholic population in Ontario had doubled mainly owing to the flood of Irish Catholic immigrants in the wake of the Great Famine. In Southwestern Ontario, the number of Catholics increased to 13,900 in 1848 and by 1851 had grown dramatically to 24,900. The bishop was also weighed down by the lack of priests and of Catholic institutions, such as schools, colleges and hospitals, and by the poverty and ignorance of the recently arrived immigrants.

Nevertheless, Bishop Charbonnel faithfully visited far-flung Catholic communities. Between June 1851 and January 1854, he visited London — where he blessed the new St. Lawrence the Martyr church on 7 March 1852 — Goderich, Ingersoll, St. Thomas, Amherstburg, Sandwich, Raleigh and Mooretown along the St. Clair River. The *Toronto Mirror* characterized Bishop Charbonnel's first trip through the western part of his diocese as "long and fatiguing."[34]

The problems in Southwestern Ontario defeated the best pastoral intentions of Bishop Charbonnel and convinced him of the need to divide the diocese of Toronto into three dioceses. He felt that the more distant Catholic settlements were too far removed from authoritative episcopal governance. For the Catholic faith to lay deep roots and flourish in those areas, the faithful there would need their own bishop who would live among them.

On 23 April 1856, Bishop Charbonnel announced with great relief that Rome had erected the new diocese of London on 21 February 1856 and that the diocese of Hamilton had been erected on 29 February 1856. Rome had chosen Pierre-Adolphe Pinsoneault of Québec as the first bishop of London and John Farrell, a native of Armagh, Ireland, as first bishop of Hamilton.

Endnotes for Part One -- From Mission to Diocese

[1] Ronald Fabbro, "Our Diocese celebrates 150 years," Roman Catholic Diocese of London website. (27 November, 2005.) http://www.rcec.london.on.ca/AnniversaryDiocese/BishopPastoralLetter.htm (accessed 8 January 2007).

[2] Bruce Trigger, *Natives and Newcomers: Canada's "Heroic Age" Reconsidered* (Kingston and Montreal: 1985), 267-71.

[3] George Paré, *The Catholic Church in Detroit 1701-1888* (Detroit: 1951), 104-5.

[4] As translated and quoted in Ernest J. Lajeunesse, ed., *The Windsor Border Region Canada's Southernmost Frontier: A Collection of Documents* (Toronto: 1960), 26-27.

[5] Reuben Gold Thwaites, ed., *The Jesuit Relations and Allied Documents: Travels and Explorations of the Jesuit Missionaries in New France, 1610-1791*, 73 vols. (Cleveland: 1896-1901), vol. 69: 51.

[6] "The Treaty of Paris." L'Encyclopédie de l'histoire du Québec / The Quebec History, Encyclopedia. http://www2.marianopolis.edu/quebechistory/encyclopedia/TreatyofParis1763-QuebecHistory.htm (accessed 18 January 2007).

[7] John P. Comiskey, *The Foundation of the Diocese of London in Canada 1760-1856* (Licentiate diss., Pontifical Gregorian University, 1997), 4-20.

[8] Ernest J. Lajeunesse, *Outline History of Assumption Parish*, 2nd ed. (Windsor: 1984), 28.

[9] Although Bishop Dignan mentions that Bishop Henri-Marie de Pontbriand visited the Huron Mission in 1755 and administered the sacrament of confirmation, there is no mention of this in Pontbriand's biography in the *DCB* or in Paré's *The Catholic Church in Detroit*. See: Ralph Hubert Dignan, "History of the Diocese of London" (unpublished manuscript, ca. 1919-1932), 20; Jean-Guy Lavallée, "Dubreil de Pontbriand, Henri-Marie," *DCB* (Toronto: 1974), 3: 193-94.

[10] "Visite de Mgr. Denaut au Détroit en 1801," *Bulletin des Recherches Historiques*, 10, no. 4 (April 1904): 97-106.

[11] *Journal des Visites Pastorales de 1815 and 1816 par Monseigneur Joseph-Octave Plessis Èvêque de Québec* (Quebec: 1903), Assumption: 44, 58; Malden: 52; St. Peter-on-the-Thames: 55-57.

[12] L.J. Flynn, *Built on a Rock: The Story of the Roman Catholic Church in Kingston 1826-1976* (Kingston: 1976), Appendix 2, 368-71. This was taken from a letter from Macdonell to Cardinal Pedicini, *Report to the Prefect of Propaganda Fide on the State of the Missions in Upper Canada, 22 June 1835*. See Comiskey, *The Foundation of the Diocese of London*, 51-54.

Endnotes for Part One -- (continued)

[13] Letter of Bishop Macdonell of Kingston to the Archbishop of Vienna, 13 February 1837, published in German in *Leopoldinen Berichte* XI (1838): 36-40, trans. by M.J. Oliver, St. Michael's College, 22 June 1922. Copy found in the papers of Father Joseph Finn. Macdonell gave not more than 5,000 as the number of Catholics in a letter of 1823. See: Macdonell to the Cardinal Prefect of the Sacred Congregation for the Propagation of the Faith at Rome, 9 May 1823, as referred to in Comiskey, *The Foundation of the Diocese of London*, 44.

[14] Macdonell to Cardinal Pedicini, *Report to the Prefect of Propaganda Fide on the State of the Missions in Upper Canada, 22 June* 1835, as quoted in Comiskey, *The Foundation of the Diocese of London*, 52.

[15] James W. Campion, "A Register of Baptisms, Marriages & Burials in Colonel Talbot's Settlement." This document was located in St. Mary parish rectory, Hamilton, in the early 1970s. A good portion of this section relies on Dignan's "History of the Diocese of London," 41-50 and 54-56, plus many handwritten inserts. Dignan obviously used the above named "Register," and he must have relied on the correspondence of Bishop Macdonell for the details of the work of the priests in the London District and the Huron Tract, from 1827 to 1841. See: AO, Bishop Alexander Macdonell Papers, MS 709 (Finding Aid 971); MS 228 (Finding Aid 963). See: Bibliographical note in Somers, *Life and Times of the Hon. and Rt. Rev. Alexander Macdonell, D.D.*," 226.

[16] Daniel J. Brock, "The Beginnings of the Roman Catholic Church in the District of London" (a talk given before the London and Middlesex Historical Society, at the London Public Library, 15 January 1974), 11-12.

[17] John Cullen, "A Register of the Baptisms and Marriages performed by Revd. John Cullen in the Mission of Niagara AD 1830." This can be located in the Chancery Office of the Diocese of Hamilton, St. Augustine's Parish, Dundas, File #1.

[18] Dignan, insert after page 46.

[19] AO, Bishop Alexander Macdonell Papers, MS 228, AB 1001, Dempsey to Macdonell, 20 November 1832.[20] As quoted in Adam Shortt and Arthur G. Doughty, eds. *Canada and its Provinces: A History of the Canadian People and Their Institutions*, 23 vols. (Toronto: 1914), 11: 47-48.

[21] *Montreal Gazette*, 13 September 1834, 2.

[22] Dignan, 55-56.

[23] Ibid., 56, insert.

[24] AO, Bishop Alexander Macdonell Papers, MS 228, AB 0507, Burke to Macdonell, 29 February 1838. Burke conducted his own census.

[25] Ibid., AB 0501, Burke to Macdonell, 26 September 1836.

[26] Dignan, 47.

[27] AO, Bishop Alexander Macdonell Papers, MS 228, AB 0502, Burke to Macdonell, 23 March 1837.

[28] Ibid., AB 0506, Burke to Macdonell, 18 October 1837. The deed to this property is dated 12 July 1839, from Rheuben Martin to Bishop Macdonell, Bishop Gaulin and Father Michael Robert Mills, who was then stationed in Dundas. See: *Ingersoll, Ontario Sacred Heart Church 1880-1980: Retrospect* (Ingersoll: 1980), 3.

[29] William Richard Harris, *The Catholic Church in the Niagara Peninsula* (Toronto: 1895), 207. Harris has Father Burke in St. Catharines in 1834, but this is clearly a mistake.

[30] Dignan, "History of the Diocese of London," 48, insert in middle of page.

[31] AO, Bishop Alexander Macdonell Papers, BB 1411, O'Dwyer to Gaulin, 1 December 1841.

[32] Daniel J. Brock, "Some Further Details Relating to the Catholic Church in Norfolk County in the Year 1843" (unpublished paper, 30 March 1978), 1.

[33] ARCAT, Power Papers, LB01.088, 3 September 1843, 103; LB01.089, 10 September, 105; LB01.090, 16 September 1843; LB01.138, 19 September 1845, 151; LB01.139, 19 September 1845, 152. For the 1844 visit, see: Comiskey, *The Foundations of the Diocese of London*, 91.

[34] *Toronto Mirror*, 26 December 1851, 3.

Part II
The Bishops of the Diocese of London

Introduction: The Diocese of London—150 Years

In 2005–2006, as the faithful celebrated the diocese of London's 150th anniversary, they could give thanks for a "graced history."[1] And, in spite of many changes and challenges in the Church, they had strong grounds for "embracing a future full of hope."[2] As Bishop Fabbro said:

> Our 150th anniversary invites us to reflect on our history and to grow in our appreciation of the enduring values of our past. These values guided and inspired our ancestors in the challenges they faced, and they continue to do so today as we encounter new challenges in a rapidly changing world.[3]

Founding of the Diocese

When the Apostolic Brief for the erection of the diocese of London was issued on 21 February 1856, Southwestern Ontario was a pioneering region. Settlers were turning the vast tracts of forest into rich agricultural lands. Villages and small towns dotted the landscape and travel was difficult.

The new diocese consisted of nine counties — Essex, Kent, Lambton, Elgin, Middlesex, Huron, Perth, Oxford and Norfolk. Scattered over this immense area were approximately 30,000 Catholics, who formed 13 percent of the population. The largest number of Catholics, mainly French-Canadians, resided in Essex County, and of these a majority was concentrated in the township of Sandwich. The other large and rapidly growing group of Catholics were Irish immigrants, who had settled at the eastern end of the diocese, mainly in the London region. The diocese's patron saints—Mary of the Immaculate Conception and St. Patrick— represent these two principal founding communities: the French and the Irish. In 1968, the diocese adopted new armorial bearings that included a fleur de lys and a shamrock to represent the two patrons and the two founding groups.

The bishops of Canada had summed up the need for the diocese when they petitioned the pope in June 1854 to divide the sprawling diocese of Toronto and erect the dioceses of London and Hamilton:

> The principal reasons for this petition are: the extraordinary and continual increase [of the population] in this part of the Province; the majority and great power of the Protestants; the need for priests, churches, schools, instruction, worship, discipline and temperance in drink; and therefore the solution of all these needs which are urgent in all parts of the diocese.[4]

When London was chosen as the See of the diocese, the city was only a year old. Although it never became the capital of Upper Canada, as Lieutenant-Governor John Graves Simcoe had envisioned, it did become an important regional centre. At the time, St. Thomas, a railway town, Sandwich (now Windsor), and the shipping ports of Sarnia and Goderich were other important centres.

The diocese had twelve parishes (generally defined by the presence of a resident priest), thirty-seven missions and mission stations, twenty-six churches and chapels and the deeds to thirty-two properties.[5] The twelve parishes were Our Lady of the Assumption, Sandwich/Windsor (1767); St. John the Baptist, Amherstburg (1828); Holy Angels, St. Thomas (1831) St. Peter-on-the-Thames, Tilbury East (1834); St. Lawrence the Martyr/St. Peter's, London (1840); St. Peter's, Goderich (1844); Sts. Simon and Jude, Belle River (1845); St. Joseph's, Chatham (1847); Sacred Heart, Ingersoll (1850); St. Patrick's, Biddulph/Lucan (1854); St. Mary's, Maidstone (1855) and St. Joseph's, Stratford (1856).[6] These parishes still exist.

The first bishop, Pierre-Adolphe Pinsoneault, established the mission of Forest in 1857 and attached it to Sarnia. During his administration, five missions matured into parishes. [7] They were Our Lady of Mercy, Sarnia (1856); St. Anne's, Tecumseh (1859); St. Anthony's (Our Lady of LaSalette), Windham (1860); St. Joseph's, River Canard (1864); and St. Alphonsus, Windsor (1865).

Twelve priests from the diocese of Toronto served in the new diocese. And there were twelve members from three religious communities: Les Dames-du-Sacré-Coeur, or Sisters of the Sacred Heart, in Sandwich; the Sisters of St. Joseph, in Amherstburg; and the Ladies of Loretto (Institute of the Blessed Virgin Mary), in London.

London's material resources were meagre, and it was encumbered with a debt of $10,000.[8] At the same time, the existing churches and missions testified to the generosity and foresight of the faithful, and were a viable inheritance on which the diocese could build.

Since its founding, the Church in Southwestern Ontario has grown with the region, responding to the needs of the people and changing conditions. Today, the diocese of London is one of the largest English-speaking dioceses in Canada, with an area of 21,349 square kilometers (8240 square miles) and a Catholic population of 622,138 in a total population of 1,944,182. Once a predominantly rural diocese, London has become much more urban because economic developments and increasing industrialization have led to a shift in population to cities and towns.

The diocese now has 138 parishes and 20 missions in seven deaneries (Windsor, Essex, Kent, Sarnia, London, Huron-Perth, and Ingersoll).

Over its 150-year history, two internal influences have played an important part in shaping the life of the diocese. The bishops' leadership style and concerns played a key role in forming London's character, while the enduring values of the faithful influenced the development of its soul.

The Ten Bishops

Although Bishop Pierre-Adolphe Pinsoneault (1856–1866) was the first of the diocese's ten bishops, many regard the second bishop, John Walsh, as the diocese's true founder. The cosmopolitan, authoritarian Pinsoneault and the pioneering diocese were not a good match, but, from Walsh on, each bishop was the right man for the

times.

The pastoral Bishop Walsh (1861–1889), a well-respected communicator and effective leader, established a viable foundation for the diocese. He presided over a remarkable increase in the number of churches, parishes, priests and religious communities in a period when the Catholic population increased by fifty-two percent. (There were 44,000 in 1861 and almost 67,500 in 1889). He also built St. Peter's cathedral, which noted architect Joseph Connolly designed.

Bishop Dennis O'Connor (1890–1899), an efficient administrator, reduced the debt, putting the diocese, which was a collection of mainly small rural parishes, on a sounder footing. A conservative, he also had a commitment to moral vigour.

Bishop Fergus Patrick McEvay (1899–1908) defended the separate school system vigorously. In spite of strong opposition, he established separate school boards in the Windsor area. Provincially, he helped formulate a compromise with the government on the certification of teachers who were members of religious orders. The bishop also had to work out differences between French-speaking and English-speaking clergy and laity as Francophones sought to protect their language and culture.

Bishop Michael Francis Fallon (1909–1931) was the author of great accomplishments and great controversy. He founded eighteen parishes, built many churches and refurbished St. Peter's cathedral. A strong believer in education, he helped make improvements in post-secondary education for Catholics by enabling three Catholic post-secondary institutions to affiliate with the University of Western Ontario. He established St. Peter's Seminary to train priests in the diocese. He defended the separate school system, but his adamant opposition to bilingual education, as then conducted in the separate schools, led to bitter conflict and attempts to have him removed. He was a gifted orator, and drew crowds of both Catholics and Protestants to sermons and lectures. Yet, the blunt-spoken bishop could also bully his opposition. During his episcopacy the number of Catholics in the diocese increased by approximately 40,000,[9] and the number of priests rose from 70 to 135. Between 1920 and 1930, the number of professed women religious grew from 504 to 710.

Bishop John Thomas Kidd (1931–1950), a careful manager, enabled the diocese to survive financially during the Depression. He strengthened its institutional foundations, providing for the social needs of the faithful. He also deepened the spiritual life of the laity. This provided comfort and stability in difficult times and prepared the way for the rise of a strong Catholic culture in the fifties and early sixties.

Bishop John Christopher Cody (1950–1963) led the diocese during a time of unparalleled growth. He established 33 parishes and 6 missions, including a number of national parishes to meet the needs of European immigrants. He streamlined the administration of the diocese and improved its charitable social services as well as the separate school system and opportunities for higher education. The pious bishop led in the development of a strong corporate devotional life, with a traditional approach to leadership as a bishop. Yet, some of his initiatives indicate openness to the growing desire for reform in the liturgy and greater involvement by the laity.

Beginning in the sixties, major shifts within and outside the Church reshaped how the Church carried out its mission. Thus, under the progressive Bishop G. Emmett Carter (1964–1978), the diocese seemed to experience constant change. Carter implemented the reforms and renewal of the Second Vatican Council, which changed the form and language of worship and shifted the Church into a more pastoral role. He also instituted reform of diocesan laws and administration, a process that increased the participation of priests and laity. An excellent communicator, the poised Carter enjoyed a high public profile because of his reforms, but could also draw criticism for his style.

During the later seventies and eighties, the Church in Canada had to adjust to a loss in status and support. While the reforms of the Second Vatican Council had made the Church more relevant, it had also resulted in the loss of a strong Catholic identity. Increased secularization, loss of regard for authority and internal Church scandals further undermined the role the Church had enjoyed. Yet, those within the Church wanted it to remain strong and vibrant.

So once again, London's bishops faced serious challenges. John Michael Sherlock (1978–2002) and his successor, Ronald Peter Fabbro (2002–) both had to wrestle with keeping the diocesan Church strong in the face of diminishing resources and declining attendance at Mass.

Sherlock, London's longest-serving bishop, found new ways to support the clergy and St. Peter's Seminary. He established a greater role for the laity, who became administrators, pastoral ministers and youth leaders. He reinstated the permanent diaconate. The number of active diocesan clergy decreased; in one five-year period (January 1993 to January 1998), numbers dropped from 232 to 197. To meet the people's needs for priests, Sherlock began restructuring the diocese to ensure the viability of parishes. He made changes in the diocese's administration. At the parish level, the diocese began clustering parishes by combining smaller parishes under one pastoral team. But, when clergy sexual abuse scandals came to light, the diocese failed to respond quickly in a meaningful way, which further eroded trust in the Church.

Bishop Fabbro courageously instituted stronger measures to ensure the health of the diocese, including closing parishes. His direct, caring approach to the sexual abuse crisis is helping rebuild trust. At the same time, the diocese faces a possible financial crisis as it settles lawsuits.

At the beginning of the anniversary year, the bishop challenged the faithful to take heart.

The theme we have chosen for our 150th comes from our pastoral plan, Embracing a Future Full of Hope. The accomplishments of the past enable us to look to the future with confidence. This anniversary year calls each of us to holiness and to greater fidelity in living our Christian vocation. It is a call to re-invigorate our parish communities, to reach out to our fellow Catholics who are not coming to church, and to tell them that we need them and welcome them. It is a marvellous opportunity for healing and reconciliation with those who feel alienated from the Church, a time to bear witness to Jesus's message of forgiveness, healing, justice, love, and peace.[10]

The Soul of the Diocese

The values that characterize the diocese have enabled it to continue the mission of Jesus, sharing the good news and reaching out to the marginalized at many levels. These ideals have helped the people sustain their faith and ensured a strong Church presence in the community.

A respect for diversity was established early,

as the founding communities, the French and the Irish, learned to live with each other, and to respect each other's cultures. The Francophone community set a standard when it fought hard to maintain its cultural and religious identity amidst a move toward assimilation.

Following its founding, the diocese welcomed immigrants in every decade. In the first part of the twentieth century many Dutch, German, Italian, Polish, and Portuguese immigrants increased the size of the diocese. Then significant waves of refugees/immigrants arrived from Asian countries, especially Vietnam, in the late 1970s. Later, people came from Latin American countries, and more recently from some African countries. The Church helped meet their spiritual and social needs by establishing national parishes and supporting groups' efforts to build places of worship. As Bishop Fabbro has said, "the diverse expressions of the common faith we profess have enriched our diocesan Church immensely."[11]

A close relationship between people and priests also characterized the diocese. In cases of "ethnic parishes," the bishop would often invite an order of priests, including Italian, Slovak and German, to staff the parish. Bishop Fallon established a seminary to train diocesan priests locally. Bishop Carter began the process of giving priests greater involvement in decision-making. He also initiated changes that increased lay involvement in ministry, a process Sherlock built on. After the Second Vatican Council, the Church did not have enough clergy to meet the needs, a problem that Bishop McEvay had experienced at the beginning of the nineteenth century.

Clergy and members of religious orders gave generously of their lives to found and run colleges, hospitals, seniors' residences orphanages, and other institutions to serve the poor. In London, women religious were very important in these expressions of social justice and in developing Catholic education. Now, members of religious orders work alongside lay people.

All the bishops have worked to ensure that the diocese of London maintains a high standard for liturgy, church architecture, and the practice of the Catholic faith. All have pushed their people to strive for excellence and for a strong Catholic presence in the community.

Support for social justice has been another

value. Because of its strong agricultural background, the diocese developed a sensitivity to farm and farm-family life justice issues. Bishop Sherlock established the Catholic Rural Life Conference to address some of these issues. Social justice for workers is also important, especially in the Windsor area with the auto-related industries. From the 1930s to the 1960s, many parishioners were involved in Catholic social action movements, including the cooperative movement, Young Christian Workers and the Christian Family Movement.

Throughout our history, diocesan leaders have emphasized Catholic education, working hard to establish Catholic elementary and secondary schools. The people have championed education at every level, making sacrifices when separate schools were underfunded. Various bishops, especially McEvay and Fallon, campaigned vigorously to defend the rights of Catholics to an equitable education. The diocese's leaders also established post-secondary educational institutions such as Christ the King College (now King's University College) and Brescia College (now Brescia University College) in London and Assumption University, in Windsor.

In general, the diocese of London was financially well off. Because of its location in a region with a strong economy, the diocese was able to collect more money than many other Canadian dioceses. That allowed it to spend more on projects, programs, and ministry offices. Prudent bishops such as O'Connor and Kidd kept the diocese stable when times were difficult.

But now, the diocese must cope with severe financial strains. Because of demographic shifts, some parishes no longer had the same level of funding; many older parishes have aging churches that require substantial funds for repair and upkeep. In addition, clergy numbers have been declining. These are the principal factors that were considered in the process of reorganization that led to the closing of some parishes. As well, the diocese has been making settlements because of the clergy sexual abuse crisis. Other factors affecting finances are the payments the diocese is making for its share of the World Youth Day, held in Toronto in 2002 and for the renovation of St. Peter's cathedral.

One other value, and the most important one, has sustained the diocese. As Bishop Fabbro has said, "the Eucharist has been the centre of the life of [the] diocese . . . It is our encounter with Christ in the Eucharist which enables us to proclaim with conviction that we embrace 'a future full of hope'."[12]

Challenges for a New Era

In one of his pastoral letters, Bishop Fabbro urged the faithful in the diocese of London, to embrace the ministry of the Good News.

The enduring values of our past will continue to guide and strengthen us. It is essential, then, for the Church to enter into dialogue with modern culture. By our words and the example of our lives we need to bring to this dialogue the light of the Gospel. The

Jesuit missionaries who came to this region in the 17th century to evangelize the native peoples continue to be a model for us. It was important for them to know the native peoples, and to understand and respect their culture and their spirituality. They teach us the way to evangelize.

We live in a secular culture which too easily forgets about God. When we enter into dialogue with our contemporaries, however, we discover that many of them are deeply spiritual. This hunger for God is an invitation to evangelize, an invitation to each of us to reach out to others, to open our hearts to them and to share with them the joy we experience through our faith in Jesus Christ.[13]

Endnotes for Introduction to Part Two

[1] Diocese of London, "Parish Reorganization in the Diocese of London," http://www.rcec.london.on.ca/reorganization/index. htm. 29 April, 2006.

[2] *Newsletter of the Diocese of London*, no. 120 (Advent/ Christmas 2005), 1.

[3] Ibid.

[4] Diocese of London, "A Brief Sketch of the Founding of the Diocese of London," compiled by John R. McMahon. http:// www.rcec.london.on.ca/founding.htm.

[5] John R. McMahon, *The Episcopate of Pierre-Adolphe Pinsoneault: First Bishop of London, Upper Canada, 1856–1866* (M.A. thesis, University of Western Ontario, 1982), 269; ARCAT, CTA01.36, "Received from the Right Reverend Francis Mary de Charbonnel, the following deeds, etc. belonging to the new Diocese of London, Canada West," 26 June 1856.

[6] McMahon, The Episcopate of Pierre-Adolphe Pinsoneault, 267; some dates revised by author.

[7] Ibid., 107. The names of the 37 missions and mission stations were Adelaide, Baby's Point (no longer exists), Bayfield, Beachville, Blenheim, Bothwell, Enniskillen, Grand Bend, Grand Point, Irishtown (St. Columban), Kettle Point, Limerick (Mt. Carmel), McGillvray, Merlin, Moore Township (Mooretown), Paincourt, Parkhill, Plympton, Pointe-aux-Roches (Stoney Point), Port Sarnia (Sarnia), Port Dover, Port

Stanley, Port Talbot (no longer exists), Raleigh/Tilbury East, Rivière-aux-Canards (River Canard), Simcoe, Sombra, St. Mary's, St. Joseph, Thamesville, Trait Carré (Tecumseh), Wallaceburg, Wardsville, Windham (LaSalette), Windsor and Woodstock.

[8] John P. Comiskey, *The Foundation of the Diocese of London in Canada 1760–1856* (Licentiate diss., Pontifical Gregorian University, 1997), 40.

[9] Catholic population figures for the diocese of London are generally unreliable. In 1911, there were 60,000 Catholics. This was substantially less than the 67,500 reported by Bishop Walsh, little more than the 59,383, according to Bishop O'Connor and the same as given by Bishop McEvay in 1905. The highest figure given by Bishop Fallon was 77,000, which did not change until 1935, when the figure of 109,581 was taken from the 1931 census. In any event, the Catholic population did increase substantially.

[10] *Newsletter of the Diocese of London*, no. 120 (Advent/ Christmas 2005), 1.

[11] Diocese of London. Bishop Fabbro's pastoral letter, "Our Diocese Celebrates 150 Years," http://www.rcec.london.on.ca/ AnniversaryDiocese/BishopPastoralLetter.htm 27 November 2005.

[12] Ibid.

[13] Ibid

1. Pierre-Adolphe Pinsoneault (1856-1866)

Pierre-Adolphe Pinsoneault was appointed as the first bishop of the Diocese of London on February 29, 1856, and the City of London was designated as his episcopal seat. The bilingual Pinsoneault, who had proven himself in Lower Canada and the diocese of Québec as a defender of Church doctrine, seemed to be the right candidate for the episcopacy, but he turned out to be the wrong choice for a developing diocese in Upper Canada.

Bishop Armand-François-Marie de Charbonnel of Toronto, who was largely responsible for Rome's choice of Pinsoneault to head the See of London, came to regret the choice.[1] The other names on the *terna* were Jean-Mathieu Soulerin, the Basilian superior of St. Michael's College in Toronto, and Jean-Marie Bruyère, the rector of St. Michael's cathedral in Toronto. As irony would have it, Bruyère would become one of London's leading priests, from 1859 until his death in 1888. Supporting Charbonnel's choice of Pinsoneault was the influential Bishop Ignace Bourget of Montréal.

According to one historian, Bishop Pinsoneault "was fitted by traditional environment, temperament and training to reign over an old, well-established French diocese in the grand manner of a French Seigneur of the old school."[2] But in 1856, the nine counties of the diocese of London were no "well-established French diocese." Bishop Pinsoneault came from a family that was wealthy and well-connected in Québec. Southwestern Ontario was still being settled, and whether the inhabitants were French-Canadians long established in the diocese, or recent immigrants from the British Isles and Europe, most were very poor. To complicate economic matters, Catholics in London were the victims of an economic meltdown caused by the end of the Crimean War in 1856; recovery would not begin until 1861.[3]

As well, the bishop had an authoritarian streak that might have passed muster in the thoroughly churched and highly structured society of mid-nineteenth-century Catholic Québec. But it had little place in the recently created rough-and-tumble diocese of London. The Catholic community, which was a minority in a largely Protestant area, was being shaped not by the culture of the Québec Church but by the dynamics of immigration from the British Isles. The bishop had so little ability to deal with anything he believed challenged his episcopal status that he was bound to fail.

Bishop Pinsoneault did not know how to govern and could not leave well enough alone.[4] This was certainly true of his dealings with women religious, with some priests and with "rebellious" parishes. While not every problem that he confronted was of his own making, according to Bishop Ralph H. Dignan, an early historian of the diocese of London, Pinsoneault "usually solved a difficulty by creating at least two new ones."[5]

Early Years and Priesthood

Born on 23 November 1815, in Saint-Philippe-de-Laprairie, Québec, Pierre-Adolphe was one of eleven children of Paul-Théophile Pinsoneault and Clotilde Raymond. The future bishop was the product of a highly structured and well-established French-speaking society that was thoroughly Catholic and firmly rooted in the traditions of Québec. After studying law for a brief period, Pinsoneault entered the Grand Séminaire in Montréal and completed his theological studies at the Séminaire de Saint-Sulpice in Paris. He was ordained to the priesthood on 19 December 1840, at Issy-les-Moulineaux, outside Paris, as a member of the Society of Saint-Sulpice. On his return to Montréal, he taught at his alma mater, the Petit Séminaire, from 1841 to 1843, and then he was put in charge of St. Patrick's church, the city's Irish congregation, from 1843 to 1849. As a result, he became fluently bilingual as part of his pastoral immersion in Montréal's Irish community. In addition, Pinsoneault's savvy in local ecclesiastical politics earned him a promotion to canon-archdeacon of the cathedral chapter. In 1849, he left the Society of Saint-Sulpice, and in 1850, he accepted Bishop Charbonnel's invitation to reorganize his chancery at the beginning of his episcopacy in Toronto. If there was a turning point in Pinsoneault's life, it was his work for Charbonnel. It confirmed him as a rising star in the Québec Church.

Pinsoneault was forty years old when he was named a bishop. His episcopal consecration took place in Montréal on 18 May 1856, at the hands of his principal patron, Bishop Charbonnel, who was assisted by Bishop Joseph LaRocque, coadjutor bishop of Montréal, and Bishop David W. Bacon of Portland, Maine.

First Bishop of London

Pinsoneault's episcopacy might have enjoyed a less turbulent and divisive start, if he had followed Bishop Charbonnel's advice of 12 April 1856 not to disturb the status quo until he had conducted a tour of Chatham, Amherstburg and Sandwich. Pinsoneault thought that a tour would be regarded as a sign of weakness and as such would lessen his authority. He wanted to be not only a father to the diocese but also its master, as he wrote to Charbonnel on 17 April 1856.

Instead, Bishop Pinsoneault made changes before he even left Montréal, squandering any good will that might have been waiting for him in London. The festering opposition in London to his election as bishop did not help matters. There had been grumbling about the Québec hierarchy foisting another French-speaking ecclesiastic onto the Irish Catholics of Canada West (Ontario). Pinsoneault would be the fourth, joining Bishop Charbonnel of Toronto, Bishop Eugène-Joseph-Bruno Guiges of Bytown (Ottawa) and Bishop Rémi Gaulin of Kingston.

The bishop ordered the Loretto Sisters in London, who were treated by their fellow Irish as indispensable to parish life, to leave the diocese, because he needed the rectory where they lived. The sisters left for Guelph in early June. Pinsoneault did

not seem to have entertained the idea of retaining the sisters and boarding them in another house. The parishioners tended to view the departure of the Loretto Sisters as an arbitrary and unjust expulsion, a blow to their fledgling community. Pinsoneault replaced them with a French-speaking community from Montréal and gave them their own house.

In his first pastoral letter to the diocese, issued the day of his consecration in Montréal, Pinsoneault changed the name of his cathedral church in London from St. Lawrence the Martyr to St. Peter. He proclaimed that the Blessed Virgin Mary in her Immaculate Conception was the first patron of the diocese and that St. Patrick was the second. These patrons reflect the diocese's two founding communities: the French and the Irish. Pinsoneault was enthroned in London at St. Peter's on 29 June 1856. Once again, Bishop Charbonnel was in charge of the ceremonial.

In London itself, opposition to the choice of Pinsoneault sprang chiefly from the popular Dean Thadeus Kirwan, a native of Ireland, and parish priest of St. Lawrence the Martyr since 1849. Into London's cozy Irish setting stepped Bishop Pinsoneault. As bishop of the new diocese, he had every right to install his own priests at St. Peter's cathedral and to take up residence in the rectory. But the way he had handled the situation revealed a serious flaw in his perception of his role as the bishop of a frontier diocese.

Pinsoneault had tried to avoid dealing directly with Kirwan, insisting in his April 1856 letter to Charbonnel that it was Charbonnel's duty to dispatch Kirwan. In that letter, he also threatened that, if London's Catholics took Kirwan's side, he would place St. Peter's under interdict, which would have deprived the parishioners of the sacraments, and that he would move to Chatham.[6] Pinsoneault had to deal with Kirwan himself, however, and he appointed the dean to Port Sarnia and made Edward Bayard the cathedral rector and Louis Musart his assistant. But Kirwan would not hand over the cathedral and rectory until the bishop had reimbursed him for the $1,100 of his own money that he had spent on the parish. When Kirwan agreed to accept $440, in July 1856, he left for Port Sarnia, an unhappy exile, and the threat of ecclesiastical punishment was lifted.

What should have remained a private matter between the bishop and the dean, however, spun itself into a controversy on the pages of the *Catholic*

Citizen and the *Toronto Mirror*, courtesy of two laymen. It was P.G. Norris, a London lawyer and Pinsoneault supporter, versus Frank Smith, a London merchant and Irish advocate, who became London's first Catholic mayor in 1867.[7] The nasty war of words between Norris and Smith left London Catholics in a foul mood and bewildered state. In 1864, Kirwan would again fight Pinsoneault, this time over his transfer to Kinkora in Perth County, claiming that, as the first parish priest in Sarnia, he was irremovable. He lost that fight and, defeated, went to Wisconsin, where he died in 1871.

Move from London

Bishop Pinsoneault did not reside long at St. Peter's in London and made a move that would lead to great friction in the diocese. Living in an Irish enclave in the midst of a Protestant majority in a little city was not to his liking. When the Christmas season of 1857 arrived, he moved to the French parish of Assumption in Sandwich, which had been established as a fur-trading post along the Detroit River and was the seat of government and courts for the region. (In 1935, it amalgamated with the adjacent City of Windsor.) Having received an ecstatic welcome from the parishioners there in September, he was determined to change the seat of his diocese from London to Sandwich.

In a letter to his fellow bishops, on 26 January 1858, Pinsoneault gave three reasons for the move. One, the Catholic population in London had never been more than 2,000, when he had been under the impression that it was closer to 5,000, and it had recently declined to nearly 1,200 (caused by the departure of labourers on the Great Western Railway when it was completed in 1853 and the resulting economic depression). Furthermore, he claimed, only 800 Catholics in London regularly practiced their faith. In 1857, there were only twenty marriages and 140 baptisms, hardly enough work for one priest. In other words, there was an insufficient number of Catholics in London to have a bishop live among them. In contrast, Sandwich with its beautiful church and 300 acres of property could easily maintain him at $1,500 a year.

His second reason was that a move to Sandwich would enable the parishioners of St. Peter's to pay down their $10,000 debt in a more timely fashion. As his third point, he said that the greatest concentration of Catholics in his diocese began at Chatham and extended southwestwards into Essex County and he could best serve them from Sandwich. Pinsoneault countered the objection that Sandwich's position at the bottom of the triangular-shaped diocese isolated it from the rest of the diocese, claiming that the four railway lines and the steamships could take him anywhere in his jurisdiction.[8]

Bishop Jean-Charles Prince of St. Hyacinthe, Québec, Bishop Bourget of Montréal and Bishop Charbonnel of Toronto objected to Pinsoneault's plans to translate the seat of the diocese to Sandwich. Prince told Pinsoneault that the poverty of St. Peter's parishioners was all the more reason for him to stay in London. When Pinsoneault asked Charbonnel to support his 29 June 1858 petition to Cardinal Allesandro Barnabo, Prefect of the Congregation of the Propagation of the Faith (Propaganda Fide), who would have to consent to any move, Charbonnel refused.[9]

Undeterred, Pinsoneault pressed ahead. As soon as Charles-François Baillargeon, administrator of the archdiocese of Québec, had given his formal, if unenthusiastic, endorsement to the petition and forwarded it to Cardinal Barnabo, Pinsoneault decided to go to Rome and present his case. He left in September 1858 and did not reappear in his diocese until June 1859, armed with Rome's permission to change the name to the diocese of Sandwich, in a decree of 2 February 1859. Bishop John Farrell of Hamilton, administrator of the diocese in Pinsoneault's absence, and the laity were under the impression that the bishop had gone to Europe to recruit much needed priests. In April, some people learned the reason for Pinsoneault's absence, and on 10 April 1859, sixteen of London's prominent Catholics signed a memorial to Pope Pius IX, in which they argued for the retention of London as the episcopal city.[10] Tensions were high on the occasion of the bishop's return to St. Peter's. The *Toronto Leader* joined the fracas, but Pinsoneault, always persuasive in moments of crisis, acquitted himself well from the pulpit. London's Catholics quickly rushed to Pinsoneault's defence. They may have regretted his decision to move to Sandwich, but they supported his right to make that decision. In a series of resolutions meant for publication they denounced the interference of the *Leader*.

Bishop Pinsoneault's Sandwich episcopate

lasted from 1859 to 1866, and was a disaster. His move to Sandwich entailed a change much lamented by Assumption's parishioners, namely, the departure of the Jesuits on 20 December 1859. Father Pierre Point and his confreres had been at the parish since 1843. They had finished the construction of the fourth Assumption church, in 1845, and conducted first-rate pastoral work in Essex, Kent and Lambton counties. The Jesuits built five other churches, organized more than a dozen schools and preached numerous missions to the faithful. They had opened Assumption College on 10 February 1857, but gave control of the college to the diocese that year. Under the leadership of Father Joseph Malbos, CSB, the first Basilian president of Assumption, the college was incorporated by an Act of Parliament, 16 August 1858, a status that provided stability, when the Benedictines, Jesuits, and diocesan clergy, in turn, directed the college. The Catholics of Chatham were fortunate that the Jesuits remained until 1874, building them a church and inviting the Ursuline Sisters.

Administrative Problems

Bishop Pinsoneault thought that he could govern his infant and impoverished diocese in the style of a seigneur, but he seemed never to have understood that this was not possible in Southwestern Ontario in the 1860s. Nothing else could explain his decision to spend the princely sum of $30,000 on an episcopal palace next to Assumption church, which was now the cathedral. Opened in 1865 and designed to look like a French chateau, local wags dubbed it "Pinsoneault's Folly."

The roof leaked so badly that umbrellas were necessary in the rooms when it rained. It was so large, rambling and poorly-built that heating it was impossible. The episcopal household in wintertime frequently awoke to find the water frozen solidly in the bedside pitchers.[11]

Slipshod construction was hardly the bishop's fault, but the misplaced desire to have a palace in the hinterland belonged solely to him. To do justice to the palace's intended setting, Pinsoneault removed the parish cemetery to its present location near the Ambassador Bridge. This upset those parishioners who had to disinter and rebury their relatives. As well, he planted several rows of chestnut trees to resemble a cloister and erected three gated archways

from the road to the palace. The palace was demolished in 1896. Only the chestnut trees remain.

The episcopal barge was another fiasco that, along with the palace and other financial blunders, helped to create a mountain of debt for the diocese.[12] The idea of visiting the diocese by boat was a good one because travel on the River Thames was common at the time. Pinsoneault spent $1,500 on a barge fitted with a chapel and an altar. But no sooner was it launched than it sank. Again, its fate was not Pinsoneault's doing, but if he had not moved to Sandwich, he might never have insisted on having a barge to visit his diocese. In any event, having ensconced himself at Sandwich, Pinsoneault had effectively removed himself from the fastest growing constellation of Catholics in the diocese. In 1860, Essex County may have boasted the largest single-county concentration of Catholics, 10,420, but Middlesex, Huron and Perth counties and the city of London combined had more than twice that number.[13]

Problems with his mail, especially that from Rome, added a comical element to Pinsoneault's mounting frustrations. Authorities in Rome were inclined to address their correspondence to Sandwich, Kent, in England, or worse, to the Sandwich (Hawaiian) Islands. Pinsoneault spilled a lot of ink trying to educate Roman bureaucrats on the existence of Sandwich, Canada West.

Pinsoneault's attitudes to raising money added to the tension between him and the faithful. At this time, most Catholics would have found the prospect of financially supporting a resident priest and maintaining a church and a rectory, no matter how humble, a burdensome sacrifice for their families. Poverty and a shortage of money were endemic, facts that the bishop did not come to fully appreciate during his tenure. He insisted that the people fulfill his directives on pastoral dues for the support of priests and pew rents for the maintenance of the churches and rectories. Pastoral dues were four dollars per year for each head of household and for single persons who supported themselves. Pews were auctioned off to the highest bidder once a year. Those without pews had to stand. Other sources of revenue were the voluntary copper collections at Sunday Mass, the twice-yearly collections for the episcopal fund that went directly to the bishop and the ecclesiastical fund for the education of priests.

Bishop Pinsoneault had every right and duty

to regulate pastoral dues and pew rents, but his expectations concerning the ability and willingness of the people to comply with the regulations were so unbending that the system fomented a tremendous amount of friction between priests and people.[14] Bishop Pinsoneault's inability to deal with finances in a sound and reasonable fashion, and to live within the means of the people that he had come to serve, was bound to destabilize his administration and lead to complaints.

Poor Judgment with People

An even greater problem was Pinsoneault's poor judgment in his treatment of women religious, in recruiting outside clergy and in handling dissident priests.[15] Bishop Pinsoneault's treatment of the Loretto Sisters was only the first episode in a pattern of behaving as if women religious were pawns. Of the three communities that had predated Pinsoneault, only one survived his administration: the Sisters of the Sacred Heart. They persevered until 1913. The Loretto Sisters were gone in June 1856, and the Sisters of St. Joseph left in 1857 and would not return until 1868. Of the five communities Pinsoneault invited into his diocese, only two remain: the Order of St. Ursula (known now as Ursuline Sisters of the Chatham Union or Ursulines) and the Sisters of the Holy Names of Jesus and Mary (Holy Names). The Ursulines arrived in Chatham in 1860 and the Holy Names settled in Windsor in 1864. The Sisters of Charity of Providence, who had replaced the Loretto Sisters in London, lasted until 1858. The Grey Nuns, who took over from the Sisters of the Sacred Heart in Sandwich, returned to their home base in Montréal in 1861. That was not all. Alarmed by Pinsoneault's tendency to meddle, the Sisters of Mercy from Pittsburgh reneged on their promise to come to the diocese in September 1861. All six women religious communities that served under Bishop Pinsoneault came from Québec and were primarily French speaking.

While Pinsoneault did invite and ordain many excellent priests to work in the diocese, he also made some very poor choices. The strong priests were stable in their personal lives, utterly loyal to their priestly vows, built churches, rectories and schools, and flourished in their vocations under Pinsoneault's successor, Bishop John Walsh. They were Paul Andrieux, Joseph Bayard, Bartholomew Boubat, Jean-Marie Bruyère, Joseph Gerard, Eugène L.M. Jahan, Edmund Burke Kilroy, Pierre-Dominic Laurent, François Marseille, James Murphy, Antoine-Phileas Villeneuve, James Theodore Wagner and Louis Auguste Wassereau. Pinsoneault also met the spiritual needs of Scottish, Irish and German immigrants by finding missionaries who could speak Gaelic and German to serve them. He also had the good sense to leave the Jesuits alone in Chatham and to invite the American Dominicans to St. Peter's in London, in 1861, where they completed St. Peter's with a spire and side galleries. Under Dominican stewardship, the parish evolved into a model of Catholic devotional life.

Bishop Pinsoneault, however, often acted out of desperation in trying to fill positions for steadily expanding diocesan populations. He was not alone among his North American episcopal contemporaries in experiencing a drastic shortage of priests and in choosing morally weak or just plain eccentric priests, wanderers and misfits who caused more grief than good. But Pinsoneault seems to have been singularly inept. Of the twenty-four priests whom he recruited, eighteen were suspended or expelled. Of the fourteen priests that he ordained, four left the diocese before he did in 1866. Only two of Pinsoneault's priests were natives of the diocese. They were James V. McLaughlin of London, who died a year after his ordination, and James Scanlon of Stratford, who was such an incompetent administrator that he was never given a permanent post after 1867.

The historical record has a great deal to say about the moral failings of Louis Bissey, Peter J. Canney, Clement Frachon, Michael Prendergast Toussaint Rouisse and Joseph Zoegel, an individual who might never have been ordained.[16] Louis Griffa, pastor of Sacred Heart parish in Ingersoll and then of Irishtown (St. Columban),was a well-meaning priest who never shirked his duties and did his best to rectify the numerous shortcomings of his predecessors in both parishes. But circumstances, stiff-necked parishioners and his own ineptitude defeated his every good intention. In 1865, just four years after he had been accepted into the diocese of London, he left, exhausted and disheartened.[17]

The greatest thorn in Pinsoneault's side was Jean Daudet, the pastor of St. John the Baptist parish in Amherstburg. A veteran from the years when London was a part of the diocese of Toronto, Daudet was a more determined opponent than Dean Kirwan, and he had the support of three powerful allies: Bishop Bourget of Montréal, Bishop John Joseph Lynch of Toronto and Bishop Peter Paul Lefevere of Detroit. All three would help to secure Pinsoneault's resignation.

Bishop Pinsoneault charged Daudet with a host of offences. He failed to supply the bishop with annual reports on his parish; he did not read his breviary and had spent months without confession; he did not say weekday Mass and was often intoxicated; and he had accused the bishop of the "illegal transfer of funds and of scandal mongering," which was an attack on Pinsoneault's integrity.[18] Daudet contested all but the first charge. In September 1862, Pinsoneault banished him from the diocese, a drastic measure. In response, 240 parishioners signed a petition in support of Daudet, and, in reaction to Pinsoneault's denunciation of Daudet from the parish pulpit, a group of them stormed the rectory.

Daudet fought back, and surprising as it may sound, he won. He appealed to Bishop Baillargeon, who forwarded his case to Rome for adjudication. Rome appointed Baillargeon as a one-man commission of the Holy See to investigate the charges and counter-charges. Pinsoneault submitted a lengthy defence, to no avail.[19] Baillargeon delivered his verdict in favour of Daudet on 28 October 1863. Pinsoneault now launched an appeal to Rome, and Pope Pius IX accepted his suggestion that a committee of three bishops judge the matter and make a final decision. Bishop Bourget, Bishop Guigues and Bishop Horan heard evidence in Kingston, from 14 to 16 July 1864, and judged that the charges against Daudet were groundless. He was reinstated but warned to submit to Pinsoneault, who for his part accepted the ruling and then transferred Daudet, on 2 November 1864, to Immaculate Conception parish in Pain Court. Pinsoneault ordered the transfer against the advice of Bishop Baillargeon, who thought that Daudet should be left where the delegates of the Holy See had placed him.[20] That started another round of appeals to Rome, but Daudet had become a nuisance. In February 1865 Rome ordered him to obey his bishop or leave the diocese. He chose to leave, moving to the diocese of Cleveland, where he served as a faithful priest until his death on 2 February 1892.

This demoralizing affair, amplified by a rising chorus of complaints from priests, heads of religious congregations, members of the laity and other bishops prompted Bishop Baillargeon to initiate an investigation into Pinsoneault's administration, with a letter to Cardinal Barnabo in October 1864. On a visit to the Vatican in the winter of 1864-65, Bishop Bourget was given the delicate task of requesting Pinsoneault's resignation. Inexplicably, he waited more than a year. In a letter of 17 August 1866, he demanded Pinsoneault's resignation and warned him of the terrible consequences of a canonical investigation if he refused. Surprised and hurt by the accusations, Pinsoneault was inclined not to comply, but obedience to the pope's wishes overcame his initial reluctance.

Resignation

Relief was followed by humiliation and bitterness. Pinsoneault submitted his resignation on 5 September 1866. Rome's acceptance of it was published in a circular to the diocesan clergy on 18 December 1866. His official reasons for his resignation were declining health, increasing deafness and the need for a younger man to head the diocese. The most compelling reason, however, was that Pinsoneault had forfeited the confidence of his fellow bishops, of a majority of his priests, including those most loyal to him, and of a growing number of lay people. He met his priests in Sandwich for a final farewell, on 15 January 1867, and he left Windsor by train for Albany, New York, a week later. At Albany, Pinsoneault lived with Bishop John J. Conroy until 1870, when he returned to the diocese of Montréal, where he assisted Bishop Bourget in confirmations and liturgical functions that required the presence of a bishop. He also spent a good deal of his retirement writing. He defended the doctrine of papal infallibility, in light of the First Vatican Council, and attacked liberalism.

Pierre-Adolphe Pinsoneault died on 30 January 1883. By then, the priests and people of the diocese of London had largely forgotten him. Pinsoneault himself may have realized that he was the wrong person for London early in his days as bishop of London. In a letter of 17 November 1857, to his friend the Abbé Petigny of Amiens, France, he confided that it might have been better for his own happiness and for the good of the Church if he had remained a canon of the cathedral in Montréal.[21] He expressed similar doubts to Bishop Bourget in 1859, when he asked for a coadjutor and a vicar general, and to Bishop Farrell in 1862.[22]

What the new diocese of London had needed in 1856 was "a man of great prudence and executive ability, full of zeal, full of energy, self-sacrificing and fearless; one whose personality would command the respect of all classes."[23] It would take an entirely different bishop to live up to this ideal.

Endnotes for Chapter 1 – Bishop Pinsoneault

[1] DLA, Pierre-Adolphe Pinsoneault Papers (hereafter PAP Papers), Box 1, Charbonnel to Bruyère, 12 August 1866.

[2] John K.A. Farrell (O'Farrell), *The History of the Roman Catholic Church in London, Ontario 1826–1931* (M.A. thesis, University of Western Ontario, 1949), 38–39.

[3] Orlo Miller, "The Fat Years and the Lean: London (Canada) in Boom and Depression, 1851–61," *Ontario History* 53 (no. 2) 1961: 73-80.

[4] DLA, PAP Papers, Box 1, Pinsoneault to Farrell, 21 July 1862; J.B.A. Allaire, *Dictionnaire biographique du clergé canadienne-français* (Montreal: 1910), 1: 310.

[5] Farrell, 38.

[6] John R. McMahon, *The Episcopate of Pierre-Adolphe Pinsoneault: First Bishop of London, Upper Canada, 1856-1866* (M.A. thesis, University of Western Ontario, 1982), 47–48.

[7] Ibid., 49–50.

[8] Ibid., 53–57.

[9] Ibid., 56–63.

[10] Ibid., 63–65.

[11] Farrell, 37.

[12] John P. Comiskey, *John Walsh: Second Bishop of London in Ontario 1867-1889* (Ph.D. diss., Pontifical Gregorian University, 1999), 42.

[13] McMahon, 273.

[14] Ibid., 146–53.

[15] Ibid., 127–30.

[16] Ibid., Chapters 4 and 5.

[17] Ibid., 166–73.

[18] Robert Choquette, "Pinsoneault, Pierre-Adolphe," *DCB* (Toronto: 1982), 11: 694.

[19] DLA, PAP Papers, Box 1, Letter Book 5, Pinsoneault to Baillargeon, 12 July 1863.

[20] Ibid., PAP Papers, Box 1, Baillargeon to Pinsoneault, 31 October 1864.

[21] Ibid., PAP Papers, Box 1, Letter Book 3, Pinsoneault to Petigny, 17 November 1857.

[22] Ibid., PAP Papers, Box 1, Pinsoneault to Bourget, 8 September 1859.

[23] Ralph Hubert Dignan, "History of the Diocese of London" (unpublished manuscript, ca. 1919–1932), 103.

2. John Walsh (1867-1889)

John Walsh succeeded Bishop Pinsoneault, and is considered the diocese's true founder. During his twenty-two years in London, Bishop Walsh built a firm foundation for the faith in the diocese. He led a diocese stunted in growth, burdened by debt and mired in controversy, to recovery and consolidation, parish by parish, mission by mission. He succeeded in having the See transferred back to London. He overhauled the administration of the diocese, regularized the liturgical and devotional life of the parishes, and developed and maintained fruitful relations with the clergy and the laity. He encouraged his priests and people to work in unity of faith and purpose and to build the spiritual and material resources of the diocese, so that they could pass on the Catholic faith to future generations.

When he became archbishop of Toronto, in 1889, he left a viable foundation on which the diocese would flourish. Walsh's legacy to the Catholics of the diocese was a direction of purpose and a sense of accomplishment in the spiritual and temporal well-being of the Church, as defined by its mission to bring the Gospel to all peoples.

The key to Bishop Walsh's success as bishop of London was his personality, gifts and experience. By all accounts, he was an affable and social person. He was described as "genial and sympathetic," a prelate who had a "universal interest in people and genuine charm."[1] One author said he possessed a "conciliatory nature and talent for finding compromise."[2] Another described him as having "great force and decision of character," a vital component in effective leadership.[3]

Walsh's gifts were extraordinary. He was a preacher and public lecturer of merit and renown, who commanded large and attentive audiences, oftentimes including Protestants. He read widely in theology, history and contemporary literature and was a prolific writer, who mastered a style that was both attractive in its presentation and authoritative in its tone and knowledge. He produced a steady stream of material that was published in the *Catholic Record*, Catholic journals in Toronto and Montréal and quite often the secular press, such as the London and Sarnia papers.

He was a pastoral bishop whose primary interest was the spiritual well-being of his people and showed a tendency to treat his nine-county diocese as one big parish. As an administrator he was known for his prudent and timely decisions.

A priest for thirteen years in the diocese of Toronto, he brought experience as a pastor in both rural and urban settings to his position as bishop. In his administrative role as a vicar general for Bishop Lynch, he was known for his prudent and timely decisions and his ability to establish peace and harmony among his sometimes unruly parishioners, and between Catholic and Protestant citizens.

Early Years and Priesthood

John Walsh was born on 23 May 1830, in Mooncoin, County Kilkenney, Ireland, one of seven children of James Walsh and Ellen McDonald. Walsh was educated at the Chapel Street School in Mooncoin, Carrick Monastery in Carrick (science and classics) and St. John's College in Waterford (philosophy and theology), where he was a student for the diocese of Ossory. In April 1852, Walsh left Ireland in the company of John F. Synnott of Mooncoin and James Hobin of Kilkenny. All three had decided to join the missions in Canada, and Bishop Charbonnel of Toronto accepted them into his diocese. Walsh completed his theological studies at the Séminaire de Saint-Sulpice in Montréal and was ordained on 1 November 1854, when he was twenty-four years old.

Walsh spent the rest of his life in Ontario and became just as Canadian as he was Irish, although he was thoroughly Irish in two important respects, his politics and his spirituality. Born the year following Catholic Emancipation, he was an Irish nationalist, an admirer of Daniel O'Connell, an Irish Catholic politician who campaigned for Catholic Emancipation and Repeal of the Union between Ireland and Great Britain. Walsh fervently supported Home Rule for Ireland. He did not, however, support Fenianism, the revolutionary Irish movement in North America that sought to secure Irish independence. Walsh had no time for the tradition in Irish politics of employing physical force. Every citizen had to respect duly constituted authority. In Canada, Walsh discreetly supported the Conservative Party of Sir John A. Macdonald, and the two became friends. He never forgot that he was essentially a missionary in the field of Ontario Catholicism and that he and his fellow clergy owed much to their predecessors for any success that they had achieved. On the twenty-fifth anniversary of his ordination to the priesthood, in November 1879, Bishop Walsh reminded his priests about those who had gone before them and the freedom the Church enjoyed in Canada:

They bore the burden of the day and the heat; they sowed in tears that we might reap in joy; "sowing they went and wept, casting their seeds, but we, coming, with joyfulness carry the sheaves" (*Psalm* 125, 6). It is for us to take up the great work they began, and as far as in us lies to carry it to a successful issue. Canada is a free and happy country; no penal law has ever soiled the virgin pages of its statute book; no state trammels hamper the action and clog the activity of the church.[4]

In religious temperament and the outward practice of his Catholic faith, Walsh was a product of the Irish devotional revolution, a movement with strong ties to the papacy of Pius IX that is referred to as ultramontane, "over the mountains." Walsh joined the priesthood "when Irish Catholicism was undergoing a tremendous spiritual transformation at the hands of an ambitious hierarchy. It was an age of great piety, self-discipline, church-building, and Catholic chauvinism."[5] As bishop of London, Walsh turned to the Irish devotional revolution to transform and strengthen the faithful of his own diocese, but he did so within the context of his adopted country, Canada.

Following a brief period of roving assignments, Father John Walsh became pastor of the Brock Mission on Lake Simcoe, beginning in December 1854. From his residence at St. Gregory the Great in Oshawa, he ministered to Catholics scattered throughout nine townships in Ontario and York counties. The work was exhausting but fulfilling and helped him understand the state of religious practice among Catholics who were isolated from each other and their priests. Father Walsh built St. Anthony the Hermit church, in what is now the village of Virginia, near Beaverton.

While at the mission, Walsh encouraged the religious vocation of Catherine Ann Campbell of Thorah Township. She became a Sister of St. Joseph, taking the name Sister Ignatia, and was one of five Sisters who came to London in 1868, at the request of Walsh. As Mother Ignatia, she would lead her community in London for more than thirty years.[6]

The priest used his solitary evenings to great advantage, studying sacred scripture and the Fathers of the Church and writing for the *Toronto Mirror* under the pseudonym "Ossory." Walsh who had nearly died in the cholera epidemic of 1854 would suffer the effects of that for the remainder of his life. Poor health forced him to move to Toronto in September 1856 and prevented him from attending the First Vatican Council (1869-70).

In the city, Father Walsh had appointments in three parishes. In April 1857, he was pastor at St. Mary's on the west side and chaplain to the Loretto Sisters' convent on Bond Street. In June 1858, he succeeded the popular Father Thomas Fitzhenry at St. Paul's and had to work hard to win the confidence of the parishioners.[7] From St. Paul's, he went to St. Michael's cathedral in March 1860, becoming rector when he was not yet thirty years of age. This assignment came courtesy of Bishop Lynch, then the coadjutor to Bishop Charbonnel and, in April 1860, bishop of Toronto in his own right.

Almost immediately, Walsh was involved in a potentially explosive social situation. Local members of the Orange Order, a Protestant Irish group that supported Protestant rule in Ireland, were insisting that during his upcoming visit to Toronto, the Prince of Wales (the future Edward VII) should walk under a series of Orange arches. Walsh appealed to Catholics not to confront the Orangemen. He asked moderate Protestants to ignore the Orange element, and he convinced Toronto's Catholic leaders to write a memorial to the Prince politely asking him to avoid the arches. John Elmsley, the most prominent Catholic of his day, delivered the Memorial to the Prince's traveling secretary, the Duke of Newcastle, who was Catholic. The pleas worked. All but one of the arches were dismantled, a brilliant victory for Walsh's diplomacy in an overwhelmingly Protestant city.

Walsh's reward for convincing the Catholic camp to stay onside with the Church hierarchy was his appointment as vicar general in the diocese of Toronto, in April 1862, and his return as pastor to St. Mary's in September of that year. During his last five years in Toronto, Walsh honed his skills as an eloquent preacher and learned public speaker, impressing "the multitudes by the strength of his convictions, especially about the pre-eminent place of the church in salvation history, and by the clarity and concision of his delivery. He was a superb rhetorician in the classical sense and no less enthusiastic about his strictly secular speeches."[8] Bishop Lynch appointed Walsh his theologian for the Third Provincial Council in Québec, in May 1863, and chose him to deliver his *ad limina* report to Pius IX, in 1864. This provided Walsh an opportunity to tour the Continent and visit Ireland; he would return to Ireland in 1876 and 1882.

Second Bishop of London

On 4 June 1867, the year of Canadian Confederation, Rome issued a brief appointing John Walsh as the Bishop of Sandwich (London). His name had appeared first on the *terna* of 18 January 1867. The other two names were John O'Brien and Rémi Ouellet. (Interestingly, Pinsoneault had tried to influence the terna, before he had left Sandwich, by submitting his own choices.) Walsh served as bishop in this diocese from

1867 to 1888 – first as bishop of Sandwich (1867-1869) then as bishop of London (1869 - 1888).

Bishop Walsh was consecrated on 10 November 1867 at St. Michael's Cathedral, in front of nine bishops, fifty priests and a throng of Toronto's Catholics, who came to salute a popular priest. Archbishop Baillargeon of Québec was the principal consecrator, with Bishop Bourget of Montréal and Bishop Lynch of Toronto assisting him and Father Patrick Dowd of Montréal preaching.

During his years in the diocese of London, Walsh presided over a remarkable increase in the number of churches, parishes, priests and religious communities that taken together transformed the diocese and remains unsurpassed. Working in his favour was the fortuitous rise in the number of Catholics in the diocese. The bishop came to London at a time of great growth in the Catholic population, from little more than 44,000 in 1861 to almost 67,500 in 1889 (an increase of fifty-two percent in twenty-eight years), during the early stages of the modernization of Southwestern Ontario's mainly rural society. He also came to a diocese that was in debt and disarray. It lacked sound administrative structures, and parish life needed to be renewed and regularized.

On his way to Sandwich, Bishop Walsh stopped in London, where he was met at the train station by a large concourse of the clergy and laity and escorted to St. Peter's church. The clergy welcomed him with an official address, followed by one from Mayor Frank Smith, on behalf of the laity. It was a splendid beginning. The next day, 14 November, Walsh was installed in the cathedral in Sandwich, in a ceremony witnessed by Bishop Horan of Kingston and Bishop Farrell of Hamilton, the senior clergy and leading members of local laity.

Stabilizing the Diocese

In order to begin a new era for the diocese, Bishop Walsh moved quickly to rectify Bishop Pinsoneault's mistake of making Sandwich the seat of the diocese. Three weeks before his consecration, Walsh had written to the Dominicans of the Province of St. Joseph, telling them that the need to liquidate the debt and to place the administration of the diocese in a central location meant that the Dominicans would have to leave St. Peter's in London.[9] (He offered them the opportunity to take another parish and was genuinely disappointed that they could not.) At the same time, Walsh lobbied the bishops to support the move. Although Bishop Lynch thought that Walsh should wait a year, since displacing the Dominicans would mean the loss of three priests,[10] Archbishop Baillargeon agreed with Walsh and convinced the Ontario bishops to support him. Baillargeon began the process with a letter to Propaganda Fide in Rome, on 14 November 1867, the day of Walsh's installation.

Bishop Walsh moved to London in January 1868, but Propaganda Fide did not issue its decree approving of the transfer until 15 November 1869, after several lengthy appeals from Walsh. Oddly, Walsh had not asked for a change in the diocese's name, but Rome changed it back to the diocese of London. In his first Pastoral Letter, dated 11 November 1867, Bishop Walsh exhorted the people to attend Mass, to receive the sacraments worthily and frequently, and to devote themselves to the Blessed Virgin Mary. He promised to visit every parish and mission, starting in the winter of 1868, and he confirmed the appointment of Jean-Marie Bruyère as vicar general of the diocese.

The promise of a diocesan visitation and Bruyère's appointment were related. Staring at Walsh was a debt of nearly $35,000, principal and interest, plus a number of private loans that Pinsoneault had contracted but not repaid. He also faced the prospect of paying Pinsoneault a pension. Pinsoneault thought that he should receive $1,200 to $1,500 per year. Bruyère thought the diocese could only afford $250 but said it would increase the pension to $400 when finances improved. Walsh supported Bruyère but, after considerable wrangling with Rome, he was forced to pay Pinsoneault an annual pension of $600.

The visitation allowed Walsh to show himself to the people and to speak about the debt, which was no secret in the diocese. Walsh had to address the financial problem in an honest and hopeful manner, using all his powers of persuasion, so the faithful would agree that until the debt was relieved it would be impossible to begin new churches or rectories and very difficult to maintain the existing ones. The plan was to raise money by means of a voluntary five-year pledge from each family. To help him, Walsh enlisted Father William Flannery, his personal secretary, as his official fundraiser. Father Flannery, who had a proven track record in raising money for

church projects, did not disappoint Walsh.[11]

Walsh also instructed Bruyère to continue with the economies he had instituted when he was administrator of the diocese in the absence of a bishop. Walsh's 1876 *ad limina* report to the diocese contains proof of his success in eliminating the debt, and renewing parish life. During the first ten years of his episcopacy, priests and people had built 28 churches, 17 rectories and a debt-free episcopal palace and enlarged five churches. The diocese also had three new convents, an orphanage at Mount Hope and a new wing at Assumption College, which the Basilian Fathers added. Bishop Walsh paid special tribute to the laity: "If they had not husbanded their resources, and instead of expending them on their families, had not put them apart for the service of God's Church, these splendid results would never have been achieved."[12]

Developing the Diocese

The generosity of the laity continued and the diocese continued to grow under the leadership of Bishop Walsh and his growing number of priests. The bishop persuaded his priests and people to accomplish big and enduring things for the Church, in particular to build Catholic houses of worship worthy of the Eucharist. One thinks of St. Peter's cathedral, St. Patrick's in Kinkora and St. Joseph's in Chatham, which were designed by the architect Joseph Connolly. One is also reminded of Bishop's Walsh's public exhortation to his priests to imitate the Eucharist which they held in their hands at Mass.[13]

From 1867 to 1885, the year the cathedral opened, the diocese and its thirty-seven parishes spent in excess of $950,000 for church and educational work. That figure included the original debt, monies for ecclesiastical education, the pension to Bishop Pinsoneault and the new cathedral. This grand sum was a marvellous tribute to the self-sacrifice of the Catholic laity. (It should be noted that many Protestants donated money to the building of St. Peter's cathedral and Holy Angels church in St. Thomas, and other churches throughout the diocese.) As well as opening the present St. Peter's cathedral, Bishop Walsh opened fifty other new churches, making an impressive Catholic contribution to the Ontario-wide boom in church construction. He established 22 new parishes; he ordained 49 priests and incardinated others, and he welcomed five religious communities into the diocese.

The religious communities Bishop Walsh invited were the Basilians (Sandwich and Amherstburg), the Franciscans (Chatham), the Sisters of St. Joseph (London, Goderich and St. Thomas), the Loretto Sisters (Stratford) and the Religious Hospitallers of St. Joseph (Windsor). The bishop gave each its own sphere of work and influence, and wisely did nothing to alienate those communities already in the diocese — the Sisters of the Sacred Heart, the Sisters of the Holy Names of Jesus and Mary, the Ursulines, the Dominicans and the Jesuits. Only two communities left — the Dominicans from St. Peter's and the Jesuits from Chatham in 1874 because of a lack of priests. Four years later, the Jesuits were successfully replaced by the Franciscans.

To a certain degree, a bishop is only as good as his priests. Walsh would have accomplished very little with the Catholic laity if he had not cultivated a positive and respectful working relationship with his priests, those already in the diocese when he came, those he ordained to the priesthood and those from outside the diocese who answered his invitation. The latter included priests from Québec to staff the French-Canadian parishes in Essex and Kent counties, Irish-born priests to take charge of Irish parishes and even a German-speaking priest for Zurich and a Scots-Gaelic-speaking priest for West Williams. Walsh's successors showed similar concern for immigrants who did not speak English. Walsh openly supported the innovative pastoral work of Dean James T. Wagner, at St. Alphonsus parish, with black Catholics in Windsor. To these people, who were descendants of escaped slaves, Wagner offered basic education, health care, and a community centre. Providing care for marginalized communities has been a constant throughout the history of the diocese.

Walsh supported the priests themselves by founding the St. John the Evangelist Society, in June 1872, to provide pensions for infirm and retired priests of the diocese. He handed the management of its assets, which were collected annually from each parish, to an executive of eight senior clergy who met once a year and reported to the bishop. The Society was incorporated under provincial law in July 1876 and remains in operation to this day.

The bishop began the needed regularization of parish life by also establishing an annual clergy retreat, at which time pastors were required to give an account of their work. The priests had to settle their cathedraticum and dispensation accounts with the diocese. They also had to provide written answers to questions concerning the number of baptisms, deaths, marriages, mixed marriages, families, apostates, converts, and those who failed to make their Easter Duty. They reported on the number of separate schools, Sunday schools, pious confraternities or sodalities (Happy Death Society, Rosary Society, Sodality of the Scapular, Congregation of the Blessed Virgin, Altar Society, St. Vincent de Paul Society, Christian Doctrine Association, Propagation of the Faith). Pastors were also asked to comment on Advent and Lenten devotions, the prevalence of drunkenness in their parishes and the last time that confirmation took place.

Many exemplary priests laboured under Walsh, and by their fidelity, longevity and loyalty to their bishop and to their parishioners, each was able to build a robust parochial life, which is the lifeblood of any diocese. The thirteen priests listed in the chapter on Bishop Pinsoneault carried on their good works under Bishop Walsh. The exemplary priests from the Walsh era were Michael J. Brady, Philip J. Brennan, John Connolly, Joseph G.E. Courtois, William Flannery, James P. Molphy, James G. Mugan, Peter McCabe, Charles E. McGee, Michael McGrath, Albert J. McKeon, Donald A. McRae, Thomas Noonan, John O'Connor, John O'Neill, John Ronan, Michael J. Tiernan, Hubert G. Traher, Bernard J. Watters, and Thomas West.

Walsh also had his share of troublesome priests. Unlike Pinsoneault, however, Walsh avoided quarrelling in public with wayward or rebellious clergy. The two main problems were intemperance and mismanagement of parish funds.[14] By March 1868, when he had been bishop for less than half a year, he suspended six priests for alcohol abuse. Father John F. Coffey was one of his more embarrassing headaches. A gifted man but an alcoholic, Coffey became a wandering priest, the scourge of the North American Church in the nineteenth century. After being ordained by Walsh on 19 December 1875, he lived in Ottawa and Almonte in the Ottawa Valley. Then Coffey became editor of *Catholic Record*, which was established in 1878, and later wrote *The City and Diocese of London*, the first history of the diocese. After leaving the diocese in 1887, he was a priest in Yonkers, New York, and then in Rondout, New York, and Dallas, Texas. He ended in Toronto, where he became a Baptist and apparently married. In 1889, he libelled Bishop Walsh in an article published in the *Toronto Mail*.

In one case, a mistaken attempt by an otherwise good priest to end a Catholic-versus-Catholic feud came close to endangering Walsh's highly successful episcopacy. The unwitting architect of this near-disaster was Father John Connolly of St. Patrick's church in Biddulph Township. A native of Sligo, Ireland, Connolly came to Canada when he was forty and was ordained when he was forty-two. He was a good priest but unaccountably naïve when it came to dealing with local Irish faction fighting. Walsh thought that only an Irish priest could bring to an end the feuding in this predominantly rural, Irish parish, which revolved around James Donnelly and his family.

One of Father Connolly's first acts as parish priest was to strike a vigilance committee and have its members sign a pledge to help control crime in the parish. Ninety-four men signed. The Donnellys did not. On 4 February 1880, an offshoot of the vigilance committee killed five members of the Donnelly family. Connolly was implicated because he had founded the vigilance committee and because he had had his own well-known differences with the Donnellys. Moreover, he did not help himself by writing a letter to the Québec press in which he stated that the purpose of the committee "was to ask my people to sign a pledge to one another, that if anything stolen should be left on their premises, that they should endeavour to find out the owner, and if possible the thief, so that he might be prosecuted according to the law."[15]

Six men were charged with murder. One was acquitted after two trials, in January 1881, and the remaining five were never brought to trial, at the request of the prosecution. At a secret meeting held in his episcopal palace, on 14 May 1881, Walsh convinced Adam Crooks, minister of education and acting premier of the province, and Charles Hutchinson, crown attorney for Middlesex County, not to proceed against Connolly. All three men were aware that a trial of a Catholic priest might never reach a verdict and, in that case, would give an excuse to the Orange Lodges in Ontario and

Quebec to stage another no-popery campaign against Catholics. Closer to home, Walsh feared that the cordial relations then existing between Catholics and Protestants in London would crumble. Mercifully, the crisis ended there. Father Connolly remained pastor of St. Patrick's until 1895, and for the last fourteen years of his life, he was pastor of Sacred Heart parish in Ingersoll, dying on 24 September 1909.

Strengthening Devotional Life

Bishop Walsh reinvigorated and sustained the devotional life of the diocese, which was central to his theology of evangelization. His priests led a variety of devotional exercises to develop the piety of the people. The *Catholic Record* reported on parish missions conducted by the Redemptorists and the Holy Cross Fathers of Notre Dame, Indiana, parish retreats, St. Patrick's Day for the Irish and St. Jean-Baptiste Day for the French, Forty Hours devotions, Holy Week services and the religious exercises of sodalities and pious associations. The newspaper gave extensive coverage to the temperance sermons of Father Michael Stafford of Lindsay, Ontario, the Jubilee celebrations in 1879, in honour of the election of Pope Leo XIII, and the well-attended public discourses of Father Joseph Henning on the Sacred Heart of Jesus, Father James Molphy on the Eucharist and Father William O'Mahoney on St. Joseph, the patron saint of Canada, Catholic education and the Christian family.

A masterful teacher, Bishop Walsh, used preaching and writing to great effect in his efforts to instruct Catholics in the faith. The *Catholic Record* (and local newspapers), contained stories on Bishop Walsh preaching at cornerstone ceremonies, blessing new churches, consecrating altars and opening new separate schools. He went everywhere in the diocese, no mission was too small or too isolated and his energy and enthusiasm never flagged. Walsh's popularity as a preacher was such that 5,000 people came to hear him, on 17 October 1886, at the blessing and laying of the cornerstone of the new St. Joseph's church in Chatham. He often delivered sermons on grand and solemn occasions outside the diocese, in Guelph, Toronto, Peterborough, Ottawa, Montreal, and even Charlottetown, Prince Edward Island.

The bishop also conducted county-by-county

confirmation tours. By 1876, Bishop Walsh had confirmed 10,000 children and adults, and, by 1889, when he left London, that number would have doubled. At every confirmation (and sometimes at First Holy Communions), he preached with sincerity, vigour and authority, leaving a profound impression of his deep attachment to the Catholic faith.

As well as having a well-earned reputation as a preacher, Walsh was a popular lecturer. He began his role as a public speaker in earnest in Toronto and continued it no less enthusiastically in London. His lectures always drew large crowds and were covered extensively in the press. He spoke on a range of topics, as four of his lecture titles demonstrate. At St. Mary's church in London, in May 1876, he lectured on "The Providential Preparation of the World for the Coming of the Redeemer."[16] At St. Peter's cathedral, in November 1879, his topic was "The Catholic Church and Divorce." A twenty-five-cent admission was collected at the door for the St. Vincent de Paul Society.[17] On 8 October 1882, he spoke in the cathedral on Home Rule for Ireland in a lecture entitled "Ireland and the Irish."[18] He lectured on the strictly secular subject of "The Rome of Augustus Caesar," in London's Grand Opera House to an audience that was a cross-section of London society.[19]

As well as being a strong speaker, Bishop Walsh wrote pastoral letters that were impressive in their number and content to teach the diocese on a range of topics that included devotion to the Sacred Heart of Jesus, loyalty to the pope, the new cathedral and Lent. The letters were published in the diocesan newspaper. One of Walsh's early biographers said, "As compositions these pastorals bear in form the impress of a polished writer; and in matter the riches of a well stored mind. Replete with Sacred Scripture, the holy fathers, the history and practice of the Church, they are pregnant with instruction upon the various subjects treated."[20]

Walsh's most substantial pastorals were the two that he wrote concerning the First Vatican Council, (which opened on 8 December 1869) and papal infallibility. The first was issued on 15 May 1869. Fifty pages in length, it explained *Aeterni Patris*, the papal bull that convoked the council. The second appeared on 2 February 1870 and was part of a larger work, also published in 1870, called *The Council of the Vatican and the Doctrines it Suggests and Illustrates*. The thirty-three page pastoral

argued that the Church was the infallible witness and interpreter of revelation and scripture. It was a living, teaching authority that was not only infallible but also imperishable and unified.[21] Both pastorals, despite their length and scholarly nature, were read from the pulpit in every parish of the diocese.

In 1875, Bishop Walsh published his last and most profound work on the subject of infallibility, in a seventy-five-page book *The Doctrine of Papal Infallibility Stated and Vindicated with an Appendix on Civil Allegiance and Certain Historical Difficulties*. Appendix A was Bishop Walsh's reply to William Ewart Gladstone, the British prime minister, who questioned the civil allegiance of Catholics in view of the definition of papal infallibility in 1870. It was his "most brilliant polemic and his closest brush with purely political controversy."[22]

Bishop Walsh's circular letters to the clergy of the diocese were often published in the *Catholic Record* and thus were matters of public record for the laity. In many of them, Bishop Walsh went out of his way to demonstrate his utter loyalty to the reigning pontiff, be it Pius IX, who ruled from 1846 to 1878, or Leo XIII, who was pope from 1878 to 1903. Walsh met Pius IX twice and Leo XIII once.

One is inclined to conclude that the religious and political events that defined the pontificate of Pius IX also shaped the priesthood and episcopacy of John Walsh and bishops around the world. The Napoleonic Wars and then the liberation movements in Europe led to instability for the Papal States. In 1848, Pius IX fled Rome and the city became a republic for a short time. Then in 1870, Italian troops occupied Rome and the Papal States collapsed. Science was questioning the wisdom of the Church and its teachings. In North America, Catholics had to take their place in a society that was still anti-dogma, anti-supernatural and very much anti-Catholic. To counteract those who questioned Church teaching and even the right of the Church to teach what it believed, the Church took a number of measures. These included the papal definition of the Immaculate Conception of the Blessed Virgin Mary (8 December 1854); the encyclical *Quanta cura* and its "Syllabus of Errors" (8 December 1864); the Vatican Council and the constitution *Pastor aeternus* (18 July 1870); the consecration of the Catholic world to the Sacred Heart of Jesus (16 June 1875), and the promotion of the rosary as a public and private prayer (1883). On the subject of the Sacred

Heart, Walsh would publish a book *Thoughts on Devotion to the Sacred Heart and also on The Life and Work of Our Blessed Lord*, in 1884. That was nine years after Pius IX's action and fifteen years before Leo XIII consecrated the world to the Sacred Heart.

Supporting Catholic Schools

Bishop Walsh's vigorous support of Catholic schools set a direction that continued in the diocese. Cardinal Newman once remarked that a church without a school was like a dove without wings. Bishop Walsh would have agreed, but he was also a realist who recognized the limitations of separate schools. Separate schools suffered from unfair laws and regulations, perennial poverty and infighting between elected lay trustees and church authorities over control of separate schools. Other problems included the reluctance of too many Catholic ratepayers to form separate school boards and the push by some Catholics for the secret ballot in separate school trustee elections. From 1876 to 1879, disputes between trustees and the clergy over the Toronto Separate School Board had practical implications for other separate school boards.[23]

In the midst of one controversy after another stood John J. Lynch, the archbishop of Toronto, a major player and an ally of Premier Oliver Mowat and the Liberal Party of Ontario. Although Lynch dominated separate school politics until his death in 1888, Bishop Walsh found room to state his opinions and take independent action, sometimes differing with Lynch and sometimes supporting him. In a pastoral letter of 1872, Walsh made his views known on the need for Catholic parents to support separate schools, for school trustees to work with local pastors, and for both parents and trustees to subordinate their opinions to those of the parish priest and the bishop. Catholic solidarity on school matters was all-important because of the perilous financial state of separate schools under the hostile administration of Egerton Ryerson, provincial superintendent of education for thirty-two years until his retirement in 1876.

During the discussion on what became "An Act to Improve the Common and Grammar Schools of the Province of Ontario" (1871), Bishop Walsh lobbied for amendments that would have established a Catholic Normal School (teachers

college), Catholic high schools and a Catholic deputy-superintendent for separate schools, obliged municipal tax collectors to collect taxes for separate schools and exempted separate school supporters from paying taxes to support Protestant high schools. Walsh was unsuccessful on all counts; but, with the exception of the demand for a Catholic Normal School, his platform for radical change to separate school legislation provided a plausible blueprint for political agitation well into the twentieth century.

In 1876, Bishop Walsh disagreed with Archbishop Lynch on the right of the department of education to inspect separate schools using public school or high school inspectors. He relayed his objections not only to Lynch but also to Christopher F. Fraser, the Catholic minister of public works who acted as an unofficial liaison between the Mowat government and the Catholic hierarchy in Ontario. Not until 1882 would Ontario's separate schools have their own Catholic inspector.

In 1885, with the support of Bishop James J. Carberry of Hamilton and Bishop James V. Cleary of Kingston, Walsh broke with Lynch on the latter's acceptance of government regulations regarding the reading of the "Ross Bible" in public schools. George W. Ross, the minister of education, invited Lynch to vet the scripture readings for public schools, so that no offence would be given to Catholic students in those schools. Lynch welcomed the invitation, without giving the project official sanction, and convinced the government to limit the readings to fifteen minutes at the end of the school day, with no commentary from the teacher. Walsh was not opposed to scripture reading in the public schools, but he told Lynch that Catholic children in those schools should be exempt automatically from any kind of participation in either Protestant prayers or Protestant scripture readings (unless required by a parent or guardian). He also said that Catholic teachers in public schools should not be forced to object to reading from the selections, since refusal to do so would mean the certain loss of employment. He argued that those public schools that had a Catholic majority should have Catholic prayers. Walsh went so far as to remind Lynch that there were fifty-seven Catholic public schools in one county alone (Essex) in the diocese of London. The message was clear: the students in these schools needed Catholic religious instruction and not Protestant scripture readings, even if they had been approved by the archbishop of Toronto.

Walsh, however, supported Lynch in his bitter struggle with the Toronto Separate School Board in 1878, publishing a circular of 2 December 1878 that included a lengthy letter from the archbishop. In the letter Lynch went to great lengths to defend himself from his Catholic critics. Walsh instructed his clergy to read Lynch's letter at all Sunday Masses.

Use of the secret ballot in elections was another highly contentious issue, and both Lynch and Walsh opposed it. A small but determined group of Catholics supported the secret ballot because they were anxious to end what they saw as clerical intimidation at open-air elections. In 1879, 1882 and 1883, Robert Bell, a Protestant member of the Ontario legislature, introduced legislation to allow a secret ballot, and on each occasion, his bill was overwhelmingly defeated. The feeling among legislators from all parties was that if Catholics did not want it, why bother irritating the hierarchy. During the debate on the 1883 bill, William R. Meredith, the leader of the Conservative opposition who sat for London in the legislature, asked Bishop Walsh to list his objections to the bill. Walsh gave four, the last one being the most political: the bill originated from people unsympathetic to Catholics; the majority of the laity did not demand a secret ballot; a secret ballot "would tend to create and foster agitation and dissension" among separate school supporters and allow a small minority among them to dominate school boards at the expense of the clergy; and Conservative support for the bill would be injurious to the party's fortunes in the next provincial election.

Walsh was willing, though, to withdraw his objections to the bill on this condition: "Were Catholics bound by law to support S[eparate] Schools as Protestants are bound to support Public Schools then, I for one, would not have the slightest objection to vote by ballot in the election of our trustees."[24] Meredith, a Protestant, did not rise to the challenge. The secret ballot did not become law until 1894, and Catholics remained unbound in law to support separate schools.

Bishop Walsh's most enduring contribution to the separate schools in his own diocese was to invite the Sisters of St. Joseph to return and assume control of St. Peter's school. They arrived in January 1869. No other religious community in the diocese contributed so many teachers and taught in so many separate schools as did the Sisters of St. Joseph of London. From three Sisters and one school in 1869 to 139 Sisters in 69 schools in 1960, the Sisters were in the classroom as late as 1997.

The bishop also stabilized the operations of Assumption College in Sandwich, which had gone through a series of administrations, when he invited the Basilians to assume control of it, in 1868. Father Denis O'Connor became president in 1870; he later became third bishop of London.

St. Peter's Cathedral

The jewel in the crown of Bishop Walsh's twenty-two-year episcopacy was the building of the current St. Peter's cathedral. Bishop Walsh announced the project at High Mass on Sunday, 15 February 1880. The architect was the renowned Joseph Connolly of Toronto, who modelled the exterior on medieval Gothic cathedrals. The first sod was turned on 10 August 1880; the cornerstone was blessed on 22 May 1881; the dedication took place on 28 June 1885; and the organ was installed in November 1885. In October 1889, prior to leaving for the archdiocese of Toronto, Bishop Walsh commissioned the installation of windows in the sanctuary, the two side chapels, the east and west transepts, and the organ loft. In the middle sanctuary window Bishop Walsh is depicted holding a cathedral, with two spires. He also commissioned the Stations of the Cross in oils and the Marian Altar.

Archbishop of Toronto

On 13 August 1889, Leo XIII named John Walsh the archbishop of Toronto. It was one of a number of significant changes to the composition of the Catholic hierarchy in Ontario precipitated that year by the death of two bishops. Bishop Carberry of Hamilton died on 17 December 1887, and Archbishop Lynch of Toronto died on 12 May 1888. As well, the English-speaking bishops in the province were exerting pressure to have Kingston raised to the status of an archdiocese. In 1889, Bishop Thomas J. Dowling of Peterborough became the bishop of Hamilton, Richard A. O'Connor was consecrated bishop of Peterborough and Bishop Cleary of Kingston became an archbishop. Working behind the scenes to secure Walsh's nomination was none other than his friend Sir John A. Macdonald.

25 The Protestant prime minister believed the Conservatives would benefit by having Walsh in Toronto.

Bishop Walsh's final Mass and sermon at St. Peter's cathedral, as bishop of London, took place on 27 November 1889, after which he boarded the train to Toronto, where later that day he was enthroned in St. Michael's cathedral in a magnificent ceremony. He had come full circle. As a token of their affection, the clergy and laity of the diocese of London gave him a farewell gift of $2,000 towards the purchase of robes and vestments.

John Walsh served as archbishop of Toronto for nine years, retaining the pastoral episcopal style that he had employed in London, seeking peace and harmony between Catholics and other Christians, regularizing the devotional life of the archdiocese, visiting parishes and missions, encouraging vocations, establishing new parishes and building new churches and chapels. At the time of his death on 31 July 1898, he was universally respected. His final act of generosity towards the diocese of London was to bequeath $1,000 against the debt on the cathedral.[26]

Endnotes for Chapter 2 – Bishop Walsh

1 John K.A. Farrell (O'Farrell), *The History of the Roman Catholic Church in London, Ontario 1826-1931* (M.A. thesis, University of Western Ontario, 1949), 64.

2 John P. Comiskey, *John Walsh: Second Bishop of London in Ontario 1867-1889* (Ph.D. diss., Pontifical Gregorian University, 1999), 11.

3 John F. Coffey, *The City and Diocese of London, Ontario, Canada: An Historical Sketch* (London: 1885), 26.

4 *Catholic Record (CR)*, 14 November 1879, 5.

5 Michael Power, "Walsh, John," *DCB* (Toronto: 1990), 12:1083.

6 Jerome Terence Flynn, *The London Episcopacy, 1867-1889, of the Most Reverend John Walsh, D.D., Second Bishop of London* (M.A. thesis, Catholic University of America, 1966), 62–67.

7 Edward Kelly, *The Story of St. Paul's Parish Toronto* (Toronto: 1922), 108–9.

8 Power, "Walsh," 1084.

9 Flynn, 48.

10 Ibid., 47.

11 Michael Power, "Flannery, William," *DCB* (Toronto: 1994), 13: 345.

12 Coffey, 33.

13 Ibid., 38.

14 Comiskey, 110–20.

15 Our Lady of Mercy Church (Sarnia), "Scrapbook," 63.

16 *Daily Free Press* [London], 15 May 1876.

17 *CR*, 28 November 1879, 5; 5 December 1879, 1.

18 Coffey, 50–52.

19 Our Lady of Mercy Church (Sarnia), "Scrapbook," 77.

20 John R. Teefy, *Jubilee Volume: The Archdiocese of Toronto and Archbishop Walsh* (Toronto: 1892), xvi.

21 Comiskey, 175–76.

22 Power, "Walsh," 1085.

23 Michael Power, *A Promise Fulfilled: Highlights in the Political History of Catholic Separate Schools in Ontario* (Toronto: 2002), 137–51.

24 DLA, John Walsh Papers, Box 1, Letter Book 1, Walsh to Meredith, 15 January 1883; Flynn, 132.

25 Comiskey, 274–75.

26 St. Peter's Cathedral, Parish Records, "Announcement Book, June 1897-1899," 11 June 1899.

3. Denis O'Connor, CSB (1890-1899)

Bishop Denis O'Connor was a cautious financial manager. His years as bishop of London were generally peaceful, and the hallmarks of his episcopacy were entrenchment, restraint and financial prudence.[1] A healthy fear of debt, coupled to a belief that a Catholic bishop should maintain existing diocesan institutions before he invested in new ones, made possible two significant achievements. Bishop O'Connor paid down a significant portion of the debt incurred during Bishop Walsh's building program, and he exerted a remarkable control over the accumulation and disposal of any new diocesan debt.

O'Connor, a member of the Congregation of St. Basil (the Basilian Fathers), a teaching order, was always a strong proponent of Catholic education for all and believed in a well-trained clergy. The new bishop also brought a conservative theological stance and a commitment to moral rigour to the diocese. A disciplinarian, he held his people to strict obedience to diocesan laws.

No one was more pleased than Archbishop John Walsh of Toronto, O'Connor's predecessor, to learn that Denis O'Connor, the efficient superior of Assumption College in Sandwich (Windsor), had been promoted to the hierarchy in Ontario. The official date of O'Connor's appointment was 18 July 1890. Writing from his summer retreat in Port Stanley, Walsh told O'Connor:

> The news is by no means a surprise to me, because it is only what I expected, but nonetheless, it gives me supreme satisfaction. I am delighted that the priest whom of all priests in Canada I would prefer to be my successor in the diocese which I love so well, has been appointed to that position by the Holy See.[2]

O'Connor's name had appeared as *dignus* (third of three names) in the 1888 *terna* for the diocese of Peterborough. In the 1890 *terna* for London, his name was listed as *dignissimus* (the first of three names) and was readily accepted by Propaganda Fide.

Unlike his predecessor, Denis O'Connor was austere and reserved, preferring obscurity to publicity. He was a priest and educator for whom the teacher-student relationship was a model by which he approached all people and all problems, often, but not always, to great effect.[3] O'Connor was humble to a fault, disliking public displays of affection on his behalf. There is only one known formal photographic portrait of O'Connor.[4] All subsequent paintings of him —a half dozen— are derived from it. He preferred to apply his abundant energy and skill to problems and opportunities without fanfare or ostentation.

Walsh had promoted O'Connor for the diocese of London for his administrative skills. Walsh had built up the diocese from very little and wanted to leave the fruit of his twenty-two years of episcopal labour in the hands of someone he knew and trusted. From this perspective, O'Connor was an excellent choice, and he lived up to Walsh's unspoken expectations.

Early Years and Priesthood

Denis O'Connor was born on 28 March 1841, the eldest of three children of Denis O'Connor and Mary O'Leary, pioneer Irish Catholics in what became St. Francis de Sales parish, in Pickering Township, east of Toronto. His mother died when he was young, and his father took a second wife, Bridget O'Callaghan, with whom he had ten children. Five of O'Connor's half-sisters entered religious life, and two nephews became priests. A second cousin, also named Denis O'Connor, was bishop of Peterborough from 1930 to 1942.

In September 1852, O'Connor left the family farm to enrol at the Basilian-run St. Michael's

College in Toronto, making him a member of the founding class. He completed his course in classical and philosophical studies, in 1859, and entered St. Basil's novitiate in June of that year. Following first vows, on 24 June 1860, he continued at St. Michael's for another year and then studied theology in France at two more Basilian colleges, Feyzin and Annonay, where his superiors noted his piety and judgment. Tuberculosis cut short his stay in France, forcing the twenty-two year-old O'Connor to return to Toronto in 1863. The disease also accelerated the date of his ordination. Having received the necessary dispensation because he was two years shy of the canonical age, Denis O'Connor was ordained a Basilian priest at St. Mary's church in Toronto, on 8 December 1863.

He spent the next five years as a semi-invalid. His stepmother nursed him back to health within twelve months, but he suffered a relapse in 1867 and had to spend a year on sick leave. On his return to St. Michael's in 1868, he was made temporary administrator of the college, in place of Father Charles Vincent, the provincial of the Basilian community and superior of the college. This gave O'Connor a chance to demonstrate "his genius for organization, economy and intelligent decisions."[5]

Father Jean-Mathieu Soulerin, the Basilian superior then living at Annonay, looked favourably upon O'Connor's efforts and instructed him to join Father Vincent in negotiations with Bishop John Walsh on the future of Assumption College, Sandwich, a private school for boys, which was struggling. Open to both day and boarding pupils, Assumption taught boys in grades seven and eight and offered the Classical course (high school), studies in philosophy for students for the priesthood and the two-year commercial course. (Eventually, Assumption divided to form Assumption College High School and Assumption University.) A Basilian, Father Joseph Malbos, had been at the school in 1857 and 1858, and Father Soulerin thought that Walsh would be amenable to having the Basilians assume control of the school once more.

Although Vincent was senior to O'Connor, the latter was the main negotiator and mediator between Soulerin and Walsh. Throughout the lengthy communications, O'Connor patiently and persistently explored all avenues of discussion, and, in the end, he was able to persuade Walsh to agree to very generous terms for a return of the Basilians.

Signed on 27 September 1869, the agreement gave the Basilians the college building and eighty acres of land for 499 years, for a nominal payment of one dollar per year, as well as control of Assumption parish.

Superior of Assumption College

Father Soulerin appointed Denis O'Connor superior of the college and placed him in charge of the temporalities (property and revenues) of the parish. Arriving in Sandwich on 20 July 1870, in the company of a half-dozen of his confreres, the twenty-nine year-old O'Connor was largely untested as a priest-administrator. He faced a formidable task. The college building, which had been opened in 1857, was in an advanced state of disrepair. Few students were registered for classes and the teaching staff was so small as to be practically non-existent. Cash on hand amounted to a paltry $300, and there was no chance of government grants for a private Catholic institution.

During his twenty-year administration of Assumption College, O'Connor kept the college solvent, tripled the number of students in any given year, drawing them from many parts of Ontario and from Michigan, Ohio and Kentucky. He quadrupled the size of the college, adding the east-west wing in 1875 and the main wing in 1884, paying for both additions in good time. Soon, the college had earned a positive reputation in Catholic circles.

In the words of Father Robert Scollard, Basilian historian, O'Connor, a micro-manager, succeeded at Assumption College where others before him had failed because of his "strict attention to business, heroic self-denial and indomitable courage."[6] Discipline was everything and everywhere; it was the lifeblood of the college.

Monsignor F.X. O'Brien, of Kalamazoo, Michigan, one of O'Connor's students in the 1870s, published a small pamphlet about O'Connor, after his death, remembering him as a workhorse around the college and a priest much respected by clergy, students and the Catholic people in Sandwich and vicinity. O'Connor was superior, bursar and professor of philosophy. He managed the bookkeeping and the correspondence and never took a vacation. He only traveled where business took him, and business could take him far from the college. A standing joke among his philosophy students was that no matter where he was, he never failed to appear on time for class. O'Connor preached frequently, heard confessions and prepared the young boys for First Holy Communion. People saw him as a priest of experience and good sense and often sought his advice. He led a busy and productive life.[7]

What emerges from this recollection is that O'Connor was a one-man show. O'Brien praised him for it. But others would be less generous in their estimation of him, seeing in O'Connor a streak of authoritarianism that, no matter how successful in a college setting, was bound to arouse opposition when exercised in a diocese.

O'Connor expended the same kind of energy and will on Assumption church as he spent on the administration of the college. He built the sanctuary and tower, in 1874, and installed the stained glass windows in the sanctuary and apse that same year. In 1882, he oversaw the installation of the stained glass windows in the nave, thereby completing the church.[8] Also, he was responsible for the Basilians taking charge of St. John the Baptist parish in Amherstburg, in 1878, and St. Anne's parish in Detroit, in 1886.

In June 1877, Bishop George Conroy, the papal delegate, visited Father O'Connor at Assumption College. Conroy was touring the country on behalf of the Holy See to investigate complaints of clerical interference in Québec politics. He had come to Sandwich to ask the highly regarded O'Connor for his opinion of the matter.[9] In 1883, O'Connor was elected to the Provincial Council of the Congregation of Priests of St. Basil (Basilian Fathers) and was re-elected in 1886 and 1889. In recognition of O'Connor's stature in Catholic education in Ontario, Pope Leo XIII conferred upon him the degree of Doctor of Divinity on 20 September 1888. O'Connor's former students bought him the cap and the ring that went with the honour.

When Bishop Walsh became archbishop of Toronto, O'Connor was appointed administrator of the diocese of London. Then, on 18 July 1890, he was appointed bishop. Such was O'Connor's stature that when he was ready to leave for his episcopal consecration, the French members of Assumption parish in Sandwich, represented by Théodule Girardot, presented him with a mitre. The Catholics of Windsor, led by Francis Cleary, QC, donated a pectoral cross and chain, and local Protestants, in the person of J.C. Patterson, MP, presented an episcopal ring.[10]

Third Bishop of London

Denis O'Connor joined the ranks of the Ontario episcopacy with great reluctance. The story is told that on taking leave of his confreres, he broke down and shed tears of sorrow. A second attempt to bid farewell to the only home that he had known for two decades also ended in tears.

His consecration took place at St. Peter's Cathedral on 19 October 1890, the first time that `the cathedral had hosted such a ceremony. Archbishop John Walsh of Toronto was the principal consecrator. Assisting him were Bishop John Foley of Detroit, who preached, and Bishop Thomas J. Dowling of Hamilton. Also attending were other bishops and at least eighty priests, dozens of whom had been O'Connor's students at Assumption College. The congregation, which crowded the nave and the aisles, used a specially printed booklet to follow the ceremony and make the appropriate responses in Latin. "All eyes were centred on the downcast eyes and solemn mien of the new Bishop," wrote the reporter for the *Catholic Record*.

After the formal consecration and enthronement of the new bishop, Thomas Coffey, publisher of the *Catholic Record*, presented an address from the laity of the cathedral parish. In the afternoon, people from Windsor and Detroit, the Knights of St. John and members of the Catholic Mutual Benefit Association and the Emerald Benefit Association, accompanied by the band of the 21st Fusiliers of Windsor, serenaded Bishop O'Connor in front of the episcopal palace. At evening Vespers, Bishop Camillus Maes of Covington, Kentucky, delivered a sermon on the office of bishop. He told the large congregation that a bishop judges, preaches, administers the sacraments and is the repository of governing authority, which is given to him by the pope, the successor of St. Peter in Rome. Following the sermon, Bishop O'Connor gave Benediction of the Blessed Sacrament. The next day, he and Archbishop Walsh paid a visit to Sacred Heart Convent in London,[11] the home of a prominent order of women religious.

In his inaugural pastoral letter, published on 24 January 1891, Bishop O'Connor discussed four concerns: two dealt with the papacy and two with the diocese of London. On the matter of Leo XIII's encyclical on the suppression of African slavery, he ordered a collection to be taken up in every diocesan parish and mission in support of the pope's work in this area. He reminded the parishes and missions about the pope's Good Friday collection, for the protection and preservation of the holy places in Jerusalem and environs, which would be taken up throughout the diocese.

Turning to more local matters, Bishop O'Connor urged all Catholic ratepayers to support separate schools by making an annual written declaration to that effect to the clerk of the municipality where they lived. This is what the government demanded, and Catholics should comply as a matter of necessity. Not wanting to put the onus of the viability of the cash-starved separate schools entirely on his fellow Catholics, however, O'Connor addressed the Liberal government of Premier Oliver Mowat. He argued that its political security, which was sufficiently strong to protect it against "hysterical fanaticism," was reason enough for it to grant to the Catholics of Ontario those rights and privileges in education long enjoyed by the Protestants of Québec.

Then came the subject of parish debt, incurred in some cases because churches were too big or too expensively decorated. Speaking directly to the priests, the bishop wrote:

> I regret to say that there are in the diocese a few churches whose revenues are so small as to render it hardly possible to pay even the interest of the debt upon them. The debt is therefore steadily increasing. To remedy this in as far as I can, I have decided to devote all fees received for dispensations to paying first the interest and then the principal of such debts.[12]

The dispensations to which he referred concerned marriage. For instance, if a petitioner hoped to be dispensed from one or more marriage banns — the official church publication of an intention to be married — he or she had to pay a fee to the diocese to have the petition considered. To help pay down parish debts, the bishop planned to apply these fees directly to the debt. Since dispensation fees were an important source of income for the central diocesan administration, applying them to parish debt would be a considerable gift from the bishop.

Bishop O'Connor's fixation with debt reduction was more than just a matter of his conservative nature. The wisdom of his preoccupation was soon justified by a decline in the Catholic population of the diocese. During the 1890s, the number of Catholic faithful dropped from 60,254 to 59,383.[13] Elgin, Huron, Lambton, Middlesex, Norfolk and Oxford, six out of the nine counties that formed the diocese, suffered net losses.[14] A decline of fewer than a thousand people was far from a crisis, but it was worrying to the bishop and his clergy as they struggled to pay down not only the interest but the principal on the diocese's collective debt. Moreover, fewer Catholics meant a greater vulnerability to attacks on their religion and their schools.

Bishop O'Connor's awareness of this downward trend in the Catholic population is shown in his working papers for his 1896 *ad limina* report to Propaganda Fide in Rome and in his submission for the 1898 *Propaganda Directory*. His careful and meticulous tabulations tell us a great deal about the state of the diocese of London six or so years after he had become bishop. (He did not present his report in person to Leo XIII. Instead, he entrusted that task to Dean James T. Wagner.)

The diocese was still a collection of rural congregations. Of the seventy-five parishes and missions, only thirteen were in cities or towns, with the remainder in the countryside. Congregations were generally small. Eight missions had fewer than 100 members. Thirty-six parishes had fewer than 500 members. Eighteen parishes had from 1,000 to 2,999 members, and only two could boast a membership exceeding 3,000. The remaining parishes claimed from 500 to 999 members. The ten largest parishes in the diocese, in terms of membership, were: St. Peter's cathedral (3,850); St. Alphonsus, Windsor (3,125); Assumption, Sandwich (2,475); St. John the Baptist, Amherstburg (2,650); St. Joseph's, Chatham (2,425); St. Joseph's, Stratford (2,050); St. Anne's, Tecumseh (1,725); Holy Angels, St. Thomas (1,637); Annunciation, Stoney Point (1,566), and Notre-Dame-du-Lac, Walkerville (1,564).

Serving the parishes and missions were fifty-six diocesan priests, three Franciscans (St. Joseph's, Chatham) and twelve Basilians (Assumption church and Assumption College, Sandwich, and St. John the Baptist, Amherstburg). Of the diocesan priests, twenty-seven were natives of Ontario, thirteen were born in Ireland, thirteen came from Québec (two were Irish) and three were from France. The dominance of Irish-born clergy was slowly ending. The French-speaking priests from Québec and those from France were in charge of the French-Canadian parishes in Essex and Kent counties.

The number of women religious was impressive: 85 Sisters of St. Joseph; 44 Sisters of the Holy Names of Jesus and Mary; 42 Mesdames (Ladies) of the Sacred Heart; 34 Ursulines; 21 Religious Hospitallers of St. Joseph, and 14 Loretto Sisters.

There was one orphanage and one home for the aged. There were 4,228 Catholic students in forty-nine separate schools; 858 Catholic students in public schools in Windsor, Sandwich and Belle River that were considered Catholic because their entire enrolment was Catholic; 3,460 Catholic students in public schools in which religion was taught after hours; and 2,212 Catholic students in public schools where no religion was taught.

The diocesan debt as of 31 December 1890, the year O'Connor became bishop, was $201,746. Additional debts contracted from that date to 1 January 1896 amounted to $102,950, for a total debt of $304,696. Bishop O'Connor, the clergy and the laity succeeded in reducing this by $159,336, leaving a diocesan debt of $145,360. Thirty-six parishes and missions had no debt on 1 January 1896.[15]

One topic in his 1896 *ad limina* report antagonized some of the clergy. Bishop O'Connor commented about intemperance among his priests, which he repeated to the clergy at their February 1896 spiritual retreat. This offended some of the senior priests to such a degree that they drafted a letter of protest to Cardinal Mieczyslaw Ledochowski, who as prefect of *Propaganda Fide* would have read the bishop's report. The letter responded to the charge of intemperance and also strongly protested the appointment of junior or favoured clergy to the more prestigious parishes, the lack of a vicar general, excessive taxation of ten percent on all revenues and the bishop's failure to give an account of the Ecclesiastical Fund.[16] The protest seems to have died with Ledochowski and was never made public in the diocese.

On 27 January 1899, less than nine years after he was appointed bishop of London, Rome selected Denis O'Connor to succeed John Walsh as archbishop of Toronto. The decision was announced on 5 April 1899.[17] Once more, O'Connor was reluctant to accept Rome's decision and only did so

out of obedience. Perhaps he recognized something of his own limitations that others in the Ontario hierarchy and at the Holy See did not yet see.

On 30 April 1899, Archbishop-elect O'Connor delivered a detailed summation of his London episcopacy in his farewell sermon at St. Peter's Cathedral. His accomplishments were meaningful but modest. He oversaw the construction of eleven churches and thirteen rectories and extensive renovations to eight churches. He consecrated seven marble altars and blessed another fifteen. He opened ten cemeteries, three hospitals and three convents. (He forgot to mention the erection of two parishes in 1896: St. Brigid, Logan, and St. Boniface, Zurich.) Eleven separate schools were built. Bishop O'Connor ordained fifteen priests for the diocese and received another six into the diocese. Nine priests had died during his episcopacy. He confirmed 13,215 people, including 359 converts.

The reduction of the cathedral debt was his biggest achievement. It stood at $64,200 when he became bishop in late 1890. He paid $37,723 on the principal and $20,638 in interest, leaving $27,000 for his successor to discharge. The beneficiaries, besides the laity, were the two bishops who followed him: Fergus Patrick McEvay and Michael Francis Fallon. Almost as an aside, O'Connor mentioned to the congregation that he had donated $15,000 towards reducing the principal. This figure elicited the greatest response in the press. He could not, however, resist chiding the congregation for not subscribing more towards the debt, and, for good measure, he brought up the subject of arrears in payments for plots at St. Peter's cemetery. This was the schoolmaster speaking.

He praised the separate schools and their teachers, separate school supporters, the Catholic Mutual Benefit Association, and those families who prayed together every evening. He warned against joining societies not approved by the Church; he bemoaned the presence of critics and faultfinders whose lack of loyalty to the Church was very damaging to unity; and he spoke of the necessity of a strict adherence to the laws and regulations of the Church.[18]

Archbishop of Toronto

Denis O'Connor ended his days as the third bishop of London with a Mass on Monday, 1 May, for the school children and a Mass early Tuesday morning in memory of the deceased members of the diocese. Immediately following the Mass, he left for Toronto, accompanied by Father John V. Tobin, a young priest, to the railway station. Twenty years later, Tobin wrote that O'Connor "burst into a flood of tears; nor did he regain his composure until he had reached the train which was to take him to his new metropolitan home."[19]

O'Connor was enthroned as the third archbishop of Toronto in an imposing ceremony at St. Michael's cathedral, on 3 May 1899.[20] The conservative archbishop's Toronto episcopacy was not happy. He lost the confidence of Archbishop Charles-Hughes Gauthier of Kingston and Archbishop Thomas Duhamel of Ottawa when he sought a compromise with the government on the teaching qualifications of religious in separate schools.

Archbishop O'Connor alienated a large number of lay people and clerics when he introduced stricter practices and attempted to isolate Catholics from the Protestant majority. These steps reflected the policies that Leo XIII and Pius X were taking to protect the Church in changing times. "While the hierarchy barricaded the Church against its perennial enemies — rationalism, secularism, and anti-clericalism — it battled internal dissent from theological liberals and cultural accomodationists."[21] In 1903, Pius X instituted a rigorous program to strengthen orthodox beliefs and practices "by reaffirming doctrinal uniformity, liturgical purity, and magisterial authority."[22] The archbishop upset lay people when he introduced Pius X's tighter controls over mixed marriages, prompting many couples to travel to Holy Angels Church in Buffalo, New York, where a young Oblate by the name of Father Michael Francis Fallon married them. O'Connor also caused considerable hardship by demanding Gregorian chant at Mass and forbidding women to sing in parish choirs. He was applying the *motu proprio* (legislative text) of Pius X on liturgical music, but was one of only a handful of bishops in North America who did so without any compromise, in all cases, at a cost of doing more harm than good. He blocked the entry of the Knights of Columbus into the archdiocese, in 1907, claiming that there were already too many fraternal societies. He tried to stop the annual parade of the Holy Name Society, fearing that any overt display of Catholic solidarity might arouse anti-Catholic hostility in Toronto.

Archbishop O'Connor's relationship with his clergy fared no better. When he introduced compulsory examinations in theology for priests who had been ordained within the last four years, the reaction from the young priests was swift and hostile. The senior clergy fought him over the sacraments, marriage dispensations, clergy salaries and even parish picnics, which the archbishop discouraged.[23] One of his most strident critics was a fellow Basilian, Father John R. Teefy, who had the ear of Archbishop Donato Sbarretti, the apostolic delegate to Canada.

Archbishop O'Connor offered his resignation in 1904 and 1905. Rome finally accepted it on 4 May 1908. He retired to a quiet life of prayer and devotion at St. Basil's Novitiate, where he lived in relative seclusion.

He died on 30 June 1911, from complications arising from Bright's disease and diabetes and was buried in Toronto's Mount Hope Cemetery among many of his Basilian confreres.

Endnotes to Chapter 3 - Bishop O'Connor

[1] John K.A. Farrell (O'Farrell), *The History of the Roman Catholic Church in London, Ontario 1826-1931* (M.A. thesis, University of Western Ontario, 1949), 83.

[2] GABF, O'Connor Papers, Folder I, Walsh to O'Connor, 5 August 1890.

[3] Farrell, 81, 82.

[4] Robert Scollard, "O'Connor, Denis," *DBB* (Toronto: 1969), 115.

[5] Michael Power and Mark McGowan, "O'Connor, Denis," DCB (Toronto: 1998), 14: 789.

[6] Robert Scollard, "Most Reverend Denis O'Connor, C.S.B., D.D.," Basilian Teacher, 4, no. 5 (1938), 89.

[7] F.X. O'Brien, *Life Work of a Saintly Prelate* (Kalamazoo, Michigan: 1914), 3.

[8] E.J. Lajeunesse, *Outline History of Assumption Church* (Windsor: 1967), 55.

[9] Michael Power, *Assumption College: The O'Connor Years 1870-1890* (Windsor: 1986), 135-37.

[10] *CR*, 18 October 1890, 1.

[11] *CR*, 25 October 1890, 4-5.

[12] *CR*, 24 January 1891, 4.

[13] Power and McGowan, 790.

[14] *Fourth Census of Canada* 1901, Vol. 1.

[15] GABF, O'Connor Papers, Folder III, Notes of Reports to Rome.

[16] DLA, Denis O'Connor Papers, Box 1, handwritten letter to Propaganda Fide, no date.

[17] *CR*, 15 April 1899; *Daily Free Press* [London], 6 April 1899, 5.

[18] *CR*, 6 May 1899, 4-5; *Daily Free Press* [London], 1 May 1899, 1.

[19] *Golden Jubilee, Assumption College, 1870-1920* (Sandwich: 1920), 67.

[20] *CR*, 12 May 1899, 4-5; *Daily Free Press* [London], 4 May 1899, 2.

[21] Mark McGowan, "'The Catholic 'Restoration' Pope Pius X, Archbishop Dennis O'Connor and Popular Catholicism in Toronto 1899-1908," CCHA, *Historical Studies*, 4 (1987), 69

[22] Ibid, 71.

[23] Power and McGowan, 792.

4. Fergus Patrick McEvay (1899-1908)

Fergus Patrick McEvay was the first choice of the bishops of Ontario, but his appointment surprised some observers. The London Daily Free Press had confidently predicted that Father John J. McCann, vicar general of the archdiocese of Toronto, would be the next bishop of London.[1] But the bishops of Ontario recommended McEvay as dignissimus, Pierre Dominic Laurent as dignior and Philip Brennan as dignus. On 25 June 1899, Thomas J. Dowling, Bishop of Hamilton, announced Monsignor McEvay's promotion.[2] In McEvay, Dowling was losing an experienced pastor and administrator, who, during his seventeen years as a priest, had excelled in every assignment and had been a model citizen.

During his nine years in London, Bishop McEvay had a fruitful administration. McEvay, who had a reputation as a vigorous and uncompromising defender of separate schools, established new separate school boards in the Windsor area, in spite of opposition. He found ways to deal with differences between French-speaking and English-speaking clergy and laity as Francophones sought to protect their language and culture. It would take years, however, for French-speaking and English-speaking Catholics in the diocese to learn to live and work comfortably together.

Early Years and Priesthood

Fergus Patrick McEvay was born on 8 December 1852, in Lindsay, Ontario, and baptized in St. Luke's church, Downeyville. His parents were Michael McEvay and Mary Lehane, both Irish immigrants. His father died young, but his mother witnessed her son's episcopal consecration in 1899 and outlived him by six years.[3] McEvay attended a rural separate school and worked for three years as a labourer and a general agent in the hamlet of Ennismore. He then entered St. Michael's College in Toronto as a student in classical studies. He matriculated in 1878 and remained for another year to prepare for theology, in the meantime winning the Thomas J. Dowling Medal for an English essay.

McEvay entered St. Francis de Sales Seminary in Milwaukee, Wisconsin, in 1879, as a candidate for the diocese of Kingston, but stayed only a year. He returned to St. Michael's for additional study in theology before he enrolled at the Grand Séminaire de Montréal in 1880. Two years later he earned his licence in theology.

On 9 July 1882, Bishop James Vincent Cleary of Kingston ordained McEvay to the priesthood, in the parish church of St. Peter-in-Chains, Trenton, two days before the erection of the diocese of Peterborough. McEvay was ordained for Kingston, but he was intended for Peterborough. Bishop Cleary "gave" him to Bishop Jean-François Jamot, who incardinated McEvay into the diocese and made him parish priest of St. Aloysius parish in Fenelon Falls, with responsibility for the missions in Bobcaygeon, Victoria Road and Galway.[4] He became a popular pastor among his scattered flock of 1,800 souls.

On 1 May 1887, when Thomas J. Dowling, a priest of the diocese of Hamilton, was consecrated the second bishop of Peterborough, he made McEvay the rector of the cathedral, also named St. Peter-in-Chains, and diocesan chancellor. Soon Dowling assigned McEvay the daunting task of building St. Joseph's Hospital in Peterborough. When Dowling was transferred to Hamilton, in January 1889, he received Rome's permission to bring McEvay with him.[5]

During his nine years in Hamilton, McEvay was episcopal secretary and then rector of St. Mary's cathedral in downtown Hamilton, which put him at the centre of Catholic life. He renovated St.

Mary's and built an impressive cathedral rectory. He oversaw the construction of a chapel and mortuary at Holy Sepulchre Cemetery and additions to St. Joseph's Hospital and the convents of the Sisters of St. Joseph and the Loretto Sisters. And he is credited with building two churches in Hamilton: St. Lawrence (1890) and St. Joseph (1894).[6]

He improved the separate school system in the city and championed the right of Catholics in general to have separate schools. In 1898, he spoke with eloquence and conviction on behalf of Manitoba's Catholic minority, who had lost their right to separate schools (the French-speaking minority had also lost the right to French-language schools). In response to what is called the Manitoba School Question, Leo XIII issued an encyclical, *Affari vos*, on the rights of Catholics to have their own schools and the legitimate means by which they could establish them. McEvay also used its publication to warn Ontario's Catholics to safeguard their schools.

In 1893, Bishop Dowling took McEvay with him on his ad limina visit to Rome, where Pope Leo XIII conferred upon Father McEvay the honour of papal chamberlain.[7] Subsequently, McEvay was designated a domestic prelate (an honorary member of the papal household) and near the end of his Hamilton career the vicar general of the diocese. In 1898, an observer wrote that Monsignor McEvay was "evidently marked out for further advancement and distinction in the Church."[8]

Fourth Bishop of London

The papal bull appointing Fergus Patrick McEvay the fourth bishop of London was dated 27 May 1899 and appeared in print on 1 July. In the opinion of one Hamilton newspaper, "No clergyman who has ever labored in this part of the country is more worthy of promotion and high honors than Mgr. McEvay …. he has been a broad-minded, progressive Hamiltonian, and this city is now and ever will be the better for having numbered him among its citizens."[9]

Bishop McEvay was consecrated in St. Peter's cathedral, on Sunday, 6 August 1899, the Feast of the Transfiguration. The principal consecrator and celebrant of the Pontifical High Mass was Archbishop Denis O'Connor of Toronto. Assisting him were Bishop Dowling of Hamilton and Bishop Richard O'Connor of Peterborough.

In his response to the priests' address, Bishop McEvay said that he was glad to hear of the good feeling that existed between Catholics and Protestants. "As Catholics," he continued, "we will always profess our faith openly, but we will also recognize the rights of others. I hope that these charitable relations may long continue for the happiness of all." To the laity, he remarked that they lived in a "beautiful section of the country where people of different races were dwelling together in unity."[10] By races, the bishop meant English-speaking and French-speaking Catholics in his diocese. McEvay's well chosen words signalled his concern with the four solitudes that defined so much of the public life of Canada in 1899: Catholic, Protestant, English and French.

At the opening of the twentieth century, the emergence of French-Canadian nationalism in Ontario meant Bishop McEvay and his fellow English-speaking bishops had to learn to cope with the sometimes conflicting expectations of English-speaking and French-speaking Catholics. Francophones were a minority and were trying to protect their identity in civic life and the Church. That led to various problems. Any attempt by the bishops to build bridges between the minority Catholic Church and the majority Protestant community in Ontario, at times a necessity, was often interpreted by Francophone Catholics as an alliance of all Anglophones against them. This was ironic, at least in Bishop McEvay's case, because he was highly suspicious of the corrosive power of the majority Protestant culture to eat away at Catholic identity and unity. In some parishes, conflicts arose because of the efforts to preserve the use of the French language and culture in the Church in Ontario.

Though the expressions of French-Canadian nationalism in the Francophone parishes in Essex and Kent countries was a largely tame affair during McEvay's tenure as bishop, he had to deal with its impact in two parishes, St. Alphonsus in Windsor and Notre-Dame-du-Lac (Our Lady of the Rosary) in Walkerville. To complicate matters further, in Essex and Kent, the Francophone Catholic community had an easy enemy — "Irish Catholics," so-called because of their Irish family names. By 1900, the typical Irish Catholic had been born in Canada and never visited Ireland. Nonetheless, many clerical and lay Francophone leaders saw the Irish as opposing their efforts to preserve their identity. In their estimation, the Irish Catholics posed a far greater threat to the viability of French-Canadian Catholicism than any opposition from the anti-Catholic Orange Lodge or a Protestant politician.

Bishop McEvay quickly asserted his authority in his new diocese. On the day of his consecration, he set up his administrative team; he chose Father Joseph Bayard, pastor of Holy Angels parish in St. Thomas, to be vicar general. Next, he appointed Father John T. Aylward as the rector of the cathedral, Father Peter J. McKeon as the chancellor of the diocese, with residence in the cathedral rectory, and Father Pierre L'Heureux as his personal secretary.[11] These four priests constituted the diocesan bureaucracy.

In September, Bishop McEvay dealt with the lack of a separate school board in Windsor during his visit to the area. He went to Assumption College, in Sandwich, where candidates for the diocesan priesthood received their classical education, and to Assumption parish in Sandwich, St. Alphonsus parish in Windsor, and the parishes of Essex County.

Separate Schools in Windsor

Bishop McEvay's visit to St. Alphonsus on 17 September 1899 led to considerable controversy. He set into motion a series of political and legal events that led to the founding of the Windsor Separate School Board and the board's acquisition of its first two schools. At times the process was divisive and acrimonious because of resistance within the parish and difficulties with the public school board. The process was further complicated by differences over language in the parish, which had both Francophone and Anglophone members. The French-speaking parishioners wanted a French-language separate school and sought to assert their "ownership" of the church, in order to have rights over the language used in the church.

In their address of welcome to Bishop McEvay, the parishioners of St. Alphonsus defended their arrangement with the public school board: "Your Lordship will also be pleased to know that the conduct of our schools is satisfactory and is based upon Catholic principles, although not under the separate school law, and that, not alone the secular but the religious training of our children is effectively cared for."[12] In 1899, Windsor had

seven public schools, one collegiate institute and no separate schools. By a gentlemen's agreement between Catholic and Protestant trustees on the public school board, two public schools were set aside for the exclusive use of the city's Catholics and were known by Catholic names: St. Alphonsus and St. Francis. (And there was one public school reserved for black children.) The public school board had purchased the site for St. Alphonsus in October 1873 and the site for St. Francis in 1890. The agreement had worked reasonably well for both sides; it gave the Catholics more money than they would have in a separate school board. But the arrangement was illegal and could have been ended at any time by the public school board, which was not legally bound to pay compensation to Catholic ratepayers.

Bishop McEvay was having none of this. He warned the Catholics of Windsor of the need to safeguard their schools. From the pulpit of St. Alphonsus church, he declared that the "Public School system of Ontario and Catholic principles are diametrically opposed on the question of religious education" and that Catholics are "bound by the law of God and His Church to follow the Separate School law whenever it is in your power to do so." Catholics needed to have their own schools, teachers and trustees. "If you cannot reach this end by agreement or arbitration," Bishop McEvay continued, "I will be compelled to close St. Mary's Academy [a private girls school next door to St. Alphonsus church] and re-open it as a Separate school, which will be Catholic in theory as well as in practice."[13] He was putting his reputation on the line.

In a private letter to Father William Flannery, pastor of St. Alphonsus, Bishop McEvay offered a solution to the debt on the two Catholic schools. He reminded Flannery that "over and above this [the debt] the Catholics are bound legally by debentures to pay thousands of dollars exclusively for the use of Protestant children. Truly such a state of affairs is most deplorable." The bishop also promised that as soon as St. Alphonsus and St. Francis were handed over to the separate school board, he would "pay the debentures due on these 2 schools so that the Board will have a clear slate to start."[14] It was a generous offer, one that he kept.

The Catholics of the nearby communities of Sandwich and Belle River heard Bishop McEvay's warning and quickly established separate schools in their communities. Since Catholics were the overwhelming majority in both places, the transfer from public to separate was relatively easy.[15] Such was not the case in Windsor, where Catholics were a minority and had to fight a protracted battle against Protestant trustees. It took two years to set up the board and another two to acquire the two schools.

Soon after his visit to St. Alphonsus, Bishop McEvay hired Francis Cleary, a lawyer and member of the parish, to report on things such as the number of Catholic students, the Catholic share of debentures, the mill rate and the value of the two Catholic schools in Windsor. Cleary's report was dated 25 June 1900. On receipt of it, the bishop instructed Father Flannery to oversee a petition in support of a separate school board in Windsor and of the just division of public school board assets. This petition was presented to the public board probably during the first half of 1901 and apparently went nowhere.[16]

The Windsor Separate School Board was formed on 18 November 1901. The three trustees, Charles E. Casgrain, chairman, Michael M. Brian and Gaspard Pacaud, presented their own petition to the public board, in early December 1901.[17] A year and a half of open conflict, negotiations and reports, including one to Justice William G. Falconbridge and another to Richard Harcourt, the minister of education, in 1903, produced no tangible results.[18] This stalemate induced the Liberal government of Premier George W. Ross to pass "An Act respecting the Property of Public and Separate Schools in the City of Windsor and other matters."[19] Given royal assent on 12 June 1903, this legislation allowed the cabinet to choose a judge of the High Court of Justice in Ontario who would arbitrate the claims of the two boards. The public board vehemently protested against the legislation, to little effect.[20]

The arbitrator, Justice William P.R. Street, rendered his judgment on 10 February 1904, awarding to the separate school board St. Alphonsus school and a majority share of the school site and building on Louis Avenue. That would have been St. Francis School, although Justice Street did not refer to it by name. The public board had to accept the judgment, but it contested the judge's evaluation of the properties and would not hand over the two schools until the end of the 1903–04 school year. In September 1904, Windsor's Catholics finally had their own separate schools. Bishop McEvay's will

had prevailed—without anyone being deprived of the sacraments or being asked to leave the church, restrictions he might have used with those who opposed his will.[21]

Language challenges

While trying to resolve the separate school issue in Windsor, Bishop McEvay also had to address differences over the use of French and English in the schools and the church. Several weeks prior to his September 1899 visit to St. Alphonsus parish, Bishop McEvay had received a petition signed by 337 French-Canadians from the parish. Gaspard Pacaud, who became a separate school trustee in 1901, headed the group. His family published Le Progrès, a local Francophone newspaper that was not afraid to challenge episcopal authority. The petition requested a French-speaking priest and instruction in French at the Sunday High Mass, in addition to that already provided at the Low Mass. Appended to the request was a brief history of the parish that attempted to prove that French-Canadians (rather than the English-speaking Irish parishioners) had donated the land, built the present church and were largely responsible for paying down its debt.[22] The "ownership" of St. Alphonsus church was crucial because the general assumption was that the group that paid the majority share in the building and ongoing maintenance of the parish church had certain language rights in connection with the sermon, the announcements and the teaching of the catechism as well as in the choice of the parish priest or his assistant. At least this contretemps took place mostly in private and did not openly engage the passions of the parishioners.

Since their request for a French-speaking priest was not unreasonable, at least on the surface, Bishop McEvay promised the petitioners that he would find one. In May 1900, Father Joseph-Napoléon Ferland arrived from Montréal. He was posted as the chaplain at Hôtel-Dieu hospital and given permission to preach in French at the Low Mass and hear confessions at St. Alphonsus. The parish records show him performing only five baptisms at the parish, from 12 July to November 1900. Bishop McEvay also asked Father Ferland to conduct a census of Francophone families in Windsor.

Father Ferland reported his findings to the bishop, in a letter of 18 June 1900. He wrote that he had visited 383 families, of which 276 were essentially French-Canadian, 65 were Francophone and Anglophone Catholic, and 40 were Francophone and Protestant. That should have been the end of the census, but Father Ferland had taken it upon himself to gather the opinions of Francophone Catholics on separate schools and the future of St. Alphonsus church.

He informed the bishop that the Francophones were willing to work with the Irish in establishing separate schools in Windsor if the following three conditions were met: 1) that the schools have teachers qualified to teach French; 2) that Francophone children should have their own classes; and 3) that daily instructional time in French should be a half-day for the junior grades and an hour and a half for the senior grades. If the board could not meet these conditions, Francophones preferred to have their own share of the school buildings.

Concerning St. Alphonsus church, Father Ferland told the bishop that the Francophones preferred to be treated as a distinct congregation and to that end they were willing to pay an indemnity of $15,000 to the English-speaking Catholics of the parish, who could use the money to build their own church. In light of this, Ferland continued, subscriptions for the new rectory, currently being collected by Father William Flannery, should be reimbursed to the donors.[23]

Bishop McEvay's response of 26 June 1901 played for time by holding out hope on both the school and church issues, with the school issue taking precedence. He pressed home the need for a unified Catholic effort on separate schools. To gain Francophone support for Father Flannery's subscription, the bishop was willing to consider the possibility that one of the two schools would become a French-language school.

The "ownership" of St. Alphonsus Church, however, was a thornier issue. Bishop McEvay had already told the people of the parish that he wanted the next church in Windsor to be neither French nor Irish but simply Catholic.[24] To placate Father Ferland, he now contradicted himself and agreed to a church for the Francophones, if they raised the $15,000 to build it. As an inducement, he offered to pay $5,000 for a rectory. If the Francophones persisted in their desire to have St. Alphonsus as their own, however, McEvay promised to have the matter adjudicated by either the apostolic delegate or the archbishops of Toronto and Montreal.[25]

In his response of 30 June 1900, Father Ferland expressed satisfaction with the offer of a French-language school, but he refused to budge on St. Alphonsus church. Instead he went to great lengths to demonstrate that it would cost between $25,000 and $30,000 to build and furnish a new church and rectory.[26] Tired of the exchange, Bishop McEvay replied in a letter of 13 July 1900 that as soon as the separate school question in Windsor was legally resolved, he would be willing to consider establishing a French congregation with its own church. On the matter of competing rights to St. Alphonsus church, he would defer to the judgment of the apostolic delegate.[27]

Father Ferland continued his campaign. He composed a "Mémoire," dated 7 October 1900, on the history of Francophone claims to St. Alphonsus church and included in it his correspondence with Bishop McEvay. He forwarded it to Archbishop Diomede Falconio, OFM, the apostolic delegate and referee in all such disputes in the Canadian church. Father Flannery wrote a thirteen-page, point-by-point rebuttal, which bore the date of January 1901.[28]

Archbishop Falconio resolved the dispute by ordering Father Ferland, the outsider, to leave the diocese. This was probably done at the request of Bishop McEvay. To appear impartial, the apostolic delegate also removed Father Flannery, the pastor of St. Alphonsus. The forced removal of a pastor was a relatively rare event. Flannery left for St. Columban's parish in St. Columban, Ontario, embittered but relieved. Although Flannery could speak French, Falconio suggested that the next pastor of St. Alphonsus be bilingual and responsible for founding a new bilingual parish. That pastor was the bilingual Father Joseph E. Meunier. The new parish was Immaculate Conception on Wyandotte Street East, which opened in December 1904, with Father Denis J. Downey, also bilingual and Meunier's curate, as the first pastor. Falconio made no mention of compensation for the Francophone members of St. Alphonsus parish, and that issue faded away.[29]

Settling the St. Alphonsus issue, however, had repercussions in another parish. The establishment of Immaculate Conception parish involved delineating new parish boundaries, which should have been straightforward. On 21 December 1904, Bishop McEvay wrote letters describing the changes to the pastors of Assumption parish in Sandwich, St.

Alphonsus and Immaculate Conception in Windsor and Notre-Dame-du-Lac in Walkerville, and he instructed them to read his letter from the pulpit.[30]

Father Lucien A. Beaudoin, the parish priest of Notre-Dame-du-Lac for the past fourteen years, objected. He was highly protective of the parish's French character and its boundaries because to lose territory was to lose parishioners. In a letter to Bishop McEvay, of 24 December 1904, Father Beaudoin claimed that at the last conference of priests the bishop told him to pay no attention to newspaper articles about impending changes to parish boundaries. In the middle of December, he heard from a fellow priest that the bishop intended to divide his parish. "I paid no attention to it," he wrote, "thinking that canon law, gentlemanship, or the word of my beloved Bishop were enough for me."[31] When he received Bishop McEvay's letter, Beaudoin felt betrayed because he had had no time to formally protest to a higher authority. He also reminded the bishop of his many accomplishments, such as separate schools and the parish cemetery. According to Father Beaudoin, it was unjust for the bishop to take away any of his territory, even if he had done so to create the bilingual parish of Immaculate Conception.

Bishop McEvay was very angry. "You accuse me," he wrote to Father Beaudoin, on 29 December 1904, "of lying, deceit, ignorance of Canon Law, ungentlemanly conduct, injustice, etc. and as these are very serious charges especially made by a priest against his Bishop, you will be called upon to substantiate them in due time and place."[32] Beaudoin backed down and apologized,[33] something he would not do later in similar circumstances.

Five-year report

His Windsor school and parish problems behind him, Bishop McEvay prepared for his first ad limina visit to Rome, which he made in November 1905. His report to Pius X says that there were 60,000 Catholics in the diocese of London spread out over nine counties, a large territory. There were fifty parishes and thirty chapels; sixty diocesan and twenty religious priests; and six communities of women religious who taught in separate schools and private academies and took care of the poor and orphaned. Bishop McEvay had founded four

new parishes: St. Patrick's in Dublin (1900), St. Joseph's in Clinton (1901), Immaculate Conception in Windsor (1904) and Immaculate Conception in Stratford (1904). In 1906 he founded St. Anthony of Padua in Harrow.

The diocese had eighty-six Catholic separate schools. There were thirty public schools where Catholic doctrine was taught after hours, but there were many public schools where no religion was taught. Parents and teachers taught religion in these schools when circumstances allowed. In May 1902, Bishop McEvay had opened St. Joseph's Nurses Training School in London.

Bishop McEvay ended his report saying that he had no complaints against his priests. He commented that the vast majority of Catholics made their Easter Communion and that there was little opposition to the pope's reform of church music. He did, however, express concerns about mixed marriages, secret societies, the inherent dangers posed by Protestants and infidels to the Catholic faithful and the scarcity of priests.[34]

The low number of vocations to the priesthood in the diocese of London was a recurring theme in Bishop McEvay's remarks at parish functions. The shortage alarmed and troubled him. While bishop of London, he ordained twenty-three priests, which was a respectable number, but death took six of his veteran and most accomplished clergymen.

Certification of teachers' crisis

During his last full year in London, Bishop McEvay was involved in the separate school question at a provincial level. The crisis was over the certification of women and men religious teachers in Ontario, a debate that had erupted in 1890, lain dormant for several years, and erupted again in 1906. The problem was the enforcement of provincial regulations concerning the uniform certification of teachers from religious communities who taught in separate schools but often lacked the proper qualifications.

The Conservative government of Premier James P. Whitney was determined to resolve the issue and was supported by John F. White, the first separate school inspector, who became the principal of Ottawa Normal School, and by the separate school inspectors. The bishops, including McEvay, held out for immediate certification based on experience and compliance with departmental regulations. Bishop McEvay wrote to Premier Whitney, telling him that he had eighty religious teachers in his diocese who were very successful in preparing their students for the all-important high school entrance examination. "No doubt the end of the proposed legislation is to secure good teachers," the bishop continued, "and if the present teachers are giving satisfaction to the inspectors, trustees and ratepayers, why not legislate accordingly and make permanent these teachers who acted in good faith and have always been obedient to the rules and regulations of the Education Department?"[35]

In 1907, the government passed "An Act respecting the Qualifications of Certain Teachers."[36] For the bestowal of permanent teaching certificates, the legislation counted years of experience up to 1 July 1907 and required one four-week session of Normal School, to be completed no later than 31 December 1908. The legislation concerned only teachers from religious communities who worked in separate schools.[37]

Bishop McEvay was satisfied with the compromise. He told Premier Whitney that he appreciated the premier's "efforts to help us out of a serious difficulty created by neither you nor me — nor by the teachers concerned. Give us what you can and we will do our best to comply."[38]

Archbishop of Toronto

After less than nine years in London, Bishop Fergus Patrick McEvay was named archbishop of Toronto on 13 April 1908. The priests and people of the diocese of London bade their bishop an affectionate farewell in St. Peter's cathedral, and Archbishop-elect McEvay was no less genuine in his feelings when he replied to their addresses.[39] Sounding an ecumenical note, the London Free Press paid him this generous compliment: "His Lordship has earned by his piety, learning and good works a large measure of the public respect in general."[40]

One of Archbishop McEvay's last administrative acts on behalf of the diocese of London was to write letters to pastors of eight parishes, reminding them that the money he loaned to build their parish schools belonged to St. Peter's cathedral.

Archbishop McEvay was enthroned at St. Michael's cathedral on 17 June 1908, in a ceremony full of pomp and splendour.[41] Archbishop McEvay, who suffered from pernicious anaemia, which left him weak, spent only three years in Toronto. He was an imaginative and modern leader of more than 70,000 Catholics in the archdiocese. He established national parishes for the Italians and for the Ukrainians of the Eastern Rite; he was one of the founders of the Catholic Church Extension Society of Canada and engineered the Society's purchase of the Catholic Register. He purchased property with the intention of building a seminary that would be national but also local. He continued to champion separate schools and was in the vanguard of English-speaking bishops in Ontario who sought to curb the influence of French-Canadian nationalists, without excluding anyone from the life of the Church.[42]

Archbishop McEvay died on 10 May 1911, at fifty-eight years of age. Bishop Michael Francis Fallon, his successor in London, preached at the funeral Mass. The two prelates had been close, and Bishop Fallon would miss McEvay's fatherly guidance and wise advice.

Endnotes for Chapter 4 - Bishop McEvay

1 *Daily Free Press* [London], 6 April 1899, 5.

2 Ibid., 27 June 1899, 7.

3 *CR*, 23 June 1917.

4 Edgar J. Boland, *From the Pioneers to the Seventies: A History of the Diocese of Peterborough 1882-1975* (Peterborough: 1976), 20.

5 DLA, Fergus Patrick McEvay Papers (hereafter FPM Papers), Box 1, Patricius F. McEvay to Cardinal Giovanni Simeoni, Prefect of Propaganda Fide, copy of exeat letter and letter of acceptance from Bishop Dowling, 25 November 1899.

6 *Daily Times* [Hamilton], 27 June 1899.

7 *CR*, 27 May 1893, 5.

8 Henry James Morgan, "McEvay, Rev. Fergus P.," *Canadian Men and Women of the Time* (Toronto: 1898), 734.

9 *Daily Times* [Hamilton], 27 June 1899.

10 *CR*, 12 August 1899, 5.

11 *CR*, 12 August 1899, 5; 19 August 1899, 4.

12 Ibid., 23 September 1899, 5.

13 Ibid.

14 DLA, FPM Papers, Box 1, "Report of Arbitration Proceedings and Division of School Property in Windsor, 1903," McEvay to Flannery, September/October 1899.

15 *CR*, 28 October 1899; *Evening Record* [Windsor], 9 October 1899, 4; 18 October 1899, 4; 26 December 1899, 4.

16 DLA, FPM Papers, Box 1, "Report of Arbitration Proceedings," Cleary to McEvay, 25 June 1900; McEvay to Flannery, 21 July 1900; "To the Board of Education for the City of Windsor," c. 1901.

17 *Evening Record* [Windsor], 4 December 1901, 4. McEvay Papers, Box 3, "Report of Arbitration Proceedings," "To the Board of Education for the City of Windsor," 5 December 1901.

18 DLA, FPM Papers, Box 1, "Report of Arbitration Proceedings," "To the Hon. R. Harcourt, 27 April 1903; *Evening Record* [Windsor], 8 July 1902, 1.

19 *Statutes of Ontario*, 1903, 3 Edward VII, c. 35.

20 *Evening Record* [Windsor], 15 May 1903, 1.

21 DLA, FPM Papers, Box 1, "Report of Arbitration Proceedings," Meunier to McEvay, 12 February 1904; *Evening Record* [Windsor], 16 January 1904, 1; 13 February 1904, 1; 22 February 1904, 1.

22 Ibid. FPM Papers,, Box 1, J.N. Ferland, "Mémoire," 7 October 1900, trans. by Sister Teresita Kennedy, CSJ, 4–7.

23 Ibid., 11-14.

24 *CR*, 23 September 1899, 5.

25 DLA, FPM Papers, Box 1, McEvay to Ferland, 26 June 1900.

26 Ibid., FPM Papers, Ferland, "Mémoire," 15–18.

27 Ibid., 18-19.

28 Ibid., W. Flannery, "Reply," January 1901.

29 Roberto Perin, *Rome in Canada* (Toronto: 1990), 203. Robert Choquette, *Language and Religion: A History of English-French Conflict in Ontario* (Ottawa: 1975), 117-19.

30 Parish Files, Immaculate Conception Parish, McEvay to Beaudoin, 21 December 1904; McEvay to Semande, 21 December 1904; McEvay to Downey, 21 December 1904; McEvay to Vicar General [Meunier], 21 December 1904.

31 DLA, FPM Papers, Box 1, Beaudoin to McEvay, 24 December 1904.

32 Ibid., FPM Papers, McEvay to Beaudoin, 29 December 1904.

33 Ibid., FPM Papers, Beaudoin to McEvay, 30 December 1904.

34 Ibid., FPM Papers, *Ad Limina* Report, 24 October 1905 and presented 14-15 November 1905.

35 Franklin A. Walker, *Catholic Education and Politics in Ontario* (Toronto: 1964), 2: 215.

36 *Statutes of Ontario*, 1907, 7 Edw. VII, c. 52.

37 Walker, 2: 220-21; Michael Power, *A Promise Fulfilled: Highlights in the Political History of Catholic Separate Schools in Ontario* (Toronto: 2002), 194–95.

38 Walker, 2: 220.

39 Ibid., 20 June 1908, 4.

40 *London Free Press*, 23 May 1908, 4.

41 *CR*, 27 June 1908, 4–5.

42 Mark G. McGowan, "McEvay, Fergus Patrick," *DCB* (Toronto: 1998) 14: 699–701.

5. Michael Francis Fallon, OMI (1909-1931)

Michael Francis Fallon remains London's most paradoxical bishop. While he held many modern ideas, he was in many respects an old style nineteenth-century Catholic churchman. He was a person of great accomplishments and great controversy. Central to Bishop Fallon's life was his unconditional love of the Church and the Catholic people and he worked hard to have non-Catholics take Catholics seriously.[1]

He left a positive lasting legacy in the diocese. He founded eighteen new parishes and financed the building of many churches, improvements to St. Peter's cathedral and the construction of St. Peter's Seminary. His episcopacy coincided with renewal and expansion. The number of Catholics in the diocese increased by approximately 40,000,[2] and the number of secular and religious priests serving in the diocese went from 70 to 135. In 1920, there were 504 professed women religious in six different communities. A decade later, there were 710 in seven different communities, an astonishing increase.[3]

Education was a mania and a mantra for Fallon and he saw in the rising generation a vibrant future for the Church. Fallon was "determined that his Catholic people, of whatever ethnic origin, would emerge from the long night of the Reformation Period, to a world of unlimited achievement of the twentieth century."[4] In his view, to become first-class Canadian citizens, Catholics had to be educated. Fallon worked to develop a properly funded separate school system and to have Catholic high schools publicly funded, a goal only achieved a few years ago. During his episcopacy, the number of separate school students had more than doubled to 14,000. Fallon also improved the opportunities for Catholic university education and founded St. Peter's Seminary in 1912 to educate diocesan priests.

Fallon's outspoken opposition to French-language schools, however, came perilously close to destroying everything that he hoped to achieve. Francophone Catholics wanted to be secure in their use of French in their churches and schools. Fallon, however, looked upon the demands for bilingual education as a potential death knell for separate schools, because the schools were at the mercy of the government to improve their funding.

A forceful preacher and an electrifying orator, Bishop Fallon attracted great crowds. His sermons made a strong impact on many, including Protestants, and he defended the faith vigorously. He was never shy about appearing on the front pages and in the editorial columns of Canada's most influential dailies. He also tended to be blunt and undiplomatic and was prone to hector his opponents into submission. He found it difficult to forgive "what he felt were slights or obstructions to his will and convictions."[5] The public loved or loathed him, venerated or vilified him.

Childhood and Priesthood

Born in Kingston, Ontario, on 17 May 1867, Michael Francis Fallon was the oldest of eight children. His parents were Dominic Fallon and Bridget Egan, Irish immigrants. He was educated at St. Mary's elementary school and at Kingston Collegiate. After one year at Queen's University, he transferred to the Oblate-run University of Ottawa and completed the five-year B.A., *cum laude*, in classical studies in 1889. He then enrolled in the Ottawa diocesan seminary as a student for Kingston and earned a Bachelor of Theology degree in 1892. He was twenty-five years old.

Fallon, the star student of his generation at Ottawa, was involved in dramatics, the English debating society, athletics, and *The Owl*, the student newspaper. Following his studies, Fallon joined the Oblates of Mary Immaculate. Father Adélard Langevin, the superior of the seminary and the future archbishop of St. Boniface, thought so highly of him that he sent Fallon to the novitiate in St. Gerlach's, Holland. In 1893, Fallon pronounced his first vows. At St. Gerlach's, the seed of his intense dislike of nationalism was planted when Fallon heard students from the German Empire talk about German domination and witnessed their rudeness towards students of other nationalities.

Because the damp climate made Fallon ill, he was transferred to Rome. On 29 June 1894, he took his final vows, and on 29 July 1894, Cardinal Lucido Parocchi, the vicar of Rome, ordained him to the priesthood. Also during July, Fallon was awarded the doctorate in theology.

Returning to the University of Ottawa, he taught English literature, coached the rugby team and was managing editor of *The Owl*. In September 1896, Fallon was appointed vice-rector, on the insistence of the rector, Father James McGuckin, OMI, who wanted Fallon to succeed him. But the French-speaking Oblates did not support the appointment, because they wanted Ottawa to return to a bilingual curriculum, in abeyance since 1874. Their English-speaking confreres wanted Ottawa to remain essentially an English university with some instruction in French.

Fallon lasted only two years during which time the French-speaking Oblates outmaneuvered Father McGuckin and in February 1898, Father Henri-Antoine Constantine, OMI, pastor of Ottawa's St. Joseph church, became the new rector. Fallon had first thought it best that he leave Ottawa,[6] but he changed his mind and moved across the street to succeed Constantineau as pastor of St. Joseph's. While there, Father Fallon developed into a celebrated controversialist and premier public speaker and debater. His pulpit-and-press tug of war with Reverend J.F. Gorman, the Anglican rector of Ottawa's Grace church, received widespread newspaper coverage. He also crusaded to eliminate "The Declaration against Certain Catholic Doctrines" from the coronation oath of the sovereign and met with success in time for the 1911 coronation of King George V and Queen Mary.

Then on 10 June 1901, Father Charles Tatin, the Oblate visitor to Canada, ordered Fallon to move to Buffalo in two weeks, probably at the behest of

French-speaking Oblates. Fallon objected, claiming not for the first time of a conspiracy against him. Although he did not publicize his unhappiness to the laity, the news spread quickly and many protested it.

Ministry in Buffalo

While parish priest of Holy Angels church in Buffalo, Fallon established the OMI Cadets, a religious and semi-military organization that had enough members to form a regiment, with a band and a field hospital. Fallon the preacher attracted large crowds. Fallon the defender of all matters Catholic asked President Teddy Roosevelt to give more consideration to Buffalo's Catholic majority when making federal appointments.[7] In November 1904, he became the first provincial of the new American Province of the Oblates of Mary Immaculate, with headquarters in Buffalo.[8]

As an Oblate, Father Fallon preached missions, which brought him into contact with Catholics in Western Canada and influenced his future ministry. In 1899, he visited Winnipeg and area; in 1902 and 1908 he went as far west as British Columbia. During his travels, he heard many complaints from English-speaking Catholics that "their interests and the interests of the Catholic Church were being sacrificed through the determination to exclude English-speaking priests from that district."[9] He also brought Protestants into the Church. In March 1908, he left a group of thirty-one people to receive additional instruction in the faith at St. Mary's, Winnipeg, and was confident that many more would join the class.[10]

Fifth Bishop of London

Even Fallon's appointment as bishop of London was tinged with controversy. The first *terna* to fill the vacant See of London was dated 25 June 1908. Archbishop McEvay stressed to Archbishop Donato Sbarretti, the apostolic delegate, that the selection by the bishops of Toronto and Kingston was unanimous and that each candidate had a working knowledge of French.[11] On being asked their opinions of the three men, however, numerous clergy delivered half-hearted or outright negative assessments. The Congregation called for a new *terna* naming candidates who were fluent in French and thus able to attend to the spiritual needs of London's French-speaking Catholics.[12] The rejection of a *terna* on the basis of language was unprecedented in the Church in Ontario.

Archbishop McEvay protested to Sbarretti that the bishops had been mindful of the needs of the French-speaking people of the diocese of London. He said that they had a reasonable supply of French priests and were encouraged to retain their language. McEvay listed what he thought were more pertinent facts to consider. The vast majority of people in Ontario were Protestants; English was the only recognized language; previous attempts to extend the use of French in the province had harmed Catholic interests, in particular Catholic education; and of the 20,000 or so Catholics in the diocese that had French surnames, most spoke English as a matter of necessity, only half spoke French, and very few were literate in the language.[13]

McEvay's protests were futile. On 25 March 1909, the bishops forwarded a different list. Father John T. Aylward, the rector of St. Peter's Cathedral in London, was *dignissimus*; Father Robert Brady of the diocese of Hamilton was *dignior*; and Father Michael F. Fallon was *dignus*. If Fallon's fluency in French was the reason for the inclusion of his name, it was his success in bringing Protestants into the Church that galvanized Sbarretti to convince the cardinals to choose Fallon.[14] On 14 December 1909, Rome appointed Fallon the bishop of London.

The Early Months of His Episcopacy

Fallon was consecrated on 25 April 1910, in St. Peter's cathedral, by Archbishop McEvay, assisted by Bishop David J. Scollard of Sault Ste. Marie and Bishop William A. Macdonell of Alexandria. Bishop Fallon began his official episcopal visit of the parishes on 1 May and in twenty-five days he visited much of the "bilingual belt" of the diocese, where he confirmed 2,115 children.[15] In September and October, he visited thirty-three parishes and confirmed seventy-six adults and 1,754 children.[16]

On the surface, things were going well. The people were impressed by Bishop Fallon's energy, presence and no-nonsense preaching. Things, however, were about to spin out of control. Francophone Catholics in the diocese wanted a greater use of French in their churches and schools. Fallon bitterly opposed them.

Francophone Catholics in Ontario were feeling vulnerable to the influence of the English-speaking population, who were now a majority. So they aggressively promoted the equality of the French and English languages under the umbrella of bilingualism and demanded bilingual education for Francophone children where numbers warranted it. They strongly believed that to lose one's language was to lose one's faith — thus the vital importance of French in the liturgies and catechism classes of Francophone parishes.

Although Ontario's other English-speaking bishops supported Bishop Fallon in criticizing bilingualism, his outspokenness made him the leader of the opposition. Fallon did not believe that the use of French in public life should be extended beyond the guarantees in the British North America Act, which covered Québec, parliament and the federal courts. And he scoffed at the notion that the survival of one's faith depended on the survival of one's language, pointing out that the Irish had lost their language but not their faith.

Fallon's opposition to the growing French-Canadian nationalism and to expanding the use of French in schools and churches brought him into bitter conflict with the Francophone establishment in Québec, Ottawa and his own diocese. Disloyal and disgruntled clergy, supported by a hostile press, mainly in Québec, were the biggest thorn in Fallon's side. This conflict dominated the first ten years, or nearly half, of his episcopacy.

Bilingual Schools and Regulation 17

The first inkling of trouble over bilingual schools, which were regularly referred to as English-French schools, came during the confirmation at St. Francis Xavier church in Tilbury, on 10 May 1910. While Fallon was catechizing the children in French, he realized that they were having trouble understanding him and replying to his questions.

In Fallon's mind, if the parish's bilingual school produced students who did so poorly on a simple catechism exercise, especially in French, such a school was doing a disservice to its students. Even if the children had spoken excellent French, Bishop Fallon would have wanted to know their degree of proficiency in English, for he believed that knowledge of English would secure them a viable future. This incident, and others like it, confirmed Fallon's worst fears about widespread illiteracy among Francophone Catholic students in his diocese.

For pedagogical reasons, Fallon believed that only one language, either English or French, should be used in educating children.[17] He was convinced that bilingual schools would never be able to teach the required subjects properly and would lead to ignorance of the catechism and to a shockingly high failure rate on the high school entrance examinations. Fallon took his argument one step further. To prepare for life, Catholic children, regardless of their mother tongue, had to have a solid command of the English language, and consequently English had to be the language of communication and instruction in the separate schools.

Adding to the tension was the problem recently created by demands for bilingual education. On 9 March 1910, the Whitney government had reneged on its promise to the Catholic hierarchy of Ontario to negotiate more favourable treatment on issues affecting separate schools. Whitney told Archbishop McEvay that the government did the about-face because of the demands of l'Association canadienne-française d'éducation d'Ontario.[18] At its inaugural meeting in Ottawa, in January 1910, which more than 1,200 delegates attended, the ACFEO had called for the government both to entrench and to extend bilingual education at all levels of schooling and teacher training. It was an ill-timed intervention in separate school business.

Bishop Fallon met the Hon. W.J. Hanna, the secretary to the provincial cabinet on Sunday, 22 May 1910, to air his opinions. Hanna sent a memorandum on their conversation to Dr. R.A. Pyne, the minister of education, and to Premier Whitney. Later, he gave one, on request, to J.O. Rhéaume, the minister of public works. According to Hanna, Bishop Fallon "had determined so far as in him lay to wipe out every vestige of bi-lingual teaching in the public schools of this diocese."[19] Fallon had said: "We are in an English speaking Province, on an English speaking Continent …. the grounding in English was absolutely essential."[20] Sometime between 23 May and 4 June 1910, Henri C.A. Maisonville, private secretary to Rhéaume, stole the memorandum. It made its way to the Québec press.

An article with the provocative title of "French and Irish War in Ontario" appeared in the *Detroit Free Press* of 5 June 1910, attacking Fallon's opinions on bilingual schools.[21] At the 14 July retreat for his priests, the bishop declared his opposition to bilingual schools because of their inefficiency and he warned that they posed a threat to future separate school legislation. Almost in the same breath, he stressed that he was in no sense opposed to the teaching of the French language and that he expected his seminarians "to be able to teach catechism in French, to hear confessions in French, to deliver in French at least a short instruction" and also to be able to demonstrate this knowledge of French before he would confer the subdiaconate.[22] Fallon had not responded publicly to the *Detroit Free Press* article, but one of the priests made sure that Fallon's comments at the retreat found their way to the Québec press.[23]

On 16 September 1910, the Windsor *Evening Record* ran a story headlined: "Wants to Abolish The French Language From Schools of Essex County."[24] The story claimed that Fallon had banned the teaching of French in the separate schools of Belle River and Walkerville. The Toronto *Sunday World* joined the anti-Fallon fray as did the French-language press, including *Le Devoir* of Montréal and *L'Evènement* of Québec[25] Several Catholic diocesan publications also criticized Fallon.[26]

Blindsided, Fallon issued a statement, dated 19 September 1910. After he called both the *Detroit Free Press* and *Sunday World* articles false and libellous, he asserted:

> I have never been by word or deed, by intent or desire, unfriendly to the interests of the French-Canadian people, and I shall never be unfriendly to them at any time or place, no matter what the provocation …. I have never issued or caused to be issued, directly or indirectly, verbally, by writing, or in any other way, any order or mandate or even expression of opinion concerning the teaching of French or of any other language in the Separate schools ….[27]

Fallon took his case to two Francophone parishes. On Thursday, 29 September 1910, he repeated his denial in Annunciation parish in Stoney Point, in front of Father Napoleon D. St. Cyr, the pastor, and Father Lucien Beaudoin, the pastor of Notre-Dame-du-Lac. Fallon did the same on 30 September at Sts. Simon and Jude in Belle River, in the presence of Father Pierre L'Heureux, the pastor.[28] St. Cyr, Beaudoin and L'Heureux did not believe their bishop and did nothing to dissuade their congregations from thinking likewise.

The day after Bishop Fallon had spoken at Belle River, he was blindsided a second time. On 1 October 1910, the Québec-based *La Revue franco-américaine* published a French translation of the Hanna-Pyne memorandum and the text of Fallon's remarks at the diocesan retreat. Eight days later, Henri Bourassa published the two items in *Le Devoir*.[29] On 13 October, the *Globe* printed an English translation of the French translation of the Hanna-Pyne memorandum. The *Globe* also published an English translation of Fallon's retreat talk, which ended with these words: "My motto is 'Justice and Peace.' There is no man on earth who wants peace more than I do, and to have it one must be armed for war, and if there is a war, it is I who will be the conqueror."[30]

A war of words followed. The French-language press denounced Fallon, declaring that he was the centre of a conspiracy in Ontario to destroy the French language and that any deficiency that existed in bilingual schools was the result of poorly trained teachers. The Conservative government was deeply embarrassed by the publication of the memorandum.

Fallon issued a combative statement on 16 October 1910. He pointed out that of the 2,000 separate school pupils in six Francophone parishes, only ten had passed the recent high school entrance examination, and that Essex County had the lowest educational standing in the diocese. The fault lay not with the children or teachers, Fallon said, but "with the system, and it is against the system and the threatened extension of it, that I protest. I base my protest on the rights of children to an education that will give them a standing in the community in which they are to live, and that will open up to them the avenues of success."[31] He scorned the contention that language is the guardian of one's religious faith: "It is a strange faith that would be preserved by the kind of English or French that is taught in the alleged bi-lingual schools of Essex, and I resent the inference that Catholicity and ignorance are convertible terms."[32]

Another uproar followed in the press. David Cheney, a bilingual school inspector, claimed that the low rate of success in the entrance exam was due more to the fact that many children were kept out of school to work on the family farm.[33]

On 2 November 1910, the Whitney government instructed Dr. F.W. Merchant, the chief inspector of public and separate schools in Ontario, to investigate the bilingual schools in Essex, Kent, Russell, Prescott, Stormont and Glengarry counties and in Ottawa. Merchant submitted his report on 24 February 1912, proposing a five-year transition period during which English would gradually replace French as the language of instruction. He also made sensible and moderate proposals on teacher qualifications, inspections and the integration of bilingual schools with the high school system.[34] Unfortunately, the government took a decidedly negative approach. On 17 June 1912, it issued Regulation [Instructions] 17, which limited instruction in French to the first three grades and placed undue restrictions on the study of French as a subject.[35]

Reaction to Regulation 17 was bitter and divisive, but Fallon let the civil authorities wrestle with the Francophone opposition. He privately directed members of religious communities who were principals and teachers in the diocese's separate schools to obey the regulations of the department of education. Benedict XV issued his apostolic letter, *Commisso divinitus nobis*, to the Canadian hierarchy on 8 September 1916, in an attempt to bring reconciliation to Catholics. Fallon accepted the pope's judgment — that all school-age children in Ontario should have a thorough knowledge of English, that Francophone children should have equitable teaching of French, that the province was within its rights to demand that all its students have a knowledge of English but that it should not contest the rights of Francophones, and that Catholics should do nothing to endanger the existence of Catholic schools.[36]

Catholics, however, kept fighting each other over Regulation 17, and in response Benedict XV issued a second letter, dated 7 June 1918.[37] Fallon, who was visiting troops in Europe, did not comment publicly. In 1927, when the Conservative government of G. Howard Ferguson took a more reasonable approach to bilingual education, Bishop Fallon remained quiet on the topic.

Francophone Priests and Parishes

While Bishop Fallon was engaged in the battle over bilingual schools, he was also fighting a war over the status of some French parishes, which turned out to be far more dangerous. A determined group of six Francophone priests challenged Bishop Fallon's authority as it affected Francophone parishes and their schools. (In all, Bishop Fallon had twenty-six Francophone priests. And thirteen parishes were distinctly Francophone at the time Fallon became bishop of London.) The six were pastors of well-established parishes and the most active was Father Lucien Beaudoin, pastor of Notre-Dame-du-Lac in Ford City. The group made excellent use of the canonical procedures open to the Catholic clergy and laity to petition the apostolic delegate to settle grievances against their bishop. Unwilling to accept the authority of Bishop Fallon, and supported by the ACFEO in Ottawa and several Québec bishops, these priests and their supporters orchestrated a campaign of complaint that drove Archbishop Peregrin-François Stagni, the apostolic delegate in Ottawa, and Cardinal Gaetano De Lai in Rome to near exasperation.

The group fired the opening salvo in the form of a 130-page *mémoire*, dated 1 February 1911 and submitted to Archbishop Stagni. The main text was an indictment of Bishop Fallon accompanied by fifty-three allegations or claims. The claims were followed by a series of sworn statements, including statistics for the years 1900 to 1910, which were generated from the registers of Francophone parishes.

Bishop Fallon waited more than two years to respond and did so only at the insistence of Cardinal De Lai. In a sixty-six-page reply, dated 30 May 1913, Fallon characterized the *mémoire* as "an unfounded attack on the Diocese of London, on my two immediate predecessors in this See, and on many of my most zealous clergy — not to say anything of myself — that if it were even partially true, it would be a discredit to the Catholic history of this Diocese during the past quarter of a century."[38] He answered each of the fifty-three allegations, saving his most scathing comments for Father Beaudoin: "He is obsessed by the conviction that he has an almost divine commission to take care of the interests of the whole population of French origin in the diocese of London."[39]

That *mémoire* was the first of many petitions to land on the desk of Archbishop Stagni. Even before it was delivered, the focus of complaint had shifted to Father Denis J. Downey, pastor of Immaculate Conception since its founding in 1904. On 2 October

1910, a committee of parishioners asked Father Downey to expand the use of French in the Sunday sermons and to give the announcements in both French and English. Accompanying their request was an unsubstantiated claim that three-quarters of the parishioners and four-fifths of the parish children were French-speaking. Two months later, Father Downey, who spoke French, told them to consult the bishop. The result was a boycott of the collection basket until Father Downey increased the use of French.[40]

A three-way stalemate ensued. Bishop Fallon spent six days in the parish, in July 1911, at the request of Archbishop Stagni, who had received a letter from two members of the parish, through Jules Tremblay, the secretary of ACFEO.[41] Tremblay's intervention galled Fallon. In his report, Fallon provided population figures that refuted the claims in the letter. He told Stagni that Windsor had a population of 17,534 people, of which 5,382 were Catholic divided between two parishes: St. Alphonsus and Immaculate Conception. Of the Catholic population,

> the people of French origin, which is a very different thing from the people of the French language, number 3,092. Fully one-third of the people of French origin do not speak a word of French, ninety per cent of them use English as the regular medium of communication, and the knowledge of French is confined to a very small number … I submit these figures in order to demonstrate the impossibility of the children retaining their French, even if they knew it, and of the uselessness of the language to them for all practical purposes.[42]

The group carried on an unrelenting crusade into 1914. By 1914, their main demand was the creation of two new parishes in Windsor for the exclusive use of Francophones.[43]

Stagni was at a loss. He told the petitioners that the right to create new parishes belonged to the bishop of the diocese.[44] At the same time, in a letter of 14 March 1914, Stagni asked Fallon to reconsider the Windsor situation for the sake of peace and the interests of souls.

But Fallon's plans for a new parish did not include the accommodation of the city's Francophones and he made the situation worse. At the beginning of December 1911, Fallon took out an option to purchase property at the corner of Richmond Street and Argyle Road in Walkerville, midway between the parishes of Immaculate Conception in Windsor and Notre-Dame-du-Lac parish in Ford City.[45] Any new parish would be carved out of Father Beaudoin's parish in Ford City. Fallon did not tell Beaudoin of his intentions because the United States Steel Corporation was quietly accumulating land in Walkerville for a plant, pushing up prices, and Fallon did not trust Beaudoin to keep the news to himself. On 19 December 1911, the four members of the bishop's council met with Fallon and gave their approval.

On 1 January 1912, Bishop Fallon announced the erection of St. Anne's parish in Walkerville, and the next day he appointed Father H.N. Robert as the first pastor. Fallon's instructions to Robert included a standard provision that allowed people to continue to attend Notre-Dame-du-Lac, the mother parish, if they wished. Father Beaudoin was shocked. He had fought Bishop McEvay on the creation of Immaculate Conception parish in 1904 but had failed to contest the bishop's decision. On 15 February 1912, Beaudoin took his case to the Sacred Roman Rota, with the assistance of Father Joseph Gignac, a canon lawyer from Laval University.

The case was decided on 5 August 1914, in favour of Fallon. The court upheld his right to divide Beaudoin's parish but ordered Fallon to pay $7,000 to Notre-Dame-du-Lac as compensation for the loss of St. Edward's school. Beaudoin's blunder was not to limit his plea to the school issue. No Church court was going to overrule a bishop's right to erect parishes. But Beaudoin used the occasion to list his many accomplishments during his twenty years as pastor of Notre-Dame-du-Lac, insult the bishop's council and attack his bishop. That opened the door for Fallon to acknowledge that Beaudoin had done great things as a parish priest but had spoiled his good works with his disobedient and scandalous conduct

Then events took a disastrous turn. On March 1913, eight priests signed a declaration on behalf of Father Beaudoin — apparently at his insistence — as part of Beaudoin's case against Bishop Fallon's decision to divide his parish. The declaration ended with these words: "Que pendant son long ministère paroissial, la seule direction épiscopal à laquelle l'abbé Beaudoin se soit opposé est celle de M. Fallon, l'Évêque actuel, défendant d'enseigner le français aux enfants des Canadiens-français et de prêcher en français aux Catholiques de cette nationalité."[46] They were alleging that Bishop Fallon had "forbidden the teaching of French to children of French-Canadians and preaching in French to Catholics of that nationality."[47]

For Fallon's Francophone critics, these words encapsulated everything that was wrong with their "Irish" bishop; for Fallon, it was the lie that became a legend.[48] In July 1913, Fallon spoke to Cardinal De Lai in Rome, who suggested that Fallon appoint a French-speaking vicar general. Fallon refused, saying that not even the pope could appoint a vicar general in his diocese. Then De Lai held up the priests' declaration. Seizing it, Fallon declared that "anything from my diocese is my property."[49] De Lai was so surprised that he made no attempt to demand the document's return.

As soon as he returned to the diocese, Fallon commenced action against the eight priests who signed the declaration. Bishop Fallon wrote to each priest, demanding that they prove the allegation or withdraw it by 10 March 1914. One must have acquiesced, because his name does not figure in the proceedings of the diocesan tribunal. Fallon convened the diocesan tribunal, whose five members owed their appointment not to Bishop Fallon but to Bishop McEvay. The tribunal met on 5 March 1912 with Bishop Fallon as the plaintiff. Each defendant challenged the competency of the tribunal. All but one filed an appeal to Rome. The final case was not settled until 1915, but in the end, one defendant offered a verbal apology, after receiving a private browbeating from Fallon. Two others signed retractions, three were suspended but reinstated after signing retractions, and one, who had not been formally incardinated into the diocese, was expelled.

Father Beaudoin was cited on 9 April 1915. He was saved from the humiliation of writing an apology because Rome had agreed to take over the case and appointed Archbishop Stagni to investigate the defendants' case.[50] Stagni took testimony in 1916 from ninety-two witnesses and because there were so many contradictions, he forwarded the dossier to Rome for adjudication. It took until 15 December 1920 for Rome to render its verdict.

Then when Father Beaudoin died, on 18 August 1917, Fallon made a decision that led to a parish revolt: he appointed Father F.X. Laurendeau as the new parish priest. Laurendeau had been the secretary of the diocesan tribunal and thus was tainted in the eyes of Notre-Dame-du-Lac's parishioners. Laurendeau begged Fallon not to send him to Ford City, but Fallon insisted.

Before the end of the memorial Mass for Father Beaudoin at Notre-Dame-du-Lac, on 23 August 1917, a group of disgruntled parishioners left the church and took over the rectory. The priests found their luggage on the front lawn and had to change out of their vestments in public. The parishioners took over the church, set up a twenty-four-hour blockade and issued a challenge in the press to Bishop Fallon — the barricades would not come down until he had removed Father Laurendeau. Fallon showed his contempt by leaving for the United States, as planned, to preach a retreat for priests. The leaders of the revolt appealed to Rome, on behalf of the parish, on 3 September.

On 8 September, when Monsignor O'Connor and Father Laurendeau reclaimed the rectory, a riot broke out, involving nearly 3,000 people, the local police and one hundred military police. By the time it was over, the mayor of Ford City had read the riot act, men were in jail and dozens were hurt. The protesters boycotted the parish until Rome announced its decision on 13 October 1918. Bishop Fallon won. He had a right to appoint Father Laurendeau, and the parishioners had a duty to accept him as their pastor. Father Laurendeau stayed at Notre-Dame-du-Lac for a quarter century and became a distinguished monsignor.

Rome may have sided with Fallon on the Ford City riot, but earlier in a private letter of 7 June 1918, Cardinal De Lai asked Bishop Fallon to resign, quoting these words from Sacred Scripture: "If they persecute you in one city, flee into another."[51] Fallon was devastated. He received De Lai's letter while in England with Canadian soldiers and was in no mood to flee. As soon as the tour concluded, he went to Rome.

During the French-language fiasco, Bishop Fallon had survived other attempts to dislodge him or to diminish his episcopal authority. Members of the Québec hierarchy tried to convince Rome that the diocese of London was too large and should be divided. Pope Benedict XV told Fallon about this in a private audience on or about 22 July 1918.

In Rome Fallon wrote a lengthy exculpatory letter to the pope, dated 22 July 1918, that marks the low point in his fortunes as a bishop. He felt obliged to defend himself against Cardinal De Lai's accusations and to pre-empt any move on the part of the Holy See to demand his resignation or to transfer him. In the end, Bishop Fallon stayed in London and the diocese remained intact, and on 15 December 1920, Rome rendered its judgment on Stagni's 1916 investigation. "So far as I was concerned," wrote Bishop Fallon when publishing what he called the Final Judgment of Rome, "there were three fundamental points at issue: 1st, the competency of the diocesan tribunal of London; 2nd, the declaration that I had forbidden the teaching of French and preaching in that language; and 3rd, that opposition to the inefficiency of Bilingual Schools meant hostility to the French language."[52] Rome vindicated Fallon on all counts and a long-sought peace fell upon the diocese of London.

Politics in the First World War

During the First World War, Bishop Fallon openly showed his support for both the British Empire and for Ireland. An ardent imperialist, Fallon argued that the Empire was a bulwark against nationalism. Yet, he repeatedly castigated England for failing to give Ireland the kind of Dominion status that Canada enjoyed.

When the British Empire declared war on Germany, on 4 August 1914, Fallon threw his full support behind the Empire's efforts. He argued for conscription as early as 1915, encouraged Catholics to enlist, and called upon Catholic voters to cast their ballots for the Unionists and conscription in the election of December 1917, an action that vaulted Fallon into the national limelight again. Many Canadians praised him for his courage, while others, including close friends, damned him for interfering in federal politics.[53] As soon as war was declared, Sir Sam Hughes, minister of militia, asked Fallon for several chaplains and on 12 October 1915, the Ontario hierarchy chose Bishop Fallon to name the English-speaking chaplains from Ontario.[54] By the end of the war, Fallon had had a hand in the appointment of half the sixty-seven English-speaking Catholic chaplains from Canada.[55] He also lobbied for a chaplain service department for Canada.

In recognition of his efforts, the Unionist government invited Bishop Fallon in 1918 to visit the Canadian chaplains and troops. He toured

France twice, and visited nearly every Canadian encampment and military hospital in England. As well as carrying out his spiritual duties, he was in constant conversation with military, government and church officials.

In the midst of his heavy schedule, the War Office asked his assistance in the campaign to recruit 50,000 Irish volunteers. Fallon said that he could not help unless Britain gave the Irish people what it had already won — self-government. Hoping that Lloyd George, the British prime minister, might change his stance and grant Ireland self-government, Fallon presented him and his cabinet a copy of Father J.J. O'Gorman's "The Irish Question: The General Principles of its Solution," to no avail.[56]

Education Revisited

In 1919, Bishop Fallon became involved in two more controversies, one theological and one political. During February and March, Fallon and Canon L. Norman Tucker, rector of St. Paul's Anglican cathedral in London, debated the doctrine of the Immaculate Conception, proclaimed by Pius IX on 8 December 1854. Tucker had started the pulpit and press war by calling the doctrine the "greatest aberration in the history of Christendom" during a sermon.[57] The bishop and the canon exchanged sermons defending their positions and wrote letters to the press that were aggressive in tone, denunciatory and at times insulting. Newspapers gave them extensive coverage.

On 13 February 1919, Bishop Fallon spoke at Massey Hall in Toronto in support of extending separate school rights. At the time, Catholics were seeking their rightful share of business, industry and utility taxes for the separate schools. They also wanted full public funding for their high schools, instead of being funded for only grades 9 and 10. "Education and salvation cannot be separated," Fallon told a large and appreciative audience.[58] His speech paved the way for a tremendous revival in the separate school agitation in 1921 and 1922. Archbishop Neil McNeil of Toronto may have initiated the campaign but only Bishop Fallon, supported by the Knights of Columbus, could have forced the issue of the constitutional right of Catholics to a publicly-funded high school education to the forefront of public debate.[59]

From May 1921 to April 1922, Bishop Fallon spoke numerous times on the topic, was part of a delegation to the Ontario cabinet and wrote an open letter to the Ontario Legislature. Fallon's finest moment was his speech at Massey Hall on 10 February 1922. Speaking for three hours without notes to 4,000 people, he was brilliant, witty and entertaining.

The lobbying and fighting led to what is known as the Tiny Township Case. In 1925, the board of trustees for the separate schools in Tiny Township launched a test case to challenge the restrictive funding for their secondary schools. The case went to the Judicial Committee of the Privy Council in the United Kingdom, which rendered its decision on 12 June 1928, declaring that separate school supporters had the right to government funding for grades 9 and 10, but did not have a constitutional right to a full school system. By the time the judges had spoken, Bishop Fallon was very sick and out of public view.

Bishop Fallon's interest in education also included post-secondary institutions. On 23 September 1912, he had founded St. Peter's Seminary, in the cathedral rectory, so diocesan priests could be trained in the diocese instead of at the Grand Séminaire in Montréal. They could have gone to St. Augustine's Seminary, which was opening in Toronto as a national seminary for English-speaking Canada under the direction of all the bishops of Ontario. Fallon had been open to this until a misunderstanding led him to view St. Augustine's as being under the direction of the archbishop of Toronto. By 1931, St. Peter's had fifty-three students. Fallon also wanted Catholic colleges to affiliate with the province's expanding secular universities, and he wanted Catholic men *and* women to obtain university degrees. Fallon promoted Western University (now known as the University of Western Ontario) and was offered the position of chancellor, which he declined. He engineered the affiliation of three Catholic post-secondary institutions with Western. They were Ursuline-run Brescia College, the Basilian-run Assumption College in Sandwich, in October 1919, and the seminary's St. Peter's School of Philosophy, in 1925. He persuaded the Ursuline Sisters of Chatham to move their liberal arts school for women to the Western campus, but failed to convince the Basilians to move from Windsor. With the affiliation, Assumption broadened its curriculum to include general and honours programs.

A year of celebration

Nineteen twenty-six was a banner year, marking the centenary of the founding of London, and it was the apex of Fallon's episcopacy. In the blessed absence of public controversy that year, he was able to use the opportunity to hold many specifically Catholic events in what became Catholic Centennial Week, held from 26 September to 1 October.

On 26 September, St. Peter's Cathedral was re-opened after having been closed for eighteen months. Fallon had added new woodwork, stained glass windows in the nave, clerestory and in the side altars, stations of the cross, communion rail, high altar, bishop's throne and electrical fixtures. The original stations from the cathedral were donated to the Martyrs' Shrine in Midland, Ontario. The Italian artist Ilario Panzironi decorated the ceiling and wall below the clerestory and painted the four scenes from the life of St. Peter in the transepts and the six angels in the sanctuary.

On 28 September, Brescia College was opened. The architect was John R. Boyde, who also designed Holy Name of Mary church in Windsor and St. Peter's Seminary.

On 29 September, 5,000 people attended a Pontifical High Mass to celebrate the opening of the main building of the seminary on the glorious sweep of Sunshine Park, which had been donated by Sir Philip Pocock, an influential London businessman and papal knight.

On 30 September, Senator Charles Murphy, a longtime friend of Fallon, spoke at the laying of the cornerstone of the new St. Joseph's Nurses Home. On 1 October, St. Mary's Church was re-opened following extensive renovations.

Illness and Death

Bishop Fallon had been ill for the last three years of his life from complications arising from diabetes.[60] Before he died, there were long periods during which he was not seen in public, rarely said Mass, or even had the strength and concentration to read his breviary.

Fallon officiated at the opening of the crowning glory of his legacy, St. Peter's Seminary's neo-Gothic chapel, on 18 June 1930. He attended the Mass but was too weak to join the photo session.

He died on 22 February 1931. Following his requiem at St. Peter's cathedral, on 26 February 1931, his remains were buried in a vault beneath the chapel of St. Peter's Seminary. His estate of $157,000 went to fund bursaries, including one for Ukrainian Eastern Rite Catholics, and chairs at the seminary.[61]

Bishop Denis O'Connor of Peterborough, who had been Fallon's vicar general for many years, described him as "an educator, an administrator, a builder for this world and for God."[62] Sir Robert Borden, the former prime minister, wrote to Joseph J. Fallon, the bishop's brother: "It always seemed to me that Bishop Fallon was endowed with the essential qualities of greatness. His passing is, indeed, an undoubted loss to the national life of our country."[63] Father J.J. O'Gorman summed up the man who after death was called the Mitred Warrior: "Bishop Fallon failed at times in patience and meekness, but God knows he did seek righteousness, piety, faith and charity."[64]

Endnotes for Chapter Five -- Bishop Fallon

[1] John K.A. O'Farrell Papers (hereafter O'Farrell Papers), Sister Paschal, RHSJ, interview by John K.A. O'Farrell, London, Ontario, 11 March 1969.

[2] Catholic population figures for the diocese of London are generally unreliable. In 1911, there were 60,000 Catholics. This was substantially less than the 67,500 reported by Bishop Walsh, little more than the 59,383, according to Bishop O'Connor and the same as given by Bishop McEvay in 1905. The highest figure given by Bishop Fallon was 77,000, which did not change until 1935, when the figure of 109,581 was taken from the 1931 census. In any event, the Catholic population did increase substantially.

[3] DLA, MFF Papers, Box 6, *Relatio*, 1920 and 1930.

[4] John K.A. O'Farrell, a review of Robert Choquette's *Language and Religion: A History of English-French Conflict in Ontario*, in *Chelsea Journal* (November-December 1977).

[5] O'Farrell Papers, Sister Pascal interview.

[6] Ibid., 133, 138-39, 140.

[7] Ibid., Fallon Scrapbook, 83.

[8] *Catholic Union and Times* [Buffalo], 10 November 1904; *CR*, 12 November 1904.

[9] Archivio Secreto Vaticano Delegazione Apostolica Canadese [ASV DAC, Papers of the Apostolic Delegate to Canada], 20, Dossier 20/20, Fallon to Stagni, 26 May 1913, 8, which is also in DLA, MFF Papers, Box 5.

[10] ASV DAC 112, Dossier 3, Fallon to P.F. Stagni, 12 June 1908.

[11] Pasquale Fiorino, "The Nomination of Michael Fallon as Bishop of London," CCHA *Historical Studies* 62 (1996), 34.

[12] SV DAC 19, Dossier 10/1,, De Lai to Sbarretti, 17 February 1909.

[13] Ibid., 19, McEvay to Sbarretti, 10 March 1909 and 1 April 1909.

[14] Ibid., 19, Sbarretti to Merry del Val, 25 May 1909.

[15] DLA, MFF Papers, Box 4, Fallon to J.E. Meunier, 25 March 1910; Bilingual Belt Confirmations, handwritten document, no date.

[16] Ibid., MFF Papers, Box 4, Confirmation Sept. & Oct. 1910, handwritten document.

[17] *Ottawa Citizen*, 17 October 1910.

[18] Ibid., MFF Papers, Box 3, Whitney to McEvay, 9 March 1910, copy.

[19] DLA, MFF Papers, Box 5, W.J. Hanna to R.A. Pyne, 23 May 1910 [Hanna-Pyne Memorandum], 2.

[20] Ibid.

[21] *Detroit Free Press*, 5 June 1910.

[22] DLA, MFF Papers, Box 3, "The Reverend Fathers L.A. Beaudoin, L. Landreville, A.D. Emery, P. Langlois, T. Martin, N.D. St. Cyr, P. L'Heureux and J.A. Loiselle versus the Right Reverend Michael Francis Fallon, Bishop of London and the

Diocesan Tribunal of the Diocese of London," no date, 8-9.

[23] Robert Choquette, *Language and Religion: A History of English-French Conflict in Ontario* (Ottawa: 1975), 88.

[24] *Evening Record* [Windsor], 16 September 1910.

[25] *Sunday World* [Toronto], 17 September 1910; *The Canadian Annual Review of Public Affairs [CAR] 1910* (Toronto: 1911), 421.

[26] DLA, MFF Papers, Box 4, Bishop Michael Francis Fallon, "French Press Controversy 1911-17."

[27] *Globe*, 23 September 1910, 2; *CR*, 1 October 1910, 4.

[28] DLA, MFF Papers, Box 3, "The Reverend Fathers … versus The Rt. Reverend Michael Francis Fallon …," no date; 7.

[29] Choquette, *Language and Religion*, 94.

[30] *Globe*, 13 October 1910, 2.

[31] *CR*, 22 October 1910, 4. The Goderich Statement was published by the *Globe* on 17 October 1910, 1-2.

[32] Ibid.

[33] *Evening Record* [Windsor], 21 October 1910, 1.

[34] F.W. Merchant, *Report on the Condition of English-French Schools in the Province of Ontario* (Toronto: 1912), 70-81. A copy of this report is in the Fallon Papers.

[35] The complete text of Regulation 17 can be found in C.B. Sissons, *Bi-Lingual Schools in Canada* (Toronto: 1917), Appendix II.

[36] For a complete text of the Apostolic Letter, see Sissons, *Bi-Lingual Schools in Canada*, Appendix III. For one newspaper's reaction, see the *Globe*, 28 October 1916, 5. DLA, MFF Papers, Box 34, "Memorandum of the Right Reverend M.F. Fallon, Bishop of London … on the occasion of their meeting at Ottawa on Wednesday, January 24th, 1917, for The Consideration of the Apostolic letter 'Commisso divinitus nobis'"; Box 5, "Points of Information …" [September 1917].

[37] *CAR 1918* (Toronto: 1919), 645-46.

[38] DLA, MFF Papers, Box 4, Fallon to Stagni, 30 May 1913.

[39] Ibid., MFF Papers, Box 4, "Reply to Allegatum," 28.

[40] Ibid., MFF Papers, Box 5, "Londinensi …," 1 February 1911, Allegatum 15.

[41] Ibid., MFF Papers, Box 3, Fallon to Stagni, 8 June 1911; ASV DAC 21, Dossier 2/1, Tremblay to Stagni, 2 June 1911.

[42] Ibid., MFF Papers, Box 5, Fallon to Stagni, 8 July 1911.

[43] DLA, MFF Papers, Box 5, Stagni to Fallon, 14 August 1911, Fallon to Stagni, 16 August 1911, Stagni to Fallon, 18 August 1911, Stagni to Fallon, 16 January 1912, Fallon to Stagni, 20 January 1912, Stagni to Fallon, 24 January 1912; ASV DAC 20, Dossier 206, Beaudoin, Langlois and St. Cyr, 12 January 1912; Ibid., 21, Dossier 2/1, petition of 9 March 1912; Dossier 3/1, Petitions of 15 February 1913; Dossier 3/2, Petition of 4 December 1913; Fallon Papers, Box 36, *La situation religieuse des Catholiques-Française* (1914), *Mémoire au subject de Paroisses Canadiennes-françaises à Windsor* (1914).

Endnotes for Chapter Five -- Bishop Fallon (continued)

[44] ASV DAC 20, Dossier 3/1, Stagni to J.D.A. Déziel, 11 June 1913.

[45] Ford City did not become a separate municipality until 1 January 1913.

[46] DLA, MFF Papers, Box 4, *Cause des curés dénoncés, diffamés, ou suspendus ab officio par Monseigneur M.F. Fallon* (1914), 3.

[47] O'Farrell Papers, "The Final Judgment of Rome," 21 March 1921.

[48] DLA, MFF Papers, Box 4, Fallon to Angelo D'Alessandri, 7 March 1916.

[49] O'Farrell Papers, Monsignor Andrew Parnell Mahoney, interview by John K.A. O'Farrell, 6 August 1968.

[50] Choquette, *Language and Religion*, 143-46.

[51] DLA, MFF Papers, Box 5, Fallon to Benedict XV, 22 July 1918. The quotation is from Matthew 11:23.

[52] O'Farrell Papers, Copy of The Final Judgment of Rome, 21 March 1921.

[53] DLA, MFF Papers, Box 3, Conscription/Union Government; *London Free Press*, 7 December 1917, 8; *CR*, 15 December 1917, 1.

[54] Ibid., MFF Papers, Box 3, "Minutes of a meeting of the Bishops of Ontario, held at the Archbishop's House, Toronto, on Oct. 12th, 1915."

[55] Duff Crerar, *Padres in No Man's Land: Canadian Chaplains and the Great War* (Montreal & Kingston: 1995), 278, fn. 32.

[56] Michael Francis Fallon, "Diary of Visit to Canadian Army in England and France at the Request of the Canadian Government," 112; copy in possession of the author; DLA, MFF Papers, Box 7, Ireland.

[57] *The Bible and the Blessed Virgin Mary: Some Correspondence* (Catholic Unity League, 1919), 3.

[58] *CAR 1919* (Toronto: 1920), 523.

[59] *CAR 1922* (Toronto: 1923), 604.

[60] O'Farrell Papers, Sister Philomena, Tourier, Precious Blood Monastery, interview by John K.A. O'Farrell, 29 March 1969.

[61] London *Advertiser*, 20 March 1931. Information on the bursary for Ukrainian Eastern Rite Catholic seminarians came in a letter from Reverend B. Dzurman to the author, 15 December 1988.

[62] *Detroit Free Press*, 27 February 1931, 1.

[63] O'Farrell Papers, Fallon Scrapbook, Sir Robert Borden to Joseph Fallon, 1 March 1931.

[64] Charles G.D. Roberts and Arthur L. Tunnell, *A Standard Dictionary of Canadian Biography: The Canadian Who Was Who* (Toronto: 1934), 1:186.

6. John Thomas Kidd (1931-1950

John Thomas Kidd, the sixth bishop of the diocese of London, was a relatively late vocation to the priesthood who profited from nine years in business and an education in Rome to rise rapidly in the ranks of the Church. He put his gifts for business administration to excellent use during three periods: when he completed the construction of St. Augustine's Seminary in the archdiocese of Toronto; when he oversaw a dramatic building boom in the diocese of Calgary; and when he kept the diocese of London solvent and functioning during the 1930s.

A man of modesty and gentleness, Bishop Kidd lived simply and worked hard to stay close to his priests and people. His piety was evident in his stately and solemn celebration of Pontifical High Mass. After the tumult of his predecessor's episcopacy, he was the right man at the right time. His combination of business skills, piety, and unassuming style ensured that the diocese remained stable and grew during a period of instability in the world. His nineteen-year episcopacy was characterized by careful management of diocesan assets, spiritual rejuvenation of the laity, and episcopal solidarity with the faithful during the Great Depression and the Second World War.

Early Years and Priesthood

John Thomas Kidd was born on 28 August 1868 in the farming village of Athlone, Simcoe County, Ontario. His parents were John Kidd and Brigid Murphy. His father was a successful entrepreneur and was held in high esteem for his unassuming charity. John junior was sent to De La Salle school on Duke Street in Toronto for his secondary education and then to the Basilian-run St. Michael's College. He was enrolled from September 1885 to April 1887, and he returned for two weeks in December 1887, likely to write his Christmas exams.

Then he moved to Wiarton in the Bruce Peninsula to manage a lumber mill, possibly owned by his father. Within three years, he was manager

and part owner of the mill, and remained for the next six years. His abilities helped him win a seat by acclamation on the local municipal council, a position he never sought. When Kidd lived in Wiarton, no more than a dozen Catholic families called it home, and for the longest time the village had no Catholic church. When one was built, there was no resident priest. Mass was celebrated at most once a month.

In such an unlikely environment — the roughhouse world of lumbering combined with the absence of a church life — Kidd, who was twenty-nine years old, decided to pursue a vocation as a Catholic priest. He returned to St. Michael's College for the 1896–97 year. When he applied to enter the seminary, he was sent, in 1897, not to the Grand Séminaire in Montréal, as was the custom, or to an American seminary, but to Rome, a privilege sparingly bestowed. He went with the encouragement and support of Archbishop John Walsh of Toronto, his first patron.

In Rome, Kidd studied philosophy at the Pontifical Urban College de Propaganda Fide and theology at the Pontifical Gregorian University, where he met Eugenio Pacelli, the future Pius XII. John Kidd was ordained to the priesthood by Archbishop J.J.F.O.Zardetti, in the chapel of the Canadian College, on 16 February 1902. Before returning home, he earned a doctorate in theology and visited the Holy Land.

On 26 December 1903, he landed in Toronto.

Archbishop Denis O'Connor immediately assigned him as curate to Father Théophile-François Laboureau, the venerable parish priest of St. Anne's parish in Penetanguishene. Father Kidd remained there from January 1904 to 14 June 1908. He came to appreciate the parish's attachment to the French language and culture, and he acted as administrator for the last two years of his assignment. (As bishop of London, Kidd always addressed French-language congregations in French.)

Archbishop O'Connor's resignation on 4 May 1908 triggered a series of events that transformed Father Kidd's life. Before his installation as archbishop, O'Connor's successor, Bishop Fergus Patrick McEvay of London, appointed Kidd as his secretary. Other responsibilities soon followed. He became an early governor of the Catholic Church Extension Society, which McEvay had founded in 1908 to nurture and safeguard Church expansion in Western Canada. In February 1909, Kidd was made chaplain of the Knights of Columbus Council 1388, the first Knights of Columbus council in the archdiocese, and in July 1909, he became McEvay's chancellor.

Rector of St. Augustine Seminary

When Archbishop McEvay died on 10 May 1911, Father Kidd was appointed administrator of the archdiocese until the installation of Archbishop Neil McNeil on 22 December 1912. McNeil retained Kidd as his secretary, and on 15 March 1913, he assigned him as the first rector of St. Augustine's Seminary, with the directive: "Go out and finish that seminary and get things started."[1] St. Augustine's had been founded to provide a national centre for seminary training in English. Prior to this, candidates for the priesthood were trained in Québec. Kidd completed construction of the building and opened the seminary in September 1913. Impressed and grateful, McNeil left Kidd at the helm for twelve years, and on 27 May 1914, he invested Kidd with the papal honour of protonotary apostolic. Ten years later, the University of Ottawa honoured him with an LLD.

Under Kidd's leadership, St. Augustine's was fashioned into a seminary that accepted candidates for the priesthood from practically every diocese in English-speaking Canada, from the China Mission Society and for a time from Eastern Rite churches. Kidd stressed the paramount importance of learning the English language to candidates destined to serve new Canadians. During and long after Kidd's rectorship, St. Augustine's "became both an expression of English-speaking Catholic independence in the area of clerical formation and an assertion of new confidence among Canadian clergy that the English-speaking Catholic Church, centred in Toronto, had a mission that extended '*a mari usque ad mare.*'"[2]

On a more personal level, one member of St. Augustine's inaugural class remembered Monsignor Kidd as a "strict disciplinarian" and a "kind and conscientious guardian," whose charity in the act of correcting one's faults was an example to faculty and students alike.[3]

Bishop of Calgary

On 6 February 1925, John Kidd was appointed the second bishop of Calgary. He was consecrated on 6 May 1925 at St. Michael's Cathedral in Toronto, by Archbishop Pietro di Maria, the apostolic delegate to Canada and Newfoundland. Assisting were Archbishop Neil McNeil and Archbishop Joseph-Médard Émard of Ottawa.[4] Bishop Kidd took for his episcopal motto the words *Deus caritas est*, which means "God is love" (*1 John* 3:8). On 13 May, he was welcomed to his new home of Calgary by citizens of all faiths. Archbishop Arthur A. Sinnott of Winnipeg officiated at the installation ceremony.

Bishop Kidd arrived in Calgary at a difficult time. His predecessor, Bishop John McNally, had endured great trouble imposing his authority on his clergy in the mission territory, and was moved to Hamilton in 1924 (he became archbishop of Halifax in 1937). Kidd skirted the problem by going to the people. After his installation, he made an extensive tour of southern Alberta, visiting Catholics in their homes, accepting simple accommodations and promising to return on a regular basis, a promise he kept.

The energetic bishop then initiated a vigorous building program. A micro-manager, he applied his extensive knowledge of the lumber business to the projects, drawing up specifications, estimating costs and often supervising construction to control costs. During his six years in Calgary, he built thirty-five parish and mission churches. Among them were

Ste-Famille for the French-speaking Catholics, St. Francis Chapel for the Hungarians and St. Stephen's for the Ukrainians. He established twenty residential parishes and added twenty-four new priests to the rolls of the diocesan clergy, many of them graduates of St. Augustine's Seminary, which he visited every year on recruitment drives. In addition, he invited the Redemptorists into the diocese in 1929, giving them a parish and a mission. To help pay for this expansion, he relied on the fundraising of the Knights of Columbus and the generosity of the Catholic Church Extension Society.

Bishop Kidd expanded health care, education and social services for Catholic Albertans. In 1929, he brought the Sisters of St. Martha of Antigonish, Nova Scotia, to the diocese, and they established hospitals in Lethbridge and Banff. The Grey Nuns, already well established in the diocese, added a chapel and a new wing to Holy Cross Hospital in Calgary. The Catholic school boards responded to Kidd's call for more secondary education by financing the construction of four new high schools, including an impressive one on the Native reserve near Cardston. Kidd introduced summertime religious vacation schools in the rural districts and organized catechetical correspondence courses for children in the diocese's most remote districts. The bishop was a pioneer in religious broadcasting on the Prairies. He convinced the owner of radio station CFCN to broadcast High Mass and Vespers from the cathedral, on alternate Sundays, and thirty-minute catechetical talks twice a week. To help him sustain parochial life, Kidd turned to the Catholic Women's League, whose volunteer work he vigorously encouraged.[5]

On 3 July 1931, John Kidd was named bishop of London. In gratitude for his superb leadership, 6,000 people gathered at Victoria Arena in Calgary, on 13 September 1931, to bid him farewell.[6] During his relatively brief time in Calgary, he had been free to build the infrastructure that a young diocese needed. In London, however, he would have to focus on keeping the diocese intact during the economic downturn of the Great Depression, which bankrupted individuals, businesses and institutions, including parishes.

Sixth Bishop of London

Bishop Kidd was installed in St. Peter's cathedral on 23 September 1931. Among those attending were Archbishop Andrea Cassulo, the apostolic delegate for Canada and Newfoundland, three archbishops, ten bishops, and four episcopal representatives.[7] The following day, described as "slight in stature and slow and dignified in his movements," he celebrated Pontifical High Mass.[8] Sixty-three years old, he was the oldest prelate to become bishop of London, and, at eighty-one, the oldest to die in office.

One of his first diocesan duties was to open the $450,000 addition to St. Joseph's Hospital in London, on 15 October.[9] That such wealth could be generated as the Great Depression began to tighten its grip surely astonished and delighted him. Kidd must have felt blessed to have been translated to such a well-established diocese. St. Peter's cathedral had been restored and St. Peter's Seminary had recently been completed. There were 135 diocesan priests, supported by a sizeable contingent of religious priests, 73 parishes, 24 missions, and nearly 100 churches. There were fifty separate schools, twelve continuation schools (grades 9 and 10), two high schools and four private academies: Assumption College for men in Sandwich, Brescia College for women and St. Thomas Scholasticate in London (Resurrectionists) and St. Alphonsus Seminary in Woodstock (Redemptorists). There were four communities of men religious and eight communities of women religious, who numbered in the hundreds. In 1931, the diocese of London had approximately 70,000 members.[10]

To ensure that the diocese remained sound, Bishop Kidd took steps to fortify its institutional foundations and deepened its spiritual life. The results allowed Catholics, both native-born and recently arrived, to flourish during his nineteen-year episcopacy and his successor's tenure.

Ensuring a sound financial future

Bishop Kidd's due diligence concerning mortgages, property ownership and estates was a hallmark of his administration. It was the prime reason that the diocese of London was able not only to blunt the most deleterious effects of the Great Depression but also to establish twenty-one new parishes and seven new missions during Kidd's episcopacy and build churches in each one. Remarkably, when he became bishop the diocese owed the banks the frightening sum of $530,500 for the new churches and renovations that Bishop Fallon, Kidd's predecessor, had undertaken during the previous seven years. The cathedral portion of this debt amounted to $181,000, half of which Kidd required the parishes to pay down in the form of regular assessments.[11] To complicate matters, the diocese felt a strong moral obligation to help separate school boards stay solvent. At times, this required parishes, if they were not already keeping sister parishes afloat, to provide emergency loans to school boards. As Canada's economy continued to deteriorate, an understanding evolved among the Catholic bishops of Ontario that no Catholic institution — diocese, college, school board or hospital — should declare bankruptcy. They feared that one bankruptcy would trigger many more and that the banks, which had been ruthless with the Church in Western Canada, would not hesitate to be as ruthless in Ontario.[12] Having been a bishop in the West, Bishop Kidd took this understanding very seriously. He realized that he needed to deal with the diocesan debt immediately and devise a plan whereby the diocese would be able to endow its own fund for good works. Otherwise he would be unable to maintain and build upon the work of previous bishops of London and would lose the confidence and generosity of the faithful.

Bishop Kidd carried out his solution in three stages over fifteen years. The opening stage involved consolidating and liquidating bank-held parish debts, by creating a sinking or reserve fund, the first of its kind for a Catholic diocese in Canada. The diocese issued episcopal corporation bonds in 1934 and 1936, to the maximum amount of $2,500,000, and gave the Canada Trust Company the right to manage the fund. (These bonds were redeemed in 1943 and replaced with a new issue at a lower rate of interest.) When Kidd floated the idea to his priests in 1933, there was little vocal opposition to this innovative approach.

For collateral, Kidd mortgaged thirty of the most valuable properties in the diocese, starting with the property on which stood St. Peter's cathedral, the cathedral rectory and the garage. To establish the true value of this collateral, he ordered a professionally conducted inventory of the holdings of each parish and mission, which produced a rich and revealing archive of the material assets of the episcopal corporation.[13] He also repeatedly warned his parish priests about the necessity of having proper insurance on all church property.

As soon as the 1934 bonds had been issued, Bishop Kidd paid the banks in full. In 1939, he examined the titles to the deeds of each episcopal property, discovering that at least four were still held in the name of the archdiocese of Toronto.[14] In 1941, in conformity to new Ontario legislation, he regularized the ownership of diocesan cemeteries.[15] As well, he supervised the management of the estates willed to the diocese, the most complicated one being that of Sir Philip Pocock, a businessman and papal knight.[16]

Kidd's financial acumen allowed the diocese to donate $1,500 a year to the archdiocese of Regina and the Francophone diocese of Gravelbourg in Saskatchewan. Archbishop James C. McGuigan of Regina, who later became the archbishop of Toronto and a cardinal, was forever grateful to Bishop Kidd.[17]

Strict economy was enforced, although at times it was carried too far. Some parishes had to live for many years with basement churches (nicknamed "Kidd's caves") until the people saved enough money to build a proper church. Also, as he had done in Calgary, Kidd immersed himself in the minutiae of property acquisition, deeds and church construction.

In September 1943, Bishop Kidd began the second stage of diocesan financial reform by lowering the rate of interest on parish debts to the episcopal corporation from four and a half percent to four percent in return for larger payments on the principal. This measure went into effect on 1 January 1944. Next, he reorganized the chancery collections, so that the burden would be carried equitably by all the parishes, in accordance with each parish's ability to pay. He continued the cathedraticum at a rate of four percent on pew rents, Sunday offertory collections, fees for baptisms and marriages, pastoral dues and the Easter and Christmas collections, pointedly reminding his priests that in other dioceses the charge was usually ten percent. There would be seven mandatory collections: African Missions, Holy Land and Peter's Pence, as ordered by the Holy See, the Catholic Church Extension Society, St. Francis China Mission Society, St. Peter's Seminary and the

Sisters of St. Joseph. The proceeds from the last-named collection were to be divided between the Sisters of St. Joseph and the Good Shepherd Sisters, in support of their work for orphans and the aged. (In 1935, he had introduced the Holy Childhood Association for schoolchildren into the diocese.)

Kidd then cancelled all other collections and assessments. In their place, he instituted a single diocesan assessment on each parish at the rate of eight percent, which included the four percent cathedraticum and the seminary collection. Collections for the Society of the Propagation of the Faith, the St. John the Evangelist Society (priests' retirement fund) and the Holy Childhood Association were not affected by the changes, since they were taken up *outside* the churches and sent directly to their respective officers.[18] These changes took effect on 1 July 1943.

These changes made possible the third and most ambitious stage of Bishop Kidd's reforms. On 16 January 1947, he announced to the clergy the beginning of the first-ever diocesan-wide fundraising campaign, "for the purpose of increasing the facilities and services rendered for Education, Youth and Charity."[19] The initiative was soon known as the Bishop's Fund Campaign and was the model for what evolved into an annual event. Kidd then addressed both clergy and laity in a lengthy and energetic pastoral letter in which he emphasized the needs of orphans and the aged, the lay retreat movement and Catholic primary, secondary and university education.

He called the campaign "a great crusade in Catholic co-operation." It was well-organized with a paid consulting firm and volunteer chairmen guiding operations at the diocesan and regional levels and in each of the ninety-five parishes and twenty-seven missions. The 6,000 canvassers from the Holy Name Society were expected to knock on the doors of every Catholic home in the diocese. Without them, the campaign would have fizzled.

The minimum objective was to raise $1,250,000 by 30 April 1949. There was no parish assessment and no quota on individuals or families. "Fair share" was the campaign slogan. People pledged an amount consistent with their ability to fulfill their pledge and paid in monthly or quarterly installments over a two-year period. Although the drive fell short by $35,000, Kidd considered the effort a success. Initial disbursements went to the Rosary Crusade, Catholic

high schools in Windsor and London, Holy Family Retreat House in Oxley, Brescia College, the Good Shepherd Sisters and St. Joseph's Manor in Windsor and campaign expenses.[20]

Ensuring a vital spiritual life

Throughout his episcopacy, Bishop Kidd was daily preoccupied with bringing the people entrusted to his care ever closer to God by means of the Eucharistic Lord and the intercession of the Blessed Virgin Mary. His spiritual leadership expressed itself primarily in Catholic education, Catholic immigration, lay retreats and the daily recitation of the rosary. Kidd's direction renewed and reinvigorated Catholic culture, which was distinctive in its day for the collective identity it fostered and sustained. That identity survived the nasty wreckage of an economic depression and the horrors of a catastrophic war in Europe and Asia. In the immediate post-war years, it had to gird itself to face a new menace — the Communist persecution of fellow believers in Eastern Europe and Asia.

The devotional re-awakening that Kidd fostered in the diocese was part of a wider movement. In the early part of the twentieth century, successive popes worked for liturgical and spiritual renewal to keep the laity strong in the face of Modernism and totalitarian movements, such as Fascism, Nazism, and Communism. They also believed that spiritual renewal would strengthen families and offer people hope in the turmoil of the twentieth century. Pope Pius X, whose motto was "To restore all things in Christ" (*Eph* 1:10), had promoted renewal centred on sacramental faith, encouraging Catholics to receive Communion more often. Pope Pius XI tried to further the deepening spirituality of Catholics that had begun under Pius X by initiating the lay retreat movement in the early 1930s and encouraging more frequent recitation of the rosary. He also promoted the Catholic Action movement to involve laity in social justice causes. These renewal movements and the greater involvement of the laity in ecclesiastical life opened up the possibility for the Second Vatican Council.

Supporting Catholic Education

Bishop Kidd fervently supported separate schools. On the provincial scene, he was a confidant of Martin J. Quinn of the Catholic Taxpayers' Association in the 1930s and participated in the work of the CTA's successor, the English Catholic Educational Association of Ontario, founded in 1942. Every year, the bishop reminded the people of his diocese of their solemn duty to assign their property and business taxes to their local separate school board and to send their children to separate schools. His reminders must have produced the desired result, since he blessed twenty-five new separate schools during his time as bishop of London.

Catholics in Ontario, however, were not receiving their rightful share of corporate taxes. When the Ford Motor Company of Windsor decided to allocate eighteen percent of its property taxes to the Windsor Separate School Board, starting in 1937, the Windsor Public School Board challenged the move in court. The case ended up at the Judicial Committee of the Privy Council in London, England in 1941. To demonstrate his support for the separate school side, Kidd dispatched Father Francis J. Brennan, then editor of the *Catholic Record*, as his observer, despite the hazards of wartime overseas travel. Typical of Kidd, he did not want anyone to know that Father Brennan had been sent to England.[21] The Privy Council upheld the appeal of the public board, a financial disaster for Windsor's separate schools.

In 1949, Bishop Kidd directed that the Bishop's Fund Campaign give nearly $70,000 to the student-rich but cash-starved Catholic high schools in Windsor and London. In January 1950, he gave his approval to the formation of Catholic parent-teacher associations.[22]

During the 1936–37 academic years, Kidd established a Newman Club at the University of Western Ontario; in 1939 he negotiated the direct affiliation of St. Peter's School of Philosophy at the seminary with Western; and in 1949, the Bishop's Fund Campaign donated $50,000 to Brescia College.

Catechetics was another one of Kidd's preoccupations when it came to the education of his Catholic flock. As one means of providing instruction in Christian doctrine, he established the Confraternity of Christian Doctrine in eighty parishes. This association of lay people who taught catechism had two main objectives. One was the religious education of children — at home under parental direction, in Catholic and public schools

and during summer vacation. The other was the provision of study groups for Catholic adults and special inquiry classes for non-Catholic adults, who were thinking of joining the Church. As well, a summer school of catechetics trained elementary and secondary school teachers in the art of teaching religion. Another avenue for catechetics aimed at elementary school children was the radio program, School of Christ, beginning on 3 December 1939, when it aired for the first time on CFPL. It was the brainchild of Monsignor West T. Flannery, a professor of dogmatic theology at St. Peter's Seminary who produced the program for its twenty-four years. The program later became a taped television show.

Responding to the Needs of Immigrants

In the post-war years, there was massive Catholic immigration to Canada from nearly every corner of Europe, and Bishop Kidd helped with the settlement process in Canada and the diocese. He co-operated with other Catholic bishops, at home and in Europe, federal immigration agents, the Catholic Adjustment Bureau and the Catholic Immigration Bureau of Toronto and the Capuchins in Blenheim and local farmers. He also worked with Father Anthony DesLauriers, SJ, of the Apostleship of the Sea, and with the Sisters of Service in Halifax, where the majority of immigrants first landed.

Catholics of many nationalities came to call the diocese their home. Among them were people from Poland, Hungary, the Netherlands, Belgium, Malta and Yugoslavia. The influx of so many new Catholics in such a short period of time, with signs that many more would follow, enriched all aspects of the life of the diocese of London, expanding the presence of the Church in Southwestern Ontario to a degree unimagined prior to the war. The numerical and thus cultural domination of the original Irish and Francophone settlers and their descendants was on the decline. The face of the diocese was changing.

Lay Retreats and Rosary Apostolate

When Pope Pius XI started the lay retreat movement in the early 1930s to make it possible for the faithful to spend time in meditation and religious exercises, Bishop Kidd advanced the cause in his own jurisdiction. Father Philip Pocock, the future archbishop of Toronto, was diocesan director. The three-day retreats were initially limited to men because they took place at Assumption College or St. Peter's Seminary. In 1937, Kidd expanded the movement to include retreats for women and French-language speakers of both sexes. In 1938, he arranged retreats for the approximately 250 female schoolteachers in the diocese, at St. Mary's Academy in Windsor and Brescia College in London.[23]

Lay retreats were so popular that Bishop Kidd, with the advice of leading laymen, purchased the Erie View Hotel at Oxley in Essex County, in 1947, and spent close to $152,000 turning it into a diocesan retreat centre. On 1 August 1948, he blessed and opened the Holy Family Retreat House, with Father Arthur L. Meloche as the spiritual director. Oxley has hosted countless retreats for men, women and school children. It stands today as a tribute to Kidd's spiritual ideals and practical foresight.[24]

In 1948, Bishop Kidd gave his blessing to the Holy Family Crusade, which would popularize the corporate praying of the rosary in the diocese. The post-war world was a time of immense anxiety over the atomic bomb and the rise of Communism. The Church had additional concerns about keeping Catholic families intact and being attentive to the call of Mary in her appearances at La Salette, Lourdes and Fatima to pray the rosary.

The crusade, the first of its kind in the Catholic world, was directed by the Father Patrick Peyton, CSC, a charismatic figure who had dedicated himself to promoting the rosary as a sure path to peace and reconciliation. He founded his ministry in 1942 in gratitude to the Blessed Virgin Mary, who had answered his prayers when he became very ill with tuberculosis during his last year in the seminary. Working from his headquarters in Albany, New York, Father Peyton had two principal ministries: the Family Theatre and the Family Rosary. With the blessing of his religious community and the help of many Hollywood friends, he was a regular on radio leading his listeners in reciting the rosary. His motto was "The family that prays together, stays together."

Father Peyton gave a rosary triduum at St. Mary's in London in 1947, at the invitation of Bishop Kidd. The three days of religious observance were a stunning success. Kidd, who prayed the rosary every day, then asked Peyton to lead a crusade for the entire diocese. The purpose was to persuade every Catholic family in the diocese to recite at least one decade of the rosary together each day. To achieve this lofty goal, Kidd assigned Bishop John C. Cody, his coadjutor since 1946, to lead a campaign modeled on the previous year's fund-raising endeavour. Again, the Holy Name Society would provide canvassers to collect signed pledges from families. The time agreed upon was 21 March to 1 May 1948. Father Peyton arrived from Hollywood on 31 March, following a special Easter broadcast of the Glorious Mysteries, and stayed until the end, preaching to large and attentive gatherings in churches, schools and movie theatres.

With ninety thousand people signing pledge cards to pray the rosary, Bishop Kidd was ecstatic. The commitment of so many Catholics to recite the rosary every day was the bedrock of a unified Catholic culture that reached its pinnacle of sophistication and influence during the episcopacy of his successor, Bishop Cody. The 1948 Family Rosary Crusade was the defining moment for 1950s Catholicism.

Other accomplishments

Other aspects of Bishop Kidd's career in the diocese of London are worth mentioning. He had a close working relationship with the Catholic Women's League and the Knights of Columbus. He attended the annual diocesan Eucharistic Congress and the giant Holy Name Society rallies. During the Second World War he encouraged his priests to serve as military chaplains; and he founded the alumni association of St. Peter's Seminary.

Bishop Kidd left the diocese spiritually vigorous and in sound financial shape. At the time of his death in 1950, he had ordained 105 diocesan priests (in 1949, the seminary was bursting with 128 resident students); he had confirmed more than 44,000 people (of these 3,400 were converts); and he had presided over a spectacular increase in the number of Catholics in the diocese, up from 70,000 in 1931 to 117,775 in 1949.[25]

Death

Bishop John Kidd died on 2 June 1950 and was interred in a vault underneath the seminary sanctuary.[26] He had enjoyed a private celebration of the twenty-fifth anniversary of his episcopal consecration, on 6 May 1950, but he did not live to witness the public celebrations planned for 11-12 June. On 12 April 1950, his old classmate, Pius XII, had named him, in a letter written in his own hand, an assistant at the Pontifical Throne.

Endnotes for Chapter Six -- Bishop Kidd

1 John C. Cody, "The Most Reverend John Thomas Kidd, D.D. Sixth Bishop of London," St. Peter's Seminary, *The Alumni Bulletin* (March 1951), 3.

2 Mark G. McGowan, *The Waning of the Green: Catholics, the Irish and Identity in Toronto, 1887-1922* (Montreal: 1999), 81.

3 Cody, "The Most Reverend John Thomas Kidd, D.D.," 4.

4 *Toronto Daily Star*, 6 May 1925, 7 May 1925; *CAR 1925-26* (Toronto: 1927), 586.

5 Diocese of Calgary Archives, "Most Rev. John Thomas Kidd, D.D., second Bishop of Calgary," two-page typescript, undated, supplied by Sister Leona Henke, OSU, assistant archivist.

6 *CR*, 19 September 1931, 1; 26 September 1931, 1.

7 Ibid., 3 October 1931, 1, 4, 5; *Toronto Daily Star*, 24 September 1931.

8 Ibid., 3 October 1931, 5.

9 Ibid., 24 October 1931, 5.

10 *Ontario Catholic Year Book and Directory 1931* (Toronto: 1932), 76-83.

11 DLA, JTK Papers 3, Box 4, Kidd to The Manager, Bank of Montreal (London), 8 May 1934; JTK Papers 4, Box 5, Pastoral Letters, 10 November 1936.

12 Michael Power, *Assumption College: The Struggle to Survive 1920-1940* (Windsor: 2000), 146-47, Kidd to Father T.A. MacDonald, CSB, president of Assumption College, 26 September 1932.

13 DLA, JTK Papers 4, Box 5, Pastoral Letters, 24 July 1933, 5 February 193417 April 1934, 1 June 1934 and 1 October 1934; JTK Papers 3, Box 2, Episcopal Corporation Investment in Bonds, "The Roman Catholic Episcopal Corporation of the Diocese of London in Ontario to The Canada Trust Company Deed of Trust and Mortgage, Dated January 2nd, 1934"; "The Roman Catholic Episcopal Corporation of the Diocese of London in Ontario to The Canada Trust Company Deed of Trust and Mortgage Made as of April 15th, 1936"; *CR*, 28 April 1934, 5.

14 Ibid., JTK Papers 3, Box 3, Title Deeds; JTK Papers 7, Box 5, Kidd to Very Rev. John V. Harris, 17 November 1939.

15 Ibid., JTK Papers 4, Box 5, Pastoral Letters, 19 March 1942.

16 Ibid., JTK Papers 3, Box 4, Estates.

17 Ibid., JTK Papers 3, Box 4, Kidd to McGuigan, 18 August 1932, McGuigan to J.C. Kelly, 3 September 1932, Kidd to J.J. Gnam, 29 October 1933, "Regina and the West Collection," 22 June 1934; JTK Papers 4, Box 5, Pastoral Letters, 8 August 1932, 16 November 1933, 30 August 1934, 31 October 1935, 25 September 1936, 9 September 1937, 6 February 1939; *CR*, 15 December 1934, 8.

18 Ibid., JTK Papers 4, Box 5, Pastoral Letters, 14 September 1943.

19 Ibid., JTK Papers 4, Box 5, Pastoral Letters, 16 January 1947.

20 Ibid., JTK Papers 4, Box 5, Pastoral Letters, 1 May 1949.

21 Ibid., JTK Papers 14, Box 6, various correspondence; *CR*, 12 April 1941, 1, 9 August 1941, 1, 4; Franklin A. Walker, *Catholic Education and Politics in Ontario* (Toronto: 1964), 2: 479-80.

22 Ibid., JTK Papers 4, Box 5, Pastoral Letters, 9 January 1950.

23 Ibid., JTK Papers 4, Box 5 Pastoral Letters, 18 July 1935, 28 April 1938, 9 June 1938.

24 Ibid., JTK Papers 3, Box 2, Holy Family Retreat House, Oxley, Ontario, various correspondence.

25 Ibid., JTK Papers 4, Box 5, Status Animarum 1949.

26 *London Free Press*, 3 June 1950, 1, 4, 8, 18.

7. John Christopher Cody (1950–1963)

John Christopher Cody, the seventh bishop of London, presided over the phenomenal growth of almost every aspect of Catholic life in the diocese, making the 1950s and early 1960s a heady time in diocesan history. The Church was sure of itself, of one mind in its goals and respected by nearly all sections of society. Perhaps the most visible demonstration of the spiritual solidarity and social standing of the diocesan Church was the annual May Day parade in Windsor. Featuring numerous floats dedicated to the Blessed Virgin Mary and a continuous recitation of the rosary, the parade ended with Benediction of the Blessed Sacrament held for thousands of the faithful.

Every initiative seemed to fall into place, not without effort, but in ways that tell us much about unity of purpose under the graceful guidance of a chief shepherd revered as a father figure. Bishop Cody relished his father image and used it to advantage.

Bishop Cody's episcopacy was favoured from the outset. The pious and gentle bishop served at a time when local Catholic culture manifested itself in popular piety and in the faithful's charitable support of diocesan institutions. The essentials of the Catholic faith and Catholic morals, the rightness of episcopal and priestly authority and the pre-eminent place of the Church in Canadian society were never seriously doubted. The diocese had benefited from Bishop Kidd's prudent financial administration and his diocesan-wide devotional re-awakening and Cody built on them. As well, the flood of immigrants from Europe during the 1950s brought many Catholics into the diocese, and immigration played a major role in determining and defining the destiny of Cody's episcopacy.

Bishop Cody's tenure also ended an era, concluding as the Second Vatican Council, that great watershed of the twentieth century, was getting underway.

Early Years and Priesthood

John Christopher Cody was born in Ottawa, Ontario, on 16 December 1899, the third of eleven children. His parents were David Patrick Cody, a CPR engineer who came from Montréal, and Maria May Tunney, who was from Ottawa. Although thoroughly Irish in family background and carefully nurtured in the Irish culture and mentality of the Ottawa Valley, John pursued his higher education in a French-speaking milieu. He attended St. Alexander's College in Québec. One of his fellow students at the college was Paul Martin Sr., the future Liberal cabinet minister, who later resided in the diocese of London. When Cody decided to become a priest for the archdiocese of Ottawa, he took his philosophy at the Sulpician seminary in Montréal and then his theology at the Grand Seminary in Ottawa under the direction of Francophone Oblates. He became fluent in French, an asset when he was bishop of London.[1]

On 26 May 1923, in Notre-Dame Basilica, Archbishop Joseph-Médard Émard of Ottawa ordained John Cody to the priesthood. Special permission was granted for him to be ordained because he had not reached the canonical age of 24. His first appointment was curate at St. Patrick's, the historic Irish parish, from 1923 to 1933. While at St. Patrick's, he taught catechetics for nine years at the Ottawa Normal School; he was in charge of the mission at Darling, near Ottawa; and he was involved in the lay retreat movement and the instruction of converts. He served as pastor of St.

Declan's in Brightside (1933), St. Elizabeth's in Cantley, Québec (1934) , and Assumption in the Francophone suburb of Eastview (1934-37). Father Cody was an excellent parish priest and particularly effective in instructing converts; his affable personality won the allegiance of his parishioners and the attention of Archbishop Joseph-Guillaume-Laurent Forbes, OMI, of Ottawa.

Bishop of Victoria

On 5 January 1937, Pius XI chose John Cody to be the bishop of Victoria, British Columbia. He was consecrated in the basilica in Ottawa, on 25 February 1937, by Archbishop Forbes, who was assisted by Archbishop William M. Duke of Vancouver and Bishop Louis Rhéaume of Timmins. At thirty-seven, he was the youngest Catholic bishop in Canada. His episcopal motto was *Victoria per Mariam*; it means "Victory through Mary" but could also mean "Victoria through Mary," a play on words relating to the name of the diocese.

Bishop Cody was installed at St. Andrew's cathedral in Victoria, on 7 April 1937. The diocese had had three bishops during the preceding twelve years, and now its 15,000 Catholics needed a bishop who would stay long enough for the diocese to prepare for its centennial in 1946 as the oldest diocese west of Toronto. He spent more than nine fruitful years as Victoria's bishop, visiting every outpost, no matter how remote, and making time for every Catholic that he met. His interest in the Native missions prompted him to raise money for that apostolic work by preaching retreats every year in Eastern Canada.

Among his accomplishments were the renovation and redecoration of the cathedral. He was instrumental in opening seven churches, nine chapels, five parish halls, three rectories, five elementary schools and two homes for the aged. He was involved in the founding of a diocesan newspaper, *The Torch*, a diocesan library and an annual summer school for religious education. He introduced five religious communities into the diocese.

In addition, Bishop Cody supported the formation of the Perpetual Help Credit Union, the Catholic Welfare Bureau, the Catholic Youth Organization, Holy Childhood Association, the Indian Co-operative and the Serra Club. He led three

diocesan Eucharistic congresses, raised $100,000 for the Centenary Education Fund and organized and directed the centenary celebrations, from 28 July to 4 August 1946.[2]

Coadjutor Bishop of London

While Cody was preparing for Victoria's centennial, Pope Pius XII appointed him coadjutor bishop of London, with the right of succession. The appointment was dated 6 April 1946, and made public on 17 April, but did not include a date for Cody's arrival. This was the first time that London was given a coadjutor or any appointed episcopal assistance. The timing prompted Cody to ask Bishop Kidd to allow him to arrive in London after 4 August, the final day of the centennial. Kidd was most congenial. He thought that if a request were made to the Holy See through the apostolic delegate, the delay would not be a problem, and he promised to cover the costs for the reception of the papal bulls for Cody's transfer.

Bishop Cody came to London on 11 September 1946 and, at Kidd's suggestion, resided at the cathedral rectory. He was happy with this arrangement because he felt that isolation would hamper his work with Kidd, who lived at Blackfriars, the bishop's palace.

Cody worked diligently on the 1947 Bishop's Fund Campaign and the 1948 Family Rosary Crusade. As well, he did his share of confirmations, was present at all major diocesan events, and always respected Kidd as the bishop of the diocese. His last public act, as coadjutor, was to represent the diocese in Rome for the 1950 Holy Year, a three-day whirlwind trip.

Seventh Bishop of London

When Bishop Kidd died on 2 June 1950, Cody became bishop of London. The next day, he ordained seven priests, and the following week, he officiated at Kidd's solemn funeral liturgy.

Cody, "a genuinely devout and very kind man," encouraged the development of a strong corporate devotional life. His piety helped shape the expression of Catholic culture in the diocese. He asked his priests to observe certain devotions and customs in parishes. During the Marian Year (1954), for example, he insisted on devotions being offered every single day in May and October, in every parish, with a sermon on each day. He asked that the cincture be arranged in the form of an "M" when setting up the vestments. (Some priests considered this "cluttered" piety.[3])

During Bishop Cody's thirteen-year episcopacy, the diocese enjoyed a robust institutional expansion not experienced before or after. "The Catholic Church is on the march in our province," wrote Father George Flahiff, CSB, the Basilian superior general, to Bishop Cody, "and you are to be complimented in giving it leadership."[4] Cody enhanced the financial well-being of the diocese. He built churches, rectories, parish halls and schools and added a wide range of spiritual and social services for Catholics of all walks of life. He warmly welcomed immigrants, defined parish boundaries, codified Catholic life in the statutes of the 1956 synod, and reached out to the Church in Peru.

During Bishop Cody's episcopacy, the diocese of London experienced impressive growth. He established 33 parishes and 6 missions; blessed 54 new churches, 40 rectories and 37 parish halls; opened two junior seminaries (Sacred Heart in Delaware and Regina Mundi in London), the College of Christ the King (now King's University College), five senior high schools, five intermediate high schools, 91 separate schools (890 classrooms) and 11 convents. He promoted higher education and completed the towers of St. Peter's cathedral and added the Lady Chapel. He brought into the diocese six communities of religious priests, one community of brothers and five communities of sisters. With his active encouragement, and sometimes with significant financial support from the diocese, two new mother houses were erected (Mount St. Joseph in London and the Pines in Chatham). Between 1951 and 1963, the aggregate number of diocesan priests increased from 202 to 254, in addition to the more than 130 religious priests working in the diocese. In 1959, there were 129 seminarians at St. Peter's Seminary. (Approximately half were candidates for the diocese of London; the others were from other Canadian and U.S. dioceses). St. Thomas Scholasticate, the seminary of the Congregation of the Resurrection, had from 20 to 30 students who took classes at St. Peter's.

Between 1950 and 1957 the diocese spent more than $9,185,593 on the following projects and programs (all figures rounded off): church construction ($4,755,191), rectory construction ($333,500), subsidies for school construction ($1,236,802), construction of other buildings ($1,739,700), and subsidies to diocesan institutions ($1,120,400).[5]

Behind these figures are some interesting stories about the development of the Church in Cody's time.

Integrating immigrants

Catholic immigration was the most significant factor that propelled Bishop Cody into his unprecedented building program. He estimated that between 1950 and 1957, the diocese built forty percent of its parish and mission churches (approximately 45) and forty-five percent of the Catholic elementary and secondary schools (approximately 85) in existence in 1957.[6]

Upwards of 70,000 Catholic immigrants settled in the diocese during Cody's episcopacy.[7] This estimate included 27,893 immigrants who arrived in 1953 and the flood of refugees from the failed Hungarian uprising of 1956. Cody welcomed the new Catholics with open arms, and set up institutions to help keep the new arrivals active in the Church beyond the first generation and to integrate them as quickly as possible into Canadian culture and traditions.

To this end, and inspired by Pius XII's encyclical *Exsul familia*, Bishop Cody founded a Diocesan Catholic Immigration Council, which was given a mandate to work with the International Catholic Migration Commission in Geneva, Switzerland, with the Catholic Rural Settlement Society of Montréal, and with the federal Department of Citizenship and Immigration. The diocese's Catholic Immigration Office, co-ordinated the Council's work. The Catholic Immigration Centre in London and in Windsor served as the primary hubs, providing short-term care such as food, clothing and furniture, assistance in finding employment and housing, and spiritual care.

The St. Vincent de Paul Society in Windsor, deaneries, parishes, social workers, welfare offices and several dozen national priests assisted in the work. The diocese had at least one priest for each of thirteen national groups: Belgian, Croatian, Czech, Dutch, German, Hungarian, Italian, Latvian, Lithuanian, Polish, Slovak, Lebanese (Maronite) and Maltese. Of these, the Dutch and the Italians were the largest in number. The Canadian Catholic Conference in Ottawa (later the Canadian Conference of Catholic Bishops) also provided annual grants.[8] It helped that Bishop Cody was chairperson of the administrative board of the Conference, in 1953, and a member of the commission on immigration established by the apostolic delegate to Canada, in January 1956.

Bishop Cody's commitment to Catholic immigration was evident in his decision to declare 29 April 1956 as Catholic Immigration Day in the diocese, as part of the diocesan centennial celebrations. Acting on a directive issued by the Sacred Consistorial Congregation in Rome, he set aside this day as a day of prayer "for the spiritual and temporal welfare of the new Canadians and the persecuted peoples of the world."[9] Each of the seven deaneries held rallies with a special 4:00 pm Mass at a church with the capacity to handle the anticipated crowds. Attending were local, provincial and national dignitaries, the executives of service clubs, immigration and employment centres and the chambers of commerce, the Knights of Columbus, the Catholic Women's League, sodalities and confraternities, school officials and new Canadians, who were encouraged to dress in traditional costume.

At the urging of the Polish people of the diocese, Bishop Cody, a fervent anti-Communist, visited Poland in August 1959. At the time, it was rare for a Catholic bishop from the West to be allowed to visit a country behind the Iron Curtain. It was a spiritually exhilarating experience for Bishop Cody, who had never witnessed such solidarity among the faithful.

In 1962, Monsignor J. Austin Roney proudly announced that the diocese had spent $2 million during the previous ten years on national parish churches, rectories, halls and additions to existing schools. Bishop Cody founded eleven national parishes, a startling number given that Cody, like many of his episcopal colleagues, was often hesitant to establish them for fear that they would be too independent of episcopal control and direction.[10]

Supporting construction and good works

Bishop Cody made changes to diocesan management, including expanded fundraising efforts and improved funding of school construction

and charities. He turned Bishop Kidd's one-time 1947 fundraiser into an annual campaign, beginning in October 1951, called the Diocesan Development Fund Campaign. The initial goal was $250,000, which was increased after several years to $300,000. Every Catholic wage earner was asked to contribute one day's pay and those with larger financial resources were asked to donate according to their wealth. The announced targets were usually met. Cody was fortunate that the faithful were willing to support his good works, at times to extraordinary lengths.

In 1952, Bishop Cody founded a modern chancery to provide a more professional and organized management of diocesan business. He introduced a new system of diocesan assessment and cathedraticum, effective 10 January 1952. Each parish was required to pay, twice a year, a fixed amount as its share of diocesan maintenance. Next, he revised the schedule of the obligatory special collections, in April 1952, limiting them to nine: African Missions, Church Extension, Holy Land, Lenten Alms, St. Peter's Seminary, Peter's Pence, St. Francis-Xavier Seminary (Scarboro Foreign Missions), Papal Charities and Propagation of the Faith. Lastly, he entered, as his predecessor had done, into a deed of mortgage and trust with the Canada Trust Company. It was dated 2 June 1952, and was for bonds worth up to $4.5 million. The buildings and property of thirty-four of the diocese's wealthier parishes, including the cathedral parish, were put up as collateral. It appears that the diocese limited its borrowing to several million dollars as Cody was anxious not to overburden the faithful or his successor with a large debt that might forestall future development.[11] Some priests and others, however, deeply resented some of these changes.[12]

A strong proponent of credit unions, the Bishop arranged for a campaign to have one founded in each parish. Some of the larger credit unions exist today as community credit unions.[13]

The subsidies for school construction helped separate school boards in Windsor and Essex County build elementary schools and urgently needed high schools. For years, banks had not been willing to loan money to those boards because some school boards had failed to meet their bond obligations during the Depression. As a result, no Catholic elementary schools were built in Windsor between 1929 and 1954. As well as funding school construction, the diocese sponsored a Catholic Building Fund Campaign for Windsor's separate schools between 1956 and 1959.[14] This placed an enormous strain on parishioners in the diocese, and particularly on those in Windsor and Essex County. But, if Bishop Cody had not come forward, one wonders how the separate schools in those jurisdictions would have survived until the Foundation Tax Plan of 1964, which increased the revenue of separate schools boards. The additional funding allowed separate school boards to extend the system to include Grades 9 and 10.

The diocese also granted generous subsidies to other diocesan institutions, many of which carried out ministries of good works and social justice. Funds went to the Immigration Centre in Windsor, and Hôtel-Dieu Hospital, Windsor, and Holy Family Retreat House. A subsidy of $20,000 went to the Federation of Catholic Charities in Windsor.[15]

In 1957, Bishop Cody established Catholic Charities as an umbrella institution to co-ordinate and streamline the charitable endeavours of all Catholic organizations in the diocese He wanted to modernize Catholic charitable work within a financial framework that the diocese could afford. The organizations were of three kinds: parish-based with traditions of service, emerging professional agencies and agencies operated by communities of women religious. They included the St. Vincent de Paul Society, the Catholic Women's League, the Legion of Mary, the Order of Alhambra, the Catholic Family Service Bureau of Windsor, the Catholic Family Centre of London, the Catholic Social Service Bureau of Sarnia and the Catholic Children's Aid Society. There was also the work of the Sisters of St. Joseph (St. Joseph's Manor House in Windsor and Providence House in London), the Sisters of Misericorde (Mercy Shelter in Chatham), the Ursulines (Glengarda in Windsor), the Religious Hospitallers of St. Joseph (Villa Marie), the Sisters of the Good Shepherd (Maryvale in Windsor) and the Daughters of Divine Charity (Loretto Hall in Windsor). Cody also founded Our Lady of London Camp (later Camp Olalondo), in 1953, for boys and girls.

Bishop Cody encouraged the appointment of men and women to the boards of directors of different agencies, knowing that one day the laity would be at the forefront of the delivery and management of social services. As well, he always insisted that Catholic Charities work closely with the broader community.[16]

Supporting higher education

In addition to funding the construction of Catholic elementary and secondary schools, Bishop Cody assisted post-secondary institutions. Subsidies went to Assumption College/University in Windsor. The lion's share of the money spent between 1950 and 1957 on the construction of "other buildings" went to the College of Christ the King, a Catholic men's college in London.

Bishop Cody played a major role in Assumption College's becoming a university. The college, which had been a Basilian school since 1870, gained university standing on 1 July 1953, through an act of the Ontario Legislature and moved from being an affiliated arts college of the University of Western Ontario to being an independent degree-granting institution. As early as 1949, when he was still coadjutor, Cody had lobbied, and eventually won over, a sceptical Father Edmond McCorkell, the Basilian superior general, to have Assumption end its affiliation with Western.[17]

Although Bishop Cody championed the establishment of a Catholic university for Windsor and Essex County, he refused to commit diocesan funds in a legally binding way to such a costly venture. As soon as Assumption had received its charter in 1953, Bishop Cody promised a one-million-dollar subsidy, in installments of $50,000 per year, to begin when Assumption announced its building campaign. He also assisted Assumption by deeding to it the land on which the college, the high school and its substantial playing fields were situated. Cody gave a total of $50,000, in 1954 and 1955, to assist in relocating the high school.

In 1956, Assumption became Assumption University of Windsor with affiliated colleges (Essex College, Holy Names College, Holy Redeemer College and the Anglican Canterbury College). The building campaign began that year and in 1957 the diocese contributed $60,000 towards the $1,250,000 drive to construct a new library, student centre and heating plant.

As matters transpired, the diocese did not have to donate the full $1 million. In 1963, Assumption University of Windsor ceased to operate as an independent Catholic university and became a federated member of the newly formed non-denominational, publicly funded University of Windsor. This was inevitable. In the 1960s, growth in Windsor and in demands for higher education meant the university needed to expand, but the Ontario government refused to fund the operations of religious colleges and universities. Moreover, the Basilians did not have the resources to sustain an independent Catholic university in Ontario. Bishop Cody realistically, if sadly, accepted Assumption's inevitable change in status, encouraging the Basilians to negotiate terms that would ensure a continuing presence and their involvement on the campus. Thus, Assumption and the non-denominational Essex College petitioned for the founding of the University of Windsor, which was incorporated on 19 December 1962. At the time, Assumption promised to hold in abeyance its right to confer the MA degree in theology. Cody was chancellor of Assumption University of Windsor for two terms and the first chancellor of the University of Windsor.

The ending of Assumption's affiliation with the University of Western Ontario in 1953 led to the founding of what is now King's University College in London. The president of Western invited Bishop Cody to establish a residential liberal college of arts for men on the campus. Negotiations began in earnest in late 1953, and the bishop announced the creation of Christ the King College in early 1954. He described it as the fulfillment of Bishop Fallon's original plan in 1919, when Fallon signed affiliation agreements with Western on behalf of the Ursulines (Brescia College) and the Basilians (Assumption College).[18] The new college would be staffed with diocesan priests and laymen and be affiliated with Western through St. Peter's Seminary College of Arts. The diocese donated a ten-acre parcel of seminary property, which is near the university campus. Cody blessed the cornerstone for a college building on 29 September 1954, and the college opened on 14 September 1955 to forty-six students, half of whom resided in the college.[19] The following year, it had 114 students. In 1955, the college offered the first year of the general arts program and has added various programs with appropriate degrees to the curriculum. Today's King's University College is a thriving Catholic institution for men and women.

To build the college, Bishop Cody estimated that he needed $1,250,000. Reluctant to tap into the annual Diocesan Development Fund, he appealed personally and in private to London-area Catholics of above-average means, to non-Catholics and to a select number of firms and foundations. Cody felt justified in appealing for money outside the church because the initial request for the college had come from the highest authorities at Western, and because the college was open to men of all faiths.

Surviving documentation does not reveal Bishop Cody's success in soliciting funds from non-Catholic sources. But the college was built, and Cody said that it cost $1,321,400.[20] He considered the college a Marian Year (1954) project and a fitting prelude to the celebration of the diocesan centennial in 1956. (The Marian Year was proclaimed to commemorate the centenary of the declaration of the dogma of the Immaculate Conception.)

Celebrating the diocese's centennial

The diocese's centennial year, 1956, was celebrated in many ways, including special parish Masses, missions, devotions, adorations and pilgrimages, sermons, a Pontifical High Mass in the Ukrainian Rite, the dedication of all newborns in 1956 to Mary Immaculate, the Joint Enthronement of the Sacred Heart of Jesus and the Immaculate Heart of Mary in family homes and a spiritual bouquet (a gift of prayers) for Pius XII.

The year also featured many special events.[21] Cardinal Paul-Emile Léger, archbishop of Montréal, was the guest of honour at the May Day parade in Windsor. Father Patrick Peyton, CSC, returned to the diocese to lead a Family Rosary Crusade, from 27 May to 10 June. The Summer School of Catholic Action was held in Windsor, 25–30 June, the first time that Catholic Action had met in Ontario and only the second time in Canada. The Holy Family Retreat House in Oxley hosted the National Workshop of the Canadian Lay Retreat Movement.[22]

The seventeenth North American Liturgical Conference met in the London Armoury, the first time that the group had convened outside the United States. Holding this event in the diocese of London suggests that Cody was sympathetic to the goals and work of the conference. This kind of group would be supportive of the Liturgical Movement, which sought reform of worship, including a return to the earlier forms of worship, and which had been slowly gaining momentum during the twentieth century. Two thousand delegates gathered to discuss "Christian Participation and the New Holy Week." Bishop Cody wholeheartedly supported the reforms of the Holy Week liturgies, which Pope Pius XII promulgated. Cody was also a prominent proponent of the "dialogue" Mass, in which the laity were allowed to say or sing the responses, and of the use of English in the celebration of some of the sacraments, such as baptism. This lay involvement was innovative for the time. In Cody's time, Mass was already offered in English at St. Mary's, London, which also had a free-standing altar facing the people.[23]

The centennial year officially closed with the first synod of the diocese of London, 27 November, at St. Peter's cathedral. The purpose of the gathering, which was attended by clergy only, was to codify Catholic life. The clergy gave their consent to 260 statutes on the following matters: diocesan clergy, religious, the laity and Catholic Action; the sacraments, sacramentals, sacred places and times and the ecclesiastical Magisterium (preaching, schools and instructions to non-Catholics); and temporalities (stipends, collections and annual reports).

The centennial may have come to a formal close but for Bishop Cody the celebration would not end until the cathedral towers had been completed, the carillon installed and the Lady Chapel opened. He blessed the towers and the carillon on Ascension Thursday, 15 May 1958, and blessed and dedicated the Lady Chapel, on the feast of the Immaculate Conception, 8 December 1958.[24]

Establishing St. Jerome's Parish

In the midst of the centennial celebrations, the division between Francophone and Anglophone Catholics in the diocese resurfaced, striking a discordant note. In 1957, a group from Windsor petitioned the bishop to erect a French-only parish in Windsor. Cody, supported by the pastors of the bilingual parishes in Windsor and Essex County, refused to agree to the petition. In response, a well-organized group of Francophones resurrected a proposal from the Fallon era to divide the diocese of London along language lines to have a French-speaking diocese for Windsor and Essex and Kent counties. The group delivered a tightly written eighteen-page *Mémoire sur le Diocese de London* to

the apostolic delegate.[25]

Annoyed, Bishop Cody replied with a lengthy "Memorandum to His Holiness Pope Pius XII Concerning the Serious Reasons Why the Diocese of London Should not be Divided at this Time."[26] It argued in favour of the territorial integrity of the diocese. At times, Cody was emotional and even accusatory, but he carefully supported his main contention with statistics.[27] The Sacred Consistorial Congregation in Rome sided with Cody, but gently asked him to reconsider the question of a national parish. Reluctantly but obediently, Cody revisited the issue and established St. Jerome's parish.[28]

Ending an era

The 1960s brought changes—small and large—to the diocese. In 1961, Catholic culture was so strong that the diocese felt confident enough to look inward and conduct the first-ever door-to-door census, called Operation Doorbell. That year, it also looked outward to Latin America and established a diocesan mission of priests and sisters in the diocese of Chiclayo, Peru.[29]

On 22 February 1962, Bishop Cody celebrated the twenty-fifth anniversary of his episcopal consecration in a magnificent liturgy witnessed by more than a thousand people at St. Peter's cathedral. In recognition of his long service, Pope John XXIII made him an Assistant at the Pontifical Throne and elevated the cathedral to the status of a minor basilica.

One of the bishops in attendance was the newly-appointed auxiliary, G. Emmett Carter. Bishop Cody introduced him to the priests and people of the diocese and appointed him vicar general with a residence next to St. Clare of Assisi Church and rectory in Windsor. Always gracious, Cody later notified the clergy that Carter would be celebrating the twenty-fifth anniversary of his priestly ordination at a Jubilee Pontifical Mass and reception on 3 June.

On 3 May 1962, Bishop Cody looked on as Archbishop Sebastiano Baggio, the apostolic delegate, turned the sod for Regina Mundi Junior Seminary. Cody was a staunch believer in preparatory high schools for boys who were deemed to be serious about the priesthood. Many priests, who thought the day of junior seminaries was over, had strongly opposed the project.[30] The junior seminary was built and furnished at a cost of $2 million, and opened on 26 September 1963.[31] It was Bishop Cody's last major work.

Other changes had much greater impact. During the sixties, the world outside the church would go through a period of significant cultural and political changes that would affect society deeply. Within the Church, the convening of the Second Vatican Council in 1962 would result in more major changes at every level. Pope John XXIII had announced the Second Vatican Council in 1959, so people knew change was coming. Some of the faithful predicted disaster for the Church, some demanded significant changes, and others had opinions in between. Many lay people, priests and bishops, in Canada and elsewhere, believed that the Church should implement major reforms in areas such as ecumenism, lay participation, and the liturgy, and later welcomed the directions taken by the Council. Bishop Cody was ahead of his time in embracing ecumenism and developed good relationships with other Christian denominations and with Jewish groups in the diocese.

The bishop attended the first sessions of the Second Vatican Council in 1962. He was elected to the commission on seminaries and education. He saw that the Church that had shaped and sustained him as a priest and bishop was about to embark on a series of major reforms, beginning with the liturgy and the role of the laity. Surely this explains his January 1963 directive to the diocesan liturgical commission to seek expert help and advice in advance of any changes in the liturgy, and his desire to have the diocese consult the laity prior to the second session of the Council.[32]

On 4 December 1963, while visiting Regina Mundi, the bishop suffered a massive brain hemorrhage. He died the following morning, eleven days shy of his sixty-fourth birthday. His Requiem Mass took place at St. Peter's cathedral, on 10 December, and his remains were interred in the seminary crypt.

To his successor, Bishop Cody left a strong and vibrant diocese, in which everything was in its appointed place. But it was not to last.

Bishop Cody was called from this life the day after the formal promulgation of the Constitution of the Sacred Liturgy, the first constitution published by the Second Vatican Council and the one that, when implemented on the diocesan level, brought about the most visible break with the past. Cody was spared having to deal with all the tension and tumult of the post-Conciliar Church and with the upheavals in society that occurred in the 1960s and 1970s. A very different bishop would lead the diocese of London into the latter part of the twentieth century.

Endnotes for Chapter Seven -- Bishop Cody

[1] DLA, John Christopher Cody Papers (hereafter JCC Papers), Box 6, File 24, "Memorandum to His Holiness Pope Pius XII Concerning the Serious Reasons Why the Diocese of London Should not be Divided at this Time" (hereafter "Memorandum"), 6.

[2] *Catholic Register*, Special Edition, 14 December 1963, L3. Additional information supplied by Wim Kalkman, volunteer assistant archivist, diocese of Victoria.

[3] Michael T. Ryan (ordained for the diocese of London in 1950), e-mail correspondence in private collection – recollections of the Cody era.

[4] DLA, JCC Papers, Box 10, File 10, Cody to J.B. Fullerton, 14 April 1954. Cody was quoting Flahiff.

[5] Ibid., JCC Papers, Box 6, File 24, "Memorandum," Schedule II-A.

[6] Ibid., JCC Papers, Box 6, File 24, "Memorandum," 1–2. The number of churches and schools are approximations that have been derived from the *Ontario Catholic Directory and Yearbook 1960* (Toronto: 1960), 9–105.

[7] A. M. Williams, "Helping 70,000 New Citizens Find Roots," in *Jubilee Magazine: John Christopher Cody, D.D., LL.D. Bishop of London* (April 1962), 33. See also, DLA, Box 6, File 24, "Memorandum," Schedule VIII, Statistics of New Canadians 1950–1957.

[8] DLA, JCC Papers, Box 5, File 10, "Report of the Diocesan Catholic Immigration Council for the Year Ended 31 December 1959."

[9] Ibid., JCC Papers, Box 7, File 19, "Catholic Immigration Day for the Diocese of London — April 29, 1956."

[10] The eleven new national parishes were London: Our Lady of Częstochowa (Polish) and St. Maria Goretti (Italian); Windsor: St. Francis of Assisi (Croatian) and St. Jerome (French); Chatham: Our Lady of Victory (Polish) and St. Anthony of Padua (Czechoslovakian); Sarnia: Our Lady Queen of Poland, Our Lady of Sorrows (Slovak) and St. Peter (Italian); Delhi: St. Casimir (Lithuanian); Courtland: St. Ladislaus (Hungarian).

[11] DLA, JCC Papers, Box 7, Files 18 and 19.

[12] Ryan e-mail correspondence.

[13] DLA, JCC Papers, Box 7, Files 18 and 19.

[14] Ibid., JCC Papers, Box 6, File 24, Schedule II-B, 2; Box 3, File 33, John Z. Noël, Catholic Building Fund Campaign Windsor, Ontario, "Executive Reports of the Campaign from June 1956 to February 1959."

[15] Ibid., JCC Papers, Box 6, File 24, Schedule II-A.

[16] P.C. McCabe, "Charities Modernized under Bishop Cody: Network of Activities Spreads in Diocese with Expert Guidance," in *Jubilee Magazine*, 22.

[17] Michael Power, *Assumption College: The Road to Independence* 1940–1953 (Windsor: 2003), 127, 181, 186.

[18] John R.W. Gwynne-Timothy, *Western's First Century* (London: 1978), 655.

[19] *London Free Press*, 13 September 1955, 13–14; *Catholic Register*, 17 September 1955, 1.

[20] DLA, JCC Papers, Box 6, File 24, "Memorandum," Schedule 1-A, 1.

[21] Ibid., JCC Papers, Box 7, File 18, Pastoral Letter, 25 November 1955.

[22] Ibid., JCC Papers, Box 3, File 3, "National Workshop of the Canadian Lay Retreat Movement, Holy Family Retreat House, Harrow, Ontario, August 3, 4 ,5, 1956."

[23] Ibid., JC Papers, Box 7, File 17, J.A. Feeney to The Clergy of the Diocese of London, 25 January 1956; Thomas Kelly, "Liturgical Renewal Strong in London Diocese: Participation of Laity Fostered in Parishes," in *Jubilee Magazine*, 27, *London Free Press*, 20 August 1956, 17.

[24] For the towers and carillon, *Catholic Register*, 17 May 1958, 1–2; for Lady Chapel, DLA, JCC Papers, Box 12, Files 14 and 15.

[25] DLA, JCC Papers, Box 6, File 26.

[26] Ibid., JCC Papers, Box 6, File 24.

[27] Ibid.

[28] Ibid., JCC Papers, Box 6, File 25, Cardinal Marcello Mimmi to Cody, 1 April 1958.

[29] Ibid., JCC Papers, for Operation Doorbell: Box 1, File 27, Circulars — Operation Doorbell 1961, Box 1, File 28, Box 7, File 21, Pastoral Letter, 8 September 1961; for the mission in Peru: Box 6, File 23, Box 7, File 21, Box 9, File 1.

[30] Ryan e-mail correspondence.

[31] DLA, JCC Papers, Box 11, File 20.

[32] DLA, JCC Papers, Box 7, File 24, Feeney to Right Reverend, Very Reverend and Reverend Fathers, January 1963; Carter to Right Reverend, Very Reverend and Reverend Clergy of the Diocese of London, 13 September 1963.

8. Gerald Emmett Carter (1964–1978)

Gerald Emmett Carter delivered a strong statement during his installation ceremony as the eighth bishop of London, on 12 March 1964. [1] "Bishop Fallon is dead, Bishop Kidd is dead; Bishop Cody is dead; but the Church lives on," he declared The message was unmistakable. The new bishop intended to shape that portion of the Church entrusted to his care — the diocese of London — according to his own reckoning of the changes coming to the Church.

During his time as a priest-educator in Québec, from 1937 to 1962, the observant Father Carter had been aware of new theological thinking on catechetics, liturgy and the laity. His embrace of that theology was affirmed by the evolving direction of the Church at the Second Vatican Council. In the Church hierarchy, some rejected the changes that resulted from the Council, or at the very least feared them, and some waited for changes and then reacted. Others, like Bishop Carter, accepted change from the outset of the Council, because they believed that it was inevitable and good. In their own dioceses, they attempted to manage that change, steering it towards acceptable outcomes.

Bishop Carter led the diocesan-wide dissemination of the formal teachings of the Second Vatican Council (1962-65), enabling the local church to accept the Council's teachings, adapt to them and carry on the mission of building the kingdom of Heaven. This was particularly true in catechetical and liturgical renewal and change. For his strong stand in these areas, he won high praise in some circles, but was a lightning rod for criticism from traditional Catholics in Canada.

Bishop Carter had a considerable intelligence, an astonishing memory, an enormous capacity for work and a willingness to listen and to delegate responsibility. He also had polish and poise, great energy and was thick-skinned. Some would say he never held grudges against those who disagreed with him. Not once did he falter in his episcopal presence or waver in his authority. If there is a paradox, it was that in temperament and style he was something of an old-fashioned Churchman. Because he relished the role, he was empowered to take a leading hand in the transformation of the Church in English-speaking Canada during the years immediately after the Second Vatican Council.

London experienced Bishop Carter in his prime as a Council Father, a mover and shaker on the local and international Church scene. His fourteen years in the diocese were a time of seemingly constant change.

Early Years

Gerald Emmett Carter was born in Montréal on 1 March 1912, the last of eight children of Thomas Joseph Carter, a typesetter at the *Montreal Daily Star*, union activist and intense Irish-Canadian, and Mary Agnes (Minnie) Kerr, who fulfilled the part of Irish-Catholic matriarch to near perfection. The children were very competitive and Emmett and his older brother Alexander spent a great deal of time arguing.

Of the seven Carter children who grew into adulthood, four entered the service of the Church. Irene and Mary became members of religious communities, while Alexander, the second youngest, was ordained a priest for the archdiocese of Montréal on 6 June 1936 and succeeded to the See of Sault Ste. Marie as the third bishop in 1958. Emmett began life on the bottom rung of the family ladder, but would rise to the top of the Church hierarchy in Canada as cardinal-archbishop of Toronto. At thirteen, the English-speaking Emmett pursued his classical studies at the cours primaire complémentaire at the Collège de Montréal, learning to speak, read and write French in fairly short order. At the seminary, Father Lawrence Whelan, a future bishop, and Father Paul Grégoire, a future cardinal-archbishop of Montréal, tutored Emmett, who seemed destined for greater things.

Emmett earned a BA (1933) from the Collège de Montréal, and then he went to the Université de Montréal, where he was awarded a Licentiate in Theology (1936).

Priesthood

Carter was ordained to the priesthood in the archdiocese of Montréal by auxiliary Bishop Alphonse-Emmanuel Deschamps, on 22 May 1937 in the Basilica of St. James. Father Carter's initial assignment was as a summer replacement at the parish of St. Hippolyte de Kilkenny on Fourteen Island Lake, his only parish posting. To Carter's surprise, Archbishop Georges Gauthier made him the Ecclesiastical Inspector of English Schools in Montréal. This appointment, gave him instant recognition in the English-speaking wing of the Church in Québec. Given authority and power to bring about change, he exercised both wisely during a career in Québec education that lasted a quarter century.

Father Carter overhauled public education for Anglophone Catholics in Montréal, including teacher training, textbooks, high school exams and catechetics. In 1939, he became a director of the English-speaking section of the École Normale Jacques-Cartier. He was involved in adult education through the Newman Club at McGill University, where he was chaplain from 1941 to 1956, and through the Thomas More Institute for Adult Education, which he established in 1946. He was its first president.

Beginning in 1948, Father Carter was a member of the Montréal School Commission (school board) and was required on occasion to deal with Premier Maurice Duplessis. Dealing with Duplessis was his first taste of power politics; he proved himself adept at lobbying the most powerful man in Québec. If he could handle the much-feared Duplessis, he could deal with practically anyone — inside or outside the Church. He quickly came to understand and appreciate "power and the ways of power," wrote Michael Higgins, "and he gravitated toward those who had it and those who knew how to use it."[2] In 1952, he founded St. Joseph's College to train Catholic elementary and high school teachers, insisting that it be open to both male and female students, a progressive move.

As busy as he was with education, Carter found the time to pursue his own academic ambitions. He earned an MA (1940) and a PhD in education (1947) at the Université de Montréal. The title of his doctoral dissertation was "The Psychological Import of Religious Education." He was three times the national chaplain, assistant director (1943) and then director (1944) of the English section of Catholic Action. He also wrote four substantial works: "The Training of Teachers of Religion" in *Lumen Vitae* (1946); *The Catholic Public Schools of Quebec* (1957); and *Psychology and the Cross* (1959), the reworked version of his doctoral dissertation, and *The Modern Challenge to Religious Education* (1961), his most influential publication, which became the standard training manual in catechetics in numerous Catholic teachers' colleges in the United States.

Father Carter's first promotion came in early 1953, when Cardinal Paul-Émile Léger, the archbishop of Montréal, made him a canon of the Basilica of Our Lady of the World. Later that year, the provincial government awarded him the Medal of the Order of Scholastic Merit. In 1958, the provincial department of education made him a Commander of Scholastic Merit of the Province of Québec. He was known as "Mr. English Catholic Education," according to his brother, Bishop Alexander.[3]

Canon Carter, not yet fifty, was at the top of his form. He was instrumental in bringing into the Church Karl Stern, the psychiatrist, and Count Robert Keyserlingk, who became editor of the *Ensign*, a Catholic newspaper, and a leading Canadian member of the Knights of Malta. He successfully lobbied for an end to the rule that priests of the archdiocese of Montréal wear their cassocks in public. He was constantly sharpening his skills as a preacher and public speaker. In 1961, Cardinal Maurice Roy, archbishop of Québec, asked him to be the first rector of the English-language St. Lawrence College in Ste. Foy.

Then on 1 December 1961, Archbishop Sebastiano Baggio, the apostolic delegate to Canada, informed Canon Carter that John XXIII had named him auxiliary to Bishop John C. Cody of

London and the titular bishop of Altiburo. Cody and Carter had known each other from the mid-1950s. London may have been a backwater compared to metropolitan Montréal and historic Québec City, but becoming a bishop on the eve of the Second Vatican Council vaulted Carter onto an international stage. He attended the first two sessions as auxiliary and was appointed the eighth bishop of London in between the Council's second and third sessions.

Emmett Carter was consecrated in a grand ceremony at Notre Dame Basilica in Montréal, on 2 February 1962, by Cardinal Léger, assisted by Bishop Cody and Bishop Alexander Carter. Cardinal Roy gave a sermon in French, and Archbishop Philip F. Pocock, a native of the diocese of London and coadjutor archbishop of Toronto, preached in English. The new bishop chose *Pax et Lux* — Peace and Light — as his motto. The procession was a spectacle of order, colour and solemnity. In addition to the Knights of Malta (Carter was an honourary Conventual Chaplain for the Order), there were "torch-bearers, stool-bearers, faldstool-bearers, provincials and generals of religious orders, honorary and titular canons, monsignori of every rank … bishops, archbishops, crozier and mitre bearers, consecrators, chaplains, familiars, gremial bearer, and the Lord Cardinal of Montreal."[4] Hindsight tempts one to see the event as rich in irony: Bishop Carter, old-school Churchman and Council Father, welcomed the end of such ornamentation in Church ceremonial and, more important, the mentality that inspired it. The Canadian version of Church triumphalism was about to end.

Auxiliary Bishop of London

Bishop Carter was an active auxiliary. Although he probably shared little in common with Cody, in terms of theology, experience and goals, he gave loyal service, never conducting diocesan business without consulting Cody. Cody made Carter his vicar general and treated him as if no one else would succeed him to the See of London. The three themes that dominated and shaped Carter's tenure as bishop of London — the new catechetics, liturgical reform and the invitation to the laity to a fuller participation in the life of the Church — emerged during this time.

As auxiliary, Carter presided over the Regional Social Life Conference at Assumption University in 1962, visited Peru in February 1963, directed clergy retreats and assisted Cody in clergy appointments and confirmations in Windsor and Essex County. Carter gave his opinions, solicited or not, on topics as disparate as the Chrysler strike, ecumenism and the Anglicans, and the custom of evening wakes in parish churches.

Carter took over, at Cody's request, the diocesan education portfolio, which included catechetics, his academic specialty. He convinced Cody to send Father John O'Flaherty to Lumen Vitae in Brussels, Belgium, also known as the International Centre for the Study of Religious Formation.[5] Lumen Vitae was a proponent of a more psychological approach to the teaching of the truths of the Catholic faith, in stark contrast to the traditional question-and-answer method of the Baltimore catechism. Many Lumen Vitae students would be involved in the publication of new catechisms and in defending them from traditionalists.

Bishop Carter was so concerned about the state of religious education that he wanted to do something radical. In a letter to Cody, dated 4 July 1963, he made one of his grand assertions. In the light of the pastoral nature of the Second Vatican Council, he wrote, "We have to admit that the presentation of the truths of our faith has tended to be somewhat conceptualized and also in some degree mummified. Without any blame for the past the Council teaches us clearly that we have to address ourselves to a more vivid presentation, finding modern man where he is."[6] Carter's ardent but sketchy proposal called for a "Crusade of Religious Education" that would reach students in Catholic high schools and universities and would make an all-out effort to reach Catholic students in public high schools. Nothing came of the scheme because of Cody's death on 5 December 1963. But as bishop, Carter developed other bold ways to engage the faithful.

Anticipating one of the major changes in how the liturgy of the Eucharist would be celebrated in parish churches, Bishop Carter redesigned the sanctuary of St. Clare of Assisi parish in Windsor. He positioned the main altar far enough from the back wall, so that it would be possible to say Mass either in the traditional way or facing the people. He also removed the tabernacle to a side altar.

In 1963, with Cody's blessing, Carter consulted

with some lay groups before the opening of the second session of the Council. The consultation was a timely initiative setting in motion a pattern of lay consultation that Carter would use to enormous advantage when he organized the second diocesan synod. By such simple yet effective means, he introduced the much-anticipated "age of the laity" into the Catholic world of the diocese of London.

Eighth Bishop of London

G. Emmett Carter was named eighth bishop of London on 22 February 1964, and installed on 12 March.

The Second Vatican Council, which was held in Rome in four sessions, between October 1962 and December 1965, was both the launching pad and the conceptual framework for Bishop Carter's episcopacy in the diocese of London. For Carter, the Council was an experience of immense personal joy and high expectations for the future of the Church as it embarked on reform and renewal and began a challenging engagement with the world. Carter was well suited to implement the decisions of the Council. He had a background in catechetics and an interest in liturgy. He was progressive, a bishop who was not afraid to dismantle past practices and mentalities if they stood in the way of the Church's twentieth-century mission to revitalize itself. Carter believed strongly in subsidiarity within the Church: if something could be best done at the local level, Rome need not interfere. At the same time, he was loyal to the pope, a firm defender of the Catholic faith and an upholder of the teaching authority of the Magisterium. The twelve reports he wrote from 26 September 1964 to 30 October 1965 to his priests on the Council's work became articles for the *Catholic Register* and still make for lively reading.[7]

The Second Vatican Council promulgated the Constitution on the Sacred Liturgy on 4 December 1963; it had been passed on 11 October 1963, by an overwhelming vote of 2,158 to 19. Its impact on "ordinary Catholics" made it perhaps one of the most contentious of the sixteen constitutions, decrees and declarations passed and published by the Council. The Constitution on the Sacred Liturgy was a statement of principles and norms for liturgical renewal. The Council Fathers wanted to promote a more active participation of the faithful in every liturgical celebration. They wanted to make the

rituals of all services and the Divine Office simpler and clearer, stripping them of all unnecessary additions and accretions; to permit the use of the vernacular in the liturgy in those countries where it would help the people's understanding; and to provide proper instruction for the clergy and the laity concerning the reforms.[8]

The changes proposed would mean radical changes in the way Mass and the other sacraments would be celebrated, changes that involved language and ritual. Except for some prayers that had been added to the end of the Mass by Leo XIII and Pius XI, the Latin Rite Church had been a fixed Latin-language Mass since 1570, thus promoting the universality of the liturgy at the expense of its organic growth and development.

While Latin remained the official language of the Mass and sacraments, permission was given to celebrate them in the vernacular, which began as early as October 1963 for baptism, confession, matrimony, extreme unction (last rites, now the sacrament of the sick) and the funeral liturgy.[9] Changes in the Mass, however, including the use of modern languages, were far more gradual.

In 1964, Pope Paul VI established the Consilium for the Implementation of the Constitution on the Sacred Liturgy to revise the Roman liturgical books (the Missal, Pontifical, Breviary, Ritual, *Cærimoniale Episcoporum*, *Memoriale Rituum*, and Martyrology), which were in Latin, the universal language of the Church. The new version of the Mass was called the *Novus Ordo Missae*, literally translated as the New Order of the Mass and sometimes referred to as the Rite of Pope Paul VI or the Pauline Mass. It was introduced at the Synod of Bishops in 1967 and made official in April 1969. The rituals of the *Novus Ordo Missae* were much simpler than those in the ornate Latin Mass (both High and Low Mass). It was still a Latin-language Mass, but the option to celebrate it in the vernacular with the priest facing the people became the norm in Canada.

The new version of the Mass also put more emphasis on the scripture readings and the homily as integral parts of the celebration and allowed the use of lay readers for scripture other than the gospel. It allowed the laity to participate to a much greater degree in the Mass, by praying aloud both responses that were formerly reserved for servers and responses and acclamations that were added in the new rite. It included the use of the sign of peace in which participants greeted each other as a gesture of reconciliation. The new Mass allowed people to receive from both the host and the cup, instead of only the host and allowed people to receive communion in the hand, instead of on the tongue, as had been the custom for centuries. The communion rail was no longer used and a greater variety of music could be used in the Mass.

After the promulgation of the General Introduction to the new Roman Missal, beginning in the autumn of 1969, Paul VI made the New Mass mandatory for the Universal Church on the first Sunday of Advent in 1971.

Although Bishop Carter was not a liturgist by training, under his leadership, the diocese of London gained a reputation for its commitment to carrying out liturgical reform at the parish level. On the international stage, Carter was a member of the Consilium in 1965 and of the Sacred Congregation for Divine Worship in 1970. He was involved with the International Commission for English in the Liturgy (ICEL) from its beginning and was its chair in 1971. (Just six days after the vote in 1963 on the Constitution on the Liturgy, eleven bishops from ten English-speaking countries had founded ICEL to translate liturgical books into English from Latin, after they were revised.)

In Canada, he was chair of the Canadian Catholic Conference's (CCC) Liturgical Commission (English-sector), in 1966, and later president of the CCC's Office of Liturgy. This gave him some influence among his brother-bishops and notoriety across the country because liturgical change could only occur after the CCC had issued the pertinent directive in its *National Bulletin on Liturgy*.[10] Its first directive, dated February 1964, concerned the use of the vernacular for the scripture readings at Mass, and its most decisive directive was its approval of the ICEL translation of the *Novus Ordo Missae* in time for its introduction in English-speaking parishes on 30 November 1969.

Soon after becoming bishop of London, Carter instituted a series of liturgical reforms. He used English in the liturgy for the diaconal ordinations of two members of the Congregation of the Resurrection.[11] And he announced on 23 February 1964, that English would be used in certain parts of the Mass beginning that week. Thus, he signalled his intentions for instituting the new Catholic liturgy.

He developed numerous administrative mechanisms to introduce and enforce changes in the liturgy and church decoration and architecture. The Liturgical Commission, Carter's liturgical administrative right arm in the diocese, was headed by Father John B. O'Donnell from late 1964 to May 1973. Carter called O'Donnell's work a "brilliant success"[12] and insisted that it was largely owing to O'Donnell that the diocese was considered a leader in liturgical renewal throughout Canada. From 1964 to 1971, the Liturgical Commission instituted changes, by means of circular letters to the clergy and directives that were endorsed by Carter, often in his circular letters.

His inaugural circular letter to the clergy on the liturgy, dated 22 January 1964, set the tone:

The morally unanimous acceptance of this Constitution by the Fathers of the Council reflected their sense of admiration and the agreement as to the importance of this document. We feel that the life of the Church can be stimulated through this new development, the first step towards a true renewal in the life of Christ in the world.[13]

He included a copy of the Constitution on the Sacred Liturgy, which he invited his priests to study with discernment and a brief explanation of its contents.

Carter also issued a stern warning against unauthorized changes to the liturgy. A certain degree of liturgical experimentation was allowed up to and including 1965, but beyond that year, mavericks in the sanctuary, clerical or lay, no matter how well meaning, were not welcome.[14] Nothing annoyed him more than the unwillingness of so many of his priests to wait for official directives on changes. During the lead-up to the long-awaited promulgation of the ICEL translation of the Canon of the Mass (Eucharistic prayer), impatient priests celebrated Sunday Mass using an unapproved English-language Canon. This caused considerable confusion among the faithful. By July 1967, the bishop was furious, declaring in a circular letter that the damage done was beyond repair.[15]

Bishop Carter had an easier time solving the problem of relocating the main altar from being attached to the wall to being freestanding and the related questions about church decoration and architecture.[16] He had concluded that for the changes to make any sense, in particular the use of the vernacular as a liturgical language, the main altar had to be situated in the sanctuary so the priest could celebrate Mass facing the people. Supported by the diocesan Liturgical Commission, he decreed that after 7 March 1965, this was the rule; no exceptions were allowed.[17]

To make the process of liturgical renewal as transparent as possible, he delegated Father O'Donnell to organize two liturgical conferences. The diocesan conference took place in London in September 1966, featured Father Bernard Häring, the German moral theologian, as a guest speaker, and offered workshops on family life, sacred music, architecture and lay readers. In addition to priests and religious, participants included lay people such as lay readers, musicians, parish councils, teachers and members of traditional apostolic movements, such as the Legion of Mary, and the St. Vincent de Paul Society.

The second was an international conference held in Windsor in October 1970. Attending were five cardinals, two-dozen archbishops and bishops, leading liturgists and nearly 1,500 delegates. The theme was "Christ Builds Community." Cardinal Michele Pellegrino, the archbishop of Turin, delivered a twenty-page lecture on "The 'New Mass' in the Christian Life and in the Pastoral Life."[18] It was the perfect window on the thinking behind and the defence of Pope Paul VI's Mass.

Another high point in Bishop Carter's seven-year struggle to implement liturgical reform was the Liturgical Commission's publication in 1970 of the *New Missal-Hymnal*, which evolved two years later into the *Catholic Book of Worship*, the official hymnal of the Church in English-speaking Canada. In the foreword, he summarized many years of thinking.

> The great strength of our liturgical renewal is in the communal expression of our worship of God. Liturgy and individualism are mutually exclusive. The appearance of the familiar language of our lives in the worship of God is simply a part of our realization that the official worship of the Church is an expression of God's children gathered in a family.[19]

Not everyone accepted Bishop Carter's apologia for the new liturgy and the use of the vernacular. The "age of the laity," which he so desired, sported its share of conservative, even reactionary, Catholics who were not afraid to take on their bishops. The overwhelming majority of people in the pews, however, welcomed their new participation in the liturgy, though many agreed the changes came too quickly and were not always sensitively introduced by enthusiastic priests. Like many things that change in the Church, it would take a generation until they were rooted in the minds of the average Catholic.

New Catechism

The introduction of a new catechism in the 1960s was also contentious. The work of thirty people, it originated in Québec and was titled *Viens vers le Père*, and was often referred to in English-Canada by the title of the Grade 1 text, *Come to the Father*. As the years went by, a new volume was added for each grade, and the entire series was popularly, but mistakenly, known as the "Canadian Catechism." The catechism was used in nearly every diocese, including that of London, and upon review in 1973, the bishops concluded that "This is our book, and we don't want any other," although the bishops' conference never formally adopted it.[20]

Bishop Carter stayed out of the debate until late 1977, when he was preparing to attend the Synod of Bishops in Rome on the topic of religious education. On the eve of the synod, Carter, who was now president of the Canadian Conference of Catholic Bishops (the CCC was now the CCCB), wrote about the catechism in the *Catholic Register*. Breaking episcopal ranks, he wrote that it contained serious errors and omissions in its psychological approach to the faith and that "clearly the authors were overly optimistic and sometimes unrealistic about the ability of anyone, particularly the immature, to bridge the gap between implicit life situations and clearly held theological positions to guide those situations."[21] He ended by claiming that the catechism was at least partly responsible for "the disastrous decline in religious knowledge."[22]

Catechetical Initiatives: the General Mission and the Divine Word Centre

Bishop Carter implemented his 1963 concept of catechizing a broad spectrum of the faithful, in light of the recent teachings of the Second Vatican

Council, with two bold initiatives. On 19 August 1964, he announced a three-year General Mission for the parishes of Essex County, including Windsor, and, in September 1966, he founded the Divine Word Centre in London. The goal of the General Mission was "renewal of the minds and hearts, of the basic attitudes, of Catholics as individuals and as a community."[23] Key concepts were "the scientific approach to human situations; the 'open' parish and 'open' organization; and personal and social responsibility."[24]

The General Mission began on 15 September 1964, with the opening of the General Mission Centre in Windsor, as the clearinghouse for all mission activities. Father Edward Boyce, CSSR, who was experienced in regional mission work, was the mission director. The mission's preparatory phase lasted for two and a half years and the preaching stage took place from 26 February to 19 March 1967. Preparations included the publication on 1 March 1965 of *A Demographic Study of Essex County and Metropolitan Windsor*, the formation of liturgy, lay apostolate and catechetics commissions as well as inter-faith activities, community involvement, and a reflection group program. The reflection group program, one of the more successful undertakings, involved nearly 8,000 lay people and was adopted by two other dioceses. The participants met in groups of eight to ten people for six months, beginning in September 1966, to share their ideas and feelings about "God, life, the Church, Faith, love, authority, attitude towards Protestants and any topics they chose."[25] The mission institutes were for those who wished to preach.

The General Mission featured eighty-four missionaries; two were lay people, the others were priests. The overall theme was "The truth shall make you free." During the preaching phase, which ran from 26 February to 4 March 1967, the General Mission sponsored thirty-four conferences on "marriage and family, work, the Bible, liturgy, ecumenism, inter-personal relationships, Faith in a changing world and the role of the layman." Missionaries spoke at convents, homes for the aged and separate schools and to young working Catholics and directed missions in the fifty-seven parishes. The bishop spoke to men and women religious, priests and missionaries and lay gatherings.

The summary evaluation of the General Mission listed eighteen positive aspects. The mission

clarified "the role of the Church and the Christian in the community"; it "fostered lay involvement in community activities and helped to make the Church more relevant"; and it sponsored the Cursillo, a renewal movement, which "encouraged lay initiative and lay leadership." The seventeen negative aspects included a failure in communication, which left many parishioners guessing at the reason for the mission; too many missionaries and conferences; the failure of the parish missions to attract many non-church-going Catholics; and lack of sufficient preparation of the laity for the preaching phase.[26]

The General Mission of Essex County was a bold pioneering effort that produced much spiritual fruit for participants, but the extent and influence of any spiritual regeneration among the faithful is impossible to measure. The General Mission was a primer for the people. Everyone who participated had a chance to experience, from the ground up, the emerging transformation of the local Church. Bishop Carter had intended that the mission be the first of a series of general missions in the diocese, but none other was held.

In September 1966, seven months before the conclusion of the General Mission, Bishop Carter opened the Divine Word International Centre for Religious Education in London, the most ambitious project of his London episcopacy. He intended it to draw scholars and students from all over the world, who would return to their home dioceses ready to engage in catechetical work. Carter had laid the groundwork for the Centre as early as October 1965, when he was in Rome for the final Council session. After an exploratory correspondence with Father G. Delcuve, SJ, the director of Lumen Vitae in Brussels, Carter invited Father Barnabas Ahern, CP, Father Charles Davis of England and Father Bernard Häring to be among the first teachers. Before leaving for Rome, Carter had appointed Father John O'Flaherty as the first director, and while Carter was in Rome, O'Flaherty worked with a catechetical team. The centre offered courses on the graduate level in scripture, liturgy, theology and doctrine, religious anthropology, sociology and psychology and religious education. In 1973, it was able to offer the degree of Masters of Religious Education, through its academic affiliation with St. Paul's University in Ottawa. A great deal of effort, good will, public relations and diocesan money was invested in the Divine Word Centre, but it closed after only thirteen years. Carter's ideal was noble and worthwhile but too rich for reality. The centre tried to teach too many things to too few students. Although men and women from thirty different countries had registered between 1966 and 1977, there was a total of only 300 full-time students; so, tuition failed to sustain the centre's operational budget. As time went on, the diocese was increasingly reluctant to spend the money needed to keep the building in proper repair.

The centre's biggest weakness, though, was the absence of strong leadership. At times, Bishop Carter was a poor judge of character, and this was true in his choice of Beryl Orris as director and in letting him remain at the helm for five years.[27] Not until the arrival of Father Marcel Gervais, in 1974, did the centre receive the leadership it needed to survive and flourish, but by then it was too late.[28]

Finally, the Divine Word Centre suffered from a perception among many of the rank-and-file clergy and faithful that it had become a place of last resort for priests and religious on the verge of abandoning their vows. Conservative critics saw the centre as a metaphor for everything that was supposedly wrong in the Church. Operations ceased in May 1979, one year after Carter had been named archbishop of Toronto.

Second Synod of the Diocese

The Second Synod of the diocese of London, which addressed renewal but also reform in the laws and administration of the diocese,[29] remains one of Bishop Carter's important contributions to the people of the diocese. Lasting from 16 February 1966 to 25 May 1969, it increased the participation of priests and lay people in the ministry of the Church. It brought the laity into the synodal process, ensured an advisory role for the laity in diocesan administration and laid a foundation for the new post-Conciliar ecclesiology.

The synod was a success for many reasons. Its central inspiration and guide was the collection of documents from the Second Vatican Council and the spirit of that council. Its fourteen commissions — the synod's basic structure — functioned in a transparent manner with a minimum of interference from the bishop, who was confident enough to allow synod members to enjoy an unprecedented freedom in assessing and formulating diocesan policy. The open and consultative forum encouraged

discussion and debate and yet was always mindful of the authority and leadership of the bishop, who would have the final say on the documents and recommendations. Carter's personality, will and theology assured a positive outcome to the proceedings of the synod.

The fourteen commissions were: liturgy, diocesan organization and affairs, priests and pastoral ministry, religious, missions, lay apostolate, ecumenism and religious freedom, communications and public relations, social life, vocations and priestly formation, universities and colleges, teachers, Christian education and the Word of God. Sitting on the commissions were 250 priests and religious, who were chosen by the executive committee, and 262 lay members. The commissions' reports, which detailed how the diocese could live out its mission, were the essential work of the synod.

During the parliamentary session, the delegates, who included 149 elected parish and four mission representatives, debated and voted on the recommendations of the commissions. After listening to tapes of the freewheeling and emotional debates, Bishop Carter felt obliged to speak at length to the synod, to calm the waters and return the delegates to the task of voting on the reports and submitting revisions.[30]

The resulting legislation, embodied in fifteen statutes designed to continue the work of the synod, was promulgated on 22 April 1969. The statutes created the diocesan pastoral council, with its four commissions (missions, higher education, liturgy and the needs of the family), and the senate of priests as advisory boards to the bishop, and parish councils to advise parish priests. An advisory board of priests and laity was established for the seminary, and two lay people were appointed to serve on the seminary's governing body. The statutes set up six new diocesan roles: director of vocations; co-ordinator of socio-economic affairs; director of information services; co-ordinator of youth; episcopal vicar for religious; and episcopal vicar for national parishes. Each of these offices had an advisory board. The statutes also established a diocesan office of religious education for Catholic students in public schools, three centres for adult faith formation (John XXIII Centre in Windsor, Christian Renewal Centres in London and Sarnia), and established the principle of financial accountability for each parish and for the diocese.

The synod's many decisions endure as a

testament to Bishop Carter's desire that the local Church accept the Council's teachings, adapt to them and carry on the mission of building the Kingdom of Heaven.

Humanae vitae

Carter became involved in the controversy surrounding the 1968 papal encyclical *Humanae Vitae.* This document, on human life and the regulation of birth engendered much discord within the Church. Episcopal conferences across the world developed statements aimed at explaining the document for the faithful. In Canada, Carter played a major role in composing the Canadian bishops' first document, the "Winnipeg Statement." Its publication began a complex and divisive chapter in the Catholic Church in Canada. Some in the Church regarded the statement as controversial for not supporting strongly enough *Humanae Vitae* and its opposition to artificial contraception . Some were very happy with the bishops' pastoral approach to a complex problem. In December 1973, the bishops' "Statement on the Formation of Conscience," which Carter wrote, renewed the storm. As vice-president of the doctrine and faith department of the Canadian bishops' conference and later as vice-president of the conference, he was a major player in the drawn-out controversy, at one point reassuring Pope Paul VI in person that the Canadian bishops were loyal to him.[31]

1970–1978

The years 1970 to 1978, the second half of Bishop Carter's tenure, continued to be hectic and occasionally controversial. But the problems, duties and opportunities that absorbed his attention often took him away from the diocese, to Toronto, Ottawa, Rome (his favourite haunt) and even to Poland.

He was vice-president of the Catholic Conference of Ontario, from 1971 to 1973, vice-president of the Canadian Conference of Catholic Bishops, from 1973 to 1975, and president, from 1975 to 1977. In that capacity, he paid an official visit to Poland in May 1977, where he befriended Cardinal Karol Wotyła, who a year later became John Paul II.[32] In addition to his collaborative work on ICEL, Carter attended the 1974 synod of bishops in Rome on evangelization, and the 1977 synod on catechetics. As part of his preparation for the 1977 synod, he wrote a "Letter to the Young People" and spoke to the students in the diocese's Catholic high schools. He received 1,500 personal responses and responded to them in a second letter, "In Response to the Young People of the Diocese."[33] More than 40,000 copies were distributed. Also in 1977, he was the first Canadian bishop elected to the administrative council of the permanent secretariat of the synod of bishops.

At home, Carter continued his campaign to change the relationship of the parishes to the diocese. As early as 1966, he wrote to his priests: "The day of the parish as the focal point of the assembly of the People of God, particularly for the liturgical celebration, has dawned. The day of the parish as a sort of ghetto or haven of isolation from the concerns of the diocese and of the Church has ended."[34]

Financial concerns increased dramatically as the diocese implemented the second synod's decisions. For example, Bishop Carter built the current chancery to house the diocesan departments, many of which resulted from the synodal statutes. Bishop Carter was grateful that the people were generous to the diocesan services fund and to the diocese's mission and charitable works.

In 1971, Carter reluctantly decided to allow the celebration of the Sunday Eucharist on Saturday evening, after the senate of priests voted 12-3 in favour of it. Other problems he faced included the continuing controversy over the ordination of women to the ministerial priesthood; the decline in vocations to the priesthood and religious life; the aging of the clergy; and the decision of some priests to leave the active ministry.

During his final years in London, Bishop Carter made decisions that produced positive outcomes for King's College, St. Peter's Seminary and Catholic secondary schools. In 1966, he had instituted the first of a major set of changes for Christ the King College, the diocesan-owned affiliate of the University of Western Ontario. These included a change in name to King's College.[35] In 1972, he granted King's College a greater degree of administrative autonomy; at the same time, he wanted to maintain and strengthen its Catholic identity. Because of the name change and a downplaying of its Catholic character in its marketing, some questioned the college's catholicity.

In 1974, Bishop Carter struck a committee to examine and report on this question. As a follow-up to the report, he participated in a 1976 symposium: "The Catholic College in Modern Society: King's College — Retrospect and Prospect."[36] This symposium, and further work, helped to build support for King's by deepening understanding of its mission as a Catholic university college — to promote Catholic studies and provide such an atmosphere for those students who wished it, while being open to students of all faiths. In 1976, he also agreed to the affiliation of the theology department of St. Peter's with King's College (and thus to the University of Western Ontario), so that the seminary's theology program could receive full grants from the Ontario government. This generated much-needed revenue and boosted the academic profile of the theology program.

He spearheaded a drive that saved Catholic high schools in the diocese from certain insolvency, with the dramatic elimination of the schools' $1.4 million capital debt. Priests and people raised this amount in record time, in 1974, an example of "wide-spread consultation" and "the pooling of minds."[37]

In June 1974, the Holy See announced the appointment of Father John Michael Sherlock, of the diocese of Hamilton, as auxiliary bishop. For the last four years of his London episcopacy, Bishop Carter was fortunate in having Sherlock to work with him in managing the ever-increasing affairs of a complex and evolving diocese.

The summation of Bishop Carter's tenure in London comes from the conclusion of the bishop's *Quinquennial Report* for the years 1974 to 1977:

The times are exceedingly troubled. Religious indifference coupled — or produced by — individualism and selfishness walk in the company of anti-authority and willful unconcern for traditional values. Our Diocese could not live in this part of the world and be unaffected. We must face the gravity of the situation and be on constant alert, ready to expend our best energies to meet the challenge. But when we look at the spiritual renewal of our priests, the faith of so many of our people who, on the whole, have remained faithful, we are aware that we are rather singularly blessed. We can only walk towards a tomorrow with hope and with the certainty that the Lord will not desert us if we do not desert Him.[38]

Archbishop of Toronto

On 29 April 1978, Bishop Carter was transferred to the archdiocese of Toronto, the fourth bishop of London to become archbishop of Toronto. John Paul II made him a cardinal on 30 June 1979, and the government of Canada invested him as a Companion of the Order of Canada on 20 April 1983. While in Toronto, he was influential in the provincial government fulfilling its promise to provide full funding to Catholic high schools. He helped establish Covenant House, a privately funded agency that provides services and shelter for street youth, in the city. In 1988, Cardinal Carter worked with the province to provide affordable housing for the elderly and those with disabilities. Cardinal Carter retired on 17 March 1990 and died on 6 April 2003, at ninety-one years of age.

Endnotes for Chapter Eight -- Bishop Carter

[1] *Catholic Register*, 21 March 1964, 1.

[2] Michael Higgins, "Gerald Emmett Carter," *The Tablet*, 19 April 2003, 48.

[3] Ron Graham, "The Power and the Glory of Emmett Cardinal Carter," *Saturday Night*, April 1983, 26.

[4] Michael W. Higgins and Douglas R. Letson, *My Father's Business: A Biography of His Eminence G. Emmett Cardinal Carter* (Toronto: 1990), 59. We relied heavily, though not exclusively, on this biography for the basic facts of Bishop Carter's life and the many insights on his character, etc., which no other source provided in such depth.

[5] DLA, Gerald Emmett Carter Papers (hereafter GEC Papers), Box 6, File 28, Carter to Cody, 23 January 1963 and 15 March 1963.

[6] Ibid., GEC Papers, Box 6, File 28, Carter to Cody, 4 July 1963.

[7] *Catholic Register*, 26 September 1964, 1; 3 October 1964, 1,3; 10 October 1964, 1, 6; 17 October 1964, 1,6; 24 October 1964, 4; 31 October 1964, 1,6; 7 November 1964, 1,6; 14 November 1964, 1,6; 21 November 1964, 1,2; 28 November 1964, 2; 25 September 1965, 1,2; 30 October 1965, 1,2.

[8] Ibid., 7 December 1963, 1 and S7; 21 December 1963, 3.

[9] Ibid., 26 October 1963, 3.

[10] Ibid., 26 October 1963, 3

[11] *The London Free Press*, 24 February 1964, 1. This was a top-of-the-page lead story with the headline, "New Bishop Authorizes Use of English in Part of Mass."

[12] DLA, GEC Papers, Box 5, Circular Letters 1973-74, Circular #4, 31 May 1973.

[13] Ibid., 1.

[14] Ibid., GEC Papers, Box 1, File: St. Peter's Seminary, Monsignor Mahoney, 17 December 1965.

[15] Ibid., GEC Papers, Box 5, Circular Letters 1967, Circular #7, 31 July 1967, Appendix, 2.

[16] *Catholic Register*, 29 August 1964, 8. The *Register* published "Excerpts from 14 Declarations on the Norms of Church Building" that were issued by Boston Liturgical Day: Worship, Art and Architecture. The declarations covered the following items: basic layout of the Church; place of those who preside; main altar; secondary or side altars; reservation of the Blessed Sacrament; ambos or lecterns; place for the choir and organ; places for the faithful; confessionals; sacred images; arrangement of decorations; and funeral art. They were meant to be a blueprint for the alteration of church interiors to accommodate the changes in the liturgy and were certainly followed in the diocese of London, beginning with the relocation of the main altar. The *Register* also featured a two-part story on the liturgical changes at St. Joseph's church in Douro, in the diocese of Peterborough. See *Catholic Register*, 22 August 1964, 8 and 29 August 1964, 8.

[17] Ibid., GEC Papers, Box 2, File: Liturgical Commission, Fr. J.B. O'Donnell, Chairman, O'Donnell to Carter, 21 February 1965.

[18] Ibid., GEC Papers, Box 19, File: Liturgical Convention 1970.

[19] Gerald Emmett Carter, "Foreword," *Catholic Book of Worship* (Ottawa: 1972).

[20] Lorene Collins, *Salvation Redefined: Catholic Parents and Religious Education in Post-Vatican II Canada* (Toronto: 2003), 131; Anne Roche, *The Gates of Hell: The Struggle of the Catholic Church* (Toronto: 1975; reprinted 1979), 128-30.

[21] *Catholic Register*, 15 October 1977, A1.

[22] Ibid.

[23] DLA, GEC Papers, Box 16, File: General Mission of Essex County, Edward Boyce, ed., *History and Evaluation of the General Mission of Essex County*, Publication No. 4 of the General Mission of Essex County, 7.

[24] Ibid., 9.

[25] Ibid., 32.

[26] Ibid., 65-67.

[27] Higgins and Letson, *My Father's Business*, 93-94.

[28] DLA, GEC Papers, Box 9, File: Divine Word Centre, Gervais to Carter, "Memo: Future of Divine Word Centre," 8 November 1974.

[29] Pasquale Fiorino, *The Second Synod of London* (M.A. thesis, Gregorian University, Rome, 1989). This is an excellent and comprehensive history of the synod and the primary source of information for this concise understanding of the synod.

[30] DLA, GEC Papers, Box 5, Circular Letters 1967-1969, "Address to the Synod by His Excellency Bishop G. Carter April 6, 1968."

[31] The twenty-minute private audience took place on 14 November 1969. See DLA, GEC Papers, Circular Letters 1967-1969, Circular #5, 24 November 1969.

[32] *Catholic Register*, 10 September 1977, A1, A3; Higgins and Letson, *My Father's Business*, 143-45.

[33] DLA, GEC Papers, Box 5, Circular Letters 1977, Circular #4, 27 September 1977.

[34] Ibid., GEC Papers, Box 5, Circular Letters, 1966, Circular #10, 1 December 1966.

[35] J.R.W. Gwynne-Timothy, *Western's First Century* (London: 1978), 657-58.

[36] DLA, GEC Papers, Box 10, File: King's College; Higgins and Letson, *My Father's Business*, 96-99.

[37] Ibid., GEC Papers, Box 5, File: Diocesan Fund Raising Campaign for the Catholic High Schools, 1974, Carter to "My dear Reverend Fathers, My dear People," 27 August 1974.

[38] Ibid. GEC Papers, Box 17, *Quinquennial Report (1974-1977)*, 20.

9. John Michael Sherlock (1978–2002)

John Michael Sherlock served as Bishop of London for nearly twenty-four years, longer than any of his predecessors, and is the only bishop of London to have retired from his position. He had an energy, style and sense of humour that radiated the prayerful hope of a shepherd deeply and lovingly committed to the Church and its people for his entire life. He made important contributions to the diocese and the Church in Ontario in education, social action and pastoral care, and in implementing the changes resulting from the Second Vatican Council. His most significant contribution to the diocese of London was helping it adapt to the new ways and realities of carrying out the Church's mission when a huge shift in the concept of ministry emerged at the administrative and parochial levels, during the 1980s. The shift affected priests, religious and laity and the viability of the diocese. He found it more difficult, however, to address the scandal of clergy sexual abuse.

Childhood

John Sherlock was born in Regina, Saskatchewan, on 20 January 1926, the second of eight children of John Sherlock and Catherine O'Brien. In 1928, the family moved to Brantford, Ontario, where John, Sr., found steady work until the Great Depression. Then the family found it a challenge to survive. But Bishop Sherlock remembers a happy and ordered childhood filled with home-centered entertainment and family prayers, devotions and regular attendance at Mass.

Eventually, John, Sr., became the church caretaker and each of his six sons served at St Mary's as altar boys under Father Peter Maloney, one of the great twentieth-century priests of the diocese of Hamilton. At age six, John Michael knew he would become at priest, while reading a story about St. Isaac Jogues, a North American Jesuit martyr who knew at a young age that he would become a priest and go to New France.[1]

After attending local separate schools, Sherlock studied at Brantford Collegiate and Vocational Institute from 1938 to 1942, where he received a watch as a prize for academic excellence. When the few Catholic students at the collegiate absented themselves from school prayers and Bible study, John usually led the walkout, believing he was standing up for the faith.

He took Grade 13 at St. Jerome's College in Kitchener, earning at least four first class honours, and in September 1943, entered St. Augustine's Seminary as a candidate for the diocese of Hamilton. (Two younger brothers, William and Philip, would follow him there and become priests.) He earned a BA in 1946, from the University of Toronto, through the seminary's affiliation with St. Michael's College, and then took four years of theology.

Priesthood

John Sherlock was ordained to the priesthood of the diocese of Hamilton at Christ the King cathedral, on 3 June 1950, by Bishop Ralph Dignan of Sault Ste. Marie. (The bishop of Hamilton, Joseph Ryan, was convalescing in Florida.) In September 1950, Bishop Ryan sent Sherlock to the Catholic University of America, in Washington, D.C., to earn a degree in canon law.

After his return to Hamilton in 1952, he began twenty-two busy and fulfilling years in the diocese. From his vocation as a priest and his commitment to serve the Church flowed the vitality and determination that he devoted to each undertaking. He was assistant pastor of St. Eugene's in Hamilton, from 1952 to 1959; assistant pastor of St. Augustine's in Dundas, from 1959 to 1963; and administrator and then pastor of St. Charles Garnier in Hamilton, from 1963 to 1974. While at St. Eugene's, he was also involved in the co-operative housing movement, 1954 to 1958, and helped to establish a pioneer co-op housing development on unserviced land in Grimsby, an inspiration to others in the co-op housing movement.

Father Sherlock breathed new life into St. Charles Garnier, Hamilton's French-speaking parish, and then replaced the old church and rectory, which were in shambles. He also led the parish through the enormous transition in the liturgy after the Second Vatican Council. Although he was "fundamentally sympathetic with the changes,"[2] as a pastor, he realized that the people needed to be prepared for its introduction or the trauma that usually accompanies change might turn into revolt. He was against the immediate cessation of the Latin Mass in the diocese, believing that each parish should retain one Sunday celebration of the *Novus Ordo Missae* in Latin to soften the shock of the liturgical reform. Bishop Ryan, who had scolded Father Sherlock for "jumping the gun" in his attempt to prepare the people of St. Charles Garnier, rejected his suggestion but later allowed one Latin Mass on Sunday at St. Mary's church.

Reflecting on the changes in the liturgy, more than forty years after their introduction, Bishop Sherlock thought that reforms of the Second Vatican Council were a great accomplishment, but that some Canadian bishops did not adopt the proper method for their implementation. Their approach was top-down and authoritarian. For example, Bishop Ryan ordered each parish church in the Hamilton diocese to have an altar facing the people by a certain Sunday. Some parishes were prepared but many were not. This resulted in hurt feelings, confusion and embarrassment, and a number of people even left the Church.

The liturgical changes were a symptom of even greater changes. According to Bishop Sherlock, prior to the Second Vatican Council, Catholic religious culture had enjoyed a homogeneity that allowed Catholics to sustain their own community, which gave them a strong identity. But this culture also had a glaring weakness: although Catholics were secure in the Faith, they possessed an unconscious arrogance in thinking that they knew all the answers. The Second Vatican Council invited Catholics to engage the world and to recognize that Catholics did not have the answers to all the questions. The distinctly Catholic identity was also affected by the hierarchy's relaxation of some of the Church's heretofore strict rules, such as abstaining from meat on Fridays. Prior to the Council, Catholic identity was closely tied to rules, practices and beliefs that differentiated them from others, such as Protestants and those of other faiths.

Attitudes changed. One result is that Catholics no longer felt obliged "under the pain of mortal sin" to attend Mass every Sunday, although it meant not having a sacramental life that is distinctly Catholic. Attitudes toward Catholics marrying non-Catholics opened up, so that inter-marriage became more common. As well, many Catholics no longer believed they must follow the Church's teachings regarding artificial contraception, or to accept uncritically other moral teachings of the Church. Another outcome is the loss of political clout exercised by Catholics as a block.

Other Responsibilities

In 1952, Bishop Ryan appointed Father Sherlock to be a lecturer in Religious Studies at McMaster University, where he taught Scripture until 1961. He was also the Newman chaplain at McMaster, from 1952 to 1963, and national Newman chaplain, from 1963 to 1969.

In 1963, the busy priest was appointed a trustee for the Hamilton-Wentworth Separate School Board, and sat on the board, from 1963 to 1974, serving as board chair in 1973. His proudest moment as a trustee was the opening of an eight-room school, in 1965, for the children of St. Charles Garnier parish.

Father Sherlock was appointed advocate and judge for the Regional Marriage Tribunal (1954-74); consultor for the diocese of Hamilton (1965-74); member of the diocesan council (1966-74) and the diocesan senate (elected in June 1974). From 1968 to 1974, he served on the board of St. Joseph's Hospital, which was next door to St. Charles Garnier church, rising to the position of vice-chair. From 1970 to 1972, he represented the Ontario bishops to the Catholic Hospital Association of Ontario when the Ontario government mandated abortion as a medical service in publicly funded hospitals. The association told the government that Catholic hospitals would rather close than provide abortions.

Then on 25 June 1974, the Holy See chose Father Sherlock to become the auxiliary bishop in London and titular bishop of Macriana in Mauritania. He was ordained to the episcopate at Christ the King Cathedral in Hamilton, on 28 August 1974, by Bishop Paul Reding of Hamilton, a seminary classmate. Archbishop Philip Pocock of Toronto and Bishop Joseph Ryan, bishop-emeritus of Hamilton, assisted. Sherlock chose *Omnia et in omnibus Christus* as his episcopal motto.[3] Translated, it means "There is only Christ: he is everything and he is in everything" (*Col.* 3:11, *Jerusalem Bible*).

Auxiliary Bishop

Bishop Sherlock reports that his appointment as an auxiliary bishop "was a shock and a surprise …. I enjoyed being a parish priest."[4] He said that he never liked administration; he did not feel sufficiently organized and tended to be easily distracted by competing ideas and emotions and could be impulsive and spontaneous. He preferred the directness and richness of human engagement. For him, the Church is a community of people, a large diverse family always united in the Gospel and the Eucharist.

Bishop Sherlock said at the time of his retirement that was thankful to have Bishop Carter as his mentor. He liked Carter's "approach and tried to imitate it in my episcopal ministry."[5] Communication, consultation, trust, and the delegation of responsibility to both clergy and laity — Bishop Carter encouraged his auxiliary to take initiatives and use his own judgment — these were the positive hallmarks of Carter's episcopacy that Sherlock made his own and refined.

Sherlock lived at St. Joseph church in Chatham for most of his time as auxiliary, moving to Windsor in late 1977, just months before being named bishop of the diocese and taking up residence in London. From the autumn of 1974 to the spring of 1975, he confirmed approximately 7,000 people at 70 confirmations. His workload increased when Bishop Carter had to spend more time away from

the diocese after becoming president of the Canadian Conference of Catholic Bishops.

On 29 April 1978, Bishop Carter was named archbishop of Toronto. Bishop Sherlock was subsequently elected vicar capitular (diocesan administrator) and moved to London. Archbishop Carter took Sherlock to Rome in May, where he introduced him to the heads of many Vatican congregations. The highlight was an introduction to Pope Paul VI.

Bishop of London

On 8 July 1978, John Michael Sherlock was named bishop of London (one of the last bishops named by Paul VI, who died on 6 August.) His installation as the diocese's ninth bishop took place at St. Peter's cathedral on 21 August 1978. Joining the diocesan clergy and 1,200 of the faithful were thirty Canadian bishops, two Anglican bishops, a rabbi and an array of other dignitaries, escorted by the Knights of Columbus.

Bishop Sherlock inherited a diocese that was strong and vibrant. London was a recognized leader in reform and renewal; finances were in good shape; the complement of diocesan and religious priests was adequate; St. Peter's Seminary continued to attract candidates; and an abundance of women religious (approximately 800 in 1977) served the diocese. Catholic separate schools had healthy enrolments, and the few Catholic high schools were prospering in spite of inadequate provincial funding. The diocese had a collaborative and participatory model of episcopal governance, with structures for consultation, including the senate of priests (later the council of priests) and the diocesan pastoral council, especially its advisory board.

Many in the diocese welcomed the changes in the Church that resulted from the Second Vatican Council and the opportunity to be more involved in the life of the Church. Sherlock was able to build on this by developing lay ministry and establishing social action ministries.

The diocese, however, was approaching a period of major transition. The number of priests and religious declined significantly, threatening to precipitate a crisis. The transition to lay ministry created upheavals. And for some the change in the culture of the Church created confusion. Some people left the Church, which had an impact on the viability of parishes. As well, changes in views of authority and values in the world affected people's perceptions of the Church.

The core of Bishop Sherlock's legacy to the diocese of London was his response to these problems. Always animated by Christian hope and trust in God's will for the Church, he would not let the shortage of priests paralyze his episcopal direction. Rather, he treated it as an opportunity to seek and implement positive change. He promoted the vital role of priests, while improving the viability of seminary education in the diocese and providing pastoral care for priests. He accelerated the development of lay ministry. During the 1990s and early 2000s, he was willing to look realistically at the health of the diocese and to reorganize the parish structure, so that the Church in Southwestern Ontario could remain viable.

But very little could have happened without open lines of communication among the bishop, the priests and the people. The days of the bishop as benign dictator were long over. Openness, transparency, dialogue and a willingness to share information — all were necessary in carrying out a successful gradual transformation of the diocese. His style of leadership was empowering, according to one of his closest advisors, Father (later Bishop) Anthony "Tony" Daniels, and was rooted in St. Paul's vision of the Church as the one body of Christ with many members who have different gifts (*Rom.* 12: 3–8). Bishop Sherlock listened to the opinions and concerns of priests, religious and laity, delegated responsibility and treated others as co-workers always dedicated to service.[6]

In response to calls for better communication, Bishop Sherlock founded the *Newsletter of the Diocese of London*, in June 1980. It began as a small-circulation publication from the bishop's office and grew over the years into a more professional-looking publication issued by the office of communications.

Supporting Priestly Vocations

During Bishop Sherlock's episcopacy, a crisis in the availability of priests to serve the diocese was developing. But it took years before it was understood and appreciated. Between 1978 and 1998, the number of retirements and deaths among the diocesan clergy far outpaced the number of ordinations. Enrolment in the seminary had declined. Accounts of clerical sexual abuse of minors and young people had begun to surface in the media; and public perception of the Catholic priesthood had become suspicious if not outright hostile.[7] Although the average number of parishes and missions remained steady at 147 and 27, respectively, there were only 197 active diocesan priests as of January 1998, compared to 232 five years earlier. The median age of active diocesan priests at the beginning of 1998 was 63 years. The number of religious priests who staffed parishes and missions had dropped from 124 to 76, between 1982 and 1998, and while in any given year a dozen or more non-incardinated priests worked in the diocese, their long-term commitment to the diocese was never guaranteed.[8]

The bishop was determined to breathe new life into vocations to the diocesan priesthood, to sustain the vocations of those already ordained and, echoing the words of John Paul II, to make the parish, where most diocesan priests exercise their ministry, "a warm and welcoming family home."[9] The shortage of priests prompted three things: diocesan programs to support priests, a financial campaign for St. Peter's Seminary and other ministries of the diocese, and an acceleration in the growth of lay ministry.

The diocese initiated measures to support its priests. In 1978, a highly successful priests' renewal program was held, but lacked proper follow-up. Additional structures were needed to support priests' growth and renewal. On 12 March 1984, the priests of the diocese adopted the Ministry to Priests program. Conceived by Father Vincent Dwyer, OCSO, of the Centre for Human Development in Washington, D.C., this program was designed to stimulate the spiritual, intellectual and emotional growth of priests by means of self-knowledge exercises, retreats, peer ministry and support groups. Bishop Sherlock, a founder of the Canadian office of the Centre for Human Development and a member of its board, appointed Father Percy Drouillard as the program's first director. Ministry to Priests continues as a vital service to the diocesan clergy. (Inspired by the successful year of renewal for priests, the diocese implemented a successful renewal program for married couples, named "I Give You Me.")

Fund-raising Campaign

By the end of the 1980s, St. Peter's Seminary,

which suffered declining enrolments, was sliding towards a financial crisis because reserve funds were being tapped to pay operating expenses. Bishop Sherlock realized that it would be incongruous to invite young men to consider the priesthood if he closed the seminary. Such a move would have been bad for morale and a public relations disaster. Instead he found a way to ensure that the training of priests and, thus the ministry of the Gospel, would continue.

After consulting the senate of priests, the advisory board of the diocesan pastoral council and several brother bishops, in the spring of 1989, Sherlock announced a fund-raising campaign, named Pentecost 2000. It was the most ambitious campaign of its kind in the history of the diocese. Its primary aim was to establish an endowment for the seminary and to purchase and renovate the former Resurrectionist seminary next to St. Peter's Seminary. Other aims included establishing endowments for the renovation of the cathedral and the special needs of parishes. The goal was $15 million.

Pentecost 2000 was concerned with more than fundraising. In a news story announcing the campaign, Bishop Sherlock remarked:

> We want to be secure in the training of our priests, who are leaders in the work of evangelization, but [the drive] is also intended to incorporate the whole Church and all the gifts of everyone in order that the work of the Holy Spirit in building up the Body of Christ might go on, and we can fulfill our responsibilities in bringing the good news of Christ to the world.[10]

The priests and people of the diocese of London responded generously. Parish chairpersons and secretaries, 5,000 volunteers and even Bishop Sherlock, gathered pledges well in excess of the original goal. In the end, Pentecost 2000 raised just over $21 million. Endowment funds were established and allocated as follows: St. Peter's Seminary, $8 million; Aquinas House, $1 million; the cathedral, $1 million; parishes, $4.85 million; diocesan programs and specialist offices, $5.31 million; campaign expenses, $850,000. The endowment funds continue to generate income.[11]

Developing Lay Ministry

Lay ministry came to the forefront of diocesan life from 1980 to 1995 when lay people became increasingly involved in the ministry of the Church at the diocesan and parish level, with differing results. Bishop Sherlock guided the development of lay ministry, assisted by the senate of priests, the advisory board of the diocesan pastoral council, the representatives of the seven deaneries, and men and women from every walk of life. Developing lay ministry was largely uncharted territory. Although the Second Vatican Council had spoken about the laity's role in the sanctification of the world — at home, at work, at school — it had made no reference to lay people working for a salary in the local church.

On one level, the ever-greater degrees of lay involvement — especially as paid pastoral assistants, pastoral ministers and parish-based co-ordinators of youth ministry — was a strictly pragmatic response to the decline in the number of active priests. On another, and more important level, the increase in lay ministry was the right response from the diocese to the call of the Holy Spirit to engage the gifts of a broader range of the faithful, in particular those of women. It built on the work of religious communities, adult faith formation and spirituality centres.

In September 1979, Bishop Sherlock approved the introduction of pastoral ministers and the program steadily grew. Pastoral ministers worked as paid employees in parishes and Catholic institutions such as hospitals, and their tasks included assisting in catechetical work such as preparing people for the sacraments. For the first five or so years, almost all pastoral ministers were women religious. By 1982, there were twenty-two women religious working as pastoral ministers: seventeen full-time and three part-time in parishes and another two women religious in hospitals.[12] In October 1983, Sherlock appointed Father Michael O'Brien as co-ordinator of lay pastoral ministers. Any parish that was interested in hiring a pastoral assistant, or any layperson who sought employment as one, needed to contact Father O'Brien's office.[13] By 1987, there were thirty-one women religious and thirteen lay persons, all full-time, employed as pastoral ministers in parishes.

At the diocesan level, the shift to lay involvement occurred gradually with people being employed in leadership and administrative positions. The administration of the following offices and programs was placed in the hands of lay people from their inception or was passed to them after having been managed for a period by a priest or a religious sister: Catholic Rural Life Conference (1981); Rite of Christian Initiation of Adults, or RCIA (1983); youth ministry to oversee the training and hiring of youth ministers in parishes (1988); director of refugees to co-ordinate the work of the parish sponsorship program (1990); Renew, a three-year parish-based program (1990-93); social justice office (1990); liturgy office (1990); office of evangelization (1990); and pro-life office (1993). (The above list also shows the extent of the bishop's work on social action issues.) In 1983, Sherlock launched pastoral health-care services. In 1994, he appointed Aurelia Hernandez, ISM, vice-chancellor of the diocese, as the first lay chancellor.

The involvement of lay people at the diocesan level was a success because it was a gradual process and because it responded to specific needs and required qualified people, whose work guaranteed continuity.

The same success initially eluded Bishop Sherlock's efforts to introduce volunteer lay ministry in parishes. He endorsed a program called the Ministries of the People of God in 1980–1981. The program was based on a principle enunciated by the Second Vatican Council that all of the baptized share responsibility for the life and mission of the Church.[14] The program had five goals: to bring the Good News to the poor and affirm the eternal dignity of each human being; to remind the People of God that all the baptized share in the ministry of Christ and the Church; to encourage everyone, in their homes, their neighbourhoods and their place of work, to be a witness of Christ; to facilitate parish life; and to assist in the formation and training of those preparing for ministry.[15]

A September 1980 report made a series of recommendations on the program. The most important were: the reinforcement of adult catechetical programs; the immediate establishment of the ministry of catechist; the appointment of a layperson to co-ordinate the development of ministries; and the continuation of discussion on the order of permanent deacon "as a distinctive course of action under the direction of the bishop."[16]

Bishop Sherlock appointed Joseph Barth as co-ordinator of the program and auxiliary Bishop Marcel Gervais as the overall supervisor. Between October 1981 and June 1982, fifteen to twenty people from each of the seven deaneries participated in a series of teaching conferences for formation and training. The bishop commissioned the 140 members of the deanery teams at St. Peter's Seminary chapel, on 5 June 1982.

The second phase was to be a process whereby the teams were to consult the clergy deaneries, the lay deaneries and the diocesan resource centres on the needs of the parishes and then provide formation programs to men and women willing to minister in their own parishes.

In spite of Bishop Sherlock's support, the careful preparation, the enthusiasm, and the support from many for overhauling parish ministry, the program petered out in the final phase. Many deaneries were unequipped to present the same type of teaching conferences and lacked other resources to continue this initiative. As well, there was less than enthusiastic support from some parish priests.

Moreover, another development added an element of confusion to the introduction of volunteer lay ministry in parishes. In the spring of 1983, the senate of priests agreed to establish the permanent diaconate, a feature of the New Testament Church, which the Second Vatican Council had restored. Father Patrick W. Fuerth was appointed director of the program.

Opposition to the permanent diaconate was immediate and intense. People wanted answers to questions such as: "How does the role of deacon differ from that of lay minister in light of the new code of Canon Law which opens so many doors to the laity?" "Is the 'Church in the pews' calling for deacons as the answer to its needs?" "Is the ordination of a few men as deacons the best way to solve the complex problem of sharing ministry, authority, leadership and decision-making within the whole Church?" And, some people wanted to know why there was no prospect of women deacons when the early Church had them. Father Fuerth's explanations that the permanent diaconate was a distinct dimension in Church order failed to satisfy misgivings about "clericalizing" lay leadership.[17]

The senate of priests and the advisory board of the diocesan pastoral council held a special joint meeting on the subject, on 15–16 February 1985. It failed to produce a clear consensus on whether the permanent diaconate would "hinder or promote the development of the vocation and role of the laity."[18] Consequently, Bishop Sherlock concluded that he would institute the permanent diaconate only if it "responded to a clearly perceived pastoral need in the diocese."[19]

The idea was shelved for almost fifteen years. Then Bishop Sherlock asked Bishop Richard J. Grecco, his auxiliary, to undertake another widespread consultation on the matter. Despite continued divisions over the issue, in December 1999, Sherlock announced his intention to implement the permanent diaconate in the diocese.[20]

In 1985, St. Peter's Seminary in London began to offer a formation program for lay people, and on 1 September 1992, Assumption University in Windsor introduced the Institute of Pastoral and Educational Ministry, to work in conjunction with John XXIII Centre in Windsor to provide training and education for pastoral ministers. The program offered Master of Arts degrees and certificates in pastoral ministry and a master's degree in religious education.

In 1986, Bishop Sherlock established the diocesan commission on women. There had been an ad hoc committee established by Bishop Carter, but Sherlock was encouraged to give it more clout by raising it to the status of a commission. Its first chair was Eleanor O'Neil, who was succeeded by Joan Lenardon, who in turn was succeeded by Connie Paré. Its primary purpose was to assess the extent of participation of women in diocesan life.

In 1987, Bishop Sherlock was one of five Canadian bishop-delegates to the synod of bishops in Rome. Its theme, "The Vocation and Mission of Lay People in Society and the Church," was a sure sign of the arrival of the age of the laity.

Following the start-up of the youth ministry office in 1988, a concerted effort was undertaken to train and hire co-ordinators of youth ministry in parishes that wanted one. By 1998, there were seventy pastoral ministers and forty-five co-ordinators of youth ministry in the diocese.[21]

Lay ministry has become an integral and necessary aspect in the life of the Church in the diocese of London. Next to the introduction of the Mass of Paul VI and the use of the vernacular in all Catholic liturgies, the rise in prominence and importance of the laity in diocesan and parish-based administration, in matters both spiritual and temporal, has been the most enduring change to have occurred in the years following the Council.

Planning for the Future

In the autumn of 1988, Bishop Sherlock established a diocesan planning commission, thus beginning a critical process to examine the future of the diocese and its viability for carrying out the work of the Gospel. Its 1992 report paved the way for reconfiguring parish structure and for the eventual closing of some parishes.

Bishop Sherlock appointed Father James M. Williams, VG, moderator of the curia, to head the commission, which was composed of clergy, religious and lay people. The mandate was to assess existing diocesan facilities, principally church buildings, to study the diocese's ability to minister to the needs of the Catholic population in the light of a growing shortage of clergy and to forecast the future needs of the diocese in terms of its churches, other properties and clergy personnel.[22] Of particular urgency was the need to examine the variegation in the roles of priests and lay ministers and to provide "support and assistance in the area of formation for people who are called to lay ministry."[23] Sherlock asked the commission to deliver "recommendations on a strategic basis that would provide an approach and format for the long range planning and development of parishes in the diocese."[24]

For the first time in the diocese of London, Catholics were enjoined by their bishop to examine and report on all facets of parochial life in a professional and objective manner, so that the diocese would be prepared to sustain its many parishes as Eucharistic communities. Two distinct possibilities came into play: some parishes, because of their dwindling congregations, would no longer have a resident pastor, or worse, would have to close.

The diocesan planning commission spent four years in consultation, discussion and debate involving the input of approximately 3,000 people. It examined population, land development and diocesan land resources, studied clergy and lay personnel, surveyed parishes and took an inventory of parish facilities. This revealed the probability that the diocese needed a fundamental reconfiguration.

The commission delivered its final report in September 1992. It focused on changes such as the re-organization of diocesan offices and establishment of new renewal adult education centres. But it could not address the need to close parishes because Bishop Sherlock had stated publicly that he would never do this.

The commission's ten recommendations were: that parishes continue to be defined geographically; that the diocese move to recognize culturally distinct communities not already served by parishes; that the diocese recognize the uniqueness of each parish and conduct periodic evaluations of them; that the diocese encourage and support parish-based strategic plans; that the diocese implement the principle of shared leadership in each parish; that increased flexibility and planning be introduced into the human resources of parishes; that the diocese institute a parish leadership model based on the principles of co-responsible ministry; that the diocese's financial and statistical policies, procedures and systems for parishes be more open to parishes; that a multi-year capital program and a capital project evaluation process be instituted; and that a permanent diocesan planning and coordination commission be created.[25]

In February 1993, Bishop Sherlock set up a committee to implement the recommendations. Restructuring the diocese may not have been the commission's original intent, but now the task was to adopt a course whereby the diocese would make the right decisions for the common good of all the faithful, parish by parish. That would take time and more discussion and debate.

The first stage of restructuring involved moving parishes into clusters. Father Tony Daniels, by that time the moderator of the curia, defined parish clustering as "a model whereby two or more parishes are associated with each other and share the leadership of a pastor together with other ministers, such as associate pastors, pastoral ministers, coordinators of youth ministry and pastoral animators." Bishop Sherlock said that clustering was important because it was "a thoughtful and rational preparation for the day when there will be fewer priests in pastoral ministry."[26]

The bishop also saw clustering as a way to increase connections and cooperation between parishes. "But the most important thing," Bishop Sherlock continued, "is that this [clustering] is a challenge to all the people in the diocese to move from a narrow parochial ministry to a catholic one. Parochialism has always been an impediment to the fullness of Catholic thought and life…. Through clustering we are asking people to begin in a very modest way to share with their neighboring parishes their human resources, expenses for shared personnel and programs, their gifts, their needs."[27]

A pilot project for clustering parishes in the Huron-Perth deanery, a mostly rural deanery that had many historic parishes, began in 1994. Two of the earliest examples were the clustered parishes of St. James in Seaforth and St. Columban in St. Columban, and St. Brigid's in Logan and St. Patrick's in Kinkora. On 3 January 1996, clustering became official policy, and Bishop Sherlock appointed Sister Shirley McAuley, OSU, a member of the permanent planning commission, to prepare parishes for the changes to come.

Clustering was a long, involved process that had supporters and critics. By the time Bishop Sherlock retired, in April 2002, the process had yet to be completed. For some parishes, especially the older and more established ones and those that had a degree of financial autonomy, it was painful and bewildering. For others, it was a lifeline and a fairly smooth transition.

The clustering of parishes proved to be Bishop Sherlock's last significant contribution to the reorganization of the diocese of London. He thought that clustering was a far better pastoral response to the shrinking number of active priests than the suppression of parishes. He did, however, close four: St. Clare of Assisi (June 2000), Immaculate Conception and Sacred Heart (December 2001), all in Windsor, and St. Joachim in Essex County (April 2000).

Celebrations and Honours

In 1981, the diocese of London celebrated its 125th anniversary with many events at the parish and deanery levels. The main diocesan celebration was a Mass celebrated at London Gardens, on Pentecost Sunday, where more than 5,000 of the faithful gathered.

In September 1983, Bishop Sherlock was elected president of the Canadian Conference of Catholic Bishops (CCCB). His most pressing task was organizing the papal visit to Canada in 1984. He made countless trips to Ottawa and Rome, reconciling conflicting desires, negotiating schedules and helping to fine-tune John Paul II's public speeches (the pope wrote his own sermons longhand).[28] As the official host, Sherlock accompanied the pope during his cross-country visit, from 9-20 September 1984, and they developed a warm and meaningful friendship which lasted well beyond 1984.

Bishop Sherlock received, in 1985, a Doctor of Law Degree, *honoris causa*, from the University of Windsor and in April 1986, a Doctor of Divinity Degree, *honoris causa*, from Huron College, London. In June 1994, he was received as a Fellow, *honoris causa*, of the University of St. Michael's College, Toronto.

In 1999, Sherlock celebrated the twenty-fifth anniversary of his episcopal ordination and, in 2000, he marked the fiftieth anniversary of his priestly ordination. He celebrated these two events at a number of Masses, to which he invited married couples, religious or priests celebrating significant anniversaries to join him and share the honour.

Sexual Abuse Scandal

During the later 1980s, the scandals of the sexual abuse of minors and young people by members of the Catholic clergy shook Bishop Sherlock and the diocese. The diocese's slowness in responding meaningfully and justly to the scandals further undermined confidence in the Church. In one sense, the situation in London became a test case in the episcopal response to criminal charges of sexual abuse laid against priests.

When Bishop Sherlock first learned of the allegations of paedophilia by priests in his diocese, he found it difficult to confront them. The initial shock overwhelmed him. His love of the priesthood made it extremely difficult for him to believe that any priest would engage in such deplorable behaviour. He was slow to appreciate the fact that the criminal personality involved in the predatory sexual exploitation of the vulnerable was always an expert liar and able to deceive many people. When the accused denied charges or said only one victim was involved, the bishop, and others, wanted to believe them. As well, the high risk of sexual offenders re-abusing was not understood.[29]

In a speech he gave as bishop-emeritus, Bishop Sherlock stated, "An early response was to protect the priesthood and the Church." He ventured that "the culture of silence" around sexual abuse cases may have resulted from priests being "victims of

their own theology." There was a belief that "a priest is a priest forever … "and should not be removed from ministry. " It took time for the protection of children to become foremost."[30]

In 1989, Bishop Sherlock started putting the proper policy mechanisms in place to deal with sexual abuse by clergy. He set up the diocesan Sexual Abuse Committee and worked with the committee to develop a protocol that includes a pastoral response to the victims and the perpetrators of sexual abuse. Now he also thinks that there needs to be a response to the parish, "the sometimes 'forgotten victim.'"[31] The bishop encouraged people not to be afraid to contact the committee, which included a civil lawyer, a canon lawyer, a psychiatrist and educators.[32] He helped write *From Pain to Hope*, a set of guidelines the CCCB released in 1992, concerning the formation of diocesan sexual abuse committees.

When more allegations were made and charges laid, however, Bishop Sherlock realized his assumptions were wrong and developed a clearer and deeper understanding of the crisis.

The bishop grew in sympathy for the victims, working hard to bring them healing and reconciliation and going out of his way to apologize personally to the victims. In his speech, Bishop Sherlock revealed that at first … he did not ask for details when speaking with victims. "This was perhaps out of a sense of delicacy … I don't know," he said. The courage to listen [for] "several hours to several victims of the same perpetrator … brought me to tears. Then it brought me to (daily) prayer for the victims, the perpetrators, and the church."[33]

In 1993, the diocese implemented a sexual harassment policy. Further, in 2001, the diocese implemented a screening program for all volunteers in the diocese: the goal was to provide a safe environment for children and other vulnerable people.

The Church began to deal more openly with the situation. Diocesan publications carried articles and the bishop wrote a letter to the priests and people of the diocese that acknowledged the incidents of sexual abuse and urged support for the victims. In his *Quinquennial Report 1993-1998*, Bishop Sherlock made a passing yet revealing reference to the impact of scandal. "[W]here failures in clerical celibacy have occurred, particularly in the area of paedophilia, the scandal is enormous and the discouragement on the part of other priests who find themselves embarrassed and shamed by the publicly revealed sins of their colleagues is a serious matter."[34]

On 27 March 2002, the Wednesday of Holy Week, Bishop Sherlock issued a letter to the priests of the diocese, which they were to read at Mass on Holy Thursday. He declared that no abuser would be returned to active ministry, that he would not forget the good work of his faithful priests, and that all those guilty of the crimes of sexual abuse deserved their prayers, since everyone, regardless of their sins, needed the saving power of Christ. "In the name of the Church," he wrote:

> I confess our sins, beg pardon of all who have suffered abuse and from their parents and families who cannot escape sharing in the suffering…. On Good Friday, my personal veneration of the cross will be an act of sorrow and repentance personally, as it is for each of you, but as Bishop [it] will be as well for the sins of ministers of the Church, which in all these scandals has been betrayed in its mission to bring the love and mercy of Christ to a suffering world.[35]

Retirement

On 27 April 2002, Rome accepted Bishop Sherlock's resignation, more than a year after he had submitted it, and after 24 years of faithful service to the diocese of London. At seventy-six years of age, he was looking forward to retirement. On the same day, Rome appointed Father Ronald P. Fabbro, CSB, the superior general of the Basilian Fathers, as the tenth bishop of London.

Since Bishop Sherlock considered the diocese his family, he stayed in London and his retirement has been active and fulfilling. He teaches homiletics at St. Peter's Seminary, conducts retreats and parish missions, and keeps in touch with university students who meet weekly in his home. He even does weekend work at parishes and the cathedral.

Bishop Sherlock never turns down an opportunity to preach the Gospel of Jesus Christ. His secret to life, he once remarked, is to spend an hour each day in prayer and then let the Holy Spirit lead him through the rest of the day.

Endnotes for Chapter Nine -- Bishop Sherlock

[1] Herman Goodden, "Asking Big Questions of Bishop John Sherlock," *Scene*, 21 September 1994, 22.

[2] Ibid.

[3] Jean LeBlanc, *Dictionnaire Biographique des Èvêques du Canada* (Ottawa: 2002), 816.

[4] *Newsletter of the Diocese of London*, no. 102 (Summer 2002), 2.

[5] Ibid.

[6] Tony Daniels, "An Occasion to Remember: London's Bishop Celebrates Double Anniversaries," St. Peter's Seminary, *Alumni Bulletin 1999-2000* (2000), 3.

[7] Daniels, "An Occasion to Remember: London's Bishop Celebrates Double Anniversaries," 4.

[8] Diocese of London, *Quinquennial Report 1993-1998*, 24; *Quinquennial Report 1998-2005*, 39. These two reports differ from each other in the number of active diocesan priests as of 1 January 1998: 149 and 197, respectively. The higher number has been taken as the more realistic of the two.

[9] John Michael Sherlock, "Keynote Address: 'Priesthood in Our Day,'" St. Augustine's Seminary Alumni Meeting, 75th Anniversary, 26 October 1988, [3].

[10] *Newsletter of the Diocese of London*, no. 37 (Pentecost 1989), 3.

[11] Diocese of London, "Pentecost 2000: What happened to the original funds?" (2001).

[12] Diocese of London, *Quinquennial Report 1978-1982*, 18.

[13] *Newsletter of the Diocese of London*, no. 17 (Summer 1984), 5.

[14] Ibid., 2 (September 1980), Appendix 2.

[15] Ibid., no. 6 (September 1981), 7.

[16] Ibid., no. 3 (December 1980), 3.

[17] Ibid., no. 14 (Fall 1983), 6-7; no. 15 (Christmas 1983), 12.

[18] Diocese of London, *Quinquennial Report 1983-1987*, 7.

[19] Ibid., 8.

[20] Ibid., no. 89 (Advent/Christmas 1999), 2.

[21] Diocese of London, *Quinquennial Report 1993-1998*, 39.

[22] *Newsletter of the Diocese of London*, no. 44 (Advent/Christmas 1990), 2.

[23] Ibid., no. 64 (Advent/Christmas 1994), 4.

[24] DLA, John Michael Sherlock Papers [hereafter JMS Papers], Diocesan Planning Commission, *Final Report of the Diocesan Planning Commission: Strategic Plan for Future Planning and Development of Parishes in the Diocese of London* (September 1992), 4-1.

[25] Ibid., 7-1 to 7-4.

[26] Quotes in this paragraph from *Newsletter*, 67 (Pentecost 1995), 5.

[27] Ibid., no. 70 (Lent 1996), 2.

[28] Bishop John Michael Sherlock, interview by Michael Power, 25 October 2006.

[29] Marie Carter, "Our former Bishop reflects on personal experience of Church's journey from pain to hope regarding sexual abuse scandals," Roman Catholic Diocese of London website, 2003, http://www.rcec.london.on.ca/abuse/Sherlock_reflects.htm.

[30] Ibid.

[31] Ibid.

[32] *Newsletter of the Diocese of London*, no. 41 (Easter 1990), 2; no. 49 (Advent/Christmas 1991), 5.

[33] Carter, "Our former Bishop reflects on personal experience of Church's journey from pain to hope regarding sexual abuse scandals."

[34] Diocese of London, *Quinquennial Report 1993-1998*, 27.

[35] DLA, JMS Papers, letter of Sherlock to "My Dear Brother Priests," 27 March 2002.

10. Ronald Peter Fabbro, CSB (2002–)

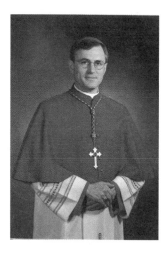

Ronald Peter Fabbro, CSB, the tenth bishop of London, is providing the diocese with servant-leadership during a period of great change and crisis, as well as celebration. During the first years of his episcopacy, Bishop Fabbro has shown his willingness to make difficult but critical decisions. He is guiding the parishes, priests and people through significant organizational changes, including the closing of parishes. He has taken a direct and firm approach to the clergy sexual abuse crisis. In 2006, he led the diocese in celebrating its 150th anniversary.

Childhood and Priesthood

Born on 6 November 1950, in Sudbury, Ontario, Ronald Fabbro is one of three children of Emile Fabbro and Ines Villa.[1] His grandparents left Italy for Canada following the First World War, and his paternal grandparents settled in Sudbury. His father was in the hotel and motel business, and later was an employee of the city of Sudbury. The young Fabbro grew up in St. Clement's parish and attended St. Albert's separate school and St. Charles College, which was run by the Congregation of St. Basil, or Basilian Fathers. Among his many fine teachers were Father Hodgson (Hod) Marshall, CSB, and Father Arthur Holmes, CSB, both of whom taught him mathematics and influenced his decision to pursue university studies in that discipline.

Before he entered the priesthood, Fabbro earned a Bachelor of Science in mathematics at Queen's University, in 1973, and a Master of Science in mathematics at the University of Toronto, in 1974. During 1974–75, he taught mathematics at St. Mary's College, a Basilian high school in Sault Ste. Marie. He lived with the Basilians that year, an experience that convinced him to join their community; he entered their novitiate in Rochester, New York, on 1 August 1975. After he made his first profession of vows, on 15 August 1976, he entered St. Basil's College in Toronto, where he completed a Master of Divinity degree in 1979.

He made his final profession in the Basilian community on 15 August 1979, and was ordained to the transitional diaconate in Sacred Heart cathedral in Rochester, on 22 September 1979, by Bishop Matthew Clark of the diocese of Rochester. He spent the next year in pastoral work with Father Thomas Mailloux, CSB, at Christ the King parish in Rochester. He was ordained to the priesthood, on 3 May 1980, by Bishop Alexander Carter of Sault Ste. Marie, in St. Patrick's church, Sudbury.

Father Fabbro's first assignment was to teach mathematics at St. Mary's College, Sault Ste. Marie, but his high school teaching career was short-lived. Having been offered an opportunity to pursue graduate studies, he opted to study moral theology at the Gregorian University in Rome. There he studied from 1981 to 1986, with residence at the Canadian College. This rich intellectual and spiritual experience changed his life in many ways and resulted in numerous lasting friendships and contacts in the Church. In addition to his course work, research and writing, he learned French, visited relatives in Italy and spent one summer in the company of his Basilian confreres at Annonay, France. He was awarded a licentiate in Theology in 1983 and a doctorate in Moral Theology in 1989. The title of his dissertation is *Co-operation in Evil*. (On November 16, 2002, he was granted an honorary doctorate of Divinity, from the University of St. Michael's College, Toronto.)

On his return to Canada, Father Fabbro taught

theology at St. Joseph's College at the University of Alberta, Edmonton, from 1987 to 1990, and at the University of St. Michael's College, Toronto, from 1990 to 1997. He was also on his community's formation team and general council, from 1993 to 1997. He was involved in the Canadian Religious Conference (CRC) as a member of its theology committee and of the administrative council of the conference's Ontario branch.

In 1997, Fabbro was elected to a four-year term as general superior of the Basilians and was re-elected to the position in 2001. In addition to carrying out his administrative duties, he taught part time. As a general councillor, he had learned a great deal about the dynamics and benefits of collaborative leadership and incorporated the principle of shared responsibility into his leadership style as general superior.

Tenth Bishop of London

On 27 April 2002, Ronald Peter Fabbro was appointed the tenth bishop of London. He is the second member of the Basilian Fathers to become bishop of London (Denis O'Connor was the first). Fabbro, who speaks English, French, and Italian, is the first bishop who represents neither of the diocese's founding groups—the French and the Irish. To the office of bishop, Fabbro has brought the gifts of a strong prayer life, a disciplined and well-trained intellect, experience of leadership in the Church, and a love of God's people. He took his motto *Secundum verbum tuum doce me* from *Psalm* 119: 169. Translated, it means "Teach me according to your word," and echoes the motto of his religious community: "Teach me goodness, discipline and knowledge."

Bishop Fabbro was ordained and installed at St. Peter's Cathedral, on 15 August 2002, the feast of the Assumption of the Blessed Virgin Mary and the anniversary of his first profession of vows in the Congregation of St. Basil. Bishop John M. Sherlock (bishop-emeritus of London), Bishop Fabbro's immediate predecessor, was the principal consecrator. He was assisted by Bishop Richard Grecco, auxiliary bishop of the archdiocese of Toronto, and Bishop Ricardo Ramirez, CSB, of Las Cruces, New Mexico, who also preached. Father Anthony Daniels read the Apostolic Letter of Appointment. The bishop's mother presented

the episcopal ring, which had belonged to Bishop Cody, and the bishop's sisters presented the mitre and pastoral staff. Father Brian Klooster, Sister Mary Diesbourg, CSJ, and Sandy Easton offered greetings on behalf of the diocesan clergy, the religious and the laity, respectively.

The new bishop was familiar with the ministry of the Basilian Fathers in Windsor and Amherstburg, but he hardly knew the diocese, and the diocese did not know him. He began getting to know his priests and people, committing himself to visiting every parish in the diocese, a promise that would take several years to fulfil. He needed to learn about the diocese's priests, people and problems and to reach out to all constituencies in the diocese.

In response to Pope John Paul II's request that each diocese create a pastoral plan, Bishop Fabbro initiated the development of a pastoral plan for London. On 30 May 2004, the feast of Pentecost, Bishop Fabbro promulgated the plan "Embracing a Future Full of Hope." It consisted of a preamble and six goals that were intended to act as the defining blueprint for decision-making in the diocese over the next five years. The goals focus on personal holiness, evangelizing and teaching, justice and compassion, liturgical celebration, formation and governance.[2]

At the same time, on the advice of the council of priests, Bishop Fabbro initiated a re-examination of the government and organization of the diocese. The committee, which had a mandate to devise a new governance model in accordance with the pastoral plan, made its recommendations to the bishop in 2004. Significant structural changes have resulted and other changes are under development.

Parish Reorganization

Bishop Fabbro also oversaw a difficult, but necessary, reorganization of the diocese's parishes to better serve the faithful. Nothing so sweeping or so potentially threatening to the diocese's parochial structure had happened in its 150-year history. The diocese knew the process was potentially divisive because some parishes would have to close and some might have to merge. The idea of losing their parish was unfathomable for some parishioners.

The need for restructuring the parishes had surfaced during the closing years of Bishop

Sherlock's administration and some of the groundwork for the changes was laid then. But more drastic changes were needed to deal with the problems created by shifting populations, aging buildings and the decline in the number of clergy.

The diocese involved each parish and mission in the process for determining change. Each one was required to justify the continuation of its existence, in an open and transparent fashion that adhered to realistic and rational expectations and outcomes.

On 29 April 2006, after a year-long study, the diocese published a four-page report on parish reorganization.[3] The result of several years of meetings, deliberations, debates and even some protests, its conclusions were radical but sensible. Six new parishes were to be established, including two with a new church building. Ten parishes were to cluster or merge with other parishes, while 36 parishes and 25 church buildings were to close. As well, 26 parishes would be involved in further studies that might lead to more changes. The process has yet to conclude, and, as Bishop Fabbro pointed out, the clustering, mergers and the closures were only the first step in the overall plan to build strong, vibrant parish communities in every part of the diocese.[4]

While significant internal changes were underway in the diocese, important changes outside the diocese also demanded Bishop Fabbro's attention. On the national level, the campaign in early 2005 to legalize same-sex unions necessitated a strong response from the Canadian bishops. Fabbro provided decisive leadership in this area within the diocese. Internationally, in the first few months of 2005, Pope John Paul II's health was declining, and his death on 2 April was a major event, in the world and in the diocese.

The Clergy Abuse Scandal

Public revelations in 2006 of more cases of clergy sexual abuse of minors in the diocese created great pain and mortification. But Bishop Fabbro's direct, firm handling of the scandal ultimately opened avenues of dialogue, healing and reconciliation.

The bishop publicly and repeatedly promised to take every action in his power to ensure that such reprehensible conduct does not happen again in the diocese. In 2006, when he appointed Father John F.

Sharp as a vicar general, he gave him responsibility for revising policies and procedures on clergy abuse, with a special emphasis on prevention. The process of revision and updating continues.

Bishop Fabbro's public apology at St. Ursula's church in Chatham, where a priest convicted of sexual abuse had served, made a strong impact. On Sunday, 6 August 2006, the packed church heard the bishop declare his intention to chart a different course for the Church. He began by acknowledging that:

It may be difficult for victims to hear people like me speak on the subject of priestly abuse. In their pain and anger, what I say can seem insincere, defensive and self-serving.

I am here to tell you that I am saying what I mean, and that I mean what I say.

He apologized to the victims and their families "for the abuse they had endured" and "for suffering the consequences of that abuse over the years." He also apologized "for the failure of the Church to protect the victims and their families." He then declared:

My goal is to protect people against abuse. My goal is also to provide a way for dealing with allegations of abuse quickly and effectively. We have learned from experience, and we have learned from science. We are now in a much better position to protect our people than we were before.

There can be no justification for abuse. There are explanations for the Church's failure to take the appropriate steps in the past to protect victims from abusive priests, but these explanations seem weak, especially with the acute vision given by hindsight.

For Catholics, it was once unthinkable that priests would abuse children. This culture of disbelief affected all of the Church from parents on to school teachers, to priests and even to bishops. So in many cases the victims were victimized twice; first by the abuse itself, and then by refusal of others to believe them. Some were made to feel guilty for making an accusation and some believe, even today, years later, that they themselves are at fault for having been abused.

There is no room left in the Church for this kind of thinking.[5]

Celebrating with Hope

The faithful have had many good things to celebrate since the arrival of Bishop Fabbro, and they have done so in style, imbued with Christian hope for the future of the local Church.

On 28 October 2004, the first Bishop's Dinner on behalf of St. Peter's Seminary took place in Windsor. Laity and clergy from Windsor and Essex County and St. Peter's Seminary Foundation conceived the idea and organized the fundraiser, under the leadership of Maureen and Emod Greff. It attracted 820 people and generated in excess of $70,000 for the seminary's operating budget. Each year, generous benefactors act as honorary co-chairs, with many others supporting the venture through businesses and personal donations. The annual event for Windsor-and-area Catholics has had up to 1,000 people in attendance.

On 9 November 2004, at a splendid ceremony at St. Peter's cathedral, the diocese received a new auxiliary bishop when R. Anthony Daniels was ordained to the episcopate.

On 5 November 2005, also at the cathedral, Bishop Fabbro ordained the diocese's inaugural class of permanent deacons. The fourteen men came from every region of the diocese.

In addition to his responsibilities in the diocese, Bishop Fabbro also has appointments on commissions and committees: the Episcopal Commission for Liturgy (2003), the Canadian Council of Churches Governing Board (2003) and the Catholic Organization for Life and Family (COLF) (2004). On the Ontario Conference of Catholic Bishops he holds appointments to the Liturgy Commission (2002) and the Education Commission (2002).

The diocese celebrated its 150th anniversary during the 2006 church year, taking a low key approach, partly because many were saddened by the impact of parish reorganization. In his letters that year, the bishop reminded his readers of their sources of hope in the face of such difficulty. In his anniversary pastoral letter, issued on the first Sunday of Advent, 4 December 2005, Bishop Fabbro wrote that our encounter with Christ is our source of strength:

The theme for the year, "Embracing a Future Full of Hope," encourages all of us to build on the good work that we have already begun through our Diocesan Pastoral Plan.

This past year, which Pope John Paul II declared the Year of the Eucharist, has been an excellent preparation for our diocesan celebrations. The Eucharist has been the centre of the life of our diocese and will be the focus of these reflections. It is our encounter with Christ in the Eucharist which enables us to proclaim with conviction that we embrace "a future full of hope."[6]

Later, in his letter on parish reorganization, issued on 29 April 2006, Bishop Fabbro challenged his readers to be encouraged by the lives of their "ancestors in the faith":

This year, we are celebrating the 150th anniversary of our diocese. During this period, we have built a strong presence across our diocese, through parishes that flourished and reached out to those in need, and through schools and hospitals, and other Catholic institutions. This graced history gives us hope as we look to the future.

The incredible sacrifices made by our foremothers and fathers continue to inspire us. The challenges we face are different from theirs, but we must be willing to tackle them with the same courage that our ancestors in the faith demonstrated.

On 16 May Bishop Fabbro presided at a solemn Mass of Thanksgiving at the cathedral, the highlight of the sesquicentennial celebrations, which concluded with a banquet for close to 1,000 people. Each of the deaneries also held special Eucharistic liturgies to commemorate the anniversary.

The bishop began his sermon at the Mass by recounting the story of Father Michel Moncoq, who had served as a missionary to both Natives and settlers living between Point Pelee and Penetanguishene. He died by drowning in the St. Clair River, on 1 January 1856, enroute from Algonac, Michigan to Baby's Point, near Port Lambton, after attending to a sick call. The faithful of the surrounding area recognized his heroic virtues, and over time his tragic death has been seen as a fitting end to the missionary era that preceded the establishment of the diocese of London on 21 February 1856.

Bishop Fabbro invited the people to be inspired

by the enduring witness of Father Moncoq as the diocese reorganized itself, confronted its many problems and looked to the future. He asked them to turn outwards, "to take up with fresh energy and enthusiasm our mission to announce the Good News of Jesus."[7]

Endnotes for Chapter 10 -- Bishop Fabbro

[1] Bishop Ronald Peter Fabbro, interview by Michael Power, London, Ontario, 7 November 2006; *Newsletter of the Diocese of London*, no. 103 (Pentecost/Summer 2002), 1, 3.

[2] *Newsletter of the Diocese of London*, no. 113 (Summer 2004), 1-3; no. 114 (Fall 2004), 1.

[3] Diocese of London, "Special Reorganization Report," 29 April 2006. See also *Newsletter of the Diocese of London*, no. 118 (Summer 2005), 10-11; no. 119 (Fall 2005), 2; no. 121 (Lent 2006), 2.

[4] Diocese of London, "Parish Reorganization in the Diocese of London," http://www.rcec.london.on.ca/reorganization/index. htm. April 29, 2006.

[5] Diocese of London, "Statement of Bishop Ronald Fabbro, CSB," 6 August 2006.

[6] *Newsletter of the Diocese of London*, no. 120 (Advent/ Christmas 2005), 1.

[7] Ibid., no. 122 (Summer 2006), 1.

11. Auxiliary Bishops

Marcel-André Gervais (1980–1985)

Marcel-André Gervais was born on 21 September 1931, in Elie, Manitoba, the ninth of fourteen children of Frédéric-Pierre Gervais and Marie-Louise Beaudry. In 1945, his family moved to Southwestern Ontario and, after he finished high school, he entered St. Peter's Seminary for philosophy and theology. He was ordained a priest for the diocese of London at St. Peter's cathedral on 31 May 1958.

Father Gervais next studied in Rome at the Angelicum (1958–59), where he obtained a Licentiate in Theology, and at the Pontifical Biblical Institute (1959–60). He then studied sacred scripture in Jerusalem at l'École biblique et archéologique française de Jérusalem and was awarded a Licentiate in Sacred Scripture.

Returning to St. Peter's Seminary, Father Gervais was a professor of sacred scripture, from 1962 to 1976, and taught there part-time until 1980. Bishop G. Emmett Carter appointed him director of the Divine Word International Centre for Religious Education in 1974. The following year, he joined the education committee of the Canadian Conference of Catholic Bishops (CCCB) and was appointed to the advisory committee of the International Commission for English in the Liturgy. From 1977 to 1980, working with a team of researchers and writers, he wrote and edited *Journey*, a course of forty lessons on the Bible, which was later translated into fourteen languages.

On 23 April 1980, Pope John Paul II appointed Father Gervais auxiliary bishop of London (and titular bishop of Rosemarkie). He was ordained by Bishop Sherlock on the Feast of St. Barnabas, 11 June 1980, at St. Peter's cathedral. Sherlock was assisted by Archbishop Charles Halpin of Regina, a cousin of the new bishop, and Bishop Aloysius Ambrozic, auxiliary of Toronto. Bishop Gervais' episcopal motto is Evangelizare, which is translated, "To evangelize," or "to proclaim the Good News."

Bishop Gervais resided in the Windsor residence that Bishop Carter and Bishop Sherlock had used when they were auxiliaries. Gervais participated actively in the Canadian Conference of Catholic Bishops (CCCB) and the Ontario Conference of Catholic Bishops (OCCB), serving on numerous episcopal commissions. In 1983, he was a member of the Canadian episcopal delegation to the Synod of Bishops — Reconciliation and Penance in the Mission of the Church.

On 3 May 1985, Gervais was named bishop of Sault Ste. Marie. Four years later, he was named coadjutor-archbishop of Ottawa, and became the eighth archbishop of Ottawa on 7 September 1989, receiving the pallium from John Paul II on 29 June 1990.

Archbishop Gervais has contributed to the fields of education, social action and dialogue with non-believers. He received the Justice James D. Higgins Award in recognition of his exceptional contributions to Catholic education in Ontario and across Canada. He retired as archbishop of Ottawa in June 2007.

Frederick Bernard Henry (1986–1995)

Frederick Bernard Henry was born in London, Ontario, on 11 April 1943, the eldest of five sons of Leo and Noreen Henry. After finishing high school, he entered St. Peter's Seminary and earned degrees from the University of Western Ontario and St. Peter's. On 25 May 1968, he was ordained to the priesthood by Bishop Carter.

Father Henry served at Christ the King parish in Windsor until 1970, when he began post-graduate work. In 1971, he earned a master's degree in philosophy from the University of Notre Dame, Indiana, and, in 1973, he was awarded a Licentiate in Theology, with a specialization in Fundamental Theology, from the Gregorian University in Rome.

On his return to the diocese, Father Henry was appointed to St. Peter's Seminary, where he taught philosophy and theology from 1973 to 1986 and was dean of theology and rector from 1981 to 1986. He was made an honorary prelate, with the title of monsignor, in 1985.

On 18 April 1986, Monsignor Henry was appointed auxiliary bishop of London (and titular bishop of Carinola). He was ordained to the episcopacy on the feast of the Birth of St. John the Baptist, 24 June 1986, in St. Peter's cathedral. Bishop Sherlock was principal consecrator, assisted by Bishop Gervais of Sault Ste. Marie and Bishop Anthony Tonnos of Hamilton. Henry's episcopal motto is *Dabo vobis pastores*, (*Jer.* 3:15) which means, "I will give you pastors." Bishop Henry resided in Windsor during the nine years he served as auxiliary.

He was named fourth bishop of Thunder Bay, and was installed on 11 May 1995. He became the seventh bishop of Calgary on 19 March 1998. Bishop Henry has served as a member of many important Church delegations, committees and organizations on the formation of priests, education, Catholic Missions and social affairs. As bishop of Thunder Bay, he opposed attempts to include sexual orientation in the Charter of Rights and protested the Ontario government's cuts in social services and its funding and promotion of casinos. In 2005, he was one of many bishops who made statements opposing the legalization of same-sex marriage. In addition, he continues to work in defence of the poor in Alberta and of workers' rights in labour disputes.

Richard John Grecco (1997–2002)

Richard John Grecco was born on 4 March 1946, in St. Catharines, Ontario, and grew up in Holy Rosary parish in the city of Thorold. He studied at St. Augustine's Seminary in Toronto and was ordained to the priesthood by Bishop Thomas J. McCarthy, on 2 September 1973, for the diocese of St. Catharines. Father Grecco's first assignment was as associate pastor of St. Denis parish in St. Catharines. In 1977, he joined the faculty of St. Augustine's Seminary and did post-graduate work at St. Paul's University in Ottawa, the Gregorian University in Rome, St. Michael's University College and the Toronto School of Theology, which awarded him the degree of Doctor of Theology in 1982. He has taught at St. Michael's and at St. Joseph's College in Edmonton, where he was professor of moral theology.

In his home diocese, Father Grecco was a leader in the field of religious education, advising the two local Catholic school boards on various matters. For four years, he directed the Renew program, training four hundred team co-ordinators. He helped found

Vineyard, the diocesan newspaper. Father Grecco's last posting in the diocese was at St. Alfred's parish, the largest in the diocese. In the words of Bishop Sherlock, Father Grecco's time at St. Alfred's was "distinguished by keen sensitivity to ethnic and cultural minorities, powerful preaching, effective team leadership and successful administration."

On 5 December 1997, Grecco was appointed auxiliary bishop of London (and titular bishop of Uccula). He was ordained to the episcopacy on the Feast of the Presentation of the Lord, 2 February 1998, in St. Alfred's church and took as his episcopal motto "Hope in the Lord" from Psalm 27: 14b. He was ordained by Bishop Thomas Fulton, bishop-emeritus of St. Catharines, assisted by Bishop Sherlock and Bishop John O'Mara, bishop of St. Catharines.

Bishop Grecco served the diocese in a variety of capacities. He was vicar general with primary responsibility for Catholics in the Windsor and Essex deaneries. (Having special responsibility for Windsor/Essex deaneries was common to all auxiliaries in Sherlock's time, and continues with Bishop Daniels, the current auxiliary bishop.) Grecco chaired the consultation committee on the restoration of the permanent diaconate, sat on the boards of Hotel-Dieu-Grace Hospital in Windsor and was a member of the diocesan personnel and finance committees.

On 27 April 2002, John Paul II appointed Grecco as an auxiliary of the archdiocese of Toronto. He has served as chair of the Christian education commission (English sector) of the CCCB and as an episcopal advisor to the Third Continental Congress on Vocations.

Robert Anthony Daniels (2004–)

Robert Anthony Daniels was born in Windsor, Ontario, on 18 June 1957, the second of four children of Robert Daniels and Barbara Fuerth. During high school, he participated in a retreat weekend for youth, after which he began to consider a vocation to the priesthood. He studied at St. Peter's Seminary, earning a Bachelor of Arts degree in 1980 and a Master of Divinity degree in 1982, from the University of Western Ontario He was ordained to the priesthood, on 7 May 1983, at St. Peter's cathedral by Bishop Sherlock.

Father Daniels' first assignment was as associate

pastor at St. John the Divine in London, a relatively new and youthful parish. From 1986 to 1989, he was associate pastor at St. Peter's cathedral. Leaving parochial work, he was appointed chancellor of the diocese in 1989. He was then appointed moderator of the Curia and vicar general in 1993. In 2003, while still moderator and vicar general, he was named rector of the cathedral. Finally, in June 2004, after fifteen years of service in the chancery, he withdrew from diocesan administration, allowing him to focus on his pastoral appointment at the cathedral.

Father Daniels played a central role in the re-organization of ministries and offices in the diocese, the implementation of parish clusters and the planning of the parish vitality survey. He represented the diocese in civil lawsuits involving clergy sexual abuse cases, becoming an indispensable support to Bishop Sherlock and subsequently to Bishop Fabbro. "In each of these positions," commented Bishop Fabbro in 2004, "[Father Daniels] has demonstrated his generosity and faithfulness, his exceptional leadership abilities, and his fervent love of the Church." He was also president of the National Federation of Presbyteral Councils.

On 21 September 2004, Father Daniels was appointed auxiliary bishop of London (and titular bishop of Scebatiana). He was ordained to the episcopate in at St. Peter's cathedral, on the Feast of the Dedication of St. John Lateran, 9 November 2004, by Bishop Fabbro. The bishop was assisted by Bishop Grecco and by Bishop Sherlock, who delivered the homily. Bishop Fabbro referred to Bishop Daniels' appointment as fortuitous because it came at a time when the diocese was about to adopt a new governance model.

Bishop Daniels chose as his episcopal motto *Duc in altum*. Taken from Luke 5:4, it is translated in English as "Put out into the deep." The bishop's choice was inspired by John Paul II's Apostolic Letter, *The New Millennium*. Bishop Daniels took up residence in Windsor. In addition to performing confirmations and presiding at special parochial celebrations, he is a member of the college of consultors, the episcopal council, the priests' personnel board and St. Peter's Seminary board, and an ex-officio member of the council of priests and the diocesan finance committee. He sits on the board of directors of Hôtel-Dieu-Grace Hospital in Windsor and St. Joseph's Health Care Society in London. Extra-diocesan appointments include membership on the liturgy commission of the CCCB and the social affairs commission and the insurance management board of the OCCB. He is also a director of the Ontario Catholic Women's League, representing the Ontario bishops.

Part III
Religious Communities

1. Society of Jesus (Jesuits, SJ)

The Jesuits were the first religious community to serve in what became the diocese of London. Although they left the diocese in 1874, their pastoral work among the First Nations and then among the French-Canadian settlers and Irish immigrants in the parishes and missions of the Western District (Essex, Kent and Lambton counties) assured the survival and flourishing of the Catholic faith in the years leading up to the erection of the diocese in 1856. Indeed, had it not been for Jesuit missionaries working from Assumption parish, the hub of their activities, in particular during their last three decades in the diocese, the progress of the faith in the southernmost part of the province would not have been nearly as robust as it turned out to be. The history of the diocese of London would be considerably different.

The work of the Jesuits can be divided into three distinct eras, each one being associated with a specific Jesuit father. The first era dates from 1728, when Father Armand de La Richardie (1686-1758) founded The Mission of Our Lady of the Assumption among the Hurons of Detroit. It was certainly a lofty name for such a small and isolated mission that took nearly twenty years to find a permanent home. Initially located on the north shore or what is now the American side of the Detroit River, Father La Richardie's mission was financed by the government, and it was understood that he and his successors would report only to their Jesuit superiors. He was completely independent of the bishop of Québec and of the Sulpician pastor of Ste. Anne's parish at Fort Detroit. Father La Richardie moved the mission to Bois Blanc Island (Bob-Lo) in 1742 and finally, in 1747, to Pointe de Montréal, which was located on the south shore or the Windsor side of the river, near the foot of present-day Huron Church Road.

Assisted by a fellow Jesuit, Father Pierre P. Potier, who had arrived in 1744, Father La Richardie constructed the first mission church in the diocese, which he opened for divine worship on 8 September 1749. Two years later, he left for Québec, never to return, and he died there on 17 March 1758. His tireless work on behalf of the Hurons figures prominently in our history, as is recounted at the beginning of this book.

Father Pierre Potier (1708-81) dominates the second era, which began when he succeeded to the mission in 1751, having already served under Father La Richardie for seven years, and which ended with his accidental death on 16 July 1781. He was alone at Assumption, except for a five-year period, 1755 to 1759, when Father Jean-Baptiste de Salleneuve was his assistant. Father Potier was the first pastor of Our Lady of the Assumption parish, which was erected by Bishop Jean-Olivier Briand of Québec in 1767 to coincide with the building of a second church. (A third church replaced this one in 1787.) Father Potier also presided over the beginning of the gradual transition of Assumption parish from a mixed congregation of Hurons and French-Canadians — each group occupying its own pews in the church — to a parish that would become a beacon of French language and customs and remain that way well into the second half of the nineteenth century.

Besides attending to the spiritual and material needs of his congregation of Hurons and recently arrived French settlers, Father Potier was a scholar in the wilderness. A voracious reader and a meticulous note keeper, he was a keen student of native languages and local customs. In the course of his scholarship, always working in isolation, he compiled five manuscripts on the Huron language, a Huron-French vocabulary and the only dictionary of the French language as it was spoken in New France just before the British took control of the colony in 1760. Father Potier also kept detailed account books for the mission and parish.

In 1773, Pope Clement XIV suppressed the Society of Jesus. Bishop Briand never promulgated the Papal Brief on the suppression, perhaps at the insistence of Governor Guy Carleton, who admired the work of the Jesuits and did not want to see them dispersed. There is no evidence that Father Potier was ever officially informed of the pope's decision. If anyone had told him, it would have been Father Pierre Gibault, a fellow Jesuit who visited him at Assumption during the winter of 1775-76. Regardless, Father Pierre Potier went to his grave a son of St. Ignatius, the only priest many of his parishioners had ever known. They would not see another Jesuit for more than fifty years.

Pius VII restored the Jesuits in 1814, and Father Pierre Chazelle was the first member of the restored Society of Jesus to return to Québec, in 1839, to preach a clergy retreat in the diocese of Montréal. In 1842, at the invitation of Bishop Ignace Bourget of Montréal, a group of eight French Jesuits arrived in Québec, with Father Chazelle as superior of the Canadian mission. The following year, Bishop Michael Power of Toronto, who had given his parish in Laprairie, Québec to the Jesuits when he became bishop of Toronto, asked for several Jesuits to work in his huge diocese, which was severely short of priests. Father Chazelle forwarded the bishop's petition to Jesuit authorities in France, and in response Father Pierre Point and Father Jean-Pierre Choné were sent to Canada.

Father Pierre Point was born on 7 April 1802 at Rocroy in the Ardennes, France. He was educated in the local Latin school and at the Jesuit school in Acheul, near Amiens, and he was ordained to the priesthood for the diocese of Rheims in 1826. He was a diocesan priest for thirteen years, rising to the rank of honourary canon of Rheims cathedral, prior to his entrance into the Society of Jesus on 1 January 1839. He and Father Choné arrived in Toronto, on 24 July 1843, where they were met by Bishop Power and Father Chazelle. The bishop made Father Point pastor of Assumption parish, and Father Chazelle selected him as superior of the Jesuit mission of Sandwich. Father Point and his confreres at Assumption were placed in charge of the Church in the Western District. For a brief period, starting

on 19 September 1845, Father Point was superior of the Jesuits in Upper Canada, and in 1846, he became dean of the Western District, an important administrative post in the diocese of Toronto that he exercised with enthusiasm and imagination for the next twelve years.

It is Father Point's work that marks the third era of the Jesuit presence in the diocese. To him goes the lion's share of the credit for rekindling the spiritual life of Assumption parish and maintaining it as the centre of French-Canadian culture, despite the parish's isolation from the mother province of Lower Canada, and the continuing dominance of the local Protestant elite in politics, the law and local government. He introduced into the parish a program of catechetical instruction for children and young people, missions for adults, annual home visitations in the months of January and February and an assortment of pious societies, such as the Archconfraternity of the Immaculate Heart of Mary and the Young Ladies Sodality, that regulated and increased the devotional life of the parish.

High Mass on Sundays and Holy Days and Corpus Christi processions were celebrated with the utmost solemnity. The topping of the church steeple with a cross (1844), the blessing of the Way of the Cross (1847), the sacrament of confirmation (1843, 1845 and 1851) and the translation of the remains of Fathers Potier, François-Xavier Dufaux and Jean-Baptiste Marchand and Sister Clotilde Raizenne from the third church to the present church (1850) — all these and other special events in parochial life were conducted in prayerful communal splendour, in the hope of increasing the faith among the people and impressing their Protestant neighbours. The long-awaited completion of the exterior of the present Assumption church, in 1845, was marked with a special High Mass on 27 July, which was one of the grandest liturgical celebrations in the history of the parish and another public opportunity for French-Canadian Catholics to assert their presence and worth in Sandwich society. From the pulpit, on many occasions, Father Point inveighed against mixed marriages, intemperance — a crippling social problem — and the proliferation of secret societies.

Father Point, always anxious about elevating the economic status of his parishioners, was also active in matters of education. He brought the Sisters of the Sacred Heart to the parish in 1852 to conduct an orphanage and a school for day and boarding students; he built Assumption College, which opened its doors to the first of many generations of students on 10 February 1857; and he convinced his parishioners to elect Catholic trustees to the Sandwich board of education, so that Catholics could turn the town's public school into a Catholic common school. In 1847, Father Point was elected a trustee, to the dismay of certain anti-clerical critics.

As superior of the Sandwich mission and later as dean of the Western District, Father Point was busy orchestrating the work of his confreres in the parishes and missions as part of his administrative responsibilities. According to Father Point's *Histoire de Sandwich*, a series of year-end letters to his Jesuit colleagues, the Sandwich Jesuits did yeoman service for the Catholics of Essex, Kent and Lambton counties. Besides Assumption parish in Sandwich, the Jesuits were in control of Maidstone, Belle River, Tecumseh, Chatham and the Indian mission on Walpole Island (which was their only outright failure). They were also active in Windsor, Stoney Point, Tilbury, Port Sarnia, Wallaceburg, Bothwell, and any number of Catholic crossroads and hamlets in between, and in times of emergency they assumed duties at St. Peter-on-the-Thames in Tilbury East Township and St. John the Baptist parish in Amherstburg. Their attention to sick calls is the stuff of legend; their desire to seek out and bring the sacraments to every Catholic family was heroic and bore great fruit for the future of the faith. By the end of 1856, they had built six churches, organized thirteen schools and preached countless missions, which earned them the respect and reverence of the faithful wherever they went.

In addition to Fathers Point and Choné, other Jesuits who worked in the Western District, between 1843 and 1874, include Fathers Dominique Chardon du Ranquet, Jean V. Jaffré and Joseph Grimot; John Holzer, William F. Gockeln and Francis C. Dumortier; Charles Conilleau, Auguste Régnier and Martin Férard; Jean M. Mainguy, Jean-Baptiste Menet and Charles Petitdemange; Alphonse Baudin, François Maréchal and Pierre J. Chazelle; Auguste Kohler, Jean-Baptiste Pédelupé and Nicolas Point, the brother of Pierre Point; and Louis J.M. Maurice and Joseph Durthaller. Assisting these Fathers were ten Jesuit Brothers. The longest serving among

them were Joseph Jennesseaux, Pierre Tupin and Sebastian Futsch.

The Sandwich mission came to an end for the Jesuits, on 20 December 1859, owing to misunderstandings among the Jesuits concerning their future at Assumption, when it became clear that Bishop Pinsoneault intended to move the seat of his See from London to Sandwich, and the bishop's unfortunate tendency to move religious communities in his diocese at will and without consultation. The Jesuits were treated no differently. They refused Pinsoneault's offer of the London parish and withdrew all of their members from the diocese, except for those attached to St. Joseph's in Chatham, where they remained until 1874. Father Alphonse Baudin was the last to leave.

As for Father Point, after a brief priestly sojourn in New York State, he served as superior of the Jesuit house in Québec for eleven years, during which time he was a zealous promoter of devotion to the Sacred Heart of Jesus. He then became spiritual director of the Jesuit-run Collège Ste-Marie in Montréal, where he lived for the rest of his life. When he died at the age of ninety-four, on 19 September 1896, he was the oldest priest in Canada.

Sources: DLA, St. Joseph's Parish (Chatham), "Sacramental Records," 1850-1855, 1855-1867 and 1867-[1878]; *Dictionary of Jesuit Biography: Ministry to English Canada 1842-1987* (Toronto: 1991), various biographies; E.J. Lajeunesse, "La Richardie, Armand de," *DCB* (Toronto: 1974), 3: 355; Francis J. Nelligan, "Father Pierre Point, 1802-1896," *Canadian Messenger of the Sacred Heart*, Part I (June 1955): 455-63, Part II (September 1955): 569-76, and Part III (December 1955): 799-806; Ibid., "Notes Taken from Father Pierre Point's *Histoire de Sandwich*," Archives of the Society of Jesus, Upper Canada (Toronto), Section C-1 Sandwich, Box C-401, Envelope 9; Reuben Gold Thwaites, ed., *The Jesuit Relations and Allied Documents: Travels and Explorations of the Jesuit Missionaries in New France 1610-1791*, 72 vols. (Cleveland: 1896-1901), vol. LXIX: 241-77, vol. LXX: 19-77; Robert Toupin, "Potier, Pierre-Philippe," *DCB* (Toronto: 1979), 4: 460.

2. Religious Of the Sacred Heart (RSCJ)

Mother Madeleine Louise Sophie Barat, who was canonized in 1925, founded the Society of the Sacred Heart in Amiens, France, in 1802, for the education of girls and young women. The Society was Mother Barat's answer to the papal suppression of the Jesuits and the French Revolution that had destroyed Catholic schools. The Society's first Canadian foundation was at Montréal in 1842. The decision to establish a house and orphanage in Detroit in 1851 led to the establishment of a convent in Sandwich the following year.

But the Sisters of the Sacred Heart, sometimes called Les Dames-du-Sacré-Coeur, would never have settled in the diocese of London if not for the wise persistence of Father Pierre Point, SJ, pastor of Assumption parish, and the co-operation of Bishop Armand-Françoise-Marie de Charbonnel, of Toronto. Father Point was anxious to have a parish school and saw the arrival of the Sisters of the Sacred Heart in Detroit as the answer to his prayers. As a French-speaking community with a proven record as teachers, they would be ideal for the needs of Sandwich Catholics. Bishop Charbonnel initially wanted the Toronto-based Sisters of St. Joseph to staff the school, but Father Point convinced him to invite the Sisters of the Sacred Heart to Assumption parish and the Sisters of St. Joseph to St. John the Baptist parish, Amherstburg.

Mother Henrietta de Kersaint, superior, Mother Connolly and Mother Limoges arrived in Sandwich on 20 April 1852 and lived at the family home of Charles Baby until the renovation of the old parish rectory was completed. The Sisters agreed to manage an orphanage, according to the terms outlined by the Beaubien family, and to run an academic boarding school and a day school for poor girls. Since boarders were the economic lifeblood of each of their schools, the Sisters made every effort, aided by Father Point, to convince prosperous Catholics to enroll their daughters as boarding students, at a rate of sixty dollars per year for tuition and board. Day students were charged the bare minimum of fifty cents per month for their instruction, and orphans paid nothing for their care and education.

The initial enrollment was six boarders, forty day students and five orphans. By 1857, the number of boarders had risen to forty-five, a remarkable achievement given that Sandwich was a small and relatively isolated town. To accommodate the growing number of pupils, the Sisters built a classroom and a dormitory in a temporary shed-like structure as they prepared plans for an entirely new convent and school.

The Sisters were very popular in the parish, not only because they taught the girls of the parish but also because they were very involved in parish life: preparing the children for the sacraments and organizing and leading the various sodalities that were so important to the moral and spiritual life of all the parish's children. What a shock it must have been for the people when without a word of warning, the Sisters departed for London on 18 August 1857. Father Point was so disheartened — a great deal of good work, earned at a steep price, vanished from the parish in an instant — that he did nothing to quell the howls of protest from his parishioners, who feared that the Jesuits would be the next to depart from the parish. Their fears were well-founded, since the Jesuits left on 20 December 1859.

The Sisters' move from Sandwich to London had been kept a secret, at the insistence of Bishop Pinsoneault, who was installed as the first bishop of London on 29 June 1856. The new bishop had a mind for machinations. Prior to his arrival in London, he had dismissed the Loretto Sisters from the diocese, and by June they had packed up and left for Guelph. Two weeks after his installation, Pinsoneault invited the Sisters of the Sacred Heart to establish a foundation in London, in addition to the one in Sandwich. He had to find a replacement for the Loretto Sisters, whose removal had caused bitter feelings, and, at the same time, he did not want to offend the people of Assumption parish. However, Mother Mary Aloysia Hardy, the superior vicar of all the Sacred Heart houses in eastern United States and Canada, strongly objected to Pinsoneault's request, on the grounds that it was impossible for the Sisters to staff two houses in the same diocese. Mother Barat agreed with her. Nevertheless, Pinsoneault got her to agree to the transfer of the Sisters to London when he told Mother Barat that he could not renege on a promise to the city's Catholics to find them another community of teaching Sisters. In the end, Pinsoneault may have appeased London's Catholics, but he did so at the cost of offending the Assumption's parishioners, at the very time when he was preparing to have the seat of his diocese transferred from London to Sandwich!

In the meantime, Bishop Pinsoneault facilitated the purchase of the London home and property of William Barker. Called Mount Hope, it was bounded by Grosvenor, Richmond and St. George streets and College Avenue and cost approximately $26,000 to $28,000, a purchase price that quickly turned into an embarrassing debt for Pinsoneault and the Sisters. As a concession to them, he allowed the Sisters to hold title to their property.

Mount Hope was the site of a convent, an orphanage, an academy for fee-paying students, a boarding school and also a free school for poor girls. The first superior of the London house was Mother Regis Hamilton, who remained for a brief transitional period. She was succeeded by two remarkable women, Mother Margaret Gilluly and then Mother Ellen Jennings. Their leadership was crucial to the survival of the Mount Hope community. Over time, and with the assistance of local Catholics, including the London Separate School Board, they began to pay down the debt and to increase their enrolment, which in 1857 was a modest seven boarders and nineteen day students. The Sisters also learned to live without the bishop, who relocated to Sandwich at the end of 1857.

Despite their best intentions and many sacrifices, the Sisters were on the verge of leaving London in 1860. In their estimation, it was taking too long to attract boarding students whose fees were vital to the economic viability of the entire operation. But Mother Barat chose the path of patience, deciding to wait another year before making a decision, by which time the American Civil War had begun. This event convinced her not to abandon Mount Hope in case the Sisters in the United States were obliged to seek refuge in Canada West (Ontario). That never happened, but by 1865-66, the same year that Mother Barat died, the Sisters and their students had outgrown the facilities at Mount Hope.

The Sisters purchased the Lawrence Lawrason property, at the north-east corner of Colborne and Dundas streets, which was more central to city life than Mount Hope. For the purchase price of $18,000, they acquired a large well-built and elegantly designed home, a stable suitable for conversion as a dormitory or school and one other building that could also be converted to school use. The grounds were spacious enough for future expansion. In 1866, Sacred Heart Academy had sixty students, and Sacred Heart elementary school, which was also private but tuition-free, had 200 students. In addition, there was a small orphanage. The Dominicans from St. Peter's church were the school chaplains.

If the academy generated much needed cash for the community's daily operations, the free school produced a wellspring of affection among London's Catholics for the Sisters' many apostolates. Their work included the promotion of devotion to the Sacred Heart of Jesus, the founding of a city-wide sodality, the Congregation of the Children of Mary, charitable assistance to all levels of society and the organization of annual retreats for young people, all the while remaining a cloistered community. In 1886, the Sisters built an addition to Sacred Heart Academy and a new Sacred Heart school on the Queens Avenue side of their property. In 1888, they opened a new chapel built at a cost of $30,000. One of its windows memorialized Bishop Walsh's success in his petition to the Holy See to keep the Religious of the Sacred Heart in London.

Walsh was not the only bishop of London to have a special affection for the Sisters. His two immediate successors, Bishop O'Connor and Bishop McEvay, also held them in high esteem. Sacred Heart convent often hosted diocesan social events, and the graduates of Sacred Heart Academy were loyal and generous to their alma mater. Moreover, a high percentage of the Sister's free school students passed the high school entrance examination, the measure by which Catholic elementary schools were often judged by their Protestant critics.

By the time of Bishop Fallon's arrival in 1910, the academy's nineteenth century finishing school courses were hopelessly outdated, leaving its students without a chance to earn the proper matriculation certificates for entry into the commercial academies, Normal School or the university. Unwilling or unable to satisfy Bishop

Fallon's explicit expectations to adopt Ontario's official high school curriculum, and to send its Sisters to Normal School for proper training, the Sisters decided to abandon their foundation in London, giving up more than sixty years of work.

The Religious of the Sacred Heart left in June 1913, to the regret of many a former student, including the mother of the future Bishop Ralph Hubert Dignan. The Sisters of St. Joseph purchased the property and turned it into their Motherhouse; they also assumed control of Sacred Heart school, which was placed under the administrative control of the London Separate School Board. Meanwhile, the Ursuline Sisters, at the request of Bishop Fallon, opened St. Angela's Academy in 1913. Located at the northwest corner of nearby Queens Avenue and Colborne Street, it opened its doors to girls from kindergarten to the end of high school.

Sources:"Barat, Madeleine Sophie, St.," *New Catholic Encyclopedia*, vol. 2 (New York: 1967), 85-86; Louise Callan, *The Society of the Sacred Heart in North America* (Toronto: 1937), 467-75; Ralph Hubert Dignan, "History of the Diocese of London" (Unpublished Manuscript, ca. 1919-1932), 157-63; John K.A. Farrell (O'Farrell), *The History of the Roman Catholic Church in London, Ontario 1826-1931* (M.A. thesis, University of Western Ontario, 1949), 104-9; John R. McMahon, *The Episcopate of Pierre-Adolphe Pinsoneault: First Bishop of London, Upper Canada, 1856-1866* (M.A. thesis, University of Western Ontario, 1982), 207-15.

3. Congregation of the Sisters of St. Joseph (CSJ)

The Sisters of St. Joseph first appeared in what became the diocese of London, in August 1853. Bishop Armand-Francois-Marie de Charbonnel of Toronto sent the Sisters to St. John the Baptist parish in Amherstburg, where they taught elementary school until their departure on December 1857. Bishop Pinsoneault had replaced them with members of the French-speaking Grey Nuns, also known as the Sisters of Charity.

On 11 December 1868, five Sisters of St. Joseph, accompanied by Mother Annette McDonald, the mother superior, arrived from Toronto to establish a Congregation in the diocese of London at the request of Bishop Walsh. They were Mother Teresa Brennan and Sisters Ignatia Campbell, Ursula Maguire, Frances O'Malley and Appolonia Nolan. Welcoming them at the London train station were Bishop Walsh, Monsignor J.M. Bruyère, the vicar general and rector of St. Peter's cathedral, Father Patrick Egan, and a delegation from the cathedral parish, who took the Sisters by sleigh to their convent on Kent Street. "Their mission was to teach children in the separate schools, to visit the sick and the poor and shortly to open an orphan asylum" (*Chronicles*, 6). In January 1869, three Sisters began to teach at St. Peter's school.

On 2 October 1869, the Sisters opened Mount Hope Orphanage in the former home of William Barker at what is now the northwest corner of Richmond Street and College Avenue. It also served as the Sisters' motherhouse for thirty-one years. In December 1870, the Congregation formally separated from Toronto "as the Bishop desired autonomy for the Sisters of his diocese" (*Chronicles*, 8). The bishop then installed Sister Ignatia Campbell, an old friend from his days as a priest of the diocese of Toronto, as superior general, a position that she held for thirty-two years. By 1888, Mount Hope was sheltering over two hundred people, including Sisters, orphans and the elderly.

The chapel at Mount Hope was the site chosen by Bishop Walsh for ordinations and other diocesan ceremonies. From 1872 to 1885, the year the current St. Peter's cathedral was opened, the bishop ordained two diocesan priests and six Basilian priests in the chapel. When the cathedral was dedicated on 28 June 1885, Bishop Walsh asked Mother Ignatia and her Sisters to host the celebratory banquet at Mount Hope for the archbishops, bishops, priests, civic dignitaries and other guests who attended the ceremony. To this day, the Sisters of

St. Joseph have hosted many formal occasions at the request of the bishops of London. Indeed, 2005 marked the twenty-ninth annual reflection day and dinner held at Mount St. Joseph for the clergy of the diocese prior to the Mass of Chrism during Holy Week.

The community of Sisters grew, and missions beyond London were established. The first was in Goderich in 1873. Next were St. Thomas and Ingersoll in 1879 and Belle River in 1889. Also, in 1884, the Basilian Fathers at Assumption College in Sandwich (Windsor) invited the Sisters "to assume care of the domestic arrangements of the house, which duties they continued to supervise for the next 20 years" (*Chronicles*, 56).

In 1888, Dr. W.T. O'Reilly asked the Sisters of St. Joseph to open a hospital in London. He had been impressed by their efficiency and compassion during his inspection of the Mount Hope Orphanage and Asylum. The Sisters responded to O'Reilly's invitation by opening a ten-bed hospital in the former residence of Judge William P.R. Street, which was opposite Mount Hope. The pioneer Sisters in this endeavor were Mother Aloysia Nigh and Sisters Herman Murphy and Martha Toohey. By 1892, the hospital was enlarged to sixty-two beds. During the ensuing years, the hospital grew until it had 700 beds. Mother Aloysia Nigh was also instrumental in founding St. Joseph's Hospital in Chatham in 1890. As well, her long experience in building large institutions was of invaluable assistance to those drawing up plans for the new St. Peter's Seminary in 1924-25. In 1946, six Sisters — Paschal Kenny, St. Stephen Dentinger, Veronica Brophy, Anna Deneau, Cajetan Van Dorrestyne and Henrietta Tyers — established St. Joseph's Hospital in Sarnia.

The Sisters of St. Joseph managed hospitals in London and Chatham for over a hundred years and in Sarnia for over fifty years. In 1993, the community decided to find an alternative means of Catholic sponsorship for their hospitals because there were not enough Sisters to carry on the work. The result was the St. Joseph's Health Care Society. It was incorporated by changing the original acts of incorporation and by-laws, and canonically established when Bishop Sherlock, with the consent of his Senate, established the Society as a public legal body. The primary aim of the Society was to maintain a Catholic presence and Gospel-based values and philosophy in each of the three St.

Joseph's hospitals. Sisters retained their seats on the hospital and Society boards. In the 1990s, however, restructuring mandated by the Ontario government led to the amalgamation of the hospital in Sarnia with the Sarnia General Hospital. In April 2003, the Society terminated its alliance with the Sarnia General.

The hospitals in London and Chatham had the distinction of also being training schools for nurses. On 4 May 1902, Sister Justina Podleski was appointed superintendent of St. Joseph's training school in London, and in 1903, Sister Monica Coyle was given charge of nurses' training at St. Joseph's Hospital in Chatham (*Chronicles*, 71). These excellent schools continued until 1970, when the Ontario government moved nurses' training to community colleges.

Between 1892 and 1905, the Sisters expanded their teaching apostolate. They accepted invitations to teach at Holy Angels, St. Nicholas, St. John and St. Martin schools in London; at Notre Dame and St. Anne schools in Walkerville; and at St. Louis school in Windsor.

At Mount Hope, the number of orphans and elderly increased, and it was deemed advisable to build separate living quarters for the old and the young. On 10 April 1899, Philip Pocock, one of London's most generous and best-known Catholics, purchased the Anglican Hellmuth Ladies' College for $13,000, on behalf of the Sisters. The transaction included thirty-one acres of land and the college, chapel and organ. The Sisters named it Mount St. Joseph and established an orphanage, a motherhouse and a novitiate.

In 1902, Mother Angela McKeogh succeeded Mother Ignatia Campbell as superior general. During the nine years of Mother McKeogh's leadership, "the community increased in numbers, the hospitals were enlarged and works of charity trebled in numbers and extent" (*Chronicles*, 131). At the time Mother Celestine McCarthy was elected superior general, in 1911, there were 118 Sisters in the community. By virtue of her strong and steady leadership, the Sisters continued to expand their hospitals and to establish new convents, as they assumed additional teaching responsibilities throughout the diocese. They were called to teach in separate schools in Kingsbridge, Seaforth, St. Mary's and Woodstock, at St. Michael's school in London and at St. Jules, St. Rose and Holy Rosary schools in Windsor.

The increase in vocations and the large number of orphans living at Mount St. Joseph prompted the Sisters to relocate their motherhouse to larger premises. The withdrawal of the Sisters of the Sacred Heart from the diocese of London, in 1913, presented the Sisters of St. Joseph with a tidy solution to their problem of overcrowding. In April 1914, they purchased from the Sisters of the Sacred Heart their property at the corner of Colborne and Dundas streets. The Sisters at the new motherhouse, known as Sacred Heart Convent, assumed the administration of Sacred Heart school and promptly added two commercial classes to the curriculum.

There followed many years of numerous vocations and fruitful activity for the Sisters of St. Joseph in the diocese of London. They founded missions in Kinkora and Maidstone and added new wings to their hospitals in London, Chatham and Sarnia.

Between 1939 and 1963, the Sisters of St. Joseph and the school children of London, under the direction of Monsignor West T. Flannery, participated in the "School of Christ" Sunday program, first on radio and later on television. It was broadcast locally and then internationally. Sisters Maureen Dalton, Marie Brébeuf Beninger and Mary Margaret Childs, accompanied by Sister Callistus Arnsby, directed the junior and senior choirs.

Over time, Sacred Heart Convent proved too small for the Sisters. In 1950, under the leadership of Mother Margaret Coughlin, the community began to build a new motherhouse on the Mount St. Joseph property. The orphans at Mount St. Joseph, being few in number, were moved to 534 Queens Avenue, which had been used to house the overflow of Sisters from Sacred Heart Convent. The Roman Catholic Separate School Board, meanwhile, purchased the convent. It housed its offices in one part of the complex and provided the remaining space for Catholic Central High School. The current Catholic Central is located on the same parcel of land.

The Sisters offered music lessons in their smaller missions as early as 1873, and they set up a music school at the Mount St. Joseph Motherhouse in 1914. Under the principalship of Sister Callistus Arnsby, the school grew in acclaim. The school's enrolment reached its peak of 400 students in 1979, when the Sisters decided to close it. From 1979 to 1993, the Sisters taught at the Western Ontario Conservatory of Music. The recital hall at Mount St.

Joseph continued to be used by many of London's music teachers.

The Sisters of St. Joseph have participated in diocesan life in many ways. In 1968, there were 468 Sisters in the diocese, the highest number in any given year in the history of the London community. From 1912 to 1980, they were responsible for housekeeping at the seminary. As well, along with seminary staff, other Sisters took on the responsibilities of teaching, counseling, spiritual direction, field education, the formation of lay students and the direction of retreats. Since the Second Vatican Council, Sisters have served on diocesan committees and commissions, on the staff of deanery renewal centres, as diocesan director of liturgy and as prison chaplain and in ministry to the bereaved at one of our Catholic cemeteries. After a career in education, Sister Edith Hogan became the first woman to work in a Marriage Tribunal as Defender of the Bond and Auditor, first in the archdiocese of Vancouver in 1972 and then in the diocese of London from 1976 to 1986. Sister Alice Marie McDonald, who held supervisory positions for many years in education, was named Tribunal Director and Auditor in the diocese of London in 1983. She served in that position until 1996.

In 1966, the Sisters of St. Joseph undertook a major renewal program. They conducted an intensive study of the Gospels and of the spirit and charism of their founder, Father Jean-Pierre Médaille, SJ. Their original charism was to respond to the needs of the people around them. As a result, Sisters ministered to the imprisoned, the poor and the marginalized, and in any social setting where needs were not being met. Sisters embraced the work of pastoral care in hospitals and parishes and participated in the Rite of Christian Initiation of Adults (RCIA program). At the same time, the laity began to participate more actively in the public life of the Church. For example, some lay people became catechists. Others gradually assumed some of the education and health care responsibilities that traditionally had been performed by the Sisters.

In 1973, under the expert hand of Sister St. Patrick Joyce, St. Joseph's Hospital opened a detoxification unit on Dufferin Avenue, which later moved to a section of the building at 534 Queens Avenue. In 1983, St. Joseph's Hospitality Centre was opened in East London to feed the poor. Joseph's House on Dundas Street was organized in 1987 to provide temporary housing to refugees, while Sister Maria van Leeuwen and others assisted them in finding a home in Canada. The Sisters also welcomed the poor and homeless at their houses on Queens Avenue and Boullee Street.

In 1969, answering the longing for spiritual deepening in an increasingly secular society, the Sisters opened Medaille House, a retreat centre for prayer and renewal, on land adjoining the Motherhouse property. Over the years, many priests, seminarians, members of religious communities and lay people have availed themselves of opportunities for retreats, reflection days and spiritual programs at this site. In 2005, Medaille Retreat House was relocated to Fanshawe Park Road.

Following the closing of Mount St. Joseph Academy in 1986, the Sisters were asked to provide accommodation as well as a place of rest and healing for families of patients, especially those who had waited for and received transplants, at University Hospital. This hospitality endeavor, known as the "Guest Wing," soon became a major work of the community. It operated for twenty-five years under the supervision of Sister Mary Lois White and her successor, Sister Stephanie Rettinger, and was closed in September 2005.

In 1988, an Associate Program was inaugurated with Sister Doreen Kraemer as director. In their lay lifestyles, Associates live the charism of the Congregation of St. Joseph. They are committed to "working to achieve unity both of neighbor with neighbor and neighbor with God," through loving, healing and reconciling services." The number of committed Associates has grown to eighty members.

At the dawn of the new millennium, the Sisters of St. Joseph entered into a strategic planning process regarding their future needs, expectations and capabilities. With few women entering religious life, and with diminishing numbers in the community, Mount St. Joseph was too large. The Sisters decided to sell their property. On 6 June 2005, the Sisters sold Mount St. Joseph to Ivest Properties Limited and London Property Corporation, which plan to develop the building as a retirement residence.

On 6 June 2007, the Sisters moved into the new Congregational Centre & Local Community on the six acres (2.4 ha) adjoining the motherhouse property.

Submitted by Sister Mary Zimmer, CSJ, and Sister Jean Moylan, CSJ. **Sources:** *The Chronicles of the Sisters of St. Joseph of London Ontario Canada 1868-1932*, ed. by Genevieve Hennessy, CSJ (London: 1932?); *Addendum 1954 Opening of Mount St. Joseph Motherhouse and Academy*, unpublished manuscript (n.d.). See also: Julia Moore, "The Sisters of St. Joseph. Beginnings in London Diocese 1868-1878," CCHA, *Study Sessions* 45 (1978): 37-55. Additional information provided by Lori Petrie.

4. Ursuline Religious of the Chatham Union (OSU)

Originating in Brescia, Italy, in 1535, the Ursuline Sisters of the Chatham Union have a rich tradition of women of courage, zeal and vision. St. Angela Merici, the foundress, was a woman of her time, a time much like the present. She invited women to meet regularly to pray, reflect on their lives and support one another while they continued to live in their homes. A woman of deep prayer, Angela was dedicated to raising the dignity of women, children and the marginalized of her society. Over the following centuries, her original ideal of religious life revealed itself in numerous ways as it spread and took root across Europe and then in North America. The Ursulines were in Quebec as early as 1639 and in New Orleans by 1727.

Another woman whose passion for the Gospel impelled her in a new direction was Yvonne Le Bihan — Mother Xavier — who established the Chatham Ursulines. She entered the Ursuline community in Le Faouët, Brittany, France, sustaining it with her large dowry. Her desire to spread the Good News took her across the Atlantic alone to Sault Ste. Marie, Michigan, then in the diocese of Detroit, which she reached on 23 May 1853. Bishop Peter Paul Lefevere asked her to open a school for girls of local families in a town experiencing a boom owing to the building of an American canal to bypass the rapids of St. Mary's River. Mother Xavier was superior, mistress of novices, class teacher and music teacher, and she became a good friend of Bishop Frederick Baraga, who became the first bishop of Sault Ste. Marie, Michigan in 1854.

Seven years later, when the canal was completed and Sault Ste. Marie began to tumble into economic decline, Mother Xavier accepted the invitation of Father Jean Jaffré, SJ, the parish priest of St. Joseph's parish in Chatham, to open a school there. She and Mother Angela Doyle were in Chatham by 9 May 1860. Mother Joseph Henry and Mother Augustine Bedard joined them in August 1860.

At the beginning, the four Sisters lived as a group in different locations and taught girls the standard academic subjects and music. On 6 February 1861, Ann McGregor, a young woman from Tilbury East Township, entered the Ursuline community as its first postulant and took the religious name of Sister Mary Theresa. On 21 May 1863, she was the first nun of any religious community to be professed in the diocese of London. Other early candidates from the diocese for religious life in the Ursulines were Jane Frances O'Grady, Mary Ann McDonald, Anne Fournier and Josephine Bouillé.

In the autumn of 1866, the Ursulines purchased twelve acres of the sixty-five-acre estate of a Dr. Robert M. Pegley, fronting on Grand Avenue in Chatham. This beautiful property, which included the Pegley family home and a barn, cost $6,500. This was the beginning of "The Pines." By 1870, the Sisters had built what became the central part of the Ursuline Academy of Chatham, for $18,000. In 1885 and 1899, they added new wings that included classrooms, an auditorium, a chapel, a community room and more accommodation for the boarding students. The magnificent west wing was constructed in the early part of the twentieth century.

Between 1860 and 1900, the Ursulines of the Chatham Foundation evolved from a strictly cloistered group dedicated to the education of young girls in their boarding school to a semi-cloistered community with foundations outside Chatham. In 1898, for example, Bishop O'Connor

chose the Ursulines to teach at St. Francis separate school in Tilbury, then in the process of being built. Their second mission was at St. Anne's school in Tecumseh, where they began teaching on 3 January 1901. By the end of the school year, the enrolment increased from 90 to 200 pupils, a remarkable achievement for this time as it was difficult, especially in the rural areas of the province, to convince Catholic parents to send their children to separate schools. The Ursulines' third mission was at Wallaceburg, in September 1906, and their fourth was in Windsor, beginning at St. Francis school in 1908. Over the years, other missions were established in Essex, Woodslee, Stoney Point, and McGregor; in Ridgetown and Blenheim; and in London, Stratford, Watford, Woodstock, Parkhill, Dublin, St. Joseph (French Settlement) and Mount Carmel.

In 1913, the Ursulines opened St. Angela's College in London, which offered a full high school course and a music department. And in 1919, Mrs. Josephine Gaukler, the mother of Mother Clare Gaukler, donated her Windsor home, "Glengarda," and eighty-five acres (34.4 ha) of land to the community. The Sisters initially used the Gaukler mansion as a residence for the teaching Sisters in Windsor and as a music school. In 1935, the Sisters opened a day and boarding school for mentally challenged children. Mrs. Gaukler and her son, Francis O. Gaukler, were instrumental in financing the construction of Brescia Hall, the Catholic women's college affiliated with the University of Western Ontario. It was completed in 1925 (see below Brescia University College).

Following the Second Vatican Council, the Ursulines gathered, in the words of Mother St. David McConnell, the superior general, "to study together and decided how certain prescriptions of the Constitutions and our way of life can and should be adapted to the changing circumstances of the times and to the teaching and norms of Vatican II." For many years, post-conciliar life in religious communities was exciting, unnerving, demanding and exhilarating. During this time of renewal, the Ursulines returned to their founder's original inspiration, heeding the words of St. Angela Merici to adapt to changing needs.

As familiar structures and patterns of living and working disappeared and new patterns slowly evolved, religious communities faced the prospect of a steep decline in the number of entrants, aging members and the phenomenon of members leaving religious life. The Ursulines were no different. At the same time that the provincial government promised full funding of separate schools, beginning in 1984 — teaching in separate schools had been a long time ministry for the Ursulines — the community began to look beyond the traditional to emerging needs among vulnerable members of society. The Ursulines became involved with affordable housing, shelter for adolescents at risk, support for women and children caught in the web of domestic violence, refugees and immigrants, people in prison, nursing home residents, the house-bound and those living on the streets. They also gave financial, moral and personnel support to the Canadian Catholic Organization for Development and Peace and to numerous inter-church coalitions that focused their collective energies on aboriginal issues in Canada, human rights in Latin America, corporate responsibility, fair trade, economic justice and militarization.

With a new awareness and a strong emphasis on social justice, the Ursulines made significant efforts to educate themselves and others and to act justly within and beyond their religious community. As a result, Ursulines took positions in justice centres, developed workshops and collaborated with others in a number of social action initiatives, from attending shareholder meetings to participating in boycotts and peaceful demonstrations concerning apartheid, just wages for workers and the nuclear arms race.

This type of activism was not entirely new to the Ursulines. In 1962, in response to a request from the diocese of London, four Ursulines (out of the fifty-seven who applied) were chosen to work in the diocese's mission in Peru. They established Colegio Santa Angela in Chiclayo, where the Sisters taught for ten years. In 1972, after much prayer, reflection and discussion, they began the process of turning over the school to the Peruvian Parents' Association. In 1975, the Sisters commenced their pastoral ministry in Urrunaga, the poorest barrio in Chiclayo. Today, only one Ursuline remains in Urrunaga, but ties with Peruvian friends are deeper and stronger than ever. Some teenagers taught by the Ursulines have matured into strong community leaders. They are working to improve health care and education and to increase social and political awareness. Regular exchanges are made between Canadians and Peruvians as all grow in appreciation of interdependence.

The Ursulines and other religious communities saved the separate school system from financial extinction, and they made many lasting contributions to Catholic elementary and secondary education during decades of dedicated service in the classroom. The last Ursuline separate schoolteacher in the diocese of London retired in 2004. Ursuline-established institutions, such as Glengarda Child and Family Services in Windsor and Ursuline College in Chatham, are now in the hands of their respective provincial ministries. Brescia University College in London is under the direction of a Council of Trustees and Principal Theresa Topic, the first non-Ursuline to head the college. The members of these three institutions carry on the work begun by the Ursulines, imbued by a passion for learning and a profound respect for the dignity of persons, which motivated the founders of the community.

As of July 2005, 117 Sisters belong to the Ursuline Religious of the Chatham Union. Today, members of the community are involved in retreat work, parish work and social work, spiritual direction, spiritual companioning, education, advocacy and justice endeavours, palliative care, chaplaincy, the visitation of prisons, hospitals and residences for seniors, ecological projects and the ministry of prayer and presence. Ursulines follow in the footsteps of St. Angela Merici, "Foundress of the first non-cloistered order available for every kind of service." This is the inscription at the base of the statue of "Angela the Pilgrim" in Brescia, Italy.

Superiors and Superiors General

1st Superior: Mother Xavier Le Bihan (1860-79)
2nd Superior: Mother Mary De Sales McDonnell (1879-85)
3rd Superior: Mother Baptist O'Grady (1885-91)
4th Superior: Mother Berchmans O'Brien (1891-97)
5th Superior: Mother Baptist O'Grady (1897-1903)
6th Superior: Mother Nativity Chevalier (1903-09)
7th Superior: Mother Clare Gaukler (1909-15)

1st Sup. General: Mother Clare Gaukler (1915-33)
2nd Sup. General: Mother Genevieve Williams (1933-45)

3rd Sup. General: Mother Kathleen Taylor (1945-57)
4th Sup. General: Mother St. David McConnell (1957-69)
5th Sup. General: Mother Dominica Dietrich (1969-77)
6th Gen. Superior: Sister Frances Ryan (1977-85)
7th Gen. Superior Sister Mary Teresa Antaya (1985-93)
8th Gen. Superior: Sister Joan Stafford (1993-2001)
9th Gen. Superior Sister Eleanor Gleeson (2001-)

Submitted by Sister Sheila McKinley, OSU.
Sources: Margaret Pray, OSU, *Pilgrims in Service: The Chatham Ursulines* (Chatham: 2001). 2 vols. See also: M. St. Paul, OSU, *From Desenzano to 'The Pines': A Sketch of the History of the Ursulines of Ontario* (Toronto: 1941).

Brescia University College

Brescia University College was founded in 1919 by the Ursuline Religious of the diocese of London as a Catholic women's college affiliated with the University of Western Ontario. Originally called Ursuline College, the institution was established to provide Catholic women in Southwestern Ontario with a university education in a setting that would support their faith and their personal development. Collaboration between Bishop Fallon of London, Mother Clare Gaukler, superior general of the Ursuline Religious, and the board of governors of the University of Western Ontario produced an affiliation agreement modeled on similar arrangements between secular and denominational post-secondary institutions in Ontario.

The affiliation agreement with Western allowed Brescia students to take some of their courses at Western and to be awarded Western degrees. At the beginning, much of the instruction at Brescia was given by Ursuline Sisters. In preparation for the opening of the college, they attended graduate schools in Canada and the United States to upgrade their credentials to the levels required for university teaching. They taught English, French, history, public speaking and mathematics. Priests from St. Peter's Seminary lectured in philosophy and apologetics. To ensure that a Catholic perspective was presented in courses considered particularly important, the curriculum at Brescia included

special sections in philosophy, religious knowledge, history and (later) psychology and economics. Home Economics was added in 1936 and attained an important academic focus at the college.

For the first five years, Brescia students lived and studied in a large house at 556 Wellington Street in downtown London. The entering class in 1919 had only seven students, but growth was on the horizon, and Ursuline leadership prepared for expansion. The Sisters purchased a large parcel of land in 1919, immediately to the west of the site to which Western planned to move its campus, and over the years they acquired additional property in anticipation of future needs. In 1923, John R. Boyde, of the Windsor architectural firm of Pennington and Boyde, was commissioned to design an imposing Gothic-style building on the hilltop to house resident students, classes and Ursuline Sisters. The London Catholic community provided strong support for the building that opened in 1925 with much fanfare highlighted by a dedicatory Mass celebrated by Bishop Fallon on the front steps of the new structure.

During the first years, most students lived in residence, were Catholic, and came from Ontario. From an early date, however, the Ursulines saw the value of a diverse student body and took active steps to recruit young women from other provinces of Canada and the world. They sought out and welcomed students from Latin America and the Caribbean and provided bursaries to those with limited means, so that they could pursue their education.

During the 1940s and 1950s, redoubtable figures such as Mother St. James Hickey, dean from 1939 to 1945 and from 1947 to 1956, and Sister St. Michael Guinan, later a renowned expert in gerontology, kept Brescia in the public eye. Brescia's operations were closely tied to the Ursuline community, which maintained a strong presence at the college and provided many faculty and staff and still do to some extent.

By 1960, there were 160 students at Brescia, and the number of fields of instruction had grown to include a full range of liberal arts programs as well as the increasingly professional home economics department. The number of lay faculty teaching at Brescia also grew, with the majority of faculty being women. The Mother St. James Building, which opened in 1967, to the east of the original building, provided much-needed space for classrooms, an auditorium, a library and offices for the college. The name of the college was officially changed to Brescia College in 1963.

At the onset of the 1990s, the Ursulines instituted a planning process for the college's future, in anticipation of a reduced role for their community in Brescia's day-to-day management. The first lay principal, Dr. Teresa Topic, was appointed in 1999, and shortly afterward a major change in organizational structure occurred when a council of trustees was created and the college was incorporated as a not-for-profit corporation. The name of the college was changed once again, in 2002, to Brescia University College. This new title clarified Brescia's status as a university-level institution whose graduates are awarded bachelor's degrees.

The college celebrated its eighty-fifth anniversary in 2004-05 with 1,043 registered students. Still small in comparison to similar institutions, Brescia takes pride in the feeling of community that its students enjoy, and as part of its Catholic and Ursuline legacies, it encourages students to involve themselves in the wider community and to consider their education as preparation "to respond with wisdom, justice and compassion to a changing world" (Brescia mission statement 2000). An addition to the library was opened in the autumn of 2006.

Submitted by Dr. Theresa Topic.
Sources: John R.W. Gwynne-Timothy, *Western's First Century* (London: 1978), 641-49; Patricia G. Skidmore, *Brescia College 1919-1979* (London: 1980).

5. Order of Preachers (Dominicans, OP)

The Dominicans of St. Rose Monastery in Springfield, Kentucky came to St. Peter's parish in London in the autumn of 1861 when Bishop Pinsoneault made Sandwich the seat of the diocese and Assumption church his cathedral; and they departed from their adopted city, seven years later, when Bishop Walsh returned the seat to London and elevated St. Peter's once again to the status of diocesan cathedral. Although the Dominicans were stellar parish priests, and Walsh could hardly afford to lose such capable clergy, the good friars had no choice but to give up their thriving parish to the bishop. The congregation that the Dominicans reluctantly relinquished owed them nearly everything for having revivified and strengthened Catholic practice and piety not only in the city, where they were stationed, but also throughout a great deal of Middlesex County and occasionally beyond it when called to officiate at church blessings and similar events. The Dominicans were victims of circumstance. Their time in London forms a curious, if all too brief, chapter in the history of the diocese.

Father Jean-Marie Bruyère brought the Dominicans to London. When Bishop Pinsoneault officially took up residence in Sandwich in mid 1859, he appointed Father Edward Bayard as parish priest of St. Peter's. Assisting him for a short while was his younger brother, Father Joseph Bayard, who became one of the great nineteenth-century priests of the diocese. The elder Bayard's appointment lasted two years, at which time he quit London for Baldwinsville, New York. Since the bishop preferred to keep his best priests close at hand at his episcopal palace next to his cathedral, he was obliged to look

outside his diocese to recruit a replacement for Father Bayard.

Fortunately for Pinsoneault, Father Bruyère, who was at Assumption cathedral, was able to convince his friends, the Dominicans in Kentucky, to assume the stewardship of St. Peter's parish. Immigrating to Kentucky as a missionary in 1840, Father Bruyère had taught dogmatic theology at the College of Bardstown and then was rector of the cathedral at Louisville from 1848 to 1854. During his time in Kentucky, he had come to know and admire the Dominicans, many of whom were natives of Ireland and England.

On 12 September 1861, Father John Augustine Kelly, provincial of the Dominican province of St. Joseph, and Bishop Pinsoneault, signed a contract, whereby in return for assuming the parish debt of $4,280, the Dominicans were granted a lease of ninety-nine years on the parish property of three acres of land, which included a church, a rectory and a school house. There were approximately 2,000 parishioners.

Father Mathew A. O'Brien was the first prior of the London community and also parish priest. He was legendary for his sermons and for traveling the back roads of Middlesex County, hearing the settlers' confessions and exhorting the faithful wherever he found them to partake of the sacraments more regularly. Assisting Father O'Brien were the American-born Father John A. Rochford and Father Hubert P. Ralph. (This Father Ralph was a good friend of the Dignan family, who for three generations honoured him by calling their eldest sons Ralph Hubert, the best known being Bishop Ralph Hubert Dignan.) Together these three priests — O'Brien, Rochford and Ralph — formed the first Dominican foundation in Canada.

The names of other Dominicans who served at St. Peter's include Fathers Stephen Byrne, who was a close friend of Henry Edward Dormer, James B. Hallisey, Denis A. O'Brien, James B. McGovern, Mathew F. McGrath and Joseph A. Kelly. This was the same Father Kelly who had signed the 1861 lease with the diocese. He was also the last prior of the London community.

The fact that St. Peter's under the Dominicans had no fewer than three priests, at any given time, and perhaps occasionally even more, made the parish a happy and flourishing anomaly among regular Catholic parishes in Ontario and helps to explain the parish's evident revival during its Dominican days. But more important than the healthy numbers of priests assigned to the parish was the spiritual genius of the Dominicans, which revealed itself in their preaching, retreats and public lectures and in their willingness to go to the people. Besides holding those who had kept their faith, they rekindled the faith in countless Catholics, bringing them back into the fold of parish life and then keeping them loyal to the local church.

The fruits of Dominican labours at St. Peter's can be measured in at least two obvious ways.

First, Father O'Brien was able to convince the congregation to make substantial investments in St. Peter's church, the city's only Catholic house of worship, so that it might shine as a beacon of the faith in the midst of London's profusion of church spires. Gently prodded by Father O'Brien, the parishioners financed the construction of side galleries along the length of the nave, which were necessary to accommodate the overflow at Sunday Masses; an impressive steeple, which made the church more visible to the entire city and surrounding countryside; and a bell for the steeple, which was christened "Patrick Dominic," in memory of St. Patrick, the patron saint of Ireland, and St. Dominic, the founder of the Order of Preachers, commonly known as Dominicans (and often referred to in the nineteenth century as the Order of St. Dominic, OSD). In effect, the Dominicans completed the church that Dean Kirwan had opened in 1852.

Second, the Dominicans attracted an impressive number of London vocations to their order. They were M.J. Egan; J.B. McLaughlin; P.A. Dinahan; J.D. Hoban; J.A. Durkin and his brother, A.A. Durkin; their first cousins, J.D. Pendergast and S.A. Pendergast; and J.J. Durkin, who was a first cousin to the Durkin brothers and Prendergast brothers. Father J.J. Durkin, who was born a year after the Dominicans had left London, attended St. Mary and St. Peter schools in London, London Collegiate and St. Jerome's College before he was professed on 15 January 1896. His Dominican cousins, no doubt, had a hand in fostering his vocation. Ordained on 7 March 1899, Father Durkin made many trips to his London home before he died on 1 July 1950. He was the last living link to the Dominican presence in the diocese that had ended almost eighty-two years prior to his death!

That presence officially came to a quiet and dignified close on 19 January 1868, when Bishop Walsh took possession of St. Peter's. It was a foregone conclusion. In a letter dated 20 October 1867, more than two weeks prior to his consecration, Walsh informed Father William D. O'Carroll, the Dominican provincial, of his intentions. He made it abundantly clear to Father O'Carroll that since Sandwich was at the extreme end of his large diocese, it was a wholly unsuitable place from which to conduct the affairs of the diocese. It appears that both the Dominicans and the bishop realized from the outset that the ninety-nine-year lease signed in 1861 was utterly worthless as a legal impediment to the bishop's claims to the parish.

To mollify the Dominicans and their many supporters and admirers, Bishop Walsh offered them the choice of St. Joseph's in Chatham or Holy Angels in St. Thomas, either one of which would have been worthy of their many pastoral gifts. Father O'Carroll thought it best, however, to concentrate his men in the Dominican province of St. Joseph (Eastern United States).

Henry Edward Dormer

The Dominicans may have packed up and said good-bye to London in 1868, but affection for their most famous parishioner, Henry Edward Dormer, who died in the odour of sanctity on 2 October 1866, continued well beyond the pale of the parish's collective memory of the man. Dormer was their lasting legacy. Pious gratitude for his life of prayer and charity was genuine enough to inspire different generations of London's Catholics to keep alive the cause for his canonization, beginning with Bishop Fallon in 1922 and 1930, continuing with Bishop Kidd in 1950 and on to Bishop Carter, during the centenary of Dormer's death in 1966.

Henry Edward Dormer was born on 29 November 1844 at Grove Park, the Dormer country home, near Warwick, England. He was the youngest child of Joseph Thaddeus Dormer, the 11th Baron Dormer, and Elizabeth Anne Tichborne. Against incredible odds, the Dormers had successfully maintained their Catholic faith during and after the English Reformation, becoming a well-known and much-respected recusant family. Henry was educated at St. Mary's College, Oscott, and also at home during a four-year period of poor health before he was gazetted an ensign in the 60th Regiment, the King's Royal Rifles, in November 1863. Two years later, his regiment, recently folded into the Royal Green Jackets, left Dublin, Ireland for London, Canada West, as part of the British government's response to the growing Fenian threat from the United States.

Dormer arrived by train in the city on 24 February 1866, where he was met by the Dominican Father Stephen Byrne. It was a fortuitous encounter. Dormer had known and admired the Dominicans for most of his life and for some time had contemplated joining the order. One of Dormer's sisters was a member of the Dominican Priory of Stone in Staffordshire, England. Seven months after Dormer's arrival, Father Byrne would give him the last rites and preach a stirring funeral sermon. Of Dormer's spiritual and charitable life that had left such a profound impression on members of his family, in the letters that he wrote to them, and on so many of his contemporaries in London, no better or more profound description of that life has been given than that by the historian John K.A. O'Farrell, in his *Dictionary of Canadian Biography* article on Dormer:

Dormer's spirituality was at once mystical and active. When off duty, and often through the night, he would worship to the point of ecstasy in either St. Peter's church or the chapel of the Sacred Heart Convent. He also attended constantly to the poor, the sick, and the inebriated. He bestowed money, his own clothes, food, and other necessities upon those in want, and gave generously of his time and effort to the poor and lonely sick. He gave religious instruction to children at St. Peter's Church and to soldiers and brother officers if they requested it. At the end of September 1866, while nursing a woman ill from typhoid fever, he caught the disease and died from it on 2 October.

No sooner had Henry Edward Dormer breathed his last than the cry went up among London's Catholics that "The saint is dead!" He was given a full military funeral, which was described in detail by the local press, and his remains were buried in St. Peter's Cemetery, London. The only known artifact from the first St. Peter's cathedral is a plaque honouring Dormer, which can be found in the west transept in the present cathedral.

Sources: The Dominicans in London: J.R. Coffey, *Pictorial History of the Dominican Province of St. Joseph U.S.A.* (New York: 1946); John F. Coffey, *The City and Diocese of London, Ontario, Canada: An Historical Sketch* (London: 1885), 14; Reginald M. Coffey, *The American Dominicans: A History of Saint Joseph's Province* (New York: 1970), 333-34, 336-37, 369; Ralph Hubert Dignan and Joseph P. Finn, "A History of the Diocese of London," ed. Guy Alden (Unpublished Manuscript, 2002), 436-46; John K.A. Farrell (O'Farrell), *The History of the Roman Catholic Church in London, Ontario 1826-1931* (M.A. thesis, University of Western Ontario, 1949), 57-59; Jerome Terrence

Flynn, *The London Episcopacy, 1867-1889, of the Most Reverend John Walsh, D.D., Second Bishop of London, Ontario* (M.A. thesis, Catholic University of American, 1966), 47-49. **Henry Edward Dormer**: Arthur C. Carty, ed., *A Thousand Arrows: Biographical Memoir of the Hon. Henry Edward Dormer Late of the 60th Rifles* (London: 1970); Dignan and Finn, "A History of the Diocese of London," 456-83; Farrell (O'Farrell), *The History of the Roman Catholic Church in London, Ontario 1826-1931*, 40-51; Ibid., "Dormer, Henry Edward," *DCB* (Toronto: 1976), 9: 215-16. See also: Val Ambrose McInness, *To Rise with the Light: The Spiritual Odyssey of Jack Chambers* (Toronto: 1989).

6. Congregation of the Sisters of the Holy Names of Jesus and Mary (Holy Names Sisters, SNJM)

Canadian-born Eulalie Durocher — in religious life Mother Marie-Rose — founded the Congregation of the Sisters of the Holy Names of Jesus and Mary in 1843, in the diocese of Montréal. Supported by Bishop Ignace Bourget of Montréal, the congregation became a papal institute, a status that gave them a fair amount of autonomy, with a novitiate in Longueuil, Québec.

In 1862, Bishop Pinsoneault of London invited the Sisters to Windsor, a town barely ten years old with a population of 3,000 and one Catholic mission, St. Alphonsus, which did not become a parish until 1 July 1865. Also involved in the invitation were the Catholic trustees of the Windsor public school board, who were looking for a teaching community to replace the Grey Sisters. Their departure from Windsor in 1861 left Windsor's Catholic children with no Catholic teachers. In addition to schoolwork, Bishop Pinsoneault wanted the Sisters to establish a novitiate in his diocese and operate under his direction, demands that were impossible to meet. It took two years of negotiations between the bishop and Mother Thérèse-de-Jésus, superior general, before four Sisters were finally sent to the diocese in 1864.

Arriving at the Windsor train station on 20 October 1864 were Sister M. Jean-Baptiste (Joséphine Lagassé), the first superior, Sister M. Mathilde (Aurélie Demers), Sister M. Alphonse (Marie-Louise David), and Sister M. Thomas (Marie Desroches). Two more sisters arrived in November: Sister M. Eugene and Sister Marie-du-Mont-Carmel. Sister M. Mathilde and Sister M. Alphonse began teaching in the Catholic elementary school four days after their arrival. The other Sisters opened up a "Select School for Girls" on 28 November 1864. Seven students formed the initial enrolment. This was the beginning of St. Mary's Academy, a bilingual school.

Vital Ouellette donated lots 81 and 82 located immediately west of St. Alphonsus church, on Park Street, to the Holy Names Sisters for a convent and school. A signatory to the leasing agreement was the diocese of Sandwich (London). Construction began in October 1865, and the Sisters and their pupils took possession in November 1867. Additions were built in 1870, 1884 and 1904, making St. Mary's Academy one of the grandest buildings in Windsor. The school offered quality Catholic education and also served as a centre of local Catholic culture that flourished under the protective hand of Dean James T. Wagner of St. Alphonsus parish.

In November 1927, news arrived that the Academy property was needed for the Detroit-Windsor Tunnel. The Ouellette family gave its blessing to the sale of the land — appraised at a staggering $1 million — but ownership of the two lots was in dispute. The Sisters claimed that the land was theirs, but Bishop Fallon counterclaimed that the diocese of London, being a signatory to the 1865 lease agreement, was entitled to a significant share of any sale monies. In any case, the transfer of the property was inevitable because of the expropriation rights of the corporation contracted to build the tunnel. Delay was not an option.

In the end, the diocese received three-tenths and the Sisters seven-tenths from the proceeds. Fallon put the diocese's portion towards the construction costs of the new St. Peter's Seminary, and the Sisters put theirs into a new St. Mary's Academy in South Windsor, which opened on 2 September 1929 and lasted until June 1971.

St. Mary's Academy may have been the principal teaching apostolate of the Sisters, but it was certainly not the only one. Beginning in 1867, the Sisters took on charitable and teaching work outside the Park Street school. They traveled on foot, by carriage or by ferry boat to staff an orphanage in Sandwich and to teach in schools on both sides of the Detroit River: St. Alphonsus (1867) and St. Francis (1879), in Windsor; and St. Joachim (1886) and St. Anne (1888), in Detroit.

A year after the Sisters arrived in Windsor, they made Amherstburg the site of their first daughter house. In 1865, six Sisters settled in St. John the Baptist parish. A hundred years later, Holy Names Sisters were still teaching in the town. Twelve of them were on the staffs of St. Anthony, St. Rose and St. John the Baptist separate schools. The last Holy Names Sister in Amherstburg was Sister Claire-Marie Durocher. In June 2003, she closed Mare-Rose Music School and moved to Windsor, where she continues to teach piano at Holy Names Residence. In total, the Sisters ministered in Amherstburg for 138 years. During that time, they worked as classroom teachers, music teachers, pastoral ministers, youth ministers and volunteers.

In 1867, the Sisters were invited to Sarnia to teach in two schools for the recently created separate school board. Six Sisters took up residence in Our Lady of Lake Huron Convent on London Road facing Brock Street. Within a year of their arrival, Father Edmund Burke Kilroy, the pastor of Our Lady of Mercy parish and a former Union Army chaplain during the American Civil War, presented to the Sisters an old friend of his, General William T. Sherman of the U.S. Army. They greeted the General and his retinue with an address and entertained them with music and songs. The Sisters taught in a private academy for girls and also in the Sarnia separate school from 1867 to 1905. When the Sisters were recalled to Montréal, 275 members of Our Lady of Mercy parish signed a letter to Mother Mary of the Rosary, superior general in Hochelaga, declaring

"the debt of gratitude we owe your Community for the two score years you have labored in the education of the younger members of the Parish and the countless acts of charity and other good deeds rendered by the Sisters of your Order at times when sickness and death visited our friends and families." In 1906, the Sisters of St. Joseph replaced the Holy Names Sisters as teachers in Sarnia's separate schools.

In 1895, Father François Marseilles, pastor of St. Joseph parish in River Canard, built a two-room schoolhouse and a convent with his own funds. This was the first St. Joseph separate school. On the invitation of Bishop O'Connor, three Sisters — M. Augustine, M. Oswald and Vincent Ferrier — arrived on 6 September 1896 to staff the school. Thus began 102 years of work in St. Joseph parish and its schools. The Sisters taught boys and girls at both the elementary and secondary levels. Numerous vocations to the religious life came from this predominantly French-speaking Catholic farming community during the twentieth century. Sister Corinne Gignac and Sister Thérèse Caron were the last Holy Names Sisters to move out of St. Joseph Convent in River Canard in 1998. Today, a beautiful garden-park planned by parishioners and young people in 2002 stands as a memorial to the Sisters' dedicated service of more than a century.

When the diocese of London celebrated its one hundredth anniversary, in 1956, students at St. Mary's Academy in South Windsor presented a pageant for clergy, parents and local parishioners. At the time, there were 160 teaching Sisters in the diocese. Along with St. Mary's Academy, their flagship school, they taught at St. Joseph's Academy in Amherstburg, at Holy Names College, the Catholic women's college of Assumption University (1934), and in separate schools in Windsor, Amherstburg, LaSalle, River Canard and Emeryville. From the 1960s to the early 1980s, the Sisters expanded their teaching presence to another twelve separate schools in Windsor.

When St. Mary's Academy closed in 1971, some of the Sisters and their students transferred to Assumption College High School. Other Catholic high schools in Windsor where the Sisters taught were Holy Names, Catholic Central, and F. J. Brennan. They also taught at St. Anne's in Tecumseh.

The Second Vatican Council brought reform

and change in the Church. Religious communities were called to return to their roots and rediscover their original charism. In 1967, the Holy Names Sisters set up their first Postulancy at St. Mary's Academy, for nine young women who came from Ontario, Québec, Manitoba and Michigan. This was in sharp contrast to earlier years when ten to fifteen women at a time from Windsor alone entered the novitiate. During the century that it took the Holy Names Sisters to establish a novitiate in Windsor, more than 250 women from Southwestern Ontario had entered the community. In 1977, the McEwan Residence became the novitiate house for women in discernment.

Another notable event in the history of the Holy Names Sisters in the diocese of London was The Trial of Evidence — the canonical process by which the Church judges the authenticity of a miracle — concerning the cause of Mother Marie-Rose Durocher, the founder of the Sisters of the Holy Names of Jesus and Mary. The Trial took place at St. Mary's Academy on 16 October 1972. It heard and recorded evidence presented by witnesses who had either direct or indirect knowledge of the 1946 cure of Benjamin Modzel, allegedly through the intercession of Mother Durocher. Father Angelo Mitri, OMI, was the postulator. The judges, notaries and Promoter of Justice were priests of the diocese appointed by Bishop Carter, who wrote in a letter of September 1972 to Sister Thérèse Bécigneul, the provincial superior: "It is a privilege for us to have this stage of the process take place in our diocese." The results of the Trial were sent to Rome for adjudication.

Although Mother Durocher's cause had commenced in 1927, it was Modzel's cure in 1946, as part of the overall examination of her life of virtue, that proved pivotal in the decisions of John Paul II to name her Venerable in 1979 and Blessed in 1982. Time will show whether Eulalie Durocher — Blessed Marie-Rose — will be formally recognized as a Saint of the Catholic Church.

During their first one hundred years in the diocese of London, the Sisters of the Holy Names of Jesus and Mary concentrated their efforts in educating Catholic youth at all levels, teaching music and participating in the arts. The community steadily grew in membership and excelled as teachers and administrators, guiding generations of Catholic children through the separate school system. The last forty years have been marked by the Spirit moving the Sisters in the direction of revitalization and renewal, as the community has sought justice for the poor, the broken-hearted, the aged and the addicted.

In 1977, the Sisters sold St. Mary's Academy and moved to a residence on Peter Street in Windsor. The Provincial Administration Team encouraged the Sisters to use their talents for the good of the whole and to live the Gospel more fully, through education in the faith, with special concern for the poor and disadvantaged. In the process, new opportunities, new risks and new women emerged in the community. As more lay people qualified to teach the young and take over the reins of principalship, some classroom-Sisters felt called to overseas missionary work in South Africa, Haiti and Brazil. After forty years, all but two have returned to the diocese. Others served as pastoral ministers in Windsor parishes or worked in hospitals and prisons, and at Brentwood and the House of Sophrosyne in Windsor for those dealing with addictions. Still other Sisters involved themselves in the inter-community Adult Spiritual Centre, which was founded in 1989 by Sister Emma Bezaire, SNJM, Sister Kathleen Lichti, CSJ, and Father Ray Earle, CSSR. After more than a decade of success, the centre closed in 2001. A similar centre, but one sponsored solely by the Holy Names Sisters, was called the Well. Sister Antoinette Janisse was the director. Lasting from 1990 to 1997, it sponsored programs for both religious and lay people.

Meanwhile, the Sisters who moved to the Holy Names Residence on Peter Street opened their home to students in need of tutoring and to weekly encounters with their elderly neighbours in the West End Golden Opportunity Club. The residence became the hub for local community meetings, gatherings and celebrations.

In June 2005, the Sisters of the Holy Names of Jesus and Mary, an international papal institute, numbered 1,356 professed Sisters and 639 Associates. Of these, 37 Sisters and 27 Associates live and work in the diocese of London. Their ministry includes refugees, a shelter for homeless women, pastoral work, parish secretarial work, spiritual companioning, Habitat for Humanity, Project Rachel and retreats and spirituality programs at the Ravine Women's Centre. Several Sisters continue to teach in schools. Though now few in number in the diocese, the Sisters and Associates of the Holy Names of Jesus and Mary remain committed to the call to be Gospel women in solidarity for liberating action.

Submitted by Sister Suzanne Malette, SNJM.
Sources: Archives of the Sisters of the Holy Names of Jesus and Mary (Windsor, Ontario); Sister John

Thomas (Helen Batte), SNJM, *Rooted in Hope: A History of the Sisters of the Holy Names of Jesus and Mary of the Ontario Province* (1982); Victor J. Dudek, *Our Lady of Mercy: A Centennial History 1878-1978* (1977); Eleanor Gignac and Laura Bondy, comps. and eds., *Led by the Shepherd: A History of St. John the Baptist Parish 1802-1992* (Amherstburg: 1992).

7. Congregation of St. Basil (Basilians, CSB)

The Basilian Fathers are the longest-serving men's religious community in the history of the diocese of London, arriving in 1857 for a year, returning in 1870 and continuing to the present day. From their ranks, at two very different times, have come two bishops for the diocese: Bishop O'Connor, the third bishop (1890-1899), and Bishop Fabbro, who was ordained and installed on 15 August 2002 as the tenth bishop.

The Basilians have served at Assumption College/University, 1870 to the present; Assumption parish in Windsor, 1870 to the present; St. Joseph's parish in Chatham, 1874 to 1878; St. John the Baptist parish in Amherstburg, 1878 to the present; Blessed Sacrament parish in Windsor, 1937 to 1968; and Star of the Sea mission on Pelee Island, various years between 1897 and 1933 and 1980 to 1988. (The Basilians also staffed and ran Assumption College High School but not as an entity separate from the college until the 1930s; the high school was located in Dillon Hall on the university campus until 1955, when a new school was built on Huron Church Road; the last Basilian principal of the school left in 1992.) Since Basilian work at the four parishes and one mission has been treated elsewhere (Part Four, Chapter One: Windsor Deanery and Chapter Two: Essex Deanery), this chapter will be devoted to the Basilians at Assumption College/University.

The Congregation of St. Basil was founded on 21 November 1822 at Annonay, in the diocese of Viviers, France, by Father Joseph Bouvier Lapierre and nine companions. The essential works of the community are teaching and preaching. In 1850, the community established a foundation in Toronto, at the behest of Bishop Armand-François-Marie de Charbonnel, who had studied at Annonay and knew some of the Basilian founders before they had formed their own community of priests. In Toronto, the first generation of Basilians built St. Michael's College and St. Basil's parish church.

In 1857, they sent one of their members, Father Joseph Malbos, to be treasurer of the newly opened Jesuit-run Assumption College in Sandwich, located in a substantial three-storey structure south of Assumption church and facing Huron Church Road. Unhappy, Father Malbos left the college on 27 October 1858.

For the next twelve years, the college experienced administrative chaos and was often closed for lack of teachers and pupils. A variety of priests and even one layman were in charge at different times, and none succeeded in turning the school into a viable institution. Following Father Malbos's abrupt departure, Father Louis Musart, a diocesan priest, became president. When the Jesuits decided to leave the diocese in September 1859, Bishop Pinsoneault appointed Father Clement Frachon, another diocesan priest, as president. His time at the college was a disaster and ended on 3 April 1860. While Théodule Girardot of Sandwich continued to direct the common school on one floor of the college building, there was no one to teach the commercial and classical courses until the arrival of the Benedictine Fathers from Latrobe, Pennsylvania in September 1861. The Benedictines departed in April 1863. Father Pierre Dominic Laurent, pastor in Amherstburg, assumed control of the college for the next seven years.

On 27 September 1869, Bishop Walsh, who wanted to salvage the diocese's only institution of higher education, and Father Mathieu Soulerin, the

Basilian Provincial, signed a concordat (agreement) that gave very favourable terms to the Basilians. It placed Assumption College (the 1857 building plus eighty acres of land) and Assumption church under Basilian direction. Terms of the 499-year lease, which called for a nominal rent from the college of one dollar per year, included a Basilian responsibility to maintain and improve the college property at their own expense and to teach free of charge three students nominated by the bishop of London. Father Denis O'Connor, not yet thirty years old, was the first Basilian superior (president) of Assumption College, and, as such, he was also head of temporalities at Assumption church.

Father O'Connor was superior, bursar and professor of theology for twenty eventful years. Arriving in Sandwich along with his confreres, on 20 July 1870, he started with $300 in his pocket, no hope of a government grant and a building in need of serious repair and renewal. When O'Connor left in 1890 to become the bishop of London, Assumption College was a bustling school that had forged strong ties of loyalty with the dioceses of London and Detroit and attracted students from other parts of Michigan and from Ohio, Pennsylvania, New York and as far away as Kentucky. By dint of superb financial acumen, O'Connor was able to build the east-west wing in 1875 and the administration wing in 1883, to increase the number of boarding students, whose fees were the economic lifeblood of the school and to leave as his legacy a school known and respected in Catholic circles for its pedagogy and piety.

Father Daniel Cushing, president from 1890 to 1901, and Father Robert McBrady, president from 1901 to 1907, carried on the O'Connor tradition of careful administration, in the process not only preserving but also enhancing Assumption's distinctive Catholic character. Father Cushing paid off the debt for the 1883 wing and did not incur any new debt. Father McBrady reformed the teaching system, published an annual *Catalogue*, laid the groundwork for an alumni association and built the chapel in 1908. But neither he nor Cushing made any significant changes to the school's curriculum or academic structure.

Assumption College was really four schools for boys under one roof. There was a preparatory school for grades five to eight, a two-year commercial course, a three-year academic course (high school

equivalent) and a four-year Arts course (university equivalent). Many students, however, finished their schooling at Assumption at the end of the second year of Arts, known as Rhetoric, which was considered the final year of one's classical education. The last two years of the Arts course were devoted to the study of philosophy and were taken almost exclusively by those considering the priesthood. In effect, aside from the four elementary grades and the two-year commercial course, Assumption College was a nineteenth century *collège classique* and a junior seminary.

But the nineteenth century had to give way to changing expectations in the field of education in Ontario. Father Francis Forster, president from 1907 to 1920, added a fourth year to high school, making it possible for Assumption students to earn junior matriculation for university entrance, and hived off the four years Arts course, so that it could function like a modern university-level program of studies. These reforms prepared Father Forster for negotiations to affiliate Assumption's Arts Department or college section with the University of Western Ontario, which were successfully concluded in October 1919, with Bishop Fallon as the chief negotiator for both Assumption and Brescia College, which became the Catholic women's college on Western's campus.

Father Forster accomplished many other things for Assumption College. He improved the O'Connor-era buildings, installed electricity, built St. Denis Hall, a gymnasium, and St. Michael's Hall, a residence, in 1915, and instituted an administrative archive for the college.

Assumption College celebrated its fiftieth anniversary in 1920 in grand style. But what should have been the beginning of a golden period for the Basilian Fathers at the college disintegrated into acrimony and isolation when Bishop Fallon and Father Forster clashed over the location of the Arts Department now that the all-important affiliation with Western had been achieved. Fallon wanted the Basilians to move it to the London campus to complement Brescia. Forster refused to be bullied into making a decision and later concluded that the Basilians did not have the resources to relocate the Arts Department and that relocation would seriously hurt the high school department left behind in Sandwich. Complicating matters was Bishop Fallon's anger at Father Forster for failing to notify him of impending changes to the Basilian constitutions.

It was a lengthy struggle that wound its way to Rome. In the end, the Arts Department remained in Sandwich, but Fallon removed his students from the college and established St. Peter's School of Philosophy at the seminary. Relations between the bishop and the Basilians were frosty for the remainder of Fallon's episcopacy, which ended with his death in 1931.

The years from 1920 to 1952 were difficult for Assumption College. The next six presidents — Fathers Joseph T. Muckle, Daniel L. Dillon, Vincent L. Kennedy, Thomas A. MacDonald, Vincent J. Guinan and John H. O'Loane — shepherded the school through the final Fallon years, a failed bid to block construction of the Ambassador Bridge, the Great Depression, the trying times of the Second World War and the exhilarating if trying days of overcrowding when returning Veterans, supported by the federal government, filled every seat on campus. During those same years the Basilians built Dillon Hall in 1927 and the Memorial Science Building in 1948, introduced evening extension courses for men *and* women teachers in 1933 and welcomed to the campus Holy Names College for women in 1934. Despite the constant worry over finances, the Basilians made every attempt to open the college to every qualified student from the Border Cities, regardless of religious background.

It was the seventh president, Father Eugene C. LeBel, who brought about the greatest changes in the history of Assumption College. From 1952 to 1964, he enjoyed the distinction of being the last president of the college when it belonged to Western (affiliation ended in 1953), the first and only president of Assumption University of Windsor and the first president of the University of Windsor. He presided over Assumption's last hurrah on 10 February 1957, when 2,000 people celebrated the college's one-hundredth anniversary.

The paradox of Father LeBel's presidency was that having guided Assumption to the zenith of its institutional life as an independent Catholic university with its own affiliated colleges (the non-denominational Essex College and the Anglican Canterbury College), he was compelled by political and economic circumstances to give up everything that he and his fellow Basilians had achieved and give it over to the new and wholly secular University of Windsor. Assumption kept its university charter (which it holds to this day) and was given the right to grant the MA degree in theology (which it promised to hold in abeyance), and to nominate its own members to the board of governors of the University of Windsor. In reality, however, Assumption became a university with no students.

Over the past forty years, the Basilian Fathers at Assumption University have worked diligently to maintain a distinctly Catholic presence on the campus through the Christian Culture Series, the student chaplaincy, academic awards and scholarships and more recently the Institute of Pastoral and Educational Ministry and the St. Basil's Institute for mental health and education. In the summer of 2005, the Basilians decided to rent the college buildings on Huron Church Road to the University of Windsor, keeping access to the chapel, the boardroom, a reception room and the Freed-Orman Conference Centre. They moved the remaining staff to St. Basil's Institute on Riverside Drive West. The long-term future of Assumption remains uncertain.

Sources: James Hanrahan, *The Basilian Fathers (1822-1972): A Documentary History Study of One Hundred and Fifty Years of the History of the Congregation of Priests of St. Basil* (Toronto: 1973); George McMahon, *Pure Zeal: The History of Assumption College 1870-1946* (Toronto: 2002); Peter M. Meehan, *From College to University: The Basilian Fathers and Assumption 1950-1963* (M.A. thesis, University of Windsor, 1991); Michael Power, ed. *A Documentary History of Assumption College*, 6 vols. (Windsor: 1984-2003).

8. The Religious Hospitallers of St. Joseph (RHSJ)

Hôtel-Dieu Hospital

In the 1880s, Dean James T. Wagner, pastor of St. Alphonsus in Windsor, was concerned about the large number of orphaned and unschooled black children in his parish. Apparently, many of them were barred from the public school; nor did they have an opportunity to enroll in a local "coloured" separate school because one did not exist. In the spring of 1887, Dean Wagner organized a catechetical mission for these children in St. Alphonsus Hall, but he lacked the necessary funds to build a proper orphanage and school. As soon as he received permission from Bishop Walsh of London, Wagner conducted a fund-raising tour in Europe, on one occasion preaching to 5,000 people in Paris, and he also sent out a circular letter in Canada asking for donations of a dime or more for his proposed mission.

A copy of his circular reached Mother Justine Bonneau, superior of the Religious Hospitallers of St. Joseph in Montréal, a cloistered community. She was so touched by his devotion to these children that she sent him two dollars and fifty cents, adding that if he ever contemplated building a hospital in Windsor, her Sisters would be happy to assist him in this enterprise. At this time, there had been some talk among civic and church leaders in Windsor about the need for a hospital, but there was insufficient interest among the people and a lack of money to pursue the project. Never one to shy away from what appeared to many others to be an insurmountable challenge, Dean Wagner seized the opportunity of Mother Bonneau's offer and invited the Religious Hospitallers to establish a hospital and take care of the black orphans.

After much deliberation between officials from the town of Windsor, Bishop Walsh, Archbishop Édouard-Charles Fabre of Montréal and the Montréal-based Religious Hospitallers, Mother Bonneau and Sister Joséphine Paquet arrived in Windsor and formally founded a community of their Sisters on 13 August 1888. The initial order of business was the purchase of six vacant lots on Ouellette Avenue, where the hospital would be built. The next was to dispatch a complement of Sisters to form a community and commence the work of building the hospital. On 14 September 1888, five Sisters of Hôtel-Dieu in Montréal landed in Windsor. They were Mother Joséphine Paquet and Sisters Joséphine Lamoureux, Philomena Carrière, Joséphine Boucher and Victoire Caron. Construction began on 10 October 1888 and was completed in February 1890.

Unlimited faith in Divine Providence helped the Sisters to survive real hardship in the early years. They never wasted a penny and spent on themselves only the absolute minimum on food and other basic necessities of life. Theirs was a genuine and heroic sacrifice. They also relied on the support of numerous benefactors who donated food, money and equipment, without which there would have been no Hôtel-Dieu hospital in Windsor.

On 18 February 1890, the Sisters admitted their first patient, Miss Kate Flynn. Soon, Hôtel-Dieu Sisters were busy not only inside the hospital but also well beyond its walls, becoming visiting nurses throughout the city. An orphanage and school for black children, built next to the hospital, opened on 2 June 1890. Because of low enrolment, however, this pioneering apostolic work was discontinued after five years. An opportunity to bring black people into the Church was lost.

On 9 October 1907, an "in hospital School of Nursing" was inaugurated under the direction of a laywoman, who had B.A. and B.Sc. degrees in nursing. In 1911, Sister Marie de la Ferre (Laura LeBoeuf) and Sister Catherine O'Donnell enrolled in the first class of eight nurses to graduate from the Hôtel-Dieu of St. Joseph School of Nursing. In 1945, owing to a significant increase in the number of students, the Jeanne Mance School of Nursing was built next to the hospital on Ouellette Avenue. This school was closed in 1973, when the Ontario government decreed that student nurses would be trained in community colleges. In sixty-six years, the Sisters trained and graduated 1,868 nurses.

Over the years, Sister Marie de la Ferre filled a variety of assignments. She foresaw future needs and encouraged Sisters to continue their studies after obtaining their nursing diplomas. Some went to university; others took post-graduate courses in various specialties. As a result, the Sisters were qualified to hold supervisory positions in departments that required specialized training. During Sister Marie de la Ferre's term as hospital administrator, a 120-bed wing was added to the hospital. Opened in 1938, it took seventeen months to complete and cost approximately $350,000.

Sister Joséphine Lamoureux, first assistant to Mother Paquet, became the first hospital pharmacist. Sister Mary McCarthy and Sister Marie Roy followed Sister Lamoureux in the pharmacy. Both Sisters held the dual roles of pharmacist and operating room supervisor. At one time, Sisters staffed and supervised every department in the hospital, including pediatrics, X-ray, laboratory, obstetrics, dietetics, general equipment, the school of nursing, surgical department, cardiac care and pastoral care. A Sister was also hospital administrator, beginning in 1890 with Mother Joséphine Paquet and ending in 1968 when Sister Cécile LeBoeuf completed her term. Roman E. Mann succeeded her as the first lay administrator.

On 1 December 1993, after two years of planning and discussion, an official alliance agreement was signed between the Religious Hospitallers of St. Joseph Health Centre (Hôtel-Dieu Hospital and Villa Maria) and the Salvation Army Grace Hospital. This alliance became effective on 1 April 1994, the first of its kind in Canada.

The retirement of Sister Rose-Marie Dufault on 1 September 2003 meant the end of an era for the Religious Hospitallers of St. Joseph at Hôtel-Dieu Grace Hospital. After 115 years, no longer would the Sisters be a daily presence in the hospital. Since 1888, over ninety Sisters served in various capacities, caring for the sick, the elderly and the most needy of Windsor. At the time of writing, the Religious Hospitallers of St. Joseph continue to own and sponsor Hôtel-Dieu Grace Hospital.

Villa Maria

In 1933, at the insistence of senior citizens and pastors of various churches, the Sisters at Hôtel-Dieu Hospital began to search for a suitable place for a home for the aged. The search continued for a decade before two friends of the Sisters, Monsignor Charles A. Parent and Father Gregory L. Blondé, found a house near the Ambassador Bridge. Sister Claire Maitre, the superior and administrator of Hôtel-Dieu, summoned a meeting of her Council and the Hospital Advisory Board. Following this, the large white brick house was purchased.

On 15 January 1944, Bishop Kidd blessed the building under the name of St. John the Evangelist Home for the Aged. The next day the bishop celebrated Mass in the home's chapel, with seventy-two Knights of Columbus, who had kindly furnished the chapel, in attendance. On that day, the doors of the home were opened for residents. Sister Marie Guévin, superior, Sister Stella Tremblay, Sister Rita Marentette and novices Eva Papineau and Aurore Beaulieu are considered the founders.

Within a relatively brief span of time, residents filled the house. The Sisters purchased a neighbouring house and very quickly that too was running at capacity. By January 1955, there were four houses in operation, all full, prompting the Sisters to consider constructing a modern single-building facility for 120 residents. In this undertaking, the Sisters benefited from the wise advice of Sir Harry Gignac and W.H. Cantelon, two members of the Hôtel-Dieu Board who used their contacts with municipal officials and the general public to the Sisters' advantage, and also from the practical advice of Ed L'Heureux, their plumber. The new home was christened Villa Maria.

On 5 August 1956, Villa Maria Home for the Aged accepted its first residents. On 1 September, Sister Blanche Garçeau was appointed superior. Up to 1971, the superior at the "Villa" was also the administrator. After that year, lay people were hired as administrators. Villa Maria closed its doors on 27 October 2003, for financial and government health restructuring reasons. At the time, Sisters Rose-Anna Tétreault, Cécile LeBoeuf, Aurore Beaulieu and Bernice Bondy lived in the convent attached to the "Villa" and volunteered their services. The building is now a privately-owned residence for University of

Windsor students.

In addition to their health care ministry, the Religious Hospitallers of St. Joseph responded to other needs in the diocese. For example, their work was essential to the early success of Holy Family Retreat House in Oxley, which opened on 1 August 1948. According to Father Jansen, in an article on the history of the retreat house, "the Religious Hospitallers of St. Joseph were asked to help with the first retreats. They came and they were not only helpful, they did yeoman work. They brought the sheets, pillowcases, towels and washcloths from Hôtel-Dieu in Windsor. They brought the cook and the kitchen staff and then a group of sisters: Mother Marie de la Ferre, Sisters Claire Antaya, Ruth Jeanette and Rita Marentette."

The Religious Hospitallers of St. Joseph, in partnership with people of all faiths, served the community of Windsor for 118 years. They persevered for so long and were able to accomplish so much in the field of health care because of their undaunted faith, strong hope and relentless spirit of service to others. Their mission continues as the torch of service is passed to men and women who are competent and compassionate and committed to the same vision of service.

Submitted by Sister Rose-Marie Dufault, RHSJ. **Sources:** Religious Hospitallers of St. Joseph, Hôtel-Dieu Hospital Archives, 1888-1943, Vol. 1, chapters, 2-4, 7 and 1943-1944, Vol. 3; Rose-Marie Dufault and Grace Dockery, "A Look at the Past to Inspire the Future" [historical pamphlet of Hôtel-Dieu Hospital, Villa Maria and the Salvation Army Grace Hospital], (1994); Adrian Jansen, "St. Peter's Seminary and Holy Family Retreat House: Another Vital Connection," St. Peter's Seminary, *Alumni Bulletin* (1996-1997), 34-36; Michael Power, "Wagner, James Theodore," *DCB* (Toronto: 1990), 12: 1077-78.

9. Order of Friars Minor (Franciscans, OFM)

The Franciscans of St. Anthony's Monastery in Cincinnati, Ohio were the third religious community to serve the Catholic people of Chatham. The Jesuits had founded the mission in 1845 and established St. Joseph's parish in 1850, building its first church and laying the spiritual and temporal foundations for a vibrant parish. They remained until 1 August 1874 and were succeeded by the Basilian Fathers of Sandwich, who were invited by Bishop Walsh to assume the pastoral charge. The Basilians stayed for three and a half years and were well regarded by the people, but a significant increase in the number of German-speaking Catholics, especially in Harwich Township, prompted Bishop Walsh to turn to the German-speaking Franciscans of Cincinnati. (In exchange for St. Joseph's parish, the Basilians accepted the parish of St. John the Baptist in Amherstburg, where they have remained as pastors to this day.)

Father Eugene Butterman was Chatham's first Franciscan pastor. Bishop Walsh asked him and his confreres to be in the parish by Sunday, 20 January 1878. Father Butterman remained for less than a year, since he understood his role as a transitional one, and he turned over the pastorate to Father William Gausepohl in December 1878. Assisting Father Gausepohl at what became St. Joseph's Friary were Fathers Innocent Bruns, Stanislaus Heitmann and Michael Hoffman and Brother Roger Molitor, who was the cook, janitor and cellarer. In addition to the town of Chatham, the bishop gave the Franciscans the care of three missions: St. Patrick's in Merlin in Raleigh Township; Ridgetown in Howard Township; and Blenheim, in Harwich Township. The Blenheim mission was the most important of the three and the one still attended by the Franciscans when they left the diocese in 1921.

During the forty-three-year Franciscan period in the history of St. Joseph's parish, thirty-nine priests, fourteen brothers and seven tertiaries were stationed in Chatham at one time or another. The three longest-serving and most productive pastors were Father Gausepohl (1878-1889); Father Paul B. Alf

(1889-1897); and Father James J. Archinger (1901-1917). Father Francis Solanus J. Schaefer, who had been parish priest from 1897 to 1900, was the last Franciscan pastor. (Each pastor was also superior of the friary.)

Father Gausepohl built the rectory in 1879 and commissioned the renowned architect Joseph Connolly to design the current parish church, a marvelous example of the Romanesque style, in 1887. It cost the handsome sum of $75,000. Father Alf orchestrated a three-day celebration of the parish's golden jubilee in October 1895 and installed a Casavant organ. That year there were 2,200 parishioners. Father Archinger built an eight-room separate school for boys and girls, at a cost of $12,000, invited the Ursulines to manage it and turned the old school into the church hall. In late 1908, he closed the church for major renovations, which included the installation of six altars, new Stations of the Cross and electrical wiring to replace the gas lighting, and the decoration of the ceiling with paintings of the life of St. Joseph. The total cost was $10,000, a debt that the parishioners, inspired by their energetic and charismatic pastor, had retired by 1914, in addition to a previous debt of $20,000. The church was formally re-opened on 12 December 1909. In 1916, Father Archinger added the twin bell towers for $17,000 and installed statues of St. Francis of Assisi and St. Michael the Archangel in niches on either side of the main entrance. That same year, the parish hosted the fifth Diocesan Eucharistic Congress. From all accounts, the public procession of the Blessed Sacrament was one of the grandest ever staged in the diocese.

The community at St. Joseph's Friary ranged from a minimum of three to a maximum of six members. In 1917 and again in 1919, there were five full-time priests on staff, an almost unheard of number for a single parish church in the diocese of London, but as it turned out, five were barely enough to keep abreast of all the parochial work in Chatham's only Catholic parish, which continued to grow at a rate that begged for the creation of a second parish. As the second decade of the twentieth century came to a close, the Franciscans had to take care of the spiritual needs not only of a large parish and at least one demanding mission but also of the Ursuline Sisters and their students at the Pines, the St. Joseph Sisters at St. Joseph's Hospital, which had its own chapel, approximately 350 separate school students, two children's sodalities and a local branch of Third Order Franciscans.

In 1919, Bishop Fallon asked the Franciscan Provincial in Cincinnati to agree to a proper division of the parish, citing the insufficient number of priests at St. Joseph's to serve its many constituents. When Fallon did not receive an answer, he turned his request into a litany of complaints, not against the Franciscan priests and brothers stationed at the parish, whose work among the people and devotion to the Catholic faith he never tired of praising, but against the Franciscan administrators in Cincinnati. He complained that various Provincials changed the staff at the parish without consulting him, and that they made far too many changes in personnel for the good of parochial life. Fallon pointedly reminded Father Rudolph Bonner, the Provincial in 1921, that no bishop of London had granted the Franciscans the inalienable possession of St. Joseph's parish, in canonical language called the *Beneplacitum Apostolicum*. In other words, Franciscan tenure at the parish was temporary, even if had lasted more than forty years, and consequently it could be revoked at will by either the bishop or the Franciscans.

As soon as Fallon was ready to divide the parish and appoint diocesan priests at St. Joseph parish (south of the Thames) and the new parish, Blessed Sacrament (north of the Thames), he instructed the Franciscans to leave. They were gone by 12 September 1921 and considered his action an expulsion. Their sudden departure came as a shock to the parish and city, forcing Fallon to take the highly unusual step (at least for him) of justifying his decision in a sermon to the parishioners on 18 September. To avoid alienating Chatham's Catholics, Fallon appointed four priests to the parish: Father (later Dean) John J. Gnam as pastor and Fathers Maurice N. Sullivan, Patrick H. Harrigan and Peter E. McKeon as assistants. A young Father Ralph Hubert Dignan was made the first pastor of Blessed Sacrament parish.

Fond memories of the Franciscans from Cincinnati lingered for many years, but the Franciscans never returned to the diocese.

Archival information supplied by Father Dan Anderson, OFM, Franciscan Archives, Province of St. John the Baptist, Cincinnati, Ohio.

10. Congregation of the
Sisters Adorers of the Precious Blood (RPB)

The Congregation of the Sisters Adorers of the Precious Blood is Canada's first contemplative community founded by a Canadian. It was established in St. Hyacinthe, Québec, on 14 September 1861, by Catherine Aurelia Caouette, who sought and received the guidance of Bishop Joseph LaRocque of St. Hyacinthe, and her spiritual director, Monsignor Joseph Sabin Raymond. Mother Catherine Aurelia died on 6 July 1905, and the opening day of the diocesan procedure of her canonization was 20 November 1984.

The young community grew rapidly, and the first foundation outside of Québec was established in Toronto in 1869. (There are currently eleven Precious Blood monasteries in the English Generalate in Canada.) The Toronto monastery sponsored the London foundation in 1913, on the invitation of Bishop Fallon. Father John V. Tobin, the first rector of St. Peter's seminary, persuaded the bishop to invite the Sisters to London. Tobin knew that the Sisters in Toronto were considering opening another monastery but had yet to decide on a location. Fallon issued the invitation and promised to take care of the spiritual needs of the Sisters. He sent them priests from the seminary, who to this day continue to make good on the bishop's promise.

On 1 May 1913, there arrived in London Mother Mary Teresa Lanphier, the first superior, and ten Sisters: Mary Agnes Fullerton, Mary of the Eucharist Herzog, Immaculate Heart McGuire, Mary Joseph Madden, Mary St. Patrick Doyle, Mary of the Precious Blood Lanphier, St. Anthony Summers, Mary Gerarda Higgins, Mary Augustine Lee and Mary Dolorosa McGinn. Viable from the very beginning, the foundation was placed under the patronage of St. Michael the Archangel.

The diocese provided the Sisters with a house at 451 Ridout Street. Since many young women entered the community in those early years, the Sisters soon had to seek larger accommodation. In early 1918, they moved into a large and beautiful home at 572 Queens Avenue, which was formally owned by the Labatt family. Subsequently, the Sisters undertook, with the help of many friends, the building of a new monastery at 667 Talbot Street. On 31 July 1923, they moved into their new home. The heavy debt on the building was finally eliminated in the late 1940s.

The Talbot Street monastery, surrounded by spacious and beautiful gardens, was for fifty-four years a haven of peace and quiet where, according to Mother Catherine Aurelia, the Sisters could "sanctify the works of their hidden solitude born of longing, prayer and sacrifice and worthily fulfill the aims of their sublime vocation" (*Sitio*, line 135). As Mother Foundress, she described the vocation of the Precious Blood Sisters, "they will work diligently in the buffeted barque of the Church, will pour the balm of prayer on her deep wounds, and burn to give their blood, their life, the very marrow of their bones to defend her holy cause" (*Sitio*, beginning at line 90).

By 1977, because of the high cost of maintenance, the need for major repairs and the loss of privacy and quiet in the neighbourhood, the Sisters sold the Talbot Street property and built a smaller monastery on land at 301 Ramsey Road donated by the Ursuline Sisters. During the long period of construction, thanks to the gracious spirit of hospitality of the Sisters of St. Joseph, the core group of Precious Blood Sisters supervising the building of the new monastery lived at Mount St. Joseph.

When the Institute began, each monastery was autonomous. In 1949, at the request of the first General Chapter, the Congregation for Religious issued a Decree to the English-speaking monasteries of Canada for the formation of a Generalate. The London monastery was chosen as the Motherhouse and Central Novitiate. The first general superior was Mother St. Patrick Doyle, who had come with the original foundation from Toronto. Along with her Council, she planted seeds for developing a centralized form of government. The initial years were difficult ones, but the community remembers the persevering efforts of that generation with gratitude.

The Sisters of the Precious Blood are devoted to a life of prayer, silence and work, punctuated each day by time for recreation. Their lifestyle has been simplified in accordance with the recommendations of the Second Vatican Council, but the essentials remain the same as in the time of Mother Catherine Aurelia. The challenge of finding new ways of expressing her unique devotion to the Precious Blood of Jesus, and her zeal for the salvation of all people in union with the redemptive mission that Jesus gave the Church, continues to this day. The *Constitutions* of the Congregation elaborate:

Mother Catherine Aurelia entered deeply into the Paschal mystery. Contemplation of the infinite love of God expressed in Christ's passion and death brought her to a unique appreciation of His Precious Blood. The Blood of the Saviour, symbolizing His love and His triumph through suffering, became the source of her spirituality. She saw in the manner of its shedding, a sign of His love unappreciated and of the gift of salvation rejected by many.

Meditating on the words of Jesus from the Cross, "I thirst," she understood that this cry expressed the thirst of God for the love of His people. In union with Jesus, she thirsted and cried out through prayer and penance for those who do not yet know the salvation of God, for those who are indifferent to what God has done for them in His Son (*Constitutions*, Introduction, 3-4).

The heart of the Sisters' life in community is their love of Jesus and their faith in him. The communal celebration of the Eucharist is their principal daily act of worship. Several times throughout the day they gather in the chapel as a community to pray the Liturgy of the Hours. Time is provided morning and evening for personal meditation, and throughout the day for visits to the Blessed Sacrament and prayers in honour of the Precious Blood. During these times the Sisters are especially mindful of all those who are relying

on their prayers that day. Each Sister makes a nightly hour of prayer in a spirit of reparation in the presence of the Blessed Sacrament. One of the special mandates left to them by their Foundress is to pray for priests: "Women committed to reparation will pray also for hearts torn by suffering and haunted by despair; they will pray for the just to be more just, the virgin to be more virginal, the priest more holy, the ardor of his zeal more living and that he be a worthy minister of the Precious Blood" (*Sitio*, beginning at line 81). The Sisters pray daily for the local Church and the priests of the diocese.

Along with their prayer life, the Sisters are occupied with various duties within the monastery and with works undertaken for their support. From their earliest days in the London diocese, they have provided the altar breads for many of the local churches. They respond to the needs of those who seek their help by offering prayers and sacrifices for them. Over the years a strong spiritual bond has grown between the Sisters and the countless friends who unite with them in adoration of the Precious Blood and who share in the fruits of their life of prayer.

Today, the general superior, other administrative Sisters and the new members of the Precious Blood community who are in formation reside at the London monastery. In the name of the Church of the diocese of London, and for the needs of the Universal Church, the Sisters keep up their work of prayer and sacrifice begun in 1913.

Submitted by Sister Carol Forhan. **Sources:** Sisters Adorers of the Precious Blood (London, Ontario), *Annals of the Community*; *Constitutions of the Congregation of the Sisters Adorers of the Precious Blood, London, Ontario, Book One* (1982); Mother Catherine Aurelia, *The Sitio: A Legacy Left to Her Daughters*, in *Constitutions*, 66-74. See also: Eileen Mary Walsh, "Linked from the Beginning – 85 Years Later," St. Peter's Seminary, *Alumni Bulletin* (1996-1997), 21-25.

11. Congregation of the Most Holy Redeemer (Redemptorists, CSSR)

During 1856 and 1857, the Detroit-based Father Francis Krutil, CSSR, a brilliant polyglot who preached in eleven languages and could hear confessions in thirteen, gave missions to Polish, Bohemian and German immigrants, as well as to French-Canadian Catholics, in the recently erected diocese of London. He preached in Port Stanley, Simcoe, Windham, Paris, London and many other villages and towns of Southwestern Ontario. Early in his episcopate, Bishop Pinsoneault offered to the Redemptorists the care of Chatham and environs where 6,000 Catholics of various nationalities lived. Despite the many tempting and repeated offers of different places in the diocese made to them, the Redemptorists judged that there were too few of them to establish a house anywhere in Canada until 1873, when the community opened one in Québec City. But missionaries from Detroit, and then from Québec City, continued to give missions and clergy retreats throughout the diocese of London.

While scouting new sites for Redemptorist foundations, in 1912, Father John McPhail, CSSR, met Bishop Fallon. A foundation in the diocese of London would be an opportunity for Canadian Redemptorists to give missions. McPhail agreed with Fallon that in the English language lay the future of the Catholic Church outside of Québec in Canada, and that English-speaking Redemptorists, rather than their more numerous French-speaking confrères, should have a presence in the diocese. Fallon then sent a formal invitation to the English-Canadian Redemptorists to establish themselves in the city of London. They were delighted to accept a new foundation in an area with so many Catholics and potential vocations and several parishes eager to host Redemptorist missions. More importantly, they were convinced that London, with its temperate climate would be an excellent place to build a house of studies — either a minor or major seminary. The London foundation was canonically erected in 1913.

The American Redemptorists loaned their Canadian counterparts the money to buy thirty acres (12.1 hectares) of land for a minor seminary, a house and a church. McPhail quickly bought land, built a temporary house and a small church and dedicated both of them to St. Patrick. Father Peter N. Doyle, CSSR, an American, was the first superior. The Redemptorists' chronicles announced, "Thus was the dream entertained [by] Redemptorist Missioners fulfilled, their fervent prayers answered." Of the four

altar boys who served the first Mass at St. Patrick's, Joseph and Wilfrid O'Donnell became Redemptorist priests. London quickly became an important missionary house, as McPhail foresaw. The small house in the city was gradually enlarged into the ideal Redemptorist parish centre, with substantial extensions to the church and the construction of a new and larger monastery, which was also intended to serve as a retirement home for English-Canadian Redemptorists. The only element missing was the minor seminary. St. Patrick's parish did not have enough land for one.

In 1929, the Redemptorists of English Canada purchased Woodstock Baptist College and turned it into a major seminary. The first community moved from Montréal to the quiet of spacious Woodstock and began teaching classes in September 1930. Thirty-six acres (14.6 hectares) of rolling pasture and woods were enough to contain the energies of a hundred students. Arthur T. Coughlan, CSSR, was the first rector of St. Alphonsus Seminary. Lack of money during the Great Depression forced the Redemptorists to turn much of the seminary into a farm managed by the Redemptorist brothers and students. Still, with houses in London and Woodstock, the community was very much a part of the growth of the Catholic Church in the diocese of London. Vocations from the diocese to the Redemptorist brotherhood and priesthood increased. Almost every English-Canadian Redemptorist after 1930 was ordained by either Bishop Kidd or Bishop Cody. Father John Keogh, CSSR, rector of Woodstock, was a cousin to Bishop Kidd, and relations between the Redemptorists and the diocese became especially close during Kidd's episcopacy.

The driving force behind an English-Canadian Redemptorist foundation in Windsor was John Lambert, CSSR, who lobbied his community and Bishop Cody to establish the Redemptorists in the city. Cody initially offered Holy Rosary parish in 1951, but the following year the Redemptorists asked for and received Lambert's home parish of St. Alphonsus. Located in the business section of the city, the parish had an eighty-five-year-old church, a hall, a large rectory and a school staffed by the Ursuline sisters.

When the Basilian-run Assumption College of Windsor became an independent university in 1953, the Redemptorists asked the Basilians to make St. Alphonsus seminary in Woodstock an affiliate of Assumption. Affiliation would allow Redemptorist students to earn Bachelor of Arts degrees, which were demanded by many diocesan seminaries, teachers' colleges and graduate schools. To effect the change in status, the Redemptorists abandoned Woodstock, long condemned as a fire hazard, and Woodstock itself, to move into Holy Redeemer College in Windsor, in 1957. Redemptorists on staff at Holy Redeemer became lecturers at Assumption University and after 1963 at the University of Windsor.

Following the suggestion of Father Martin Foley, CSSR, that either London or Windsor would be an appropriate centre for a regional mission, so that additional Redemptorists and other missionaries, such as the Passionists and the Vincentians, could reach more people on an individual basis, the Redemptorists wrote to Bishop Carter in the spring of 1964 about holding a General Mission. Carter welcomed the proposal and made known his desire for a catechetical centre in the diocese. Father Edward Boyce, CSSR, led a General Mission to update the diocese according to the recent teachings of the Second Vatican Council, and Father Emmanuel Demerah, CSSR, was the first director of the Divine Word Centre.

Boyce, Demerah and the missionaries stationed at St. Alphonsus in Windsor prayed, "Just as Pope John described the [Second] Vatican Council as a second Pentecost so we hope that the General Mission will be a second Pentecost on the local level." Redemptorists from across Canada were invited to participate in the mission, as soon as the sociological studies and other preparations were completed in 1967. The diocese successfully adapted the studies, grouping parishes into pastoral zones, each one having different pastoral approaches. It was hoped that such groupings would lead to more effective diocesan planning and better-informed local leadership. Bishop Carter then asked the Redemptorists to give a General Mission to the parishes of Middlesex County.

The Redemptorists sent their missionaries to the Divine Word Centre in London for further training. The missionaries were grouped into bands of four men, and the first such band was stationed at Holy Redeemer College in Windsor. It served as a model mission band and also assisted the General Mission in the diocese of London.

The Windsor mission band transferred to St. Alphonsus parish and later to a private home in the city to avoid conflicts between its own missions and the work of Holy Redeemer College and St. Alphonsus parish. The mission team traveled throughout eastern Canada, wearing secular clothes, encouraging school children to call them by their first names and introducing audio-visual materials, new liturgical songs and a lighter atmosphere to the entire mission. Controversies erupted when some parents and diocesan clergy questioned the Redemptorists' orthodoxy and such practices as late-night meetings, group confessions, communion in the hand, a more casual approach to church authority and an increased emphasis on personal conscience. Some wondered why so little time was spent on heaven, hell and original sin, which had been prominent topics in traditional missions. Although the team felt that it was preaching in the spirit of the Second Vatican Council, and initially had Bishop Carter's protection, the complaints continued, leading the bishop and the Redemptorists to agree to remove the mission from the diocese.

Because of a decline in the number of vocations and a significant exodus of religious in the wake of the Second Vatican Council, the Redemptorists decided to concentrate on missions rather than parish work. They withdrew from St. Patrick's in January 1975 and from St. Alphonsus in June 1984. Holy Redeemer College ended its seminary and arts teaching and reinvented itself as a retreat centre.

But the effort to manage the buildings and programs with so few Redemptorists at hand convinced the community to close the college in 1991. It was sold in 1994 to a private Catholic school. Since then, one Redemptorist, Father Desmond Scanlon, CSSR, continues to live and work in the retreat movement in the diocese of London. When invited, Redemptorist missionaries from other parts of Canada give missions, renewals and retreats to

parishes, schools and other Catholic groups in the diocese, continuing a tradition begun by Father Krutil in 1856.

Submitted by Paul Laverdure. **Sources:** Paul Laverdure, *Redemption and Renewal: The Redemptorists of English Canada, 1834-1994* (Toronto: 1996).

12. Sisters of the Good Shepherd (RGS)

Known initially as the Religious of Our Lady of Charity of the Refuge, the Sisters of the Good Shepherd have as their origin a group of women who were brought together by St. John Eudes in Caën, France in 1641, for the purpose of rescuing young women from a life on the streets. At the time of the French Revolution, there were seven autonomous Houses of Refuge in France, but none survived the anti-Church violence and general upheaval of the Revolution. The community experienced a second founding at a House of Refuge in Tours, France, in 1814, under the inspired leadership of Rose-Virginie Pelletier. In religious life, she was known as Sister Maria Euphrasia, and she was canonized in 1940.

The Good Shepherd Convent in Toronto is responsible for the Windsor foundation. Late in 1928, Bishop Fallon invited the Sisters to the diocese of London. Fallon had been promised ten acres (4.5 hectares) of land in South Windsor and $10,000 in cash, on condition that the Sisters start to build their convent on the property prior to May 1930. He sweetened the enticement by promising the Sisters an additional $5,000.

Five Sisters came in May and June 1929: Mother Alphonsus Sullivan, superior, Sister Juliana Holland, Sister Mary Immaculate Heart Todd, Sister Gerard Higgins and Sister Mary of the Incarnation Clancy. Their first convent was the old and substantial McEwan mansion, at 9 (now 131) McEwan Avenue in Holy Name of Mary parish. Father John A. Rooney, his housekeeper and the ladies of the parish went to extraordinary lengths to welcome the Sisters in their new home. Several families provided dining room furniture and food and took care of the gardens and lawn. On 7 June 1929, the Feast of the Sacred Heart, Father Rooney celebrated the convent's foundation Mass. By August, there were in residence five Sisters, four girls and one candidate for the

community.

Shortage of room was a problem from the start, and soon the Sisters had to turn away girls recommended to their care. To compound their problems, they were told that they would be unable to take possession of the gift of land in South Windsor because of a prolonged dispute between Bishop Fallon and the realty company that held title to the property. On 6 May 1930, Father Rooney and Father Ralph H. Dignan, sensing an impending disaster for the Sisters, approached a dying Bishop Fallon and asked him to help the Sisters find new accommodations. He approved a loan of $50,000 at five percent per annum to buy three buildings on four acres of property at the corner of Prince Road and College Avenue, the former site of the Essex Golf and Country Club. This was no gift, but it was the only solution at hand.

The Great Depression had already begun, and the decade leading up to the Second World War was an anxious time for the community. Very quickly, the number of girls increased to twenty-four. The Sisters opened an on-site laundry as an employment opportunity for the older girls while they taught the younger ones the regular school curriculum. One of the community's greatest assets during these years of penury was the superior, Mother Alphonsus. She had a friendly nature and a genuine spirit of gratitude for even the smallest gifts sent to the convent. Her own spirit of poverty and her deep faith endeared her to the countless people in Windsor who became generous benefactors of the Sisters' work.

On 24 September 1937, the convent at Windsor was received into the Generalate of the Sisters of the Good Shepherd.

Following the Second World War, the Sisters adapted to changing social circumstances, providing an institutional setting for teenage girls who had no other place where they could deal with their problems. They received a well-balanced program of specialized education, including practical courses in business, home economics and hairdressing, and a range of up-to-date social services designed to meet their specific psychological and spiritual needs. This was the beginning of Maryvale.

In 1968, at the request of the Ontario government, the present cottage system with a completely open setting was inaugurated. The Sisters oversaw the construction of six split-level homes, chapel, convent, administration offices, school gymnasium, indoor swimming pool and infirmary. The property was expanded from the original four acres, purchased in 1930, to 17.5 acres (7.08 hectares). Regular government grants financed an expanded curriculum and the engagement of professional lay staff.

Owing to a decline in vocations to the religious life, the Sisters of the Good Shepherd withdrew from Maryvale and Windsor in May 1988, after fifty-eight years of selfless service. Although the word pioneer is overused, the Sisters of the Good Shepherd at Maryvale definitely took the lead in the provision of educational opportunities for troubled girls and young women who did not fit into the regular school system. Remaining behind in Windsor was a band of Sisters from the contemplative branch of the community. In 2005, there were seven Sisters at Maryvale, assisting the poor and needy in their midst and praying daily for the success of the worldwide Good Shepherd apostolate. They also continue to be a positive and generous presence among the girls at Maryvale, who appreciate the Sister's work on their behalf at Thanksgiving, Christmas, Easter and other times during the school year.

Submitted by Sister Therese Alice, RSG.
Sources: Sisters of the Good Shepherd, Toronto, Ontario, Archives and *Annals of the Community*; "Good Shepherd, Sisters of Our Lady of Charity of the," *New Catholic Encyclopedia*, vol. 6 (New York: 1967), 627; Windsor Roman Catholic Separate School Board Centennial Committee, *Gift of Catholic Education: Contribution of Religious Orders to the Windsor Area 1816-1992* (1992), 61-62.

13. Other Religious communities

Brothers of the Christian Schools (FSC)

The Institute of the Brothers of the Christian Schools, known popularly as the Christian Brothers, was founded in Rheims, France in 1680 by a young French priest, Jean Baptiste de La Salle (died 1719). From its earliest days, the Institute steadily grew until it became the largest non-clerical Congregation of Religious men devoted to Catholic and Christian education and is now found in some eighty countries.

The Christian Brothers came to Montréal in 1837. Having established themselves there, they were able to send a few Brothers to begin an apostolate in Toronto. In 1920, a small band of Brothers from Toronto settled in London, Ontario and began teaching at Sacred Heart school and the following year at St. Peter's school. Brother Tatian Edward was the superior. His confreres were Brothers Victor, Edwin, Jerome, Theobold, Ambrose and T. Bernard. Their residence was Brendan Hall on Ridout Street. A few years later, the Sisters of St. Joseph took over St. Peter's school, and the Brothers moved their high school classes into the parish hall of St. Peter's cathedral at 520 Richmond Street and named it De La Salle High School.

During the more than thirty years that the Christian Brothers were in London, there were some notable superiors and exceptional teachers among them. The third superior was Brother Roger Philip (1923-26), who was also a visiting professor at the University of Western Ontario. In 1956, he set up the department of psychology at Assumption University and was its head until he retired in 1962. He was president of the Ontario Psychological Association in 1960 and was named an honourary president of the association in 1971; and he was granted an honourary doctorate by the University of Windsor in 1964. Another interesting superior was Brother Francis (1926-29). He brought distinction to himself and his school, as well as to the Brothers, not only in the field of academics but also in the area of music, especially Gregorian Chant. Brother Ignatius Powell (1932-38), a gentleman and a scholar, gave great service to the students in the field of English literature. Two others worthy of mention are Brother Romauld (1944-47), and Brother Stanislaus (1938-44 and 1947-52), who was the last Brother who was principal at De La Salle High School when the Brothers withdrew from London in 1952.

Other Brothers left their mark as capable teachers and as ambassadors for the Christian Brothers in the diocese of London. These include Brothers Edwin, Herman, Raymond, Alphonse (also called Alexander) and the two Benedicts, Brother Benedict McAvoy and Brother Benedict Taylor. As well as being excellent classroom teachers, they were involved in after-school sports, puppetry and public speaking, in the parishes and the wider community. They were also catechists. In 2005, only two Brothers who worked in the London high school remain. Living in retirement are Brother Martin O'Connell, who was a student at De La Salle High School and later a teacher there, from 1947 to 1952, and Brother Edmund Coates, who was on staff in 1938 and 1939.

In 1969, Brother Sylvester (Edmund Miner, PhD) began a thirty-year career as an English professor at King's College, University of Western Ontario. After his official retirement, he continued to teach and tutor students on a part-time basis. His brother, Brother Bonaventure (John Miner, PhD), was head of the history department at the University of Windsor and a well-liked professor of the university's European summer school program. He wrote *The Grammar Schools of Medieval England*, but he died very suddenly in May 1987 before he had completed it for publication. Brother Sylvester edited the manuscript, which was published in 1990.

In 1924, a second group of Brothers were sent to teach in Sandwich East (now a part of Windsor). They lived on Marentette Avenue in Immaculate Conception parish. The first superior was Brother Gregory Green. On staff were Brothers Leo, Bernard, Andrew, Clement, Arthur and Gerald. For many years, the Brothers taught in four elementary schools and, from 1961 to 1969, at St. Gabriel High School. Good schoolmen and coaches, they took charge of extra-curricular activities, such as sports, in particular basketball, glee clubs and chancel choirs. They were also active members of the Ontario Education Association and the Ontario English Catholic Teachers' Association (OECTA), serving on the executives at the local and provincial levels of both professional organizations. Superiors, such as Brothers Camillus, Jerome, Maurice, Norbert, Alban, Edgar and Xavier, were admired and long remembered by the Catholic people of Windsor. Brother Jerome, who was superior from 1933 to 1951, was principal of St. Angela's school for eleven years and was so popular among students and parents alike that he was pressed to run for mayor of the city!

The Brothers, once their careers in the classroom ended, pursued other apostolates in Windsor. From 1960 to 1973, they managed a scholasticate on Riverside Drive West, near the campus of the University of Windsor, for young Brothers in their community who were pursuing degrees. Next, it was used as an International Novitiate to train American and Toronto novices. This lasted from 1973 to 1983, when the dwindling number of candidates prompted the Brothers to lease the building for several years to a secular organization. They then reclaimed the building, renovated it and called it The Lasallian Centre. It was a place for teacher colloquiums, student retreats and adult prayer days. The Centre lasted for approximately ten years, at which time the Brothers sold the building and property to the Basilian Fathers of Assumption University and relocated to Toronto.

Submitted by Brother Walter Farrell, FSC.
Sources: Archives of the Brothers of the Christian Schools, Toronto: *Book of Personnel for the Community of Brothers*; *Annals of the Community of Brothers in London*; *Annals of the Community of Brothers in Windsor*.

Brothers of St. Louis (CSA)

The year 2005 marks the fiftieth anniversary of the Brothers of St. Louis in the diocese of London. They have lived in Aylmer and St. Thomas and still have a residence in Sarnia. The Brothers are known for their dedication to Catholic education, their active participation in the life of the local church, their work in Africa and their financial support of many projects in Indonesia, where their confreres from the Netherlands work among the poor.

The Brothers of St. Louis was organized in March 1840 in the Dutch village of Oudenbosch by Vincent Huybrechts (Brother Vincent), Aloysius Fryters (Brother Aloysius) and the parish priest of Oudenbosch, Father Hellemons, who was their longtime chaplain. The new congregation, devoted to the welfare of boys, was dedicated to St. Aloysius Gonzaga, a young Jesuit who died at the age of twenty-three while caring for the sick. He became the patron saint of youth, and his feast day is 21 June.

From the very beginning, Brothers Vincent and Aloysius established a catechism and music school for boys and gave food and shelter to the poorer students. This led to the formation of a boarding school. In 1850, there were 250 boys enrolled in the school. As membership in the community grew, the Brothers had the resources to set up schools in other cities and towns in the predominantly Protestant Netherlands, and in 1864, to send four of their members to Indonesia, then a Dutch colony, to commence the congregation's missionary work.

A century after the Brothers of St. Louis was founded, the occupation and liberation of the Netherlands during the Second World War devastated the country. Between 1946 and 1961, nearly 150,000 Dutch people immigrated to Canada, the bulk of them settling in rural Ontario. At the same time, Pope Pius XII was urging religious orders to send members to Africa. The Brothers of St. Louis initially saw Canada as a place where their future missionaries could learn English as part of their preparation for service in the British colony of Tanganyika (Tanzania).

In 1954, Bishop Cody, who was aware of the intense shortage of teachers for boys and young men, invited the Brothers to serve in the diocese of London. The Dutch-speaking Sacred Heart Fathers of Delaware facilitated the negotiations. Brothers Herbert and James arrived in Canada in March 1955. They purchased a home in Aylmer and were joined in April by Brothers Ambrose, Peter and Francis. Experienced teachers in the Netherlands, and already speaking English, they acquired Ontario teaching qualifications and began to teach in Aylmer-area Catholic schools in September 1955.

The initial group of Brothers was augmented in October 1955 by Brothers Arthur and Aloysius, who attended English classes in St. Joseph High School in St. Thomas, and later by Brothers Anthony, Gregory and Sebastian. The Brothers built Notre Dame House in Aylmer as their community home, and they taught in separate schools in Aylmer and at St. Joseph High School in St. Thomas. They launched a popular Saturday sports program at St. Joseph's, and Brother Peter produced his first operetta, *The Marquis*, in Aylmer.

In the autumn of 1958, Brothers Herbert, James and Ambrose took teaching positions at St. Patricia Junior High School, Sarnia, which added a new wing the following year. More members arrived from the Netherlands, bringing the total in Canada to sixteen. To meet the growing demand for Catholic secondary school education in Sarnia, the Brothers constructed a large junior seminary in 1963. Known as the Juniorate, it was situated on Murphy Road and is currently the front wing of the Twin Lakes Terrace Nursing Home. It enrolled twenty-two boys from Sarnia, Southwestern Ontario and Michigan for its inaugural year. By day, the boys attended St. Patricia's, where the Brothers were members of the staff. By night, they returned to the Juniorate, where the Brothers supervised their studies and recreation. This dedicated but demanding twenty-four-hour routine continued for the next ten years. Brother Patrick came from the Netherlands in 1963 to assist.

In the early sixties, the Brothers embarked on their first missionary activity from Canada. Several Brothers, including Peter and Herbert, left to teach in Tanganyika. Brothers Sebastian and Peter spent some twenty years in Liberia, West Africa. They were expelled during the country's civil war and returned to the Netherlands. Brother Joseph founded an agricultural centre in Liberia, which taught the local population to grow produce for their own use and to sell the surplus in the local markets.

Despite their best efforts, the Brothers of St.

Louis did not attract the Canadian vocations that they so fervently sought. In 1968, they closed Notre Dame House in Aylmer, and in 1975, they sold the Juniorate, which signaled new directions for them. The General Chapter discussed but voted down a proposal that would have given the Brothers the option of ordination to the priesthood while remaining members of the community. Brother Arthur, however, chose to leave and join the diocesan priesthood. He was ordained in 1975 as Father Paul Beck and served the diocese of London until his sudden death on 17 May 2003.

The Brothers taught at St. Patricia and St. Patrick high schools in Sarnia until 1998. In the meantime, they participated in the work of a host of Catholic organizations, such as the Knights of Columbus, Catholic Family Movement, Cursillo, COR youth movement, the Children's Aid Society, the St. Vincent de Paul Society (summer camp at Camlachie), the Mission to Seafarers, the Canadian Catholic Organization for Development and Peace and the Rayjon Foundation that assists Caribbean and Latin American communities. The Brothers had a positive impact on each of these organizations, despite their relatively small numbers.

Today, there are five Brothers of St. Louis in Canada — all in Sarnia — and about another fifty are in the Netherlands.

Submitted by Dennis DesRivieres.

Capuchin Friars (OFM, Cap)

In 1927, Bishop Fallon decided that the Capuchin Fathers from Belgium were particularly suited to the spiritual needs of Flemish and Dutch Catholics who had recently settled in the Blenheim area of Kent County. The bishop's request to the Capuchin Minister General in Rome was referred to the Flemish Capuchins in Belgium, who immediately accepted the invitation. As a result, Father Willibrord Penninckx and Father Ladislaus Segers were the first to be sent to Canada. They were welcomed at the Chatham railway station on 14 September 1927. Their arrival marked the elevation of St. Mary's mission in Blenheim to parish status. On 18 September 1927, Father Ladislaus celebrated the Capuchins' first Mass in their new home.

Father Damas Van Dycke and Brother Marius

Vereecke came in 1928. The addition of these two members helped to establish regular community life in the Blenheim foundation. In great demand wherever Flemish people had settled, the Capuchins spent the opening years of their Kent County ministry giving catechism lessons, regularizing marriages, baptizing children and preparing young people for the sacraments. Their aim was to bring the people back to the Church, and, to a large extent, they were highly successful. Also in 1928, Father Willibrord and Brother Mansuetus Constandt left for St. Boniface, Manitoba.

In the meantime, so many Czechs were immigrating to the area that a morning Sunday Mass was introduced for them at St. Mary's. Father Ladislaus spent considerable time learning the Czech language and even went to study it more intensely in what was then Czechoslovakia.

In 1929, Sacred Heart church in Princeton closed. Bishop Kidd re-opened it in 1941 as a parish and placed it in charge of the Capuchin Friars with Father Damas as pastor. By the end of the 1940s, the parish numbered over 100 families, much to the credit of Father Damas and his successor, Father Masseo Bogaert. Father Otger DeVent was the last Capuchin pastor when the parish returned to the care of diocesan priests on 10 June 1961.

On 27 August 1933, Bishop Kidd blessed St. Anne of the Lakes church in Erieau on the shores of Lake Erie and made it a mission of St. Mary's parish in Blenheim. Father Polycarp Christiaens had been celebrating Mass at various locations in Erieau prior to the opening of the church. Soon, St. Anne's church became the site of an annual pilgrimage for the area's Dutch, Flemish and Czech Catholics. In June 1958, Bishop Cody made St. Anne's a parish and appointed Father Cyrinus Nieuwlandt as the first pastor. The parochial territory included Cedar Springs, Pardoville and Dealtown, where the Southwest Regional Centre was under construction. It opened in June 1961 and over the years would house 1,200 mentally and physically handicapped residents and employ over 2,500 staff.

Father Nieuwlandt seized the moment by building a small church in Pardoville. On 24 June 1962, Bishop Cody blessed the church of Our Lady of the Angels, made it a mission of St. Anne's parish in Erieau and celebrated the mission's first Mass. Four years later, the church needed an addition to accommodate the many Catholics who made it their spiritual home. The priest who served the Pardoville mission was also the chaplain at the Southwest Regional Centre.

In 1967, Bishop Carter gave the Capuchins charge of the combined Essex County parish of Our Lady of Lourdes in Comber, Holy Redeemer in Staples and Star of the Sea on Pelee Island. After the suppression of the parish in Staples, in 1971, the Capuchins remained in the Comber parish until 1972.

Besides parish work, in 1939, the Capuchins built St. Francis Minor Seminary, to educate candidates for the Capuchin community in the high school curriculum as prescribed by the Ontario Department of Education and in accordance with the spirit of the Order. The community purchased a house in Blenheim and opened its doors to the seminary's first four students. Father Eleutherius Olivier was the founder. The Second World War, however, severed all connections with the mother province in Belgium, which cut off the main source of seminary recruits and delayed any chance to build up the seminary staff.

The conclusion of the war was welcomed by all and was a blessing for the Capuchins in the diocese of London. In 1947, four priest-friars from the Flemish Province arrived in Canada; in 1948, a friar from Czechoslovakia joined them; in 1949, the Dutch Province sent four of their own friars; and in 1950, the Dutch sent another. Each of these Capuchins was assigned to St. Francis Minor Seminary. During the next two years, four Canadian-born priest-friars returned to Canada, having completed their theological studies.

The future of St. Francis Minor Seminary was bright. The Capuchins built a new seminary building that was large enough to house twenty-five to thirty students. By 1960, there were five professors and thirty students at the seminary. The following year, the Capuchins determined that the building was too small and built a larger seminary just south of Orangeville in the diocese of Toronto.

Today, the Capuchin Friars remain in charge of St. Mary's in Blenheim and of St. Anne of the Lakes parish, which reverted to mission status in May 2007.

Submitted by Father Paul Duplessie, OFM, Cap.

Congregation of the Resurrection (Resurrectionists, CR)

In 1930, the Resurrectionists (CRs) of the Ontario-Kentucky Province purchased five acres of land adjacent to St. Peter's seminary and commenced construction of St. Thomas Scholasticate, now called Aquinas House. Prior to 1930, Resurrectionist scholastics from this Province studied alongside their American confreres either in Rome or at St. John Cantius Seminary in St. Louis, Missouri, earning their degrees through St. Louis University. The Ontario Ministry of Education, however, did not recognize their qualifications for teaching in Ontario, so the community decided to establish a Canadian house of studies that would be linked to a major seminary affiliated with a university. St. Peter's Seminary, which was affiliated with the University of Western Ontario, was the obvious choice. Bishop Fallon gave his blessing to the project, perhaps one of the last significant decisions of his episcopacy before dying.

On 22 September 1930, Father Fred Arnold, the rector, two priest assistants, three lay brothers and sixteen scholastics moved into St. Peter's seminary, while the scholasticate was still under construction. It opened on 29 November 1930. Father Arnold wrote to Father Michael Jaglowicz, the superior general, that "The reception accorded to us by the seminary Fathers was 'to say the least' wonderful. They seem not to be able to do enough for us. They certainly have shown how glad they are at our entry into the diocese." The philosophy students took their courses at the seminary and Western (and later at King's College), and the theology students did their work at St. Peter's. Many scholastics came from Ontario, after graduating from Grade 13, while others had graduated from St. Mary's College in Kentucky, a Resurrectionist minor seminary. To fit into the Ontario university program, these scholastics enrolled in a preliminary year at Western. Fathers Ernie Schumacher, Carl Fritz and Charlie Schoenbacchler followed this route. Also, many scholastics, earmarked for the teaching apostolate, were able to take summer courses in their teachable subjects at Western.

St. Thomas Scholasticate was built during the first full year of the Great Depression, making it one of the few grand projects in the diocese for many decades (another project, St. Peter's seminary chapel, opened on 18 June 1930). Money was scarce, and the scholasticate had to be as self-sufficient as possible. The students, who remained at the scholasticate year round, were very busy every summer and autumn, growing and canning their own fruits and vegetables and raising their own chickens. One summer, they hauled enough clay from the bed of the River Thames to construct two tennis courts. They also served Mass for the priests at St. Peter's, in the days before concelebration, and they waited on tables at the seminary during retreats.

The first Resurrectionists from St. Thomas Scholasticate to be ordained were Norbert Dentinger and Fabian Dietrich, on 21 June 1931, in Woodstock. Bishop Gerald C. Murray of Victoria, British Columbia, was the celebrant, in lieu of a bishop from the diocese of London, Bishop Fallon having died the previous February.

During the 1950s, there were so many vocations that St. Thomas Scholasticate could no longer house all their students (in 1959, there were three priests, thirty-two students and three lay brothers living there). To relieve the overcrowding, some theology students were sent to Rome and others to St. John Cantius in St. Louis, Missouri, an ironical solution that did not last very long. The American Resurrectionists also had numerous vocations and were unable to cope with an additional influx from Canada. A new solution was sought. In 1964, the philosophy program was moved to St. Eugene's College, to the west of St. Jerome's College on the campus of the University of Waterloo. Left behind were twelve theology students, their rector, Father John F. Miles, his two assistant priests and three Brothers. In the 1970s, St. Eugene's amalgamated with Resurrection College, a college-level seminary located in Kitchener, also run by the Resurrectionists, which provided pre-theology courses to candidates for the diocesan priesthood. The new college retained the name Resurrection, with most seminarians, both Resurrectionist and diocesan, proceeding to St. Peter's seminary for their theology.

In 1982, the Resurrectionists left St. Thomas Scholasticate and sold the building to the diocese of London. By this time, with a decline in vocations, it had become too large for the number of theology students resident there. The community decided to send their students to the Toronto School of Theology.

The scholasticate produced three bishops — Bernard Murphy and Brian Hennessey in Bermuda and Nino Marzoli in Bolivia — two superiors general of the Congregation of the Resurrection — Hubert Gehl and Sutherland MacDonald — two presidents of St. Jerome's College — Cornelius Siegfried and John Finn — and one of the founders of Laurentian University in Sudbury — Norman Weaver.

Besides St. Thomas Scholasticate, the Resurrectionists were involved in high school teaching, albeit briefly, and parochial work in the diocese of London. From 1953 to 1956, Fathers Dominic Kirwan and John Miles taught at Catholic Central High School and lived at the scholasticate. In 1972, Bishop Carter asked the Resurrectionists to assume pastoral responsibility for St. Joseph's parish in Kingsbridge, which was near their summer residence, "Huronia," and the parish's two missions: St. Augustine in East Wawanosh Township and St. Mary in Lucknow. Father Edward Dentinger and Brother Carl Voll formed the first pastoral team. Father Harry Reitzel was the last Resurrectionist pastor of St. Joseph's, from 1989 to 2003. When he departed, seventy-three years of a Resurrectionist presence in the diocese of London came to an end.

During those years, priests and seminarians of the Congregation of the Resurrection assisted in parishes and pastoral programs, did chaplaincy work in hospitals and on military bases, gave spiritual direction and heard confessions in convents and conducted retreats with Sisters and students — always sharing with others the Resurrectionist charism of hope. The scholastics learned a great deal about friendship and sportsmanship in their games of baseball, football, basketball and hockey with their counterparts at St. Peter's seminary. On countless occasions, St. Thomas Scholasticate offered hospitality to the faculty and students of the seminary, in return for the hospitality received at St. Peter's by the Resurrectionists beginning on the first day they had set foot in the seminary, in 1930. Those Resurrectionists who lived, studied and served in the diocese of London recognize that their lives were enhanced by their relationships with the bishops, priests, religious and laity of the diocese. Special in the memory of many Resurrectionists is the fine education that they had received at St. Peter's seminary.

Submitted by Father Paul Voisin, CR, and Father Charlie Fedy, CR. See also Charlie Fedy and Paul Voisin, "St. Thomas Scholasticate: a 50-Year Partnership with St. Peter's Seminary," St. Peter's Seminary, *The Alumni Bulletin* (2004), 19-23.

Congregation of St. Michael the Archangel (Michaelite Fathers, CSMA)

Blessed Bronisław Markiewicz, the founder of the Congregation of St. Michael the Archangel, was born on 13 July 1842, in Prochnik, a small town in southeastern Poland, and was ordained a priest, on 15 September 1867, by Bishop Antoni Monastyrski for the diocese of Przemyśl. From the beginning of his priestly life, he was recognized and credited for his tireless and devoted work for the poor, especially for children and youth. He spoke boldly against social injustice and national vices, and he believed that the proper upbringing and education of children and young people was the solution to all social problems.

Father Markiewicz went to Turin, Italy, on 30 November 1885, and stayed there for seven years, working closely with St. John Bosco, the great nineteenth-century educator who died in 1888. While there, he became a member of the Salesian Fathers. After returning to Poland in 1892, he began to organize social services for orphans and underprivileged children, in addition to his regular pastoral duties at Miejsce. He established orphanages and a complete system of education, including vocational schools. His goal was to teach young people Christian values and to prepare them in a practical way for life and work, guiding them to God and pointing them in the right direction as they came to make decisions concerning their future.

On 23 September 1897, Father Markiewicz applied to the bishop of Przemyśl and to Pope Leo XIII for permission to found the Moderation and Work Society, a forerunner of the Congregation of St. Michael the Archangel. That same year he left the Salesian Fathers, with their approval. Although the statutes of Father Markiewicz's Society were affirmed in 1898, and Leo XIII gave his blessing to its work, Father Markiewicz did not live to see the formal establishment of the Congregation. He

died on 29 January 1912. Archbishop Adam Stefan Sapieha of Kraków is credited with founding the Congregation on 29 September 1921. The Holy See gave its approval with a *Decretum Laudis* (Decree of Praise), on 15 January 1966. Pope Benedict XVI beatified Father Markiewicz on 19 June 2005.

The spirituality of the Congregation of St. Michael the Archangel is expressed in two mottos: "Who is like God" and "Moderation and Work." The first motto, the call of St. Michael the Archangel, is a manifestation of God's greatness, His love and His goodness, and also of one's readiness to fight and to die for Him. The Congregation has two martyrs among its members: Blessed Father Władysław Błazdinski (1908-44) and Blessed Father Wojciech Nierychlewski (1903-42). They were beatified on 13 June 1999. The second motto stresses the virtue of work and embodies the simplicity and modesty of its members' way of life. They are constantly striving towards excellence in all three human dimensions — spiritual, intellectual and physical — which is necessary in order to honour and to serve God and His people to the best of one's ability.

As of November 2007 the Congregation had 358 members, including 257 priests, 17 brothers, and 62 seminarians. (A Congregation of Sisters of St. Michael the Archangel was founded in 1928, and there are two apostolic groups for both the clergy and the laity.) Twelve priests, 17 seminarians, and 2 novices were from countries other than Poland. Members of the Congregation can also be found in Ukraine, Belarus, Germany, France, Austria, Switzerland, Italy, Australia, Paraguay, Argentina, Papua New Guinea, the Dominican Republic and Canada.

In 1956, Bishop Cody of London visited Poland. At the time, Polish Catholics, in particular religious orders, were severely persecuted by the Communist government. There was a great concern that many religious would not survive the oppression. When Bishop Cody met with Cardinal Stefan Wyszynski, the Polish Primate, he asked the cardinal what the Church in Canada might do to help alleviate the situation. The cardinal suggested that Bishop Cody invite members from some of the religious communities into his diocese. The bishop then extended an invitation to the Michaelite Fathers, but it took several years before any of their members could leave Poland for Canada.

The Congregation of St. Michael the Archangel

was established in the diocese of London on 22 July 1962. Father Bartlomiej Slawinski was the first to arrive, followed by Father Ed Mucha and Father Stan Soltysik in 1968. Since then, many more members of the Congregation have come to serve the people of the diocese. Some arrived in Canada already ordained to the priesthood, and others came as seminarians, who completed their studies at St. Peter's Seminary and were ordained by the bishop of London.

At the beginning, members of the Congregation worked only in Polish-speaking parishes, but as time passed, they became more acclimatized to their new home and took up pastoral work in English-speaking parishes. Besides their custody of Our Lady of Częstochowa parish in London, the Congregation has sent priests to St. Mary's parish (London), St. Agnes parish (Chatham), St. Joseph's parish (Stratford), Holy Cross parish and Holy Trinity parish (Woodstock) and Queen of Peace parish (Sarnia). The community house is located on Sunningdale Road West in London.

Submitted by the Michaelite Fathers of London.

Little Flower Congregation (CST Fathers)

On 19 March 1931, Father Thomas Panat, later known as Father Basilius, established a society of Brothers under the title of Little Flower Brotherhood in Kerala, India. In 1945, the society was reorganized and renamed the Little Flower Congregation, so that not only Brothers but also priests could be members. Father Basilius wrote the Constitution, which was approved by Archbishop Mar Kandathil on 8 October 1947. Nine years later, the Congregation welcomed the first priest ordained for the community.

The Brothers expressed a desire for greater autonomy, and, after careful study and mature discussion, the Holy See decided to erect two distinct Congregations *juris eparchialis*. The community of the priests was canonically erected as a Clerical Congregation *juris eparchialis* on 8 December 1978 and named Little Flower Congregation (CST Fathers). Pope John Paul II raised the Congregation to the status of a Religious Institute of Pontifical Right on 21 December 1995.

Little Flower Congregation has provinces in Kerala, South India, North India and Nepal. Its members are engaged in various ministries in numerous dioceses. In 2000, Bishop Sherlock invited the Congregation to serve in the diocese of London. Father Francis Thekkumkattil, who had been in the archdiocese of Toronto since 1994, was the contact person and was subsequently appointed as the pastor of the clustered parishes of St. Boniface in Zurich and St. Peter in St. Joseph, effective 28 June 2001. Following the death of Father Paul Beck in 2003, Father Francis also became the pastor of Immaculate Heart of Mary parish in Grand Bend, bringing the clustering of the three parishes into full implementation.

In November 2002, Father Thomas Kuriacko Cherusseril joined Father Francis as associate pastor of St. Boniface and St. Peter. In December 2003, Father John Joseph Kulathinkal joined Father Francis and Father Thomas. Beginning on 1 March 2004, Father Thomas has been associate pastor of St. Peter in Goderich and Father John has been associate pastor of the parishes in Zurich, St. Joseph and Grand Bend.

Submitted by Little Flower Congregation.

Missionary Oblates of Mary Immaculate (OMI)

The Oblates of Mary Immaculate is a religious order of priests and brothers founded at Aix-en-Provence, France, in 1816, by Bishop Charles-Joseph-Eugène de Mazenod. The Oblate motto is "He has sent me to preach the Gospel to the poor. The poor will be evangelized." The community's first mission foundation was Montréal, where they arrived in December 1841, and very quickly the Oblates were in charge of Native missions. Within a decade, they had brought the Gospel to the remotest regions of northern Canada, from Labrador in the east to Hudson Bay in the north to the Alaskan boundary in the west. They are credited with "conquering" Western Canada for the Church, and in nearly every instance they were named the first vicars apostolic and bishops in Western dioceses.

The only Oblate bishop in the diocese of London was Bishop Fallon, from 1909 to 1931. Before he became bishop, he had been a student and then a professor at the Oblate-run University of Ottawa and provincial of the American Oblate province headquartered at Holy Angels in Buffalo, New York. During his lengthy episcopate, he built St. Peter's seminary, helped to found Brescia College for Catholic women and was instrumental in its affiliation with the University of Western Ontario and redecorated the interior of St. Peter's cathedral.

The Oblates of St. Peter's Province, Ottawa, returned to the diocese in 1962, with a residence on Dufferin Avenue in London, and took up high school teaching, social work and parish ministry. Father Harold J. Conway was the first superior, principal of Catholic Central High School and subsequently a recipient of the Order of Canada in recognition of his many contributions to Catholic education. Other Oblates at Catholic Central over the years were: Father Peter A. Sutton, who in 1974 was named bishop of Labrador-Schefferville and later as archbishop of Keewatin-LePas, Manitoba; Father William B. Thompson; Father Frank Kavanagh, who, like Conway, became president of OECTA; Father Frank Hennessy, Father Paul Howard and Father Joe Redmond.

The Oblates also taught at John Paul II high school and St. Thomas Aquinas high school in London. In addition, they were social workers at the Catholic Family Agency in the city; established Mary Immaculate parish under the direction of Father Cornelius Herlihy, who was succeeded by Father Kevin McNamara and Father John O'Connor; worked on behalf of COR, a weekend retreat movement for high school students that recently celebrated its eightieth weekend in the London deanery; and managed Camp Oskiniko, a cultural exchange for parents and students from London and Southwestern Ontario and the Cree children from the diocese of Moosonee. Founded by Father Sutton, Camp Oskiniko was subsequently directed by Father Redmond.

There are currently three Oblates of Mary Immaculate in the diocese of London: Fathers William Thompson, Joe Redmond and Alessandro Costa.

Submitted by Father Joe Redmond, OMI.

Priests of the Sacred Heart of Jesus (SCJ)

Father Léon Dehon founded the Priests of the Sacred Heart of Jesus in 1884, in France, and moved the motherhouse to Brussels, Belgium in 1901, when France outlawed religious communities. In 1910, Father Dehon attended the Eucharistic Congress in Montréal. During the congress, he spoke with several Canadian bishops about the possibility of sending members of his community in Europe to work in Canada. These bishops were only too happy to have more priests as there was a special need for Catholic priests in the Prairie Provinces, which were then opening up to new immigrants. Soon, six French-speaking Sacred Heart Fathers were in Canada, serving Catholics in a string of parishes and missions along the Grand Trunk Railway and its recently completed extension into the West, the Grand Trunk Pacific Railway, form Montréal to Edmonton.

Over the years, the community's presence became largely concentrated in Montréal. The year 1948 witnessed the beginning of large-scale immigration of Dutch Catholics to rural Southwestern Ontario, and the arrival in Canada of two Sacred Heart Fathers from the SCJ province in Holland: John R. Van Burren and Alphonse Vandervorst. They initially lived with their French-speaking confreres in Montréal, but, on 2 January 1950, they were officially accepted in the diocese of London, where many Dutch-speaking Catholics had settled, with many more to come. Fathers Van Burren and Vandevorst then purchased a 300-acre (121 ha) property with an imposing manor house and farm buildings near the village of Delaware. Afraid that they might encounter anti-Catholic hostility, they wore old clothes and never revealed that they were priests when they viewed the property.

The house turned out to be suitable for a modest junior seminary for high school students. It opened in September 1950 with eighteen students. There were nine in grade nine and nine in the remaining grades. Their teachers were Fathers John Van Burren, Adrian Marijnen and Evert Baay. Father John Van Damme, who is now a diocesan priest, was enrolled in grade nine in the class of 1950 and was the first student from the junior seminary to be ordained for the Sacred Heart Fathers in the diocese.

As part of the negotiations between Bishop Kidd and the Sacred Heart Fathers was the bishop's insistence that the junior seminary should be open to any student who felt a call to the priesthood or religious life — he should be completely free to choose a vocation in his own diocese or in any other religious community. During the twenty years that the junior seminary was in operation, the Sacred Heart Fathers faithfully adhered to this stipulation. Fewer than a dozen students joined the Sacred Heart Fathers, while more than a dozen became diocesan priests or members of other religious communities.

Sunday Masses at the seminary chapel were the beginning of Sacred Heart parish in Delaware, which was established in 1951, apparently with Father Van Burren as the first pastor. Parishioners came from a handful of old Irish families, Belgian tobacco farmers and recently arrived Dutch families, who very quickly became a majority in the parish. In 1956, the people built a new church and a separate school in Delaware.

Meanwhile, other Sacred Heart Fathers set up and managed the Catholic Immigration Centre on Kent Street in London. The Centre provided spiritual care for thousands of immigrants and arranged marriage preparation courses, First Friday devotions and picnics for the Dutch. Also, Father John Van Wezel founded the St. Willibrord Credit Union, which became so successful that branches quickly opened in different parts of the diocese. (It is still in business under the name Libro Financial Services.) Father Peter Renders and Father Martin Grootsholten were Father Van Wezel's assistants and each subsequently succeeded him as head of the credit union.

Another apostolate that occupied many Sacred Heart Fathers was the steady provision of weekend assistance in the celebration of Mass in numerous parishes, especially those in the tobacco belt, such as Delhi, Tillsonburg and Aylmer. The Catholics in these towns, if they were not Hungarian, were usually Dutch or Flemish. In addition to presiding at the Eucharist, the Sacred Heart Fathers also heard confession at these parishes — the 1950s and 1960s being a time when frequent confession was the norm — and also at parishes in LaSalette, Langton, West Lorne, Parkhill, Forest and Grand Bend. Lastly, they provided assistance at parishes in Stratford and the surrounding area and in Essex County as needed,

particularly in the days leading up to Christmas and Easter.

It was the policy of the Sacred Heart Fathers never to establish national parishes, since the Dutch were eager to adapt to Canadian ways and parish life. Therefore, ironically, by the 1980s, the community was no longer needed for its ethnic work. They retired from the diocese peacefully, mission accomplished.

Submitted by Father Herman Falke, SCJ. Additional information supplied by Father John Van Damme and Dan Brock. **Sources:** "Dehon, Léon Gustave," *New Catholic Encyclopedia*, vol. 4 (New York: 1967), 721; "Sacred Heart of Jesus, Priests of," *New Catholic Encyclopedia*, vol. 12 (New York: 1967), 826.

Sisters of Loretto (Institute of the Blessed Virgin Mary, IBVM)

The Sisters of Loretto, formerly the Institute of the Blessed Virgin Mary, first arrived in London in November 1855, on the invitation of Dean Thadeus T. Kirwan, the pastor of St. Lawrence the Martyr parish. Three teaching Sisters and one lay Sister moved into the rectory and took up a ministry of teaching and general assistance. The arrangement lasted a mere eight months. Although the Sisters were extremely popular in the parish, the creation of the diocese of London, on 21 February 1856, and the arrival of Bishop Pinsoneault for his installation on 29 June, meant that the Sisters had to leave not only the rectory but also the diocese because Pinsoneault preferred French-speaking religious communities. Father John Holzer, SJ, welcomed the Sisters to the parish of Our Lady in Guelph in the diocese of Hamilton.

The Loretto Sisters returned to the diocese of London twenty-two years later and enjoyed a much longer and more fruitful ministry. In February 1878, Father Edmund Burke Kilroy, pastor of St. Joseph's parish in Stratford, asked Bishop Walsh to invite the Sisters to make a foundation in Stratford. In anticipation of their arrival, Father Kilroy purchased the P.R. Jarvis estate at a cost of $11,000, which he offered to the Sisters at half price. They accepted. The property comprised two acres of land on which the Jarvis home had been built in 1850. It stood at the corner of Waterloo and Grange streets and was the nucleus of the Loretto convent and academy for the next eighty-five years.

On 15 August 1878, five Sisters left Toronto by train and were met at Berlin (Kitchener) by Father Kilroy and Father John J. Ronan, his assistant, who escorted them the rest of the way on the train to Stratford. Waiting for them at the Stratford station was a contingent of prominent Catholics, who welcomed the Sisters and conducted them to the Corcoran family home at 158 Church Street, where they were supposed to remain until their convent was ready. But the Sisters were anxious to be in their new home and decided to move in on 17 August.

In Stratford, three Sisters taught in St. Joseph's separate school, which was not a proper school building but a three-room rented house, with no plaster on the walls. It opened on 2 September 1878, with an enrolment of one hundred girls and seventy boys. The other two Sisters opened Loretto Academy, a private or select school, in the convent on 9 September, with twenty-nine day students but no boarders since the convent was too small at the time to accommodate them. For the students at both schools, the Sisters taught regular subjects and catechism classes every Sunday on the convent verandah and organized sodalities.

Over the next few years, the enrolment at both the separate school and the academy increased steadily, prompting Loretto Abbey in Toronto to send four additional teachers. In 1886, the average attendance at the separate school ranged from 175 to 180, and the academy had seven boarders and thirty-eight day students. In June 1888, there were twelve boarders and forty-five day students at the academy.

In August 1892, the Sisters were put in charge of the ninety boys who made up the senior boys' school at the parish. On 18 November 1892, these boys joined the other grades at a new separate school on Grange Street. There were now six Loretto Sisters teaching both boys and girls, juniors and seniors, at St. Joseph's separate school. The Sisters taught at St. Joseph until June 1973. Other separate schools in Stratford where they taught were Immaculate Conception (1922-23); St. Aloysius (1955-70 and 1971-73); St. Ambrose (1960-73); and St. Michael's Intermediate (1963-66, 1970-71).

As the convent was enlarged and its facilities improved, Father Kilroy continued his financial support. In 1881, he donated $2,000, which kept the convent and academy solvent; on 10 December 1887, as a gift for the feast of Our Lady of Loretto, he supplied a telephone for the school; and at Midnight Mass that year, his Christmas greetings to the Sisters contained a cheque for $600. This enabled the Sisters to pay off the mortgage, obtain the deed to the property and borrow $2,000 to add a third storey to the convent, which was completed by September 1888. Father Kilroy's last substantial donation to the academy was $4,000 towards the cost of a new chapel in 1893.

In 1909, the Sisters financed a major addition to the academy that cost $15,000. They added a classroom, a science room, dormitories, a kitchen and a laundry room. The boarding school attracted pupils from all over Ontario and the Eastern United States and even several from Latin America. In addition to courses in elocution, painting and music, they took the prescribed curriculum in the high school and commercial school, as set by the provincial department of education. Also boarding at the school were students from the recently opened Normal School in Stratford.

In 1956, the Sisters had to close the boarding school because of the deteriorating condition of the building. Overall enrolment at the academy declined in the 1950s, owing to a decision by the provincial government to divide high school students into three streams, prompting many young women to choose the Stratford Collegiate over the academy. In 1960, the Sisters decided to retain Grades 9 and 10 and the commercial course but discontinue the upper grades. Two years later, rising maintenance costs forced them to abandon Loretto Academy.

St. Joseph's parish agreed to build the Sisters a modern, three-story convent next to the church. It was completed in Christmas 1962, but of the twelve Sisters who had lived in the former convent, only five moved into the new Loretto Convent. The separate school board, meanwhile, convinced the public board of education to provide rooms for the academy's Grades 9 and 10 students, while St. Michael's Intermediate School (Grades 7-10) was being built. The original academy was demolished in January 1963, and St. Michael's opened its doors in September 1963, with a Sister of Loretto as principal. In 1965, the separate school board opened a new St. Joseph's school on St. Vincent Street South and demolished the old St. Joseph's to make room for an addition to St. Michael.

In June 1972, the Sisters vacated their convent. Three of them remained in a private residence to finish their teaching obligations: Rosemary Albon, the last Loretto principal at St. Joseph's school; Mary Van Hee, the last Loretto principal at St. Ambrose school; and Anacleta Miles, a remedial reading teacher at St. Aloysius school.

Between 1969 and 1971, five Sisters attended the University of Windsor, and between 1971 and 1973, Sister Sheila Zettel and Sister Judith Kidd were members of a downtown community begun by Father Marcel Gervais of St. Peter's Seminary. While there, the Sisters taught at St. John's school in St. Mary's parish. Their return to Toronto in June 1973 brought to a close the presence of the Sisters of Loretto in the diocese of London.

Submitted by Sister Juliana Dusel, IBVM. **Sources:** Loretto Sisters (IBVM), Canadian Province Archives.

Sisters of Service (SOS)

In response to an influx of immigrants to Western Canada, Catherine Donnelly founded the Sisters of Service in 1922, on the advice of her spiritual director, Father Arthur Coughlan, a Redemptorist, and with the approval of Archbishop Neil McNeil of Toronto. Working as public school teachers, rural nurses and social workers, the Sisters brought the message of the Gospel to people who were often difficult to reach because of their isolation from major population centres. Headquartered in Toronto, the community grew rapidly. Within ten years, the Sisters had missions from Halifax to Vancouver. In more recent years, the Sisters have taught in small communities in Newfoundland, Northern Ontario, Saskatchewan and Alberta.

The Sisters of Service mission in the diocese of London began in August 1988, being warmly welcomed by Bishop Sherlock. At that time, the Sarnia Separate School Board hired three Sisters to teach at Holy Rosary school in Wyoming: Sisters Colleen Young, Patricia Flynn and Peggy McFadden. Sister McFadden taught one year; Sister Flynn taught two years; and Sister Young taught until June 1994, when she retired from teaching. During her retirement, Sister Young has served as a lector and Eucharistic minister at Holy Rosary parish

in Wyoming and St. Philip parish in Petrolia and has contributed to the preparation of music and liturgies for special occasions.

Sister Anita Hartman taught in St. Joseph school in Sarnia, from January to June 1990, replacing a lay teacher on maternity leave, and in St. Peter Canisius school in Watford, from September 1990 to June 1991. She also taught Grade Two at St. Michael school in Brights Grove for ten years, from September 1991 to June 2001, at which time she retired from the St. Clair Catholic District School Board. Continuing to reside in Brights Grove, Sister Hartman set up a music program in her residence, offering instruction in piano and guitar to forty-five children from kindergarten to high school.

Sister Bernice Anstett came to the SOS Wyoming mission in November 1992 and has served as a VON volunteer in palliative care since 1994. She has also assisted in pastoral care at Holy Rosary and St. Philip parishes, working in the RCIA program, serving as a lector and minister of Communion and acting as leader of the Liturgy of the Word and Communion services at nursing homes and seniors residences. Since 1994, Sister Anstett has been the leader of the Little Rock Scripture Study group.

As Eucharistic ministers, Sister Young and Sister Anstett have attended to the sick and shut-ins at Holy Rosary parish. Also, both Sisters attended St. Paul's University in Ottawa for six summers and earned certificates in pastoral liturgy. They have led liturgies at CWL meetings, conducted retreats and served for three years as members of the liturgy committee in connection with the proposed Holy Rosary parish complex. On 31 May 2005, Sister Young and Sister Anstett were honoured at an appreciation Mass and social at Holy Rosary church.

Submitted by Patricia Burke, SOS, and M.C. Havey. **Sources:** Archives of the Sisters of Service, Toronto, RG 6-51, Annals of the Wyoming Missions (1988-2005). See also Jeanne R. Beck, *To Do and To Endure: The Life of Catherine Donnelly, Sister of Service* (Toronto: 1997).

Sisters of Social Service (SSS)

The Society of the Sisters of Social Service was founded in Budapest, Hungary in response to

Pope Leo XIII's 1891 encyclical, *Rerum novarum*. The Sisters settled in Stockholm, Saskatchewan in December 1923, at the invitation of Archbishop Olivier Mathieu of Regina. Their purpose at the time was to help pioneering Hungarian immigrants in the West to establish a new life in a new land without losing their Catholic faith and Hungarian culture. The Sisters served Hungarian "New Canadians" in Saskatchewan and Alberta and then in Toronto, Montréal and Hamilton prior to their arrival in the diocese of London in 1949.

In the diocese of London, the Sisters worked in Courtland, Delhi, Langton and Tillsonburg, which were in the "Tobacco District." At first, their ministerial field of labour was the organization of the Hungarian Catholic population, this being the foundation for the establishment of St. Ladislaus Hungarian parish in Courtland, where the Sisters conducted social ministry and religious education. They also assisted in the founding of Our Lady of Fatima school on the church property. Two Sisters were the school's first teachers, and members of the community taught there from 1959 to 1968.

Several people from the "Tobacco District," who attended the 1948 blessing of St. Stephen Hungarian church in Hamilton, came away convinced of the need for a Hungarian Catholic parish in their part of the diocese of London. Their conviction was inspired in part by the significant role that Sister Mary Schwarz, SSS, played in the early history of St. Stephen's parish in Hamilton. They immediately began a petition for signatures that they intended to present to Bishop Kidd of London. Concrete action, however, did not begin until 1949, when Father John Uyen, pastor of St. John Brébeuf parish in Delhi, spoke to one of his parishioners, a Mrs. Racz, about the need for services in Hungarian. She referred him to the Sisters of Social Service, being familiar with their work in Hamilton and Montréal.

Armed with the addresses of 200 Hungarians, given to her by Father Uyen, Sister Mary Schwarz conducted an extensive survey of Hungarian farmers that produced 860 addresses. George Bakos provided transportation, and the Sisters of St. Joseph gave her accommodation. Sister Mary encouraged families to attend two eight-day missions to be preached by Father Ladislaus Cser, SJ, in Langton and Tillsonburg. The success of the missions convinced Father Ujen, Father Cser and Sister Mary to suggest in a report to Bishop Kidd, who had kept in regular

contact, that the Hungarians needed their own territorial parish in a central location. On 1 January 1950, minutes before the beginning of 11:00 Mass in Delhi, Father Cser received a phone call from Bishop Kidd, giving permission for a Hungarian parish.

The Sisters of Social Service who worked in St. Ladislaus parish were Sisters Mary Schwarz, Magdolna Heczke and Scholastica Rakay. Sisters who kept house for them and assisted in other ways were Sisters Julia Lampert, Valerie Nagy and Stefania Horvath. Sisters who taught in Our Lady of Fatima school were Sisters Sylvia Rakay, Theresia Miskolczi, Philomena Orosz and Ernestine Miskolczi.

The Sisters of Social Service withdrew from the diocese in 1968 as a result of a shortage of members in their community.

Submitted by Sister Gabriella Petoniak, SOS. **Sources:** Archives of the Sisters of Social Service, Toronto: minutes of meetings, correspondence with parishioners, notes and reports by Sister Mary Schwarz, SOS, and others.

Congregation of the Holy Ghost (Spiritans, CSSp)

During the decade immediately following the Second World War, the Spiritans enjoyed an abundance of vocations in the "home countries," such as France, Germany, Holland, Belgium, Ireland, Portugal, the United Kingdom, the United States and even Québec. The congregation also experienced the first generation of vocations in their community from the "mission countries." In 1952, the General Chapter of the Spiritans decided to found missions in third-world regions where the Spiritans had yet to establish themselves and to place members in new "home countries" where they could augment their ranks with even more missionaries.

The Spiritans in Ireland were chosen to set up a foundation in English-speaking Canada. Father W. Leo Brolly, fifty years of age, who had spent a quarter century in Nigeria, travelled to Detroit, Michigan, and with the assistance and advice of his Spiritan confreres there made contact with Bishop Cody of the diocese of London. A former student at the Spiritan-run St. Alexander's College in Gatineau,

Québec, Bishop Cody was immediately sympathetic to Father Brolly's request for a parish in the diocese and awarded the Spiritans the new parish of St. Rita of Cascia in Woodstock.

It was an interesting gift on the part of the bishop. St. Rita was a parish in name only, not yet carved out of St. Mary's parish. There was no church, no rectory and no roll of parishioners. To make a start on the parish, the diocese purchased an old house and property at the corner of Dundas Street and Clarke Avenue. Six Irish Spiritans arrived on 18 October 1954. Accompanying Father Brolly were Father Paddy Walsh, who had been a vicar general, superior and seminary professor in Nigeria, Father Garry McCarthy, a former teacher and coach at St. Mary's College in Dublin, Father Bob Hudson, an experienced vocations preacher, Father Nick McCormack, a parish priest for twenty years in Trinidad, West Indies, and Father Des McGoldrick, who had been a retreat master and spiritual director in Kenya.

Father McCormack became St. Rita's first pastor, with Father McCarthy as his assistant. They celebrated Sunday Masses in the gymnasium of the local separate school and weddings and funerals at St. Mary's church. A very simple wooden chapel served as the parish church until a fine brick church replaced it three years later. Meanwhile, Fathers Walsh, Hudson and McGoldrick preached parish missions and school and convent retreats in numerous dioceses across Canada, spreading the Spiritan missionary message. Each succeeding year saw more Irish Spiritans come to St. Rita's parish. In 1958, there were enough members to open Neil McNeil High School in Toronto, at the request of Cardinal James McGuigan.

On 17 May 1998, the Spiritans celebrated forty-five years at St. Rita parish, in the presence of Bishop Sherlock. It was a bittersweet anniversary because the occasion was used to announce the end of their presence at the parish, because of a shortage of personnel. Over the years, sixty-six Spiritans from fourteen different countries (including fifteen from Canada) have called St. Rita parish in Woodstock their home. The last three were Fathers Jimmy Dunne, Jude Ogbenna and Martin Brennan. Fondly remembered by many of the parishioners are Fathers Mick Wasser, Kiernan Keena, Hugh Roach, John Cunningham, Gerry Scott, Jack Sheppard, Bill Dwane and Pat Smyth. Only Fathers Hudson and McCarthy of the original six are still alive. Father Dunne, who is stationed at St. Bernard's church in Waterford, maintains the Spiritan presence in the diocese.

Submitted by Father Gerald Fitzgerald, CSSp.
Sources: *Spiritan Missionary News* (May 2004), 4-5; (February 2005), 22.

Ursuline Religious of Ireland (Irish Ursulines, CSU)

In late August 1956, six Ursulines from Waterford, Ireland arrived at St. Peter's parish in Sarnia. They had come in response to a personal invitation from Bishop Cody of London, with the approval of Bishop Daniel Cohalan of Waterford and Lismore, to teach in the city's separate schools. Four of the Sisters were choir nuns and two were lay sisters (who returned to Ireland in 1958). Sister Peter Beadon, who had been a medical doctor in London, England, was appointed superior of the mission, and Sister Ignatius Heffernan was made bursar. Sisters Sacred Heart, Martin, Perpetua and Lelia made up the rest of the contingent.

Father Aloysius Nolan, pastor of St. Peter's, welcomed the sisters at the train station and lodged them in the rectory until their convent, next to the church, was completed in November. In the meantime, Father Nolan lived in the parish gymnasium. In exchange for annual salaries of $2,000 for each of the three teaching Sisters — which was double the salary paid to other religious teachers in the separate schools — the Irish Ursulines agreed to purchase the convent and grounds from the diocese on a mortgage amortized over twenty-five years. The parish agreed to furnish the convent. They began teaching at St. Peter's school in September and remained there for the next ten years.

The Sisters, however, were unable to teach in Ontario on a regular basis. To do so, they had to attend the Toronto Normal School for two successive summers and also the London Normal School for a full school year to earn valid teaching certificates. Father Nolan facilitated the process by offering to pay one half of the cost of tuition and board for three Sisters, not to exceed $2,500 in total. While studying in London, the Sisters lived at Mount St.

Joseph. Within three years, three Sisters earned their qualifications to teach and came on staff at St. Peter separate school.

The community needed a minimum of seven teaching Sisters to pay down what was a substantial mortgage. The goal was to have twelve members in the Sarnia convent. This never happened. During the ten-year life of the Sarnia community, there were never more than six members. The Waterford Motherhouse was unable to furnish additional members for several reasons. Many of its members were over fifty years of age and therefore too old to make the difficult transition to a new country and new climate (the Sisters found the summer heat and humidity almost unbearable, one Sister had already returned to Ireland because of the cold winters). No arriving Sisters were qualified to teach in Ontario schools, and the expense involved in retraining them would be prohibitive. That three of the Sisters in Sarnia had earned their teaching certificates was due to the largesse of Father Nolan and his parishioners. Lastly, the bishop of Waterford was adamant that no Ursulines in his diocese could be spared for Sarnia schools.

Except for one choir nun, Sister Francis Xavier, and one Irish postulant, Joan Stafford, the Motherhouse ignored the repeated requests of the Sarnia convent for Sisters. Because the Sarnia convent was only a mission or a branch house, with so few members, establishing a Novitiate was out of the question, but the absence of a Novitiate made it virtually impossible to build up their community with local vocations. In an attempt to remedy this situation, the Ursulines of Sarnia became a separate foundation on 20 April 1962. Sister Peter Beadon was the first (and only) Superior. Rome gave its definitive approval on 31 July 1964.

Independence allowed the Ursulines of Sarnia to open a Novitiate and to send several members to university to earn their Bachelor of Arts degrees and to qualify to teach high school. With the encouragement of Bishop Carter of London, two Sisters attended the International Catechetical Centre, Lumen Vitae, in Brussels, Belgium, from September 1964 to June 1965. On their return to the diocese, they worked with school boards and teachers who requested in-service training in the new approaches to scripture, liturgy and catechesis, as mandated by the Second Vatican Council. The Sisters also began a catechetical centre in Sarnia,

which housed a library and acted as a centralized catechetical workshop.

Despite their ability to adapt as an independent foundation, the Ursulines of Sarnia failed to attract enough vocations to remain viable. Although the Sisters had resisted uniting with another Ursuline foundation, after several years of negotiations, with Bishop Carter acting as mediator, they finally acquiesced to Rome's desire and formally applied to join the Ursulines of the Chatham Union. Signing the petition, on 28 January 1966, were Mother Peter Beadon, Mother Ignatius Heffernan, Mother Martin Lynch, Mother St. Andrew O'Hanlon and Sister Mary Patricia Stafford. They were accepted into the community of the Ursulines of the Chatham Union on 4 June 1966.

Sources: DLA, Bishop John C. Cody Papers, Box 1, Files 12 and 13. Additional information supplied by Sister May O'Hanlon, OSU.

Ursuline Sisters of the Agonizing Heart of Jesus (USAHJ)

On 8 December 1965, the closing day of the Second Vatican Council, ten Ursuline Sisters of the Agonizing Heart of Jesus, with Sister M. Górska as superior, arrived in Canada from Communist-controlled Poland. Bishop Carter had invited them, and Monsignor Lawrence Wnuk, pastor of Holy Trinity parish in Windsor, arranged the details of their emigration and welcomed them to his parish. The Sisters, popularly called the Polish Ursulines, settled in their first convent at 1430 Pierre Street, and in the following year they moved to 1381 Hall Avenue. They are currently located at 1371 Langlois Avenue. In 1975, Father Peter Sanczenko, pastor of Our Lady of Częstochowa parish in London, invited the Sisters to establish a house in the city. Sister Kinga Lewicka was the first superior, and Polish Ursulines still work in the parish.

From the beginning of their foundation in the diocese, the Sisters' two primary ministries have been education and pastoral work. Starting in 1967, Sister Ursula Wolniewicz taught at Brennan High School in Windsor, where she was joined in 1968 by Sister Paula Ryniec and in 1969 by Sister Magdalen Budniak. They taught French, English, German, Polish and World Religions. Prior to full funding for Catholic schools, the Sisters donated a portion of their salaries to the daily operational expenses of Grades 11, 12 and 13 (as did other religious communities who taught in Catholic schools). In addition to regular classroom work, the Sisters were involved in the extracurricular life of the school, conducted heritage classes, oversaw several youth organizations, such as the Eucharistic Crusaders and parish camps, and assisted numerous immigrant students and their parents as they adjusted to life in Canada. Their work increased dramatically during the 1980s and 1990s, a time of sustained emigration from Poland. In 1971, the Sisters opened a highly successful day nursery. Other ministries include parish secretarial work and assistance to the sick and needy. Wherever their work takes them, the Polish Ursulines carry on the mission of simplicity and joy of St. Ursula Ledóchowska, their Foundress.

Julia Ursula Ledóchowska was born in 1865. In her twenty-first year, she entered the Ursuline community in Kraków, Poland. In 1907, she organized a convent in St. Petersburg, Russia. There, she conducted a boarding school for girls and assumed various apostolic and ecumenical undertakings. When Sister Ursula was exiled from Russia in 1914, she went to Sweden and did not return to her native land until 1920. Joining her in Poland were the Sisters from the St. Petersburg convent. Sister Ursula received permission from the Holy See to establish a new congregation, the Ursuline Sisters of the Agonizing Heart of Jesus.

In the decades following the First World War, Sister Ursula immersed herself in rebuilding the spiritual and intellectual life of Polish youth. She successfully devoted the bulk of her community's energies and talents in the establishment of schools and in the delivery of pre-school and after-school programs. She also introduced religious instruction in the public school system. During the remainder of her life, Sister Ursula witnessed the flourishing of her Congregation and the respectful admiration of the people for the work of its members.

Sister Ursula Ledóchowski died in Rome in 1939 and was buried there. Pope John Paul II beatified her on 20 June 1983, during his pilgrimage to Poland. After a ten-day journey across Europe, in 1989, the relics of Blessed Ursula arrived in Pniewy, Poland, and were laid to rest in the chapel of the Motherhouse of the Ursuline Sisters. On 18 May 2003, John Paul II proclaimed her a saint for the whole Church.

St. Ursula, as foundress, wrote a constitution for the community, which includes the following two points: the work of the Congregation is to spread the good news of Jesus Christ and the love of His Agonizing Heart by means of the nurturing and education of children and youth and by being of service to the most needy among us; and in their evangelization of the world, coupled with their pursuit of human dignity, the Sisters offer spiritual and material assistance to those in need, regardless of national, religious or cultural borders.

Faithful to their foundress' call, the Ursuline Sisters of the Agonizing Heart of Jesus work in Argentina, Belarus, Brazil, Canada (Windsor, London and Ottawa), Finland, France, Germany, Italy, the Philippines, Poland, Tanzania and Ukraine.

Submitted by Sister Magdalen Budniak.

Part IV
Cathedral, Parishes and Missions

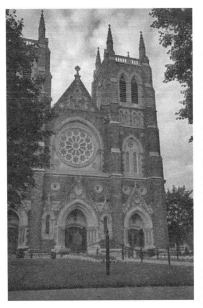

1. St. Peter's Cathedral Basilica

Bishop Alexander Macdonell of Kingston, whose diocese covered the entire province of Upper Canada, visited Port Talbot and St. Thomas in July 1827 and instructed Father James W. Campion, missionary of Niagara and Dundas, and Campion's successor, Father John Cullen, to make regular visits to the Catholics of the London District. In 1831, Macdonell severed London and St. Thomas from Dundas and sent Father Laurence Dempsey to St. Thomas. In August of that year, Dempsey opened St. George's chapel, the forerunner to Holy Angels, and became pastor, with London as a mission. He also ministered to tiny bands of Catholics in Adelaide, Stratford and Goderich.

In 1834, Father (later Dean) Daniel Downie succeeded Dempsey and opened London's first Catholic church, St. Lawrence the Martyr, on 10 August 1834. It was 30 feet by 40 feet (9 m by 12 m) and was located on the southwest corner of Richmond Street and Dufferin Avenue. The church was close to the corner, with the churchyard to the south on land presently occupied by the Grand Theatre. This church burned to the ground on the morning of 24 August 1851.

Other priests who served London and St. Thomas and their outlying stations during this period — up to 1850 — include the Franciscan Father Joseph Maria Burke, Father Michael Robert Mills, Father James O'Flyn, Father Constantine Lee, Father James D. Ryan and Father Patrick O'Dwyer. St. Lawrence the Martyr became a parish in 1840.

Dean Thadeus T. Kirwan built the second church, which was opened and dedicated by Bishop Armand-François-Marie de Charbonnel of Toronto, on 7 March 1852. Designed by architect John Wright, and constructed of white brick, it was located on the northeast corner of Richmond and Dufferin, facing Richmond, and completed within a year at a cost of £5,000. The Dominican Fathers (1861-68) added the steeple and galleries, which increased seating capacity to as high as 800 people.

The overall design was very similar to St. Patrick's in Lucan and First St. Andrew's United Church in London.

Bishop Pinsoneault made this church his first cathedral in 1856 and changed the name to St. Peter's. When he moved the seat of the diocese to Sandwich, in 1859, St. Peter's reverted to the status of a parish church. This lasted until 1869, the year that Bishop Walsh convinced Rome to restore the seat to London. That same year, Bishop Walsh contemplated alterations to St. Peter's that would have extended the cathedral north, south and east into a cruciform shape and raised the roof for the addition of stained-glass windows. The $60,000 cost, however, was prohibitive. In 1873, Walsh commissioned Edward Welby Pugin, eldest son of the more famous Augustus Welby Pugin, to draw up plans for an entirely new cathedral, but nothing came of his efforts. Subsequently, a London architect, George F. Durand submitted two large drawings, but Durand was Protestant, and Walsh chose Joseph Connolly, a Toronto architect and a Catholic. Walsh announced his decision to the people on 15 February 1880.

It took five years to complete the present St. Peter's cathedral, which was dedicated on 28 June 1885. The cost escalated from Walsh's $60,000 to Connolly's $75,000 to a final tally of more than $136,000. The debt was not retired until Bishop Fallon's time.

The design is French Gothic Revival, with the façade modeled on Notre Dame in Paris. The proportions are the same: three strong horizontals, three strong verticals and three gabled doorways. The foundation stone came from the quarry at Queenston; and the pink sandstone came from Medina, New York; the stone for detailing or trim (i.e. tracery) is blue Ohio sandstone; and the granite columns are from Scotland. The interior features a vestibule, a nave, a main aisle and two side aisles, an apsidal sanctuary, east and west transepts, two side chapels and a sacristy. The total length is over 200 feet (60 m); the width, measured from transept to transept, is 115 feet (34.5 m); the height, from the ground to the ridge of the main roof is 90 feet (27 m); with the flèche, at the conjunction of the nave and transept roofs, the height rises to 185 feet (55.5 m). The only known artifact from the second church and first cathedral is the memorial plaque to Henry Edward Dormer in the west transept.

In 1889, Bishop Walsh commissioned the seven large windows, four clerestory windows and two medallion windows in the sanctuary, the roundels and the six windows in the two side chapels, the large lancet (creedal) windows and rose windows in the transepts, which were paid for by John Wright (who had come out of retirement to supervise the construction of the cathedral), and the rose window in the organ loft. Walsh also commissioned the Stations of the Cross in oils and the Marian altar. Left unfinished were installation of the remaining stained-glass windows in the nave and clerestory and the completion of the towers topped with spires, as originally planned by Connolly.

Bishop O'Connor made enormous progress to reduce the debt on the cathedral, and Bishop McEvay continued this task. During his episcopacy Bishop McEvay added the southernmost stained-glass window on the east wall of the nave. Directly across from McEvay's window is a double stained-glass window donated by the Patriotic Citizens of London, in 1901, in memory of private John Donegan, who died in the Boer War.

Bishop Fallon completed the interior decoration. He removed the existing woodwork, with the exception of the beams, doorways, wainscoting, choir loft and flooring. Globe Furniture produced new Stations of the Cross, carved in oak at $1,000 each, new communion rails, and in the sanctuary, new choir stalls, high altar and bishop's throne.

Stained-glass windows were installed in the nave and clerestory. Fallon replaced the six windows in the side chapels, keeping the same themes, and donated the 1889 originals to the Martyrs' Shrine in Midland. Also given to the shrine were Walsh's Stations of the Cross. The artist Ilario Panzironi of Rome and New York decorated the ceiling of the nave, the walls below the clerestory windows, the frieze below the Stations of the Cross (now painted over), the ceilings in the transepts and the six angels in the sanctuary. Added were new electrical features and a three-manual organ with 59 stops and 3,869 pipes by Casavant Frères Ltée of St. Hyacinthe, Québec. The cathedral was re-opened in September 1926, after being closed for eighteen months.

Bishop Kidd dedicated the Shrine to Our Mother of Perpetual Help, in December 1949. Designed by Mario Licceoli, the Italian agent for the New York-based Rambusch Decorating Company, the shrine is on the north wall of the east transept and features a copy of the well-known painting of Our Mother of Perpetual Help, nine angels, two of which hold a crown, and a canopy with a cross, all gilded in a burnished gold and polished with agate. A parishioner donated the cost of $5,000.

Bishop Cody dedicated the baptistry in September 1952. It was located on the east side of the vestibule. The baptismal font, donated by the Sansone family of London, was made of Botticini and Verdi antique marble with a cover of hammered bronze. Behind it was a woodcarving depicting the baptism of Our Lord, surrounded by seven medallions on the wall that were painted by Philip Aziz. This baptistry no longer exists.

Under Bishop Cody, St. Peter's underwent another round of extensive renovations and even expansion, in 1958. Peter F. Tillmann, architect, completed the two towers and added new tracery, using Medina stone from the recently demolished St. Thomas post office, but he was unable to add the spires because the foundation lacked the strength to carry the additional weight. Carillons of twelve bells, each named for an apostle, were installed in the towers, and a consecration bell was placed in the flèche. Cody also installed new stained-glass windows, designed locally by Christopher R. Wallis of Edwards Glass, in the narthex, both towers and the sacristy. Philip Aziz was commissioned to turn the Sacred Heart chapel into the Christ the King chapel, featuring his wall painting of the Tree of Jesse; the Marian chapel into the St. Joseph's chapel; and what was the 1885 sacristy into the Lady chapel, which was the gift of the diocesan priests to mark the 100th anniversary of the diocese in 1956. The original sacristy was enlarged and became the chapel, and a new sacristy was added. Aziz is also responsible for the two sets of crosses and candlesticks at the side altars. Pope John XXIII made St. Peter's a minor basilica, in December 1962, in honour of Bishop Cody's twenty-fifth anniversary as a bishop.

The liturgical reforms of the Second Vatican Council called for more changes to the interior of the cathedral. Bishop Carter extended the sanctuary into the nave, which necessitated the removal of the communion rail and several rows of pews, and he removed the high altar, reredos, canopy, choir stalls and paneling between the sanctuary and the side altars. A new altar was situated directly beneath the flèche. The architect was David C. Stevens of London. The firm of Thompson, McCance & Pigott Limited supplied the designs. The four Evangelist panels were later relocated to the rear of the nave, and Aziz's Tree of Jesse was painted over.

The three-phase, multi-million-dollar Campaign 2002 funded the replacement of the original slate roof, the restoration of the flèche and work on the masonry and woodwork. Future projects include painting the interior of the cathedral, replacing some mechanical systems, and repairing the roof of the Lady chapel and the cathedral entrances.

In the summer of 2004, the cathedral rectory, the old episcopal palace, was closed and subsequently demolished. Opened in the autumn of 1872, it was the bishop's home until Bishop Fallon received Blackfriars as a gift. The rectory served as the first St. Peter's Seminary from 1912 to 1926.

St. Peter's was the only Catholic church in London until St. Mary's mission church was opened in 1874 and the only parish in the city until St. Mary's became a parish in 1899. Today the cathedral and fifteen other parishes serve London's Catholics.

Sources: *Canadian Illustrated News*, 27 May 1871, 323, 325; *Catholic Record*, 20 February 1880; 9 July 1880; 20 May 1881; 3, 10, 17 January 1985; 19 April 1885; 4 July 1885; 14 November 1885; 12 October 1889; John F. Coffey, *The City and Diocese of London, Ontario, Canada: An Historical Sketch* (London: 1885), 43-48, 54-60; John P. Comiskey, *John Walsh: Second Bishop of London in Ontario 1867-1889* (Ph.D. diss., Pontifical Gregorian University, 1999), 261-69; Jerome Terrence Flynn, *The London Episcopacy, 1867-1889, of the Most Reverend John Walsh, D.D., Second Bishop of London* (M.A. thesis, Catholic University of America, 1966), 96-10, 108-13; John R. MacMahon, *St. Peter's Cathedral Basilica London, Canada* (London: 1985). Additional information supplied by Dan Mezza and Dan Brock.

2. Windsor Deanery

Assumption

The parish of Our Lady of the Assumption is the mother parish of the Catholic Church in Ontario and the oldest parish west of Montréal in Canada. It has belonged to the dioceses of Québec, Kingston and Toronto and holds pride of place in the diocese of London. Its eighteenth century history is linked to the founding of Fort Pontchartrain (Detroit) by Antoine Laumet Lamothe Cadillac, on 25 July 1701, Cadillac's invitation to the Hurons (Wyandots) of Michilimackinac to settle near the fort, the Huron request for Jesuit priests and the French settlement of the south shore of the Detroit River. Interestingly, the Michilimackinac Hurons were descendants of those Hurons who encountered the Jesuit missionaries in mid-seventeenth century Huronia and fled with them after the Iroquois massacres.

Father Armand de La Richardie, SJ, arrived in the summer of 1728 and ministered to the Hurons, first on the north shore, then on Isle du Bois Blanc (Bob-Lo Island) near the mouth of the Detroit River, starting in October 1742. Father Pierre Potier, SJ, came as an assistant in September 1744 and succeeded La Richardie two years later. In 1748, La Richardie returned and moved the Huron mission to the south side of the river, at La Pointe de Montréal, where the Ambassador Bridge begins its arch over to the United States. He and Potier built a church, and when the French began to settle on the south side, in 1749, they started to minister to their spiritual needs. Father La Richardie departed for Québec in 1751 and did not return, leaving Father Potier as his successor. On 3 October 1767, the Huron mission became Assumption parish and a new church was built, measuring 60 feet by 30 feet (18 m by 9 m). Father Potier died on 16 July 1781. For the next sixty-two years priests from the diocese of Québec and Kingston were pastors of the parish.

Assumption

Father Jean-François Hubert, a future bishop of Québec, constructed a rectory and parish hall in 1784, which lasted for more than a century, and Father François-Xavier Dufaux supervised the construction of the third church, in 1787. It was made of squared timbers and measured 90 feet long by 50 feet wide (27 m by 15 m). Located on Vista Place, this church is featured in Dr. Edward Walsh's 1804 painting, "A View of Detroit and Straits Taken from the Huron Church." A pulpit was installed in 1793 and can be seen in the current church. It is the only eighteenth century parish artifact to survive.

The churchwardens approved plans for a fourth church in 1835, to be made of brick, but the cornerstone was not blessed until 21 July 1842, by Bishop Peter Paul Lefevère of Detroit, and not opened for public worship until 20 July 1845. The church had two-foot thick walls and was 120 feet by 60 feet (36 m by 18 m). This is the present church at the corner of University Avenue West and Huron Church Road. On the west wall, at the rear of the nave, there hangs a copy of Murillo's "Assumption of the Blessed Virgin Mary." It was executed by the Canadian artist Antoine Plamondon, in 1846, at the request of Judge Phillipe Panet, of Québec, whose daughter Rosalie was married to Charles Baby, a prominent member of the parish.

The Jesuits were at the helm of Assumption when the fourth church was opened. They had returned in July 1843, led by Father Pierre Point, SJ. Under his leadership, the Jesuits built a thriving French-Canadian parish in Sandwich, attended to missions in Essex and Kent counties and founded Assumption College, which opened its doors on 10 February 1857. Their fine work came to an abrupt end in 1859, when Bishop Pinsoneault decided to make Assumption his cathedral.

In 1870, the Basilian Fathers assumed control of both the parish and the college. Father Denis

O'Connor, CSB, who became the third bishop of the diocese, added the tower and the sanctuary in 1874, at a cost of $25,000, and the stained-glass windows in the nave in 1882. The Basilians have remained in charge to this day. Various pastors have restored, renovated and even added to the fabric of this historic and attractive church. The major works include the Stations of the Cross (1883); the high altar (1887); new bell in the tower (1893); the demolition of the bishop's palace and the construction of a new rectory (1896); Rosary chapel and sacristy (1907); new organ (1919); stained-glass window in the narthex (1920); side altars and communion rail (1925); Marian Statue (1950); Donlon Hall (1959); temporary altar and lectern facing the people (1965); new rectory (1970); repointing of the brick, attic insulation and new electrical wiring (1979); releading and recasting of the stained-glass windows (1982); repainting (1983); permanent oak altar and lectern (1984); roof (1993); and the repointing and repainting of Rosary chapel (1998).

Eight people are buried beneath the floor, from 1846 to 1905. They are Rosalie Panet, Fathers Potier, Dufaux, Jean-Baptiste Marchand and Antoine Phileas Villeneuve, and three nuns, Clotilde Raizenne, who was the first nun in Upper Canada, Mary Connally of the Sisters of the Sacred Heart and Marie Martine Sirois of the Sisters of the Holy Names of Jesus and Mary.

Today Assumption parish has 650 registered families as well as many students from the University of Windsor.

Sources: E.J. Lajeunesse, "The Coming of the First Nun to Upper Canada," Canadian Catholic Historical Association, *Report* (1955): 27-37; Ibid., *Outline History of Assumption Parish* (1967, rev. ed 1984); Ibid., *The Windsor Border Region: Canada's Southernmost Frontier* (Toronto: 1960); E.C. Lebel, "History of Assumption, the First Parish in Upper Canada," Canadian Catholic Historical Association *Report* (1954), 23-37.

Atonement

Atonement

In June 1970, the General Chapter of the Franciscan Friars of the Atonement, held at Saranac, New York, recommended that the community visit different cities in Ontario where new foundations might be established. After an interview with Bishop Carter, the friars accepted his invitation to settle in Windsor. On 1 September 1971, three friars — Father Timothy MacDonald, SA, Father Walter Gagne, SA, and Brother Paschal Breau, SA — inaugurated the Forest Glade Mission. Forest Glade, a new housing subdivision in east Windsor, was in need of its own Catholic parish.

The first Mass took place in St. Anne's, Tecumseh, but starting Sunday, 16 October 1971, the Eucharist was celebrated in the gymnasium of L.A. Desmarais separate school on Eastcourt Drive, with weekday Masses held in the small chapel of the friars' residence. This practice continued until April 1979. On 30 March 1975, Bishop Carter created the Parish of the Atonement, from territory belonging to St. Anne's, and appointed Father Wilfrid Brennan, SA, as the first pastor. There were already three separate schools in the parish but no church!

In the autumn of 1977, the diocese hired the architectural firm of J.P. Thompson Associates and Kehl Construction as general contractors. Bishop Sherlock turned the sod on 2 July 1978, and he presided over the solemn dedication on 10 June 1979. The church is modern theatre in design and seats 1,000 people. "The interior combines warmth with dignity. The restricted palette of materials — redwood, brick, and a self-coloured carpet — is well handled, and gives a sense of calm and competence," according to a 1981 Award of Merit citation from the

Ontario Masons' Relations Council. The cost was $1.2 million. The 1,200 families in the parish retired the debt by 1993.

As Forest Glade grew, so too did the parish. Soon the relatively new parish could not accommodate the needs of the various ministries of this busy suburban Catholic community. As early as 1989, the congregation realized the urgent need to expand the parish centre and office. But since there was still a debt, and Bishop Sherlock's Pentecost 2000 campaign was slated to begin in the near future, the parishioners wisely decided to wait several years. On 11 May 1991, the parish organized a Collaboration Day. It was a grassroots informal affair that was designed to encourage maximum participation from the pew.

Following considerable discussion and deliberation, the parish decided to pursue the option of expansion. More meetings, visits to other parishes which had expanded their facilities, discussions with the parish council, a referendum in June 1992 and the formation of building and finance committees — all this collective activity led to the construction of the Parish Family Centre. Once again, J.P. Thompson was the architect. The centre was opened and blessed on 9 April 1995. Bishop Sherlock wrote to the parish, on 1 March 1995, that by building the parish centre, the people had committed themselves to the renewal of their parish community, not only in mutual service in charity but also in the building up of their faith. "It is my prayer," he continued, "that this new facility will be a constant inspiration for each of you to commit yourselves to the building up of that edifice which is constructed of living stones with Jesus Christ as the cornerstone."

After nearly thirty-two years of faithful service to the Catholics of Forest Glade, the Franciscan Friars of the Atonement surrendered the parish to diocesan priests, on 30 June 2003.

Sources: DLA, Parish Files; Paschal Breau, *Atonement History in Canada* (Windsor: 1997); The Ontario Masons' Relations Council Unit Masonry Design Awards 1981 (1981).

Blessed Sacrament

During the 1930s, there lived in the west end of Assumption parish several hundred families who felt cut off from the parish because of the Great Depression, which left them impoverished and prone

Blessed Sacrament

to the influence of local communists. To bring these people back into the Catholic fold, Father Edward Allor, CSB, Assumption's pastor, decided to build them a church of their own. He purchased eight lots, across from St. Edward school (1929), at the corner of Prince Road and King Street. The city had appropriated the property for tax arrears and sold it to the diocese for fifty dollars.

On 23 June 1937, Father G. Harvey Wilbur, CSB, turned the sod for the church and rectory, in the presence of the children from three separate schools — St. Edward, St. Francis and St. Anthony — and a large number of parishioners. Construction proceeded quickly. On 11 July 1937, Bishop Kidd laid and blessed the cornerstone and bestowed the name Blessed Sacrament upon the church. By 19 October 1937, the church was ready for its inaugural solemn High Mass, which was sung by Bishop Kidd. The total cost was $9,929.

Built of brick, the church looked as if it were plucked from nineteenth century rural Ontario. It was simple and straightforward in design, six windows deep, a truncated tower and front doors opening directly onto the sidewalk. In 1957, the tower was demolished and the front of the church was extended by 20 feet (6 m), using the gable design and an extensive door to roof window. Hanging in front of the window is a cross and positioned on the wall to the right of the entrance is an attractive oversized monstrance. In 1964, the parish built a new rectory. In the late 1980s, Father Joseph Langlois and the parishioners, on the advice of David McNorgan, adapted the sanctuary to the changes in the liturgy, striking a balance in their design between the liturgy of the Word and the liturgy of the Eucharist. They also created a baptistry and greeting area at the entrance of the church through the rearrangement of several rows of pews. Imaginative frugality was at work during the entire process. By keeping the existing furnishings, everything was completed for $23,000. The ceiling in the church collapsed in 2000 but was repaired in time for Christmas 2001. Mass was held in the basement until the work was completed.

Father Wilbur was the first pastor of Blessed Sacrament. He stayed for ten years and helped to establish the Harvey Credit Union, a pioneering effort in Windsor to bring financial stability to families struggling to overcome economic hardships. Blessed Sacrament parish produced 125 men for the armed services during the Second World War, a remarkable number for such a small parish. Eight of those men died. The Basilian Fathers served the parish until 1968. When the parish celebrated its fortieth anniversary, in 1977, there were 1,200 families in the parish. Records show that during those forty years, there were 3,800 baptisms and 1,139 marriages.

In recent years, the parish has been a beehive of activity. It initiated a food and clothing distribution program in co-operation with Christ the King parish; it is a meeting place for people from Central America and Rwanda; and it has an ecumenical friendship with Reverend Owen Burey of Sandwich First Baptist Church. Although the closure of St. Edward's school was a blow to the parish, Blessed Sacrament continues to be an effective presence in the west-side neighbourhood that it serves. It is slated for closure, however, in 2012.

Sources: DLA, Parish Files; *Our Parish: Church of the Blessed Sacrament* (Windsor: 1947). Additional information supplied by Father Joe Langlois.

Christic the King

On 21 July 1926, Raymond B. Marentette, a Windsor businessman, met with Bishop Fallon in London to request the erection of a parish on Grand Marais Road in South Windsor. Fallon advised Marentette that he would act upon the

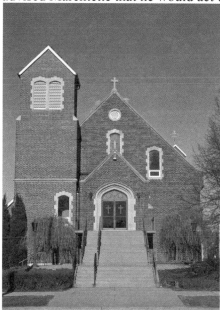
Christ the King

request if he received a formal petition from the area's Catholics. Blanche Marentette, Raymond's wife, collected the necessary signatures, and the petition was in Fallon's hands within a week. It was not until November 1928, however, that the bishop assigned the bilingual Father John E. Pageau, CSB, as the first pastor.

The delay may have been caused by a lack of property. The 1920s was a time when lots in South Windsor fetched high prices and were often in the hands of American speculators. Joseph B. Sherwood, a Detroit attorney, was one such speculator, but he decided to help local Catholics. He donated to the diocese a parcel of land south of Grand Marais Road between Curry Avenue and Dominion Boulevard, on the stipulation that construction of a rectory would commence no later than 1929 at a minimum cost of $8,000. The parish agreed to the terms concerning the rectory and planned to build a church on the southwest corner of Curry and Grand Marais. Father Pageau celebrated the first Mass in Notre-Dame-de-Bon-Secours separate school, located at the northeast corner of Dominion and Grand Marais, in December 1928. (This is the location of the present Christ the King school.) There were sixty families in the parish.

The Great Depression forced the parish to scuttle plans for a church and convinced Father

Remi Durand, the second pastor, to rent the rectory and board at St. Alphonsus. Land values collapsed, forcing many owners to forfeit their property, a severe deflation in wages occurred and money was generally scarce. In 1936, however, the parish generated enough profits from its weekly bingos, card parties and dances to acquire, at cost, land next to Notre Dame school. Time passed and progress was further impeded by the Second World War. Only the post-war building boom allowed the parish to begin construction, and the boom was so extensive that the parish was subdivided four times in ten years: St. Paul's on Malden Road, 1952; Our Lady of Mount Carmel, in 1953; St. Gabriel's, in 1959; and St. Martin de Porres, in 1963. Also, on 23 June 1952, parishioners founded the Christ the King Credit Union.

In 1946, Father Hubert Roy, the third pastor, and a building committee, contracted Sterling Construction to build the church basement, which flooded just in time for Easter. Father Roy then built a rectory adjacent to the church, in 1948, at times giving a hand in the construction work. His successor, Father Philip A. Mugan, hired the architectural firm of J.C. Pennington and Damien Construction to complete the church, in 1954, at a cost of $100,000. Bishop Cody blessed the cornerstone and opened the church. A distinguishing feature of the church is the elevated height of the floor of the nave. This was done purposely in order to avoid any possibility of flooding from the Grand Marais ditch. The debt was eliminated in 1963.

For more than two decades, Monsignor Mugan shepherded the parish through every major change, from the last vestiges of the pre-conciliar church to the beginnings of the liturgical renewal. Working with various committees, he oversaw the decoration of the sanctuary, in 1956, by enlisting the Peach Festival Committee, the CWL and the Ushers to purchase the main altar, the tabernacle and the communion rail, respectively, and by encouraging individuals and families to pay for items such as the main altar crucifix, the sanctuary lamps, the monstrance for the exposition of the Blessed Sacrament, ciboria for Holy Communion, candlesticks, etc. Other parishioners bought holy water fonts and the Stations of the Cross.

In 1964, Father Mugan built a new rectory and office for $111,000 (the 1948 rectory was sold and moved). Thomas L. Gemmel of the firm G.A.

McElroy was the architect, and A. Lombardo and Son Ltd. was the contractor. A committee of men superintended the project, and a committee of women furnished the rectory. Immediately following the 1966 Diocesan Synod, a parish council was formed, and in 1969 the parish hired Thompson, McCance and Pigott to redesign the sanctuary. This was the same firm that executed the changes to the sanctuary of St. Peter's cathedral. In 1977, Mark Construction, assisted by Bernard Rondot as a design consultant, renovated the church basement. Other additions and renovations include Our Lady's Shrine (1981), front steps (1981) and elevator tower and lift (1989).

From 1928 to 2002, there have been 3,714 baptisms, 1,155 marriages and 762 funerals. In 2001, Christ the King parish clustered with St. Martin de Porres parish. Both were suppressed in January 2007 and in their place, the new parish of Corpus Christi was erected.

Sources: DLA, Parish Files; *Christ the King Church 50th Anniversary 1928-1978* (Windsor: 1978); *Faith Community of Christ the King 75 Years 1928-2003 St. Martin de Porres 40 Years 1963-2003* (Windsor: 2003).

Holy Name of Mary

Bishop Fallon founded Holy Name of Mary, originally called Our Lady of Prompt Succour, on 27 May 1917, and he chose a young and untested Father John A. Rooney as parish priest. Monsignor Rooney was pastor for fifty-one consecutive years, a diocesan record, and at the time of his death, on 14 May 1982, he had been a priest for seventy-one years.

The first church was located at the corner of Curry and Martin avenues and was dedicated on 28 October 1917. It was a simple frame structure, which exists today as an apartment building. The second and present church was built on McEwan Avenue, south of Wyandotte Street West. The laying of the cornerstone took place on 17 October 1926, and Bishop Fallon opened and blessed the church on 20 June 1927. The architects were Pennington and Boyde (John R. Boyde was a member of the parish), and Blonde Construction Company of Chatham was the general contractor.

Built of Georgetown (Credit Valley) stone in

the English Gothic style, according to Bishop Fallon's wishes, Holy Name of Mary is 72 feet (21.6 m) wide across the front, 64 feet (19.2 m) across the nave and 108 feet (32.4 m) across the transepts. It is 169 feet (50.7

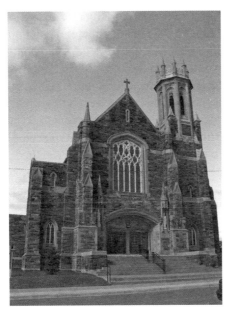

Holy Name of Mary

m) in depth from the front steps to the rear of the sanctuary. This cathedral-size church seats 1,100 people and features nearly 100 stained-glass windows. Those in the north and south transepts are of particular artistry and value. The total cost of the church, rectory, garage, windows and church furnishings was in excess of $300,000, a staggering sum, but the debt was paid off in 1946. Decoration of the interior was completed in 1950, and Bishop Cody blessed the bells on 24 October 1954.

During Monsignor Rooney's lengthy pastorate, Holy Name of Mary was known for its liturgical and social life. The parish sponsored an annual Corpus Christi procession and hosted the diocesan Eucharistic Congress in 1938 and ordinations to the priesthood in 1965. Its drama club and baseball teams were known throughout the city. At one time, there were four schools attached to the parish: Holy Name, Sacred Heart, St. John and École St-Robert. Holy Name of Mary was instrumental in founding St. Patrick's parish in 1950.

Under Father James L. Doyle, who became bishop of Peterborough, the sanctuary underwent extensive renovation in 1969. Included was a new main altar that was modeled on a fourteenth-century altar in Lincoln cathedral in England. Also renovated were the two side chapels and the alcove in the north transept where the parish's first proper baptistry was installed.

The last two decades have been challenging for Holy Name of Mary parish. Death claimed the founding families, the parish's working class neighbourhood declined and the number of children decreased. Holy Name (renamed J.A. Rooney) and Sacred Heart schools closed. The church spire had to be removed in 1997, and the rectory was demolished in 2001. The parishioners funded the repointing of the mortar around each stone, replaced the roof and installed a $125,000 organ in 2000 after the church and rectory were struck by lightning. The Vietnamese apostolate came to the parish in 1990, with Father Thomas De Nguyen-Dang as the first pastor. In July 1999, Holy Name clustered with St. Patrick's parish, its old mission, and continued to boast a highly successful choir. Holy Name of Mary will close effective 30 June 2008.

Sources: Michael Power, *A History of the Parish Church of Holy Name of Mary, 1917-1984* (Windsor; 1984); Additional information supplied by Robert Langlois.

Holy Trinity

By 1915, there were approximately 300 Polish families living in Windsor, enough to attract the attention of Father (later Bishop) Ralph H. Dignan, an assistant at Immaculate Conception parish. Father Dignan celebrated Mass for them in the church basement and designated people to translate his sermons into Polish. Władek Kwapisz, Francis Wandor and Andrew Jakubiak shared the translation duties. As dedicated as Father Dignan was to Windsor's Polish Catholics, who dearly appreciated his efforts, what was needed was a Polish priest who could establish a Polish parish.

Father Jan J. Andrzejewski was that priest. He arrived in Windsor on 29 September 1916, from the parish of Our Lady of Częstochowa in New Castle, Pennsylvania. Forty-two-years-old and a native of Milwaukee, Wisconsin, he was ordained on 30 November 1896. Father Andrzejewski was well prepared for the difficult task that lay ahead of him. He celebrated Mass at Immaculate Conception on 2 October 1916 and was involved in the preparation of nearly 100 children for confirmation. When Bishop Fallon saw the large number of Polish children, he agreed to set up a parish, the first ethnic or national parish in the diocese of London. The only concern between Fallon and the Polish people surfaced in

1919 when Fallon had to remind them that the right to found a national parish resided exclusively with the bishop and that at minimum there had to be twenty families or 100 adult parishioners for the parish to be viable.

There was a parish but no church and precious little money among the Polish people to build one. A door-to-door campaign collected $137.50. Disappointed but not discouraged, sixty-two parishioners met and agreed each to donate a dollar a month and to form a building committee composed of Joseph Samborski, Ignatius Leskiewicz, Francis Wandor and Andrew Jakubiak. But one cannot build a church without land. It was at this juncture that Walter Bourg, who was neither Polish nor a Catholic, entered the picture and changed the fortunes of the parish. His admiration for Father Andrzejewski led him to donate seven lots at the corner of Langlois Avenue and Ellis Avenue East. There was one condition: construction had to begin by 1 June 1918 and be completed within a year or the donation would be forfeited.

Although the lots were situated on farmland isolated from populated parts of the city, the parishioners accepted the challenge. Since they had only $2,000 at hand, they hand dug the foundation themselves and carted building materials to the site by horse-drawn wagon. Impressed by their tenacity, Bishop Fallon blessed the cornerstone stone on 27 October 1917 and loaned the parish $18,000 to finish the church. By Easter 1918 it was ready for Mass and was officially blessed and opened by Bishop Fallon in 1919. The cost was $32,982. The parish had approximately 100 families or 500 hundred souls. Attached to the parish was a mission at St. Mary's in London. Holy Trinity remained the diocese's only Polish parish until 1953.

As soon as the church opened its doors, the parishioners organized many different societies and clubs, such as the Holy Trinity Society, the Holy Rosary Society, the St. Cecilia choir, the Dramatic Circle and the Holy Name Society. In subsequent years, parishioners joined the Third Order of St. Francis of Assisi and the Catholic Women's League. They also purchased vestments, chalice, monstrance and two bells. When the basement had been converted into a hall, Holy Trinity quickly became the centre of the cultural and social life of Windsor's Polish community, a role that it successfully fulfilled for many decades.

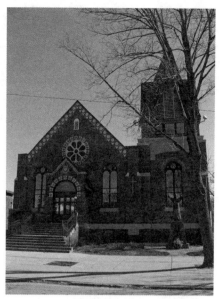

Holy Trinity

In anticipation of the fortieth anniversary of the parish, in 1956, the fourth pastor, Father Ludwik F. Kociszewski, who had come from England in 1949, organized the redecoration of the church. Work was done on the main altar, the two side altars, the baptismal font and the statue of St. Theresa the Little Flower. Statues of St. Joseph and St. Francis, the Nativity Crib and the Stations of the Cross were imported from Italy. Polychrome, the art of painting in various colours, was applied to the entire interior. Father Kociszewski was also responsible for the parish credit union that began in 1954.

Monsignor Wawrzyniec Wnuk was pastor from 1961 to 1983. He brought the Ursuline Sisters of the Agonizing Heart of Jesus to Windsor, in 1965, established the Copernicus Fund at the University of Windsor and spearheaded the development of Polonia Park housing project. More than 1,000 immigrant families joined the parish between 1988 and 1991. In 2000, the parish erected a statue of Pope John Paul II and held a special memorial Mass for him when he died in April 2005. On 28 January 2006, Bishop Ronald Fabbro, CSB, blessed and opened a two-million-dollar renovation and expansion of Holy Trinity Church.

Sources: DLA, Parish Files; *75 lat Parafii Św. Trojcy Windsor, Ontario, Kanada 1916-1991* (Windsor: 1991). Additional information supplied by Father Roman Waszkiewicz.

Immaculate Conception

Immaculate Conception parish was born at the start of the English-French language disputes in Essex County and spent the first decade of its existence as one of several parochial pawns in the local French-Canadian struggle against Bishop Fallon. Bishop McEvay established the parish in 1904, to relieve

Immaculate Conception

overcrowding at St. Alphonsus, and he claimed territory from it and Our Lady of the Lake for the then city of Windsor's second parish. The site for the church was the southeast corner of Marentette Avenue and Wyandotte Street East. The parishioners were French-Canadian and Irish and many of their descendants populated the parish rolls for decades to come. Father Denis J. Downey, who was bilingual, was the first pastor.

Williams Brothers was the architect and Blonde Brothers of Chatham was the contractor. The outer dimensions of the church are 145 feet in length and 56 feet in width (43.5 m by 16.8 m), an imposing structure for an inner city neighbourhood. The seating capacity was 700 people. The vestry is 50 feet by 31 feet (15 m by 9.3 m). Built of brick with stone trimming, the overall style of the church is Gothic. The original design called for two towers, the one on the east smaller by a third than the one on the west, with both towers topped by spires. The tower on the east and the two spires were eliminated. Mrs. Edward Chandler Walker, a Catholic, donated the church bell. The total cost of construction ranged from $30,000 to $40,000.

Bishop McEvay blessed the cornerstone on 3 July 1904, the fiftieth anniversary of the proclamation of the dogma of the Immaculate Conception, and he blessed and opened the church,

in the presence of the apostolic delegate and a huge throng of local Catholics, on 8 December 1904, the feast of the Immaculate Conception. A rectory was built in 1907, the same year that Father Downey reported that 364 families or 1,607 souls belonged to the parish.

It took about two decades to decorate the interior of the church. The parish hired Rambusch Decorating Company, which chose thirteenth-century Gothic as the dominant feature. The contract was for approximately $60,600. For this rather large sum, the church received antique oak stalls, carved pulpit, communion railing, twenty-three stained-glass windows, murals of St. Paul and St. Peter in the sanctuary, new candlesticks, sanctuary lamps, lantern lighting fixtures, polychrome painting of the walls and polychrome trimming of the woodwork. Another $16,000 was spent replacing the altars. Many years passed before the debt for this work was retired.

In the meantime, the congregation grew to such an extent that not even five Sunday Masses were sufficient to accommodate everyone. In 1924, Bishop Fallon erected Sacred Heart parish on Ottawa Street. This brought relief to the overcrowding at Immaculate Conception, but the parish was so bustling with people that it did not adversely affect it as a model of Catholic parochial life. The parish hosted a variety of societies, sodalities and associations: St. Vincent de Paul, Altar Society, the archconfraternity of St. Ann, Young Ladies Sodality, Happy Death Society, League of the Sacred Heart, St. Angela's Society, Holy Name Society, St. John Berchman's Sanctuary Society, the Catholic Order of Foresters and the Catholic Mutual Benefit Association. There were also the ushers, drama groups and sports teams. The CWL was formed in 1923, and the Legion of Mary came in 1944. The years 1935 to 1945 might have been the busiest decade in the history of the parish. There were 570 marriages, 1,511 baptisms, 434 deaths and 185 converts.

The parish had three schools: St. Francis (now Immaculate Conception), St. Edmond's and St. Joseph's (later De LaSalle and then C.G. DeSantis). At one time or another, three religious communities lived in the parish to teach at these schools. They were the Ursulines, Grey Sisters of the Immaculate Conception and the Christian Brothers.

In 1954, the fiftieth anniversary of the parish,

there was another round of renovations and repairs, this time to the roof, front steps and communion rails. Money was also spent on the grounds, the kitchen and washrooms. Total cost was $60,000. The 1960s witnessed many changes to the sanctuary of the church, including the removal of the high altar, the communion rail, the side altars and some of the statues; the gradual disappearance of devotional traditions, such as benediction and novenas, and many revisions to the Mass.

Outside the church, the neighbourhood that had sustained the parish was also undergoing a radical alteration. No longer was the parish the preserve of the French-Canadians and the Irish, and no longer was the neighbourhood so Catholic. Beginning 1 January 1981, the number of Masses was reduced to three for the 550 people who came to church. Over the next two decades, that number slowly but steadily dwindled. In 1997, Immaculate Conception was clustered with Sacred Heart parish. The church closed on 25 December 2001 and it was sold to the Chaldean Catholics of Holy Family parish.

The last parishioners of Immaculate Conception parish joined those of Sacred Heart parish, in 2002, to form Immaculate Conception and Sacred Heart Faith Community. As of January 2007, this community is the new parish of Immaculate Heart.

Sources: DLA, Parish Files; *Evening Record* (Windsor), 4 July 1904, 12 December 1904; *History of Immaculate Conception Church 1904 70th Anniversary 1974* (Windsor: 1974). Additional information supplied by Father James F. Roche.

Most Precious Blood

On 15 October 1929, Bishop Fallon appointed Father John J. White as the first pastor of Most Precious Blood parish. Thirteen days later the stock market crashed and the Great Depression began. It would take twenty-five years for the parish to build its own brick church. Father White celebrated the first Mass at the old St. Bernard's school at Meldrum Road and Milloy Street, on 24 November 1929. Church and school would share the same building until a new St. Bernard's opened in September 1930. The school was made of wood and measured 90 feet by 23 feet (27 m by 6.9 m). Territory for the new parish was taken from Our Lady of the Rosary (Our Lady of the Lake). There were 165 founding

Most Precious Blood

families.

During Father White's pastorate, 1929 to 1936, there were on average 210 families, of which 110 regularly attended Sunday Mass. Only three families in the entire parish had a full time worker. Some had part time jobs; everyone else was on welfare. Despite the appalling economic conditions, parish volunteers ran weekly bingos, setting $50 profit per week as their goal. With this money, Father White paid down all debts and left $9,000 in the bank for his successor, Thomas P.C. Donnellan, who guided the parish through the remainder of the Depression and the Second World War.

Like other parishes in the diocese that were erected just before or during the 1930s, Most Precious Blood had to wait for the post-war boom years to lay permanent foundations. Father Michael J. Dalton, a decorated war chaplain, became pastor in 1946. Energetic and unabashed, he ushered in an era of intense activity and achievement, which gave the parishioners a more solid identity of themselves as a distinct community of the faithful. In 1947, Bishop Kidd allowed Father Dalton to purchase eight lots at the corner of Meldrum Road and Tecumseh Road East for $500 and to build a basement church covered by a flat tar roof. He also built a rectory at a cost of $16,000. Father Dalton emphasized church attendance, family worship and Marian devotions. He promoted group retreats at Oxley and conducted parish missions in 1948 and 1949, sending out a small army of volunteers to individual households and into the streets armed with loudspeakers to broadcast the date of the next mission. A champion of the rosary, he invited Father

Patrick Peyton to the parish to lead a rosary crusade.

Father Dalton had saved $75,000 for a new church to be erected on the basement church, but it was the next pastor, Father John M. Fogarty, who was given the opportunity to preside over the construction of a more recognizable house of worship. Bishop Cody blessed the cornerstone on 16 May 1953 and opened the church on 14 December 1954. Constructed of Cooksville brick, it cost $130,000 and seated 600 people. A bell was blessed on 9 December 1962, and seating was increased to 750 with an addition in 1964. That year there were 950 families in the parish, a healthy number. Actually, the congregation of Most Precious Blood had grown so quickly immediately after the war that it had already given birth to another parish, St. Christopher's, in 1951. There have been three schools in the parish: St. Bernard's (1930), Most Precious Blood (1955) and St. Andrew's (1957).

Father Paul Charbonneau, better known as the director of Brentwood, and Father Larry Brunet, guided the parish through the changes to the liturgy called for by the Second Vatican Council, the accompanying alterations to the sanctuary and the introduction of new people and practices in the Mass, such as lay readers and ministers of Holy Communion.

On 14 November 1978, a massive fire destroyed the front entrance, the nave, the roof and parish hall. The rectory and sacristy were spared, but smoke damage to the basement and the rectory was extensive. It was back to St. Bernard's for Sunday Mass. Under the leadership of Father Larry Brunet, the present church was completed and opened in June 1980. The architect Robert Langlois designed a semi-circle theatre church that cost $937,000. Although the insurance covered less than half this amount, the parishioners were committed to rebuilding, and, in the process, they emerged from the ordeal a stronger and more unified Catholic community. When St. Joseph the Worker parish was closed in 2002, many parishioners from there joined Most Precious Blood parish.

Sources: DLA, Parish Files; *Most Precious Blood at Fifty 1929-1979* (Windsor: 1979). Additional information supplied by Father Larry Brunet.

Our Lady of Fatima

Our Lady of Fatima

Our Lady of Fatima on Elinor Street began as a mission of St. Anne's in Tecumseh, on 26 July 1947. For the next three years, one of Monsignor Gilbert P. Pitre's assistant priests celebrated Mass on Sundays at Ste-Thérèse school. Bishop Cody made Our Lady of Fatima a parish on 11 November 1950 and appointed Father Lawrence C. Paquette as pastor. Father Paquette was a good choice. As an assistant at St. Anne's, he had taken care of the people of the new parish for more than seven years, compiling a census, visiting the sick and teaching catechism in the school. He was also eager to have his own parish. He told Bishop Cody, in a letter of 14 November 1950, that since a portion of the western part of Our Lady of Fatima was made up of people from St. Rose of Lima, he was anxious to visit them.

Father Paquette built a prefabricated church and rectory, a familiar approach to church building during Bishop Cody's days. Having a church as quickly as possible was uppermost in the bishop's way of thinking, and having one at minimum cost was the ideal.

Father Edgar H. Robert was the second pastor. His appointment began in July 1952, and he stayed for twelve years. A kind and hard working priest, he took care of the church and property, even mowing the four and one half acres (1.82 ha) of lawn with a push mower! After Father Robert there came Father Edward P. Forton (1964-67), Father Herman R. Reardon (1967-81), Father Joseph P. Langlois (1981-88), Father J. Douglas Mercer (1988-94) and Father Joseph N. Bagatto. Under Father Bagatto, the parishioners financed a series of renovations to the church and rectory, from 2002-2005, under the guidance of an in-house architect, Greg McLean. They spent in the neighbourhood of $100,000 and never borrowed a penny.

In June 2005, Father Bagatto retired but remained in the rectory to serve the parish. The administration of Our Lady of Fatima passed into the hands of St. John Vianney parish. On Pentecost Sunday, 4 June 2006, Bishop R. Anthony Daniels, auxiliary bishop of the diocese of London, celebrated the last Mass in the church.

Sources: DLA, Parish Files; Paula B. Bajamic, "Gather us in ... Our Lady of Fatima and St. John Vianney parishes unite," *Newsletter of the Diocese of London*, no. 123 (Fall 2006), 8. Additional supplied by Father Joseph Bagatto and Diane Adair.

Our Lady of Guadalupe

In 1919, the Windsor Separate School Board asked the Ursulines to provide additional teachers. Mother M. Clare Gaukler, OSU, agreed to the request but needed to find larger living quarters for the Sisters. Her mother, Mrs. Josephine Gaukler, and her brother, Frank, purchased the McGregor property in the 5000 block of Riverside Drive East and transferred it to the Ursulines on 29 April 1919. The property had 98 feet (29.4 m) of river frontage and encompassed 70 acres (28.5 ha) from Riverside Drive to Tecumseh Road East. There was also a mansion, which became Glengarda. In 1951, the Ursulines donated a parcel of land from this property — south of Wyandotte Street East, between Raymo Road and Westminster Boulevard — to the diocese of London for a church and rectory.

In May 1951, Bishop Cody selected Father T. Gordon Dill as the first pastor of Our Lady of Guadalupe parish. Territory for the parish was taken from the parishes of Our Lady of the Rosary and St. Rose of Lima. Beginning on 8 July 1951, Father Dill celebrated two Masses in the Glengarda auditorium for the parishioners. The first church (now the parish hall) measured 110 feet by 40 feet (33 m by 12 m). It was one of many similar prefabricated churches built in Cody's time. Men from the parish cleared the property. The groundbreaking ceremony took place on 3 October 1951. A contractor was hired to erect the church, and the parish men worked alongside the paid labourers. The first Mass was celebrated on

Our Lady of Guadalupe

Christmas Day 1951. The men also assembled and varnished the pews, built two altars, a confessional and Stations of the Cross and installed a church bell. The women provided the altar linens and drapes. The total cost, including furnishings and sidewalk, was $35,000, which was paid in full by 1 January 1953.

The church was a simple building. It was cold and drafty in the winter, unbearably hot in the summer and, as the congregation grew, crowded and uncomfortable all year round. Father Dill lived behind the sacristy. Since it was impossible to provide living quarters for an assistant, a two-storey rectory was opened in December 1953, at a cost of $40,000. It was more expensive than the church but built to last longer. The parishioners paid off the rectory debt in four years.

By 1962, the parish needed a new church. The architectural firm of Sheppard, Mason, Brand and Langlois won the competition, submitting a thoroughly modern design that had none of the Gothic about it. This was a significant departure from past practice in the diocese. The triangle, not the perpendicular, is the basic geometric shape. Three oversized identical gables, with steep-pitched roofs and plenty of glass, form the basic look of the church. The gables above each entrance converge where the flèche can be seen, which is directly over the altar in the sanctuary. The floor plan is in the shape of the cross. All the pews, including those at the side entrances, face the altar. Seating capacity is 750. There is a stark simplicity to the sanctuary. The alterations to it, in order to accommodate the liturgical changes that were introduced in 1965, a year after the church opened, were relatively minimal.

Monsignor J. Austin Roney turned the first sod on 19 May 1963. Bishop Carter blessed the cornerstone on 21 November 1963 and officially opened the church on 7 June 1964. The first Mass had been celebrated on 3 April. Fifty years later, Our Lady of Guadalupe is clustered with St. Rose of Lima, where the priest for both parishes resides. The parish has three schools: St. Joseph, St. Thomas and F.J. Brennan High School.

Sources: DLA, Parish Files; *Twenty-Fifth Anniversary of Our Lady of Guadalupe 1951-1976* (Windsor: 1976).

Our Lady of Mount Carmel

Our Lady of Mount Carmel

Bishop Cody founded Our Lady of Mount Carmel parish on 4 July 1953 and appointed Father Patrick J. Donovan as the first pastor. He remained at the parish for seventeen years. Raymond J. Durocher Sr. donated the land at the corner of Cousineau Road and Mount Royal Drive for the church and rectory. The inaugural parish Mass was said at Our Lady of Mount Carmel school, on 12 July 1953. Approximately 150 people attended. Monsignor J. Austin Roney turned the first sod for the church on 18 October 1953. It was an all-wood prefabricated structure that seated 320 people. The first Sunday Mass was celebrated on 14 February 1954. The church with its attached rectory was subsequently covered in aluminum siding. Mike Lahoud, contractor, added a parish hall.

In 1966, the parish sponsored a "mission" at St. Jude's school for those parishioners who lived east of Howard Avenue from Cabana Road to Highway 3 and the 6th Concession. Father Joseph Langlois started this mission, which lasted ten years. It came to an end when the new church was built.

On 20 March 1976, fire completely destroyed the church. A passerby rescued Monsignor Charles W. Carrigan and his housekeeper, Alice Ouellette, from the rectory. It was a sad day in the history of the parish — twenty-five years of hard work and sacrifice vanished in the flames and smoke — but Monsignor Carrigan and the parishioners looked upon the calamity as a fortuitous opportunity to build a better, larger and more permanent church for their expanding congregation. The parish did not waste time. The sod turning ceremony took place on

11 March 1977. Bishop Sherlock, as the auxiliary bishop, blessed the cornerstone on 2 October 1977, and after he became bishop of the diocese, he consecrated the altars and officially opened the church on 17 September 1978. At the cornerstone ceremony, he told the people, "The building of the church is a sign that our faith remains strong." The first Mass had already taken place on Christmas Eve 1977.

Robert Langlois, architect, employed the hexagon in the design of the church. It has two main sections under one roof and connected by a foyer that runs from the front entrance to the rear. As one enters at the front, the church is on the left and the vestry, rectory, and parish hall are on the right. The church seats 610, there are no pillars, and the pews are arranged so that no one is far from the sanctuary. The church and hall cost $685,000; the furnishings were another $29,000; and the pews, made of red oak and purchased from Valley City Company in Dundas, Ontario, cost $27,000.

The crucifix in the sanctuary and the statues of the Blessed Virgin Mary and St. Joseph are made of fiberglass and were imported from Italy. The stained-glass windows also come from Italy and are notable for their raised glass. The baptismal font and the tabernacle are hammered bronze. The Stations of the Cross are also bronze and the gift of the Ursuline sisters. The altar is made of red oak. The Baldwin organ was purchased in Windsor for $15,000. A list of the donors and their donations was compiled for a special souvenir book.

Sources: DLA, Parish Files; *Windsor Star*, 19 June 1976, 3 October 1977, 14 January 1978.

Our Lady of Perpetual Help

On 19 October 1945, Father William E. Dillon of Sacred Heart parish recommended to Bishop Kidd that the diocese establish a new parish in the Remington Park district of Windsor and that it be called Our Lady of Perpetual Help. Sacred Heart would provide the parishioners and territory. There were 225 founding families. Bishop Kidd agreed with the recommendation but proceeded cautiously, as was his custom. In December 1945, the diocese purchased property from A.R. Marentette, at the corner of Parent Avenue and Grand Marais Road East, close to Our Lady of Perpetual Help school. On 22 July 1946, the bishop appointed Father Charles Carrigan as administrator. The next day, he instructed Father Carrigan to erect a basement church, the dimensions of which would be 100 feet in length, 42 feet in width and 10 feet in height (30 m by 12.6 m by 3 m). The roof would be made of cement covered in roofing material and be ready to support a superstructure at some later date. John R. Boyde was hired as the architect and Meyers Construction Company was awarded the contract.

Father Carrigan estimated that the basement church would cost $28,000 and that another $7,500 would be needed for a six-room rectory, the upper part of which would remain unfinished. In anticipation of a start date in August 1946, Father Carrigan asked the bishop for a loan of $30,000 and permission to use a reserve fund of $10,000. In the meantime, he informed the bishop, the parish had converted the old separate school into a hall and would use that as a church and that an announcement concerning the new parish would be made from the pulpit of Sacred Heart church on 1 September 1946. The bishop loaned the parish $25,000 and told Father Carrigan to have the parishioners pay for the church furnishings.

A sod-breaking ceremony for the church took place on 24 August 1946. The rectory was ready by 3 March 1947, and Bishop Kidd blessed and opened the basement church on 27 June 1947. Sixteen years passed before the superstructure was added. Mark Construction did the work in 1962-63, at a cost of $110,000. Two decades later, the parish financed several major renovations to the church: a new sanctuary (1984-85); a new front entrance, including the installation of an elevator for handicap access, and a new washroom (1989-90); and removal of

Our Lady of Perpetual Help

the front entrance canopy, new heated stairs, a walkway to the road and elevator, new boiler, an air conditioning unit and electrical work (2002).

Our Lady of Perpetual Help is an ethnically diverse parish with a strong sense of community and close ties to the parish school, which has 600 students.

Sources: DLA, Parish Files. Additional information supplied by Shirley Robillard.

Our Lady of the Rosary

Our Lady of the Rosary parish was originally called Our Lady of the Lake (Notre-Dame-du-Lac) and is now commonly referred to as Holy Rosary. The parish has had a long and venerable history, punctuated in 1917 with the diocese's only parish riot and yearlong boycott of the parish priest. Over the decades the fortunes of the parish have mirrored those of the neighbourhood that it has served, evolving from a largely French-Canadian rural enclave to a crowded industrial urban landscape dominated by waves of immigrants in search of work in the auto industry.

In 1881, Father James T. Wagner of St. Alphonsus began to minister to the sixty to seventy Catholic families in Walkerville and Sandwich East (Ford City, 1913-1935). After three years had passed, he convinced Bishop Walsh to elevate the mission into a parish. The bishop took territory from St. Anne's in Tecumseh and St. Alphonsus in Windsor and directed that a church be built facing the Detroit River, on the southeast corner of what is now Riverside Drive East and Drouillard Road. On 18 May 1884, Bishop Walsh blessed the cornerstone; on 12 June 1884, he appointed Father Bartholomew Boubat as the administrator; and on 3 November 1884, he blessed and opened the church, which was described as "a lovely little white wooden church with a beautiful little steeple."

Our Lady of the Rosary

At some later date, this wooden church was covered with a brick façade. The first pastor was Father Alexandre M. LaPierre, who arrived on 25 April 1885.

Father Lucien A. Beaudoin was the second pastor, from 18 June 1891 until his death on 19 August 1917. Father Beaudoin's accomplishments were many. He established Our Lady of the Lake cemetery on 17 July 1892; he decorated the interior of the first church in 1893; he founded four separate schools: Notre Dame (1894), St. Louis (1895), St. Anne's (1905) and St. Edward's (1908); he invited the Sisters of St. Joseph to the parish in 1901; following the destruction by fire of the first church, on 16 March 1907, he organized the building of the present church.

The cornerstone was blessed on 27 October 1907. The three bells, one of which was donated by Mrs. Edward Chandler Walker, were blessed on 20 September 1908, and Bishop McEvay dedicated the church under the new name of Our Lady of the Rosary on 11 October 1908. The architectural firm of William Brothers designed a Romanesque-style church. It is built of brick and trimmed in stone, is 165 feet (49.5 m) in length and seats 1,000 people. The twin dome bell towers are its distinguishing feature. The cost was $45,000. The front steps were revamped into their current circular shape in 1923, and the interior was decorated in stages from 1925 to the early 1930s. During this period the dome of the sanctuary was decorated with a painting that

depicts the Blessed Virgin Mary giving the rosary to St. Dominic. Also featured in the painting is St. Catherine of Siena.

Monsignor François-Xavier Laurendeau was pastor from 1917 to 1942. He survived the anti-Bishop Fallon riot of September 1917 and the yearlong protest against his appointment to the parish to become one of Holy Rosary's most beloved parish priests. Monsignor Wilfrid J. Langlois, a native son of the parish who sang at the church dedication in 1908, was the next pastor, from 1942 to 1956 and again from 1958 to 1965. The Catholic population of east Windsor had grown so large that out of Holy Rosary nine new parishes were formed. They were Immaculate Conception (1904); St. Anne (1912), St. Rose of Lima (1924), St. Theresa (1928), Most Precious Blood (1929), Sts. Cyril and Methodius (1940), St. Joseph (1943), St. Francis (1950) and Our Lady of Guadalupe (1951).

After Monsignor Langlois retired, the administration of the parish passed into the hands of the LaSalette Fathers of Attleboro, Massachusetts. Father Arnold E. Sillery, MS, was the first LaSalette pastor. He was assisted by Father George S. Morin, MS, Father Maurice Viens, MS, and Brother Aloysius Machabee, MS. The LaSalette Fathers faced a huge challenge. In 1900, there were 303 families in the parish; by 1924, that number had risen to 1,000; but by 1965, it had declined to 300. In the face of a shrinking congregation, they had to revivify parish life, implement the liturgical reforms and restore the fabric of the church.

To celebrate the centennial of the parish in 1984, the parish financed the restoration of the two towers, the front steps, the stained-glass windows and the Stations of the Cross, the redecoration of the church hall, upgrading of the kitchen, landscaping for the parking lot, new wiring, heating and sanctuary drapes and lighting, handicap access and the construction of a new rectory and parish office.

Holy Rosary was clustered with St. Anne's in Walkerville on 1 July 2001. The LaSalette Fathers left the parish on 30 September 2004. Holy Rosary was closed on 31 October 2007.

Sources: DLA, Parish Files; Mary Kate Brogan, *Our Lady of the Rosary Parish Windsor, Ontario 1884 Centennial 1984* (Windsor: 1984).

Sacred Heart

Although nine lots on the south side of Ottawa Street at Benjamin Avenue had been conveyed to the diocese of London, in 1914 and 1916, Bishop Fallon did not appoint Father Denis L. Brisson as the first pastor of Sacred Heart of Jesus parish until 24 June 1924. The new parish immediately went to work. By August 1924, it had erected a temporary wooden church for $7,500. It measured 80 feet by 40 feet (24 m by 12 m) and seated 500 people. Bishop Fallon blessed and opened this church on 7 September 1924. Within three years, there were 363 families in the parish. The first church had already outlived its usefulness.

On 31 March 1927, construction of a new church commenced. John R. Boyde was the architect, and Blonde and Ibbetson were the contractors. Total cost, not including the furnishings, was $185,000. The style is Romanesque, and the basic dimensions are 150 feet in length and 85 feet in width (45 m by 25.5 m). Compared to Holy Rosary on Riverside Drive (1907), Sacred Heart is a grander and larger version of that church, with higher vertical proportions and greater architectural details. It was a huge parish church, an example of the kind of Ontario Catholic triumphalism promoted by Bishop Fallon, who blessed the cornerstone on 22 May 1927 and presided at the church's solemn dedication on 11 December 1927. Ten years later, there were 1,000 families in the parish.

Father Brisson died on 23 November 1938 and was succeeded by Father William E. Dillon, who remained as pastor until his death on 22 August 1954. During Monsignor Dillon's pastorate, the parish significantly reduced its debt of $106,500, renovated and decorated the interior of the church, saw 700 Sacred Heart men join the Canadian armed services during the Second World War, seventeen of whom died, and led all parishes in contributions to the 1947 bishop's campaign. The renovations and decoration took place from 1941 to 1947 and included three new altars (the main altar being designed by Rambusch Decorating Company of New York and executed by the Ontario Marble Company of Peterborough), a marble communion rail, stained-glass windows, sanctuary furniture and three bells that were blessed by Bishop Cody on 29 June 1947. These bells were purchased from the Meneely Bell Company in Troy, New York. One

was 3,000 lbs. (1,875 kg.) and named St. Michael in honour of Bishop Michael Francis Fallon; the medium-sized bell weighed 1,200 lbs. (750 kg.) and was given the name St. Denis in memory of Father Denis Brisson, the founding pastor; and the smallest one at 1,000 lbs. (625 kg.) was christened St. William, the patron saint of Monsignor William Dillon.

The spiritual statistics for Sacred Heart's first twenty-five years are impressive. There were 4,162 baptisms, 335 converts, 1,270 marriages, 2,888 confirmations and 764 funerals. Adding to an already

Sacred Heart

busy parochial life was the fact that the parish actively supported diocesan efforts to minister to the growing number of Italian, German and Hungarian Catholics in Windsor. Beginning in 1929, priests for these different national groups often resided at the parish. In 1946, the people of St. Anthony of Padua, the Hungarian parish, publicly thanked Monsignor Dillon for assisting them as they struggled to pay the mortgage on their church. Joseph Cardinal Mindszenty also thanked Monsignor Dillon.

Alterations to the sanctuary, in conformity to the liturgical renewal, were modest. Much of the rest of the interior was left untouched. As time passed, however, the parish began to decline in the same way as its nearest sister parish, Immaculate Conception. The surrounding neighbourhood experienced many transformations; the first generation of parishioners had either died or moved away and their children and grandchildren lived elsewhere. In 1997, Sacred Heart was clustered with Immaculate Conception and closed its doors on 31 December 2001. The diocese sold the church to the

Coptic Orthodox Patriarchate (Egyptian), which renamed it Saint Mary and St. Moses.

Sources: DLA, Parish Files; *Windsor Star*, 9 August 1997; *Sacred Heart Church, Windsor, Ontario, Église du Sacré Coeur, 124-1949, 25th Anniversary* (Windsor: 1949); *Sacred Heart Church, Windsor, Ontario, 50th Anniversary 1924-1974* (Windsor: 1974). Additional information supplied by Father James F. Roche.

St. Alphonsus

In 1854, Windsor became a village and the Canadian terminus for the Great Western Railway, bringing in its wake numerous Irish Catholic navvies who settled in the village alongside the already established French-Canadians. That same year, Samuel Smith Macdonell donated three lots on Goyeau Street south of Park Street to Bishop Charbonnel of the diocese of Toronto. Bishop Pinsoneault of the new diocese of London imparted the episcopal blessing on the site on 18 September 1856, and the first church was duly dedicated in the autumn of 1857. Facing Goyeau Street, this church was a simple frame building with a plain interior that quickly needed an addition to accommodate a steadily growing congregation. Added were a combination gallery and organ loft and a much larger sanctuary and the removal of the sacristy further to the rear of the church.

St. Alphonsus was a mission of Assumption parish in Sandwich until 1 July 1865. On that day, Bishop Pinsoneault appointed the twenty-seven-year-old Father James T. Wagner as the first pastor. Dean Wagner's accomplishments were many during the next thirty-one years of the parish's history. He built the first rectory; he sponsored the building of the first St. Mary's Academy, 1865 to 1867, on property west of the church donated by Vital Ouellette; he purchased the church bell, named Maria Theresa Philomena, in 1869; and he went to Europe to raise funds to build the present St. Alphonsus church. In 1887, Dean Wagner set up a catechetical mission for black children, and in 1888, he invited the Religious Hospitallers of St. Joseph to Windsor, where they opened up Hôtel-Dieu Hospital on Ouellette Avenue. As dean of Windsor, Wagner helped to found St. Clement's in McGregor, Essex County, Notre-Dame-du-Lac (Our Lady of

the Rosary) on Riverside Drive East in Windsor and Star of the Sea on Pelee Island.

Bishop Walsh blessed the cornerstone of the second church on 3 September 1871, and he officially opened it on 1 July 1873. It cost $30,000. Free of debt

St. Alphonsus

on its completion, thanks to the generosity of Vital Ouellette, St. Alphonsus was the first church in the diocese to be formally consecrated. The interior decoration by Edwards of Detroit was completed on 25 September 1892 and featured a main altar that resembles the one at Assumption church and paintings of St. Alphonsus Ligouri, scenes from the life of Christ and various saints and Doctors of the Church. The wooden ceiling consists of twelve panels and eight medallions; the stained-glass windows are rich in colour and detail; and each of the fourteen Stations of the Cross is 8 feet (2.4 m) high. The dimensions of the Norman-style church are 125 feet by 60 feet (37.5 m by 18 m), and from floor to ceiling, at its centre, 45 feet (13.5 m), with walls 3 feet (1 m) thick. The steeple rose to 204 feet (61.2 m).

Succeeding Dean Wagner, who died on 26 August 1896, was a long line of outstanding diocesan priests: Joseph Bayard, William Flannery, Joseph E. Meunier, Denis J. Downey and Frank. P. White.

The Redemptorists took charge of St. Alphonsus on 5 October 1952. Under their direction, the parish attracted a large number of people for confessions, noon-day Masses, Mother of Perpetual Help devotions and Saturday evening Bible vigils in preparation for Sunday Mass. The Redemptorists left the parish in 1984.

Recent years have witnessed a reinvigoration

of the parish. It sold the property on which stood the rectory and St. Alphonsus Hall to the Windsor Tunnel Corporation, on 4 August 1993. The money from the sale financed parish offices, a boardroom, a parish hall with a capacity for seventy-five people and air conditioning for the hall and church. In 1999-2000, the parish also restored the tower, installed a carillon and erected a spire to replace the one that had been removed eighty years ago. The church bell was displayed in public. The second spire rises to 164 feet (49.2 m). In 2002, the restoration of the stained-glass windows began.

St. Alphonsus parish was clustered with St. Clare's parish in June 1997. When the diocese sold St. Clare's to St. Peter's Maronite community in August 2000, the statue of St. Clare that adorned the front entrance of the church was moved to the courtyard at St. Alphonsus. Today the parish serves an ever-changing downtown population, including many recent immigrants to Canada.

Sources: Michael Power, "Wagner, James Theodore," *DCB* (Toronto: 1990), 12: 1077-78; *St. Alphonsus Church MDCCCLXV-MCMLXV Centennial Celebration* (Windsor: 1965). Additional information supplied by Father Vincent J. Gleeson.

St. Angela Merici

In December 1927, Bishop Fallon commissioned a census of Italian Catholics in the Border Cities, at the request of Archbishop Andrea Cassulo, the apostolic delegate. The census, which was taken by Fallon's priests, counted 1,531 Italians. Of these, 496 regularly attended Mass in the different parishes and 517 attended only occasionally. There were 309 children under seven years of age. Loyalty to the separate schools was sporadic, a sore point with the bishop. Also, many Italians were in transit to the United States. In a letter to the apostolic delegate, dated 30 December 1927, Fallon concluded, "There seems to be no disposition and no desire on the part of the Italian Catholics in this district to have or to support a national Italian church." He promised, however, that he would provide an Italian-speaking priest to these people in the very near future.

Fallon made good on his promise. He stationed Father Alphonse N. Page, who had recently returned from Rome, to Sacred Heart church. Father Page arrived on 13 January 1929 and quickly set up

St. Angela Merici

an Italian chapel at Sacred Heart. He sponsored a mission on 7-14 April 1929, which was given by Father Raphael D'Alfonso. A Holy Name Society was formed on 14 May 1933. These men were involved in fundraising for a church and later had a hand in building it. During the 1930s, the Benedictine Fathers of Detroit often assisted at the Italian chapel. Since they were Italian, their presence helped to unify the Italian Catholic community at a time when work was scarce and poverty was endemic.

In 1938, the apostolic delegate intervened a second time. He convinced Bishop Kidd to accept Father Costantino DeSantis, the administrator of St. Michael's parish in Atlantic City, as pastor of St. Angela Merici in Windsor, a national parish for Italians. No other priest is so closely identified with the early history of St. Angela's than is Father DeSantis.

He arrived on 22 December 1938 and celebrated Mass at Holy Trinity on Christmas Eve. Fundraising for a church began on 1 January 1939. Between that date and 30 June 1939, the parishioners had donated almost $616. Every penny of that modest amount was a sacrifice. At the same time, Father DeSantis organized the CWL, the Catholic Youth Organization (CYO) and St. Angela's Ladies Society. Along with the Holy Name Society, these organizations became the backbone of the parish and continued the campaign to raise money.

The northeast corner of Erie Street and Louis Avenue was selected as the site for a church. Since money was so scarce, Father DeSantis persuaded Keystone Construction to excavate the basement and pour the foundation at no cost and Sterling Construction to discount the cost of building materials. He secured a loan from the diocese and set up a building committee headed by Boldo Camilotto. Work began immediately, with many men from the parish doing the actual construction work. Bishop Kidd blessed the cornerstone on 29 October 1939, and Father DeSantis celebrated the first parish Mass in the basement on Christmas 1939. On Palm Sunday 1940, the church was officially opened. Romanesque in design, the church is a distinctive addition to the heavily commercial appearance of Erie Street.

Wartime considerations prompted Father DeSantis to return to the United States in the summer of 1940. He resumed his pastorate in December 1942. He opened the youth hall next to the church, on 11 December 1949, and built an addition to it in 1952 for kindergarten classes. Father DeSantis was made a monsignor in 1956, retired in 1960 and died on 14 March 1966.

Bishop Cody signed an agreement with the Benedictine Fathers, on 1 September 1955, to assume the administration of the parish when Monsignor DeSantis retired. But it was the Missionaries of St. Charles, known as the Scalabrini Fathers, who came to the parish on 18 December 1957 and have been the parish priests since then. The Sisters of the Holy Family have worked at various ministries in the parish since 1963. The church was remodeled and expanded in 1958, in 1975 for the liturgical changes and in 1989 for the fiftieth anniversary. The parish tore down the youth hall in 2005 and will build a new one.

St. Angela Merici parish remains a robust Catholic presence in Windsor's "Via Italia" on Erie Street.

Sources: DLA, Parish Files, Bishop Fallon Papers, Box 5, Fallon to the Apostolic Delegate, 30 December 1927; *St. Angela Merici Parish and The Italian Community of Windsor* (Windsor: 1956); "Celebrating the 60th Anniversary of Sant' Angela Merici, a church for the millennium 1939-1999."

St. Anne

St. Anne's parish began in controversy, another example of the local French-English language debate in the diocese of London. Bishop Fallon was determined to establish an English-speaking parish in the Border Cities, the first of its kind, and

St. Anne

he chose to found St. Anne's in Walkerville. In December 1911, he took out an option to purchase property at the corner of Richmond Street and Argyle Road, and on 1 January 1912, on the advice of his council, he announced the creation of St. Anne's parish. Territory for the new parish was taken from Father Beaudoin's Notre-Dame-du-Lac (Our Lady of the Rosary), and St. Edward's school, financed by Father Beaudoin, also went to St. Anne's. On both counts, Father Beaudoin sued Bishop Fallon in ecclesiastical court, and in 1914 Rome ruled that Bishop Fallon had a right to found parishes but that he had to pay Notre-Dame-du-Lac $7,000 in compensation for the school.

Father Hubert N. Robert was the first pastor. Mass was said at St. Edward's school until the church was opened. In November 1912, Bishop Fallon blessed the cornerstone. J. Jacques and Company, architects, designed a simple but attractive church. Built of brick, it blended into the neighbourhood and could have been mistaken for a schoolhouse. The church was completed in 1913, and the bell, donated by Mrs. Edward Chandler Walker, was blessed on 28 June 1914. There were thirty-five founding families, a very small number, who were saddled with a $39,000 debt, which increased several years later when the walls had to be straightened and secured by the Canadian Bridge Company.

Father James B. Neville came to the parish in 1916 and remained until 1950. He built the rectory in 1923 at a cost of $20,000, which was paid in full by the parishioners when the rectory was ready for occupancy. In 1940, the people retired the parish debt, and, ten years later, they responded to Father Neville's call to fund major repairs to the church and rectory. To galvanize his parishioners, Father Neville pointed to the generosity of the congregation at neighbouring St. Mary's Anglican church. Money was raised to fix the tower, roof, eaves, down pipes, electrical wiring and plastering in the church. The interior and the trim on the exterior were painted. The rectory was renovated and painted, after twelve years of neglect.

Monsignor Francis J. Brennan was pastor from 1953 until his death on 21 April 1964. He oversaw the construction of a new and much larger St. Anne's school, the cornerstone of which was blessed on 21 June 1959. (The name of the parish school had been changed from St. Edward's to St. Anne's in 1921.) Father J. John McCormick succeeded Monsignor Brennan in 1964. Bishop Carter instructed Father McCormick to build a new church. The 1913 church had been built in a hurry, and restoration could not save it. Moreover, it was situated at the eastern edge of the parish territory, which made it difficult to attract and keep parishioners.

The old church was demolished. While the new one was being built, parish Mass was celebrated in the auditorium of Walkerville Collegiate. The architect was Robert J. Langlois. He designed a church in keeping with the liturgical reforms. The seating capacity is 450, and skylights light the sanctuary. The cost was $225,000. The church opened on 16 August 1970. The parish's 535 families also paid for air conditioning, a new parking lot and church furnishings. On 30 June 1976, the debt stood at $52,000. On 1 July 2001, St. Anne's was clustered with Our Lady of the Rosary. The parish was closed on 31 October 2007.

Sources: DLA, Parish Files; *Evening Record* (Windsor), 24 June 1914, 2; Patricia Horvath, "History of St. Anne's Church Windsor (Walkerville)," (Windsor: 1976); *St. Anne's Yesterday St. Anne's Today 1950-1951* (Windsor: 1951).

St. Anthony of Padua

On 25 September 1927, Windsor's Roman Catholic Hungarians held a meeting and founded a "parish" under the guidance of the Hungarian priests stationed at Holy Cross church in Detroit. They organized themselves by selecting twelve curators (trustees) and twelve collectors

St. Anthony of Padua

(ushers). Mass was said at St. Peter's Syrian church on Parent Avenue. About a thousand of the approximately 1,800 Hungarians then living in Windsor and vicinity were Roman Catholics. Others were Presbyterians, Lutherans, Greek Catholics or of no religious affiliation.

The parishioners published a parish constitution on 31 October 1928, and the first entry in the baptismal records is dated 1 January 1929, considered to be the official inauguration of the parish. Father John Matty was the founding parish priest. He had been a chaplain in the Austro-Hungarian Army during the First World War. When the army was dissolved and the Empire dismembered, by virtue of the Versailles Treaty, Father Matty was left with no parish and no country and so immigrated to the United States. He sought the help of Monsignor E. Eordogh of St. Stephen's Hungarian parish in Toledo, Ohio. He accepted Father Matty's ecclesiastical papers and recommended him to the bishop of Toledo, who gave Father Matty a Slovak parish at Rossford, Ohio. From the diocese of Toledo, he made his way to Windsor.

In 1931, the parishioners decided to build their own church. They chose a site at the corner of Parent Avenue and Shepherd Street East, but they had only sixty dollars in the parish coffers. It was the Great Depression. Money was scarce and unemployment was widespread, but the 1930s was also a time of steep deflation, when a sum of money paltry by today's standards could be used to buy land and build a church. The diocese of London loaned the parish $11,000 to purchase the property and acquire building materials. The men of the parish promised to help in the construction. The cornerstone was laid in 1931, and Bishop Kidd blessed and opened St. Anthony of Padua, a national parish for the Hungarians, on Pentecost Sunday 1932.

The parishioners were unable to pay a penny on the debt for the next nine years, and the debt rose to $21,000. Their inability to pay was a source of irritation and embarrassment, which was only made worse by Father Matty's increasingly erratic behaviour. He was involved in an unfortunate dispute with the pastor of the local Hungarian Lutheran church, in 1935, and the next year a large number of the parishioners signed a petition to have him removed as their pastor. The upshot of the rebellion was that Father Matty left Windsor and returned to the diocese of Toledo. From 1937 to 1940, there were three priests: Father Jacob Wildinger, who encouraged Hungarian-speaking Germans to join the parish, Father N. Wesselenyi and Father George Hetenyi.

From 1940 to 1948, there was no Hungarian-speaking pastor at St. Anthony of Padua. Monsignor Dillon of Sacred Heart parish and his assistants took charge of the Sunday liturgies and paid off the parish debt by 1 October 1946. The Basilian Fathers from Assumption College also helped. To maintain the parish's Hungarian identity, the Daughters of Divine Mercy, a teaching religious order from Hungary, moved into the parish and took over language classes and looked after the school-age children. At one time, they had fifteen members in their Windsor community. Their work saved parish life.

On 1 September 1948, Father Martin Gaspar became the pastor. He stayed at St. Anthony of Padua for more than thirty years, providing a much-needed stability to the parish. He organized the construction of Mindszenty Hall on Marentette Avenue, which was blessed by Bishop Cody on 8 October 1951; he was instrumental in securing diocesan patronage of a Church Art Exhibition at Mindszenty Hall, on 13-15 December 1953; and he was involved in resettling Hungarian refugees in 1956 and 1957, whose presence revitalized the parish for many years. Father Gaspar took part in an ecumenical worship service at Mindszenty Hall on 20 August 1970, which saw members of the different Hungarian churches gather together in a sign of spiritual unity.

Today, St. Anthony of Padua has a small but active congregation of approximately sixty families. A recent influx of Hungarian-speaking Catholics from Transylvania in Romania has tipped the balance in favour of the young.

Sources: DLA, Parish Files. Additional information supplied by Father Louis Angyal.

St. Casimir

There were Lithuanian immigrants in Windsor as early as the 1920s. The bulk of them, however, came between 1948 and 1952. Catholic Lithuanians had to wait many years for a priest of their own. In 1950, Father Bronius Dagilis from Detroit said Mass on Sundays in Sts. Cyril and Methodius Slovak

St. Casimir

church. The first resident priest was Father Joseph C. Danielius. He celebrated Mass at St. Francis of Assisi Croatian church. Father Vincent Rudzinskas was the third Lithuanian priest. He stayed until 1962, when he suffered a heart attack and then paralysis.

Shortly before Easter 1962, Father Victor Kaleckis arrived from the United States. Although small in number, and grateful for the hospitality of other churches, the city's Catholic Lithuanians felt that it was time to have a parish and church of their own. In June 1962, Father Kaleckis approached Bishop Cody about the possibility of forming a parish and buying a church. The bishop agreed and promised to loan the Lithuanians the lion's share of any mortgage. At the end of August 1962, Father Kaleckis had raised $3,000 and put a down payment of $300 towards the purchase of the Lebanese Hall at 808 Marion Avenue. The cost of the hall was $12,000. The diocese loaned the parish $9,000, making good on its promise.

In October 1962, Father Domininkas Lengvinas succeeded as parish priest and continued the pioneering work of Father Kaleckis. On 15 May 1963, Bishop Cody officially established St. Casimir's Lithuanian national parish.

Father Lengvinas remained parish priest until 22 May 1982, when he collapsed and died at a parish wedding. Since then, there has been no resident priest in the parish. In order to preserve a regular liturgical life, the parish formed a committee that looks after the church and rectory and invites Lithuanian priests from Detroit to celebrate Mass on Sundays and holy days and at the occasional funeral. In effect, St. Casimir's is unofficially clustered with Lithuanian parishes in Detroit. Priests who have served the parish in this fashion have been Fathers Casimir Simaitis, S. Maziliauskas, Casimir Butkus, Aloyzas Volskis and A. Babonas.

St. Casimir's has suffered the fate of other national parishes. As the younger generation moved on and the founding members died, the parish rolls dwindled. In St. Casimir's case, there are about thirty devoted parishioners, most of whom are on pension.

Sources: DLA, Parish Files; *Pranash Gaida, Lithuanians in Canada* (Toronto/Ottawa: 1967), 64-65. Additional information supplied by Ronald Dumcius and Frank Kairys.

St. Christopher

Claiming territory from St. Mary's parish in Maidstone and Most Precious Blood parish on Tecumseh Road East, Bishop Cody erected St. Christopher's parish in 1951, in what was then Sandwich East. The boundaries were the Canadian Pacific Railway on the north, the Michigan Central Railway on the south, Pillette Road on the east and Lincoln Road on the west. Father Victor C. Côté, the first pastor, conducted a door-to-door campaign and, after a good deal of door knocking, he found approximately forty Catholic families. When he came to the home of Frederick and Hazel Robinson of 3507 Walker Road, he asked them if they were Catholic. They replied, yes. He then asked them about the hall close to their home. The hall belonged to them and was used for Saturday night dances. They agreed to turn it into a temporary parish church. It was renovated and enlarged and ready for

St. Christopher

the first Mass on 17 June 1951. The first baptism in the parish also took place on that day. The inaugural bulletin appeared on 2 September 1951.

Within eighteen months, there were four Sunday Masses. Assisting Father Côté on a regular basis was Father J. Stanley Murphy, CSB, of Assumption College. The converted dance hall was unequal to the task of accommodating the parishioners almost as soon as it had opened its doors. In August 1952, Monsignor Wilfrid J. Langlois, dean of Essex, turned the sod for a permanent church on Woodward Boulevard, next door to St. Christopher's school that opened in September. Plans indicated a one-story frame church. The contractor was Gerry Provost, a member of the parish. The diocesan loan was $52,000. Construction went quickly enough for Father Côté to sing High Mass in the church on Christmas Eve 1952. Bishop Cody blessed and opened the church on 15 March 1953. A parish hall was opened in September 1954. The parish grew to 175 families and then to more than 275 families.

Raffaele L'Europa, a twenty-three-year-old carver from Italy, designed and executed the mahogany and oak main altar, the main altar tabernacle and two side tabernacles, in January 1953. His work was featured in the *Windsor Daily Star*.

In 1993, the parish decided to renovate the church in three stages — a new façade, the sanctuary and the main body of the church — and to proceed without borrowing any money. To do this, the parishioners formed a twenty-five-person bingo team and a small army of volunteers, such as plumbers, electricians, roofers and drywallers. By June 1992, they had raised $40,000. Working together under the direction of Lino Silvaggi, the people of St. Christopher's tore down the old entrance and built one the entire width of the church, in the process creating enough space for bathrooms, a baptistry at the entrance door and parish meetings. Saverio Galli, known for his work at the Caboto Club in Windsor, designed the two windows: St. Christopher and the Holy Family. In 1999, the parish renovated the sanctuary at a cost of $28,000.

In June, 2007, the St. Christopher parish was suppressed and the church was closed.

Sources: DLA, Parish Files; *Windsor Daily Star*, 24 January 1953, 18; *Windsor Star*, 14 March 1997, 20 July 2001. Additional information supplied by Fred Robinson.

St. Clare of Assisi

Bishop Fallon founded the parish of St. Clare of Assisi on 26 June 1924, taking territory from St. Alphonsus parish, and he appointed Father Edward G. Doe as pastor. Father Doe had been a First World War chaplain who had risen to the rank of major and suffered from shell shock. He celebrated the parish's first Mass at St. Clare school on 20 July 1924 and built the first church on land leased for five years from the Windsor Separate School Board, at the northwest corner of Bruce and Shepherd avenues. A simple wooden frame structure, this church measured 80 feet by 40 feet (24 m by 12 m) and was blessed and opened by Bishop Fallon on 7 December 1924. There were 169 families in the parish. This number rose to 315 by 1931. Immediately after the opening, the parish organized a dozen societies, establishing a well-earned reputation as an extraordinarily active parish. St. Clare's was also known for a rich liturgical life that not only attracted many people but also fostered a sense of long-term loyalty to the parish.

On New Year's Day, 1929, there was a fire in the church. On 4 August 1930, another fire destroyed the building. The parish had already bought land at the northwest corner of Shepherd and Victoria avenues for a new church, but the neighbours objected and the parish purchased property at Victoria Avenue and Tecumseh Road West. It was farmland owned by a Mr. Bedford and was considered to be on the outskirts of the city but central to the slowly emerging urban development. Even though it was the onset of the Great Depression, the parishioners were determined to build. Albert J. Lothian was the

St. Clare of Assisi

engineer and architect, and Blonde Construction, a well-known Catholic firm, was the general contractor. It had submitted the lowest bid at $89,000. Father Doe turned the first sod on 10 November 1930; Monsignor Andrew P. Mahoney blessed the cornerstone on 1 February 1931; and Bishop Kidd blessed and dedicated the church on 13 June 1931.

Lothian's design of St. Clare of Assisi was a significant and daring departure from the conventional. It was the diocese's first and only art deco church. In a publication commemorating the dedication of the church in 1931, we read: "The Structure of the Church proper is that of a twelve sided figure, approximating an elliptical form with the long axis east and west, and not quite parallel to Tecumseh Boulevard; with the Sanctuary openings from the north side of the ellipse; and the two Naves, the main entrance, the Choir loft and Tower opening from the south side of the ellipse and looking towards Tecumseh Boulevard." A clerestory with stained-glass windows on the east, south and west sides was created by the fact that the ceiling in the elliptical or main section of the church was 10 feet (3 m) higher than the rest of the church. The central focus was the main altar, from which no one seated in the main section was more than 35 feet (10.5 m). The church seated up to 800 people.

It was the parish's great misfortune that the roof of their stunningly beautiful and quite original church leaked from the day it opened. The diocese won a protracted lawsuit against Blonde Construction, which as a result was forced into bankruptcy, but a victory in court did not solve the problem of the leaks. Indeed, during the next seventy years, the rain kept coming in. Despite this constant and expensive irritation, the parishioners considered their church a work in progress. It was said that Father Doe (1924-36) built the church; that Father John J. White (1936-53) paid off the debt; and that Father Frank J. Walsh (1953-69) and Bishop Carter, when he was auxiliary and living at the parish, decorated it for the revised liturgy. In 1962, the parish purchased the Stations of the Cross by the Dutch artist Felix Heerkens, and in 1965 it installed three new altars.

By the 1970s, the parish was experiencing a drastic reduction in the size of its congregation, as the elderly died and the young moved to the suburbs or out of town. Sunday Mass attendance declined from 2,000 in 1953 to 1,000 in 1976 and continued to drop during the next two decades. In the late 1990s there were 200 families remaining. The parish clustered with St. Alphonsus in June 1997. When faced with the prospect of spending $900,000 to fix the roof, repair other parts of the church and replace the boiler, the diocese decided to suppress the parish. It was formally closed on 15 June 2000. The church was saved from the wrecking ball when the diocese sold it to a congregation of Maronite Catholics, who renamed the church St. Peter's and successfully restored it.

Sources: DLA, Parish Files; *Windsor Star*, 25 June 1999; "History of St. Clare of Assisi Parish 1924-1979"; *In Commemoration of the Dedication of St. Clare's Church Windsor, Ontario* (1931).

Sts. Cyril and Methodius

Sts. Cyril and Methodius parish, a national parish for Slovak Catholics in Windsor, was established in the latter half of 1940. The founding pastor was Father Francis J. Kurta. A late vocation and student at St. Peter's Seminary, he was ordained in 1935 and remained pastor until 1974, when he officially retired. Father Kurta died on 20 July 1980.

Assisting Father Kurta in the erection of the parish were approximately 184 Slovak families. Generally speaking, Bishop Kidd was reluctant to allow any national group to build a church for its own exclusive use. He relented in the case of the Slovaks, because they were eager and organized and had a priest, but he stipulated that prior to any construction, they had to raise sufficient funds

to purchase property and build at minimum a basement church. By 25 October 1940, the Slovaks had met these requirements. For around $1,305, a wartime bargain, they had acquired from the city of Windsor seventeen lots bounded by Alexis Road, Seminole Street, Chandler Road and an alley, on the understanding that any building erected on the property would be permanent, have exterior walls of stone, brick or stucco and cost no less than $3,000. In the meantime, Bishop Kidd petitioned for and received a special Indult, dated 15 February 1941, from the Holy See to sanction his decision to give the Slovaks of Windsor a national parish.

Sts. Cyril and Methodius

Interestingly, as of 11 November 1941, Bishop Kidd instructed Father Kurta to co-operate with an elected lay committee of four men in the financial administration of the parish. This was anything but standard practice in the management of parish finances in the diocese of London. Normally, every parish priest was responsible to the bishop for keeping and safeguarding the records and supplying the diocese with a report every June and December. Father Kurta, however, was required to work with a committee of lay people, who were allowed to collect and count parish funds before they were handed over to the pastor and to receive a duplicate copy of deposit slips from the bank. And although all funds were deposited in the name of the Episcopal Corporation of the Diocese of London — a legal requirement for every parish and mission — no withdrawals from the Sts. Cyril and Methodius account could be made without the signatures of Father Kurta and two members of the committee. This set a pattern of lay control at Sts. Cyril and Methodius that in the future would generate unseemly conflict between Father Kurta and his parishioners.

Windsor's Catholic Slovaks built and furnished a simple but solid brick church, six bays deep, for a total cost of $32,084. It was opened in 1943. The money for the church came from loans from a parishioner and Father Kurta, totaling almost $13,000, parish savings, cash on hand, small donations made by individual parishioners and monies raised by bazaars and the Altar Society. Father Kurta certainly did his part to see his parish succeed. He lived an austere life on a monthly salary of fifty dollars, and his parishioners, few of whom could have been described as middle class, made considerable sacrifices to have their own church.

In 1951, Father Kurta purchased an additional eight lots from the city for $2,900, which would act as a buffer against unwanted development near the church; in 1957, the three marble altars that had been purchased in 1943 were formally consecrated; in 1956, the church interior was decorated for the first time, at a cost of $4,000; and in 1960, the rectory was renovated. By far the biggest and costliest development to take place in the parish, during Father Kurta's lengthy pastorate, was the construction of a much needed parish hall, St. Cyril's Slovak Centre. Opened on 18 April 1973, the hall cost $165,372. J.G. Hreno and Associates was the architectural firm, and A. Lombardi & Son was the contractor.

What should, however, have been a time of rejoicing in the parish soon degenerated into a bitter public quarrel between Father Kurta, who was on the verge of retirement, and the parish's advisory board, which had been approved by Father Kurta. Two things prompted the conflict: a significant discrepancy between two versions of Father Kurta's financial report concerning the hall and the apparent popularity of his assistant, Father George Kadlec, who came to the parish in 1971 and was understood by many to be in line to replace Father Kurta. Once before, as far back as 1950, the parishioners tried to have Father Kurta replaced, but Bishop Cody, who had recently become the bishop of the diocese, refused to bow to their demands and nothing came of the protest. In 1973, a more determined band of parishioners, led by the advisory board, demanded that Father Kurta resign in favour of Father Kadlec and that the diocese audit the parish's books.

Bishop Carter took a dim view of the advisory board's aggressive politicking and came down firmly on the side of Father Kurta. The bishop forced Father Kadlec out of the parish, abolished the advisory board, and reaffirmed the rule that only Catholic Slovaks in Windsor could belong to Sts. Cyril and Methodius parish. (Several of the leading dissidents lived in Detroit.) Vindicated, Father Kurta retired as pastor in 1974 and was replaced by Father William S. Lacko, a Slovak-speaking Jesuit.

Peace returned to the parish, which continued to grow and prosper under effective pastoral leadership. Over the last thirty years, Sts. Cyril and Methodius has continued to serve the spiritual and community needs of the city's Slovak Catholics. In 2005, the parish celebrated its sixty-fifth anniversary.

Sources: DLA, Parish Files; *Windsor Star*, 14 October 1940, 3.

St. Francis of Assisi

On 25 September 1948, Bishop Kidd appointed Father Lujo Ivandic, OFM, a war refugee, as the founding pastor of St. Francis of Assisi Croatian parish. Father Ivandic, a Franciscan of the Croatian province, worked in the parish for seventeen years, during which time he purchased a Baptist church at Albert and Seminole streets and converted it into the parish's first church. It was blessed and opened on 20 August 1950. Father Ivandic's pastorate was marred by many struggles with certain post-war members of the Croatian community who were openly hostile towards the Church and refused to welcome Father Ivandic when he visited their homes.

That same hostility disrupted the work of the second pastor, Father Milos Culin, a priest from the Sibenik diocese who arrived in Windsor in September 1965. Father Culin built a second, slightly larger, church, at the corner of Turner Road and Seneca Street. Officially blessed on 5 November 1967, it held 250 people. Attached to the rear of the church, off the sanctuary, were a modest rectory and office. Unfortunately, the spirit of peace and generosity that allowed Father Culin to work with a parish committee to build a new church did not last. Parochial life degenerated into constant quarrelling and dissension that became so acrimonious that the diocese was obliged to appoint Monsignor Philip A. Mugan to preside over parish meetings. The result was the departure of Father Culin in

St. Francis of Assisi

June 1973, and an invitation that same month from Bishop Carter to the Croatian Franciscans of the Holy Family Custody, in Chicago, to assume the administration of the parish. They accepted.

Father Ferdo Skoko, OFM, became the third pastor. In only three years, he initiated catechism and Croatian language classes, liquidated the parish debt, organized the parish's twenty-fifth anniversary and accumulated a parish fund of $41,000, in itself a remarkable achievement. Father Zvonimir Kutlesa, OFM, succeeded him on 20 August 1976. He established the children's choir, which evolved into the Kardinal A. Stepinac Kolo and Tamburica Group (dance and music); he was instrumental in bringing to the parish the Franciscan Sisters of the Immaculate Conception, who arrived from Dubrovnik, Croatia, on 27 February 1980; and he oversaw the purchase of property on Turner Road and the construction of the third and present church complex. Monsignor Jean Z. Noël turned the sod on 1 June 1980. Bishop Sherlock led the dedication ceremony on 4 October 1981, the 800th anniversary of the birth of St. Francis of Assisi, and left the congregation with these words: "You are Catholic, Canadian and Croatian."

The parishioners built a church with a capacity for 500 people, a rectory, a convent, a basement hall large enough to hold 800 people, a cultural centre with eight classrooms, and an impressive and attractive plaza in front of the church and rectory. The architect was Predrag Kovacevic and the general contractor was Martinac and Sons, Inc. The design incorporates traditional Croatian and modern elements of architecture. John Tomac of Majestic Tool & Mold Ltd. designed the crosses over the entrance and on the tower. The church bell came from the old St. Anne's church in Walkerville. The Roko Juricic family purchased and donated it.

In 1989, the parish built a choir loft and vestibule inside the main entrance to the church and erected golden Gothic arches over the main altar. In 1990, Branimir Dorotic of Croatia installed his painting of the crucifixion on the sanctuary wall, and the 450 families eliminated the parish debt, fourteen years ahead of schedule. The parish established a branch of the Knights of Columbus in 1997, hosted the twenty-fourth Canadian Croatian Folklore Festival in 1998 and celebrated its golden anniversary on 1 October 2000.

Sources: DLA, Parish Files; *1950-2000 The Golden Anniversary of the parish of St. Francis of Assisi Croatian Catholic Church Windsor, Ontario Canada* (Windsor: 2000); "A Short History of the Croatian Catholic Parish of St. Francis of Assisi in Windsor, Ontario," (1981).

St. Gabriel

St. Gabriel's parish is one of a string of parishes that runs in almost a straight line through South Windsor: St. Martin's, Christ the King, St. Gabriel's and Our Lady of Mount Carmel. Bishop Cody established St. Gabriel's in June 1959 and named Father Aloysius L.J. Nolan as the first pastor. Sunday Masses were celebrated in the gymnasium of St. Gabriel's elementary school for two and a half years, beginning with the inaugural Mass on 1 July 1959.

The altar was an old side altar from Christ the King. To encourage participation in the liturgy, Father Nolan situated it in the "round." Other innovations introduced by Father Nolan during his five-year pastorate were a hymn board, the placement of offertory collection baskets and unconsecrated communion wafers at the entrance of the church, lay readers and adult Mass servers. He promoted tithing, congregational singing, silent prayer after Mass, parish picnics and summer camps for the children. One Palm Sunday he rode into church on a donkey. It was not uncommon for Father Nolan to scoot around the neighbourhood on his motorbike.

In 1960, the parish initiated a Spiritual and Financial Campaign. The aim was threefold: to compile a parish census, to have parishioners meet and work with each other outside of Sunday Mass and to raise one-third the cost of building a permanent church and rectory. All aspects of the

St. Gabriel

campaign were very successful.

Land was purchased at the corner of Curry Avenue and Cabana Road East, next to St. Gabriel's school, and Monsignor Wilfrid D.J. Langlois performed the sod-breaking ceremony in June 1961. The cornerstone was blessed later the same year. The cost of the church and rectory was $170,000. An additional $20,000 was spent on church furnishings. The architect was Blackwell & Haggarty of London; the general contractor was Ascon Construction Ltd.; the electrical contractor was Ebbinghaus Electric Ltd.; and the heating and plumbing contractor was Hussey Plumbing & Heating Ltd.

A front entrance lobby connects the church to the hall and rectory to form a ground-level complex under one roof. The decoration of the interior of the church was kept to an austere minimum. St. Gabriel's had a crucifix on the wall of the sanctuary, Stations of the Cross, two statues — one of the Virgin Mary and the Infant Jesus and one of St. Joseph — and three altars — an altar of sacrifice, an altar for the Blessed Sacrament and an altar of God's Word. Philip Aziz, the London artist who worked for Bishop Cody at St. Peter's cathedral, designed the baptismal font. Absent from the interior were vigil candles and a communion rail. The most striking piece of liturgical art can be found on the façade of the church, high above the entrance. It is a brilliant white sculpture of St. Gabriel the Archangel, the parish's patron. Professor Joseph N. Delauro of Assumption University designed the sculpture, which is readily noticeable from the road and is surmounted by a large cross.

In 1959, St. Gabriel's parish had 535 families and two schools: St. Gabriel's (1956) and St.

Hubert's (1958). Twenty-five years later, the number of families nearly doubled to 1,055. On 9 February 1964, a flash fire destroyed the sacristy and its contents. The parishioners restored the sacristy and replaced the contents at a cost of $21,600.

Reflecting the changing demographics of South Windsor, a group of seniors from the community formed the St. Gabriel's Seniors on 6 April 1990. They enjoy a weekly social gathering in the church community room and have use of storage space for their craft supplies. In exchange, they do sewing projects requested by the parish.

In 2005, St. Gabriel's was clustered with Christ the King and St. Martin de Porres to form one new parish. In January 2007, it was suppressed and absorbed into the new Corpus Christi parish.

Sources: DLA Parish Files; Mrs. Gerard Marchand and Mrs. J. Barney Reaume, manuscript history of St. Gabriel's parish (1965); "St. Gabriel's Parish Twenty-fifth Anniversary 1959-1984" (1984). Additional information supplied by Alice Mykytiuk and Judy Bertram.

St-Jérôme

Unlike the historic French-Canadian parishes in the city, from the outset St-Jérôme was founded as a French-language (not a bilingual) parish, whose territory is the entire city of Windsor. It received that specific designation not from the bishop of London but from Rome, on 29 May 1958. As a result, the pastors and people of the parish have happily avoided the kind of language controversies that dogged parishes such as St. Alphonsus, Our Lady of the Rosary and Immaculate Conception at the beginning of the twentieth century.

Bishop Cody met with the founding members of the congregation at the Centre Canadien-français on the first Sunday of Advent 1958 and bestowed the name St-Jérôme to the fledging parish, in honour of the fourth-century saint who gave the Church the Vulgate (Latin) Bible. On his 1959 *ad limina* visit to Rome, the bishop was able to secure relics of the parish's patron and of St. Ambrose for the church's main altar. Father Léo E. Charron was appointed the first pastor.

There was a parish with a priest but no church of its own and not many parishioners. The parish needed people and would have to scour the city to

St-Jérôme

find them, and from the people would come the money to buy the land and build a church. To that effect, Albert Cousineau, the president of La Société St-John Baptiste, headed a recruitment drive from July to October 1958. By mid August, he had 200 families on the parish rolls and had organized several parish societies and a choir under the direction of Maurice Lacasse and organist Charlotte Mongenais.

Father Charron celebrated the first Mass in August 1958 in the basement of Holy Rosary school. This arrangement lasted for several months. Next, the parish was allowed to set up a Sunday Mass chapel in the basement of Sts. Cyril and Methodius Slovak church, on the invitation of its pastor, Father Francis J. Kurta. Weekday Masses were held at the Centre Canadien-français. Official diocesan recognition of the parish came on 8 December 1958. Bishop Cody declared that St-Jérôme was a national parish set aside for French-Canadians from Québec and bilingual French-Canadians from territorial parishes in the city where little or no French was spoken. Other members of the faithful who attended the parish would be treated as visitors. (Bishop Carter lifted this restriction in 1964.) Lastly, French-Canadians in Windsor were not required but certainly encouraged to make St-Jérôme their parish.

In a letter to Father Charron and the parishioners, dated 21 April 1959, Bishop Cody expressed his reservations about building a basement church. If the parish raised $25,000 and paid for the land by the end of 1959, it could proceed to build a proper church. Not mentioned in the bishop's letter was the possibility of receiving dowries from neighbouring parishes or a diocesan loan, as was the diocesan custom. From 7 September to 3 October 1959, the parish conducted a subscription campaign.

The goal was $75,000. The final tally was almost $89,000, which was subscribed by 225 people.

Following a celebratory banquet on 15 October 1959, the diocese allowed Father Charron to enter into contracts for the construction of a church on the south side of Ypres Avenue, between Westcott Road and Central Avenue. The architectural firm was Trace and Glos of Windsor; the general contractor was Damien Construction; the cost was $115,022. The church, which resembles the one for St. Vincent de Paul, was completed by 21 August 1960. The solemn blessing took place on 30 September 1960.

Father Oscar A. Martin, pastor from 1964 to 1969, built the rectory for $46,000, which increased the parish debt to over $116,000. He went without a salary for eighteen months, donated $7,643 to the parish, bought the rectory furniture with his own money, went begging to people who had money and ran a weekly bingo to help pay down the parish debt. He never had more than 250 families. That number doubled for his successor, Monsignor Jean Z. Noël, who was pastor from 1969 to 1982 and appears to have experienced a more prosperous time in the parish's history.

On 30 November 1969, the parish wrote a constitution that established structures and norms and set up its first parish council. During the parish's first twenty-five years, there were 755 baptisms, 178 marriages and 158 funerals. Members of three religious communities have contributed to the spiritual and cultural welfare of the parish: one from the Sisters of the Holy Names of Jesus and Mary; one from the Ursulines; and eighteen from the Sisters of Charity of Ottawa. On 12 June 1988, the parishioners celebrated in grand style the fiftieth anniversary of the ordination of Monsignor Noël, a priest who played a large role in the founding of four French-language elementary schools in Windsor and L'Essor secondary school in Essex County.

Sources: DLA, Parish Files; Hugette Parent, "Historique Paroisse Saint-Jérôme de Windsor: Un Quart de Siècle de Vie Communautaire," (1985); "Paroisse Saint-Jérôme," (1988).

St. John Vianney

St. John Vianney

Correctly anticipating a building boom in the eastern part of St. Rose of Lima parish, the diocese purchased property in 1952 for a future church, at the corner of Dieppe Street and what is now Cedarview Street. On 28 June 1954, Bishop Cody erected the parish of St. John Vianney, taking 225 families from St. Rose and appointing Father Melvin J. Quenneville as the pastor. The parish used St. Cécile school as their "church" commencing Sunday, 5 September 1954. The ground floor was turned into a chapel, and Father Quenneville's living quarters were on the upper floor. He later moved into St. Rose's rectory.

Monsignor J. Austin Roney turned the sod for the first church on 25 September 1955. Construction began on 21 October 1955. The architectural firm was Blackwell & Haggarty, and the contractors were Martin Glass and Sons. Monsignor Roney blessed the cornerstone on 26 February 1956, and Bishop Cody presided over the solemn blessing and opening on 10 June 1956. The church was rectangular in shape and seated 450 people. Father Wilfrid P. McNabb, the second pastor, renovated the sanctuary in marble and installed a marble main altar. The entire church was destroyed by fire during the early morning of 25 June 1965. Saved were the chalices, the consecrated hosts, the tabernacle, the sacred oils and the pyx.

Sunday Mass moved to St. Wilfrid's school gymnasium, an arrangement that lasted two years. In the meantime, the parish, led by Father Aloysius Nolan since October 1965, had to build a second church. Bishop Carter declared that St. John Vianney would conform, in spirit and interior design, to the norms of the Second Vatican Council, in terms of liturgy, parish councils, ecumenical dialogue with local Protestant churches and lay involvement in parish ministry.

Construction began in March 1967. J.G. Hreno of Windsor was the architect; Aronne Brothers was the general contractor; and the firm Thompson, McCance and Pigott collaborated with the architect in the design of the altars, the celebrant's chair and lectern in the sanctuary and the baptismal font to the left side of the sanctuary. Hreno was also responsible for the oak pews.

Hreno designed a theatre-style church for 850 people that "emphasized the participation of the laity in the liturgical action at the Altar of Sacrifice. The pews form a semi-circle around the sanctuary. The laminated wood beams of the roof rest on staggered masonry walls and gently rise towards the centre of the nave. The lines of the centre aisle roof also rise gradually from the narthex to the sanctuary, and then soar to the tower. This space over the sanctuary is further emphasized by the brick wall extending to the top of the tower, which forms a backdrop to the sanctuary. One side of the tower is constructed of cathedral glass. As a result this wall and the sanctuary itself are flooded with natural northern light."

Father Nolan celebrated the first Mass in the second church on 30 July 1967. Bishop Carter dedicated it on 21 October 1967. The cost of the church, rectory, committee room, offices (all one complex), property and furnishings was approximately $350,000. From 1970 to 1979, the parish spent a further $86,000 on such items as extending and paving the parking lot, electrical and heating work and roof repairs.

During the past twenty-five years, St. John Vianney parish has provided for the spiritual and sacramental needs of the Catholic people in the Riverside neighbourhood of Windsor. It has also developed and maintained a wide range of parish activities, such as youth ministries for elementary school and high school students, weekly euchre card parties and social outings for seniors, twice-a-year (autumn and winter) parish breakfasts sponsored by the Knights of Columbus, dinner dances, excursions to out-of-town plays, concerts and an annual parish picnic every September. Bishop Fabbro celebrated a fiftieth anniversary Mass on 14 November 2004.

In 2005, St. John Vianney and Our Lady of Fatima were clustered. In June 2006, the latter was absorbed into St. John Vianney parish.

Sources: DLA, Parish Files; "St. John Vianney Church," (1969); "St. John Vianney Church Windsor, Ontario," *Canadian Catholic Institutions* (May-June 1968), 23-24; "Twenty-Fifth Anniversary St. John Vianney 1954-1979," (1979). Additional information supplied by Betty Ann Lyons.

St. Joseph the Worker

St. Joseph the Worker began as a mission of Our Lady of the Rosary in the early 1940s. Monsignor Wilfrid Langlois and his two assistants, Father Jean Noël and Father Lawrence J. Coughlin, celebrated Mass at the home of Leo Lafrance at 151 Aubin Road and afterwards at Noë Bontront's workshop at 1449 Rossini Boulevard. The diocese purchased property for a church at the corner of Rossini Boulevard and Seminole Street in July 1943, and Bishop Kidd elevated the mission into a parish on 1 October 1943.

Father Coughlin became administrator of the parish in July 1944. By then, construction of the basement church had already begun under the supervision of Monsignor Langlois. It was 40 feet by 90 feet (12 m by 9 m), a space that was large enough to hold 300 people, and it had wooden floors, hard wooden benches for pews and a stove right next to the sanctuary in full view of the congregation. At least this version of a Bishop Kidd basement church had a proper roof and even a bell tower, although the whole structure looked as if it had sunk into the ground. "Primitive" best describes the look of the first St. Joseph's church. Sterling Construction built it for around $12,000. Bishop Kidd blessed the cornerstone on 1 September 1944, and the first Mass was celebrated at Christmas.

In 1950, Mousseau Construction built an addition for $20,000, including a new heating system. On 13 March 1955, fire came close to destroying the entire church. Parishioners working with Damien Construction rebuilt it in record time. Terrazzo replaced the wooden floors, which were hazardous for fire, and proper pews with homemade kneelers took the place of the old benches. By 1959, there were five Sunday Masses to accommodate the spiritual needs of a growing congregation. Capacity was increased to 500 people by removing the wall behind the sanctuary and tearing down the choir loft. The church was also completely redecorated. Plenty of volunteer labour from the parishioners and no-

St. Joseph the Worker

charge work by Eastern Construction kept the cost to $3,200, which the parish paid out of its savings.

While these necessary improvements were being made, Father Mark J. Wildgen, the second pastor, initiated a building fund for a new church. He called it "Crusade for Completion." Seventy-five canvassers began their five-week, door-to-door campaign in April 1959. People were asked to sign a pledge for 150 weeks, so that the parish could raise the minimum one-third amount required by the diocese to build a church. It was a difficult challenge because half the parish had been out of work for almost five years. Pledges were very modest, even by the standards of the 1950s, but they were plentiful in number. The collective spirit that had animated the parish since its inception was the same spirit that was determined to have a church worthy of the thrift and imagination of the congregation.

On Easter Sunday 1961, Bishop Cody announced plans for a new St. Joseph's church. After additional property near the first church was acquired, construction began on 21 May 1962. Monsignor J. Austin Roney blessed the cornerstone on 19 May 1963, and Bishop Carter, as auxiliary, blessed and opened the church on 26 May 1963. That evening, he confirmed 150 children.

The second church was strikingly different from the first one. The overall design resembled that of Our Lady of Guadalupe. The triangle predominates, outside as well as inside. Three large size gables with steep pitched roofs met to form a cross. Inside, all lines, in particular the laminated triangular wood arches, led to the altar in the sanctuary. Above the altar, framed by a slight recess in the brick wall of the sanctuary, was a crucifix of four aluminum bars on which hangs a "line drawing" presentation of the crucified Christ. Behind the sanctuary wall, built as a single structure and attached to the church, were the rectory, offices, instruction rooms and a meeting room on a lower level. The total cost was $180,000. Father Charles C. Campbell, the third pastor, was a constant source of inspiration to the parishioners during the fund raising and construction.

In 1982, the parish successfully petitioned the diocese to have its name changed to St. Joseph the Worker, to reflect more accurately and openly the neighbourhood that it served. For example, Father Francis L. Murphy, who came as pastor in 1981, celebrated Mass in Spanish the first Saturday of every month for parishioners from Central America. Sister Cecile Thibault, SNJM, became the pastoral assistant in 1987. She gave instruction to those preparing for Baptism, First Holy Communion and the Sacrament of Reconciliation and also taught classes in Scripture. The parish kept close ties with the two parish schools: Holy Family (1957) and Our Lady of Lourdes (1959).

What was once a dynamic parish fell on hard times in the 1990s. The familiar pattern of a changing neighbourhood, the gradual disappearance of the founding families and a decline in regular participation in the liturgical and charitable work of the Church led to the clustering of St. Joseph the Worker parish with Most Precious Blood parish and then to its closure on 14 October 2002. Father Matthew R. Kucharski was the last pastor. The church and rectory were sold to a Chinese Baptist congregation.

Sources: DLA, Parish Files; "History of Parish," (1963); "St. Joseph the Worker Parish Established 1944: Celebrating 25th Year of our New Church 1988," (1988).

St. Martin de Porres

Bishop Cody established St. Martin de Porres parish on 28 June 1965. He appointed Father Louis L. Ouellette as the first pastor. Members of Father Ouellette's family were pioneer parishioners in Christ the King parish, and he was the first priest to come from the parish.

On 16 June, the bishop announced a dowry of $35,000 for St. Martin de Porres, which was to be paid by the parishioners of Christ the King, in installments of $10,000 the first year and $5,000 for each year thereafter until the amount was paid down. The bishop chose the name St. Martin de Porres for

St. Martin de Porres

two reasons: St. Martin was a native of Peru, where the diocese had a mission, and Pope John XXIII recently canonized him, on 6 May 1962.

Father Ouellette lived at Christ the King rectory (he had a pull-out bed in the living room!) and celebrated the new parish's first Mass on 30 June 1963 in the basement of Christ the King church. He wasted little time in establishing his parish. Assisted by Abe Renaud, who was able to persuade the municipality to rezone a parcel of land in a residential area, Father Ouellette purchased property for a church, rectory and hall on Labelle Street, west of Dominion Road. The deal closed on 23 August 1963. Two days earlier, he had received permission from the diocese to hire an architect. The total cost for all three buildings was estimated at $150,000.

Meanwhile, Father Ouellette rented a house at 3034 Avondale Crescent and began to celebrate Sunday Masses at Notre Dame school, on 2 November 1963. Approval for the architect's plans came on 9 April 1964, and a contract was awarded to Ascon Construction Ltd. The final cost, including architect's fees, changes, pews and furnishings was in excess of $201,000. Work on all three buildings was completed on 15 December 1964; Monsignor Vito H. Grespan consecrated the altar on 22 December 1964, placing in the altar stone relics of St. Prosper, St. Clare and St. Pius X; the inaugural Mass in the new church was celebrated on Christmas; and Bishop Carter dedicated the church on 1 May 1965.

Father Ouellette left the parish on 15 May 1974. The parish's 300 families struggled to pay down the debt, but the congregation did not grow in number as originally expected. All the same, at Father Ouellette's departure, the parish debt stood at a little over $51,000, the difference between the original estimated cost and the final cost. Father Lawrence W. Paré, the second pastor, introduced bingos to help reduce the debt. During his four years, the debt declined by seventy-five percent. At the same time, the parish funded new storm windows, the paving of the parking lot and sanctuary renovations. In 1977, the number of families in the parish rose to 385, but, oddly enough, enrolment at Notre Dame and St. Hubert's declined from a total of 600 to 340 students. Three years later, St. Hubert's closed.

Father Percy V. Drouillard, the third pastor, completed the sanctuary renovations, built a Confession room, installed ceiling fans and eliminated the debt in time for the parish's fifteenth anniversary, on 28 June 1978. On its twentieth anniversary, in 1983 the parishioners financed a facelift to the facade of the church, hall and rectory; on its twenty-fifth anniversary, in 1988, they purchased a new pipe organ, lighting system and air conditioning.

Father William F. Kornacker was the last pastor of St. Martin de Porres before it was clustered with Christ the King in 2001. While he was on sabbatical, Father Gerald J. Craig, OFM Cap. was the administrator from July to December 2000. In 2005, the parishes of St. Martin de Porres, Christ the King and St. Gabriel were clustered to form one new parish. The sacramental registers for St. Martin de Porres, from 1963 to 2002, record 1,200 baptisms, 460 marriages and 264 funerals.

St. Martin's was suppressed in January 2007, and absorbed into the new Corpus Christi parish.

Sources: *Faith Community of Christ the King 75 Years 1928-2003 St. Martin de Porres 40 Years 1963-2003* (Windsor: 2003).

St. Michael

Following the Second World War, the German-speaking Catholics of Windsor needed a priest, a parish and a church. They found their priest in Father Koloman Moullion, a Danube Swabian refugee who had escaped a communist prison in the old Yugoslavia. Father Moullion arrived in Windsor in early 1949. After he was introduced to Monsignor William E. Dillon, pastor of Sacred Heart parish who was in charge of the city's German Catholics, he began to learn English at Assumption College and

to organize a parish, with Bishop Kidd's approval.

Father Moullion was an energetic and creative organizer, a priest blessed with pastoral qualities that brought out the best in his congregation, especially at a time of transition. Having found each other, priest and people established a parish and built a church. Father Moullion celebrated Mass for his new congregation on 31 March 1949, at the Hungarian church of St. Anthony of Padua. This is the date

St. Michael

on which the parish was founded. On 24 April 1949, 212 persons gathered under his leadership and subscribed $10,000 in pledges and cash. The next month, they purchased eight lots on Parkwood Avenue, south of Tecumseh Road East. Monsignor Dillon turned the sod for a church on 14 August 1949.

The money generated from dances, raffles, picnics and bingos financed the construction of a hall or basement church for Sunday Masses, a rectory and a chapel in the rectory for weekday Masses. Bishop Cody blessed the basement church on 23 July 1950. The parish flourished as a result of waves of post-war immigration, rising to its peak enrolment of 600 families in the 1950s, and it was able to complete the church. To begin, the basement had to be widened to accommodate a side nave for the proposed superstructure. J.C. Pennington was the architect; F. Wetzel Contractor was the builder; and the parishioners were directly involved, donating almost 6,000 hours of volunteer labour. The total cost was $250,000.

Bishop Cody blessed the cornerstone on 10 October 1954, and the first Mass was celebrated on

Easter Sunday, 10 April 1955. It took ten years to complete the interior of the church. As money was available, the parishioners purchased pews, pulpit, baptismal font, marble altar and communion rail, floor tiles, marble for the walls, statues of Mary the Mother of God, St. Joseph and St. Anthony, Stations of the Cross and the impressive artwork. Monsignor Vito Grespan consecrated the altar on 20 December 1961. Incredibly, the parish was debt free by 1965.

The person responsible for the paintings, mosaics and stained-glass windows was Sister Antonia Moullion, a sister of Father Moullion. Trained in the academies of Budapest and Vienna, she began to work at the parish in 1955. She painted the symbols of the liturgical year on the ceiling and designed seven large mosaics — a crucifixion scene flanked by twelve apostles on the wall behind the main altar; St Boniface and St. Elizabeth on the walls to either side of the main altar; the seven joys and seven sorrows of the Blessed Virgin Mary on the wall of the side altar; St. Michael over the side entrance; and the symbols of original sin and the Holy Spirit over the baptismal font. Sister Antonia is also responsible for the glazed tile in the baptismal area and for the thirty-two stained-glass windows, which were executed in Innsbruck, Austria. On one side of the nave, the widows depict the six days of creation, and on the other side, they depict the seven sacraments. Michael Benzinger described her work as "remarkable specimens of modern, and yet intelligible art, as they adorn what is probably the last major Danube Swabian church edifice in the whole world."

Like most ethnic parishes of the 1950s, St. Michael's strove to retain the religious customs and cultural heritage of the old country while it participated in the parish-based organizations of the Church in Canada. The parish had its theatre and music groups. For many years German was the language of the majority of its Sunday Masses and the outdoor Corpus Christi procession with its four portable altars was a centrepiece of parish devotional life. At the same time, parishioners joined the CWL, the Holy Name Society and the St. Vincent de Paul Society.

The parish register from 1950 to 1975 records 788 baptisms, 375 marriages, 309 funerals, 365 First Holy Communions and 319 confirmations. Over the past thirty years, assimilation, along with other factors, has reduced the congregation to about 100 people for the one German-language Mass on Sunday.

In January 2007, St. Michael parish was suppressed, and the church is now home to Immaculate Heart parish.

Sources: DLA, Parish Files; "History of St. Michael's Roman Catholic Parish, Windsor, Ontario," (1986); Michael Benzinger, "The Parish of St. Michael's Windsor"; Robert Benzinger, "St. Michael's Church, Windsor, Ont.," (Windsor: 1982).

St. Patrick

In 1949, Monsignor John A. Rooney, pastor of Holy Name of Mary, alerted Bishop Kidd to the need to establish a parish south of Tecumseh Road West. The bishop responded to Monsignor Rooney's petition by setting up a committee to choose a name and boundaries and appointing Father Hillsdon B.A. McManus, an assistant at Holy Name of Mary since 1942, as the administrator. In a letter dated 18 April 1950, Bishop Kidd formally accepted the committee's choice of St. Patrick as the parish's patron and its proposal for the boundaries. Territory for the parish was claimed from Holy Name of Mary parish and from Assumption parish. On 17 July 1950, Father McManus became St. Patrick's first pastor. Sadly, he died two years later, on 10 April 1952.

Well before Bishop Kidd's letter of 18 April 1950, the parish was busy looking for a new church. Monsignor Rooney and the parishioners of Holy Name of Mary donated $5,000 towards the purchase of a temporary church at 1564 Tecumseh Road West. The building had been a two-room school and later a bakery. St. Patrick's parishioners quickly turned it into a church and later tore down the front porch and built an addition for confessionals on the first floor and a choir loft on the second. Father McManus celebrated the first parish Mass on Easter Sunday, 9 April 1950. The parish purchased a small frame house next door to the church for a rectory.

Father Charles E. Sullivan, the second pastor, opened St. Patrick's school in 1954, and the next year he supervised the construction of the current rectory on Partington Avenue. To save money, Father Sullivan acted as his own general contractor and convinced the men in the parish to work as volunteer labourers on the project. The rectory was

St. Patrick

completed in March 1955, and the parish was free of debt. Soon, however, it became apparent that the parish also needed a much larger and permanent church for its expanding congregation, and an assistant priest. Four Sunday Masses were necessary to accommodate everyone. The parish's first assistant priest, Father Richard L. Morse, arrived immediately after his ordination in June 1954.

Monsignor Rooney came to the rescue of St. Patrick's parish once again. By November 1953, his parishioners had raised $11,500 for a new church. This money was used to purchase four acres of property next to the rectory, in 1954 and 1955. Monsignor Rooney had the honour of turning the first sod on 4 December 1955; Monsignor J. Austin Roney blessed the cornerstone on 12 February 1956; and the church was ready for the first Mass of Father Lawrence Paré on 3 June 1956. Bishop Cody blessed and opened St. Patrick's church on 23 September 1956.

From its very beginning, St. Patrick's parish has been a busy Catholic community. For the first two years, the ushers club (now called ministers of hospitality) and the altar society were the only parish societies. In 1952, the Legion of Mary was established; in 1953, the Holy Name Society began its work with 110 members; in 1955, the Junior Legion of Mary started. The St. Vincent de Paul Society also came on board. Other parish groups and societies, which have appeared during the years and reflect changing patterns of participation in parochial life, are the parish council, the finance committee, ministers of Holy Communion, lay readers, liturgy committee, music ministry, the St. Patrick's seniors club and the St. Patrick's Community Association. The last named was established as an umbrella

organization of different groups whose main purpose was to foster and strengthen the relationship between church, school and community.

In 1975, the Missionaries of St. Charles (the Scalabrini Fathers) came to St. Patrick's. After a two-year transition period, Father Ermet Nazzani, CS, became parish priest. The appointment of the Scalabrini Fathers, who had been parish priests at Windsor's St. Angela Merici church since 1957, was in response to the large number of Italians in St. Patrick's parish. Soon a special relationship formed between St. Angela Merici and St. Patrick's. Although the Scalabrini Fathers are no longer at St. Patrick's, one Sunday Mass is still celebrated in the Italian language.

In July 1999, St. Patrick's and Holy Name of Mary clustered, reuniting the former mission and its mother parish after a half-century, with the parish priest living at St. Patrick's.

Sources: *40th Anniversary St. Patrick Church 1956-1996* (1996); Michael Power, *A History of the Parish Church of Holy Name of Mary, 1917-1984* (Windsor: 1984), Ch. 10; "Souvenir Programme Solemn Opening and Blessing of St. Patrick's Church by His Excellency J.C. Cody, LL.D., D.D." (1956).

St. Paul

Two separate but related developments led to the formation of St. Paul's parish on Malden Road. The first development concerns the establishment of a mission at Highway 18 and Chappus Street (where the E.C. Row Expressway ends in west Windsor). The diocese bought a building and hired John R. Boyde, architect, and Damien and Larose Construction to turn it into a two-room school with a chapel. The name of the mission and the school, which opened in September 1948, was St. Thomas Aquinas. There was also a rectory.

But the mission attracted too few local Catholics to build a stand-alone church. As a result, the diocese decided to move the mission and chose Malden Road, where it already had purchased property for a school, on 26 November 1947. Bounded by Malden Road, Elliott Road (now Sprucewood Avenue) and Maple Avenue, the land cost $2,750. Additional costs to close two alleys pushed the price over $3,100. A portion of this land was then sold to the separate school board for $1,800, with the money returned to the school board after it had received its legislative grant for the purchase of property. The board built a three-room school with a chapel and named it St. Paul. The architect was John R. Boyde. Opened in 1949, the school had an initial enrolment of fifteen children, the minimum number. The Sisters of the Holy Names of Jesus and Mary assumed the administration of the school.

Now to the second development. The diocese chose the Malden Road site because of a prior decision by the priests at Blessed Sacrament parish to send a catechist to that part of the city. Father G. Harvey Wilbur, CSB, and Father Roger F. Debilly, CSB, asked Velda Ostrowski of Sprucewood Avenue to teach catechism to the Catholic children of Malden Road Public School. She began to teach sometime before she was married in 1945. She naturally came to know the Catholic children in the area and realized that there were enough of them to qualify for a separate school. When it came time to move the mission from Highway 18, she had fifteen children for St. Paul's school, which did double duty as the Sunday church for the mission.

St. Paul's became a mission of Christ the King parish in 1950 and a parish in 1952. Father Herman R. Reardon was the first pastor. One of the first collections netted $8.97. Undaunted, Father Reardon and his small band of parishioners pressed ahead with plans to build a church. On 1 August 1952, assisted by Bishop Cody's Diocesan Development Campaign Fund, the parish signed a contract for a church. The cost was $26,833. It was one of many similar prefabricated churches built in Cody's time. The plans for St. Paul called for a church, offices and rectory. John Drobitch was the building contractor, and Gerry Supply and Lumber Company of London manufactured the prefabricated portions. Solomon Morencie, a parishioner, dug out the basement with a horse and drag, and Ernest Morencie, his son, laid the cement blocks, shingled the roof and secured a bell for the church from the fire hall on Mill Street in Windsor.

Monsignor Wilfrid Langlois, dean of Essex, presided over the sod turning ceremony on 18 August 1952. Father Reardon and John McKernan, described as a senior member of the congregation, assisted him. Bishop Cody blessed and opened the church on 25 January 1953, the feast of the conversion of St. Paul. Above the main altar hung an interesting icon-like triptych. The central panel

St. Paul

showed St. Paul wrapped in a banner stenciled with the words: "Who shall separate us from the love of Christ" (Rom. 8:35). Behind him stands Our Lord. A single halo surrounds their heads, demonstrating the union of Paul with Christ. The two side panels feature scenes from the life of St. Paul.

St. Paul's remains a small but very active parish. It took many years for the parishioners to retire the initial debt. Bingos and bazaars were regular features of its ongoing fund-raising activities. In 1965, there was a great deal of talk about building a new church. One option was to purchase property directly across the street from the church, which would free up much needed land for St. Paul's school. The other option was to acquire those lots adjoining the current church property, approximately three acres (1.2 ha), as they became available on the market. The diocese chose the second option, completing the purchase in 1967. But no new church was ever built. There were not enough families to shoulder the burden of debt that a permanent church would entail. In 1965, there were only eighty-five families that regularly attended Mass. Over the years, that number did not increase to any great degree. However, there was never any lack of commitment on the part of the parishioners to keep their "temporary" church in good repair. New condominium developments in the parish might have a positive effect on the parish's future.

In 2006, the parish was transferred to Essex deanery.

Sources: DLA, Parish Files. Additional information supplied by Velda Ostrowski.

St. Rose of Lima

St. Anne's parish in Tecumseh and Our Lady of the Rosary parish in Ford City provided the territory for St. Rose of Lima parish, which included historic riverfront lands that were settled by the French in the latter half of the eighteenth century. Father François X. Laurendeau, pastor of Our Lady of the Rosary, established a mission in the eastern section of his parish in 1922, and he and his assistants — Fathers Wilfrid Langlois, Albert J. McNabb and Gregory L. Blondé — celebrated Sunday Mass for about 150 families in a chapel in the basement of St. Peter's school. Although warmly welcomed by the people, this arrangement was understood by all to be temporary.

A move to erect a parish and build a permanent church began when the families of Alphonse St. Louis and Eugene Mailloux donated the land. The architect was John R. Boyde; the contractor was Blonde Construction; and the contract price for the 450-seat Romanesque-style church was $69,700. Father Laurendeau was in charge of the project. Bishop Fallon liked to build big and to build often. In his way of thinking, the church of St. Rose of Lima was a testimony in brick and stone to the solidity of the Catholic faith of the people who built it and to his own rock-solid sense of the triumphant Church. It was the first church of any denomination to have been built in what was then Riverside. Holy Name of Mary on McEwan Avenue and the former Sacred Heart on Ottawa Street, both of which were opened in 1927, are two more examples of "Fallon churches."

Bishop Fallon blessed the cornerstone of St. Rose of Lima on 22 June 1924 (the inscription on the cornerstone reads 1 June 1924), in front of 2,500 people. He returned on 16 November 1924 to bless and open the church. St. Rose of Lima, the parish's patron was the first canonized saint in the Western Hemisphere. Father Langlois, its first pastor, was a relative of Jean-Baptiste Langlois, who was the recipient of the original grant of land that became the site for the church. Langlois remained pastor until 1942, when he transferred to Our Lady of the Rosary.

The church was furnished within a year of its opening for $15,811. Ulysse G. and Leonard Reaume donated the faux-marble high altar; Adolphe Janisse purchased the altar to the Blessed

St. Rose of Lima

Virgin Mary; and Charles Montreuil and the Altar Society gave the 2,200 lb. (1,375 kg) church bell, in December 1926. The interior was decorated in 1935, for $570.50, a reminder that small sums of money went a long way during the Great Depression. To mark the parish's twenty-fifth anniversary, in 1949, a large three-section mural depicting a crucified Christ, the Last Supper and a priest elevating the Host at Mass was painted on the sanctuary wall, and Bishop Cody consecrated the high altar. The parishioners had successfully retired the debt.

The parish grew tremendously during its first quarter century. From November 1924, there were 2,062 baptisms and 583 marriages. In addition, there were 262 funerals. Growth can also be measured in the number of parish schools. St. Louis had operated from 1895 to 1922 and was replaced that year by St. Peter's, which received an addition in 1950. Next there was St. Thomas (1925), which had an addition built in 1951. It was followed by St. Cecile (1926) and St. Rose de Lima (1953), which was an eight-room intermediate school. It was built with a $108,000-bond issue completely paid for by the parishioners.

In 1950, a section from the east side of the parish was given to Our Lady of Fatima parish; in 1951, eight blocks from the west side went to Our Lady of Guadalupe parish. In 1951, the parish built a rectory. The architect was J.C. Pennington, and the contractor was Cleve Mousseau; in 1953, the parish built an entrance on the west side of the church; in 1960, it financed the construction of a parish hall; and in 1995, it renovated the church hall and added a much needed elevator.

From January 1971 to Easter 1972, the church

experienced a three-stage renovation. In the first stage, the vestibule was altered and a vestry and rest rooms were built. In the second stage, in order to adjust to the changes in the liturgy, the sanctuary was remodeled and on either side of it there was built a chapel for the Blessed Sacrament and a chapel for baptism. The communion rail and many of the statues and paintings were removed. The cost was $84,934. Father Percy V. Drouillard, the pastor, described, explained and justified the changes, in a six-page printed document dated 3 July 1972. It helped many people accept the changes.

Over the years, St. Rose of Lima has provided many vocations to the priesthood and religious life and has been known for its fine choirs, led by first-rate organists and directors. In August 2002, it clustered with Our Lady of Guadalupe.

On 30 June 2008, St. Rose of Lima, along with St. Thomas, will be closed and absorbed into Our Lady of Guadalupe parish.

Sources: DLA, Parish Files; Percy Drouillard, "St. Rose of Lima Church Windsor, Ontario," (1972); Charles V. McNabb, "St. Rose Parish, Riverside, Ont.," (1953); *St. Rose of Lima Church Golden Jubilee 1924-1974* (1974). Additional information supplied by Father Dino Salvador.

St. Theresa

Father F.X. Laurendeau founded the mission of Ste. Thérèse of Lisieux on 27 May 1925, ten days after the canonization of Ste. Thérèse. There were 133 families. It was a mission without a church, but not for long. Sacred Heart school, a simple wood frame structure, was moved from the corner of Westminster Boulevard and Empress Street to property owned by the Ursuline Sisters on Tecumseh Road East near Princess Avenue. Assisted by several carpenters, the people quickly turned it into a church, serving in that capacity for twenty-three years. It seated 266 people. When the new church opened, the building reverted to its original use as classrooms, this time for St. Jules school.

On 2 December 1928, Bishop Fallon erected St. Thérèse into a parish and appointed Father J. Isaac Ducharme as the first pastor, who remained for fourteen years. Father Isidore J. Poisson succeeded him, on 18 December 1942. He built the present church and rectory. The cost was $150,000, all

of which had to be borrowed from the diocese and the bank. J.C. Pennington was the architect; Meyns Construction of Windsor was the general contractor; and Canadian Bridge Company provided the structural steel. The church is 59 feet (17.7 m) in width and 143 feet (42.9 m) in length. It was built with a concrete block foundation, brick and stone walls, asbestos shingle roof and an aluminum sided spire.

St. Theresa

The stained-glass windows in the nave are devoted to scenes in the life of Ste. Thérèse, beginning with her childhood. Bishop Cody, as coadjutor, blessed and opened Ste. Thérèse church on Norman Road and Empress Avenue, on 23 December 1948. The rectory was opened earlier, on 8 August 1948. It had been in three previous locations: 2325 Arthur Road, 2328 Princess Avenue and 1895 Pillette Road. To put an end to the rectory's peregrinations, the architect attached it to the church!

Parish records from 1928 to 1968 reveal a busy and growing parish on Windsor's east side. During the parish's first forty years, there were 4,300 baptisms; 3,618 First Holy Communions; 3,093 confirmations; 1,134 marriages; 380 funerals; 23,210 Masses celebrated and 2,880,000 Communions. In 1967, there were more than 1,000 registered families in the parish—in 2005, the number was higher by almost 200— and four schools: St. Jules (1924), Ste. Thérèse (1951), St. Joan of Arc (1957) and St. Alexander (1961). The parish outgrew itself by the mid 1950s. On 25 June 1956, the diocese erected St. Vincent de Paul parish, to the east of Ste. Thérèse, on Balfour Boulevard.

A measure of the parish's dynamism was its 1958 publication of *Catholic Guide Book*. Fifty-eight pages in length, it describes among other things each society then active in parish: Ushers Club (the first organized group), Boosters' Club, the Christian

Family Movement, Legion of Mary, the Apostleship of Prayer, Altar Boys Society, Parent-Teacher Association, CYO, Regis Club, Young Christian Workers, Holy Name Society, CWL, St. Anne Altar Society and Saint Vincent de Paul Society. There was a parish credit union, established in 1952. The *Catholic Guide Book*, if examined with care, offers a revealing window onto the world of 1950s Catholic parochial life in the diocese of London.

Bishop Carter, as auxiliary, consecrated the two side altars on 12 March 1963, thirty-five years after the church was opened. This ceremonial was the final act in the completion of the church as it was before the implementation of the liturgical changes stemming from the Second Vatican Council. Monsignor Noël, pastor from 1949 to 1969, initiated those changes and the necessary renovations to the sanctuary. On 30 September 1967, Monsignor Philip A. Mugan blessed the new main altar. Renovations continued under Father Clement W. Janisse, the fourth pastor. He built a new confessional room in 1975, renovated the chapel in 1976 and oversaw the installation of new carpets, vinyl kneelers and a baldachino in the sanctuary, painting of the interior and the replacement of the front steps in time for the fiftieth anniversary celebrations on 5 March 1978.

Other changes include the formation of a parish charismatic prayer group in July 1970, the introduction of a Saturday evening Mass on 7 August 1971 and the departure of the Sisters of St. Joseph from St. Jules school on 30 June 1975. Perhaps the biggest change to occur was the gradual disappearance of a French-language Mass. Although the parish was named after a popular French saint, and the first three pastors were French-Canadians, Ste. Thérèse was never intended by Bishop Fallon or by any of his episcopal successors to be a French-Canadian parish. At best, it was a bilingual parish. Evidence for its bilingualism can be found in the use of the French language in sermons and catechesis when Mass was in Latin and the scheduling of a French-language Mass when the vernacular replaced the Latin in the liturgy. Also, many items produced by the parish were published in both English and French.

On 11 July 1971, the people at the French-language Mass, reflecting the changing cultural landscape, decided that, beginning in August, their Mass would be in English with hymns in French and English and the occasional sermon in French. If specifically requested, weddings and funerals would be celebrated in French.

Sources: DLA, Parish Files; *Catholic Guide Book for the Parishioners of St. Theresa's Church* (1958); "Paroisse Sainte-Thérèse," (1981); *St. Theresa Church La Paroisse Ste. Thérèse* (1968); *St. Thérèse Parish 1928-1978* (1978).

St. Thomas the Apostle

St. Thomas the Apostle

As part of its planned expansion on the east side of Windsor, the diocese purchased property on the north side of Edgar Street, between Lauzon Road and St. Paul Avenue, from Blaise and Florence Rivard, who lived next door and became loyal parishioners. The transaction was closed on 4 November 1963, but the property lay undeveloped for more than three years. On 28 May 1965, Bishop Carter chose Father Douglas F. Boyer as the pastor of the new parish of St. Thomas the Apostle; and on 24 June 1965, he finalized the boundaries, taking territory from the parishes of St. Rose of Lima and St. John Vianney. Both these parishes also agreed to provide a dowry for start-up costs. St. Rose donated $30,000 and St. John Vianney $10,000.

St. Thomas the Apostle began with 400 Catholic families. Sunday Mass was celebrated in St. Maria Goretti school gymnasium — the parish's inaugural Mass took place on 25 June 1965 — and the first rectory was a house at 1228 Matthew Brady Boulevard.

Father George J. Zimney became the second pastor in June 1966, and he oversaw the construction of the church, rectory and hall. The sod-turning ceremony took place on 15 January 1967. The architectural firm was Sheppard, Masson, Brand, and Langlois; the builder was Woodall Construction, a local firm. Woodall built a church, rectory and hall, all in one fourteen-sided unit, for $321,682. The first Mass in the new church was on 24 September 1967, and the project was completed by July 1968. The mortgage was liquidated in full in November 1993.

The parish celebrated its fortieth anniversary on the 20 April 2005, with Bishop Fabbro celebrating the Mass. It was a bittersweet moment. During the past decade, attendance at Sunday liturgies had declined to the point where Mass was celebrated only twice on the weekends, once on Saturday evening and once on Sunday morning. Other problems included the absence of a school and the fact that St. Thomas is very near to the parishes of St. John Vianney and St. Rose of Lima, both of which could easily absorb the congregation at their own liturgies. St. Thomas' weak financial viability and the shortage of priests prompted the diocese to recommend its closure by 31 December 2006.

St. Thomas is to close on 30 June 2008, and, along with St. Rose of Lima, be absorbed into Our Lady of Guadalupe parish.

Sources: DLA, Parish Files. Additional material supplied by the parish.

St. Vincent de Paul

Father Jean Noël, pastor of St. Theresa's church, founded St. Vincent de Paul as a mission on Sunday, 20 November 1955, when he celebrated Mass at the recently built St. Vincent de Paul school. On 23 June 1956, Bishop Cody erected the mission into a parish and appointed Father Clifford J. Girard as the first pastor, slicing off territory from St. Theresa's and asking the people there to support the new parish with a substantial dowry.

The location of the Sunday Mass was changed to the Sandwich East Community Centre on Jefferson Boulevard, in September 1956, in order to accommodate the rapidly increasing congregation. Soon there were three Sunday Masses. Volunteers came rushing in. So, in no time, three societies were functioning: the Women's Committee, which later became the St. Anne Altar Society, the Ushers Club and the Boosters Club. Each one would have a profound and positive impact on parochial life.

With the help of Gilbert Trudell, the parish

St. Vincent de Paul

purchased property at the corner of Balfour Boulevard and Empress Street, plus an additional 20 feet (6 m) from another property owner, for a churchyard and parking, and arranged with a next-door neighbour to build a comparable home in exchange for his current residence, which was earmarked as the rectory. The exchange was completed in December 1956.

Father Noël turned the first sod and blessed the site on 25 November 1956. Norman Drouillard immediately began the excavation for the basement, donating his time and expertise. Blackwell & Haggarty of London was the architectural firm. Brockenshire Construction was the contractor. Work on the superstructure began in March 1957, and Mass was celebrated for the first time in the church basement on 9 June 1957. On 19 July 1957, Monsignor Roney officiated at the blessing of the cornerstone; on 4 August 1957, Mass was celebrated in the church proper; on 22 September 1957, Bishop Cody dedicated the church.

The parish sponsored an innovative way to raise funds to pay down the parish debt. It built and raffled a three-bedroom ranch-style home on a large lot on Ferndale Avenue, valued at $12,000. The raffle was a huge success. It was one of many moneymakers during the parish's first ten years. At a gala dinner on 29 May 1967, which was attended by 500 people, the parish celebrated the final payment on the original debt of $113,350.

During the 1970s, when Father Christopher S. Quinlan was pastor, the parish financed the painting and roofing of the church, the replacement of the front doors and extensive work on the basement, including a heating system, a new floor, painting and ceramic tile for the washrooms. Additional renovations took place in 1987. Improvements were made to the roof, foyer, sacristy, family room, basement meeting rooms and kitchen. Also, storage space in the garage was provided for the St. Vincent de Paul Society.

In 2004-05, the parishioners financed the installation of stained-glass windows as part of their fiftieth anniversary. Themes are biblical and modern. There are windows to Moses, Elijah, the Blessed Virgin Mary, the Baptism of Jesus, the Resurrection, Canadian Martyrs, John XXIII, Mother Teresa, Fr. Michael McGivney (the founder of the Knights of Columbus), St. Margaret D'Youville, Kateri Tekakwitha, Zacchaeus, and St. Vincent de Paul as the Good Samaritan in the Choir loft.

As of 30 May 2005, St. Vincent de Paul parish had approximately 30 ministries that serve a stable population of workers and retirees, mainly from the automobile industry, as well as people in three housing projects; cumulative statistics for the parish were: 3,239 baptisms, 897 marriages, and 788 funerals.

On 19 November 2005, Bishop Anthony Daniels inaugurated the parish's fiftieth anniversary celebrations with the celebration of the Eucharist.

Sources: DLA, Parish Files; *St. Vincent de Paul Parish Twenty-Fifth Anniversary 1957-1982.* Additional information supplied by Frances Conway.

3. Essex Deanery

Amherstburg: St. John the Baptist

On 1 May 1800, Bishop Pierre Denaut of Québec founded the missions of St. John the Baptist in Amherstburg, Malden Township, and St. Peter-on-the-Thames, Tilbury East Township, Kent County. Jean-Baptiste Marchand, pastor of Assumption parish, was put in charge of both missions. During a visit in June 1801, Bishop Denaut negotiated the purchase of a site for a chapel on Bathurst Street, Amherstburg, for the Malden mission, which was completed in the autumn of 1802. Separate parochial records for the mission were begun on 26 June 1802. By June 1816, when Bishop Joseph-Octave Plessis toured the Western District, St. John the Baptist mission had a church, a small rectory and 300 members, many of whom belonged to the British garrison at Fort Malden.

Father Joseph Crévier was given jurisdiction over the two missions but continued to live at Assumption. He built the second church in Amherstburg, also on Bathurst Street, in 1820, when there were 500 Catholics in the mission. The church was 30 feet (9 m) in length and held 220 people. According to the 1827 census of the Catholic population of Essex and Kent counties, the number of Catholics in the Malden mission had increased to

600 people.

On 23 May 1828, Bishop Macdonell of Kingston erected Amherstburg into a parish and appointed Father Louis J. Fluet the first pastor. The parochial territory covered Kent County, including the French-Canadian

St. John the Baptist

mission of St. Peter-on-the-Thames, to Pelee Island and the southern half of Essex County. It was time to build a bigger and more permanent church on a larger parcel of land. On 31 January 1834, the Crown granted to Bishop Macdonell five acres (2 ha) for a church and rectory. The grant was bounded by Brock, Gore, Kemp and Richmond streets in Amherstburg. The Wyandotte Indians donated 115 tons (126.8 t) of stone for a new church from their quarry in Anderdon Township, but construction did not commence until the arrival of Father Louis Boué in January 1844. Bishop Peter Paul Lefevere of Detroit blessed the cornerstone on 3 July 1844, and the church was opened for worship during the latter half of 1844 or sometime in 1845. The cost was $9,200.

Father Jean Daudet (1850-65) built a rectory and purchased property on the Third Concession of Malden Township for a much larger cemetery. Father Pierre D. Laurent (1863-76) built the stone tower and spire and installed two bells. He also built a stone convent for the Sisters of the Holy Names of Jesus and Mary, a parish hall on King Street and the "Lake Chapel" on old Highway 18A, for Catholics in Malden Township and Colchester South Township. This chapel gave way to St. Anthony's church in Harrow in 1906.

In 1878, the year that Amherstburg became a town, Bishop Walsh conveyed the administration of the parish to the Basilian Fathers. A succession of Basilian pastors have added to the fabric of the church and overseen many renovations to the interior. Father Patrick J. Ryan, CSB (1878-1901) installed the main altar, which was designed by Detroit architects Mason and Rice and built by Patrick Navan of Amherstburg, three side altars and the Stations of the Cross, which were probably painted by the artist Edouard Cabane. Father Ryan added twelve stained-glass windows, removed the side galleries, extended the rear one and commissioned the frescoes of the Joyful Mysteries. In 1887, he built a small church on Pelee Island, and in 1899 a new rectory in Amherstburg. By 1901, the parish had 450 families or 1,750 members, 190 rented pews and three schools.

Father Luke L. Beuglet, CSB (1925-32) added a new vestry as well as a side entrance and vestibule to the east side of the church. Father Vincent A. Thomson, CSB (1940-54) added an entrance to the north side. Father Robert E. Lowery, CSB (1954-58) replaced the seventy-three-year-old altars with marble ones, which were designed by Joseph Cincik of Cleveland and installed by J. Horvath Company of Windsor, and installed a new communion rail. During Father Lowrey's pastorate, there were 904 families or 3,500 members, four elementary schools, one high school and seventeen Sisters of the Holy Names. Father James E. Martin, CSB (1959-71) presided over the massive $150,000 renovations to

conform to the norms of the Second Vatican Council. As well, the parishioners financed a new $86,000 parish centre that connected the church and the rectory. Father Robert J. Duggan, CSB (1983-89) carried out further renovations. The parish restored eight pre-1894 stained-glass windows in 1995, opened a climate-controlled Heritage House in 2000 and rebuilt the tower and steeple in 2004.

On 5 October 1978, the parish purchased the Malden United Church on Highway 18 and re-christened it the St. Theresa of the Little Flower Chapel. The first Mass was celebrated on 18 February 1979 and the last Mass in June 1995.

Sources: *Amherstburg Echo*, 10 August 2004; *Catholic Register*, 8-15 August 2004, 8, 26 December 2004, 28; Eleanor Gignac and Laura Bondy, comps. and eds., *Led by the Shepherd: A History of St. John the Baptist Parish 1802-1992* (Amherstburg: 1992); John Robert McMahon, *The Episcopate of Pierre-Adolphe Pinsoneault: First Bishop of London, Upper Canada 1856-1866* (M.A. thesis, University of Western Ontario, 1982), 103-21. Additional information supplied by Eleanor Gignac-Warren.

Belle River:
Sts. Simon and Jude

Belle River is an historic late eighteenth century French settlement, on the south shore of Lake St. Clair. It was formally surveyed in 1793, and in the first half of the nineteenth century Irish Catholic immigrants augmented the local population. Equidistant from Assumption parish in Sandwich and St. Peter-on-the-Thames parish in Tilbury East Township (34 km either way), the parish of Sts. Simon and Jude was a station and then a mission for the priests from Assumption. Among their number we count Father Jean-Baptiste Marchand, Father Joseph Crévier, Father Angus MacDonell and Father Pierre Point, SJ.

The first chapel was built in 1826. Its location is unknown. The second one was constructed in 1834 and was situated on land that is now a part of the parish cemetery. The donor was Joseph Reaume, who was also the first person buried in the cemetery. Bishop Michael Power of Toronto visited Belle River in 1843, the year the Jesuits returned to Assumption, and again in 1845. Father Point and his fellow Jesuits are responsible for the third church and the first rectory, both of which were erected near the second church. Father Point's church was a simple frame structure. He blessed and opened it on 7 February 1849 and erected the Stations of the Cross

Sts. Simon and Jude

on 4 November 1850. Father Joseph Grimot, SJ, was the regular priest for the St. Jude mission for seven years, but he did not reside in Belle River. He blessed the bell, named Angélique, on 25 March 1855, and he welcomed Bishop Armand de Charbonnel of Toronto to the mission in the summer of 1855.

Bishop Pinsoneault of London appointed Father Eugène L.M. Jahan, a native of France, as the first resident priest in 1857. Father Jahan was pastor until 1876. During his tenure, the parish received an influx of French-Canadians from Québec, which helped to solidify and enhance the French character of the parish. Their welcomed addition to the parish rolls convinced Jahan of the need for a new and more permanent church, one made of brick. He purchased the property for the fourth and present church as early as 1861, but he had to wait at least a half dozen years before he accumulated enough money to begin building. In June 1868, the cornerstone was laid and construction was completed by the end of the year. The cost was $12,000, a sizeable sum. Jahan designed the main altar, and Antoine Lemoine and Joseph Legace of the parish executed the design. Bishop Walsh opened and blessed the church on 11 January 1869 and bestowed upon the parish its present name, Sts. Simon and Jude.

Father Joseph Gerard, the second pastor (1876-91), purchased the stained-glass windows on a trip to France, redecorated the church and built a brick school in 1889. He invited the Sisters of St. Joseph

to staff the school and thus began a long and fruitful relationship between the Sisters, the parish and Catholic education. Father Pierre L'Heureux, the fifth pastor (1904-28), added the tower, replaced the roof on the church and rectory and decorated the altars in gold and white. A tornado of 30 November 1919 demolished the tower and damaged the west side of the convent. The tower was rebuilt and the convent restored. Father L'Heureux played a major role in the founding of a high school in 1922.

Father Charles H. Laliberté, pastor from 1928 to 1945, remodeled and redecorated the church, installed a new heating system, erected new Stations of the Cross and either established or reorganized numerous parish societies such as the Ushers Club, the Altar Society and the CWL. Father Laliberté presided at the centennial celebrations for the parish in 1934, and he was instrumental in the founding of St. James High School in 1945. His successor, Father Alvin P. Marentette, was pastor for twenty-three years. He redecorated the church in 1947, built a new parish hall in 1949 and a new rectory in 1951 and founded the parish of St. William in Emeryville. In 1968, he built a new foundation and floor for the church and began the renovation of the sanctuary, which was completed by the next pastor, Father Lawrence Paré, a former secretary to Bishop Carter.

Today, the parish of Sts. Simon and Jude has more than 1,700 families and is a strong and vibrant francophone presence in the community. It is known for its French-language choir and ministry to youth.

Sources: DLA, Parish Files; E.J. Lajeunesse, *Outline History of Assumption Parish* (1967, rev. ed. 1984); Ibid., *The Windsor Border Region: Canada's Southernmost Frontier* (Toronto: 1960); *The Parish Family of St. Simon and St. Jude 1834-1984 La Famille Paroissiale de St. Simon et St. Jude* (1984). Rose-Marie Roy, "La Paroisse St-Simon et St-Jude de Belle Rivière," *Newsletter of the Diocese of London*, no. 109 (Autumn 2003), 13.

Comber: Our Lady of Lourdes

Comber was a mission of the French-Canadian parish of Holy Redeemer in Staples as early as 1914 and always was treated by the diocese as a French-speaking congregation. Parish priests from Staples celebrated Mass in different homes in Comber before settling on the home of Joseph Lefevre. This custom continued until June 1943, when Bishop Kidd purchased the house of Adam Fenner and turned it into a rectory with a chapel. Father Achille A.E. Rondot of Staples said the first Mass in the rectory on 11 July 1943.

In anticipation of the construction of a church, in 1947, Father Jean Noël of Our Lady of the Rosary parish in Windsor and a committee of

Our Lady of Lourdes

Comber Catholics helped to organize the mission. Bishop Kidd met with the people on Sunday, 20 October 1947, which cleared the way for the diocese to enter into a contract. It was signed a week later. The architect was John R. Boyde, and the contractor was Mousseau Construction. The cost for the mission-style stucco church was $24,700. Moreover, the contractor was obligated to supply altars, altar railing, confessionals and vestment case but no pews or electrical fixtures. Those were considered extras! Work began immediately and the church was enclosed in time for Christmas but not completed until June 1948. Parish correspondence indicates that in addition to the church Mousseau built a rectory.

Father Herman R. Reardon of Most Precious Blood parish in Windsor celebrated Christmas Eve Mass and was appointed administrator. Father Léo E. Charron of St. Francis Xavier parish in Tilbury succeeded him in 1950 and became the first pastor in June 1952. The following year, the parish built a grotto in honour of Our Lady of Lourdes, between the church and rectory, and, in 1960, it acquired three acres (1.2 ha) of land for a cemetery.

In 1967, the Capuchin Fathers, who had been stationed at St. Mary's parish in Blenheim for many years, were put in charge of the combined parish of Our Lady of Lourdes and Holy Redeemer, with residency in Comber, as well as the mission of Star of the Sea on Pelee Island. Holy Redeemer, was suppressed in 1971, and the church and rectory were sold in 1974. The Capuchins stayed in the Comber parish until the death of Father Anselm Spacey on 12 June 1983. Other Capuchins who served at Our Lady of Lourdes include Fathers Vitus H. Van Olffen, Leopold C. Nieuwlandt, Gerald J. Craig, Aurelius

B. Prefontaine, and Ivo S. Tommeleyn.

In 1979, under the direction of Father Spacey, the church underwent a major renovation, which included new doors, windows, roof, carpet, central heating and a fresh coat of paint. In 1982, the congregation commissioned a painting of the apparition of Our Lady to St. Bernadette, by the Montréal artist George DiCarlo. In 1983, to honour the work of the Capuchins, a branch of the Franciscans, the parish dedicated and hung a copy of the Byzantine-style crucifix that hangs in San Domiano church in Assisi.

In 1986, Father Robert D. Warden covered the church façade in brick, installed new windows and added handicap access. The cost was $135,000, which the parish, although always small in numbers, paid off in several years. The generosity of the people was evident during Bishop Sherlock's Pentecost 2000 campaign in the late 1980s. The parish goal was $35,000. This was exceeded by more than $17,000. In 1997, however, the parish built an addition to the parish hall, creating a debt of almost $54,000, which proved too difficult for the 137 registered families to manage in a timely fashion. In 1999, the diocese estimated that it would take a quarter million dollars to renovate the church.

In 2000, Our Lady of Lourdes was clustered with St. Joachim parish and Annunciation parish in Stoney Point. In December 2002, its fiftieth anniversary as a parish, Our Lady of Lourdes was closed. The church and property were purchased by a Mennonite community in 2005.

In 2006, the new paroisse de la Visitation parish, comprising the three former parishes, was established in Comber, and its newly-constructed church was dedicated by Bishop Fabbro on 2 December 2006.

Sources: DLA, Parish Files. "Paroisse de la Visitation Parish church dedication," *Newsletter of the Diocese of London*, no. 124 (Advent/Christmas 2006), 1.

Emeryville:
St. William

St. William's parish began with St. William's school. On 4 July 1950, at the invitation of Monsignor Gilbert P. Pitre of St. Anne's parish in Tecumseh, the Catholic ratepayers of Emeryville gathered in Belle River and formed a new separate school section for their community and chose three trustees. They were William Ellwood, Ernest Pike and Louis Morneau. As soon as the ratepayers made clear their intentions, Monsignor Pitre announced that Mary and Sadie Ellwood, the aunts of William Ellwood, had donated five acres (2 ha) of land for a school and church on what became Church Street. They had done so following a personal visit from Bishop Cody. In August, the diocese acquired from Joseph Ellwood an additional five acres (2 ha). The school board built a three-room school, which opened in 1951, and an addition two years later. By 1959, St. William school had seven teachers, including two Sisters of the Holy Names of Jesus and Mary, and 225 pupils. The Sisters lived in a convent built for them by the parish.

In 1953, there were 150 year round families in Emeryville, who attended Mass at Sts. Simon and Jude parish in Belle River. That number increased to 250 families during the summer months. The pressure to form a parish was strong. On 1 October 1953, Father Alvin P. Marentette and the St. Vincent de Paul Society of Sts. Simon and Jude parish began a recitation of the rosary each evening in St. William's gymnasium. Their main petition was a new parish for the Catholics of Emeryville. At the same time, the Parent-Teacher Association at the school became a very active proponent of the establishment of a parish next to the school, which continued to grow in enrolment.

Bishop Cody established St. William's parish in 1955 and appointed Father Felix M. Bezaire as the founding pastor. He celebrated the parish's first Mass in the school on 10 July 1955. Father Bezaire lived in the rectory in Belle River and oversaw the construction of the church hall, which was formally blessed by Bishop Cody on 9 July 1956, but he was too ill to continue as pastor for more than a year. Father Léo E. Charron succeeded him that same year.

Although there were diocesan plans to build a proper church, they were never implemented.

St. William

Instead, the parish turned the hall into a church. Over the years, chairs gave way to pews, a proper sanctuary was constructed, the walls were plastered and stained-glass windows were installed. Added to the original hall were a new entrance, vestibule and a second hall with a kitchen.

Father Charron proved to be the right priest to guide St. William during the early years of its formation. It was a parish divided into two linguistic factions. The Anglophone parishioners were closely allied with the Parent-Teacher Association and the four English-only classes at St. William's school. When the church was opened in 1956, the PTA was asked to confine itself to school matters and allow the formation of traditional parish-based societies, such as the Ushers Club, the CWL and the St. Vincent de Paul. The PTA agreed. The Francophone parishioners, however, organized a branch of the French version of the PTA, in view of the fact that two of the classes were bilingual. They had the support of Father Charron, Monsignor Noël and the local school inspector. This infuriated many of the English-speaking parishioners, to the point where they actively opposed their French-speaking counterparts on parish matters.

St. William's might have self-destructed over language if not for Father Charron's patience, diplomacy and repeated calls for everyone in the parish to practice charity. He was a true leader who led by example. By 1958, the people had put aside their differences. When Father Charron was transferred in June of that year, parishioners, as well as some non-Catholics in the neighbourhood, pleaded with Bishop Cody not to move him. Even the school children signed a petition. Father Charron left for his new assignment, but not before expressing his own misgivings to the bishop, and the parish carried on.

From 1970 to 1991, the Missionary Fathers of St. Paul were in charge of the parish. They had come from Malta and had been in the diocese since 1961. The parish council was heavily involved in overseeing the improvements and renovations to the church, and the Usher's Club supported the diocesan mission in Peru, adopting a new parish there in 1967. Also active in the parish are the St. Vincent de Paul Society and the CWL.

When the parish celebrated its fortieth anniversary in 1995, Bishop Sherlock remarked in a letter to Father Raymond J. Masse and the parishioners that "Anniversaries are times of looking back with nostalgia and gratitude for the pioneers whose faith and dedication enabled the parish to begin. It is also a time for looking forward and renewing the commitment of all members of the parish in the mission of the Church, which is to share the Gospel and the life of Christ with others."

St. William's marked its fiftieth anniversary in 2005.

Sources: DLA, Parish Files; *St. William's Church Emeryville, Ontario 40th Anniversary 1995* (1995).

Essex: Holy Name of Jesus

The parish of Holy Name of Jesus, originally called St. John, spent fifty-six years as a mission before it became a parish. It was a mission of Maidstone from 1880 to 1920, of Leamington from 1920 to 1930 and of Woodslee from 1930 to 1936. The reason for this odd state of affairs is simple. For many of those years, the Catholic population of Essex Centre was too small to support a resident priest but just large enough to warrant mission status and its own church.

Local tradition suggests that Mass was celebrated in 1880 in a second storey hall above a store at the northwest corner of Centre and Talbot streets. In a letter to Bishop Walsh, dated 21 March 1886, twenty-one people affixed their signatures to a subscription list for a Catholic church, raising $765 in cash and pledges, including $100 from Gordon Wigle, a Protestant. They used $500 of this money to purchase a lot from Wigle, on the condition from him that they build a church on it. In a second

Holy Name of Jesus

letter to Bishop Walsh, dated 16 January 1887, the Catholics of Essex Centre informed their bishop that they had $500 in the bank, $200 in notes from Catholics and $500 in subscriptions from non-Catholics, who promised to honour their pledges as soon as building materials were purchased. They proposed to build a frame church on substantial posts, 60 feet by 30 feet (18 m by 9 m), with a sacristy in the rear, 12 feet by 16 feet (3.6 m by 1.8 m). The church would be "plain but well finished, and painted in a neat and becoming manner, the gable end to be surmounted by a cross." They also left open the option of using brick on a stone foundation and hiring a local architect by the name of Alexander Lang.

In the end, the first Catholic church in Essex Centre was built of brick and located at the corner of Centre and Russell streets. It seated 138 people. The cornerstone was laid in August 1887, and Bishop Walsh blessed and opened the church on 1 January 1888. Although this church was damaged in the nitroglycerine explosion of 1907, it functioned as the mission church until 1942.

Bishop Kidd appointed Father M. Ignatius O'Neil as the first pastor on 25 September 1936. He remained for twenty-two years. Unable to afford the purchase of a site for a badly-needed new church, Father O'Neil turned to one of Assumption parish's most generous and active Catholics, Sir Harry Gignac, who bought property at the corner of Fairview Avenue and Talbot Street, the site of the present church. Bishop Kidd allowed the parish to build a temporary church. To save money, the parishioners tore down the first church and used the bricks and timbers from it for their new church, which looked more like a hall than a church. To pay for the construction and furnishing of the church, Father O'Neil turned to his brother priests in an appeal dated 28 August 1942. He asked them to cover the cost of bricks, cement, water, lumber, crushed rock, sand and gravel, plaster, shingles, floor, windows, doors and frames, paint, electric lights and pillars. To each request was attached a prayer. A rectory was added to the rear of the church and was replaced in 1959.

The first Mass in the second Holy Name of Jesus took place on 4 September 1942. What was considered temporary lasted for nearly thirty years.

Father O'Neil established the first separate school in the town, in September 1931, when he was a curate in Woodslee in charge of the Essex mission. The school was located on Russell Street next to the original church and placed in the hands of the Sisters of St. Joseph. Eleven years later, he purchased a school bus by borrowing money against an insurance policy and drove it twice a day for several years. A new school on Talbot Street opened in 1948 and was expanded in 1955 and 1967. Other parish schools, all located outside the town and now closed, were St. Pius X (1951), St. Christopher (1957) and St. Imelda (1961). A convent for the Ursuline Sisters was opened on Talbot Street, on 22 August 1957. Next to it was St. Ignatius Hall, the parish, which was completed in 1949-50.

Father Francis S. Mulkern built the third and present theatre-style church for $136,000. It seats 550 people, with no one in the congregation more than 70 feet (21 m) from the sanctuary. The architectural firm was Haggarty, Buist, Breviko and Milic from London, and the contractor was Matassa Construction. The second church was demolished in October 1973, and Bishop Carter dedicated the new one on 2 June 1975. In 1991, the rectory was renovated and attached to the church and garage. Marchevechio Construction did the work for $274,000. In 1998, the parish expanded the church by adding new offices, a large gathering space that serves as the narthex, two meeting rooms, a kitchen, hall and a basement for future expansion. Gregory McLean of Windsor was the architect.

In 1900, there were eighteen families in the mission church in Essex Centre. Today, the parish has 1,400 families. Holy Name of Jesus is a very active parish. One of its special works is the Life Teen Ministry for high school students. Holy Name Council 3305 of the Knights of Columbus and the CWL have a high profile in the parish and community.

Sources: DLA, Parish Files; *Holy Name of Jesus Parish, Essex, Ontario 1887-2000* (2000). Additional Information supplied by Wendy Halford and John Fahringer.

Harrow:
St. Anthony of Padua

St. Anthony of Padua parish was a mission of Amherstburg for sixty-four years, from 1869 to 1933. Father Pierre Laurent, pastor of St. John the Baptist, built a small frame lake chapel on County Road 50 (18A Highway), near the Malden and Colchester South township lines. We do not know exactly when the chapel was constructed, but we do know that William Caldwell, Jr. leased the land — 100 square feet (30 m²) on Lot 60, Malden Township — for one shilling per year, in a 999-year lease dated 1 March 1869. Sunday Mass was celebrated once a month. Bishop O'Connor erected Stations of the Cross that were taken from St. John the Baptist church, in March 1899.

A second chapel was built in 1906, this time in Harrow, affording a more central location. Dr. William J. Campeau, brother of Monsignor J. Norman Campeau, purchased property from Alfred Munger (Munger Avenue) for $200 and donated it to the diocese of London, on 9 May 1905. The property was 264 feet by 175 feet (79.2 m by 52.5 m). Father Luke Renaud, CSB, decided to build with Essex County fieldstone and sand taken from Lake Erie. Local Catholics began collecting and delivering the stone in August 1905. William Brothers of Detroit was the architectural firm. The general contractor was Blonde Brothers. The original plan called for a church 90 feet by 40 feet (27 m by 12 m), but Bishop McEvay reduced the plans to the size of a vestry, believing that the debt of a full-scale church would have been too heavy to bear for the twenty-five families. Father Renaud and Theodore Marentette turned the first sod on 25 June 1906. The vestry chapel was constructed for $4,000, was opened and blessed by Bishop McEvay on 18 November 1906 and given the name St. Anthony of Padua.

Parishioners donated the vestments, liturgical articles, sanctuary furnishings, windows and organ. James Campeau constructed the altar. Separate sacramental records began on 26 May 1907. Stations of the Cross were erected in 1928, and the CWL was organized on 29 March 1929. Although there were only fifty year-round families, the influx of summer residents made it necessary to have three Sunday Masses in July and August.

On 7 April 1933, Bishop Kidd appointed Father Albert J. McNabb as the first resident pastor. He stayed until June 1944. During his pastorate, he built an addition to the vestry chapel in 1933, at a cost of $6,500. John R. Boyde was the architect and Charles Beaudoin was the contractor. Father McNabb paid the workers and bought the construction materials. He also acquired a rectory. Father Remi J. Durand, the second pastor, purchased eight lots on Munger Avenue for a separate school, which opened in September 1946. The following year, the Ursulines came to teach. Father Durand also had the northern part of Colchester Memorial Cemetery reserved for Catholics. It is called St. Anthony's Plot.

From 1950 to 1956, the parish financed a wide range of renovations to their church, bought a new organ in 1953, eliminated the debt in 1955 and built a new rectory in 1956, the fiftieth anniversary of the church in Harrow and the 100th anniversary of the diocese. At the time of the diocesan jubilee, the parish had 200 families, many of whom were recent European immigrants, and eleven societies, sodalities and confraternities.

In 1956, the parish decided to build a rectory on church property and fund a major expansion of the church. The 1906 church had never been more than a chapel in size. It had been left unfinished from the outset and a half- century later was too small to accommodate the "cottage Catholics." Father Francis J. Bricklin, who had arrived in the parish in 1950, organized a parish committee of canvassers. The campaign began with benediction on Sunday, 8 April 1956. Monsignor Roney, the chancellor, spoke to the canvassers.

The contractor was William Pimiskern Construction. The total cost for a new rectory and

St. Anthony of Padua

an expanded church, which incorporated the 1906 chapel, was $114,983. The diocese loaned the parish $75,000. The diocese's reluctance to loan a greater amount was dictated by an unwritten rule not to place too great a debt on the shoulders of a small congregation. The parish saved $19,000 and in 1959 sold the old rectory and a vacant lot adjacent to it, putting the proceeds against the cost of the church. Father Bricklin explained to Monsignor Roney that St. Anthony's first priority was seating. The decoration would come later. In November 1957, the parish paid $8,000 for pews that could accommodate approximately 400 people.

St. Anthony of Padua remains a summer parish for the cottagers and a year-round parish for the locals. During the past fifty years, the different pastors and the people have worked well together to promote an active parish life in the community and to maintain their church.

In June 2007, the clustering of St. Anthony's with St. Jean de Brébeuf and Companions, Kingsville, was brought to full implementation when Father Richard K. Janisse was named pastor.

Sources: DLA, Parish Files; Eleanor Gignac and Laura Bondy, comps. and eds. *Led by the Shepherd: A History of St. John the Baptist Parish* (Amherstburg: 1992), 32-33; "Golden Jubilee Canvass St. Anthony's Church 1956, Harrow, Ontario," (1956); Gerald Pollard, "The History of St. Anthony's Church," (no date); J. Scott Turton, "A History of St. Anthony of Padua Church, Harrow, Ontario," (1984). Additional information provided by Father Edward Gatfield.

Kingsville: St Jean de Brébeuf and Companions

In the summer of 1930, Fred Alice, Sr., donated a parcel of land on Highway 18, about a mile (1.6 k m) west of Kingsville, for a Catholic chapel. Father J. Arthur Finn, pastor of St. Michael's in Leamington, was given the task of building the chapel and managing the mission, despite the fact that his own parish was experiencing severe financial distress during the first full year of the Great Depression and desperately needed a new separate school. Monsignor Andrew P. Mahoney, the vicar general, blessed the cornerstone of the chapel, which was given the name St. Jean de Brébeuf and Companions, in August 1930. Pope Pius XI had canonized St. Jean de Brébeuf and his seven Jesuit companions, all martyrs, on 29 June 1930, hence the choice of name. The chapel was opened in the autumn and seated 125 people. It lasted for fourteen years.

In 1943, Father Peter E. McKeon, who succeeded Father Finn in Leamington, purchased two adjoining properties in Kingsville. The first was a large home at 8 Spruce Street South, and the second was at the corner of Main Street and Spruce Street South. In July 1944, Bishop Kidd raised the mission to the status of a parish and chose Father Frederick M. Doll as the administrator, resident in Kingsville. Father Doll, however, waited until 1950 to become the first parish priest.

In the meantime, there was a church to build. The Highway 18 mission church was closed in September 1944, after the tourist season concluded, and a temporary chapel with the Blessed Sacrament was opened in the Spruce Street South home. In June 1945, Sterling Construction of Windsor began work on a basement church, completing the structure in time for Bishop Kidd to bless and open it on 26 September 1945, the Canadian feast day of St. Jean de Brébeuf and Companions. For the occasion, Bishop Kidd celebrated Mass and erected the Stations of the Cross. Two years later to the day, Bishop Kidd blessed the cornerstone of the superstructure. Eansor Steel Company of Windsor had the contract. The structure was enclosed and roofed over by November 1948. On 18 May 1949, Bishop Cody, as coadjutor, blessed the bells, and on 29 May 1949, he blessed and opened the church in the morning and held confirmation in the afternoon. The topping of the tower with a crucifix on 23 September 1949 and the erection of new Stations of the Cross on 15 October 1949 completed the construction of the church. The next year the

St Jean de Brébeuf and Companions

patient and hard working Father Doll was appointed pastor of Kingsville.

The total cost of the church was $80,000. J.C. Pennington was the architect and Clyde Vinzant of Kingsville was the contractor and builder. In 1955, individuals, families and three Sisters of St. Joseph donated the following: several stained-glass windows, altars, tabernacle, monstrance, chalices, ciboria and marble communion rail. Beginning in 1954 and extending into 1955, the front steps were added, the ceiling was finished and glass doors, lighting and pews were installed. In recognition of the success of the parish in bringing to a close the construction and decoration of its church, Bishop Cody chose Kingsville as the site of the 1955 Diocesan Eucharistic Congress.

Father Michael J. Dalton, MBE (Member of the British Empire), became pastor in 1959 and oversaw the payment of $100,000 towards the parish debt and carried out work on the church, rectory and hall. He promoted parish retreats at Oxley Retreat House. Father L.C. "Mike" Langan, the pastor starting in November 1970, established committees for liturgy, building and maintenance, parish spirit, adult education, youth and retreats. He also supervised major renovations to the interior of the church in 1975. Father Christopher S. Quinlan came to the parish in May 1982. During his pastorate, the church brickwork was restored, the roof was replaced and air conditioning was installed. He was also instrumental in persuading the parishioners to finance the building of a $400,000 parish centre, which opened on 10 September 1989. The parish had 150 families in 1948 and more than 1,000 families in 1989.

Integral to the history of the parish is the history of St. Jean de Brébeuf and Companions elementary school. The school section was formed in April 1943. Classes began at the parish house on Spruce Street South in September 1945, continued in the basement church, as soon as it was ready, and finally in a proper three-room school at Easter 1947. More classrooms were added in 1965 and 1969.

In June 2007, the clustering of St. Jean de Brébeuf and Companions with St. Anthony's, Harrow, was brought to full implementation when Father Richard K. Janisse was named pastor.

Sources: DLA, Parish Files; Michael Dalton, *Parish History* (1968); "St. John de Brébeuf and Companions Parish Main Street East, Kingsville, Ontario," (1989); "Silver Jubilee Canvass St. Jean de Brébeuf and Companions Kingsville, Ontario," (1955).

LaSalle: Sacred Heart

Sacred Heart parish in LaSalle is the Catholic centre of the historic French-Canadian community originally known as Petite Côte. Settlement of the area began as early as 1749. Although Petite Côte was fairly close to St. Joseph's parish in River Canard, which was founded in 1864, the people belonged to Assumption parish in Sandwich. Father François X. Semande, CSB, pastor in Sandwich, organized a separate school board in Petite Côte, on 26 December 1901. With the financial assistance of Bishop McEvay, the board of trustees purchased a lot on Gary Street and built a two-room frame school, which was blessed on 3 November 1902. In the diocese of London, where there was first a school, a parish church often followed. This would hold true for LaSalle.

Twenty years later, the Catholics of Petite Côte petitioned Bishop Fallon for a priest and permission to erect a church. Dated 27 June 1921, and signed by the heads of 106 families, their lengthy letter pointed out that since they had to travel anywhere from four to seven miles (from 6.4 to 11.2 k m) to attend Sunday Mass in Sandwich, and had to rely on the electric tramway to take them there, many Catholics in Petite Côte had a difficult time participating in the sacramental and social life of the parish. Attendance at Sunday evening vespers and benediction was impossible. Also, there was no Sunday school for their children. The petitioners then pointed out to the bishop that the presence in the area of the Canadian Steel Corporation would spur population growth and development, and that the American Realty Company had offered free land for a church, rectory, convent and school. The land offer was substantial. It is bordered by the present day Sacred Heart Drive, Divine Street, Kenwood Boulevard and Michigan Avenue.

After a council of three priests — Dean Downey, Father John Rooney and Father Alfred J. Côté, CSB, — approved the proposed site, Bishop Fallon established the parish on 20 July 1921. He named it Sacred Heart of Jesus, drew the boundaries

Sacred Heart

as Turkey Creek and Martin's Lane and appointed Father J. Magloire Baillargeon, who was bilingual, as the first pastor. Father Baillargeon stayed for seventeen years.

The first Mass was in the schoolhouse. One of the altar boys was Ernest Lajeunesse, the future Basilian and historian. The parish built a wooden church, understood by all to be temporary, and began to raise funds for a permanent and substantial house of worship. Impressed with the new parish's enthusiasm and generosity, Bishop Fallon hired John R. Boyde, architect, and Blonde Brothers of Chatham, contractors, to construct a Romanesque-style 560-seat church for $84,000 and a rectory for $12,000. The bishop opened and blessed the church on 17 June 1923, at which time he administered the sacrament of confirmation.

That same year, the Sisters of the Holy Names of Jesus and Mary began to teach at Sacred Heart school. In 1925, the school board opened a new four-room school on Gary Street, which was subsequently expanded to six rooms. A new school designed by J.C. Pennington, architect, was built on Divine Street between Delaware Avenue and Kenwood Boulevard and named Immaculata school. Bishop Cody blessed it on 15 May 1954. All the students from Sacred Heart school on Gary Street were transferred to a much-expanded Immaculata, in 1964, and the two schools became the new Sacred Heart.

In 1924, Father Baillargeon bought a Casavant organ for $6,000 and purchased land for Sacred Heart Cemetery. Father Leo H. Marchand, the second pastor, was known for his Christmas pageants. Father Oscar A. Martin, the third pastor, hired Roland Jobin of St. Joachim to redecorate the interior of the church in 1952, and Father Martin printed the first parish bulletin in January 1954. Father Raymond G. Forton, the fourth pastor, built St. Raymond Convent on Divine Street in 1960, for the Sisters of the Holy Names of Jesus and Mary, who had been commuting from Windsor since 1923. The 600 or so parishioners paid for the entire project, raising the money at annual parish picnics.

Between 1956 and 1969, the parish financed the redecoration of the parish hall, the renovation of the organ, repointing of the mortar and repairs to the stone and brickwork, a new roof and lightning rods, and the repainting of the interior after a fire in 1969.

Sacred Heart has always been an active congregation. The names of its members can be found on the rolls of many organizations: the Sodality of the Blessed Virgin Mary; the Holy Name Society; the Ushers Club; St. Vincent de Paul Society; Legion of Mary; the Confraternities of the Blessed Sacrament, Christian Doctrine and the Holy Rosary; and the CYO and St. Francis Youth Conference. Parishioners joined rosary and Eucharistic crusades and held annual Corpus Christi processions. After the Second Vatican Council, the people built a new altar that faced the people, sent delegates to the Diocesan Synod (1966-68) and participated in the General Mission for Essex County, from 26 February to 4 March 1967. As a follow-up to the mission, fifty parishioners took the "Vatican and You" course at the John XXIII Centre in Windsor.

Sacred Heart parish has produced fourteen vocations to the priesthood and thirty-three vocations to the religious life.

Sources: DLA, Parish Files; *Sacred Heart Church Église du Sacré-Coeur LaSalle, Ontario 1921-1971* (1971).

Leamington: St. Michael the Archangel

Father Jean J.M. Aboulin, CSB, the first Basilian pastor of Assumption parish in Sandwich, visited Leamington in 1874, when it was known as Gainsville. He said Mass at the home of William Farren, who lived near the present church on Elliott Street. Father Aboulin's census listed the names of twenty Catholic families, enough for the village to be considered a mission. It was originally called St. Andrew.

From 1874 to 1882, St. Andrew's mission belonged to the Basilian-run parish of St. John the Baptist in Amherstburg; from 1882 to 1886, it belonged to the parish of St. Mary's in Maidstone. Under the direction of Father John G. O'Connor, pastor of St. Mary's, a small white frame church was built on Elliott Street in 1882. It was three windows deep and two windows and a door across the front. Phillippe Delaurier and other Catholics of Pelee Island provided the lumber; a Mr. Delisle donated the land; and Patrick Navan of Amherstburg constructed it. This church lasted for forty years. From 1886 to 1900, St. Andrew's was a mission of the parish of St. John the Evangelist in Woodslee. The parish priest was Father Edmond J. Hodgkinson.

In 1900, Bishop McEvay created Leamington a parish with Staples and Point Pelee as its missions and appointed Father Joseph Hermas Colin as the first pastor. But Leamington did not remain a parish for long because Father Colin chose to reside in Staples, which had sixty families, the largest number of any mission in the area. Also, the people in Staples were building a new church. When Bishop McEvay asked Father Hodgkinson to suggest boundaries, he replied that Staples was the centre of Catholic settlement in the area that included Comber and Leamington. As things turned out, Staples became the parish, with Leamington as its mission and Comber, Point Pelee and Kingsville as its mission stations.

In 1919, Bishop Fallon erected Leamington into a parish, arising from a substantial influx of immigrants to the area immediately following the end of the First World War. The majority of them were from Belgium. The bishop chose St. Michael the Archangel as the parish's patron and Father Jeremiah P. Gleeson as the first pastor. To the new parish he attached Holy Name of Jesus in Essex as its mission.

Father Gleeson's first order of business was to purchase a rectory across the street from the church. His second was to build a replacement church, one big enough to cope with a steadily growing congregation plus the annual influx of summer visitors. The architect was John R. Boyde, and the contractor was Blonde Brothers of Chatham. The cost for the 400-seat, Spanish-style church was $24,000, more than half of which Father Gleeson had collected from the people before the church was completed. The church had white stucco walls, high small windows, no overhanging eaves and a red tiled roof. Monsignor Denis O'Connor, the vicar general, blessed the cornerstone in early 1922, and Bishop Fallon blessed and opened the church on 10 December 1922. One of Father Gleeson's last decisions as parish priest, before he was moved in 1928, was to secure the Sunday assistance of the Flemish-speaking Capuchin priests from Blenheim, whose regular presence would help to keep the Belgian parishioners loyal to St. Michael's.

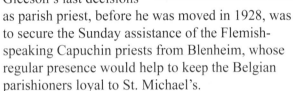

Father J. Arthur Finn was the second pastor, from 1928 to 1939. In the midst of the Great Depression, he built a church for the Kingsville mission in 1930, and he opened a separate school in the basement of St. Michael's church in early 1932. It attracted seventy-five students. The first teachers were three Sisters of St. Joseph, who rented a house near the church. St. Michael's school operated in the church basement until Easter 1941, when a stand-alone school was opened on church property. In 1956, a second storey was added. Other separate schools in Leamington are Queen of Peace, St. Louis, École St-Michel, which was first located in the St. Michael's school, after it ceased to function, and Cardinal Carter Secondary School.

Father Peter E. McKeon, the third pastor, paid off the church debt of $10,000, purchased a modern heating system and an electric Minshall organ, and installed a new high altar. During, his pastorate, Pelee Island became a mission of Leamington, in place of Kingsville, which had become a parish.

Monsignor Louis J. Phelan was pastor from 1951 to 1969. He built the current rectory and the 600-seat St. Joseph's church. Ben Bruinsma Sons Ltd. was the contractor. Bishop Carter blessed it on 24 May 1970 and declared that the parish would remain intact but maintain two churches. Monsignor Phelan was proud of the fact that the congregation had grown to more than 1,100 families

and included people from at least ten different ethnic communities, making it the most diverse parish in the diocese.

In 1993, the parish purchased the old St. Michael's school/École St-Michel from the separate school board, converted it into parish offices and meeting rooms and connected it to the church. Today, Mass is celebrated at St. Michael's parish in English, Italian, Portuguese and Spanish. The parish offers a special ministry to Mexican farm labourers.

Sources: DLA, Parish Files; *Leamington Post*, 15 December 1922; P.E. McKeon, "A History of St. Michael's Parish, Leamington, Ontario"; *The People of God: St. Michael's Parish Family 1993* (1993); Frances Selkirk Snell, *Leamington's Heritage 1874-1974* (1974). Additional information supplied by Jack Boyde.

Maidstone: St. Mary

St. Mary's parish in Maidstone is the enduring centrepiece of the Irish Catholic settlement of Maidstone Township, beginning as early as 1828 when all of Ontario belonged to the diocese of Kingston. Two nearby but distinct tracks of settlement took shape along the Talbot Road (Highway 3) and the Middle Road (County Road 46). By 1831, Maidstone Cross, the original name, was a mission of Assumption parish in Sandwich and was intermittently served by Fathers Angus MacDonell, John Foley, J. Lostrie, Peter Schneider and Jean-Baptiste Morin. Father Michael McDonell, an Irish priest of the diocese of Toronto, lived in Maidstone from 1841 to 1844. He was replaced by the Jesuits, who had returned to Assumption in 1843, at the request of Bishop Michael Power.

In addition to Assumption parish, the Jesuits were in charge of all the missions in Essex County, including Maidstone. The names of Fathers Pierre Point, SJ, Pierre J. Chazelle, SJ, Jean Jaffré, SJ, and Charles Conilleau, SJ, can be found in St. Mary's sacramental records. In December 1845, Father Jaffré gave an eight-day retreat at the mission, which attracted more than 600 people. The overwhelming success of the mission may have influenced the decision to keep separate records for St. Mary's, starting in 1846. During the latter half of the 1850s, Father Conilleau ministered to Maidstone Catholics from his base at St. Joseph's in Chatham. Bishop Pinsoneault appointed St. Mary's first resident pastor, Father Robert Keleher, Jr., on 7 March 1860, the day when St. Mary's became a parish. Father Keleher may have already been posted to St. Mary's as Father Conilleau's assistant, in response to the problem of intemperance in the parish, which aroused the ire of the bishop in 1857 and again in 1862.

St. Mary

The parish has built three churches. The exact date for the erection of the first one is unknown, but it may have been built by Father MacDonell, the Irish priest, since he lived in the settlement. It was a log church, 40 feet in length by 20 feet in width (12 m by 6 m) and 10 feet (3 m) high in the corners. It had a pitched roof surmounted by a cross, four or five windows on each side and a door and two windows on the entrance side. Patrick Tumbleton donated the land, two acres (0.8 ha) just west of the present church.

The second church, along with a rectory and a cemetery, was completed in 1848. Constructed of brick, it was 75 feet by 35 feet (22.5 m by 10.5 m) and had five large windows on both sides and a rose window. On the roof was a six-foot high cross. Instead of pews, which would have been a luxury, there were ten- to twelve-foot-long benches. Later on, the parish added a fifteen-foot (4.6 m) mission cross and a stand-alone belfry on the church property. Peter McLaughlin added a vestry. This church was located 70 feet (21 m) from Talbot Road and 20 feet (6 m) from Middle Road.

It took three different pastors to build the third and present church and two to pay off the debt. Father Patrick J. O'Shea and Thomas Moran, the village storekeeper, raised subscriptions for a new church in 1872. The pastor signed a construction contract for $14,000. His successor, Father Edmund Delahunty, purchased the site for the church and

blessed the cornerstone in August 1874. He also laid out a new cemetery and beautified the church grounds but failed to finish the church. That was left to Father James P. Ouellette. He completed the church, which seated 500 people, installed the stained-glass windows and started what became a parish tradition of choral music. Charles Kavanagh purchased the second church and turned it into a carriage shop.

Father Ouellette was greatly troubled by the church debt and felt unequal to the task of reducing it. The next pastor, Father Joseph P. Molphy, built a new rectory for $4,000 and pared down the debt by selling the old one at a "Grand Bazaar and Drawing of Prizes" held on 26-28 December 1882. Father John O'Connor retired the debt shortly before his death on 3 May 1890. Father Peter McCabe, the longest serving pastor (1904-28), plastered and decorated the interior of the church, installed steam heating and a new lighting system and added a belfry to the tower. In 1928, Father Anthony M. Stroeder built a convent for the Sisters of St. Joseph. Following a fire in 1947, Father Jeremiah P. Gleeson, with the assistance of John R. Boyde, redecorated the church.

During the twentieth century, the priests and people of St. Mary's made numerous sacrifices to preserve and enhance the beauty of their historic church, a beacon of the Catholic faith in Essex County. The parish has been attentive to the past, producing two histories, and has worked hard to fashion a viable future for itself as a rural church; it has produced many vocations and founded several separate schools; and it continues to participate in the liturgical and charitable life of the diocese.

St. Mary's was clustered with St. John the Evangelist, Woodslee in 2005.

Sources: DLA, Parish Files; *Windsor Star*, 15 October 1983; Rosemary Halford, "The Irish Settlement: Some Aspects of Growth in Maidstone 1825-1855," unpublished paper (1982); Ibid., "Maturation of the Irish Settlement: Maidstone 1850-1900," unpublished paper (1983); *St. Mary's Parish Maidstone, Ontario 1846-1996*, ed. by Rosemary Halford, with assistance from Carolyn Collins and Peter W. Halford (1996).

McGregor: St. Clement

In 1879, Father J. Pierre Grand, CSB, a priest at St. John the Baptist parish in Amherstburg, convinced Bishop Walsh to erect a new parish for French-Canadians in Essex County with Colchester North Crossing, now McGregor, as its centre. Taking territory from the parishes in Amherstburg and River Canard, the bishop gave St. Clement's 38½ square miles (69.6 km²) of land, which drew Catholics from six townships, and he designated Father Grand as the first pastor.

St. Clement

Work began on a church on 30 November 1879, and it was completed in quick order, on 22 February 1880, the date of the inaugural Mass. The builder was Patrick Navan of Amherstburg. The church cost $2,512, of which $300 was spent on furnishings. The church was situated at the northeast corner of the present church parking lot. Horse sheds were constructed to the right of the church. Dean James T. Wagner of Windsor dedicated the church on 6 June 1880 and named it in honour of St. Clement, the fourth pope (c. 91-101). The church bell, named "Ave Maria," was installed in 1883. Designed by Vanduzen and Tift Company of Cincinnati, and cast by the Buckeye Bell Foundry, it measures 2 feet, 3 inches (0.7 m) high and 9 feet, 3 inches (2.8 m) in circumference.

Father Grand was in the parish for only six months. Father Auguste P. Schneider succeeded him on 12 July 1880 and stayed for eight years, a time of tranquility and steady growth. Father Schneider purchased three acres (1.2 ha) of land on Texas Road for a parish cemetery. Father Alfred Béchard was the third pastor, from 1888 to 1900. By the time he turned the parish over to Father Charles A. Parent, in 1900, there were 700 to 800 people in the parish. The 1880 church had outlived its usefulness.

Father Parent built a 400-seat church. The walls were made of stone blocks from a local quarry. The 100-foot (30 m) tower and spire was topped with a four-foot (1.2 m) cross, making St. Clement's an impressive landmark on the flat lands of Essex County. The church has fifteen stained-glass windows in the nave, six more in the sacristy chapel, fourteen statues designed by Carli Ltd. Montréal, a high altar, and two side altars, one to St. Joseph and one to the Blessed Virgin Mary, Stations of the Cross that are made of plaster and hand painted and a marble baptismal font that was the gift of Father Denis L. Brisson, pastor from 1922 to 1924. The bell from the first church was installed in the tower.

Father Joseph D. Pinsonneault was the fifth pastor, from 1905 to 1922. He had a reputation for outspokenness and ruling the people of St. Clement's with a firm and sometimes iron hand. He built a new rectory in 1913 and established the parish's first separate school, St. Ursula's, in 1917, in the face of considerable opposition from local public school supporters. To teach in the school, he invited the Ursuline Sisters, who opened a convent on 31 August 1917.

Father Romeo J. Lefaive, the longest serving pastor, from 1945 to 1963, eliminated the debt on the convent that the parish had built for the Ursulines in 1947, and built a new St. Ursula's school in 1956. He was a remarkable financial manager, successfully keeping the parish out of debt, even though a June 1947 tornado destroyed the tower and steeple and the church hall. The rebuilt tower is shorter than the original, and instead of a steeple, it is completed by a cupola-like-dome. An entirely new hall had to be built. A second tornado, in 1971, ripped away a portion of the church roof and sent it crashing into St. Louis Hall.

Renovations following the Second Vatican Council included the removal of the communion rail, the lowering of the pulpit and the installation of a stand-alone altar that faced the people. The high altar, the two side altars and the fourteen statues have remained in place. Over the years, there have been other renovations as well as numerous repairs and improvements, all aimed at preserving and enhancing this historic 100-year-plus church. The parish replaced the front steps, covered the stained-glass windows with protective outdoor windows, purchased a new furnace, reinforced the bell housing, re-mortared the stone work and installed electric bells and an alarm system. In 1997, the church roof was copper plated, as part of a series of renovations that cost $500,000.

St. Clement's 820 families celebrated the parish's 125th anniversary on 25 June 2005. At the same time, it was clustered with St. Joseph's in River Canard, with full clustering in June 2007.

Sources: DLA, Parish Files; *Windsor Star*, 17 March 1999; Augustin J. Caron, "A Short History of St. Clement Parish, McGregor, Ontario," (1965); *La Paroisse St. Clement's Parish 1880-1980* (1980); Theo Martin, "History of the Parish of McGregor," (1930); "St. Clement's Church McGregor, Centennial 1903-2003: Sharing the Spirit of Our Faith," (2003). Additional information supplied by Father William Kornacker.

River Canard: St. Joseph

Father Pierre Potier, SJ, pioneer priest of the Huron mission, visited Rivière-aux-Canards on 28 October 1744 and again on 22 September 1745. During the nineteenth century, a French-Canadian community evolved along the river and its environs, with Catholics attending Mass at either Assumption parish in Sandwich, 10 miles (16 k m) distant, or St. John the Baptist parish in Amherstburg, 7 miles (11.2 k m) distant. Either direction was a hardship. In 1864, Bishop Pinsoneault established St. Joseph's parish and appointed Father François Marseilles, a native of France, as the first pastor. He remained until 1910 and was buried in the crypt of the present church in 1914. His pastorate is one of the longest in the history of the diocese.

On land donated by Alexandre Bénéteau, which was at the centre of the parish, Father Marseilles built a wooden plank chapel that measured 16 feet by 14 feet (4.8 m by 4.2 m). Honoré Petrimoulx and others assembled the building, which was located on the site of the current rectory driveway. The first Mass was celebrated in October 1864. Six years later, Father Marseilles oversaw the construction of the first church. It was 80 feet by 45 feet (24 m by 13.5 m), with a vestibule that was 15 feet by

12 feet (4.5 m by 3.6 m). The walls were vertical boards with molding over the joints; the roof was made of pine shingles; there was a full steeple; and the windows were long and narrow. On the inside, there were large oaken pillars to support the roof, plastered and painted walls, three altars and five statues. The cost was $400. Father Marseilles also built a rectory. Attached to it was the chapel, which he turned into a kitchen. In 1895, he built St. Joseph's bilingual separate school and a convent with his own money. The cost was $3,000. Three

St. Joseph

Sisters of the Holy Names of Jesus and Mary began to teach in the school in September 1896.

Father Joseph A. Loiselle was the second pastor, from 1910 to 1928. He built a new rectory for $7,000 and then a new church, which was a grand and noble achievement for the parish. Five years passed from the demolition of the first church in 1911 to the dedication of the present church in 1916. In the meantime, Mass took place in the St-Jean-Baptiste Hall. J.O. Turgeon of Montreal was the architect; Joseph Wilson of Amherstburg did the brickwork; and Urgel Jacques did the woodwork. Parishioners hauled crushed stone from the Amherstburg quarry, gravel from Leamington and brick from Windsor. They also helped to excavate the basement. Built of brick and stone, with a cathedral-like façade that features impressive twin towers, St. Joseph's church seats 782 people on the ground floor and another 250 people in the choir loft. Its dimensions are 158 feet (47. 4 m) in length on the outside, 153 feet (45.9 m) on the inside and 68 feet (20.4 m) to the roof above the wall plates. The cost was $75,000.

Bishop Fallon blessed the cornerstone on 15 June 1913. The basement opened on 18 April

1915. And Bishop Fallon returned to the parish to dedicate the completed church on 22 October 1916, delivering a memorable sermon on the "Holiness of the Church" and "This is the House of God and the Gate of Heaven," in both English and French.

In the early 1950s, Charles Malczyk and his wife, Polish immigrants, decorated the interior of the church. They spent a year designing and painting seventeen biblical and doctrinal themes on the walls and ceiling of the church. At the same time, Austin Meloche, a member of the congregation, built three new altars of solid walnut. Using plans drawn up by Arthur Schilling, a Detroit-based German architect, Meloche spent four months constructing them. The main altar and backdrop are 17 feet (5.1 m) in height and each of the two side altars with backdrops are 15 feet (4.7 m) in height. All three altars still exist. Father Eugène P. LaRocque, who later became bishop of Cornwall-Alexandria, began the implementation of the liturgical changes mandated by the Second Vatican Council, beginning in 1968, and Father Edouard P. Forton, pastor from 1975 to 1988, superintended numerous renovations and alterations to the church, including the extension of the sanctuary steps from wall to wall, and also to the rectory and grounds. The parishioners financed everything without going into debt.

From 1995 to 2005, the people of St. Joseph have spent $1.7 million in restoration work. The three main projects have been storm windows for the stained-glass windows, the repointing of the brickwork and the addition of braces and steel rods to reinforce the rear of the church, where the walls were separating from the roof. The parish plans to spend an additional $1.5 million to restore the interior in time for the parish's sesquicentennial in 2014.

The pastors and people of St. Joseph's have worked diligently to maintain and enhance the French-Canadian traditions and bilingual character of their parish.

In June 2007, St. Joseph's was clustered with St. Clement parish, McGregor.

Sources: DLA, Parish Files; *Paroisse St-Joseph Parish Rivière-aux-Canards, Ontario 1864-1989* (1989). Additional information supplied by Don Soulliere.

St. Joachim: St. Joachim

Although Patrick McNiff had surveyed the lands that bordered the Ruscom River as early as 1793, it took nearly a century of settlement before there were sufficient French-Canadian Catholics in the area to petition for a parish and a priest. Arriving in 1824, Louis Quenneville and Isidore Carré are considered the first settlers. More settlers followed with the introduction of transportation links, such as the Deerbrook stagecoach on Highway 2, in 1827, which was superceded by the Great Western Railway, in 1854. The St. Clair Siding became a GWR station in 1875. The availability of arable land and the growth of the potash industry were other inducements. Prior to the establishment of St. Joachim parish, local Catholics attended Mass and received the sacraments at either Sts. Simon and Jude parish in Belle River or Annunciation parish in Stoney Point.

By 1880, there were 100 families along or near the Ruscom River. Father Joseph Gérard, pastor of Belle River, advised Bishop Walsh of the necessity of a new parish between his parish and that of Stoney Point. After interviewing two delegations, one led by Désiré Dupré of Deerbrook and another supported by Father Gérard, which wanted a more central location, the bishop toured the area and chose the intersection of County Road 42 and the 5th Concession. On 3 June 1880, the diocese purchased three and a half acres (1.4 ha) from Alexander Cameron.

To the Catholics of Ruscom, Bishop Walsh said, "Build a church, and I will send you a priest." Local memory also has him saying, "Build, you have the land, and God will help you." Bishop Walsh was buying time, since he had no French-Canadian priest at his disposal for the new parish. He would have to find one.

In the meantime, the parishioners had to build a church. In the autumn of 1881, Elzéar Jacques and his two sons, Adam and Gustave, of Tecumseh, were put in charge of construction. Financing came from a two-day picnic that raised $3,000. The Jacques family built a frame church of white oak, 80 feet in length and 500 feet in width (24 m by 15 m), which rested on a foundation of local fieldstone. Bundles of eight-inch (20.3 c m) oak posts, placed every sixteen feet (4.9 m) below the floor, support the columns that held up the roof. The family also constructed pews made of ash, a balustrade, a confessional and two simple altars. Interestingly, the church was put together in a fashion similar to a barn-raising bee.

St. Joachim

As the church neared completion, Bishop Walsh wrote to Bishop Edouard-Charles Fabre of Montréal for a priest. He sent thirty-six-year-old Father Ambroise Lorion, a native of Epiphany, Assumption County, Québec. Father Lorion toured the parish in the company of Norbert Sylvester, church treasurer, and accepted the invitation. He was parish priest for twenty-eight years.

Father Lorion celebrated the first Mass in the parish on 5 March 1882. The offertory collection was $9.80. Monsignor Jean-Marie Bruyère, the vicar general, blessed the church on 17 June 1882. There were ninety families in the parish, according to pew rent tabulations.

In 1883, Father Lorion finished the rectory, which was a stone-and-brick palace in the middle of Rochester Township, and purchased an Angelus bell for the church. In 1891, he added to the length of the church, which increased the seating capacity to 425, and he added a sanctuary, 24 feet by 18 feet (7.2 m by 5.4 m) and a sacristy, 24 feet by 32 feet (7.2 m by 9.6 m). He covered the exterior walls with brick. The total cost was $10,610, which was paid in full by the congregation by 1895. Father Lorion was scrupulous about not leaving unmanageable debt and was known for priming the more affluent of his flock for donations. Bishop O'Connor consecrated the enlarged and more solid looking church on 27 October 1891.

Father Lorion added a bell tower, a permanent high altar and a side altar, in 1896, a second altar in 1897, red oak pews in 1898, and a new roof in 1903.

The pews were the gift of a Mme Taylor, a hotel owner in Belle River. The oak was locally harvested and cured and sent to the Globe Furniture Company in Walkerville.

Father Joseph G.E. Courtois, the second pastor, conducted a parish census. Dated 12 October 1911, it listed 164 households, 895 souls and 10,900 acres under cultivation. Father Charles Laliberté, third parish priest, from 1912 to 1928, commissioned the Sacred Heart monument in front of the church, installed electricity in the church and rectory, repainted the interior walls, varnished the pews and erected the Stations of the Cross, which came from the chapel of the Petit Séminaire de Montréal. Bishop Fallon blessed them on 28 September 1916. Roland Jobin decorated the interior of the church in 1935, during the pastorate of Father Joseph E. Emery.

For more than a century of parochial life, the pastors and people of St. Joachim have worked diligently to sustain the French-Canadian heritage of their parish.

In 1996, St. Joachim was clustered with Annunciation parish in Stoney Point and Our Lady of Lourdes in Comber. St. Joachim church was closed in April 2000. The 270 registered families would have had to spend nearly $1 million to refurbish it. St. Joachim's was absorbed into Annunciation parish.

In 2006, the new paroisse de la Visitation parish was established, comprising the three former parishes, and its new church, located in Comber, was dedicated by Bishop Fabbro on 2 December.

Sources: DLA, Parish Files; Jeanne d'Arc Barrette, "La Paroisse de Saint-Joachim," *Newsletter of the Diocese of London*, no. 103 (Summer 2002), 13; Joseph Emery, "Histoire de la Paroisse Saint Joachim a St. Joachim Rivière Ruscom, Comté d'Essex, Ont." (1943); *Histoire de la Paroisse St-Joachim 1882-1982* (1982).

Staples: Holy Redeemer

Holy Redeemer parish in Staples, at the junction of Highway 77 and County Road 8, became a parish in 1901 by default. Leamington was Bishop McEvay's choice as a new parish, with Staples and Point Pelee as missions, but the first parish priest, Father Joseph Hermas Colin, decided to live in the village of Staples because it had the largest Catholic population in the area — sixty families — and the people were building a church. Consequently, Staples became the parish; Leamington was its mission; and Kingsville, Comber and Point Pelee were its mission stations. As time passed, Leamington (1919), Comber (1950) and Kingsville (1952) evolved into parishes, establishing their own identities. Point Pelee, however, remained a mission, and Comber would decide the fate of the parish in Staples.

Holy Redeemer

From its inception, Staples was two things: French Canadian and a quiet country parish that experienced few opportunities to grow and expand. The 1903 parish report to the diocese recorded 115 families, 500 souls, 64 pew holders and 150 children of school age. Pastoral dues were calculated at 10 cents per acre. The church was valued at $2,500. The 1913 parish report listed 80 families, 400 souls, 65 pew holders and 70 school age children. Pastoral dues remained the same, although labourers were expected to contribute four dollars. Parish organizations included the Altar Society, Holy Name Society, Propagation of the Faith and the League of the Sacred Heart. Curiously, the parish owned nine acres (3.6 ha) of land, but it never developed this land for anything connected to the work of the parish, such as a cemetery. In 1914, the total receipts for the parish were $1,801.

Apparently in the 1930s, the parish constructed a new church. Built of brick, it was four windows deep and two windows and a front door wide, with a "tower" and a steeple. According to the 1934 diocesan evaluation, there was seating for 260, but parishioners interviewed in 1974 claimed that the church could hold only 100 people. In 1965, Roland Jobin decorated the church interior. His previous work included St. Joachim and Sacred Heart in LaSalle. The original 1901 church was turned into the rectory.

By 1959, there were seventy-five to eighty families. In 1967, the diocese combined the parishes of Comber and Staples. There would be

two churches under one pastor who would reside in Comber. This was a novel solution, one that did not sit well with many parishioners from Staples, who were now in a minority and thus not in control of the future of their parish. Father Roger J. Bénéteau, a diocesan priest, was the last resident pastor. Bishop Carter passed the administration of the new combined parish to the Capuchin Fathers, who also celebrated Mass on Pelee Island.

Then there arose the question of the French-Canadian status of Holy Redeemer. Was French still the language of the parish? Matters came to a head on this thorny question in 1971. Father Eugène P. LaRocque, then the dean of Essex, reported to the diocese that Staples had 95 families, of which 53 were French-speaking, but only 35 families attended church regularly, and of these, fifty per cent were French-speaking. Only two families could not understand English. Comber had 145 families (53 envelope users), and Pelee Island had 11 families (5 envelope users.) On Sunday, 14 February 1971, the collection at Staples was $69.50, and at Comber it was $116.

Father LaRocque made three recommendations: 1) that the present schedule of Masses in English at Comber, Staples and Pelee Island remain unchanged; 2) that that those families who wanted Mass in French be allowed to become full members of either St. Joachim or Annunciation in Stoney Point; and 3) that Mass continue to be celebrated in French at the bilingual Ste-Bernadette school. In addition, he commented that the ongoing upkeep of both the Comber and Staples parishes was questionable, given the small revenue that each one generated and the fact there was a steady flow of people between the two parishes.

This last comment convinced the diocese to close Holy Redeemer in 1971. The five-person advisory board of the combined parish (two from Comber and three from Staples) agreed. In December 1974, the parishioners decided by a vote of 73-2 to sell the church and rectory.

Sources: DLA, Parish Files; *Tilbury Times*, 14 March 1974, 18.

Stoney Point: Annunciation

Annunciation parish was the third of four nineteenth-century French-Canadian parishes established on or near Lake St. Clair. The others are Belle River, Tecumseh and St. Joachim. It began and has remained a rural parish. There are several traditions concerning its origins. One tradition has Father Eugène Jahan of Belle River building a chapel in Stoney Point in 1860, in response to the growing Catholic population of Rochester Township, and saying Mass there once a month until the parish was established. This was probably true, but no one today can ascertain the location of the chapel, and no such chapel played a role in the parish history. A second tradition claims that Bishop Pinsoneault founded the parish in 1865 and appointed a Father David as the pastor, who purchased land for a church and a cemetery but left the area after a year. Although a land purchase did take place, Father David remains an obscure figure.

A more promising start to the parish was made in 1867, when Father Paul Andrieux, a native of Lagniole, France, was appointed parish priest. Parish records begin on 15 September 1867, ten months after Bishop Pinsoneault left the diocese and nearly two months before the consecration of Bishop Walsh. It seems likely, therefore, that Monsignor Jean-Marie Bruyère, the administrator, was responsible for sending Father Andrieux from St. Joseph parish, Corunna, to Annunciation in Stoney Point.

Father Andrieux was an energetic and imaginative priest. He convinced his parishioners to build a large frame rectory, which served as his home and the parish chapel, and he actively took part in the construction of the first parish church, working alongside his parishioners without distinction of rank. He stayed in the parish until 1872, when he was called by Bishop Walsh to build a new church in Tecumseh. Father Pierre Fauteux was the second pastor, from 1872 to 1882, and Father Joseph Bauer, who served only two years but built a three-story classical college, was the third pastor. The college had a brief life but did have

Annunciation

among its students two future priests of the diocese: Father Emile C. Ladouceur and Father Achille Rondot.

Father Napoléon D. St. Cyr, a native of Nicolet, Québec, was the sixth pastor. He arrived in the diocese on 9 December 1892, at the invitation of Bishop O'Connor, who made him parish priest of Stoney Point the following year. Father St. Cyr revitalized parochial life and rallied his parishioners to embark on a period of renewal and expansion. They built a substantial rectory for $5,000, which was paid for by subscription. To save money, they collected the foundation stones from the lakebed and traveled to Chatham where they were given free construction material.

Next, they built the second and current church. Bishop McEvay blessed the cornerstone on 23 October 1905. For the occasion, Bishop Joseph-Simon-Herman Bruneault of the diocese of Nicolet preached the sermon. Louis Caron of Nicolet was the architect, and Blonde Lumber Company was the contractor. The price was $23,000. Built of brick, the church is 143 feet (42.9 m) in length and 55 feet (16.5 m) in width. A two-tiered pagoda-like spire tops the tower, which contains the 1889 bell from the first church. Two smaller towers flank the front of the church and a third is located in the rear. The foundation is ten feet (3 m) high. The full-sized basement included a hall below the nave and a winter chapel below the vestry. Annunciation church was a fitting testimony to the faith and determination of the parish's 200 families.

Father St. Cyr was a gifted amateur musician, who directed the parish choir, making it one of the best in Essex County, and he purchased a $9,000 organ. He was also an ardent French-Canadian nationalist who ran afoul of Bishop Fallon and was expelled from the diocese on 10 July 1914. His abrupt expulsion came as a shock to his parishioners and made life difficult for Father Gilbert P. Pitre, his young and inexperienced successor. Father Pitre stayed for nineteen years. During that time, he won over his parishioners, and with their assistance and generosity, he accomplished many things. In 1920, the Ursulines came to teach in the separate school; in 1922, electricity was installed; in 1930, Louis Jobin of Montreal decorated the interior of the church (in 1960, he decorated the church a second time); also in 1930, Louis Brisson of Detroit installed a new heating system; the rectory was renovated; and by 1931, the parish debt was reduced to $13,000.

Succeeding generations of Annunciation parishioners, in concert with their pastors, have been unflagging in their efforts to maintain their parish church and keep alive their French-Canadian traditions. Substantial has been the sacrifice, and long is the list of renovations and repairs. It includes the 1976 reconfiguration of the sanctuary, the 1981 repointing of the brickwork for $66,000 and the 1989 restoration work by Windsor architect Gregory McLean, which cost $470,283. Bishop Sherlock rededicated the church on 1 June 1989.

In 2000, Annunciation parish, with more than 775 registered families, was clustered with the parishes of Comber and St. Joachim. It was the last of three to remain open but was suppressed in 2006 and absorbed into the new paroisse de la Visitation parish. The new parish church, located in Comber, was blessed by Bishop Fabbro in December 2006.

Sources: DLA, Parish Files; Hélène Chauvin, "Historique"; Ursule Leboeuf, "Histoire de la Paroisse de l'Annonciation," *Newsletter of the Diocese of London*, no. 92 (Summer 2000), 11; *Paroisse de l'Annonciation 1867 ... 1967* (1967); *Paroisse de l'Annonciation Pointe-aux-Roches 125th Anniversary 1867-1992* (1992); G.P. Pitre, "A Short History of the Parish of the Annunciation Pointe-aux-Roches, Ont." (1931).

Tecumseh: St. Anne

St. Anne's parish is the second oldest French-Canadian parish in Essex County. In 1857, Catholics east of Pillette Road petitioned Bishop Pinsoneault to erect a mission. The bishop consented, and the diocese purchased land for a church and rectory at the corner of Tecumseh Trail (Tecumseh Road East) and Lesperance Lane (Lesperance Road). The first church was tiny. Its dimensions were 20 feet by 40 feet (6 m by 12 m) and 18 feet (5.4 m) at the highest point. It had a peaked roof, wooden shingles, a squared-lumber frame, walls of upright boards and a double-door entrance. The interior was rustic — a small altar, crucifix, no tabernacle, a single-plank communion rail and benches for pews.

A mission of the Jesuit-run Assumption parish in Sandwich, the church was dedicated on 9 January 1859 and given the name Ste-Anne in honour of Ste-Anne de Beaupré in Québec. Father Nicolas Point, SJ, celebrated the first Mass and baptized two children. On 20 October 1859, twenty-seven children received First Holy Communion, and Bishop Pinsoneault confirmed them and twenty-four adults later the same

St. Anne

day. In December 1860, the bishop appointed Father Pierre Fauteux as the first pastor.

From 1860 to 1970, St. Anne's was blessed with six long-serving pastors: Father Fauteux (1860-71); Father Paul Andrieux (1871-88); Father Antoine P. Villeneuve (1888-1905); Father Pierre Langlois (1905-33); Father Gilbert Pitre (1933-58); and Father Charles E. Lanoue (1958-70). Immediately following Father Lanoue was Father Eugène LaRocque (1970-74), who was consecrated bishop of Alexandria-Cornwall on 3 September 1974, in St. Anne's church.

Father Fauteux opened the cemetery in 1861, blessed the church bell, named "Marie Louise," in 1865 and oversaw the building of the foundation for the current church. Father Andrieux completed the church, which was opened in 1874 and seated

900 (some sources say 600) worshippers. Elzéar Jacques was the builder. Father Andrieux taught plainchant to the parish's young people, organized a choir and purchased a hand-pumped Casavant organ in 1887. His successor, Father Villeneuve, completed the steeple, which rose to 125 feet (37.5 m), in 1891, and he transferred the "Marie Louise" bell from its original setting on the church lawn to the church tower. He paid for the construction of two separate schools and invited the Ursulines to assume their administration. Bishop O'Connor blessed the cemetery on 15 October 1893. Interestingly, the first English announcements at Mass were not made until 1905.

Father Langlois was parish priest for twenty-eight memorable and productive years. He constructed a permanent sacristy (1908); installed steam heating (1911), improved the electrical lighting (1913); built the Sacred Heart of Jesus monument, as a memorial to the parish men who fought in the First World War (1919-20); covered the church's deteriorating brick and mortar work with a heavy application of cement made to look like cement block, which is the appearance of the church today (1921); purchased a new organ (1930); and redecorated the interior of the church (1930-31). A highlight of the redecoration was the new Stations of the Cross that were painted on canvas and glued to the walls.

The month of July 1927 was a grand time of celebration in the history of the parish. On 17 July, the three new bells were christened "Pierre," "Paul" and "Ste-Anne" and installed in the tower next to the original bell. (All four bells were cleaned and restored in 1992.) On 24 July, the cemetery mausoleum was blessed; on 26 July, 5,000 people took Holy Communion on the Feast of Ste-Anne; and on 28 July, Bishop Fallon presided at the Diocesan Eucharistic Congress.

Father Pitre, the fifth pastor, led the parish for twenty-five years. To him was given the unenviable task of eliminating the debt during the Great Depression and later on of rebuilding the rectory that was severely damaged by fire. He was a fervent supporter of separate schools, founding St. Anthony and St. Pius X elementary schools and co-founding St. Anne's High School in Tecumseh, in 1946. Father Lanoue, the sixth pastor, was known for his deep devotion to St. Anne, and he shared that devotion with countless others on CHYR radio broadcasts of the St. Anne Novena.

St. Anne's territory has been divided three times to form the parishes of Our Lady of Fatima (1950), St. Gregory the Great (1958) and Atonement (1975). Although St. Anne's has been substantially reduced in size, the loyalty and generosity of the remaining parishioners has not diminished. Indeed, the rededication of the entire church on 21 January 1995, which brought to a close a massive $800,000 restoration, marked the beginning of a renaissance in parish life that continues today.

Sources: DLA, Parish Files; *Catholic Register*, 13 June 1992; *Windsor Star*, 23 January 1995; *Église Ste Anne Church 1859-1984: 125 Years* (1984); Adrien Letourneau, "History of Our Parish," in *Saint Anne, Mère de Marie* (1959).

Tecumseh: St. Gregory the Great

During the 1950s, the village of St. Clair Beach, which was located in the east end of St. Anne's parish, underwent a building boom that attracted families with young children. At the same time, a significant number of Catholics in the village were involved in the Christian Family Movement. The CFM was a type of Catholic Action involved in the building of Christian community. Father Gerald J. Freker, of St. Anne's, was their chaplain. He urged CFM members to organize a separate school section and build a school. By June 1958, there was a school board in place, and the trustees purchased property near what is now the corner of St. Gregory Road and Arlington Boulevard, with the financial assistance of the diocese.

Where there is a school, a church will follow. This was a pattern of parochial development often repeated during the time of Bishop Cody, and the establishment of St. Gregory the Great parish was no exception. On 20 June 1958, the bishop founded the parish and chose Father Victor C. Côté as the first pastor. Father Côté was known and appreciated in the diocese as an organizer, builder and administrator.

In July 1958, construction began on a two-room school and church hall, side by side, as if they were one project. The diocese decided to build a hall and use it as a temporary church in order to give the parish's two hundred families time to find their financial feet, so to speak. The bishop was reluctant to place too great a mortgage on St. Gregory's small band of parishioners and also expect them to contribute their full share for St. Anne's High School — $25,000 over three years — and for the Diocesan Assessment, which was recently instituted to take the place of the traditional cathedraticum. In the meantime, Father Côté celebrated Mass at Lakewood Golf Club. This lasted from June to early December 1958.

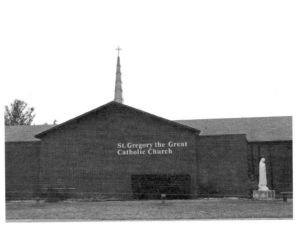

St. Gregory the Great

The architect of the church hall was J.P. Thomson Associates of Windsor, and the contractor was H.T. Reaume. The design was very basic: long and narrow in shape, concrete block construction with an extensive use of glass, including coloured cathedral glass, on all four walls, and laminated arches in the interior that eliminated the need for columns. Capacity was 400 persons. Pews were individual hall seats. A small rectory and offices were part of the structure. The total cost was $43,389, plus interest of $18,724, which the parishioners paid in full by 2 June 1967.

The first Mass at St. Gregory's took place on 7 December 1958. In April 1959, Father Côté organized a parish fundraiser that netted $68,500 in pledges from 158 people. The people were not only generous with their money but also with their time. St. Gregory's parish experienced a high rate of participation in the Holy Name Society, the Ladies Auxiliary of St. Gregory, the 1959 canvassers, altar boys, the parish council and the building committee. First Holy Communion took place for the first time on 31 May 1959, and Bishop Cody confirmed thirty-three children and eight adults on 15 May 1960.

St. Gregory's never did build a stand-alone church. Instead, over a period of twenty years, additions and renovations transformed the hall into a church and another hall was built. In 1968, a proper rectory was added. In 1977, the parish turned the temporary church into a permanent one, spending $201,798, or three times as much as the cost of the original hall. The work was long overdue,

since the number of parish families was steadily climbing and would reach more than 1,000 in 1984. The architect was Robert Langlois, and the builder was a parishioner, Ted Brotto of Suburban Builders. The pastor at the time was Father Raymond G. Forton; the head of the parish building committee was Dennis Drew. Subsequent work included a parking lot in 1979, a parish hall addition in 1984, a new rectory in 1993 and stained-glass windows for the east and west ends in 1998.

Two years later, there was intense discussion about the future of St. Gregory's church. Four options were considered: ongoing care of the present facilities; relocation and the construction of a new church, hall and rectory; the construction of a new rectory and office on the present site; the exchange of properties with the separate school board coupled with the sale of the parochial buildings to the board. In the end, the status quo, as represented in the first option, was retained. In 2006, however, the diocese recommended that St. Gregory the Great and St. William in Emeryville become a new parish with a new name and build a new church in a place more central to the needs of the shift in population.

Sources: DLA, Parish Files; *Silver Anniversary Year of St. Gregory's Parish Family 1958-1983* (1983).

Woodslee: St. John the Evangelist

The parish of St. John the Evangelist is located in both Rochester and Maidstone townships and was founded at the request of Irish Catholic settlers. Pioneer missionary priests to the area included Father Angus MacDonell, pastor of Assumption in Sandwich who ministered to the people of the future parish on his visits to Maidstone and Belle River, and Father Jean Jaffré, SJ, who was in charge of the Irish in Essex and Kent counties, from 1845 to 1857, when he was posted to Chatham. Thereafter, the local custom was for Catholics on the Maidstone side of the Middle Road to attend Mass at St. Mary's, an Irish parish, and for Catholics on the Rochester side to participate in the Sunday liturgy at Sts. Simon and Jude in Belle River, a French-Canadian parish.

In the spring of 1873, a delegation of Woodslee Catholics, headed by John Conway, met Bishop Walsh on a confirmation stop at Maidstone. The delegation asked Bishop Walsh for permission to build a church. He granted their request but only after the petitioners, whom he had called to the altar rail at the end of the confirmation ceremony, pledged their financial support to the project. John Conway donated two acres (0.8 ha) of land, and others subscribed $1,500. On 23 September 1873, two more acres of land, at $60 per acre, were added to the parochial property.

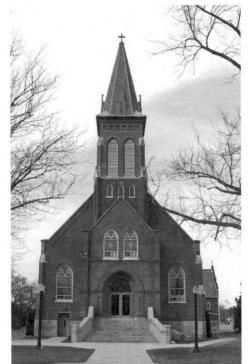

St. John the Evangelist

Construction on the church began in the spring of 1874 and was completed in the autumn of the same year. Robert Moon, a non-Catholic, was the contractor, and Father James P. Ouellette, pastor of Maidstone, was the supervisor. Local sawmills supplied the lumber, and the people purchased finishing materials in Chatham. The church was a frame structure with a peaked roof, six windows deep and two windows and a doorway wide. A small porch was attached to the front, and another porch was part of the sacristy at the rear.

The church was officially opened on 15 April 1875, and Bishop Walsh appointed Father Patrick Fitzpatrick as the first pastor. During his pastorate, which lasted eighteen months, Father Fitzpatrick built a two-story, brick rectory, encouraged his parishioners to pay down the debt and opened a school in the sacristy in 1874, one of the earliest in the diocese of London. The next year, he built a

stand-alone school on church property. This school lasted until 1902, when a larger one replaced it.

Father Edmond J. Hodgkinson, pastor from 1887 to 1914, is responsible for the second and current church. Construction commenced in May 1900 and was completed in December of the same year. Benjamin Blonde of Chatham was the contractor. Bishop McEvay blessed the cornerstone on 17 June 1900. The final cost was $10,983. The foundation was of stone and the walls were made of brick. The seating capacity was 440 people. Father Hodgkinson also planned and fenced the cemetery at the rear of the church and was responsible for the Leamington and Pelee Island missions, which had been given to the parish in 1887.

His successor, Father Thomas J. Ford, was pastor for twelve busy and productive years. In 1915, he built a new rectory; in 1918, he purchased the Schooley Store (originally a Methodist church) and turned it into a parish hall, which was later enlarged; from 1919 to 1922, he renovated the church and improved the cemetery and church grounds; in 1923, he invited the Ursulines to teach in the parish school, and the parish purchased the Hogan Estate and converted it into Marymount Convent; in 1924, the church hall was turned into the temporary home of St. John's continuation school (grades 9 and 10), which lasted until 1962; and in April 1930, the parish was given the mission of Essex.

As St. John the Evangelist parish grew and developed, beginning in the 1920s and continuing well into the 1950s, it became a centre for local public speaking, dramatics and debates and sponsored team sports such as baseball, lacrosse and lawn tennis. Father Gerald J. Labelle, pastor from 1926 to 1936, and Father Earl J. McMahon of Maidstone, founded the North Essex Baseball League in 1928. The parish, never large but always active, was also known for its numerous vocations to the priesthood and religious life. From 1909 to 1995, sixteen men were ordained to the priesthood, and from 1884 to 1941, twenty-four women entered religious life.

Other notable events in the life of the parish include the formation of the Woodslee Credit Union in 1943, by Father E. Gordon Doe; renovation to the interior of the church in 1958, by Father Michael Dalton, MBE; repairs to the roof and interior of the church and the rearrangement of the pews and altar in 1991-92, by Father E. Carl Keane; and the structural reinforcement of the roof and steeple, and the renovation of the main entrance in 1999-2000, by Father Chris Quinlan.

In 2000, St. John the Evangelist parish celebrated its one hundred and twenty-fifth anniversary. In 2005, owing to the scarcity of priests, the declining number of enrolled parishioners and the proximity of parishes in Essex, Maidstone and Belle River, the parish was clustered with St. Mary parish, Maidstone.

Sources: DLA, Parish Files; Edward Gordon Doe, "A History of the Parish of Saint John the Evangelist and Woodslee, Ontario," (1942); Thomas J. Ford, "History of Woodslee Parish," (4 October 1923); *Sharing Our Memories: A History of St. John the Evangelist Church and the Woodslee Area*, ed. Georgine Willemsma (2000).

Leamington:
Portuguese Mission

As the priest in charge of the Portuguese mission in London, since October 1974, Father António Seara, O de M, felt that it was also his duty to minister to the Portuguese communities throughout the diocese. Twice a year he visited Windsor, Harrow, Leamington, Wallaceburg and Sarnia. By the autumn of 1975, there were Portuguese-speaking priests in both Strathroy and Sarnia, in addition to Father Seara in London. Meanwhile, the Portuguese of the Windsor area asked for a resident Portuguese-speaking priest. Windsor had some 100 Portuguese families, Harrow 125, Leamington 250 and Wheatley 135. At this time, it was suggested that a second priest was needed in London and one in Windsor.

In October 1976, Father Henry G. Kea, CSSR, a native of the Netherlands who had been serving in the diocese of Peterborough, was placed in charge of the Portuguese mission of Essex County, which included Windsor. His main concern, however, was for the Portuguese living outside the city. By early November 1976, Father Silvio Gasparotto, CD, had arrived from Rome. A friend of Father Ugo Rossi of

St. Michael's parish in Leamington, he had a sister living in Windsor. Besides Italian, Father Gasparotto spoke Portuguese and was given the spiritual care of Windsor's Portuguese community. He lived at Sacred Heart rectory and was also appointed associate pastor of that parish, leaving Father Kea to look after the Portuguese in the county outside the city.

Like Father Gasparotto, Father Kea had learned to speak Portuguese in Brazil, which was different in certain respects from the Portuguese spoken by their parishioners in Windsor and Essex County, most of whom came from the Azores. For both men, this inevitably produced some tensions and difficulties in communication, which were compounded by their unfamiliarity with some of the people's customs and traditions.

When Father Kea was transferred to London, in April 1977, Father Gasparotto was placed in charge of Windsor and Essex County and, in August 1979, changed his residence to the rectory of Our Lady of Blessed Sacrament in Wheatley. In 1982, he moved to Leamington. As a result of the restructuring of the Portuguese mission, about 1987, Father Kea succeeded Father Gasparotto, and the mission was renamed the Kent and Essex Counties: Portuguese Mission. On 1 June 1989, Father Manuel Cardoso succeeded Father Kea.

While the Portuguese Mission, as such, ceased about this time, the Portuguese Catholics of the area continue to be served by a Portuguese-speaking priest from St. Michael parish, Leamington.

Sources: DLA, Portuguese Missions File, Gerald Emmett Carter Papers, Box 23; "The Official 1989 Pastoral Appointments," *Newsletter of the Diocese of London*, no. 37 (Pentecost 1989), 17; "Rev. H.G. Kea," *Newsletter of the Diocese of London*, no. 63 (Fall 1994), 5.

Pelee Island:
Star of the Sea Mission

Bishop John Walsh placed Dean James T. Wagner, parish priest of St. Alphonsus in Windsor, in charge of Pelee Island Catholics, in the autumn of 1886. Prior to that date, Mass had been celebrated only twice on the island: on 22 August 1862 by Father Jean Daudet, pastor of St. John the Baptist parish in Amherstburg, and in August 1878, by a priest from Kelly's Island, Ohio. In October 1886, Dean Wagner sent his assistant, Father Charles McManus, to Pelee Island to take a head count of Catholic families and to celebrate Mass, which he did at the home of the island lighthouse keeper, James Cummings. Father McManus discovered only six families but sufficient enthusiasm to recommend the construction of a chapel.

In response to Father McManus's report, the people of St. Alphonsus raised $385 at a parish bazaar. In the spring of 1887, Father Michael McGrath, the new assistant at St. Alphonsus, celebrated Mass at the Cummings' home and counted thirteen families, who began a subscription drive for the chapel on the heels of James Cummings' donation of an acre (0.4 ha)of land on the eastern end of the island for a church, rectory and cemetery. On 3 May 1887, Dean Wagner shipped the building material from Windsor to Point Pelee and accompanied J.B. L'Heureux, the designer and builder, and five carpenters, who completed the basic structure of the chapel in four weeks.

Christine Langlois donated a church bell weighing 300 pounds (135 kg); Louise Montreuil gave the Stations of the Cross; and Mrs. Bernard Fox provided a statue of Our Lady Star of the Sea. All three donors were from St. Alphonsus parish. Their donations have survived and can be seen at the chapel today. On 5 June 1887, Dean Wagner blessed the bell, also transported by boat from Windsor, and celebrated the first Mass. In attendance were eighty people, many of whom were Protestant.

The interior of the church was not plastered until 1909. For the next eight years, the chapel, which was used only part of the year, fell victim to vandals, who caused so much damage that Mass had to be celebrated at the home of Gerry Mahoney at the south end and at the home of Gil Ouellette at the north end of the island. Extensive repairs were made in 1917. Ten years later, the parishioners paid for kneeling benches, a new roof, repairs to the foundation and exterior painting in green and white. The shingles had to be replaced in 1937 and the windows and the foundation in 1947. A rectory was opened in June 1944. The entire church was renovated once again, in 1987, to commemorate its one hundredth anniversary.

Star of the Sea has been at different times a mission of the parishes in Amherstburg, Blenheim, Leamington and Comber. For the mission's inaugural decade, different diocesan priests served the people on Sundays during the summer months, when the navigation season was open, and sporadically, if at all, during the rest of the year. In 1897, the Basilians from St. John the Baptist in Amherstburg, were given responsibility for the mission. In the Star of the Sea registers, Fathers Luke Renaud, Gabriel Fuma, Vincent I. Donnelly, Luke L. Beuglet, M. John Ryan, and G. Harvey Wilbur are recorded as serving the people of the mission. Father Wilbur conducted a highly successful mission on Point Pelee in 1927, with Father Donnelly as the preacher.

Administration of Star of the Sea reverted to diocesan priests in 1933, when it became a mission of St. Michael parish in Leamington. The parish priest was Father J. Arthur Finn. In 1943, Star of the Sea became a parish, with Father Francis J. Walsh as the resident pastor, who was succeeded by Father T. Gordon Dill in August 1945. Fathers Stanley A. Nouvion and John A. Achtabowski followed, but since they chose to live in Leamington, instead of on the island, the diocese listed them as administrators. In 1952, Star of the Sea was once again a mission, this time of St. Ignatius parish in Bothwell, which was run by the Capuchin Fathers of St. Francis Friary. Except for Father Simon E. White (1962-64) and Father Robert Warden (1967-68), who were diocesan priests, the Capuchins from Blenheim and then Comber, beginning in February 1967, administered the parish until 1980.

That year saw the return of the Basilians to Pelee Island in the person of Father John R. Dougherty, who was the longest serving and arguably the most successful priest in the history of the mission. He remained until Easter 1996 and died on 9 August 1996.

In June 2007, Star of the Sea became a mission of the clustered parishes of St. Jean de Brébeuf, Kingsville, and St. Anthony of Padua, Harrow.

Sources: DLA, Star of the Sea File; Mary E. Hamel, *A Short History of The Star of the Sea Parish Pelee Island, Ontario 1887-1987* (1987); Ibid., "Our Lady, Star of the Sea Church; Continuation of History," (1996).

4. Kent Deanery

Chatham: Blessed Sacrament

The Catholics on the north side of the Thames River in Chatham and area were served by St. Joseph's prior to the establishment of Blessed Sacrament Parish on 30 October 1921. Its pastor, Father Ralph H. Dignan (1921-29), offered the parish's first Mass in "The Pines" chapel. The Malcomson estate, originally the home of Hugh Malcomson, a former mayor of Chatham and proprietor of the New York House on King Street West, was purchased. The Italianate-style, mid-1870s home, at 145 Victoria Avenue, with its centre tower, double-entrance doors and decorative pressed-metal hoods over the windows, was converted into a rectory. On the property, the firm of Benjamin Blonde built a church "along modern lines," but the facade was of Medieval French Gothic style. The rose window was the work of master carpenter David Hamon, a native of the Isle of Guernsey. On the morning of 4 February 1923, Blessed Sacrament was officially opened and blessed by Bishop Fallon. In the evening he administered the sacrament of confirmation for the first time.

Father Dignan, appointed bishop of the diocese of Sault Ste. Marie on 22 December 1934, was succeeded at Blessed Sacrament by Father J. Norman Campeau (1929-39), who in turn was succeeded by Father Gerald J. Labelle (1939-46). During the pastorship of Father Vincent W. Walsh (1946-58), the northwestern part of the parish was detached to form St. Agnes Parish. When Monsignor John Uyen (1958-67) was pastor, a fire completely destroyed the interior of the church on 6 January 1964. Chatham architect, Joseph Storey, and Rambush of Canada, liturgical designers, were commissioned to carry out the necessary repairs, producing a more unified space that focused on the sanctuary and its liturgical functions. Over the next eighteen months, Mass was celebrated in the church basement.

Monsignor Uyen was succeeded by Fathers Charles Campbell (1967-80) and Joseph J. Padelt (1980-96). During the pastorate of Father James M. Williams (1996-2001), Blessed Sacrament hosted the first National Catholic Parish Mission, 5-7 March

Blessed Sacrament

2000, which was broadcast nationally on the Vision Television Network. Bishop Paul-André Durocher, then auxiliary bishop of the diocese of Sault Ste. Marie, led the mission which was filmed entirely in the church. Among those who participated in this mission were Michael Burgess, star of *Les Miserables*, Juno Award winner Natalie MacMaster, renowned violinist from Cape Breton, and Adele Kozak of the Vancouver Opera Company.

Father Jan Burczyk, CSMA (2001-02), succeeded Father Williams, and was in turn succeeded in 2002 by the present pastor, Father Joseph J. Nevett, who ministers to more than 1,300 families in a parish that prides itself on the tremendous faith and support of its people.

Of special interest at Blessed Sacrament are the church grounds, which are known for their colourful show of beauty and originality. Over the years the parish has won many landscaping awards from various clubs. The origins of the distinct features of the grounds may be traced to the pair of ginkgo trees on the front lawn, mementos of the Malcomsons' tour of the Orient about 1900. These trees have been identified as the largest and among the oldest of their species on the continent.

Blessed Sacrament was slated to be clustered with St. Agnes effective June 2008.

Sources: Parish Files, "The History of Our Church," "Our Parish History" and "Parish Highlight." Additional information supplied by Lynda Cadotte.

Our Lady of Victory

In the mid-1940s many of the Poles in the Chatham area gravitated to the periodic visitation of the Czech Jesuit priests. Thus, it was natural for these same recent immigrants to attend services at St. Anthony's church in Chatham, after the establishment of this Czechoslovakian national parish in 1949. In November 1951, Bishop Cody formally granted permission for Poles and other Slavs of the Latin Rite in the parish and outside its boundaries to become members. The presence of their Slavic cousins in ever-increasing numbers was not without its problems, however, and in the summer of 1956, the leadership among the Czech laity declared that Poles were guests only at St. Anthony's

Our Lady of Victory

and, while they should continue to contribute to its support, they should have no part in the management of the parish.

This was probably a leading factor in the establishment of a Polish parish in Chatham. Father Wawrzyniec (Lawrence) A. Wnuk (1957-61), a former prisoner in a German concentration camp, was introduced as the pastor at a Mass held for the Polish people at St. Joseph's church on 16 June 1957. For the time being, Father Wnuk lived at St. Joseph's rectory and held services for his people in its church. On 1 October 1967, a ten-acre (4 ha) property, with a farmhouse, along Highway 40, was acquired for $21,000. Monsignor E. Ambrose O'Donnell, dean of Kent, blessed the grounds on 20 October. The title selected for the new parish was Our Lady of Victory, because many of the parishioners were veterans of the Polish Army who had gone through the same ordeals as Our Lady of Kozielsk. This was a painting of Our Lady holding the Child Jesus that was executed by the Polish lieutenant T. Zielinski, a Soviet prisoner of war in the concentration camp in Kozielsk, USSR, near the eastern border of Poland. This work of art, on a piece of lime-tree board, was smuggled out of the Soviet Union by a group of released prisoners following the German declaration of war against the Soviets. The

painting then travelled with the Second Polish Army from the USSR through Persia (Iran), Iraq, Egypt and Palestine and was with the army of General Władysław Anders in its victory at Monte Cassino, Italy. After the demobilization of the Polish Army in Great Britain, in 1945, the image was placed in the Brompton Oratory, in London, England. The first replication of Our Lady of Kozielsk for the Chatham church was painted by Mr. Z. Kośceiuszko of Detroit.

During the pastorate of Father Peter A. Sanczenko (1963-73), 5.5 acres (2. 2 ha) of the church property was sold off. The present rectory was built in 1970 with the proceeds of the sale and the old farmhouse was demolished. The parish numbered some 125 families at the time Father Mitchell S. Kaminski (1973-83) succeeded Father Sanczenko. During Father Kaminski's pastorship, the parish hall was enlarged and central air conditioning installed in both the church and hall. The sanctuary was rebuilt in March 1976. Father Kaminski himself designed the church's bell.

In March 1977, the painting of Our Lady of Kozielsk was replaced by a carving of the same. This was the work of Stanisław Bałos of Poland. The painting was then hung in the choir loft. So well received was Bałos' work that he was commissioned to carve a statue of the body of Christ on the Cross, the Stations of the Cross and the Last Supper. These works were blessed by Bishop Carter on the occasion of the twentieth anniversary of the parish in June 1977.

From the beginning, this active and closely-knit Polish community was generous in its support of its culture and faith. Presently, the parish also serves those of non-Polish origin. The parish was canonically suppressed, effective June 2007, and re-established as Our Lady of Victory Polish Catholic Community, with former pastor Stanisław Kuczail, SCH (2004-07), as priest-chaplain.

Sources: DLA, Parish Files for St. Anthony of Padua, Chatham and Our Lady of Victory, Chatham; *"20 – Lecie Parafii Matki Boskiej Zwycięskiej 1957 – Czerwiec – 1977* 20th Anniversary of Our Lady of Victory Parish Chatham, Ont." [n.d.]. Additional information supplied by Father Mitchell S. Kaminski.

St. Agnes

St. Agnes

In July 1957, St. Agnes Parish was established by Bishop Cody to relieve the overcrowding at Blessed Sacrament Church. As Father Ralph Dignan, the first pastor of Blessed Sacrament had done some thirty-six years earlier, Father Douglas F. Boyer (1957-59), St. Agnes' first pastor, celebrated the first Mass of his parish in "The Pines" chapel on 14 July 1957. The parish boundaries were the Thames River on the south, St. Clair Street on the east, the Eleventh Concession of Dover on the north and Bear Line on the west. In October 1957, Mrs. Mary Genevieve (O'Brien) Fidler donated land on Croyden Street for the new church. A private home at 241 Grand Avenue, immediately behind the new church site, was purchased for the rectory and chapel. On 20 February 1958, Monsignor Ambrose O'Donnell and Father Boyer participated in the sod-turning ceremony. The new church cost $115,500, and the first Mass was celebrated in August 1958. Bishop Cody blessed St. Agnes church on 23 November 1958.

Father Clifford J. Girard (1959-65) succeeded Father Boyer and was in turn succeeded by Father Lionel C. Morand (1965-74), who encouraged his parishioners to pay off the debt. With the debt paid off, Father Joseph Bagatto (1974-79) oversaw the installation of the stained-glass windows.

Father F. John Hurley (1979-89) oversaw the building of a new rectory and office, a larger church and the installation of an air-exchange and air-conditioning system, meeting rooms and a nursery in the basement. Construction began in the spring of 1981 and was almost completed by the end of the year. The church had a seating capacity of 575 and the old rectory was demolished.

During the pastorship of Father John F. Sharp (1989-90), the parking lot was paved. A vision statement was developed by the pastoral council and a new music system, with organ, key board and speakers, was installed in 1992 under the direction of Father Alan A. Momney (1990-94). The $500,000 debt, incurred through the necessary building and renovations of the early 1980s, was paid off in 1997 during the pastorate of Father Melvin G. MacIsaac (1995-99). Since the early 1980s it has been the practice to have signing for the deaf at one of the Sunday Masses. An FM system was acquired for the hard-of-hearing during Father MacIsaac's stay, and in 1998, an elevator was installed. Father Andrzej (Andrew) Kowalczyk, CSMA (1999-2005), oversaw the renovations to the kitchen in the basement, completed in 2002, just in time for the parish to host pilgrims to the World Youth Day in Toronto. These consisted of young people from Mexico and Nunavut. The latter were accompanied by their bishop, priests and sisters. Once a week the basement facilities are used for a soup kitchen.

Father Terrence R. McNamara (2005-06) succeeded Father Kowalczyk on 30 June 2005, the same year in which a Wellness Ministry was initiated. With 1,000 registered families, St. Agnes is described as "a vibrant and active parish striving to meet the needs of all."

St. Agnes was slated to be clustered with Blessed Sacrament parish, effective June 2008.

Sources: *Chatham Daily News*, 11 July 1957; 21 September 1957, 3; 21 February 1958, 6,9; 24 November 1958, 13. Additional information provided by Father Andrew Kowalczyk.

St. Anthony of Padua

In the mid-1940s a number of Moravian farmers, who retained strong political ties with the Czechs, were living in the Chatham and Dresden areas. There were also some Slovaks. Occasionally, they were ministered to by Father Francis A. Dostal, SJ, a native Czech stationed at Batawa, east of Belleville. In June 1947, the Czechoslovak community of the district formally requested of Bishop Kidd that Father Dostal conduct regular monthly visits to the area or, if agreeable to Dostal's Jesuit superiors, that he be transferred to Chatham. In December 1948, with the backing of the diocese, the Sts. Cyril and Methodius Society purchased the Evangel Tabernacle at 93 Centre Street.

St. Anthony of Padua

By May 1949, Father Dostal (1949-56) was residing in Chatham and the national parish of St. Anthony of Padua was established to serve the local Czech and Slovak community. Bishop Cody blessed the church on 14 August 1951. In November of that year, he granted permission for Poles and other Slavs of the Latin Rite in and outside the parish boundaries to become members of St. Anthony's. In the autumn of 1952, the parish purchased 80 Centre Street and turned it into a rectory, which was replaced by 84 Centre Street in October 1955.

Meanwhile, on 13 September 1953, the parish celebrated the 900th anniversary of St. Prokopius, patron saint of Czechoslovakia. An addition was built at the back of the church in the spring of 1955. The latter part of that year, however, saw discord between Father Dostal and his assistant, Father Jaroslav Popelka, SJ, which led to tension among the parishioners.

St Anthony's church was destroyed by fire in the spring of 1956. By this time the search for another site for the parish was already in progress. It was decided to build the new church on the back portion of the grounds of the Mercy Shelter (a home for unwed mothers). The architect engaged to design a church, parish hall and rectory was Frank J. Stalmach of Toronto, a Czech native. In December 1956, Father Dostal, who was suffering from fatigue, took a leave of absence after introducing his replacement, Father Adolph Pelikan, SJ (1956-58), of the Czech Province, to the administration of the parish. The ruins of the church and two adjacent houses on Centre Street were sold in February 1957. In April, Oakwood Street – the site of the new church – was renamed St. Anthony Street. Before the church was completed, an extension to the back was approved in June. The church was blessed by Bishop Cody on 11 August 1957

In October, Father Bohuslav Janicek, SJ, was appointed administrator for Father Pelikan who was in poor health. Like his predecessors, Father Janicek was confronted with a lay committee which believed that it, and not the pastor, was responsible for the running of the parish. There was also conflict between the pre-Second World War immigrants and those who arrived after the war. In June 1958, Father Janicek (1958-59) was appointed pastor, following Father Pelikan's resignation. By this time, however, the Czech Jesuits were so disheartened and their status at St. Anthony's so low that the Jesuit provincial, Father Gordon George, SJ, advised Bishop Cody that a different course of action be taken.

Consequently, in the spring of 1959, Father Longin I. Gaborik, CC (1959-64), pastor of Batawa and a member of the Consolers of the Sacred Heart who escaped from Czechoslovakia after the Communist takeover, replaced Father Janicek and the Jesuits. After the pastorship of Father Damian A. Mlynsky, CC (1964-66), Father Gaborik again served as pastor until his death in September 1977. He was succeeded by Father Charles D. Moravèik, CC (1977), and Father Stephen Rus, CSB (1978-80).

Father George Kadlec, who arrived in August 1980, oversaw the celebration of the fortieth anniversary of the present church on 8 June 1997. With his retirement, and no later than June 2008, St.

Anthony's is currently slated for closure.

Sources: DLA, Parish Files; Lyle A. McCormick, comp., *The History of St. Ursula's Parish: "A Labour of Love" 1951-2001 Chatham, Ontario* (Chatham: 2001). Additional information provided by Father George Kadlec.

St. Joseph

Although it is reported that Mass was offered on the site of Chatham even before the War of 1812, the first documented liturgical celebration in what is now Chatham was in 1827, with Father Joseph Crévier of Assumption parish in Sandwich as the celebrant. For many years to come, Catholics of Chatham and the surrounding area would generally attend Mass at St. Peter-on-the-Thames. Its pastor, Father Jean-Baptiste Morin (1834-44), appears to have periodically visited Chatham. In 1836, the Catholic Church was granted a large parcel of land, now bounded by Queen, Wellington, Raleigh, and Richmond streets. In the autumn of 1845 Father Jean Jaffré, SJ, came out from Sandwich to minister to the people of this area. Mass was celebrated at various sites within the town until a church was built in 1847. St. Joseph was elevated to parish status in 1850. The following year, the bell, weighing 1,000 pounds (453.6 kg) and imported from Croydon, Kent, England, was placed in the bell tower. The parish's first rectory was built in 1857, by which time the church was renovated. Before leaving St. Joseph's, in 1860, Father Jaffré was instrumental in persuading the Ursuline Sisters to establish their first community in the London diocese at "The Pines" in Chatham. Although St. Joseph's originally had burials in its churchyard, eight acres (3.2 ha) were purchased outside the town in 1869 and became St. Anthony Cemetery.

In 1874, the Jesuits were succeeded by the Basilians, then in charge of Assumption College in Sandwich, and the Basilians by the Franciscans,

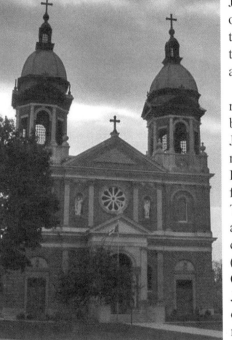

St. Joseph

beginning with Father Eugene Butterman, OFM (1878) in January 1878. A new rectory was built in 1879 during the pastorship of Father William Gausepohl, OFM (1878-89). Joseph Connolly, the renowned Toronto architect who had designed St. Peter's cathedral in London, was selected to draw up plans for a new church. Bishop Walsh blessed the cornerstone on 17 October 1886, and he returned to bless and officially open the new Romanesque-style edifice on 23 October 1887. During the pastorate of Father Paul Alf, OFM (1889-97), the Casavant pipe organ was installed. St. Joseph's celebrated its golden jubilee in Chatham in October 1895. The church was renovated in 1909 under the direction of Father James J. Archinger, OFM (1901-18). The scenes depicting the life of St. Joseph were probably painted on the ceilings at this time. The twin bell towers were added to the church structure in 1916 at a cost of $17,000.

The Franciscans were replaced by diocesan priests, beginning with Father John J. Gnam (1921-34), who was named the first rural dean of Kent County. He was also the first pastor to die in office. The rectory was refurbished and the auditorium built during the pastorship of Father (later Monsignor) Ambrose O'Donnell (1950-66). Father James M. Williams (1966-67) oversaw the restoration and repair of the church's exterior. The repair and decoration of the church and implementation of the changes decreed by the Second Vatican Council were undertaken during the pastorate of Father John B. O'Donnell (1967-70). Bishop Sherlock, while auxiliary bishop of the diocese, served as pastor between 1974 and 1978, followed by Father John M. Michon (1978-81).

The centennial of the present church was celebrated in 1987. In 1995 Father Stanley E. McGuire (1981-98) initiated the restoration of the exterior of the building from the roofline up. Father Gregory J. Bonin (1998-2004) continued both exterior and interior restoration in 1999. The 122-

year-old rectory was demolished in 2001.

St. Joseph and St. Ursula parishes were slated to be clustered, effective June 2008.

Sources: *Dictionary of Jesuit Biography Ministry to English Canada 1842-1987* (Toronto: 1991), 152-53; John R. McMahon, "St. Joseph's Chatham, Celebrates Centennial," *Newsletter of the Diocese of London*, no. 28 (Lent/Easter: 1987), 1,3; Louis Boulet, "The Roman Catholic Church in Kent County" [n.d.]; Joseph A. Campeau, "History of St. Joseph's Parish, Chatham" (paper presented at the Windsor Clergy Conference, Windsor, October 1947); P.J. Waters, "History of St. Joseph's Parish" [n.d.]; Ralph Hubert Dignan and Joseph P. Finn, "A History of the Diocese of London," edited by Guy Alden (unpublished manuscript, 2002).

St. Ursula

St. Ursula's was formally established on 9 June 1951, and the pastor, Father A. Joseph Schwemler (1951-55), took up residence at "The Pines." The parish's first Mass was celebrated in the Chatham Memorial Arena on 1 July. Later, Masses were shifted to the Kinsmen Auditorium. The sod-turning ceremony for the church, at the corner of Lacroix Street and Tweedsmuir Avenue, took place on 19 July. The building, which contained the rectory and sanctuary and could accommodate up to 450 persons, was the third prefabricated church in the diocese. Like that of St. Gabriel's, Rondeau Park, Gerry Supply & Lumber Company of London was responsible for the structure. With only the subfloor in place, Mass was held for the first time on 16 September 1951. In December, the church was officially dedicated by Bishop Cody, who also blessed St. Ursula school.

With Father Schwemler's death, on 12 October 1955, Father J. Bartley Clark (1955-67) became St. Ursula's second pastor. The mortgage was paid off in 1961. On 21 September 1965, during the pastorate of Father Charles E. Sullivan (1965-67), St. Ursula's Roman Catholic Parish Association was formed as a laypersons' organization to organize and coordinate the temporal affairs of the parish. It was the first association of its kind in a Catholic parish in Ontario to encompass an entire congregation. The parish offices were also built during this time.

Father Paul F. Mooney, the assistant pastor,

St. Ursula

guided the parish from October 1967 until the following year when a new pastor arrived, who remained for the next thirteen years. In 1969, St. Ursula's parishioners became the first in the city to receive communion in the hand. Father Phil Tétreault, of the Society of the White Fathers of Africa, arrived at St. Ursula's, in May 1972, to gain experience in parish work. He remained until June 1974. In October of that year final approval was given for a new church and rectory. The architect was Bruno Apollonio, and the general contractor was Ampath Construction of Leamington. The groundbreaking ceremony took place on 8 December 1974. The church, of theatre-style construction, seated 730 people, with no seat being more than forty feet (12.2 m) from the altar. The estimated cost of the church, rectory and furnishings was in the neighbourhood of $501,300. Bishop Carter blessed the new building on 7 November 1976. In 1977, the old church was dismantled and reassembled as a recreation building at the St. Vincent de Paul Society summer youth camp near Bothwell.

On 23 April 1987, during the pastorship of Father John J. Devine (1980-99), the Knights of Columbus Council No. 9551 received its charter. A former parishioner, Father Michael L. Dwyer, was ordained on 2 May 1987. It was also during Father Devine's time that the original church bell from the first Annunciation church (1865-1906) at Stoney Point was installed in St. Ursula's entry hall.

About 1906, the old Annunciation church was relocated to the farm of Wilfrid R. Dauphinais. When the Dauphinais family moved to Raleigh Township they took the church bell with them.

Wilfrid's son, Henry, was the owner of the farm in the early 1950s, when Frank Mindorff noticed the old bell and suggested that St. Ursula's could make use of it. For a few decades, however, it was stored for safekeeping on Louis Schneider's farm.

Father Murray W. Sample (1999-2005), who had previously served the parish as a seminarian and later as an associate pastor, was appointed pastor and dean of Kent in 2001. The fiftieth anniversary of St. Ursula's was marked that same year with a dinner and dance at Club Lentina on 26 October, and a history of the parish was published. In July 2005, Father Daniel M. Vere succeeded Father Sample.

St. Ursula and St. Joseph parishes were slated to be clustered, effective June 2008.

Sources: Lyle A. McCormick, comp. *The History of St. Ursula's Parish: "A Labour of Love" 1951-2001 Chatham, Ontario* (Chatham: 2001). Additional information provided by Father Dan Vere, Father John Devine, Kathy Bunker and Jean Dauphinais.

Blenheim: St. Mary

In 1872, George Halleck, a French-Canadian, and his family moved to Blenheim. A man of initiative, he arranged for Father Francis Maréchal (Marshall), SJ, to come from Chatham to celebrate Mass for the few Catholic families in the area. Soon the Halleck home proved to be too small for these monthly services, and two acres (0.8 ha) of land for a church site, on the west side of Chatham Street North, were donated by Harold Labatt of Chatham. Meanwhile, in 1874, the Jesuits were succeeded by the Basilians in Chatham.

The church was completed in 1876, blessed by Father F. Régis Hours, CSB, the pastor of St. Joseph's, and dedicated to the Blessed Virgin Mary. The following year Bishop Walsh administered confirmation in the new church. In 1878, the Basilians were succeeded by the Franciscans of Chatham, who continued to minister to the Blenheim mission, perhaps only four or five times a year. When the Franciscans left Chatham in August 1919, St. Mary's was transferred to the Ridgetown parish.

Owing to the influx of Flemish and Dutch families into this area, following the First World War, Bishop Fallon decided that the Capuchin Fathers of Belgium were particularly suited for the

St. Mary

needs of these immigrants. Thus, Fathers Willibrord Pennincx, OFM Cap, and Ladislaus Segers, OFM Cap, were the first Capuchin Fathers to arrive in Blenheim, on 17 September 1927. St. Mary's was now a parish with Father Willibrord as its pastor. By the following year the numbers of the Capuchin Fathers had doubled and a regular communal life had been established. Father Willibrord and Brother Mansuetus Constandt, OFM Cap, who had arrived in November 1927, were transferred to St. Boniface, Manitoba, in 1928, and Father Polycarp Christiaens, OFM Cap (1928-39), became St. Mary's second pastor. In 1930, to accommodate the growing number of parishioners, an annex was attached to the existing church, constructed in such a way as to open onto the sanctuary for Sunday Mass and, when closed, to serve as a parish hall. In 1933, a mission church was built at Erieau, and in September 1935, a separate school was opened in St. Mary's church hall.

Father Segers (1937-50) succeeded Father Willibrord as pastor in September 1937. In 1939, a former Methodist Church on Chatham Street was purchased and converted into the second St. Mary's church. It was blessed by Bishop Kidd on 5 May 1940. Because of the large number of Czechs farming in the Mull area, a small Protestant church, on the east side of the Mull Side Road, was purchased. This mission church was blessed and named in honour of St. Isidore, patron saint of farmers, and the first Mass was celebrated by Dean J. Norman Campeau on 4 July 1943. This church remained the meeting place for the Czechs until 1971 when the mission was suppressed owing to a lack of parishioners.

During the pastorate of Father Vitus H. Van Olffen, OFM Cap (1950-57), many Dutch families settled in the parish. A new parish hall was built and blessed by Bishop Cody on 17 August 1952, coinciding with the celebration of the parish's silver jubilee. During the second term of Father Bernard A. Robert OFM Cap as pastor (1962-69), construction began in November 1964 on the third St. Mary's church. Bishop Carter officiated at the opening of the current Marlborough Street building, on 26 September 1966.

In 1977, during the pastorate of Father Omer DeRoo, OFM Cap (1971-78), Bishop Sherlock opened the golden anniversary celebrations of the parish with a Solemn High Mass. The congregation later marked the sixtieth, seventieth and seventieth-fifth anniversaries of their parish. With the retirement of Father Martin A. Johnston, the pastor of St. Michael's parish in Ridgetown, on 8 August 2005, the Blenheim and Ridgetown parishes were clustered, with the Capuchin Fathers serving both parishes. The current pastor is Father Paul Duplessie, OFM Cap, who had previously been pastor of St. Mary's between 1986 and 1991.

Sources: *Parish of St. Michael the Archangel Centennial Calendar 1880-1980*; "St. Mary's Parish History 1875-1927" [c 2005].

Bothwell: St. Ignatius

The home of Francis Cartier is credited as being the site of the first Mass in Bothwell in 1855. A boomtown after the discovery of oil in the area in 1865, the bubble had burst by 1867 and Bothwell was almost a ghost town. In May of that year the Bothwell Land and Petroleum Company, Ltd. donated several lots to the Catholic Church for the customary legal fee of one dollar.

A wooden frame church was then built on this site by William Lavin, a local carpenter, merchant and church trustee. The structure had neither a sanctuary nor a bell tower. The seats and windows were plain and the building was heated with two box stoves at the entrance to the building, with flues running the full length to the front and the chimneys on either side of the sanctuary. Dedicated to St. Ignatius, the church was blessed, on 26 June 1867, by Monsignor Jean-Marie Bruyère, vicar general and

St. Ignatius

administrator of the diocese of Sandwich. Father Joseph A. Kelly, OP, a Dominican stationed at St. Peter's, London, preached the sermon. For many years, the Catholics in the Bothwell area would be served by priests from Chatham and London, the latter having a mission in Adelaide Township, Middlesex County.

St. Ignatius was elevated to parish status in July 1873 with the appointment of Father Patrick Fitzpatrick (1873-74), "a gentleman of small stature, kindly, amiable, and very devoted to his far-flung flock," who was ordained in May 1872. His pastoral field extended to the missions of Wardsville, Glencoe, Thamesville and Alvinston. That same year the parish's first rectory was built at a cost of $15,000. Father Fitzpatrick was succeeded by Father Martin Kelly (1874-79), "a striking figure – tall, rugged, athletic," who was entrusted with the task of building a church in Alvinston. Father Michael McGrath (1879-81), Bothwell's third pastor, engaged the architectural firm of Tracy & Durand of London and oversaw the addition of the sanctuary, sacristy, vestry, choir loft and bell tower to the church, as well as the complete bricking of the facade. The renovated church was blessed by Bishop Walsh on New Year's Day 1881. Father John J. Ronan (1881-82) succeeded Father McGrath.

Father Albert J. McKeon (1882-89) was given the task of repaying the parish debt of $25,000 to the diocese. To this end, he organized the church picnics and successfully persuaded the town council to fund them. The picnics in turn were the inspiration for the Old Boys & Girls reunions that continued for many years after Father McKeon's departure.

During the pastorate of Father Daniel Forster

(1900-04), who had previously been pastor at his home parish of St. Mary's, Simcoe, a new church was built in the mission of Thamesville.

St. Ignatius reverted to mission status in May 1920, when Father Frank McCarty went to reside permanently in the newly purchased rectory in Thamesville. The Bothwell rectory was then sold. In 1952, Bothwell was again elevated to parish status, with Wardsville and Glencoe as missions. In 1960, St. Ignatius and St. Charles Garnier separate schools were opened in Bothwell and Glencoe, respectively. An annex to St. Ignatius Church was built in 1972 and, under Fr. Paul F. Mooney's direction, St. Vincent de Paul Camp was opened.

Through the efforts of the Local Architectural Conservation Advisory Committee, St. Ignatius Church was designated an historic site in 1991 by the Bothwell Town Council. A grant from the Ontario Heritage Foundation was received to help offset the cost of restoration of the exterior of the church and a total of $275,000 was raised over the next seven years to upgrade the interior and restore the stained-glass windows.

In 2000, St. Ignatius was clustered with St. Paul's, Thamesville. It was canonically suppressed on June 2007, and its territory absorbed into St. Paul's.

Sources: Ralph Hubert Dignan and Joseph P. Finn, "A History of the Diocese of London," edited by Guy Alden (unpublished manuscript, 2002). Additional information provided by Marion Matt and Father John Van Damme.

Dresden: St. Michael

The first known Mass to be celebrated within the present boundaries of St. Michael's parish was in 1864, at the home of Henry Ennett on the Lindsay Road at Turnerville. The celebrant was Father F. Wilhelm Gockein, SJ, then stationed at Chatham, whose primary responsibility was the mission at Wallaceburg. Prior to this time the Catholic families from Chatham Township attended St. Joseph's, Chatham, while other families living in Dawn and Sombra townships fulfilled their spiritual obligations in Algonac, Michigan. For a short time, the Dresden-area Catholics attended Mass at Sacred Heart mission church at Baby Point, near present Port Lambton, and later the mission church at

Wallaceburg. Starting in 1864, Mass was celebrated once a month in the homes of such settlers as Henry Ennett, Michael Mahoney, Simon Burns, James McGuire and Michael Lonergan.

When it was brought to Bishop Walsh's attention how difficult it was for these scattered Catholic families to attend Mass because of distance and the

St. Michael

deplorable roads, he urged them to build a church and promised them that he would return to bless and dedicate it. In 1872, a frame church was built at Dresden and dedicated to St. Michael the Archangel on his feast day, 29 September 1872. A serious illness prevented Walsh from officiating, and his place was taken by his vicar general, Monsignor Jean-Marie Bruyère. With the establishment of Our Lady Help of Christians in Wallaceburg as a parish in 1878, the Dresden mission was transferred from Chatham to Wallaceburg.

In 1904, Father Michael J. Brady of Wallaceburg oversaw the enlargement of the church. The entire structure put onto a stone foundation, the exterior was covered with a brick veneer and a steeple was added. The current stained-glass windows were installed at this time and a choir loft added to increase seating capacity.

The aftermath of the First World War saw the Catholic population of the parish augmented by the arrival of Belgian and Czechoslovakian families. Consequently, in 1927 Bishop Fallon was able to detach St. Michael's from Wallaceburg and erect it as a separate parish. He also mandated the building of a rectory for Father Thomas J. Ford (1927-33), who was appointed the first pastor on 4 December 1927. Father Alphonse N. Page (1939-66) is especially remembered for his ministering to the immigrants who arrived in the area following the

Second World War. In 1947, the church and statues were redecorated and both the church and rectory re-roofed. Also, the spire, which had become unsafe, was reduced in height. Father Donald G. Allaster (1966-81) oversaw the changes prescribed by the Second Vatican Council, the enlarging of the church, the excavation under it to establish a hall and the installation of modern washroom facilities. Upon completion, St. Michael's was rededicated, on 9 June 1974, by Monsignor Andrew P. Mahoney, a son of the aforementioned Michael Mahoney, on the occasion of the sixtieth anniversary of Monsignor Mahoney's ordination.

Under the pastorship of Father J. Henry Cassano (1986-90), a youth group and a Council of the Knights of Columbus were formed. The parish celebrated its sixtieth anniversary on 19 July 1987, at which Bishop Henry officiated. The interior of the church was renovated and a new heating system installed during the pastorate of Father Andrew Sipek (1990-98). He was succeeded, on 26 June 1998, by the present pastor, Father John H. Betkowski. Under his pastorship, the rectory has been restored, further structural improvements as mandated by the diocese have been made to the church, the entire building has been re-bricked and the stained-glass windows of 1904 returned to their original condition.

St. Michael's merge into one parish with St. Paul's, Thamesville, effective June 2007, and the church at Dresden remains as a second non-parochial church site of St. Paul's.

Sources: Dargan Burns, "St. Michael's Parish Dresden - Ontario 1927-1987 Sixtieth Anniversary" [1987]; Marie DeBruyn, "St. Michael's, Dresden, 60th Anniversary," *Newsletter of the Diocese of London*, no. 30 (Fall 1987), 19; Ralph Hubert Dignan and Joseph P. Finn, "A History of the Diocese of London," edited by Guy Alden (unpublished manuscript, 2002); "St. Michael's Parish, Dresden, Ontario" [n.d.].

Erieau: St. Anne of the Lakes

In 1930, Thomas J. and Anne Bresnahan of Detroit donated a cottage near their summer home at Erieau in Howick Township, to the Capuchin Fathers of St. Mary's, Blenheim, so that they might have a place to celebrate Mass during the summer for the

Belgian and Slovak farmers of the area. They soon outgrew this remodeled cottage, and a chapel was established on the second floor of an old building, known because of its construction as the "Wedding Cake." Then, in 1932, the Bresnahans donated land for the Capuchins to construct a small mission church. Bishop Kidd approved the construction. The architect was a Mr. Thompson, and the contractor was Neale R. Ibbetson of Walkerville. In July 1933, Kidd laid the cornerstone for the St. Anne of the Lakes mission church. In the construction of the

St. Anne of the Lakes

building, the three Gothic roof braces were salvaged from the former Blessed Heart of Mary, Mother of God mission church in Wardsville, which had been torn down by the Ibbetson firm late that spring.

Since 1933, St. Anne's Day, on the last Sunday in July, has been the high point of the liturgical year for the community. Originally, there was the carrying of the statue of St. Anne in procession to the lakeshore, with the congregation following in their native Belgian, Slovak or Polish costumes. The priest would recite prayers to the patron saint of fishermen and sailors, ending with the blessing of the boats gathered at the shore. The procession would then return to the church for the celebration of an outdoor Mass. It was a young Father Francis McCarroll, OFM Cap, who originated the custom of having an outdoor chicken barbeque after the Mass to accommodate the large crowd. Although the traditions of the processions and costumes have ceased, the barbeques still continue, thanks to the work of the Father Ladislaus Council No. 7744, Knights of Columbus, which was established in

1981. Parishioners of St. Mary, Blenheim and St. Anne, Erieau enjoy the barbeques.

On Easter Sunday 1958, Father Bernard A. Robert, OFM, Cap, pastor of St. Mary's, wrote to Bishop Cody, stating that there were sixty-four families in Erieau and vicinity. Owing to the large number of American summer residents, two Masses were needed in Erieau in the summer. He urged a resident priest for Erieau in order to solve the problem of fallen-away Catholics in the area and to serve the increase in the number of Catholics anticipated in the Cedar Springs area once the new Ontario Hospital was up and running. Bishop Kidd concurred and, later that spring, St. Anne of the Lakes was detached from St. Mary's and elevated to parish status with Father McCarroll (1958-59) as its first pastor. The church basement became his living quarters, which in the winter was both damp and very cold. Consequently, his successor, Father Leopold Nieuwlandt, OFM, Cap, who became pastor in September 1959, urged Monsignor J. Austin Roney, chancellor of the diocese, to grant permission to build a proper rectory. Permission was granted on 31 August 1960.

In 1962, a stained-glass window was erected above the church entrance in memory of its first priest, Father Ladislaus, who died on 19 August 1961.

After a succession of eight pastors in eight years, Father Ivo Tommeleyn, OFM Cap, arrived in 1975 and has been the shepherd of this small country parish with its mission church ever since. On Labour Day weekend in September 2005, the parishioners paid tribute to the Bresnahan family for their many years of work on behalf of St. Anne of the Lakes. In their honour, the Bresnahan Memorial Rock Garden was dedicated.

The parish was canonically suppressed in September 2006. Its territory was absorbed into St. Mary parish, Blenheim. St. Anne's remains open during the months of May to September under the care of the pastor of St. Mary's.

Sources: DLA, Parish Files; "St. Mary's Parish History 1875-1927" [c 2005]. Additional information supplied by Jerry Dalton.

St. Charles Garnier

Glencoe:
St. Charles Garnier

With the establishment of a parish in Bothwell in 1873, Glencoe became a mission of St. Ignatius. Prior to this, the area was probably served by priests from Chatham and London. By 1955 it had ceased to function, and the local Catholics attended services in Wardsville and Bothwell.

Then, on 3 May 1956, the diocese purchased ten building lots in Glencoe, and on 30 October 1957, Bishop Cody blessed the new St. Charles school. Sunday Mass was first celebrated in the school on 12 August 1962, and again Glencoe had mission status, this time within St. Ignatius' parish. That same year, two barracks in Aylmer were purchased from the Canadian Department of Defense, dismantled and transported to Glencoe. Work on the foundations for the proposed house of worship began in December 1962. On 4 February 1963, Mass was first celebrated in the church, dedicated to St. Charles Garnier, one of the North American martyrs honoured in the title of the chapel in Wardsville. Some of the statues, holy water fonts, brass candlesticks and the baptismal font came from the Wardsville chapel; twenty pews came from Blessed Sacrament Church, Chatham; and thirty more pews, the Stations of the Cross and the Communion rail came from "The Pines" in Chatham.

Initially, the St. Charles Men's Group and the Women's Group operated separately but, from 1962 until 1992, they met as the St. Charles Adult Group. An active youth group was in operation between 1968 and 1974, and in 1981, Stepping Stones, a drop-in centre for youth was established. On 12 April 1992, the Catholic Women's League began at St. Charles and chose to continue the charter of the Chapel of the North American Martyrs' CWL, Wardsville, which dated from 1953.

Father William J. O'Flaherty was the priest connected with Glencoe in the late 1950s. His successors included Fathers Charles T. McManus, Robert A. Charbonneau, Paul F. Mooney, William E. Capitano, Terrence R. McNamara, Joseph A. Kannath and Gary G. Ducharme. In 1990, it was decided to build a new church in Glencoe rather than put money into the repair and maintenance of the old building. Two years later, however, the diocese investigated the possibility of closing the churches in Glencoe and Bothwell and building one in Newbury. This proposal appears to have met with too much opposition from the parishioners of St. Charles and St. Ignatius and instead architectural plans for a new church in Glencoe were produced. With the arrival of Father Ducharme's successor, Father John C. Van Damme, in 1995, the building project moved forward. Architectural plans were drawn up in 1998 by the firm of Walter Fedy Partnership, and on 16 August 1998, the groundbreaking ceremony was held and the blessing given by Bishop Sherlock. The general contractors were Reid and Deleye Ltd., and the new structure cost $1.2 million.

The last Mass was celebrated in the old church, on 4 July 1999, and the tabernacle was carried in procession to the new church at 244 Stella Avenue. On 12 September, Bishop Sherlock officiated at the solemn dedication of the new church. In 2001, the parishes of St. Charles, Glencoe and Sacred Heart, Delaware were clustered, with Father Peter W. Poel as pastor, assisted by Monsignor Isidro Payan-Melendez. Father Francis L. Murphy succeeded Father Poel as pastor in 2004.

Sources: Fr. John C. Van Damme, "St. Charles Garnier, Glencoe, dedicated," *Newsletter of the Diocese of London*, no. 88 (Fall 1999), 15. Additional information provided by Marion Matt.

Grande Pointe: St. Philippe

By the 1820s, pioneer French-Canadian families were settling near a section of land that jutted out into Lake St. Clair. This area soon became known as Grande Pointe or Big Point. On 5 March 1829, nineteen families who had already settled in the area signed a petition requesting that the lieutenant-governor grant them permanent title to these lands. Realizing that they should have presented their application before they had moved onto the land they had occupied, the petitioners cited dire poverty and distress as reasons for not paying the small registration fee required for this transaction.

From time to time, these families were ministered to by priests from Sandwich and later from St. Peter's, Tilbury East. Under the direction of Father Claude Antoine Ternet, the pastor at St. Peter's, a small chapel was built at Grande Pointe, blessed on 11 May 1852, and named in honour of Father Ternet's patron saint, St. Anthony the Hermit. On 3 September 1852, Ternet caused an imposing

St. Philippe

wooden cross to be raised near the church. In 1858, Bishop Pinsoneault transferred the mission of Grande Pointe from St. Peter's to the newly established parish of Immaculate Conception, Pain Court. With the increase in the Catholic population in the northern part of Dover Township, Father Joseph Bauer, then pastor at Pain Court, was authorized by Bishop Walsh to build a larger church on the Ninth Concession. On a site donated by Möise Martin and Joseph Cheff, a new structure was built at a cost of $6,000 and opened in 1882. Since both the Martin and Cheff families came from St. Philippe, Québec, at their request the church was dedicated to St. Philippe the Apostle. A cemetery was likewise established the same year, behind the church.

In 1886, Bishop Walsh elevated the mission of St. Philippe to parish status with Father Antoine Carrière (1886-87) as pastor and declared the public road dividing the sixth and seventh concessions of Dover Township to be "the line dividing the Parishes of Paincourt and Big Point." Father Carrière's successor, Father Pierre Langlois (1887-91), completed the construction of both the church and the rectory, the latter having been begun by Father Carrière. It was in 1916, during the pastorate of Father Lucien Landreville (1908-18), that the debt on the church was liquidated.

Father Joseph E. Emery (1918-28) was appointed administrator in 1918 and prepared to build a new church to replace the 1882 structure, which he claimed to be in a dangerous state and about to collapse. To this end, in 1925 he purchased a 10-acre (4 ha) plot of land from Emile Pinsonneault for $1,700. Although Father Emery did succeed in gathering considerable funds for a new church, it would not be built until more than two decades later. The parish hall was constructed in 1946 during the pastorate of Father Oscar A. Martin (1945-49), and funds were raised for the construction of a new rectory. In 1949, the old church was dismantled and the present Gothic-sytle structure was situated in the more central location, one mile (1.6 k m) away on the Ninth Concession at the Winter Line on land originally purchased by Father Emery. It fell to Father J. Euclide Chevalier (1949-55) to complete the building of the new rectory and church. This was done in March and October 1950, respectively. Bishop Cody blessed the church on 29 October 1950. Renovations to the parish hall and rectory were made during the pastorate of Father Roger J. Bénéteau (1967-70). His successor, Father Charles E. Lanoue (1970-77), oversaw improvements and repairs to both the church and parish hall. The latter renovations were completed during the pastorship of Father Louis H. Rivard (1977-94), in time for the parish's centennial celebrations in 1986.

On 1 August 1997, with Father Robert L. Champagne as pastor (1997-2006), St. Philippe parish was fully clustered with Immaculate Conception parish in Pain Court. St. Philippe's was canonically suppressed effective June 2007, and its territory absorbed into Immaculate Conception.

Sources: *"La Paroisse Saint-Philippe de Grande Pointe," Newsletter of the Diocese of London*, no. 97 (Easter 2001), 11; Louis Boulet, "The Roman Catholic Church in Kent County" [n.d.]; [Rev. Louis Rivard, et al.], *"Église St-Philippe Church Grande Pointe, Ontario Centenaire* – Centennial 1886-1986," [Tecumseh: 1986]; Ralph Hubert Dignan and Joseph P. Finn, "A History of the Diocese of London," edited by Guy Alden (unpublished manuscript, 2002).

Merlin: St. Patrick

The first Mass in what became St. Patrick parish is said to have been celebrated in 1833 by Father Jean-Baptiste Morin of Amherstburg. With Father Morin taking up residence at St. Peter's, Tilbury East, in 1834, he was able to visit the Irish community in this part of Raleigh about twice a year. Father Jean Jaffré, SJ, and some of his brother Jesuits from Sandwich visited the area two to four times a year between 1844 and 1853. In 1853, Father Jean T. Raynel, SJ, pastor at St. Peter's, became convinced that a church and cemetery were needed in Raleigh. Accordingly, Timothy Dillon and Peter McKeon each donated 2.5 contiguous acres (1 ha) for these purposes. A frame church was then constructed, and, on 26 August 1855, it was formally consecrated to St. Patrick, in accordance with Bishop Charbonnel's instructions. The cemetery was consecrated on 15 November. Apart from the presence of Father Bartholomew Boubat for a few months in the late 1850s, the mission continued to be served by Jesuits from Sandwich or Chatham. Bishop Pinsoneault first visited St. Patrick's in 1862 to administer confirmation and, it would appear, he promised a resident priest once a dwelling was built.

In 1863, the newly ordained Father Peter P. Mazuret took up residence at Buxton, as the station was then denoted, and St. Patrick's was elevated to parish status. Against the advice of his parishioners, however, this headstrong young priest insisted on moving the church closer to the road and enlarging it into a cruciform shape. Being structurally unsound, the roof collapsed the following year and Father Mazuret prudently took leave of the parish. St. Patrick's then reverted to mission status and was served by the Jesuits from St. Joseph's, Chatham. By this time, the congregation was outgrowing its little church. A new church was built, under the direction of the Jesuit fathers, and opened in 1868. Between 1874 and 1878, St. Patrick's was served by Basilian priests from Chatham and, from 1878, by the Franciscans.

In 1876, Father Patrick J. Ryan, CSB, an assistant at Chatham, oversaw the building of a new brick rectory at St. Patrick's. Two years later, Father Thomas T. West (1880-84) took up residence,

St. Patrick

thereby becoming St. Patrick's second pastor, and he took charge of St. Michael mission, Ridgetown. Father Thomas Quigley became pastor in March 1889 and oversaw the addition of a sacristy and bell tower as well as interior repairs to the church. In August 1901, Father James G. Mugan (1901-06) was transferred to Raleigh to erect a new church.

The first order of business, however, was to construct a drive shed. In November 1901, a forty-eight-stall horse shelter was completed. With Father Mugan's example and encouragement, work on the new brick church commenced in October 1902; the cornerstone was laid in April 1903 and the church was dedicated by Bishop McEvay on 17 September 1903. The present brick rectory was built during the pastorate of Father James J. Hogan (1908-14). During the administration of Father Carl G. Walsh (1949-55), the church and rectory were renovated in time for the centenary of the Raleigh church in 1955. Father Lawrence J. Coughlin (1967-72) oversaw the sweeping changes in the church in the wake of the Second Vatican Council. After the departure of Father Raymond T. Buchanan (1989-91), the parish reverted to mission status and was served by priests from St. Joseph's and Our Lady of Victory in Chatham. Talk of closing St. Patrick's ended with the arrival of Father Michael L. Dwyer (1992-2005). In 1999, however, the parishes of St. Francis, Tilbury, St. Peter, Tilbury East, St. Charles, Stevenson, and St. Patrick were clustered with Father Eugene G. Roy as pastor and Fathers Jan Konieczny and Dwyer as assistants. The following year, Father Dwyer was again named pastor of the clustered parishes of St. Patrick, St. Peter and St. Charles.

Effective 30 June 2005, Father Michael J. O'Brien was appointed pastor of the clustered parishes of St. Patrick and St. Peter parishes. These parishes were slated to be clustered with St. Francis parish effective June 2008.

Sources: Ralph Hubert Dignan and Joseph P. Finn, "A History of the Diocese of London," edited by Guy Alden (unpublished manuscript, 2002). Additional information supplied by Ray Cocteau.

Pain Court: Immaculate Conception

Pain Court derived its name from the terse French expression "pain court" (bread is short), in reference to the difficulty in the early days of acquiring flour in the area, the nearest gristmills being some distance away and travel long and difficult.

By the mid-1840s, the French Catholics in the southern part of East Dover Township were being ministered to by Father Pierre Point, SJ, and his assistants from Assumption parish in Sandwich. A Catholic school is said to have been established at Pain Court during this time. In 1851, Father Claude-Antoine Ternet became pastor at St. Peter's, Tilbury East, and the surrounding missions, and that same year he was directed by Bishop Charbonnel to build a chapel in Pain Court. Mass was first celebrated in the new St. Joseph's chapel on 1 March 1852. Ternet's successor in June 1853 was Father Jean-Thomas Raynel, SJ, who undertook the building of a school and presbytery at Pain Court as well as a church proper. On 31 August 1854, the footings and cornerstone were blessed by the vicar general, Father Pierre Point, SJ, of Sandwich. Bishop Charbonnel selected the name Immaculate Conception in honour of Our Lady, who revealed herself to Bernadette Soubirous at Lourdes, France as the Immaculate Conception just months earlier. At this time, the mission of Immaculate Conception was served by Father Jean Jaffré, SJ, pastor of St. Joseph's in Chatham. On 29 April 1855, Father Point returned to bless the new church.

The mission of the Immaculate Conception was elevated to the status of a parish by Bishop Pinsoneault on 10 April 1858, with Father Bartholomew Boubat (1858-59) as its first pastor. Father Paul Andrieux, OMI, appears to have been the pastor between 1861 and 1864, although, in

Immaculate Conception

February 1863 it was Father Raynel who assisted Father Charles Conilleau, SJ, of Chatham in blessing the Stations of the Cross at Pain Court. Bishop Pinsoneault blessed the new church bell, christened Marie-Thérèse, in September 1864. It can be seen today in front of the present church.

Father J. Calixte Duprat (1869-81) was sent to Pain Court in December 1869. The following year saw the completion of the church begun in 1854 at the site of the present cemetery. The structure was destroyed by fire, the work of an arsonist, on the night of 4 May 1874. On 30 May 1875, the first High Mass was celebrated in the new brick church facing Winterline Road. Father Duprat was compelled to retire at the end of 1881, owing to profound deafness. His successor, Father Joseph Bauer (1882-86), renovated the church and rebuilt the rectory. Father Andrieux (1888-1901) returned to Pain Court and, in September 1900, celebrated his fiftieth anniversary as a priest and was named archdeacon of the diocese by Bishop McEvay. Bishop Fallon assigned a native son, Father Alfred D. Emery, as pastor, in January 1911, for the specific purpose of building a new church and rectory. Fallon blessed the cornerstone of Pain Court's third church on 11 June 1911. The Gothic- style church was blessed and opened for worship on 3 March 1912. The brick rectory was built the same year.

On the morning of 2 January 1937, the church was destroyed by fire. A new edifice, the fourth and present church, was built on the existing foundation and with the retention of most of the old walls. It was blessed by Bishop Kidd on 8 December 1937.

Immaculate Conception parish was fully

clustered with St. Philippe's parish, Grande Pointe, on 1 August 1997. A family tradition ended in 2002 when Amédée Emery retired as organist at Pain Court. His mother, Marie Emery (née Cheff), had been the church's organist before him from 1905 until 1962.

Sources: A.D. Emery, Album *Souvenir de la Pariosse de L'Immaculée Conception de Pain Court, Ont. 1851-1926* [n.d.]; Mrs. J.P. Dunn, "The Roman Catholic Church in Kent County," Kent Historical Society, *Papers and Addresses* (Chatham: 1914), 22-23; Ralph Hubert Dignan and Joseph P. Finn, "A History of the Diocese of London," edited by Guy Alden (unpublished manuscript, 2002). Additional information supplied by Louis Boulet and Rose-Marie Roy.

Pardoville: Our Lady of the Angels

By 1958, work was underway for the construction of an Ontario Hospital School, in the Cedar Springs area for mentally challenged children. The potential increase in the Catholic population that this would bring to the area was one of the factors contributing to the elevation of St. Anne of the Lakes, Erieau, to parish status late that spring. The provincial institution was opened near Pardoville in 1961.

Meanwhile, by early 1960, catechism classes were being held at the old Pardo estate, and Father Leopold Nieuwlandt, OFM Cap, pastor of St. Anne's, saw the need to establish a mission in the area to serve the ever-increasing flow of Catholics. By early 1961, an unused Reorganized Church of Latter Day Saints church, 38 feet by 24 feet (11.6 m by 7.3 m), with a potential seating capacity of 120, was on the market in Erie Beach. Walter Dalton of Windsor, a summer resident of Erieau, donated a half-acre (0.2 ha) parcel of land facing the highway at Pardoville for a church. It was planned that the mission church would serve area communities, catechism classes would be set up in the church and Mass would be celebrated there once a week. Through Monsignor J. Austin Roney, chancellor, the diocese furnished a loan for the purchase of the building in October1961. During the first half of January 1962, the church was

Our Lady of the Angels

transported to Pardoville and placed on a concrete block foundation. A steeple, containing a bell, and surmounted by a three-foot (2.7 m) high cross, was added, as well as a lobby and some concrete steps leading up to the church entrance. Much of the work had been done by volunteer labour under Joseph Van Meerbergen's direction. Three persons particularly noted for their fine work, in addition to Van Meerbergen, were Gil Vanthuyn, Jac Woodward and Con DeCorte. Even so, the cost of the excavation, foundation, renovations, and other expenses, drove the cost to over $7,700, by the end of June 1962, above and beyond the original purchase price of $1,500 and the mover's wages of $250. On 24 June, the mission, dedicated to Our Lady of the Angels, was officially opened and blessed by Bishop Cody to serve the Catholics from Cedar Springs to Dealtown, including Highbanks, Sleepy Hollow and Pardoville. By late July 1963, the debt on the church had been paid down to an even $6,000 and a benefactor had given a gift of close to $2,000 for additional seating and a pulpit. By this time, the congregation during the summer season had outgrown the capacity of the little church and Father Neuwlandt was on the lookout for an addition to it. A building on the RCAF base in Aylmer was assessed in October but found wanting. Finally, in 1966, Glenwood United Church was purchased, moved to Pardoville, and joined perpendicular to the existing structure by late summer.

Harmonious relations between the church at Erieau and its mission at Pardoville did not always prevail. By the spring of 1975, Father Anacletus A. Mennen, OFM Cap, the pastor, had been compelled to separate the finances of the two entities. Matters

went from bad to worse, however, between the members of Our Lady of the Angels and their pastor, and Father Mennen had to seek recourse to the diocesan chancellor, Monsignor Fergus J. Laverty, who called upon Father Charles C. Campbell, dean of Kent, to mediate the situation.

Father Ivo Tommeleyn, OFM, Cap, succeeded Father Mennen as pastor of St. Anne of the Lakes later in 1975. Our Lady of Angels continued to be a mission of St. Anne of the Lakes under the pastorate of Father Tommeleyn, until it was closed on 29 January 2006, more than a quarter of a century later.

Source: DLA, Parish Files.

Ridgetown:
St. Michael the Archangel

By the 1850s, the Catholics of Howard Township were being ministered to by Father Jean Jaffré, SJ, pastor of St. Joseph's, Chatham. On 17 March 1858, he led the people in building a log chapel, 32 feet by 20 feet (9.8 m by 6.1 m) with a roofline of 10 feet (3 m). It was located on two acres (0.8 ha) of land that had been donated by John Cosgrove and is on lot 3, concession 7, now the site of the present cemetery. The finished structure was dedicated to St. Joseph the Carpenter. In 1863, a cottage was constructed as Saturday night lodging for the monthly visits of a priest. Bishop Pinsoneault administered confirmation in the chapel for the first time on 23 September 1864. In 1874, the Basilians replaced the Jesuits in Chatham and served St. Joseph mission in Howard. The Franciscans succeeded them in 1878.

By the late 1870s, it was decided to relocate the mission church to the more populous Ridgetown. A three-day bazaar in February 1880 raised $1,000 in support of the proposed building program. On 30 May 1880, the cornerstone for the new church was laid and blessed by Monsignor Jean-Marie Bruyère, vicar general of the diocese, the priest in charge of the mission being Father Michael Hoffman, OFM. The light-red brick church was blessed by Bishop Walsh, on 3 July 1881, and dedicated to St. Michael the Archangel. About this time, Ridgetown was detached from Chatham and attached to Merlin with the elevation once again of St. Patrick's to parish status.

St. Michael's was elevated to parish status in 1897. Its first pastor, Father Daniel P. McMenamin (1897-99), arrived on 1 February 1897. Two years later, he oversaw the building of a rectory to the east of the church. This rectory was designed and built by James O'Connor, the same person responsible for the church's

St. Michael

1880 altar. In order to assist in the payment of the rectory, Father McMenamin generously gave up half of his salary during his pastorate. His successor, Father Bartholomew Boubat (1900-06), ministered to some twenty-five Catholics in Muirkirk, Orford Township, usually at the home of Frederick Deshaw, which was located on lot 14, concession 4. The church's stained-glass windows were installed in 1908 while Father James J. Mugan was pastor (1907-14). Beginning in August 1918, the priests of Ridgetown served the mission at Blenheim. This continued until 1927 when St. Mary's was raised to parish status. Father Edward G. Doe (1918-24) had a verandah built on to the rectory at St. Michael's. With the parish debt retired by the 1920s, the congregation concentrated on such improvements as installing natural gas heating and more stained-glass windows. During the pastorship of Father M. Joseph Fallon (1924-26), excavations took place beneath the church for a basement/hall. Father William T. Moran (1926-42) permitted the local Rotary Club to hold its meetings in the church basement and was elected its first president. Father Leo W. Power (1942-49) oversaw the strengthening and reconstruction of the tower but died before the bell was installed. His successor, Father Carl A. Pettit (1949-60), re-organized the Catholic Women's League in 1950. The mission of St. Gabriel was opened in 1952 in Rondeau Provincial Park within St. Michael's parish. Father T. Gordon Dill (1963-68) carried out

the reforms of the Second Vatican Council. In 1971, Father Ulysee A. Lefaive (1968-79) oversaw the formation of the first advisory board and in 1975 the extensive remodeling of the church. The church's centennial was celebrated during 1980. With the retirement of native son and pastor, Father Martin A. Johnston, on 8 August 2005, St. Michael's parish was clustered with St. Mary's and is served by the Capuchin Fathers who have been in Blenheim since 1927.

Sources: *Parish of St. Michael The Archangel Centennial Calendar 1880-1980* [1980].

Rondeau Park:
St. Gabriel the Archangel

In 1951, during the pastorship of Father Carl A. Pettit of St. Michael the Archangel parish, Ridgetown (1949-60), the decision was made to erect a mission church in Rondeau Provincial Park. Gerry Supply & Lumber Company of London assembled the prefabricated structure, the first of its kind in the diocese. The outside measurements were 40 feet in width by 110 feet in length (12.2 m by 33.5 m). There were two Gothic-style windows on either side of the main entrance and nine main windows each on the two side sides of the building. Inside the church there were thirty-eight 14-foot (4.3 m) fir pews. The building was topped with a belfry 4 feet by 4 feet by 6 feet (1.2 m by 1.2 m by 1.8 m). By early June, the site had been leveled and the footings were poured. The church was named in honour of St. Gabriel the Archangel, a fitting touch considering this would be a mission within a parish dedicated to St. Michael the Archangel. The total cost of construction was $18, 908.86, which included foundation and walks, construction labour, electrical work, plumbing, painting and incidental expenses, in addition to the payment of $11,709 to Gerry Lumber for the building, seats, altar, altar railing and confessionals. The church seated 360 adults and was opened to the summer residents and tourists in 1952.

Over the next couple of years, similar prefabricated churches, also erected by Gerry Supply & Lumber Company, sprang up in Chatham, Windsor, Sarnia and London, and they were affectionately known by the clergy and laity alike as "Cody's Cabins," for Bishop Cody. As for St. Gabriel's, it was used for the celebration of Mass between mid-June and mid-September only and had no heating or insulation. In the words of its pastor, Father Pettit, for the rest of the year it was

St. Gabriel

"hermetically sealed."

In 1959, the parish spent $727.92 on kneeler cushions and soundproofing of the confessional. St. Gabriel's was valued at $33,734.80 for insurance purposes in 1965, but as Monsignor Fergus J. Laverty, the chancellor, informed the pastor, Father T. Gordon Dill (1963-68), it would be impossible to replace the building for that sum.

Up to this time, persons who came to Rondeau Park to attend Sunday Mass did not have to pay the entry fee, but by the early 1970s, an increasing number of persons used the Mass exemption as a ruse to enter the park for free. Consequently, beginning on 28 May, 1972, everyone had to pay $1.50 to enter the park. Those legitimately coming into the park for Mass were naturally irate, and the matter ended up on the floor of the Ontario Legislature. Leo Bernier, the minster concerned, later wrote to Bishop Carter and Darcy McKeough, M.P. for Chatham-Kent, to assure them that fees would not be charged to persons who wished to attend church and some means would be found for screening those persons misrepresenting their intentions. Ironically, in 2006, an entrance fee to the park was re-established for churchgoers.

Today, St. Gabriel's remains a mission of St. Michael's, and is open from May to September.

Sources: DLA, Parish Files: St. Michael the Archangel, Ridgetown, and St. Gabriel's Mission, Rondeau; Gerald Emmett Carter Papers, Box 23.

Stevenson: St. Charles

Prior to the establishment of a mission church in the Stevenson area, the faithful travelled to either St. Patrick's, Raleigh (Merlin) or St. Francis Xavier, Tilbury. The increased population in the late 1920s led Monsignor Charles A. Parent, pastor of St. Francis, to convince Bishop Fallon of the need to build a church in that part of Romney Township. On 15 January 1927, Albert Regnier donated 8.5 acres (3.4 ha) for the site of a new church.

On 4 January 1934, Father Isidore J. Poisson (1934-42), curate at St. Francis, was appointed pastor of Stevenson. The first sod was turned on 25 May 1934; the cornerstone was laid on 17 June; and Bishop Kidd blessed the new church dedicated to St. Charles Borromeo, on 16 September. While most of the ninety-four families were French-Canadian, others were of Belgian, Irish, Dutch and German origin, with one family being Polish. The first church picnic was held on 8 September 1934, and the Holy Name Society convened its first meeting on 18 November 1934.

The families of Dan Phillips and Camille Benoit donated the $252 needed to purchase and install the bell. It was blessed by Father Pierre L'Heureux, on 11 September 1938, and named St. Helen in honour of Father Poisson's mother.

The Ladies Altar Society was formed in 1942. With Father Poisson's transfer to St. Theresa's parish in Windsor, on 15 November 1942, St. Charles reverted to mission status attached to the parish of St. Francis Xavier. Parish status was restored in September 1944 with the pastoral appointment of Father J. Euclide Chevalier (1944-49). He lived in the sacristy of the church until a proper rectory was built. This was officially opened on 24 February 1946. In 1949 a parish cemetery was opened.

Father Chevalier's successor, in June 1949, was Father Oscar A. Martin (1949-51). On 26 June 1951, he was succeeded by Father Ovila E. Charbonneau (1951-52), who supervised the installation of stained-glass windows and the renewal of the Stations of the Cross. Father Charles E. Lanoue (1952-58) oversaw the painting of the church interior. On 31 May 1953, Father Louis H. Rivard, the only native son to be ordained a priest, celebrated his first Mass at the parish. In 1955, Father Lanoue established Our Lady of the Blessed Sacrament mission in Wheatley. Father Ulysee A.

St. Charles

Lefaive was appointed curate of Stevenson in June 1956. A new organ, which cost $1,230, was purchased in 1957, replacing "St. Cecilia," purchased for $1,000 on 3 December 1947.

During the pastorate of Father Earl D. Paré (1958-63), the parish celebrated its silver jubilee on 4 November 1959, the feast day of St. Charles Borromeo. In 1962, Wheatley was elevated to parish status and detached from Stevenson. The redecoration of the church interior was completed in February 1964, during the pastorate of Father Linus F. Bastien (1963-70). Between 1968 and 1970, Wheatley was once more a mission of St. Charles.

Father Henri Masse (1973-77) is remembered for holding ceramic classes, open to all in the community, in the rectory basement. At this time, guitars and folk music were introduced into the Masses, and many young people joined the choir. In the summer of 1976, he provided Sunday Masses at Camper's Cove. When Father Masse was transferred to Grande Pointe, on 5 May 1977, St. Charles once again became a mission of St. Francis and Masses at the Cove were discontinued. Over $8,000 was spent on repairs to the church roof in 1981. The tradition of the Living Rosary was initiated in November 1982. Beginning in the fall of 1983, St. Charles was served from Belle River. A high point of the community's history was the golden jubilee of the church, which was celebrated throughout 1984. Stevenson was a mission of St. Patrick's in Merlin when it was suppressed in 2005, the last Mass being celebrated at St. Charles on 26 June.

Sources: DLA, Parish Files; St. Charles Anniversary Committee, "St. Charles Mission-Stevenson 50 Anniversary 1934 – Golden Jubilee-1984."

Thamesville:
St. Paul

It was probably in the latter half of the 1840s that Father Jean Jaffré, SJ, of Sandwich, who was ministering to the people of Chatham, first offered Mass in what became St. Paul's parish. In 1853, Father Thadeus Kirwan, who served the Wardsville mission from London, was an occasional visitor to the Thamesville area. Father Michael Prendergast visited the area about 1857, about the same year in which the first Mass in Thamesville, then called Tecumseh, was held in Bernard Broderick's shoe store. During this time, however, Father Jaffré continued to minister to the Catholics of the area about once a month from St. Joseph's, which had been established as a parish in Chatham in 1850.

Father Jaffré's successor in Chatham in 1860 was Father Martin Férard, SJ. He inspired the Catholics of Thamesville to acquire land and build a church. The land was purchased in June 1861, and a small, white-frame church, with a little tower facing

St. Paul

Railroad Street, was built. In 1873, Father Patrick Fitzpatrick was appointed pastor at Bothwell, and the mission of St. Paul, Thamesville, was transferred from Chatham to St Ignatius parish. The church was remodeled in 1888, and a sanctuary, sacristy and choir were added. Father Albert J. McKeon was then the pastor at Bothwell.

A new, Gothic-style brick church was built, facing Alice Street, during 1903-04. Father Daniel Forster, the pastor of St. Ignatius and a farm boy from Norfolk County, is reported to have travelled daily from Bothwell to assist in the church's construction. Moore & Henry of London was the architectural firm.

The old St. Paul Cemetery was situated by what became Highway 21, along the Thames River, and was in use from at least 1870 until 1909, at which time one and a half acres (0.6 ha) were purchased for the present cemetery.

In 1920, the brick house next to the church was purchased for $5,000 and was converted into a rectory. St. Paul's was elevated to parish status in May 1920 when Father Frank McCarty (1919-33) transferred his residence from Bothwell to Thamesville. In 1925, the interior of the church was redecorated and a basement/hall excavated beneath the church the following year.

In 1952, Bishop Cody detached St. Ignatius from St. Paul parish and elevated the former once again to parish status with Wardsville and Glencoe as its missions. During the pastorate of Father Jan A. Achtabowski (1954-59), the beautiful church paintings were produced by Polish-born Benny Ryll, the carving of Christ was executed in Oberammergau, Bavaria, and the cross was carved from two oak trees by a gentleman from Chatham. Father Achtabowski celebrated his twenty-fifth anniversary as a priest in December 1957. During the pastorate of Father Frederick M. Doll (1959-64), St. Paul's school, which cost $37,210, was opened in September 1960. By 1969, two additions had been made to the school.

The seventy-fifth anniversary of the present St. Paul's church was celebrated on 1 April 1978, followed on 4 June with a celebration of Father Leo A. Larivière's twenty-fifth anniversary as a priest.

In 2000, St. Paul's was clustered with St. Ignatius, Bothwell. Effective June 2007, the boundaries of St. Paul's were adjusted to take in the former St. Ignatius and St. Michael's, Dresden. The 100th anniversary of St. Paul church was celebrated in 2004 during the pastorate of Father Andrew A. Dwyer (2000 to present).

Sources: Ralph Hubert Dignan and Joseph P. Finn, "A History of the Diocese of London," edited by Guy Alden (unpublished manuscript, 2002). Additional information supplied by Marion Matt.

St. Francis Xavier

Tilbury: St. Francis Xavier

The first Mass in the Tilbury area was celebrated in 1845, in the log cabin of Jean-Baptiste Duprat, located opposite the present parish cemetery. The priest was probably Father Jean-Baptiste Morin, who was pastor of St. Peter's, Tilbury East. It was to St. Peter's that the Catholics of the area would generally trek Sunday after Sunday, both before and after 1845. For the next ten years, however, priests came on average once a month from Chatham, Pain Court, or Belle River, as well as Tilbury East. On 2 March 1855, local Catholics met to purchase property for a proposed chapel. One of the group, François-Xavier Lanoue, offered to donate five acres (2 ha) of land for this purpose, on one condition, that the chapel be dedicated to his patron saint. Under the direction of the pastor of St. Peter's, Father Jean Raynel, SJ, a log chapel was built near what became the Middle Road, later Highway 98 and now Essex County Road 46. A sacristy was added sometime afterwards.

The mission of St. Francis Xavier attained temporary parish status in November 1861 with the arrival of Father F.M. Ruitz, the first priest to take up permanent residence in Tilbury. Once a month, he would minister to St. Peter's, which had reverted to mission status, and to the mission of St. Patrick's in Raleigh. Bishop Pinsoneault visited the chapel in August 1862, confirmed eighty-nine persons and blessed the recently completed log rectory and newly acquired church bell. With Father Ruitz's transfer to another parish in July 1864, St. Francis Xavier once again reverted to mission status and was attached to St. Joseph's parish in Chatham.

When Bishop Walsh visited the chapel, on 19

January 1871, the congregation urgently requested a resident priest be sent to them. Walsh promised this on condition that a proper church and new rectory be built. Under the direction of Father Francis Maréchal (Marshall), SJ, of St. Joseph's, Chatham, a frame church, 100 feet by 40 feet (30 m by 12 m), was erected and the bell, formerly hanging on a frame in the open air alongside the old chapel, was installed in the belfry. Father Antoine P. Villeneuve was appointed pastor in September 1872, and the mission of St. Peter's was attached to St. Francis. In 1876, the first separate school in the parish was built. Father Louis A. Wassereau succeeded Father Villeneuve in November 1882 and ministered to the parish until his sudden death in April 1890. Two years earlier, a separate school was opened in the then village of Tilbury Centre.

In time, the congregation outgrew the small church. Since it was two miles (3.2 k m) from the centre of the village to the church, the pastor, Father Pierre Langlois (1891-1905), persuaded Bishop O'Connor of the need to relocate in Tilbury. Thus, on 24 May 1894, the cornerstone of the new church was laid and blessed by O'Connor, who returned on 1 May 1895 to officially open and bless both the church and the new rectory.

Many parish milestones took place during the pastorate of Father Charles A. Parent (1905-44). Electric lights were installed in the church and its interior walls adorned with the tableaux and paintings of the European artist Alexander Theurbieun in 1916; the Eighth Diocesan Eucharistic Congress was held there in 1919; a Casavant two keyboard pipe organ was installed in the church and the Calvary Monument erected in the parish cemetery in 1923; land was purchased for a mission church at Stevenson in 1930; and the golden jubilee of Monsignor Parent's ordination was celebrated in 1941.

Originally a French-language parish, for many decades St. Francis Xavier has been truly bilingual. It celebrated its centenary in 1955 and its 150th anniversary in 2005.

St. Francis Xavier parish was slated to be fully clustered with St. Patrick, Merlin, and St. Peter, Tilbury East, effective June 2008.

Sources: "Historical notes – St. Francis-Xavier Parish, Tilbury, Ont. 1855-1979" [1979]; Lynda Montminy, "La paroisse Saint-François-Xavier de Tilbury," *Newsletter of the Diocese of London*, no. 105 (Advent/Christmas 2002), 11; Lynda Montminy, "From seeds scattered and sown Paroisse St. Francis Xavier celebrates a harvest of 150 years," *Newsletter of the Diocese of London*, no. 111 (Lent 2005), 13; Ralph Hubert Dignan and Joseph P. Finn, "A History of the Diocese of London," edited by Guy Alden (unpublished manuscript, 2002); "St Francis Xavier Parish," (2005); "Souvenir of the Centennial Celebration of Saint Francis Xavier Church, Tilbury, Ontario" (1955).

Tilbury East: St. Peter

Originally known as St-Pierre sur-la-Tranche, the French-Canadian mission of St. Peter-on-the-Thames, East Tilbury Township, Kent County, was founded on 1 May 1800 by Bishop Denaut of Québec. During the same visit, he also established the mission of St. John the Baptist in Amherstburg, Malden Township. Father Jean B. Marchand, PSS, the pastor of Assumption parish, was put in charge of both missions. In late 1796, Father Marchand had counted twelve Catholic families living along the lower Thames River. On 8 July 1802, he blessed and dedicated the first chapel to St. Peter the Apostle and made the first entry in its register. Interestingly, and to add to confusion and debate ever since, Marchand described the register as being for "la chapelle de la nouvelle paroisse" — the chapel of the new parish — when, in fact, he resided in Sandwich and both St. Peter's and St. John the Baptist were missions of Assumption parish. In 1824, a new church was built to replace the original one, which had been demolished by a windstorm. With the erection of Amherstburg as a parish, in May 1828, St. Peter's was detached from Assumption and became a mission of St. John the Baptist under the pastorate of Father Louis J. Fluet. It was only with the arrival of its first resident priest, Father Jean-Baptiste Morin, in 1834, that St. Peter's became a parish. Father Morin died in December 1846. According to his wishes, he was interred beneath the epistle side of the altar. His successor, Father Joseph M. Billow (Billon) (1847-50), was the first priest at St. Peter's to describe himself as curé (pastor) in the church register, in September 1848.

In 1859, St. Peter's once more reverted to mission status and was served about once a month by the pastors of St. Joseph's in Chatham and St.

St. Peter

significant historical value of the church and its site, not only to its parishioners but also for the entire province.

In 1999, the parishes of St. Peter, St. Francis Xavier, Tilbury, St. Patrick, Merlin, and St. Charles, Stevenson, were clustered, and Father Eugène G. Roy was named moderator, assisted by Fathers Michael L. Dwyer and Jan Konieczny, CR. The following year, Father Roy became pastor of St. Francis Xavier only (1998-2006). St. Charles was suppressed in 2005.

Effective June 2008, the parishes of St. Peter's, St. Patrick's, and St. Francis were slated to be fully clustered.

Sources: DLA, Church Register, St-Pierre-sur-la-Tranche; "History of St. Peter's Parish 1802-1947" [1947]; E.J. Lajeunesse, CSB, *Outline History of Assumption Parish* (Windsor: 1967); "Honouring Our Past" [1985]; Louis Boulet, "The Roman Catholic Church in Kent County" [n.d.]; Mrs. J.P. Dunn, "The Roman Catholic Church in Kent County," Kent Historical Society *Papers and Addresses* (Chatham: 1914), 22-23; Rose-Marie Roy, "Pariosse Saint-Pierre....sur la Tranche La deuxième paroisse," *Newsletter of the Diocese of London*, no. 112 (Easter 2004), 13; Théo Martin, "History of the Parish of St. Peter Diocese of London" (paper presented at the Theological Conference, Chatham, Ontario, 24 Oct. 1928). Additional information supplied by Paul Giroux and Father Eugène Roy.

Francis Xavier in Tilbury. From 1872, the mission was attached to Tilbury, between 1885 and 1886 to Pain Court, and between 1886 and 1892 to Grande Pointe. After thirty-three years, St. Peter became a parish for the second time, in 1892, with Father Charles A. Parent (1892-1900) as pastor. One of his first tasks was to build a rectory, after which he transferred the church registers and other documents, a most fortuitous decision. On 28 October 1895, the white-frame church, erected in 1824, was destroyed by fire; only the chalice and a few records were saved. The present brick structure, measuring 80 feet by 40 feet (24 m by 12 m), was completed the following year and the remains of Father Morin re-interred beneath the epistle side of the altar in the new church. It was during the pastorship of Father Emile C. Ladouceur (1900-10) that the debt incurred for the building of the rectory and the new church was liquidated. In 1920, Father Théo Martin (1910-28), commissioned the renowned painter, Marie Joseph Georges Delfosse of Montréal to produce eighteen ecclesiastical paintings, which still adorn the ceiling and walls. In 1952, the church was restored to its original beauty and a new parish hall was built through the efforts of the parish community and its pastor, Father Anthony F. Scalisi. During the pastorship of Father Louis L. Ouellette (1953-56), Mass in French was discontinued, the vast majority of the parishioners now being of Dutch and Flemish background.

St. Peter's celebrated its centenary in 1902, its sesquicentennial in 1952, its 175th anniversary in 1977 and its bicentennial in 2002. The Ontario Heritage Foundation unveiled a plaque on the church grounds, in 1985, in further recognition of the

Wallaceburg: Holy Family

In December 1945, during the pastorate of Father Edward F. Goetz of Our Lady Help of Christians, Wallaceburg, property was purchased on Murray Street at a cost of $8,500 from Joseph and Sarah Reaume. The land was for the building of a parish church in the southern part of the town. During the winter of 1947-48, it was decided to build a hall to be used for church purposes and a school, as it was deemed too expensive to build a proper church. In June 1948, several men dug the footings for the foundation. The building was 105 feet by 46 feet (32 m by 14 m) and contained, in addition to the hall, living quarters for the priest, a kitchen and a furnace room. It was erected by Pete Prisner, as contractor, with the help of the parishioners.

In July 1948, Father Bernard R. Laverty became

Holy Family

administrator of the yet unnamed new parish. He was subsequently appointed its pastor (1948-55) and offered the first Mass in the new building on Christmas 1948. After some consultation with the diocese, the name Holy Family was selected for the parish. This name was revealed to the parishioners when Bishop Cody blessed the church on 27 February 1949. The baptisms of Remi Verberckmoes and Martin Hebert, performed on 20 March 1949, were the first in the parish. These were followed by the first wedding, that of Arthur Gervais and Anna Bogaert, on 23 April 1949. Until 1950, the back part of the church was used as a school. The initial class receiving the Blessed Eucharist for the first time was held here in 1951. Father Cyril A.J. Doyle (1955-57) oversaw the completion of the parish annex begun during the pastorate of Father Laverty. The church, choir loft and annex seated a little over 600 people. Father Lawrence J. Coughlin (1957-61) succeeded Father Doyle and was followed in turn by Fathers William E. Morris (1961-70), Paul D. Milne (1970-72) and J. Hubert (Hugh) Fleming (1972-78).

With the arrival of Father Wilfred J. Bourque (1978-89), a new confessional room and crying room were added to the church and a kitchenette to the annex. In the autumn of 1978, a new office and garage were built. All the work was done by Skinner & Laprise at a cost of $20,500. The parking lot was extended in the summer of 1979, at a cost of $43,595. Large flowerbeds were added and the church exterior was painted.

Major renovations, costing $470,892, were undertaken in 1982. Through the efforts of the CWL, formed in 1949, a new storage room was built and an outdoor statue of the Holy Family was purchased

and erected at a cost of $23,900 and $10,000 respectively.

Father Bernard A. Robert as pastor and Father J. Bartley Clark as associate pastor arrived in June 1989. During this time the Renew program was introduced. A joyous event occurred on Sunday, 14 May 1989 when Father Randy Foster, a native son, celebrated his first Mass at Holy Family.

Father Dennis J. Wilhelm was appointed pastor in 1993. During his stay, the carpets in the church were replaced, the walls painted and the sound system upgraded. To mark the parish's fiftieth anniversary in 1999, a new photo album was produced and a dinner dance was held at the Wilkesport Hall. The parish credit union, begun in 1952, ceased operations in 2003.

In 2004, under the pastorate of Father Gregory J. Bonin, assisted by Father John P. Jasica, Holy Family was clustered with its mother parish, Our Lady Help of Christians, and Sacred Heart parish in Port Lambton to form one community.

Sources: DLA, Parish Files; Gregory M. Blonde et al., *History of the Church of Our Lady Help of Christians Wallaceburg, Ontario 1871-1978* (Wallaceburg: [1978]).

Wallaceburg:
Our Lady Help of Christians

The Wallaceburg area was probably visited a couple times a year, beginning in 1845, by Father Jean Jaffré, SJ, of Sandwich, who ministered to the Catholics in Essex and Kent counties. By 1856, the need for a mission church at Wallaceburg was evident, and in March 1857, land was purchased. It appears, however, that this site was not suitable, because in 1861 property was purchased on the northwest corner of Duncan and Elgin streets on which a church was opened the following year. From 1862 until 1868, Father F. Wilhelm Gockein, SJ, stationed at Chatham, had the primary responsibility for the Wallaceburg mission. On his confirmation tour in June 1871, Bishop Walsh put the mission under the patronage of the Sacred Heart of Jesus.

In 1874, the Basilians replaced the Jesuits in Chatham, and in April 1877, the present church site was purchased, under the direction of Father J. Pierre Grand, CSB. On 14 January 1878, Father

James Ryan (1878-86), a diocesan priest, became the first pastor at Wallaceburg with Dresden as his mission. One of Father Ryan's first tasks was to begin work on the construction of the new church. George Waddle of Grand Rapids, Michigan,

Our Lady Help of Christians

was the architect. The cornerstone was blessed and laid on 11 August 1878, and the Gothic-style, red-brick church was dedicated to Our Lady Help of Christians by Bishop Walsh, on 23 May 1880, the day before her feast day.

Tragedy, however, befell the last Jesuit priest who served the Sacred Heart of Jesus mission. It is said that, at the request of his former parishioners, Father Francis Maréchal (Marshall), SJ, then stationed in New York, had gone to Troy, New York, to select a bell for Our Lady Help of Christians church. The railway car in which he was travelling caught fire, and as a result he died on 13 January 1882. The bell, on the other hand, made its way to Wallaceburg and was blessed by Bishop Walsh on 5 February 1882.

In May 1897, during the pastorate of Father John J. Ronan (1886-1901), the organ, manufactured by the Scribner Organ Manufacturing Company of London, was installed. Father Ronan's successor, Father Michael J. Brady (1901-19), supervised the construction of a new rectory, "The Palms," on the northeast corner of Creek and Elgin streets, which was blessed by Bishop McEvay on 8 May 1902. Previously, the priests had apparently lived in a house on the southwest corner of Creek and Wall streets. With the opening of the new separate school in 1905, the old school, housed in the former mission church, was moved behind the rectory and converted into a stable for Father Brady's horses. Later it

became the rectory garage. In 1931, it was bricked over and converted into the first St. Angela Merici High School. In 1906, the church was completely renovated.

On 7 October 1920, during Father John P. Brennan's pastorship (1919-33), a parish hall was informally opened in the former Bank of Montreal building at the northwest corner of Nelson and Wellington streets. This landmark building was demolished in 1964.

During Father Edward F. Goetz's pastorate (1933-44), a side entrance was added (1933), the twenty-third Diocesan Eucharistic Congress was hosted by the parish on 11 September 1935, a new pipe organ was installed (1939), the church was redecorated (1941-43), the fortieth anniversary of Father Goetz's ordination was celebrated in 1944, and plans were undertaken to establish a new parish on the south side of the town. The interior of the church was refurbished in 1995, and work on the exterior was completed in 2002.

In 2004, Our Lady Help of Christians parish was clustered with Holy Family parish in Wallaceburg and Sacred Heart parish in Port Lambton.

Source: Gregory M. Blonde et al., *History of the Church of Our Lady Help of Christians Wallaceburg, Ontario 1878 -1978* (Wallaceburg: [1978]).

Walpole Island: Sacred Heart Mission

Bishop Michael Power of Toronto, shortly after his installation, invited French Jesuits to work in his diocese, and he entrusted to them the Indian missions. As a result, Father Dominique du Ranquet, SJ, and Brother Joseph Jennesseaux, SJ, arrived on Walpole Island on 23 April 1844. While awaiting permission to settle on the island, the two men pitched their tent on the shore and raised a temporary chapel constructed of canvas and rush matting. On the first Sunday there was only one Indian present at Mass, along with a few French-Canadian and Irish settlers from the area. In time, the government gave leave for the missionaries to live on the Reserve and to build a church, house and school.

A few months later, Sacred Heart mission church, which was built of logs and measured 50 feet by 25 feet (15.2 m by 7.6 m), with a 45-

foot-high (13.7 m) steeple, was raised and almost completed when, in September 1844, notice was received from the provincial government that work stop. From the beginning, the Jesuits had been opposed by the non-Christian Indian leaders, who used the slightest pretext to drive the missionaries from the island. Meanwhile, as he made the rounds of his missions, Father du Ranquet offered Mass for a disparate crowd of French-Canadian and Irish Catholics, Protestants and non-Christian Indians on the island. Hymns were sung and a sermon was delivered in two or three languages.

Opposition to the missionaries continued, even within the Indian Department and Bishop Power addressed the matter to a succession of governors general, but without any satisfaction. In 1847, the final orders arrived from the government for the Jesuits to vacate Walpole Island. Both Bishop Power and the Jesuit superior, Father Boulanger, SJ, saw the futility of further appeals to provincial officials and decided to abandon the Walpole mission. In the early morning hours of 22 March 1849, while Father du Ranquet and Brother Jennesseaux were absent from the island, the church, house, school and all their contents were consumed by flames. By June, a mere hut served as a chapel, and an adjoining bark cabin served as a dwelling for the missionaries.

The missionaries then removed to Baby Point on the mainland where a combination church and residence was built. The mission on Walpole Island was virtually abandoned in August 1850 when du Ranquet and Jennesseaux were transferred to Holy Cross mission on Manitoulin Island.

From time to time, however, missionaries would visit the island and offer Mass for the few Catholics living there. In making his confirmation tour of the western part of his diocese in the early 1850s, Bishop Charbonnel visited the abandoned mission and described it as "a poor mission without a resident priest, a poor church of bark and poor planks, a still poorer cabin, which was just a lean-to against the church; all in the worst possible state." While the natives begged the bishop to provide them with a priest to teach their children, it appears that neither Charbonnel nor his successors were able to comply with this request. The church appears to have survived until the early 1900s, being visited occasionally by missionaries.

Source: Gregory M. Blonde et al., *History*

of The Church of Our Lady Help of Christians Wallaceburg, Ontario 1878 -1978 (Wallaceburg: [1978]).

Wardsville: North American Martyrs

By the mid-1840s, Mass was celebrated in the area about once or twice annually, first at the home of John Hurley and then that of James Cunningham. The priest probably came from London. The newly ordained Father Augustine Carayon was stationed at Wardsville for a time in 1852. By 1853, Wardsville was served from London and had a church but no altar. It was during the pastorate of Father Thadeus Kirwan of London (1849-56) that a mission church was built in Wardsville on land purchased from John O'Brien Ward for £7 10s. The timber for the frame church was pre-framed in London and floated down the Thames River. The night before the people were to erect the frames, someone cut loose the boom and the frames floated away. The faithful had to assemble new frames on the ground. They were assisted by recently arrived railway workers, who were building the extension of the Great Western Railroad (now a branch of the CN) between London and Sandwich. The church, dedicated to St. Thomas of Canterbury, was opened in 1853, opposite the present Canadian Martyrs cemetery along the ravine, on the northeast corner of what was euphemistically called Church and King streets. The latter was a dirt path and is now known as Ontario Street. Dean Kirwan noted, however, that the church did not have an altar. Father Michael Prendergast was the priest in charge during 1857-58. Between 1861 and 1873, St. Thomas mission was served by the Jesuit priests from St. Joseph's parish in Chatham.

With the appointment of Father Patrick Fitzpatrick as the first pastor at Bothwell, Wardsville became a mission within St. Ignatius parish. By the late 1870s, the congregation had outgrown the small building and a new one was needed. Initially, there was much opposition to erecting a new church at Wardsville because a larger number of Catholic families had settled in Glencoe and to the east of that village. An influential gentleman from England with the surname English, however, was able to persuade Father Michael McGrath, the pastor of

North American Martyrs

St. Ignatius, that the church should be built at Wardsville. Constructed as an "exact counterpart" to the church in Alvinston, the new church of white brick, with stone capping to all the projections and pillars, was completed at a cost of $5,500. The main part was 58 feet by 40 feet (17.7 m by 12.2 m), with a chancel 20 feet by 30 feet (6.1 m by 9.1 m), which contained vestry and confessional rooms on each side. The 70-foot-high (21.3 m) tower was surmounted with a cross and other ornamental work. Inside, the ceiling of the nave was covered in pure white plaster and supported by oak arches, and the roughcast walls were covered in imitation stone. In the west end, there was a large semi-circular gallery for the choir, which was panelled with oiled and varnished oak. The church was dedicated by Bishop Walsh to the Blessed Heart of Mary, Mother of God, on 28 December 1879. The old building was then torn down, and the site is now occupied by the foundations of former tobacco kilns.

Although still active as a mission church within St. Ignatius parish as late as 1918, Blessed Heart church was no longer in use by 1933. Over the years an underground stream had undermined its foundation. It was described as in a very precarious condition and in need of demolition for safety's sake. Accordingly, N.R. Ibbetson, engineers and contractors of Walkerville, tore it down late that spring at a cost of $250.

In 1935, the local bank manager, J.P. Dougherty, pleaded with Bishop Kidd to build a new church in Wardsville. The bishop assented, assigning a recent bequest of $5,000, which sum completely paid for the small chapel on the north side of the main street (Highway 2). Although privately referred to by some

as "Kidd's Cave," its official title was the Chapel of the North American Martyrs. In 1969, during the pastorship of Father William E. Capitano of Bothwell, Wardsville was closed as a mission. The well-built structure, consisting of an outer layer of dark red brick and two inner layers of softer yellow brick, was demolished in 1987 during the pastorate of Father Terrence R. McNamara. Today, the only Catholic presence in Wardsville is the cemetery.

Sources: DLA, Parish Files; "Dedication Service To Mark Alvinston Church Anniversary," 1 Oct. 1949, unidentified newspaper clipping; "Mark 70th Anniversary Of Church Consecration At Alvinston Parish," [c. Sept. 1949], unidentified newspaper clipping; Ralph Hubert Dignan and Joseph P. Finn, "A History of the Diocese of London," edited by Guy Alden (unpublished manuscript, 2002). Additional information supplied by Marion Matt and Father John Van Damme.

Wheatley: Our Lady of the Blessed Sacrament

Winnifred Hanson was the main force in the establishment of a church in Wheatley. Her husband, a Baptist, had died in 1953, leaving her without transportation to Sunday Mass at St. Michael the Archangel parish in Leamington. Like the woman in the parable of the persistent widow (Luke 18:1-5), she bombarded the diocese with requests for Mass to be celebrated in her village for the sake of the Catholics there, until she was listened to by the bishop. With the assistance of Mrs. Madge Daudlin, and the co-operation of Father Charles E. Lanoue of St. Charles parish in Stevenson, Mrs. Hanson enumerated thirty-one Catholic families — "good, bad & indifferent" — in the Wheatley area.

On 13 July 1954, Father Louis J. Phelan of St. Michael's oversaw the purchase of 1.2 acres (0.5 ha) of lot 161, concession 2, Romney and Erie Street North, from Howard and Gladys Moody for $1,000. The first Sunday Mass in Wheatley was celebrated by Father Lanoue in the Kinsmen Community Hall on the afternoon of 11 December 1955. Sunday Mass continued to be offered there until 11 November 1956.

In May 1956, Bishop Cody authorized the building of a church in Wheatley. The architect was Wm. J. Hilliker, the designer was W.C. Crosbie and L.L. Odette, Jr. of Eastern Construction Co. was the contractor. The first sod was turned by Monsignor E. Ambrose O'Donnell, dean of Kent, on 4 July 1956. Bishop Cody blessed the church, constructed of concrete block and brick, on 18 November 1956. It was dedicated to Our Lady of the Blessed Sacrament and attached to St. Charles parish. The first Mass was celebrated by Father Phelan.

Our Lady of the Blessed Sacrament

Father Ignatius Lenckowski (1962-67) was Wheatley's first pastor, effective 3 March 1962. Until the rectory was completed in 1963, his living quarters were located at the back of the church. With the departure of Father Robert A. Van Vynckt (1967-1968) in June 1968, Our Lady of the Blessed Sacrament once again became a mission of St. Charles.

In 1970, however, with 135 Catholic families, Wheatley became a parish for the second time. Father Charles V. McNabb (1970-75) was appointed as pastor on 3 June 1970. In 1971, he was joined by his brother, Monsignor Albert J. McNabb, who had retired from St. Francis Xavier parish in Tilbury several years earlier. During the years of the McNabb brothers, the church and rectory were painted, and the upstairs of the latter was finished and furnished. Being horticulturists, they beautified the grounds with new trees, shrubs and flowers. During the summer months, between 1970 and 1975, the McNabb brothers celebrated Mass at Campers'

Cove, three miles (5.1 k m) east of the church. The sixteenth anniversary of the church was celebrated on 16 November 1972. By this time, the parish had adopted the mission at Mocupe, Peru.

Father Stanley A. Nouvion (1975-85) was appointed pastor on 15 October 1975, at which time there were 150 families. Between 1986 and 1988, the parish spent $220,000 on renovations to the church. Father Silvio Gasparotto (1990-91) unselfishly donated his salary to help pay off the parish debt.

Our Lady of the Blessed Sacrament was slated to be clustered with St. Michael's in Leamington, in 1997, but Father Ugo Rossi (1997-2002) agreed to come to Wheatley. He too was eager to pay off the debt and donated generously to the parish. During the pastorship of Father Francis L. Murphy, Our Lady of the Blessed Sacrament was fully clustered with St. Michael's. Since 2004, Father Patrick W. Fuerth was pastor of the two parishes. Our Lady of the Blessed Sacrament celebrated its fiftieth anniversary on 18 November 2006. The parish was canonically suppressed in January 2007, and its boundaries were absorbed into St. Michael's, Leamington.

Sources: DLA, Parish Files; "Our Lady of the Blessed Sacrament 1956 Anniversary 1981 Wheatley Ontario" [1981]; *Wheatley Journal*, 22 November 1956; 27 November 1975.

5. Sarnia Deanery

Sarnia:

Our Lady of Mercy

The first Mass in the Sarnia area is said to have been offered by Father Louis J. Fluet, in 1827, at the home of Joseph LaForge. In succeeding years the Jesuit missionaries from Sandwich periodically ministered to the needs of Catholics in the area. In 1844, Fathers Pierre Chazelle, SJ, and Dominique du Ranquet, SJ, arrived, ostensibly to visit the French-Canadian and Irish settlers but in reality to attempt a mission among the more than 400 Indians on the nearby reserve. While at Port Sarnia, Father du Ranquet guided the people in building a small frame mission church dedicated to St. Michael the Archangel.

In 1856, Bishop Pinsoneault appointed Dean Thadeus Kirwan as the first pastor of St. Michael's (1856-64). Under his guidance a new and larger frame church, facing London Street, was completed by the summer of 1857 and dedicated to Our Lady of Mercy. The former St. Michael's church building then served as the rectory. Kirwan was especially attentive to the Indians of the area and also worked actively to bring Irish immigrant families into the parish.

Father Edmund B. Kilroy was appointed pastor in 1864 and remained until 1869, but Father Kirwan refused to relinquish the parish until monies owed to him were paid. The matter went to mediation. Meanwhile, for a few Sundays in August 1864 Kirwan continued to celebrate Sunday Mass in the church while Father Kilroy was obliged to offer Mass in the town hall.

A new rectory and schoolhouse were constructed under Father Bartholomew Boubat (1874-77). The new white-brick church, designed by George Wadell of Sarnia, was built during the pastorate of Father Joseph Bayard (1877-97) and originally placed under the protection of St. Joseph. When Bishop Walsh laid the cornerstone on 9 June 1878, however, he placed the parish under the protection of Our Lady of Mercy. Bishop Walsh returned to bless the edifice on 1 February 1880. Its steeple, identified by sailors as Our Lady of Good Hope, was a landmark visible for miles from out on Lake Huron during the

late nineteenth century. Under Father Bayard, the parish cemetery was transferred from the church grounds to its present location further north on Michigan Avenue.

When Monsignor John T. Aylward was pastor (1914-33), the rectory was altered,

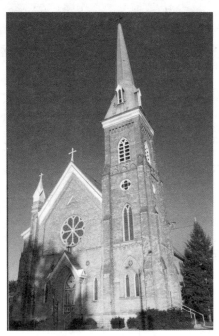

Our Lady of Mercy

the convent was enlarged, a massive redecoration of the church was undertaken in 1923 by Daprato Statuary Co. of Montreal and St. Patrick's high school was opened in 1930. On 24 September 1925, the Diocesan Eucharistic Congress was held at OLM for the first time. Father Lorenzo P. Lowry, a native of Ireland, served as pastor from 1934 until his retirement in 1965. Known affectionately as "Pop" Lowry, this kindly priest, who later became a monsignor, was a product of the Great Depression and noted for his frugality.

As administrator, Father Gerald J. Freker (1965-68) had the altar repositioned and simplified, and the communion railing, some statuary and one of the side altars removed. The parish council was organized in 1966. The large Victorian-style rectory of 1893 was demolished and replaced by a new rectory and office attached to the north transept of the church. Father John P. Boyde, son of the architect John R. Boyde, was the next pastor (1968-76). He began planning for the centenary celebrations of the present church. With Father James F. Blondé as pastor (1976-79), exterior floodlighting was installed to highlight the architectural features of the church during 1978, the year of its centennial. Father

Douglas Boyer (1987-91) oversaw the re-roofing of the church and repairs to the interior, including some re-decoration. Father Daniel A. Rocheleau (1991-2003) made improvements to the rectory and installed a more efficient furnace in the church, new flooring in the nave, a security system and new sound system. He also had the interior repainted.

The 125th anniversary of OLM was celebrated during 2004. Considerable redecoration and renovation of the parish building were undertaken during that year, and the beautification of the grounds was enhanced through the installation of a watering system.

Sources: Victor J. Dudek, *Our Lady of Mercy A Centennial History, 1878-1978* [Sarnia: 1977]. Additional information supplied by Jim Cassin and Father Len Desjardins.

Our Lady of Sorrows

From at least the late 1920s Slovak immigrants were moving into Sarnia. By 1957, there were some ninety-five families. In that year the former Anglican church at 652 Lakeshore Road came on the market and was purchased by the Slovak community for $15,000. It was subsequently resold to the diocese to be used as a Slovak national church. Under the direction of John Chrapko, a Slovak contractor, extensive renovations and additions were made to the church at a cost of $12,000. Frank Durco replastered the interior. John Kukura did the brick work and finished off the front of the church with limestone that he salvaged from the former Sarnia jail. When completed, the building had a seating capacity of 110. Initially, Sunday Mass was celebrated by Father Joseph Dragos, curate of St. Matthew parish, Alvinston, from 1951 until 1964. Father Dragos was ordained a priest in 1936, in his native Czechoslovakia (now Slovakia) and immigrated to Canada after the Second World War.

Our Lady of the Seven Dolours was raised to parish status in 1959 with the arrival of its first pastor, Father Charles D. Moravèik (1959-63), a member of the Order of the Consoler Fathers of Gethsemane of Vienna. Bishop Cody had met him in Israel. When Father Moravèik was in his twenties, he left his native Czechoslovakia for the Holy Land. There, he studied Hebrew and Arabic and was ordained in 1950 in Jerusalem. A teacher in Jordan

Our Lady of Sorrows

for several years, he was a close friend of King Hussein I.

He left Sarnia to establish a junior seminary in Brights Grove in 1963, and was succeeded by Father Hieronym Havlovic, CC (1963-64), also a native of Czechoslovakia and ordained in 1939. He was succeeded by Father Longin I. "Long" Gaborik, CC (1964-66), formerly of St. Anthony of Padua parish in Chatham. Father Gaborik was ordained in 1935 and came to Canada in 1948, after the Communist takeover of Czechoslovakia. Before moving to Chatham he served as pastor of Czech-language Sacred Heart church in Batawa. Father Gaborik died on 5 September 1977. Both he and Father Moravèik, who died on 22 April 2003, were interred in adjoining graves in Chatham.

Father Havlovic served a second term from 1966 to the end of 1970, when he departed for Vienna, Austria. Our Lady of Sorrows church had no pastor until February 1972. During this period Father Jan Sprusansky, SJ, of the Slovak Jesuit mission house in Galt (now Cambridge), came to celebrate Mass on Sundays. Father Havlovic returned and served a third term, from 1972 to 1976, before taking up residence in St. Joseph's parish in Chatham. Father Sprusansky was appointed interim pastor in May 1976. With his departure at the end of 1977, Our Lady of Sorrows was again without a priest. In June 1978, Father George Kadlec, the present pastor, was appointed.

Under the Communist regime in Czechoslovakia, Father Kadlec was refused admittance into a seminary. While in Rome, in 1960, with his soccer team from the city of Trnava, he sought and was granted asylum by the Italian government. Subsequently, he entered a seminary in Rome, was ordained in 1967 and immigrated to Canada in 1970. Before coming to Sarnia, Father Kadlec was pastor of Sts. Cyril and Methodius parish in Windsor. Since August 1980, he has also been pastor of St. Anthony of Padua parish in Chatham, where he has taken up residence. Our Lady of Sorrows parish will close, effective June 2008 or at the retirement of Father Kadlec, whichever comes first.

Sources: Information supplied by Father George Kadlec and Emile Varsava.

Queen of Peace

The small Polish community in Sarnia was augmented by the arrival of some 120 Poles after the Second World War. Most of these newcomers joined the local branch of the Polish Alliance of Canada. A Polish hall, which served the social and patriotic needs of the community, was built in 1951. Pope Pius XII's encyclical *Exsul Familia* recommended the establishment of national parishes to meet the needs of immigrants scattered around the globe as a consequence of the War. Thus, the Polish community was able to obtain Bishop Cody's permission to establish a Polish mission in Sarnia.

Queen of Peace

Father Franciszek A. "Francis" Bardel came from Orchard Lake, Michigan, on 17 August 1952, to celebrate Mass in Our Lady of Mercy school and continued to serve the Polish mission in Sarnia on Saturdays and Sundays until 1956. A church committee was formed to prepare plans, raise funds, select a church site and obtain Bishop Cody's permission to establish a parish. In 1957, the former Lutheran church on College Street, was purchased, remodelled and decorated to serve as a place of worship. An icon of Our Lady of Częstochowa, sculpted by Mrs. Zofia Trzcinska-Kaminska and blessed in Warsaw, Poland, by Cardinal Stefan Wyszynski, was placed in the church. The building was blessed on 4 May 1958 by Bishop Cody, who was assisted by Fathers Bardel and Joseph Pucka.

Father Bardel had requested Father Pucka to replace him in order that he might return to Poland permanently.

Ordained in Poland, in June 1939, Father Pucka spent most of the Second World War in a slave-labour camp in Dachau, Germany. On Christmas Eve, 1944, a German-Catholic priest was permitted to visit the camp, and at the risk of his own life, he gave Father Pucka some altar breads. Thus, at 3:00 Christmas morning, he silently celebrated Mass on his bunk and the Blessed Eucharist was passed quietly from bed to bed in the large barracks. It was the first and only time during his imprisonment that Father Pucka was able to celebrate Mass and receive Communion.

Now, more than thirteen years later, with Father Pucka as its first resident priest (1958-81), the Polish mission in Sarnia was raised to parish status and dedicated to Our Lady Queen of Poland.

In 1960, four large lots on Rosedale Avenue in the north end of the city were purchased as the future parish centre. A parish rectory was built in 1961. Seven years later, diocesan permission was granted to build a new church with the proviso that the parish become an ethnic-territorial parish and be renamed Our Lady Queen of Peace. Father D. Kenney McMahon officiated at the sod-turning ceremony on 20 June 1969, and Bishop Carter blessed the new church on 14 December 1969.

During the pastorate of Father Zbigniew Rodzinka, CSMA (1989-98), the loans were paid off in 1997 and work commenced on the remodelling of the church, according to the design prepared by Roman Kuczma of London. A new floor, pulpit and altar were installed. On the sanctuary wall, behind the altar, was placed a scene of Golgotha, sculpted by Mrs. M. Filarski of Windsor. The icon of Our Lady of Częstochowa was moved to the left of the altar, with the tabernacle on the right. A new pipe organ was installed in the choir loft at the upper rear of the church, and the choir room was furnished.

In later years, the parish was made up of those of

both Polish and non-Polish origin. This was reflected in the fact that two of the three weekend Masses were in English and weekday Masses are celebrated in both Polish and English. Queen of Peace parish was canonically suppressed effective June 2007, and was re-established as Queen of Peace Polish Catholic Community, with Father Rodzinka as priest-chaplain.

Sources: DLA, Parish Files. Additional information supplied by Jack Boyde.

Sacred Heart

In 1948, Bishop Kidd commissioned Father T. Gordon Dill to establish a parish from the northern part of Our Lady of Mercy Parish, in what was then Sarnia Township. In April, fourteen lots were purchased on Lecaron Avenue for $1,400. Kenwick-on-the-Lake Dance Hall in Bright's Grove was rented for Sunday Mass from July to Labour Day. Meanwhile, Father Dill was living in rented quarters on Colborne Road.

Bishop Cody turned the sod and blessed the ground for the basement church of the newly establish Sacred Heart parish on 5 September 1949. By the following month, Sunday Mass was being offered in the new four-room Sacred Heart school. Meanwhile, work on the church continued. On Palm Sunday in April 1950, Mass was celebrated in the new church, located on the south side of Charlesworth Avenue. In February 1951, Father Dill was able to move into the new rectory, adjacent to the church. He was succeeded by Father J. James E. Kelly (1951-56) in June.

The interior of the basement church was gutted by fire on 16 January 1959, and once again church services were held in Sacred Heart school. Meanwhile, owing to the rapidly increasing Catholic population within the parish, thirteen lots were purchased in 1956, on the northwest corner of Charlesworth Drive and Lecaron Avenue, for a church of slab construction with an attached rectory. The sod-turning ceremony was held on 7 September 1958 in the presence of Bishop Cody. The opening Mass was celebrated in the new building on 1 November 1959, and the former basement church was refurbished for use as a parish hall.

On 1 August 1965, Father P.J. McHenry of the Scarboro Foreign Missions was ordained by Bishop Carter at Sacred Heart Church. Father D. Kenney McMahon (1965-82) remodelled the sanctuary in 1968 and opened a new rectory, attached to the church, on 21 June 1968. The old rectory then became the residence of the parish's first full-time custodians, Arnold Bongers and his wife. In the summer of 1974, the old parish hall was demolished in order to expand the schoolyard and to provide for parking, and the old rectory was moved north of the new one. On 4 December 1976, Father Paul J. Beck, formerly Brother Arthur Beck of the Brothers of St. Louis, was ordained in Sacred Heart Church by Bishop Carter.

Sacred Heart

Between 1962 and 1986, three parishioners of Sacred Heart were honoured with the title Knight of the Order of St. Gregory the Great. They were Gregory Hogan (1962), Ray Wyrzykowski (1978), and Joseph Pace (1986). Gregory A. Hogan school was opened in 1978 in honour of an individual who was an active leader within his parish and the city of Sarnia. Ray Wyrzykowski's "dynamic, hardworking enthusiasm extended beyond the parish to the community, the diocese, and even Third World countries." In 1986, together with John Barnfield, he established Rayjon, a charitable organization to help the poor of Haiti. Twice a year, groups composed of young people, adults and medical professionals travel to Haiti to assist with ongoing projects. According to Bishop Sherlock, "No one individual in the London Diocese has worked harder and achieved more, for the true goal of Catholic Education" than Joseph Pace.

Meanwhile, Father Paul E.F. Crunican (1982-87) and Sister Patricia Hogan, CSJ, the pastoral minister, initiated the RCIA program. Stella Burns has been pastoral minister from 1984 to the present. Father Thomas J. Lever (1988-98), a native of Sarnia, was spiritual advisor to the local Cursillo movement and established both the Stephen and bereavement ministries, staffed by trained members of the laity. Mary Valiquet introduced youth ministry in 1990, and her work has been continued by Cathy Smith, from 1993 to 2001, and by Joanna Giresi, from 2001 to the present. Father Leonard G. Desjardins, who succeeded Father Lever in 1998, is best known for his love of liturgy and creative decoration of the sanctuary for various liturgical celebrations.

In 2006, the parish consisted of 1,385 families, forty-eight ministries, three elementary schools and two high schools.

Sources: [Anne Hummel], "Historical Highlights of Sacred Heart," (1999); Pauline Dixon, "History of Sacred Heart Parish, Sarnia, Ontario: 1948-1979" [n.d.]. Additional information supplied by Father Len Desjardins and Larry Scully.

St. Benedict

In the late 1950s, land was purchased in the Coronation Park subdivision by both the diocese of London and the Sarnia separate school board for a church and school. In 1959, Father Raymond J. Groome was appointed pastor of the new parish and found temporary residence at St. Peter's rectory. Church services were held in the St. Patrick high school gym. Father Groome had his own chalice but relied on the goodwill of other city and county parishes to supply him with such items as a temporary tabernacle, vestments, altar candles, ciborium and a processional cross. The new parish comprised former members of St. Peter, St. Joseph and Our Lady of Mercy parishes. The first parish bulletin appeared on 1 November. Parish branches of CWL, Knights of Columbus and St. Vincent de Paul Society were formed in rapid succession. In December, the majority of parishioners voted for a cruciform design for the new church. The architectural firm of Blackwell and Hagarty of London drew up plans for a church, rectory and parish hall that would cost $190,000. Curran and Herridge of Sarnia were general contractors.

Monsignor Joseph A. Cook, assisted by Father Groome, partook in the official sod-turning ceremony on 18 June 1961. Monsignor Andrew P. Mahoney blessed and laid the cornerstone on 15 October 1961, and the first Mass in the new

St. Benedict

church was celebrated that Christmas Eve. Bishop Cody blessed St. Benedict's church on 29 January 1962. The large wooden cross suspended from the ceiling in the sanctuary was a gift of the general contractors. The parish room extended to the west behind the sanctuary and led to the rectory on the north. In 1964, the position of the altar was changed to allow the celebrant to face the congregation. It was about this time that Father Michael O'Connor, CP, conducted the parish's first mission. Meanwhile, in September 1961, the custom of having lay readers was introduced. The statue of St. Benedict was installed in front of the church, on the north side, on 3 September 1967.

The church interior was remodelled in 1973. A new parish centre and foyer on the south side of the church was built in 1993. The old parish hall is now used to accommodate the breakfast program for pupils at St. Benedict's school, the children's liturgy and other activities. A five-year capital improvements program, between 1999 and 2004, financed a new roof for the church, repairs to the parking lot surface, a driveway behind the rectory and upgrades to the interior of the church. Air conditioning was installed in both the church and rectory. In order to accommodate weddings and funerals and provide much-needed space in front of the sanctuary, seating capacity was reduced from 620 to 520 in 2005. The original Stations of the Cross have been retained. On the railing of the choir lift is a mosaic of St. Benedict, flanked by wooden statues of St. Joseph and Mary and the Child Jesus.

From the beginnings of the parish in 1959 until July 2005, the parish has recorded 3,555 baptisms, 3,352 first communions, 2,960 confirmations, 1,143 marriages, and 842 deaths. During the same period, St. Benedict's had grown from 378 to 1,500 families. Father Groome was succeeded as pastor by Fathers Adrian P. Jansen, Joseph J. Padelt, Donald G. Allaster and Richard G. Dales. Father Richard K. Janisse, who arrived in 1996, had been an assistant pastor at St. Benedict's between 1975 and 1980.

Sources: St Benedict parish records. Additional information supplied by Angie Gibson.

St. Joseph

With the increase of the Catholic population in Sarnia, the Albert Street Presbyterian church property was purchased for $925, on 16 May 1904, and used as both a church and school. This South Ward church, also known as the Little Church, became a mission of Our Lady of Mercy parish and was dedicated to St. Joseph, on 28 August 1904, by Bishop McEvoy. Father Joseph Kennedy, pastor of Our Lady of Mercy, superintended the installation of new pews and rails that were made by Blonde Bros. of Chatham. Monsignor John T. Aylward, another pastor of Our Lady of Mercy, put a new roof on the church.

In 1923, St. Joseph's was elevated to parish status with Father Thomas J. McCarthy as its first pastor. Although property at the corner of Stuart and Devine streets was purchased in 1901, for a church, one was not built until 1928. Designed by the architect John R. Boyde of Windsor, and constructed of red and brown tinted brick, it measured 120 feet (36.6 m) in length and 65 feet (19.8 m) in width. The bell weighed 1,280 pounds (580.6 kg) and cost $1,000. It was cast in Baltimore, Maryland, and blessed by Monsignor Denis O'Connor, vicar general of the diocese, who later became bishop of Peterborough. The first Mass was celebrated in the new church at midnight on Christmas Day 1928. During Father McCarthy's tenure, a school, rectory and convent were built. Father McCarthy, who was an overseas chaplain in both world wars, was promised that St. Joseph's would be his parish until he retired. He died

St. Joseph

suddenly at a hockey game on 21 February 1950, and he is one of many priests of the diocese interred in the priests' plot in St. Peter's cemetery in London.

Monsignor Francis J. Brennan (1950-53) succeeded Father McCarthy. In 1950, the two matching side altars were imported from Italy. Monsignor Brennan was followed as pastor by Fathers Joseph L. O'Rourke (1953-55), Bernard R. Laverty (1955-68), John J. Devine (1968-80) and later priests.

St. Joseph's church is noted for its beautiful stained-glass windows, the painting of the ascension of Christ in the apse, and its white carrara marble altars, altar railings and baptismal font. These remain as a testimony to the sacrifices made by previous generations of parishioners.

The seventy-fifth anniversary of the present church was celebrated in 2003 in the presence of Bishop Fabbro, together with many priests and sisters who had served in the parish. Over the years several young men from St. Joseph's became priests: Fathers Joseph F. Paquette, Carl G. Walsh, Francis J. Walsh, Lester A. Wemple, T. Lawrence McManus, James F. Summers, F. John Hurley and Thomas J. Lever. All, with the exception of Fathers Hurley and Lever (ordained in 1955 and 1957, respectively), are now deceased and represent the older generation of priests.

On 30 June 2007, St. Joseph's was amalgamated into Our Lady of Mercy parish, with its church remaining open as a second worship site within the parish.

Sources: St. Joseph parish records.

St. Peter

The post-war growth of Sarnia led to the establishment in 1949 of St. Peter's parish. Its territory was formed from what had been the northern and eastern boundaries of Our Lady of Mercy parish. Father Aloysius L.J. Nolan was appointed pastor of St. Peter's in the summer of 1949 and remained until 1959. The church, erected on the corner of Maxwell and Rayburne streets, was blessed by Bishop Cody in September 1949. That fall also saw the construction of a school and rectory.

St. Peter

On 14 May 1954, only the tabernacle and altar escaped damage by a fire in the church. Undeterred, Father Nolan had a big top tent erected, and on 23 May, sixty young people received their first holy communion. The new church, at 756 Maxwell Street, was blessed on 22 February 1955. By now the number of families had increased from the initial eighty to 400. In 1956, a convent was built, just west of Oxford Street, for the Irish Ursuline sisters who taught at St. Peter's school for ten years.

In order to meet the needs of the Italian community, Bishop Cody invited the Society of St. Charles (the Scalabrini Fathers) to minister to the Italians at St. Peter's parish. The first to arrive, in December 1957, was Father Angelo J. Calandra, CS, and henceforth a Mass was celebrated in Italian every Sunday. In 1959, Father Calandra (1959-71) succeeded Father Nolan as pastor. It fell to the former to guide the parish through the liturgical changes of the 1960s. Also, during this time, an Italian CWL, St. Frances Cabrini, was established, in addition to the existing English-speaking CWL.

Father Calandra's successor, Father Nicholas Marro, CS (1971-80), was a gifted homilist and strong communicator. He developed visitation teams to local seniors' homes and coordinated events for the youth. He was an active spiritual leader of Cursillo and, together with Rev. Dennis Clarke, pastor of St. Andrew's Presbyterian Church, was instrumental in the development of inter-denominational Cursillo. The parish's first pastoral assistant, Marjorie Scully, was hired during the pastorate of Father Emil Donanzan, CS (1981-87). She built an RCIA program and developed sacramental preparation programs. Meanwhile, in co-operation with the rector of Canon Davis Anglican church, Father Donanzan co-founded a chaplaincy for seafarers visiting the city. Many renovations in the church and rectory took place during the pastorship of Father Louis Piran, CS (1987-91), who had served as associate pastor from 1983. Father Piran was succeeded by Father Ermet "Herm" Nazzani, CS (1991-1994). Father Leno Santi, CS (1994-97), is especially remembered for his innovative Christmas scenes, one being a replica of the new railway tunnel, using mirrors to see the Nativity at the tunnel's end. The last of the Scalabrini fathers to serve at St. Peter's was Father Albert Corradin, CS (1997-2000), and his assistant Father Guerrino Ziliotto, CS. In 1999, the parishioners celebrated the fiftieth anniversary of St. Peter's and its selection as the home parish for the deanery-wide Perpetual Adoration chapel.

The parish has produced three priests. The late Father Richard Dochstader was ordained a Scalabrinian priest in 1975 and later became a diocesan priest in Chicago. Father Brian Christie was ordained for the Companions of the Cross in 2005. And Father Tomasso V. Ferrera was ordained on 29 April 2006 for the diocese of London.

In 2003, under the leadership of Fathers Terence W. Runstedler and Alessandro M. Costa, OMI, St. Peter's and St. Thomas Aquinas became clustered parishes.

On 30 June 2007, St. Peter's was canonically suppressed. Its boundaries were absorbed into St. Benedict's and Our Lady of Mercy parishes.

Sources: St. Peter's Parish Records. Additional information provided by Jim Lathen, Larry Scully and Gerry Tobin.

St. Thomas Aquinas

During the Second World War, the Canadian government established a Crown company, the Polymer Corporation, to manufacture synthetic rubber. Owing to a shortage of labourers, a large number of French-Canadians, most of whom were Catholic, settled in Sarnia to work in the plants. Consequently, Father Thomas J. McCarthy, pastor of St. Joseph's parish, and his curates, began to celebrate Sunday Mass in the Polymer dining hall. The community was located some two miles (3.2 k m) south of Sarnia and became known as Blue Water. In 1951, it was annexed by Sarnia. In the meantime, the educational and spiritual needs of the local Catholics were provided, through Father McCarthy's efforts, with the construction of St. Thomas Aquinas school-chapel on Kent Street in 1944. Because the school was bilingual and initially taught by the Sisters of St. Joseph, it attracted a very large number of French-Canadian families.

St. Thomas Aquinas

Soon, the pastor of St. Joseph's was overwhelmed with the number of Catholics in his parish, and Bishop Kidd appointed Father J. Césaire Levacque as administrator of a new parish in Blue Water, to be known as St. Thomas Aquinas. He arrived in October 1944. His successor, Father Raymond G. Forton, arrived as administrator on 1 July 1945, and he completed the rectory on the corner of Windsor Avenue and Kent Street. Unfortunately, on 24 October 1945, the school was destroyed by fire. For the next eight years, a Polymer bunkhouse served as the chapel and as classrooms until a new school was built. The first Mass was at midnight on 25 December 1945. Four years later, four Masses were celebrated in the parish on Sundays, and, on 25 June 1950, Father Ulysee A. Lefaive was appointed as the parish's first curate.

About 1953, seven acres (2.8 ha) of land were purchased in the Coronation Park subdivision for the church and school. Knowland & Stevens was selected as the architectural firm. Bishop Cody turned the first sod, on 14 May 1953; he also blessed the parish's Jacques Cartier Cooperative Store and the new offices of the Credit Union. The materials for the prefabricated church, patterned after St. Ursula church in Chatham, were also supplied by Gerry Supply and Lumber Co. Limited of London. On 6 December 1953, the new church was blessed.

Its estimated cost was $97,000. By this time, however, Blue Water was hemmed in by the petrochemical industries on three sides and the Sarnia Indian Reserve on the fourth. It had been agreed that the entire Blue Water community would be relocated in another part of the city, but no action was immediately taken.

On 1 January 1960, the expropriation of Blue Water by the city of Sarnia took place. Families began leaving the community and their homes were purchased by the petrochemical companies. Father Clement W. Janisse was appointed pastor in February 1962 and supervised the transition of the parish to a new location. On 27 May 1963, it was decreed that a new church, rectory and hall would be built in St. Albans Park. William E. Andrews of Sarnia was the architect. The last Mass at the Blue Water site was celebrated on 14 December 1963, and the next day, the first Mass was offered in the new church. It was officially opened and blessed on 15 March 1964. The parish was unique: it was both a territorial and national parish and completely bilingual.

Effective 29 June 2007, St. Thomas Aquinas parish was designated as the Francophone parish of Sarnia and Lambton, under the name of St-Thomas D'Aquin. The territory was absorbed into Sacred Heart parish.

Sources: DLA, Parish Files; "*Eglise St. Thomas D'Aquin* St. Thomas Aquinas Church Sarnia Ontario 1965"; "*La Paroisse Saint-Thomas-d'Aquin de Sarnia,*" *Newsletter of the Diocese of London,* no. 94 (Advent/Christmas: 2004), 11. Additional information supplied by Rose-Marie Shoniker.

Alvinston: St. Matthew

In the early 1850s, a group of Irish-Catholic immigrants settled on the second concession of Brooke Township. They were visited occasionally by priests from Chatham. When St. Ignatius parish in Bothwell was established in 1873, Brooke became one of its stations. At the time, Mass was celebrated in various homes in "Little Ireland," some seven miles (11.5 k m) southwest of the present Alvinston, and in the home of Edward Donnelly in the village. By 1877, the Irish settlers were pressing for the erection of a church in their community, and, after much heated discussion, the choice of Alvinston won out. Frank Wagner donated land for the church site on the west side of River Street. A church, built of brick fired in the local Alvinston brickyard, was erected under the direction of Father Michael Magrath, then the curate at Bothwell. Illuminated with kerosene lamps and heated by wood-burning stoves, it was solemnly consecrated by Bishop Walsh on 12 January 1879.

St. Matthew

On 21 February 1886, the Alvinston mission was detached from Bothwell and attached to Holy Angels parish in St. Thomas. In 1895, property for a Catholic cemetery was purchased from James Cook adjoining the north side of the Alvinston public cemetery. This cemetery was consecrated by Bishop O'Connor on 17 June 1896. Previously, interments had been in Wardsville. Meanwhile, in April 1894, St. Matthew's became a mission of St. Peter's cathedral.

By 1914, St. Matthew's was again a mission of St. Thomas, and in 1928, it was a mission of Our Lady Help of Christians in Watford, with Father E. Raphael Glavin (1928-39) as the first pastor. Father Leon M. Blondell (1942-52), however, chose to reside in Alvinston, where he moved in November 1942, thus elevating St. Matthew's to parish status. The shrine, dedicated to Our Lady of Fatima, was blessed by Bishop Cody on 2 October

1949. Meanwhile, between 1937 and 1943, Father Ladislaus Segers, OFM Cap, pastor of St. Mary's, Blenheim, came to Alvinston twice a year to preach to the Slovaks at a Sunday Mass. He also presided over Slovak burials. Father Francis A. Dostal, SJ, stationed in Batawa and, from 1949, in Chatham, succeeded Father Ladislaus in this role, until 1951, when Father Joseph Dragos, curate at St. Matthew's, was sent to minister to the Slovaks of the area.

During the pastorship of Father Laurent P. Lacharité (1952-55), the rectory was further improved and refurnished. On New Year's Day, 1955, however, all but the four walls of the church were destroyed by fire. Young Steve Janicek risked his life by climbing through a window to rescue the Blessed Sacrament. Church services were then conducted in the nearby Slovak Cultural Home. After St. Matthew's was rebuilt, it was decorated by Benny Ryall of Windsor. Bishop Cody blessed the church on 30 June 1957. Also in 1957, the rectory, which had been purchased in 1943, was exchanged for Jim Esselment's residence next to the church, and three rooms were added to the rear of the building.

June 1969 saw the appointment of Father Bernard A. Robert (1969-73) as pastor of the twinned parishes of St. Matthew's and Our Lady Help of Christians. He selected Watford as his place of residence. Whereas two Masses were celebrated at St. Matthew's in the mid-1960s, only one was offered on Sundays by 1971. Beginning with the pastorship of Father Michael J. O'Brien (1989-2003), St. Matthew's has become very much involved in the ecumenical movement in the community, which is noted for its Ecumenical Canada Day celebrations, Ash Wednesday services, and in particular its "Cross Walks" on Good Friday. St. Matthew's, which celebrated its 125th anniversary in 2004, was canonically suppressed on 1 November 2005, and the church was closed on 30 June 2007.

Sources: DLA; Ralph Hubert Dignan and Joseph P. Finn, "A History of the Diocese of London," edited by Guy Alden (unpublished manuscript, 2002). Additional information supplied by Pat Triest and Father John Van Damme.

Baby's Point: Sacred Heart

Local tradition claims that the first Catholic church in Lambton County was erected in 1827 when the local French-Canadian lumber merchant François Baby decided to build a church on Baby's Point, a little to the south of the present Port Lambton. It also claims that this church was constructed of squared logs with a brick facade, and that Bishop Macdonell administered confirmation at Baby's Point in 1836, at which time Chief Wawanosh and many other Indians were confirmed.

The continuous history of Sacred Heart, however, begins with the abandonment of the Sacred Heart mission on Walpole Island and the establishment of a new mission of the same name at Baby's Point in 1849. With the help of neighbouring settlers, Father Dominique du Ranquet, SJ, and Brother Joseph Jennesseaux, SJ, constructed a combination church and residence. It is more likely that this was the building constructed of hewn logs with a brick facade. In August 1850, Father du Ranquet and Brother Jennesseaux were transferred to Holy Cross mission on Manitoulin Island. The Jesuits continued in charge of the St. Clair missions until August 1852 when Father John J. O'Doherty replaced them. But he deserted his post the following year, and the missions were attached to Sandwich. This arrangement lasted until the summer of 1854, when Father Michel Moncoq arrived. He had charge of the Indian mission field from Point Pelee and Malden to Penetanguishene. Tragically, this dedicated missionary drowned in the St. Clair River while returning from a sick call at Algonac, Michigan, on the evening of 1 January 1856. The body was found on 23 July 1856 and interred at Baby's Point. On 11 June 1878, it was transferred to a crypt in the new church at Port Lambton.

Between the death of Father Moncoq and the transfer of jurisdiction to Dean Thadeus Kirwan of Sarnia, Father Jean Raynel, SJ, of St. Peter's in Tilbury, served the missions along the St. Clair River. Father Kirwan arrived at Baby's Point in early November 1856 and continued to minister to the faithful in the area until the arrival of Father Bartholomew Boubat (1860-64). With the appointment of Father Boubat to the St. Clair

missions, on 1 April 1860, Baby's Point was served first from Mooretown and then from Corunna. On 21 May 1866, during the pastorship of Father Paul Andrieux of St. Joseph's in Corunna, Bishop Pinsoneault confirmed fifty-seven persons at Baby's Point. After the departure of Father Andrieux, and at the request of Bishop Walsh, Father Edmund B. Kilroy of Sarnia visited Baby's Point on 19-20 January 1868, and he made three more visits between February and June 1868. Father F. Gauthier (1868-69) took charge of St. Joseph's on 20 July 1868 and periodically visited Baby's Point. So too did his successor, Father Ferdinand A.J. Ouellet (1869-73). By this time, the old church had become too small for the Catholic population and was also showing its age. The newly built mission church in the village of Sombra some four miles (6.5 k m) upriver, was dedicated to St. Mary in June 1871. Although this did not lead to the complete disuse of the church at Baby's Point, the building of the new church at Port Lambton, also dedicated to the Sacred Heart of Jesus, when Father Bernard J. Watters of Corunna (1873-80) was pastor, certainly did.

It is said that the little French church was later moved to Port Lambton and used as a blacksmith shop. But it is also claimed that some of the stone or concrete salvaged from the church was used in a breakwater along the banks of the river at the Point.

Sources: DLA, Parish Files; Maxine Devin, *Our Parish History Sacred Heart Port Lambton, Ontario St. John's Sombra, Ontario 1880-1980* [n.d.].

Bright's Grove: St. Michael

Like its mother parish, Sacred Heart in Sarnia, St. Michael's has its origins in Kenwick-on-the-Lake Dance Hall, which was first rented for Sunday Masses in June 1948. For the next several years, from July through Labour Day, it served as a mission church of Sacred Heart. After the dance hall was destroyed by fire in the mid-1960s, services were held until 1967 in Our Lady of Sorrows Minor Seminary on Lakeshore Road, which was run by the Consoler Fathers of Gethsemane. Thereafter, Sunday Mass was celebrated in St. John-in-the-Wilderness Anglican church. As soon as the present St. Michael's school opened in 1985, weekend Masses were held in its gymnasium. When Bishop Sherlock came to bless the school, he announced that a new parish, also dedicated to St. Michael, would be established.

Masses continued to be held in the gym: the basketball hoops were covered, the portable altar was rolled out, and chairs were arranged around the altar. After the last Mass, everything was put away until the next Sunday. A great sense of community was built

St. Michael

on this need to transform the school gymnasium into a sacred space for weekend worship. The volunteer time of many parishioners was required to do this work. This community spirit was much in evidence during fund-raising time for the new church. There were cabaret nights, fashion shows and a calendar lottery, the format of which has been adopted in many other places.

Father James M. Higgins (1986-92) arrived on 23 May 1986 as St. Michael's first pastor, and Mrs. Janet Oliver was hired on 2 September 1986 as pastoral minister. Sunday Masses continued to be celebrated at St. Michael's school and weekday Masses in the basement of the rectory.

J.P. Thompson & Associates of Windsor was selected as the architectural firm; Peter Kapteyn was chosen as the general contractor; the ground-breaking ceremony for the church was held on 19 April 1990; and the new $1.6 million structure, with a seating capacity for about 656, was dedicated by Bishop Sherlock on 3 February 1991. James Marshall of Medicine Hat, Alberta, crafted the central Crucifix and Stations of the Cross, a notable aspect of the church's interior. When they were installed, each class from the school came to hear a presentation by Canada's only brick sculptor. Behind the crucifix was placed a time capsule containing photographs, contemporary news items, paintings, poetry and memorabilia provided by the children. The four stained-glass windows were designed and fabricated by Father Graham R. Keep while he was a seminarian at St. Peter's seminary. The stone in the present altar contains the relics of two martyrs – St. Clare and St. Prosper. It was consecrated by Monsignor J. Austin Roney on 12 August 1955 and

transferred from the portable altar used at the school to the permanent altar in the new church.

Father John C. Van Damme succeeded Father Higgins in October 1992. The next pastor was Father Gary G. Ducharme, who came in August 1995. Father Iheanyi Enwerem, OP, from Nigeria, assumed the duties of parish administrator in February 2004, and was succeeded as pastor by Father Joseph S. Snyder in August 2006.

A distinct feature of the parish is its high percentage of young families. When the church was first opened only five people who registered were over sixty-five years of age. In the ensuing years, the demographics have changed, and the congregation at St. Michael's now has people of all ages. St. Michael's prides itself on being a welcoming parish, and this is reflected in its twenty-six different organizations and committees.

Sources: Father J.M. Higgins, "St. Michael's, Bright's Grove," *Newsletter of the Diocese of London*, no. 44 (Advent/Christmas: 1990), 16. Additional information provided by Janet Oliver.

Corunna: St. Joseph

The church at Mooretown, erected in the 1840s, had been primarily an Indian mission. By 1860, however, and with European settlers in the majority, it regained parish status with the appointment of Father Bartholomew Boubat (1860-64). Because the building was now too small for the congregation, plans were made for a new church. But the more numerous Catholics in the northern part of Moore Township argued that since the southern part would never be anything but a swampland, the new church should be erected at Corunna. Bishop Pinsoneault agreed.

St. Joseph's in Corunna was dedicated by Bishop Pinsoneault on 21 September 1862. Meanwhile, by 10 June 1861, the settlers had claimed the remains of their loved ones from the Mooretown cemetery and reinterred them in the new St. Joseph's cemetery. Of course, a few unidentified graves were missed. In 1863, Father Boubat first convened classes in the church's sacristy until a log schoolhouse was erected the following year on a parishioner's farm. This served as the parish school, some two miles (3.2 k m) from the church, until 1907. Bishop Pinsoneault confirmed forty-one persons at St. Joseph's on 23 May 1866, two days after he had confirmed a larger number at Baby's Point mission.

The first rectory at Corunna was built in 1873 during the pastorate of Father Bernard J. Watters (1873-80). As the St. Clair missions to the south were still part of St. Joseph's parish, Father Watters often travelled as far south as Baby's Point, on the little steamer *Hiawatha* that plied the waters between Sarnia and Wallaceburg. In 1880, the Indian Reserve to the north in Sarnia Township was detached from St. Joseph's and given to the Sarnia parish. When Father John J. Ronan was pastor (1882-86), the frame church received a stone foundation and the interior walls were plastered and painted. The building was re-opened and rededicated on 9 December 1883. Father Ronan also devised a water system for the rectory. An 810-pound (367.4 kg) bell was installed in the church's tower while Father James G. Mugan (1889-1901) was pastor. Bishop O'Connor blessed the bell on 10 June 1891. It was named Annie Roberts, Maud Stanley and Jennie McLaughlin after the three little girls who had collected a considerable sum of money towards its purchase. In January 1901, Father Mugan reported that there were thirty-six families attending St. Joseph's church and the revenues for 1900 were $517.00. He also noted that the parish included the mission at Courtright and a station at Brigden, ten miles (16.1 k m) to the east.

Father John P. Brennan (1901-05) directed the building of the present rectory in 1901. Father Gerald J. Labelle (1913-26) oversaw renovations to the church, improvements to the cemetery and the establishment of a separate school. Monsignor Francis J. Brennan (1949-50) was largely responsible for the planning and completion of the school building, which at present serves as the parish centre. Major renovations to the church took place in 2000 when Father Dikran G. Islemeci was pastor (1996-

St. Joseph

2002). The entire church was raised and concrete footings were poured for the new foundation. The original wooden beams that supported the floor were replaced by steel beams. The building was extended 25 feet (7.6 m), thereby increasing the seating capacity to 350. The parishioners donated and installed new stained-glass windows. At the same time, the integrity of the board-and-batter exterior was maintained because St. Joseph's is considered one of the few churches of this style on the continent. As has been the case since 1862, its doors continue to open on to the St. Clair River.

Sources: Father Gregory M. Blonde et al., *History of The Church of Our Lady Help of Christians Wallaceburg, Ontario 1878 -1978* (Wallaceburg: [1978]); Ralph Hubert Dignan and Joseph P. Finn, "A History of the Diocese of London," edited by Guy Alden (unpublished manuscript, 2002). Additional information provided by the parish office.

Courtright: St. Charles

The relocation of the church at Corunna from Mooretown meant that the parishioners in the southern part of Moore Township had to walk an extra four miles (6.4 k m) to attend Mass. Some people went to St. Clair's parish on the Michigan side, especially in winter, and after the opening of St. Mary's (St. John's) in 1871, some trekked southward to Sombra. Fortunately, these extreme hardships were offset by the zealousness and understanding of a pastor who was aware of the sacrifices made by his flock. On occasion he visited the various neighbourhoods on horseback, carrying his vestments, altar stone and sacred vessels, and celebrated Mass in private homes. As soon as the priest arrived at a home, usually in the afternoon, the children of the family would notify the neighbours, who would pass the word along. Those living close by came to confession in the evening, and those who lived at a distance arrived early the next morning.

The construction of the St. Clair Division of the Canada Southern Railway, passing through Brigden to the St. Clair River, brought Courtright into existence in the 1870s. Mass was celebrated in the village's English Hall in the 1880s. By this time, however, the faithful of the area were clamoring for a church of their own. Charles Bedard and William Cassin took their pastor at Corunna, Father Charles E. McGee (1886-88), on a tour of the southern portion of the township in order to obtain subscriptions for the building of a church. The result was the construction of a church in Courtright. A church, named in honour of St. Charles Borromeo, one of the chief architects of the decrees of the Council of Trent, was dedicated on 10 June 1888. Because Bishop Walsh was in Europe at the time, Dean Edmund B. Kilroy of Stratford took his place at the dedication. He was assisted by Father James Walsh of London and Father Philip J. Gnam of Wyoming. Exactly three years later, on 10 June 1891, Bishop O'Connor was present at St. Charles to confirm fifty-seven members.

In 1900, the revenues collected from the congregation, numbering forty-five families, was $877.02. Father James G. Mugan, pastor at Corunna (1891-1901), celebrated Mass at Courtright every second Sunday, on Easter, Pentecost and Christmas, and on some Holy Days, by 1901. On his departure, he estimated the value of the church building at $2,300.

Since its founding, St. Charles has continued to be a mission of Corunna, with the exception of a short while in the 1950s, when Father Paul R. Sargewitz was appointed pastor at Courtright. He returned, however, to St. Joseph's as pastor and remained there until 1960. His successor at Corunna, Father Cameron F. McMartin (1960-73), did not endear himself to the parishioners at St. Charles when he publicly stated that the Courtright people

St. Charles

did not deserve a church because they did not support it sufficiently to maintain it. On the other hand, the members of St. Charles mission believed that all the money was being spent in Corunna and, as a result, their church was unfairly neglected. Thus, on his arrival as pastor of St. Joseph's in June 1976, Father Paul D. Milne saw it as his duty to begin "a simple program to restore some dignity to St. Charles Church." Using donated labour and $15,000, he supervised a number of renovations that made the church more presentable and consequently uplifted the spirit of the congregation. On the eve of the church's 100th anniversary in 1988, the people again donated their labour, this time to make a few minor changes at minimal cost.

The mission of St. Charles, Courtright was canonically closed, effective June 2007. As was the case some 120 years earlier, the faithful are part of St. Joseph's in Corunna.

Sources: DLA, Parish Files; Ralph Hubert Dignan and Joseph P. Finn, "A History of the Diocese of London," edited by Guy Alden (unpublished manuscript, 2002).

Forest: St. Christopher

Tradition has it that French missionaries visited this area in the seventeenth century and that the ruins of a large building, some 60 feet by 40 feet (18.3 m by 12.2 m) with a stone fireplace and chimney, which was discovered along the Ausable River in the 1820s, belonged to the Jesuit mission of St. François. Be that as it may, in the nineteenth century, prior to the mid-1850s, local missionaries from Sandwich periodically visited local Catholics. Between 1854 and 1855, Father Michel Moncoq, the first pastor at Mooretown, ministered to this area. With the establishment of St. Michael's parish, now Our Lady of Mercy, in Port Sarnia, the Catholics of the Forest area had Dean Thadeus Kirwan (1856-64) as their priest, and then Kirwan's successor, Father Edmund B. Kilroy (1864-69). Mass was said to have been celebrated monthly in the homes of James and Bridgette Hubbard and John Phelan and in the railway freight shed in Forest. Under

Father Kilroy's direction, the first Catholic church in Forest was built in 1866, on lot 5, West James Street. It is now the corner of James and Jefferson streets and runs through to Washington Street. This property, owned by William Stacey, was never deeded to the diocese. The long one-storey frame building was simply referred to by the locals as the Roman Catholic Church of Forest. By the latter months of 1867, the Forest area was served by Father Henry Japes (1867-72), Wyoming's first pastor. Father Francis Xavier Darragh (1872-74), Wyoming's second pastor, supervised the 20-foot (6.1 m) enlargement and renovation of the mission church in Forest at a cost of $325. The church was rededicated on 11 December 1873.

St. Christopher

When Father John Ansboro (1875-79) was pastor at Wyoming, Mass was celebrated at Forest every third Sunday and Sunday school was conducted every Sunday afternoon. The Forest mission was attached to Parkhill in 1884. On 6 October 1886, the congregation observed the church's twentieth anniversary with a jubilee service.

During the pastorship of Father Donald A. McRae of Parkhill, the cornerstone of a new church was laid on 30 May 1893, by Bishop O'Connor, who returned to dedicate the debt-free church on 1 December 1893. The church was named St. Christopher to honour Christopher Murray, a parishioner and the biggest benefactor of the new church. In 1897, the mission was detached from Parkhill and attached to Sarnia. This lasted until 1907 when it was attached to Corunna. Between 1924 and 1934, St. Christopher's was a mission of St. Peter's seminary, and was ministered to by Father J. Brian Ffoulkes. In 1934, Forest was again attached to Our Lady of Mercy parish in Sarnia.

St. Christopher's was elevated to parish status in June 1939, with Father Leo J. Kelly (1939-45) as its first pastor. Parish numbers dropped during the

1940s, owing to the Second World War and the shift of people from the rural areas to the cities. This trend was halted and reversed, however, with the arrival of new immigrants from The Netherlands in the 1950s.

The centennial of the church was celebrated in 1993, and St. Christopher's was rededicated by Bishop Henry on Thanksgiving Sunday 1993. Meanwhile, Fathers Douglas F. Boyer (1969-87), Charles T. McManus (1987-93) and John F. Sharp (1993-98) each proposed additions to the church, but the project, being beyond the parish's financial capabilities at the time, was always put on hold. The situation changed under Father Michael R. Michon (1998-2001). The parishioners voted in 2000 to purchase land in the northwestern part of the town and build a new church. The new complex contains a 450-seat church, a hall and offices, and was dedicated and opened by Bishop Fabbro in October 2002. At the time, Father Julius B. Frondosa was administrator (2001-03). Incorporated into this post-conciliar church are stained-glass windows, Stations of the Cross, statues and altar furnishings from the previous church.

Sources: [Janis McCahill, et al.], *Our Heritage The History of St. Christopher's Parish Forest, Ontario,* [1993]; Ralph Hubert Dignan and Joseph P. Finn, "A History of the Diocese of London," edited by Guy Alden (unpublished manuscript, 2002); Gladys Dewey, "St. Christopher parish, Forest, centenary," *Newsletter of the Diocese of London,* no. 59, (Advent/Christmas 1993), 16. Additional information supplied by Father David Rankin, SJ, and Larry Scully.

Mooretown: St. Joseph

Father Joseph Crévier of Sandwich is believed to have ministered to the Indians and the few white settlers on the left bank of the St. Clair River, near what became the village of Mooretown in Moore Township, in 1826. He was followed by Father Louis J. Fluet in 1829. Mass was celebrated at the home of Louis Gallerneau, who had settled at Mooretown on land granted him for government service. It was probably shortly after his appointment as first pastor of St. Peter's in East Tilbury, in 1834, that Father

Jean-Baptiste Morin began to visit Moore Township. Bishop Macdonell is said to have administered the sacrament of confirmation to the Catholics of Moore Township in 1836. The Indians greeted him with great ceremony, the chief wearing a high silk hat. On 12 June 1838, 100 acres (40 ha) of land — lot 43 along the riverfront — was granted by the government of Upper Canada for the use and benefit of the Catholics in the township. It is believed that under the direction of Father Morin, a Catholic cemetery, possibly the first in Lambton County, was established on this grant. Many of the early residents along the river, from Sarnia to Sombra, were buried there in the ensuing years. One account states that on the northern boundary of this lot, between the St. Clair River and the River Road, Father Morin oversaw the erection of a small frame church that was dedicated by Bishop Gaulin on his way to the Lake Superior missions late in 1838. According to another tradition, in 1842-43 Father J. Baptiste Pédelupé, SJ, assisted Father Morin in building the church, which was dedicated by Bishop Power in 1843.

A highlight of the period was a week-long Grand Mission that took place in about 1841 at the home of Joseph LaForge, which was some four miles (6.2 m) upriver at what became Froomfield. A large timber platform with a canopy over the outdoor altar was erected. Father Morin and three other priests preached and administered the sacraments. It is said that hundreds of Indians and white settlers, some from as far south as both sides of the Detroit River and as far north as Sault St. Marie, participated.

Starting with the arrival of Father Dominique du Ranquet, SJ, and Brother Joseph Jennesseaux, SJ, in April 1844, other Jesuit priests periodically visited the missions along the St. Clair River until 1852. Father John O'Doherty actually resided at Sarnia and Moore Township in 1852-53, and Father M. Jean Mainguy, SJ, again visited the mission after Father O'Doherty's departure. In the summer of 1854, Father Michel Moncoq assumed responsibility for the St. Clair missions. Taking up residence at Mooretown, on 15 October 1854, which elevated the mission to a parish, Father Moncoq ministered to the Indians from Point Pelee and Malden, in the east, to Penetanguishene, in the west, and three other missions in between. Mooretown reverted to mission status when Father Moncoq drowned in 1856. It was again attached to St. Peter's in East Tilbury

and this time placed in the care of Father Jean Raynel, SJ, who was given the added responsibility of the missions along the St. Clair River. When St. Michael's, now Our Lady of Mercy, was established as a parish later in 1856, the St. Clair missions were served for the next few years by Dean Thadeus Kirwan of Sarnia.

Mooretown briefly regained parish status on 1 April 1860 with the arrival of Father Bartholomew Boubat (1860-64), who was placed in charge of the St. Clair missions. A larger church was needed, however, and rather than building one at Mooretown, a site in Corunna was selected.

Today, an historical plaque, on the west side of Highway 40 near Baby Creek, south of Corunna, commemorates this early mission church in Lambton County.

Source: DLA, Parish Files; Ralph Hubert Dignan and Joseph P. Finn, "A History of the Diocese of London," edited by Guy Alden (unpublished manuscript, 2002).

Oil Springs: St. Anne

Dean Thadeus Kirwan, pastor of Our Lady of Mercy in Sarnia (1856-64), ministered to local Catholics on horseback and celebrated Mass in the log home of the Powers family and in O'Grady's cooper shop on Main Street in Oil Springs. In 1866, his successor, Father Edmund Kilroy (1864-69), purchased a small frame Wesleyan Methodist church, the first church built in Oil Springs. This building was moved to Roady Park Street and dedicated to St. Anne. In October 1867, the mission at Oil Springs was transferred from Sarnia to the newly formed parish of Wyoming. In 1889, Father Philip J. Gnam, the pastor at Wyoming (1886-1910), initiated substantial renovations to St. Anne's church, and in December 1889 it was dedicated by Father Albert J. McKeon of Strathroy (Bishop Walsh had been translated to Toronto in August 1889). Father McKeon, an eloquent preacher, delivered a sermon at the morning Mass and at Vespers. He spoke for more than an hour on both occasions and held his audience spellbound the entire time.

St. Anne's became a mission of St. Philip's, with the transfer of the pastor's residence from Wyoming to Petrolia in 1910. In 1915, Father J. Norman Campeau, the pastor in Petrolia (1913-26), had the frame church in Oil Springs torn down and replaced by a small brick one on the same location. The cornerstone for the new church was laid on 27

St. Anne

July 1915. At the time, Mass was celebrated every five weeks in Oil Springs. Father Harry J. Laragh, pastor of Petrolia (1953-61), redecorated St. Anne's.

Only four marriages were ever conducted in this small church, which consisted of three rows of pews and two aisles. The first marriage was between Terrance Callaghan and Margaret Mackesy in September 1938, and the last was between Lance Evoy and Anne-Louise Moran in June 1967. Most couples from Oil Springs were married in Petrolia. The church was sold in 1974 when Father Martin A. Johnston (1971-80) was pastor and is now a private residence.

Sources: Ralph Hubert Dignan and Joseph P. Finn, "A History of the Diocese of London," edited by Guy Alden (unpublished manuscript, 2002). Additional information supplied by Ursula Johnson.

Petrolia: St. Philip

The Petrolia station was detached from Sarnia and given to Holy Rosary in Wyoming when it became a parish in October 1867. Father Henry Japes (1867-72), Wyoming's second pastor, oversaw the construction of a frame church. This was located on England Avenue in the east end of Petrolia, on land donated by the Hon. Ronald MacDonald. The first baptism was recorded on 26 December 1867. Under Father Philip J. Gnam (1886-1910), pastor at Wyoming, the London architect George F. Durand of the firm of Durand and Moore, drew up plans for a white-brick church with red-brick and cut-stone trim on a stone foundation. This was erected at the corner of King and Victoria streets on a parcel of land purchased for $1,000. The contractor for the Gothic-style church was William Reath of St.

Thomas. Bishop Walsh blessed the cornerstone, on 5 June 1887, and he dedicated the church to St. Philip, Apostle of the Lord, in honour of Father Gnam, on 16 October 1887. Described as the most costly and elaborate structure in town, which cost of upwards of $9,000, the church seated 410 people, was 105 feet long by 45 feet wide (32 m by 13.7 m) and had a spire that rose to a height of 120 feet (36.6 m).

In recognition of the pre-eminence of St. Philip's, Wyoming and Oil Springs became missions

St. Philip

of Petrolia in 1910. The following year, Father Thomas P. Hussey built a rectory on Victoria Avenue behind the church. His successors as pastor were Fathers J. Norman Campeau (1913-26) and Francis G. Powell (1926-29), the latter being a native of London and a former Basilian superior of St. Michael's College, Toronto. During the pastorship of Father Patrick J. Harrigan (1929-48), Father Francis J. Kurta visited two or three times a year to minister to the Slovaks in the parish. Father Harrigan was succeeded by Fathers Leo J. Kelly (1945-48), D. Kenney McMahon (1948) and Francis S. Mulkern (1948-53).

While Father Harry J. Laragh was pastor (1953-61), the two-room St. Philip's school was opened in 1956, the church was redecorated and the parish received its first curate, Father Mitchell S. Kaminski (1960-63). Father Kaminski also assisted Father James F. Summers (1961-65), as did Fathers Louis H. Rivard (1962-63), Patrick J. Mellon and David L. Chisholm (1964-68). Father Anthony F. Scalisi (1965-70), who died at the rectory on 23 March 1970, established the parish council. By the time of Father Martin A. Johnston (1971-80), the church in Oil Springs was no longer used for services and was sold in 1974. Father Johnston was very much involved in the Charismatic movement. In 1979, a hall was built on King Street next to the church to serve the social, religious and educational needs of the parish. During the centenary of St. Philip's in 1987, a new sign was placed in front of the church and a ramp was constructed to make the building wheelchair accessible.

There are many active organizations in the parish. The Youth Ministry has groups from Grade 3 to high school. The Knights of Columbus host a monthly breakfast. The CWL, together with that of Holy Rosary, Wyoming, sponsors bursaries and hosts card parties, luncheons, special dinners and an annual bazaar. A choir, cantors, readers, liturgical ministers, Sunday school, the RCIA and the Little Rock Scripture group are all active in the two churches, along with the St. Vincent de Paul Society.

Sources: Helen Heisler and Frances Jenniskens, "Holy Rosary Church Wyoming, Ont. St. Philip's Church, Petrolia, Ont. St. Anne's Church Oil Springs, Ont. A History – 1866-1980" (1980); Ralph Hubert Dignan and Joseph P. Finn, "A History of the diocese of London," edited by Guy Alden, (unpublished manuscript, 2002). Additional information supplied by Ursula Johnson.

Point Edward: St. Edward the Confessor

With more and more Catholic families settling in Point Edward, St. Edward separate school was built in the village in 1955. The opening of the school on the east side of Louisa Street, north of Helena, coincided with the need to establish a parish in the area. In 1957, Father Cameron F. McMartin (1957-58) was appointed the first pastor.

For the next several months, Father McMartin lived at Our Lady of Mercy rectory and celebrated Mass at St. Edward's school. With a grant from the mother parish, Our Lady of Mercy, and a $100,000 loan from the diocese, work proceeded on the construction of a church. Land immediately north of the school was purchased from the separate school board, the first sod was turned by Monsignor Lorenzo P. Lowry, dean of Lambton, on 18 March 1957, and the cornerstone was laid by Monsignor J.

St. Edward the Confessor

Austin Roney, chancellor of the diocese, on 30 June 1957. The general contractor for the church, rectory and hall was Westmass Construction. The new church, dedicated to St. Edward the Confessor, was blessed on his feast day, 13 October 1957, by Bishop Cody. With Father McMartin's transfer in 1958, Father J. William Farrell was named administrator. Later that year, Father Charles E. Sullivan was appointed the parish's second pastor. Meanwhile, the men of the parish laid sidewalks and completed the landscaping. In the fall of 1958, Father Sullivan had to leave and Father Farrell (1958-64) returned.

In his early thirties, Father Farrell was then the youngest pastor in the diocese. Under his guidance, the parking lot was finished, the garage and driveway were built, sewers were installed, the hall was painted, the concrete floor was tiled and a porch was added to the front entrance of the church. In June 1964, Father Farrell, who was also Catholic chaplain to the Sarnia Militia Garrison, accepted Bishop Carter's request to join the Canadian Army forces as a captain in the Padres' Corps. Father Ulysee A. Lefaive (1964-68) was appointed St. Edward's fourth pastor. When he was transferred to St. Michael's parish in Ridgetown, Father John F. Lynch (1968-73), who was chaplain at the Ursuline Motherhouse at Chatham, became pastor and remained in the parish until his death from cancer on 25 March 1973. Monsignor Joseph A. Cook (1973-78), who had worked for decades in family counselling and teaching, and who was more than seventy years old, was asked by Bishop Carter to become St. Edward's sixth pastor.

After Monsignor Cook fell terminally ill, St. Edward's had a succession of pastors. During this time there was a decline in membership. Finally, in

1983, Father Farrell, who had been chaplain at St. Joseph's Hospital for several years, was "dragooned" by Bishop Sherlock to return a third time to St. Edward's, despite acute and constant suffering from a broken back and five spinal operations, the result of a faulty parachute drop while with the Canadian Army. While Father Farrell had to face another long cleanup and repair job in a badly neglected and financially troubled parish, he was spurned by many of the very parishioners whose folly had led to the present crises. He found enough support, however, from within the parish and from "outsiders," who began attending and contributing to the church

The parish was suppressed on 6 April 2004, and its boundaries were once more absorbed by Our Lady of Mercy parish, where its sacramental records are now located.

Sources: DLA, Parish Files; Orlo Miller, *The Point: A History of the Village of Point Edward (Incorporated 1878)* (Point Edward: 1978); *Parish of St. Michael the Archangel Centennial Calendar 1880-1980* (1980).

Port Lambton: Sacred Heart of Jesus

Sacred Heart of Jesus parish can trace its roots to Sacred Heart mission on Baby's Point and to Sacred Heart mission on Walpole Island. When the Baby's Point church became too small for its congregation, another church was built in Sombra in 1870-71. When subscriptions were raised for the building of a rectory there, it was obvious that, as in the case of the building of the church in Sombra, the bulk of funding had come from Catholics in the southern part of Sombra Township. This led to the diocesan-approved decision to scrap the plans for a rectory in Sombra and, instead, to erect a church in Port Lambton to replace the small and aging structure at Baby's Point.

The cornerstone of Sacred Heart church was laid in late July 1877. The remains of Father Michel Moncoq, which had reposed at Baby's Point since 1856, were re-interred, on 11 June 1878, beneath the floor of the new church in front of the St. Joseph side altar.

On 29 September 1880, Port Lambton was detached from Corunna and elevated to parish status with Father Peter H. Feron (1880-81) as its first pastor. St. Mary's in Sombra, which was renamed St. John's, was its mission church. During the pastorate of Father John T. Aylward (1890-99), the church interior was remodelled for the first time. Upon the departure of Father Aylward, Sacred Heart parish was placed under the care of the Basilians for ten years. Continuing the custom of earlier years, the Catholics of Algonac and Marine City, Michigan, attended Mass in Sacred Heart parish on the Canadian side of the St. Clair River. Father Francis J. Odrowski (1912-26) also ministered to the Catholics on Walpole Island. On occasion, when the road between Port Lambton and Sombra proved

Sacred Heart of Jesus

impassible, he would cross the river by ferry to Robert's Landing on the Michigan side, catch the electric train to Marine City, cross the river again to Sombra and walk to St. John's church. After hearing confessions and celebrating Mass, he would retrace his steps to Port Lambton, usually arriving in the late afternoon. In 1915, he purchased a piece of land on lot D, concession 7, Sombra Township for a cemetery. Previously, interments were in St. John's Cemetery in Sombra or in Wallaceburg, Dresden or Mooretown.

On 4 June 1954, when Father D. Kenney McMahon was pastor (1950-60), Sacred Heart parish hall, originally a Quonset hut, was dedicated by Bishop Cody. By the early 1960s, the 1877 church was too small and too old for the growing congregation, and it was decided to replace it with a new structure. Father McMahon drew up the plans, and Father Carl A. Pettit (1960-69), was able to carry them out with bequests from the estates of two widows, Kathlyn Kerwin and Alice Dalton. Construction on the new church began in 1964. In the meantime, the old church had been torn down to make way for the new one on the same site, and Masses were celebrated in the parish hall and at St. John's in Sombra. Curran and Herridge of Sarnia were the contractors for new church, which cost around $100,000. The doubled-bricked structure was officially opened and blessed by Bishop Carter on 4 April 1965.

In 2004, Sacred Heart parish was clustered with Our Lady Help of Christians and Holy Family parishes in Wallaceburg. With the priests living in Wallaceburg, the 1910 rectory in Port Lambton was put up for rent.

Sources: DLA, Parish Files; Maxine Devin, *Our Parish History Sacred Heart Port Lambton, Ontario St. John's Sombra, Ontario, 1880 -1980* [1980]; Wayne Stubbs, "History of parish rich in religious devotion," *Catholic Register*, 17 October 1992, 13.

Sombra: St. John

Catholics in this part of Sombra Township attended Mass on Walpole Island in the mid-1840s and at Baby's Point thereafter. By the late 1860s, however, the faithful had outgrown Sacred Heart church and a new church was needed. Under the direction of Father Ferdinand A.J. Ouellet of Corunna, ten acres (4 ha) were purchased on lot B, concession 12, in Sombra Township from James Dawson, a lumber merchant. Apparently, Dawson and another man donated board for board the lumber for construction of a frame church with a high-domed ceiling. The cornerstone was laid by Father Ouellet on 26 June 1870, and the church was blessed and consecrated by Bishop Walsh on 25 June 1871. It measured 80 feet by 40 feet (24.4 m by 12.2 m) and was surmounted by a 120-foot (36.6 m) spire. It was probably named St. Mary's.

Father Bernard J. Watters (1873-80), Father Ouellet's successor, quickly paid off the debt on the chapel at Sombra and turned the southwest corner of the lot into a cemetery. Previously, burials had taken place in Corunna. The next step for the mission was to procure a resident priest, which meant building a rectory. Because the bulk of subscriptions for the proposed rectory came from the southern portion

of the township, the rectory was not built and the monies went towards the construction of a church in Port Lambton.

St. John

The church at Sombra faced the St. Clair River and was known as the Sailor's Church because it was a landmark for vessels plying the Great Lakes. It was detached from Corunna and became a mission of Port Lambton on 29 September 1880. In his July 1886 report to Bishop Walsh, Father Nicholas J. Dixon (1885-90), the pastor of Port Lambton, noted that about thirty-five families and eight individuals comprised the congregation at St. Mary's. Mass was celebrated every second Sunday, and Holy Day celebrations alternated between Sombra and Port Lambton.

By 1903, St. Mary's mission was renamed St. John Evangelist mission. Around 1912, however, it was known as Our Saviour mission. Mass was still celebrated every second Sunday and also every Holy Day. Father Francis J. Odrowski (1912-26) made various improvements to the church and had sidewalks built around the church and the house. By the end of 1916, the congregation consisted of thirty families or about 150 individuals. In 1920 or thereabouts, the mission church was once more dedicated to St. John. Later, it was known as St. John the Apostle and at other times as St. John the Evangelist. The total valuation of the church, its contents, and surrounding land, in February 1934, was placed at $9,068. At the time, the church seated 208 persons. The bequest of the estate of the widow Katherine Mullen and that of her husband George financed the renovation of the church.

Because the building was not insulated, the congregation made Sacred Heart their winter place of worship. St. John's was used between the 24 May weekend and Labour Day and finally closed in 1986. The last Mass was celebrated in this wooden structure on 1 November 1987. The roof was ripped off by a tornado, on 28 March 1991, and the rest of the building was torn down on 5 May 1991. A large white cross and cairn now mark the site of the mission church of St. John, while St. John's cemetery in Sombra remains open for use.

Sources: DLA, Parish Files; Maxine Devin, *Our Parish History Sacred Heart Port Lambton, Ontario St. John's Sombra, Ontario, 1880-1980* [1980]; Wayne Stubbs, "History of parish rich in religious devotion," *Catholic Register*, 17 October 1992, 13.

Warwick: Mission Church

The Potato Famine of the 1840s drove tens of thousands of Irish Catholics to seek a new life in North America. Among these, a few settled on small farms in Warwick Township. It is believed that Jesuit missionaries visited this area and that Fathers Michael R. Mills and Patrick O'Dwyer of London had Warwick Township as a station in the late 1830s and early 1840s. It is said that Father Dominique du Ranquet, SJ, came to Warwick from Walpole Island in 1844 and that the Jesuits continued to make periodic visitations until 1854. What is certain, however, is that, as pastor of London (1849-56) and then of Sarnia (1856-64), Dean Thadeus Kirwan ministered on horseback to the Catholics of the Warwick area. The earliest record of his visiting "Warwick Town" was on 24 November 1849, when he baptized a child. It was probably Dean Kirwan who oversaw the 1850 grant of land to the Catholic Church in the settlement of Warwick on the southeast corner of the junction of the London or Egremont Road (later Highway 22) and the Ninth Side Road.

Although one secondary source claims that a Father O'Donovan built a log church and laid out a cemetery in Warwick in 1855-56, and another source that a log church was built there in 1859, it would appear that the first Catholic church in Warwick was a frame church large enough to seat approximately 200 persons. It was still unfinished at the time of the 1861 census and was then valued at $400. This church probably drew additional families from Plympton Township. It is not presently known, however, to whom it was dedicated.

In 1867, Warwick became a mission of Wyoming when Father Henry Japes (1867-72) became its first pastor. Warwick Township itself had a population of eighty Catholics in 1869.

Meanwhile, with the completion of the Sarnia branch of the Great Western Railway in December 1858, Watford, some five and a quarter miles (8.4 k m) to the southeast, surpassed Warwick in importance because the local population, trade and commerce gravitated to Watford on the rail line. On 28 August 1871, Father Japes purchased two acres (0.8 ha) for a new Catholic cemetery, on the southeast corner of lot 18, concession 3, south of Egremont Road, about a mile (1.6 k m) north of Watford.

The Warwick mission was detached from Wyoming and given to Strathroy in 1875, and its pastor, Father Henry B. Lotz (1874-76), celebrated Mass every second Sunday in Warwick. This was only for a short time, however, as the increase in the Catholic population in the Watford area necessitated the building of a new church there. It was probably in late 1875 that the church in Warwick was closed. It was sold by public auction on 3 May 1878.

Over time, the remains of some deceased family members were removed from the cemetery at Warwick to the new Catholic cemetery north of Watford. Timothy and Annie,

The ten gravestones remaining from the Catholic cemetery in Warwick

the children of Andrew and Annie McDonnell, had died in 1875 and were buried in the Warwick cemetery. When their remains were re-interred in the Watford cemetery, on 10 June 1884, the "bodies were found to be petrified, every feature being as true as when interred."

After many decades, the abandoned cemetery at Warwick became overgrown. In recent years, the lot was cleaned up and the ten remaining gravestones were mounted on a brick wall, the only evidence that a Catholic cemetery and mission church were once located in the village. Based on the dates of death on the gravestones, it would appear that the cemetery was in use as early as April 1858 and as late as August 1876.

Sources: DLA, John Walsh Papers, Box 1, The

Status Animarum for the Diocese of Sandwich, 12; [Janis McCahill, et al.], *Our Heritage The History of St. Christopher's Parish Forest, Ontario* [1993]; *Our Lady Help of Christians 1875 -2000 Watford, Ontario* [2000]. Additional information supplied by Julia Geerts.

Watford:
Our Lady Help of Christians

Prior to 1875, the mission church of the faithful of Watford and area was in the village of Warwick. The passing of the Sarnia branch of the Great Western Railway through Watford, rather than Warwick, had assured the ascendancy of Watford. On 28 August 1871, the pastor of Wyoming, Father Henry Japes (1867-72), purchased two acres (0.8 ha) of land, about a mile (1.6 m) north of the village for a local cemetery. By this time, it was also evident that a church was needed in Watford, which had become the centre of Catholic population. In 1875, the Warwick mission was detached from Wyoming and transferred to Strathroy, and a church was built on land donated by John Roche, on the corner of Warwick and Victoria streets in Watford. On 6 July 1875, the cornerstone was laid and blessed by Bishop Walsh, who returned on 5 December to dedicate the church under the title of Our Lady Help of Christians. The pastor of All Saints parish in Strathroy, Father Henry B. Lotz (1874-76), now travelled to Watford every second Sunday. By the early years of the twentieth century, a priest came to celebrate Mass three Sundays a month, travelling by horse and buggy and later by automobile. One of those priests who came to Watford by car was the curate Father E. Raphael Glavin (1927-28).

Our Lady Help of Christians ceased to be a mission of Strathroy when it was elevated to parish status in 1928. Father Glavin (1928-39) was the first pastor. By the early 1940s, however, the population of the parish had declined markedly as families left their farms for larger centres. Father Leon M. Blondell (1942-52) remained in Watford only two months and then transferred his residence to St. Matthew's in Alvinston. Our Lady Help of Christians became a mission of St. Matthew's.

The late 1940s and early 1950s witnessed an influx of new Canadians, mainly from the Netherlands. In 1956, Watford was once more a parish with Father Peter A. Oostveen (1956-69), a Dutch-speaking priest, as pastor. During his pastorate, two Masses were celebrated on Sundays, the church was renovated and enlarged to a seating capacity of 320 and a new rectory was built. Bishop Cody blessed the church, rectory and St. Peter Canisius separate school on 18 January 1959. On 9 December 1967, Father Peter Sanders, SCJ, became the second member of the parish to be ordained. The first was Father John A. Ruth, CSB, who was ordained on 15 August 1942.

Our Lady Help of Christians

During the last quarter of the twentieth century further renovations and improvements were made to the church. These included new stained-glass windows, a domed sanctuary, lighting, new pews, carpeting, steps and a ramp for handicapped access. New office facilities were constructed in the church basement, together with a new kitchen and renovated meeting room. The 100th anniversary of the church was celebrated during 1975 and its 125th in 2000.

Since 1969, the parishes of Our Lady of Help and St. Matthew, Alvinston have been served by one pastor. The first pastor of the twinned parishes, Father Bernard A. Robert (1969-73), selected Watford as his residence. Father Michael J. O'Brien (1989-2003) further strengthened the clustering of the two parishes through joint weekly bulletins, parish council meetings and yearly celebrations. In 2007, Our Lady Help of Christians absorbed the boundaries of St. Matthew's.

Sources: *Our Lady Help of Christians 1875-2000 Watford, Ontario* [2000]. Additional information supplied by Julia Geerts, Helen Green and Father John Van Damme.

Wyoming: Holy Rosary

The first priest mentioned as having celebrated Mass in Plympton Township was Father Patrick O'Dwyer, in 1838, who came into the area on horseback. As he was not in the London-St. Thomas area until 1842-43, and if the year 1838 is correct, the priest in question, however, would likely have been Father Joseph Maria Burke, OFM (1836-38), or Father Michael R. Mills (1838-39). It is possible that missionary priests from Sandwich, East Tilbury or Chatham may have ventured into this area. Certainly, the Catholics of this part of Lambton County would have come in contact with the priests of the St. Clair missions in the 1840s and early 1850s.

The picture becomes clearer in 1856 when Dean Thadeus Kirwan, pastor at London, was transferred to Sarnia as the first pastor (1856-64) of St. Michael's (now Our Lady of Mercy) church. He too ministered to the Catholics of inland Lambton on horseback. It was his successor, Father Edmund Burke Kilroy (1864-69), who oversaw the erection of a frame chapel in Wyoming. It faced the Second Line of Plympton Township and was situated directly behind the present church. The graveyard was at the rear of the church.

Father T.J. Quin, the assistant priest at Sarnia, was appointed the first pastor of Wyoming in October 1867, but he died shortly thereafter. He was succeeded in the latter part of 1867 by Father Henry Japes (1867-72), who had a house purchased to serve as his rectory. His parish also included the missions of Petrolia, Oil Springs, Warwick and Forest. Wyoming's second pastor was Father Francis Xavier Darragh (1872-74), who was followed by Fathers John Murphy (1874-75), James Scanlon (1875) and John Ansbro (1875-79).

In 1875, the Warwick mission was detached from Wyoming and given to Strathroy. A white-brick rectory in Wyoming was built in the mid-1880s during the pastorship of Father M. McCauley. Father George R. Northgraves, who assisted Father McCauley from time to time between 1880 and 1885, mapped out Mount Calvary cemetery in the southeast part of Wyoming. Bodies from the first cemetery were transferred to this new location. Meanwhile, in 1884, the Forest mission was detached from Wyoming and attached to Parkhill.

Holy Rosary

Before the end of 1888, under the direction of Father Philip J. Gnam (1886-1910), the old frame church in Wyoming was replaced by a white-brick structure. Dedicated to the Holy Rosary, and similar in style to St Philip's in Petrolia, it cost a little more than $7,000. A 600-pound (272.2 kg) bell was installed in the cupola tower. The beloved Father Gnam also oversaw extensive improvements to the rectory and the construction of a barn and drive shed. During the latter part of his tenure, the drive shed became a garage for his Model T Ford, Petrolia's first automobile.

Wyoming became a mission of St. Philip's in 1910 when the pastoral residence was transferred to the more populous and prestigious town of Petrolia. Some twenty years later, the interior of Holy Rosary's former rectory was renovated and used as the parish hall. The two-roomed, Holy Rosary school was opened in 1957, while Father Harry J. Laragh was pastor at Petrolia (1953-61). He also oversaw the redecoration of the church.

On 30 June 2007, Holy Rosary was canonically suppressed, and its boundaries and parishioners incorporated into St. Philip's parish.

Sources: Ralph Hubert Dignan and Joseph P. Finn, "A History of the Diocese of London," edited by Guy Alden (unpublished manuscript, 2002). Additional information supplied by Ursula Johnson.

6. London Deanery

London:

Blessed Sacrament

In 1948, Father Arnold F. Loebach, assistant pastor at St. Michael's church, celebrated Mass in a classroom in the new Blessed Sacrament school. This classroom was used as a chapel for more than three years. Blessed Sacrament parish was formally established, on 9 June 1951, from portions of St. Michael and St. Patrick parishes, with Father J. Bartley Clark (1951-55) as pastor. The first sod for the new church, at the southwest corner of Oxford and Spittal streets, was turned by Father J. Austin Roney, on 24 September 1951. Modelled after St. Ursula's in Chatham, it was the fifth prefabricated church in the diocese supplied by Gerry Supply & Lumber Company, and was intended to have a life of some twenty-five years. Mitchell & Sons were the contractors. The Christmas Midnight Mass was the first Eucharist celebrated in the partially completed church. Since there were no pews, chairs were brought in from the school. The church was completed in May 1952 and blessed by Monsignor Mahoney on 15 June.

On 15 October 1959, during the pastorship of Father John B. O'Donnell (1959-63), the first Sunday evening Mass was celebrated for the convenience of shift workers and parents with large families. This Mass was replaced by a Saturday evening Mass, beginning 3 July 1971.

On 15 October 1962, the house immediately to the northwest of the church was donated by William English for use as a rectory. Prior to this, the priests had lived in quarters behind the sanctuary, on the south side of the church. In 1968, aluminum siding was installed on the church, the interior of the church and that of the rectory were painted, and the kneelers in the church were covered.

There were 550 families registered at Blessed Sacrament in 1972, a drop from the 1,000 registered in 1965 when Bishop Carter established St. Andrew's parish. A charismatic prayer group was established in the parish in June 1974. Two years later, on 9 June 1976, the parish's twenty-fifth anniversary was celebrated with a Mass of

Blessed Sacrament

Thanksgiving by Bishop Sherlock.

The years 1973 to 1999 saw several renovation projects and changes on the church property. In 1973, during the pastorate of Father Arnold F. Loebach (1971-77), Bontje Construction was contracted to renovate the church hall and remodel the kitchen, for a total of $38,000. In 1975, the rectory was refinished with full bathrooms on both the second floor and the basement and the kitchen was enlarged. In the church, the ceiling tiles were replaced and bathrooms installed. The kitchen in the hall was refurbished and part of the basement was excavated to build storage areas. In 1976, the church entrance was widened. New roof shingles and eavestrough were installed on the rectory in 1980. The church roof was reshingled in 1982, and air conditioning was installed in the church in the summer of 1986. Then, in 1991, during the pastorate of Father John H. Betkowski (1988-98), a total of $305, 241 was spent in renovating the church's interior and in structural roof repairs.

One of Blessed Sacraments more interesting and longtime parishioners was Leonard Howard. He was superintendent of St. Peter's cemetery in London, for more than a half-century, and he trained lay readers in Middlesex County.

In August 2000, Blessed Sacrament was clustered with St. Patrick's, with Father Robert G. Couture as pastor of both parishes. Since Father Couture was also pastor of Ste. Marguerite d'Youville, a number of priests were paid a weekly stipend to lead weekend and weekday liturgies at Blessed Sacrament. Bishop Fabbro announced, on 28 April 2006, that Blessed Sacrament would be suppressed as a parish and, on 25 June, he celebrated the last Mass in the church.

Sources: Information supplied by Dan Brock and Father John Van Damme.

Catholic Latvian Mission

The Catholic Latvian Mission was established by 1965, with Father Stanislaus Mozga as director. Father Mozga was born in 1918 in Latvia and was ordained in 1947 in Rome, Italy. Between 1949 and 1952 he worked with Latvian immigrants in England and followed them to Canada in 1952, having been accepted into the diocese of London. Between 1955 and 1965, he was chaplain of St. Mary's Hospital in London, where he lived before moving, by 1966, to the residence of John Mozga, his brother, at 137 Huron Street. The receipts for this mission in 1965 were $815.25 and the expenditures were $703.50. From 1 July 1968 until 1978, Father Mozga resided at the Precious Blood Monastery at 667 Talbot Street, with the diocese paying his salary of $165 per month. In addition, as chaplain at the monastery, he was provided with room and board, plus $100 per month by the Precious Blood Sisters. As of March 1969, the $100 was to be remitted to the diocese and would be included in the monthly $165 paid to him by the diocese. Father Mozga, who spoke Italian and German, in addition to Latvian and English, also ministered to the Latvians in the dioceses of Hamilton and St. Catharines from 1968 to 1969.

In 1972 and again in 1973, Father Mozga visited Riga, Latvia, where he had a sick brother in hospital. He himself took a three-week sick leave in February 1973, having been advised by his doctors that he required a complete rest. In 1978, he again took up residence with John Mozga. Father Mozga was still in charge of the Latvian mission at the time of his death, on 9 January 1983. His funeral Mass was celebrated by Bishop Sherlock at Our Lady of Częstochowa church in London, and his remains were interred in St. Peter's cemetery, London.

His successor was Father Peter Paul Bojars. Born in Berzgale, diocese of Ręzekne, Latvia, he was ordained a priest in 1924 in Riga. Both his parents were in concentration camps during the Second World War. His father escaped to Poland in 1944, but his mother died in the camp. Father Bojars was permitted to celebrate her funeral Mass and bury her. He came to the United States in 1950 and served in St. Ann's parish, Chicago, for thirty-two years. In 1982, he came to Hamilton, Ontario, where his sister lived. Father Bojars came to live at Mount St. Joseph Motherhouse, in 1983, where he served as chaplain. In addition to ministering to the Latvian community of London, he served those in Windsor and Detroit. Father Bojars died suddenly in the parking lot near his car at Mount St. Joseph, on the evening of 28 June 1991. His funeral Mass was celebrated at Mount St. Joseph chapel by Bishop Sherlock, followed by another Mass the next day in Hamilton. From there, his remains were entombed in Holy Sepulchre mausoleum, Burlington. Although the address for the Latvian mission is given as Mount St. Joseph, as late as 1993 in the *Directory of the Diocese of London Canada*, it would appear that the mission closed with the death of Father Bojars.

Source: DLA, London: Latvian Mission File.

Communauté Catholique Ste Marguerite d'Youville

Mass has been celebrated in French over the years in London, but the origins of the Communauté Sainte-Marguerite-d'Youville began with a Mass celebrated in 1982, in the gymnasium of St. Lawrence separate school, by Father Donald J. Thériault of St. Peter's Seminary. The occasional Mass in French soon became a monthly event. In 1985, the fledgling congregation, known as *Communauté catholique francophone de London*, was transplanted to St. Stephen of Hungary church, which it shared with the Hungarian and Spanish communities until 1999. After 31 March 1990, the number of Masses in French was increased to twice a month.

The pastoral council, elected in 1985, asked Bishop Sherlock to name a priest to minister to the francophone Catholic community and, in June 1990, Father Robert G. Couture, who was also assistant pastor at St. Patrick's in London, accepted this position. In order to accommodate his duties at St. Patrick's, he celebrated the French-language

Mass at St. Stephen's at 5:00 p.m. on Saturdays. A building fund started, and Father Couture and his congregation continued to collect, salvage, make, sew, order and commission the necessary furnishings for their future chapel.

The construction of *Centre scolaire communautaire de London*, later named *Centre Desloges*, was finally allowed to begin in the summer of 1998, on the site which had given birth to the *Communauté* at 920 Huron Street. With sixty families officially registered, the chapel was completed and opened in September 1999. By the time of *Centre Desloges'* official opening, on 19 November 1999, a second Sunday Mass was added. Through the generous donations of its members, the spiritual home of *Communauté Sainte-Marguerite-d'Youville* was debt free by that Christmas. With Father Couture's transfer to St. Anne's, Tecumseh, effective 7 August 2002, Father Murray K. Watson was appointed as both administrator of the Communauté and a member of the faculty of St. Peter's Seminary. By the spring of 2002, the official membership had risen to 100 families.

Effective 15 August 2004, Father Maroun Aboujaoude, OAM, superior of St. Charbel Monastery, was appointed with special responsibility to the pastoral care of the French community in London. Shortly thereafter, Father Charles Zichella, OFM, Cap., became administrator and resided at Holy Cross rectory before being appointed administrator of St. Michael's. After 1 July 2005, with Father Zichella's transferral to St. Nicholas of Bari parish, Toronto, the Communauté was served by the priests from St. Peter's seminary, until the appointment, in June 2006, of Father Richard D. Charrette as chaplain for a term of at least three years.

From its humble beginnings in an English-language Catholic school, *Communauté Sainte-Marguerite-d'Youville*, the only Francophone "mission" in the eastern part of the diocese, shares space in *Centre Desloges* with Monseigneur-Bruyère and Gabriel-Dumont secondary schools and the *Centre communautaire régional de London*, on the northwest corner of Huron and Barker streets in northeast London. Presently, the *Communauté* consists of more than 135 families. As early as 1982, its liturgical celebrations were enhanced with both adult and children choirs and, since 2000, throughout the school year at the Sunday Mass, "*les Amis de*

Jésus" has provided activities for children aged four to eight.

Sources: "*Ouverture et historique de la chapelle Sainte-Marguerite-d'Youville,*" *Newsletter of the Diocese of London*, no. 89 (Advent/Christmas 1999), 15; *Diocese of London Directory*, various years. Additional information supplied by Jacqueline Hétu.

Holy Cross

The post-Second-World-War boom necessitated the establishment of a mission in the Ealing district of St. Patrick's parish, in East London. Father Cyril A.J. Doyle (1946-55) was appointed administrator, and the house at 1104 Trafalgar Street became his residence. On 21 July 1946, the first Mass was celebrated in the front room, which was designated as Holy Cross chapel. The choir was forced to sing from the kitchen. In September 1947, Holy Cross school was opened on the east side of Elm Street, and, from January 1948, the school basement served as Holy Cross chapel. By 1949, because of limited space, three Masses were said each Sunday. About October 1949, this was increased to four. Between 1948 and 1950, Father Doyle was assisted by the Resurrectionists from St. Thomas Scholasticate.

Bishop Cody elevated Holy Cross to parish status in 1950. Its boundaries were formed from portions of the parishes of St. Mary's and St. Patrick's and comprised about thirty-five families. Construction on the new church, immediately north of the school, began in 1951. About the same year, Father Doyle moved to the new rectory, immediately north of the church. As soon as the basement auditorium of the church was finished, it was used for the celebration of Mass. On 11 October 1953, the church, of traditional Gothic-style design, was opened and solemnly blessed by Bishop Cody, although it was unfinished. It fell to Holy Cross's second pastor, Father Albert P. Spencer (1955-67), to oversee the changes wrought by the Second Vatican Council. It was during Father Paul D. Milne's pastorate (1972-76) that the London Portuguese mission began using Holy Cross church for services, and the priest in charge, Father Orlando Fazzenaro, took up residence at Holy Cross rectory. Meanwhile, population shifts saw a decline in the number of families in Holy Cross parish while, at the same

Holy Cross

time, there was still the need to find a permanent home for the London Portuguese mission. As early as 1973, the Portuguese community promoted the concept of Holy Cross as a co-parish, but this idea was not encouraged by Father Milne and the parish council. Finally, however, Bishop Sherlock decreed on 25 May 1984 that the two faith communities would be amalgamated as one and the new parish, centred at Holy Cross church, would be known as Holy Cross-Santa Cruz parish community. Father Manuel Cardoso, who was in charge of the Portuguese mission, was named pastor (1984-88), and Father John P. Comiskey was appointed assistant pastor (1984-88). Both worked to make the parish an example of the unity and diversity to be found within the Catholic faith community.

Under the direction of Father Cardoso's successor, Father John J. Mendonça (1988-91), the church's interior was renovated. He organized catechetical formation sessions for the community at large and focused on establishing a wholesome integration of the new Canadians into the life of the parish. Father José F. Seminati (1991-98) continued the work of his predecessors and oversaw the task of making the church accessible to the elderly and physically challenged. The next pastor, Father Lucio X. Couto (1998-2006) re-established the parish council and revived many of the existing pastoral and liturgical committees, such as stewardship and ministry to young families. For the Portuguese-Canadian seniors, a group was established to offer them a place to gather and share their valuable resources. In October 1978, the twenty-fifth anniversary and, in 2003, the fiftieth anniversary of the opening of Holy Cross church were celebrated.

Sources:"Church marks 25th anniversary," *London Free Press*, 24 October1978, C1; *Holy Cross Church 2003* [London: 2003]; "600 Witness RC Dedication of New Church," *London Free Press*, 12 Oct. 1953, 15.

Holy Rosary

On 17 October 1948, Holy Rosary was established as a mission of St. Martin of Tours parish. Father Stanley A. Nouvion (1951-58) was appointed the first pastor of Our Lady of the Rosary on 24 May 1951. The sod-turning ceremony was performed by Monsignor J. Austin Roney on 1 June 1952. The church, a prefabricated building identical to that of Blessed Sacrament church on Oxford Street and also erected by Mitchell & Sons, was solemnly blessed and dedicated by Bishop Cody on 8 February 1953.

From the very inception of Holy Rosary, fruitful parish organizations were established. The CWL and the Altar Guild/Altar Society were formed in 1951, followed by the Confraternity of the Most Holy Name in 1952, the St. Vincent de Paul Society in 1957, the RCIA in 1989, the Social Justice Committee in 1999, and the Knights of Columbus in 2001. The CWL was one of the most enduring and active groups in the parish and was well known for its annual bazaar in October. In later years, it was responsible for supplying the necessary funds for the redecoration of both parish halls and a complete new kitchen in the rectory. The parish was generous to refugees, sponsoring a family from Kosovo and working with the Glen Cairn Community Resource Centre. Youth groups have come and gone, the most enduring being the Youth and Adult Three Pitch Church League, formed in the late 1970s, which continued for more than ten years. One early parish organization, the Holy Rosary Bowling League, formed in 1956, still exists, and for years has had members beyond its territorial and religious boundaries. In 2007, it was renamed the High-Fivers Bowling League.

Father John G. Winter (1981-85) oversaw major structural changes to the church in 1985. The altar was transferred to the north side of the building and the pews were arranged in a semicircle around the sanctuary. A larger, second entrance was opened on the south side of the church. Later, this entrance was made wheelchair accessible. Bishop Sherlock

Holy Rosary

blessed the newly renovated church in December 1985.

In 1990, at the suggestion of the CWL and under the direction of the pastor, Father John P. Comiskey (1988-91), the project of installing stained-glass windows in the church was initiated. The windows were designed and crafted by Rosemary Fleming, a parishioner. The last window, which commemorated Father Nouvion, the parish's founder, and Father Joseph J. Hennessey, was installed in 1992.

Pastors, associate pastors and resident priests came and went over the years, but the parish's "perennial assistant," Father Hennessey, helped out at Holy Rosary from its founding in 1951 until a few months before his death in September 2001. Renowned for his brief and to-the-point homilies, he was beloved by all, from the very young to the elderly. He was also the chaplain at the Veterans' hospital in London. On 22 May 1994, the parishioners hosted a celebration in honour of his sixtieth anniversary as a priest.

The parish celebrated its twenty-fifth anniversary on 23 May 1976, and its fiftieth anniversary on 26-27 May 2001. In November 2004, however, the church was declared to be structurally unsound and was closed. Mass was again celebrated in the gymnasium of Holy Rosary school. While there were 700 registered families in the parish, only some 150 were regular supporters. Faced with high repair costs, a declining population and a scarcity of priests, it was decided to canonically suppress the parish. This took effect on 15 May 2005, with Bishop Fabbro celebrating the closing liturgy. The territorial boundaries of the former parish were then absorbed into the mother parish of St. Martin. The building became the Rowntree Park Early Childhood Learning Centre in June 2007.

Sources: Father Stan Soltysik, "Stained glass windows installed at Holy Rosary, London, *Newsletter of the Diocese of London*, no. 52 (Pentecost: 1992), 20; Norman de Bono, "Raging blaze hits day care in London," *London Free Press*, 3 December 2006, 6. Additional information supplied by Gertrude Roes and Mary Kay Butler.

Holy Spirit

Holy Spirit parish grew out of the University of Western Ontario Newman Club and the London Newman Alumni. Bishop Kidd had set up the Newman Club on Western's campus in the academic year 1936-37. The first chaplain was Father William J. Phelan (1936-39). With the establishment of the Canadian Federation of Newman Clubs in 1942, the London club was one of the first charter members and its chaplain, Father Joseph A. Cook (1939-47), was selected as the Federation's first chaplain. In 1967-68, a rented house at 984 Richmond Street became the new Newman Centre. Previously it had been in the Colonnade, later the Somerset Apartments, on Richmond Street North, and, before that at 76 Albert Street, on the corner of Ridout.

Bishop Carter's experience as chaplain at McGill University convinced him that a pastoral ministry on campus should "get a better break" than was possible through a club and chaplaincy. Consequently, in the fall of 1966, the university parish was established on a trial basis. It proved a success and on 10 October 1967, with the sympathy and willingness of the priests of the diocese to co-operate, Bishop Carter appointed Father Richard T.A. Murphy, OP, chaplain of the Newman Club and a teacher at King's College, as "Vicarius Curatus" of the new Holy Spirit University parish, effective 15 October. Sunday Masses, for this "bold new venture" – the establishment of a personal as compared with a territorial parish – were celebrated at the theatre in Middlesex College. Father Murphy was chaplain from 1965 to 1974.

In 1968, the house at 211 Broughdale Avenue was acquired as the parish rectory and centre and the Newman Club house and given the name Holy Spirit Centre. By January 1972, Sunday Masses were celebrated at Brescia and King's colleges and at Saugeen-Maitland residence and Middlesex College. Weekday Masses were held at Holy Spirit Centre and at Brescia and King's colleges. Father

Paul E. Crunican, a diocesan priest and professor of history at King's College, succeeded Father Murphy as pastor in 1974. The Basilian Fathers began their ministry at Holy Spirit on 1 July 1982, the first pastor being Father Paul M. McGill, CSB (1982-85). Father J.J. Kenneth O'Keefe, CSB (1985-91), who had been appointed an associate pastor of Holy Spirit, effective 1 July 1982, was appointed pastor for a six-year term, beginning on 1 July 1985. He was followed by his associate pastor, Father Angelo Bovenzi, CSB, in 1991.

On 24 October 1992, the twenty-fifth anniversary of the parish was celebrated at St. Pius X church, with more than 200 persons in attendance. By the following year, Sunday Masses were celebrated at Middlesex College, Brescia College chapel and St. Luke's Anglican church. Daily Mass was celebrated at Brescia chapel, and students met Wednesday evenings at Holy Spirit Centre for Mass and supper.

Nine years later, in June 2000, Holy Spirit ceased to function as a parish when it was amalgamated with the faith community at King's University College to form the Office of Campus Ministry at King's. Father Michael D. Béchard was installed as chaplain of this new ministry. In addition to serving the liturgical and sacramental needs of the faithful of the University of Western Ontario and King's University College, this faith community celebrates in common with the Congregation of the Sisters of St. Joseph of London on Sundays. During the academic year, two Sunday Masses are celebrated, a morning Mass with the Sisters of St. Joseph in the Chapel of the Immaculate Conception at Mount St. Joseph and an early evening Mass in Elizabeth A. "Bessie" Labatt Hall at King's University College. Between 1968 and 2005, the parish celebrated 383 baptisms, 192 confirmations, 256 marriages and thirteen funerals.

Sources: DLA, St. Pius X parish, London; Jack Briglia, "Holy Spirit Parish, London, celebrates 25th anniversary," *Newsletter of the Diocese of London*, no. 54 (Advent/Christmas: 1992), 8. Additional information supplied by Father Michael D. Béchard and Andrea Rector.

London German Apostolate

In February 1964, the London German parish was established, with Father Isidore Risse, OFM, as pastor, and it was soon known as St. Francis German Catholic Church in London. Father Risse resided at St. Peter's cathedral rectory, and, from 13 February 1964 to 9 September 1966, the diocese subsidized this parish to the amount of $4,696.45. Because he also spoke Portuguese, Father Risse ministered to the London Portuguese community. In the summer of 1965, the collection dropped to less than twenty-five dollars. This was probably the result of the arrival of Father Manuel A. Louro to take care of the newly established Portuguese mission. By the end of February 1966, numbers had increased slightly, but there were still only ten to twelve families regularly in attendance at the German mission. Father Risse left London on 9 September 1966. Father Jenö Boday, SJ, then residing at 525 Queens Avenue and ministering to the Hungarian community, was also serving the London German mission by May 1969. During these years, services were held in various locations in the central and northeastern parts of the city.

Meanwhile, the German community continued to beseech Bishop Carter for a pastor of its own and to use St. Joseph's church as its place of worship. On 1 July 1970, Father George M. Svoboda, formerly of St. Anthony's parish, Elma, Manitoba, assumed responsibility for the German Catholics of the London area. Bishop Carter gave approval for the mission to be called St. Boniface German Catholic Mission. On Sunday, 13 September 1970, Father Svoboda celebrated Mass in German at St. Joseph's church, which was attended by about 150 people. Thus, the German Catholic congregation was re-established in London, but soon after, it was formally known as St. Joseph's German Speaking Congregation in London, Ontario. It was estimated that the German ministry would not occupy more than half of Father Svoboda's time and that he would spend the other half in service to St. Mary's parish, to which he had been appointed assistant pastor on 13 July. In late October 1971, the number of Sunday Masses to the German-speaking congregation was reduced to one evening Mass a month, owing to the financial hardships facing the congregation, which was already being subsidized by the diocese at the rate of $150 per month.

By January 1972, the number of German-speaking families had levelled off to thirty. In April, Bishop Carter concluded that since most of the families were rapidly integrating into their geographical parishes, there was no need for a full-time priest. The occasional visit from a German-speaking priest would be sufficient to care for their pastoral needs. Another reason, however, was the financial drain of this mission on the diocese. Consequently, after two years, Father Svoboda was released back to the jurisdiction of the archdiocese of St. Boniface, Manitoba, and he left in July 1972.

The German apostolate was then under the care of Father Martin Grootscholten, SCJ, who celebrated Mass twice a month. But he proved incapable of carrying out any work among the German families or continuing the bimonthly Mass in conjunction with his full-time family apostolate duties. In October 1972, an appeal was made for a priest from Germany for the some 400 German-speaking families in London, but none could be spared, owing to the shortage of priests in Germany. Father K. Zarnowiecki, CSMA, of the Michaelite Fathers of Hyde Park commenced serving the German community in January-February 1973. Father John Van Wezel, SCJ, of the Sacred Heart junior seminary in Delaware, was in charge of the German apostolate by October of the same year, which appears to have been terminated with the departure of Father Van Wezel in 1979 or 1980.

Source: DLA, Latvian Mission File and Gerald Emmett Carter papers, Box 23, London German mission. Additional information supplied by Anna Arndt.

London Portuguese Mission

Father I. Risse, OFM, arrived in London in February 1964 to minister to the German community. Interestingly, because he also spoke Portuguese and had worked with Portuguese immigrants, the diocese established a Portuguese mission in London on 1 September 1965.

Father Manuel A. Louro, a native of Portugal, was placed in charge and conducted services in St. Mary's church hall. The Portuguese community then comprised some 340 individuals, most of whom lived within the boundaries of St. Mary's parish. The church was filled for the community's first Our Lady of Fatima procession, held on 12 October 1965. In August 1966, Father Louro was appointed assistant priest at St. Mary's. In addition to overseeing to the needs of the Portuguese people of London and area, he also ministered to the Portuguese communities in Strathroy, Woodstock, West Lorne and Sarnia. With Father Louro's leaving, about September 1967, Father Luis Amado, who was from Latin America and a student at the University of Detroit, ministered to the community on weekends. In October, he transferred the celebration of Mass to the Divine Word Centre.

Father António M. Martins, SJ, of Lisbon, Portugal, became Father Louro's replacement in July 1968. His insistence on a place for weekday Masses led to the purchase, in late December 1970, of the house at 634 Dufferin Avenue. Father Orlando Fazzenaro, of the diocese of Lins, Brazil, succeeded Father Martins in July 1972. By the end of 1972, Father Fazzenaro had transferred his residence to Holy Cross parish and was celebrating weekday and Saturday evening Masses there and two Sunday morning Masses, at the Divine Word Centre. Effective 4 March 1973, the Sunday morning Mass was held in the church basement and the afternoon Mass in the church. The Sunday morning Mass was transferred to the church in June. On Sunday, 29 July 1973, the Festa Señor des Milagros was held. The procession started at 1:00 p.m. from St. Mary's Church and made its way to the Western Fair Grounds. After the procession, an outdoor Mass was celebrated, followed by a dinner.

Father António Seara, O de M, of Madrid, Spain, succeeded Father Fazzenaro in October 1974. Owing to the cramped quarters at Holy Cross and the friction between Father Fazzenaro and the pastor, Father Seara moved to St. Patrick's rectory but continued to hold services at Holy Cross. Like his predecessors, Father Seara felt the need to minister to the Portuguese communities beyond the London area and began to collect funds for the building of a Portuguese church in London. A few years later, when this project fell through, Father Seara made it a point to refund all the money to those who had given to the cause.

In April 1977, he was succeeded by Father Henry G. Kea, CSSR. While given jurisdiction over the Portuguese communities within only the London deanery, Father Kea, like Father Seara before him, tended to overextend himself in assuming responsibility for all the Portuguese in the diocese. In May 1978, the property at 204 St. Julien Street in London was purchased as a rectory for the London Portuguese mission, and, in November, Father Manuel Cardoso succeeded Father Kea, who was transferred to Sarnia. On 25 May 1984, the London Portuguese mission was elevated to parish status and amalgamated with Holy Cross parish to form the new parish of Holy Cross-Santa Cruz.

In 2000, Father Nelson M. Cabral was the first to be appointed, for two years, as co-ordinator of the Diocesan Portuguese Community and took up residence at Holy Cross rectory. The main focus was the organization of the Portuguese-speaking clergy to oversee the administration of the various Portuguese communities in the diocese on a regular basis.

Sources: DLA, London: Portuguese Mission File and Gerald Emmett Carter papers, Box 23; Holy Cross Church 2003 [London: 2003]; "Rev. H.G. Kea," *Newsletter of the Diocese of London*, no. 63 (Fall 1994), 5.

Mary Immaculate

On 15 August 1965, Father Cornelius P. Herlihy, OMI (1965-74), was appointed pastor of a new parish dedicated to Mary Immaculate in southeast London. Its west-east boundaries extended from Vancouver Street to the Middlesex-Oxford county line. On 20 August, Father Herlihy finalized arrangements with the London Public School Board to celebrate three Masses each Sunday in the gymnasium of Sir Winston Churchill Public School. The first Mass was celebrated at the school on Sunday, 29 August. The first offertory collection amounted to $330.17, of which $75 went to pay for the rental of the premises. In the mean time, Father Herlihy, and his assistant, Father Kevin McNamara, OMI, were living at St. Patrick's rectory and arrangements had been made to purchase a house at 225 Admiral Drive as a temporary rectory. As the building was still under construction by Mason Brothers, plans were altered to include two additional rooms and a bathroom. The parishioners soon outgrew the public school location and Sunday Masses were transferred to the auditorium at Clarke Road Secondary School.

A site for the new church was obtained in the

Nelson Park subdivision, and a loan of $40,000 was provided by St. Patrick's parish. On 3 October 1966, the first sod was turned by Monsignor Fergus J. Laverty, the chancellor. The architect for the

Mary Immaculate

new church was Tim A. Murray of Ottawa, and the general contractor was Ellis-Don Ltd. of London. The cost was $350,000. The church and rectory were connected by a walled-in courtyard. It had been decided that the church should not have a front-and-back-door look to it. The amphitheatre-style provided seating for 750 people, with the furthest seat only 70 feet (21.3 m) from the semicircular sanctuary. The interior received controlled daylight. The altar, baptistry and confessionals were designed by Ottawa artist Gerald Trottier. Mary Immaculate was one of the few churches at that time not to have a communion rail. Shortly after its completion, the building won an award of merit for its design. The parish had approximately 500 families. The building was completed in August 1967 and solemnly blessed by Bishop Carter on 19 December 1967.

Mary Immaculate's second pastor was Father John O'Connor, OMI (1974-78). After serving the parish from its inception, the Oblates were compelled to relinquish Mary Immaculate in August 1978, owing to a lack of priests in their community. The parish was then placed in the hands of the diocesan clergy, with Father T. Francis O'Connor as pastor (1978-80), followed by Fathers Paul A. Roy (1980-86) and Martin A. Johnston (1986-88). During the pastorate of Father Richard P. Bester (1988-97), the twenty-fifth anniversary of the parish was celebrated with a Mass on 15 June 1991. Bishop Sherlock was main celebrant. Father Bester was succeeded by Fathers Lance W. Magdziak (1997-98), Jan Burczyk, CSMA (1998-2001) and Joseph F. Hardy (2001). Under Father Graham R.J. Keep, a three-phase construction project was undertaken, beginning with the building of a new rectory, which was completed in September 2004. Father Keep commissioned Ellen Erenberg, a parishioner and local artist, to produce an oil painting of the Blessed Mother.

Among the groups serving the parish are the CWL, Knights of Columbus, Life Teen, Mission and Social Justice Committee and St. Vincent de Paul Society.

Sources: "Church to Rise," *London Free Press*, 4 October 1966, 5; "Congregation and sanctuary united in new R C church," *London Free Press*, 17 August 1967, 23; "The Church of Mary Immaculate...," *London Free Press*, 28 September 1968, 38. Additional information supplied by Chris Bray.

Our Lady of Częstochowa

Polish immigrants started arriving in London before the end of the nineteenth century, though not in significant numbers. By October 1908 they were served at St. Mary's church by Father Paul Sobczak, CR, pastor of the Poles in Berlin (now Kitchener). As of September 1906, Father Jan J. Andrzejewski ministered to the Poles of London from his base in Windsor. The Polish mission at St. Mary's was attached to Holy Trinity (Polish) parish in Windsor with the establishment of that parish in 1918. Father Francis R. Nowak, appointed chaplain of St. Joseph's hospital about 1930, celebrated Mass for the Polish community each Sunday at St. Mary's. Father Paul R. Sargewitz (1933-39) expanded the work among the Polish people, and an early morning Mass was celebrated in Polish at St. Mary's each Sunday.

A new wave of Polish immigrants arrived after the Second World War, and Father Jan A. Achtabowski, who ministered to the community in London and was himself a native of Poland, urged them to establish their own parish. In this endeavour they were encouraged by Bishop Cody, who established a Polish parish named in honour of Our Lady of Częstochowa. Father Franciszek Pluta, a pastor in Shickley, Nebraska, agreed to become the

Polish pastor in London. Bishop Cody conducted the groundbreaking ceremony on 12 December 1953. The first Mass was celebrated in the yet-unfinished church on 15 August 1954, the feast of the Assumption, the day of the annual pilgrimage to the church of Our Lady, in Częstochowa, Poland. On 12 September 1954, the new church was blessed by Bishop Cody. On 11-12 September 1969, the parish hosted Karol Cardinal Wojtyła, who in 1978 was

Our Lady of Częstochowa

elected pope and took the name John Paul II.

Monsignor Pluta retired in 1973 and was succeeded by Father Peter A. Sanczenko (1973-83). Among Father Sanczenko's many accomplishments was the initiation of the annual Corpus Christi procession in 1975. That same year, he arranged for the Ursuline Sisters of the Agonizing Heart of Jesus to establish a small community on Adelaide Street. This, in turn, allowed for the formation of the Eucharistic League in 1976. Its purpose was to deepen the faith of its young female members and to form a circle of friendship among them. The two Ursuline sisters who have continued to enhance the spiritual life of Our Lady of Częstochowa parish are Sisters Kinga Lewicka and Ursula Bruzik. In 1984, during Father Mitchell S. Kaminski's pastorship (1983-92), parts of the church were rebuilt and the parish hall was modernized. Father Kaminski is probably best known for his sponsorship of many refugee Polish families in the wake of the imposition of martial law, on 13 December 1981, and the suppression of the Solidarity Trade Union in Poland by the Communist government. As well, he and the parishioners have extended a helping hand to many to get settled and adjust to a new country.

During the pastorate of Father Adam Gabriel, CSMA (1992-2005), renovations were made to the rectory and parish offices, the parish bulletin was redesigned and the parish website was launched. His greatest project, however, was overseeing the complete rebuilding of the church between October 1995 and June 1996. Seating capacity was doubled to 600 to accommodate approximately 2,300 families, who are served by six Masses on the weekends. On 12 September 2004, the Polish community celebrated the fiftieth anniversary of the parish. The extremely important contribution of the Michaelite Fathers to the diocese was demonstrated in 2005 when they were given custody of the parish.

Sources: Mary Turner, *St. Mary's Parish London, Ontario 1872-1942* [London:1942]; "Our Lady of Częstochowa celebrates 50th anniversary," *Newsletter of the Diocese of London*, no. 114 (Fall 2004), 14.

Our Lady of Šiluva

In 1949, Father Vincent Rudzinskas was the first to minister to the needs of the Lithuanians of London in their own language. In the early 1950s, Father Francis Jokubaitis briefly ministered to the Lithuanian community, and was in turn succeeded by Father Joseph C. Danielius. Some 150 Lithuanian families lived in London and, during this period, Sunday Mass was celebrated at St. Joseph and other London parishes. Language classes were conducted at St. Peter's school on Saturdays. Owing to his advanced years, Father Danielius retired in the early 1960s, after serving the London Lithuanian community for more than ten years, and the search for his successor began. Through the efforts of John Butkus, Sr., president of the local Lithuanian council, the services of Father Boleslovas Pacevièius were obtained. He arrived in London on 18 January 1964.

Within weeks, Father Pacevièius convinced the leaders of the Lithuanian community that they should organize a parish of their own in their own building. With the willingness of the community to support such a venture, full agreement was reached on 14 February 1964, and, two days later, Bishop Carter formally founded a Lithuanian national parish with Father Pacevièius as its first pastor (1964-76). A week later, the former St. Mark's Anglican church, located at 1414 Dundas Street East, was acquired for $25,000. The diocese loaned $15,000

for its purchase and, within three months, more than $17,000 was raised by seventy families, together with the help of their neighbours, some of whom were non-Catholic. The redesigning of the church's interior was undertaken by the Toronto architect, Dr. Alfredas Kulpavièius, with much of the work being done by parishioners. The dedication and first Mass in the renovated building was celebrated on 14 June 1964, the anniversary of Soviet mass murders and deportations of Lithuanians to Siberia in 1941. The church was renamed Our Lady of Šiluva in honour of the apparition of Our Lady in 1608, in the village of Šiluva, Lithuania.

The parish hall, which could not accommodate

Our Lady of Šiluva

all 600 guests at the dedication, soon became the community's cultural centre for such groups as the CWL, the Baltija folk ensemble, the Tauras sports club, Saturday Lithuanian language classes, scouts and guides, three choir groups, a folk-dance group, a pensioners' club, a financial aid club and a library.

In 1981, while Father Jonas Staškus was pastor (1976-81), $2,600 was raised and sent to Lithuanian Catholic Religious Aid. In 1984, during the pastorship of Father Ignas B. Mikalauskas, OFM (1981-89), Our Lady of Šiluva celebrated its twentieth anniversary with the publication of a history booklet, which noted that, since its inception, the parish had spent $299,917.25 and was debt free. The number of active parishioners consisted of thirty-nine families and an additional forty individuals. Father Mikalauskas was still pastor when the parish commemorated its twenty-fifth anniversary in 1989. Since 1989, Father Kazimieras

Kaknevicius has been parish administrator.

The number of families attending Our Lady of Šiluva has decreased, owing to deaths and migrations, but the parish remains the centre of the Lithuanian Canadian community in London. The library, museum and community archives are still housed in the parish hall. The community continues to hold a special meeting on the first Sunday of each month, and the London Lithuanian Pensioners Club meets every third Wednesday of the month. Pašvaisté, the Lithuanian choir, still leads the congregation in singing at Sunday morning Mass. All religious and national festivities are regularly celebrated in the parish hall. Moreover, the generosity and sacrifices of the community ensures that the large funds necessary to operate the parish are raised, as it puts into practice the words of the Lithuanian national hymn: "For the benefit of our country and welfare of all the people we must work united and work hard."

Our Lady of Šiluva was canonically suppressed as a parish, effective 30 June 2007, and established as Our Lady of Šiluva Lithuanian Catholic Community, with Monsignor Jonas (John) Staškevićius as priest-chaplain.

Sources:. "*Šiluvos Marijos Parapija Londone 1964-1984*" [London: 1984]; "*Šiluvos Marijos Parapija Londone 1964-1989* Our Šiluva Lithuanian Parish, London, Ontario, Canada" [London: 1989]. Additional information provided by Dana Chainauskas.

St. Andrew Kim Korean Apostolate

In September 1975, Father Hyoshin M. Kim was placed in charge of the Korean Catholic Community and held services in St. Martin of Tours church. He had been invited to look after the spiritual needs of the Korean Catholics in the diocese of London and was paid $250 monthly — $150 for room and board and $100 for maintenance. Father John Y.S. Lee took over from Father Kim, on 9 January 1976. The previous year he had served the Korean Catholics in the archdiocese of Toronto. He was given the same $250 monthly allowance from the diocese, plus car expenses of $100 per month. Receipts in 1976 were $2,866.33 and expenditures

were $2,448, exclusive of the monthly diocesan allotment to Father Lee. As his three-year leave expired in April 1977, he had to return to the diocese of Jeonju, South Korea.

Father Joseph C. H. Yu succeeded Father Lee in March 1977. By the end of 1978, his monthly allotment from the diocese consisted of $150 for maintenance, $143 for car expenses and $150 for room and board. In August 1977, the Korean Catholic Community in London was registered with the Federal Government as a charitable non-profit organization. The fifth anniversary of the Korean apostolate in London was celebrated on the weekend of 27-28 September 1980 at St. Martin's. Young Chug Lee and Christine Lee received plaques and special thanks from the congregation of some forty families for keeping alive the traditional values of their religious and ethnic community. By 1981, a Korean Catholic Language Heritage school was located in the adjacent St. Martin's school. In 1981, Father Yu returned to Korea and was succeeded by Father Benedict P. Kim.

On Sunday, 4 September 1983, Father Kim offered a special Mass at St. Martin's in memory of the 269 people killed in the shooting down of a South Korean airliner by a Soviet fighter plane on 1 September. Father B. Kim returned to Korea in April 1985 and was succeeded by Father John P-H. Kim. Like all his predecessors, he resided at St. Peter's cathedral rectory. In March 1987, Father John Kim returned to Korea, and for the next few years the Korean Apostolate had no resident priest in London, the contact person being Jungsik Lee.

In 1989, the Korean apostolate in London again had a resident priest, this time in the person of Father James P-H. Kim (1989-91), who lived at St. Martin's rectory. By now the apostolate was dedicated to St. Andrew Kim Taegon, the first Korean-born priest who in 1846 was the first priest to die for the faith in that country. Along with 102 others martyred in Korea between 1839 and 1867, he was canonized on 6 May 1984 by Pope John Paul II.

Father Kim was assigned outside the diocese in September 1991, and was succeeded by Father Mark K.Y. Lee. In 1994 or 1995, Father Lee took up residence at 75 Four Oaks Crescent. Henceforth, this was to be home for those in charge of the Korean apostolate. In February 1997, Father Lee was succeeded by Father Paul Y. Park. At this time, the Korean-language Sunday Mass was celebrated, at

1:00 p.m., at St. Martin's. The apostolate celebrated its twenty-fifth anniversary on 28 September 2000. On 30 June 2007, it was established as St. Andrew Kim Korean Catholic Community with Father Jacobus J. Hong as priest-chaplain.

Sources: DLA, London, Korean Mission File; "Koreans keep native customs," *London Free Press*, 25 September 1980, D1; "London's Koreans react with shock and anger," *London Free Press*, 3 September 1983, A6; "Korean children keep Yule tradition alive," *London Free Press*, 23 December 1983, B1.

St. Andrew the Apostle

St. Andrew the Apostle

On 1 August 1965, a new parish was established in the northeastern part of the city, with Father John K. McMaster as its first pastor (1964-73). The Masses were celebrated initially at St. Stephen Anglican Church and Evelyn Harrison Public School, while a rectory was set up at 1295 Sorrel Road. The new parish was named St. Andrew the Apostle in recognition of the many years of service to the diocese by Monsignor Andrew P. Mahoney as rector of St. Peter's seminary and vicar general of the diocese. The first Christmas and New Year's Masses were celebrated at the Ontario Vocational School (now Fanshawe College) on Oxford Street.

Joseph J. Fallon donated land on Packs Lane for the new church, and Philip Carter Johnson was hired as architect. On 8 May 1966, Monsignor Mahoney turned the first sod, and, on 26 December 1966, he blessed and laid the cornerstone. The Ellis-Don Company was the general contractor. By this time, because of the large numbers of parishioners, Sunday Masses were celebrated at Huron Heights Public School. Father McMaster moved into the new rectory in late February 1967, and, on 11 June 1967, Bishop Carter blessed the new church.

The parish was saddened by the death of their beloved pastor on 13 May 1973. Father Marcel L. Leboeuf was appointed the second pastor. In the summer of 1974, extensive repairs were made to the church and the parish hall was completely renovated. In March 1981, the church organ was overhauled. The spire was removed in November 1984 to solve an ongoing problem of water leaking into the church. Bishop Sherlock participated in the twenty-fifth anniversary celebrations on 17 June 1990.

In June 1989, Father Patrick J. Mellon succeeded Father M. Francis White as pastor and served until 1993. By November 1991, the parish had put a new roof on the church and rectory, replaced the entrance doors, repaired the furnace and kneelers, installed a new sound system and replaced the sign on the front lawn. At the same time, the parish debt was reduced from over $93,000 to $46,000. The debt was completely eliminated in April 1992. In January 1993, Father Mellon suffered a brain aneurysm and died one year later.

Meanwhile, the Order of Discalced Carmelite Friars, established in the diocese on 15 August 1989, were given St. Andrew's parish effective 25 June 1993. Father Manuel Schembri, OCD, assumed the duties of pastor, from 1993 until 1996, with Father Raphael Bruzzone, OCD, as associate pastor. In recognition of the donation of the church property by Joseph Fallon, the street was renamed in August 1995 and St. Andrew's became 1 Fallon's Lane.

Father Dominic Borg, OCD, who had been associate pastor since October 1994, was named pastor in June 1996 upon Father Manuel's recall to Malta. Later the same year work began on additions to the church and rectory and a major renovation of the parish hall. The cost was covered by the generosity of the parishioners and a donation of $137,000 from the friars themselves within the diocese. A major bequest in the amount of $40,000 from the John Mestick estate was received in September 1998, and a new sound system was installed that December. In 2000 the parish was debt free.

A high point, not only for the parish, but for the entire Catholic community of London, was the visitation of the major reliquary of St. Thérèse of the Child Jesus at St. Andrew's on 18-20 October 2001. The thirtieth anniversary of Father Dominic's ordination was celebrated on 9 July 2002; this coincided with the visit of the Father Provincial of the Order, Father Alfred Grech, OCD.

Sources: Information supplied by Ann Anderson and Father Dominic Borg, OCD.

Sts. Cyril and Methodius Mission

Beginning in January 1968, a period of political liberalization known as the Prague Spring, occurred in Communist Czechoslovakia. This was crushed, however, by the invasion of the forces of the Soviet Union and most of its Warsaw Pact allies on 20-21 August 1968. As a result, thousands of Czechs and Slovaks sought asylum in Western Europe, the United States and Canada. By September, political refugees from Czechoslovakia were arriving in the diocese of London. On 15 September 1968, Father Francis A. Dostal, SJ, the founding priest of St. Anthony of Padua parish (for the Czech and Slovak communities) in Chatham, began offering Mass at St. Mary's Hospital for the arriving Czechs. Before the end of the month, thirteen refugees were in London. Father Dostal left London at the end of September 1968 but, from time to time, returned to celebrate Mass.

Soon, however, the number of the refugees in London began to increase, and, at the beginning of 1969, Bishop Carter established the Sts. Cyril and Methodius mission for the Czechs and Slovaks and placed Father Dostal in charge. Our Lady of Częstochowa church, which served London's Polish community, became the host church for Father Dostal's mission. The first baptism in this mission, that of Henry Edward, son of Zdenek and Janina Karasek, was performed at Our Lady of Częstochowa church on 9 February 1969. Over the next few years, Father Dostal's mission also extended to St. Thomas, Blenheim, Windsor and Kingsville. The first of only two marriages performed by Father Dostal in this mission was that of Tomislav Tomljenovic and Marija Vzelac, on 5 September 1971, at Holy Angels church, St. Thomas. The second was also celebrated there on 3

November 1973. Bishop Carter conducted the only confirmation of members of this mission on 21 May 1972. On this occasion three individuals received the sacrament.

In 1970, Mass was celebrated on Sunday evenings at Our Lady of Częstochowa church, preceded by confessions, beginning at 5:30 p.m. Also, a Slovenian school, in connection with the mission, was being operated on Saturdays at St. Mary's school. In 1971, Holy Week and Easter Sunday services were held at St. Peter's seminary, where Father Dostal was living. In Father Dostal's absence, in late 1971 and early 1972, Father George M. Svoboda offered Mass for the Czech and Slovak communities at St. Mary's church. On 5 March 1972, Mass was offered by a Slovak Jesuit priest from Galt. By March 1974, the Czechs and Slovaks were served by two Sunday Masses in London: 3:00 p.m. at Our Lady of Częstochowa church and 6:15 p.m. in the main chapel in St. Joseph's Hospital.

The revenues for Sts. Cyril and Methodius mission in 1971 were $1,243.61, including offerings at Masses in St. Thomas, Blenheim, Windsor and London. Expenditures were $915.51. In 1972, revenues had increased to $1404.76, including Mass offerings from Kingsville, and expenditures were $1,189.95. In 1973, revenues for the mission, including London, Alvinston, Chatham, Dresden and Ridgetown, were $1274.02, and expenditures were $1270.05. The charge of $875.30 for room and board at St. Peter's seminary was, as in other years, paid by the diocese of London. This mission appears to have ceased sometime after August 1974, with the death of Father Dostal.

Source: DLA, London, Sts. Cyril & Methodius Mission File.

St. Francis of Assisi Hispanic Catholic Community

With Bishop Sherlock's appointment of Sister Helen Diesbourg, CSJ, to minister to the Spanish-speaking refugees in London, the Catholic Centre for Latin Americans was established at 533 Clarence Street. Father M. Francis White celebrated a Spanish Mass at 2 p.m. on the last Sunday of the month at Holy Rosary church, and Father Clare J. Coleman was the community's spiritual director.

With the arrival of Father Francis E. Brown in London, on 1 October 1988, and his taking up residence at St. Martin's rectory, Father Coleman, the pastor, gave permission for Father Brown to offer Mass on Sundays at St. Martin's church. Prior to coming to the city, Father Brown had spent twenty-three years in Ecuador with the Society of St. James.

His congregation in London was largely from Chile, Nicaragua, Guatemala and El Salvador. On their arrival in the city, the Spanish-speaking immigrants were approached by evangelical sects, which tried to lure them away from the Catholic Church.

After 31 March 1990, the Catholic Hispanic community was transferred from St. Martin's to St. Stephen of Hungary church at the corner of Bruce Street and Wortley Road. By the late 1990s, Father Brown's persistence and hard work was paying off and his congregation was filling St. Stephen's every Sunday for the 11 a.m. Mass.

After the closure of St. Stephen's church in January 2002, the Catholic Hispanic community returned to St. Martin's for services. In addition to ministering to the Hispanic community at St. Martin's, Father Brown started in December 2002 to celebrate a Spanish-language Sunday Mass at Blessed Sacrament church. The fifteenth anniversary of the community was commemorated in 2003, with Bishop Fabbro as celebrant of the Mass. Father Brown retired, effective 31 March 2004, and was succeeded by Monsignor Isidro Payan-Melendez. A native of Mexico, he was previously assistant pastor at Sacred Heart, Delaware. He continued to celebrate weekend Masses on Saturday and Sunday evenings at St. Martin's. For health reasons, Monsignor Payan-Melendez returned to Mexico at the end of 2004.

The Hispanic Charismatic Renewal Group began the tradition of holding annual overnight Easter vigils in 1992. Catholic Congresses, aimed at celebrating and keeping the faith alive, were held at Centennial Hall, from 1999 to 2001 and in 2003. Anywhere from 400 to 600 people participated. The seventeenth anniversary of the Charismatic Renewal Group was celebrated in conjunction with the Catholic Congress in late October 2005, and a dinner was held.

During January 2006, Father Francis L. Murphy, pastor of Sacred Heart, Delaware, and Father T. Francis O'Connor, of St. Peter's seminary,

ministered to the Spanish community in the interim. Both had served for a number of years in the diocese's mission in Peru, and Father O'Connor had previously filled in for Father Brown when needed.

Throughout 2006, Father Cleber Fernandez, OP, came from Toronto to celebrate weekend Masses. This arrangement lasted until the end of August.

On 27-28 May 2006, a retreat for the mission was conducted by Brother Felix Colon of the Divine Mercy Religious Association of Puerto Rico. Permission was granted to celebrate Mass at 11:30 a.m. on Sundays at St. Martin's during the months of July and August.

At the time the mission had some 325 families registered. There were fifteen active ministries, groups and committees, involving over 150 individuals, in this vibrant faith community.

On 30 June 2007 the community was established as St. Francis of Assisi Hispanic Catholic Community, with Father Pedro Delgado as priest-chaplain.

Sources: DLA, Catholic Hispanic Community of London File; Fred Pitt, "Meet the Pastor of London Hispanic community — Padre Francisco," undated newspaper clipping; "London's Catholic Centre for Latin Americans," *Newsletter of the Diocese of London*, no. 34 (Fall 1988), 15. Additional information supplied by Martin Jimenez.

St. George

The parish of St. George was established in village of Byron by Bishop Cody, on 9 July 1955, and Father Raymond J. Groome (1955-59) was appointed pastor for the parish's one hundred families. Mass was initially celebrated in the auditorium of Byron public school. The groundbreaking ceremony for the new church was held on 1 January 1956. The first Mass was celebrated in the completed church basement on 2 September and in the church proper on 28 October. The church was blessed and dedicated by Bishop Cody on 4 November 1956.

In 1980, during the pastorship of Monsignor J. Austin Roney (1964-84), the church was upgraded with a new entrance on the south side. In December 1982, the building was extended on the north side to accommodate the growing parish community. The wooden beams on the outside of the A-frame structure were enclosed. During the pastorship of Father Richard K. Janisse (1990-96), the new position of pastoral minister was established and filled by Sister Mary-Ellen Kenny, OSU. She continued as pastoral minister until 2006.

St. George

Serious deterioration in the wooden beams supporting the church's structure was noticed in 1992, and Parker Consultants recommended against their replacement owing to prohibitive costs. Moreover, a ten-fold increase in the number of parish families since 1955, together with the anticipation of future growth in the west end of the city, raised the question whether to repair or to replace the church. After much discussion and consideration, eighty-three percent of the parishioners voted in 1993 to build a new church. Initially, it was believed that the existing location was too small for a much larger church, and efforts were made to acquire property west of Byron. Most parishioners, however, showed little enthusiasm for this proposal. Also, there were environmental concerns at the proposed new site, which convinced the building committee to re-examine the possibility of using the existing site. Following negotiations with the London District Catholic School Board regarding parking concerns, the committee concluded that the new church could indeed be built on land occupied by the existing church. Father Janisse's successor, Father Gary N. Goyeau (1996-2004), threw himself wholeheartedly into the planning of the new building, a task made easier by the active participation of many talented lay people who served on the building committee. In late 1996, the parish selected the architectural firm of Walter Fedy Partnership of Kitchener. Two of the partners, Roger Farwell and Bill Krohn, consulted with the parish's building committee and the diocesan Liturgical Commission at the beginning of 1997. In the summer of 1997, Achim Klass was retained to design the worship space, altar and statues. On 10-11 January 1998, the final Masses were celebrated in the old church. The building was taken down and the cornerstone was preserved for placing in the new building. For more than a year, Mass was

celebrated at St. Thomas Aquinas secondary school on weekends and at St. George Catholic school during the week. The first service in the new church and community centre, which cost $3.2 million, was celebrated at the Easter Vigil on 3 April 1999. Bishop Sherlock blessed and dedicated the church on 23 April, the feast of St. George the Martyr, the parish's patron saint. Two unique features of this church are its Renaissance style of architecture and the place of repose for the Blessed Sacrament in a chapel rather than in the church proper.

Father John M. Pirt arrived in June 2004 and was soon involved in the planning of the celebration of the fiftieth anniversary of the parish in 2006. Various events were held during that year, including an anniversary banquet at the Hellenic Community Centre on the evening of 7 May. This was attended by Bishop Fabbro and many of the former pastors of St. George's. Today, the parish serves over 1,500 registered families and three nursing homes.

Sources: *Celebrating 50 Years 1956 - 2006* [London: 2006]; James Reaney, "A new perspective on the art of worshipping," *London Free Press*, 24 July 1998, A2; Robert Barlow, "A marriage of form and function," *London Free Press*, 19 June 1999, F8. Additional information supplied by Peter Myers, Sister Mary-Ellen Kenny and Father John Pirt.

St. John the Divine

Bishop Carter founded St. John the Divine parish in May 1965. It was one of four parishes established in London that year. Its boundaries were the Thames River on the north, the present Wonderland and Southdale roads on the west and south and a line extending roughly south, from the Thames through the Coves on the east. While the area was formerly a part of St. Martin of Tours parish, a number of families of the newly founded parish had been attending St. George parish in Byron. Father Stanley E. McGuire (1965-76) was named the first pastor, and Mass was first celebrated in July in the auditorium of Westminster secondary school. During its first year of operation the congregation numbered some 175 families and the average Sunday attendance at Mass was 600. Many parishioners opened their homes for weekday Masses. With no church building available, study groups also moved from house to house.

St. John the Divine

On 16 April 1967, the first sod for St. John the Divine church was turned by Monsignor West T. Flannery, pastor of St. Martin's, the mother parish. Monsignor Fergus J. Laverty, the chancellor, laid the cornerstone on 1 October 1967. Meanwhile, the number of families had swelled to 450, and on average 1,100 people attended the three Sunday Masses. On 4 February 1968, the first Mass was celebrated in the new church. On 5 May 1968, Bishop Carter solemnly blessed the complex.

David Stevens of London was the church's architect. Murray McCance, a former Trappist monk, was the liturgical consultant and designer. The church was designed to allow all parishioners to be as close to the altar as possible. Standing out against the blue sanctuary wall was a resplendently jewelled Resurrection Cross, designed by Christopher Wallis. Emphasizing the Risen Christ, its fused glass and quartz, in red and white, reflects light from above and around. The altar of French marble was designed and produced in Toronto. The sanctuary lamp, with its seven lamps, recalls the seven lamps mentioned in the opening chapter of Revelations. This lamp was designed by the sculptor George Wallace, who was also responsible for the statue of St. John the Divine that stands outside the church, the Crucifix in the chapel and the church's candlesticks. The entrance facade was designed along the lines of the basilica of St. John Lateran, the pope's cathedral in Rome.

Over the years St. John the Divine parish has been one of the most progressive in the diocese in the wake of the Second Vatican Council. Many of the changes, which we take for granted today, were first introduced in this parish: Communion in the hand; the distribution of Holy Communion by lay persons; women lay readers; folk choirs; and a parish advisory board. In 1980, Father John P. Boyde, the pastor (1976-81), hired Julie Harrison as the first lay pastoral minister in the diocese.

By 1975, there were an estimated 800 families within the parish boundaries. Sunday attendance at Mass averaged 1,800, with four Masses being celebrated. By 1990, the twenty-fifth anniversary of the parish, the number of families was in excess of 1,200, the average attendance at Sunday Masses was 1,700 and the average weekly collection was about $5,600.

As the church mezzanine became too small for meetings and social gatherings, the second floor of the neighbouring St. Albert's separate school was converted into parish rooms and the school gymnasium was used for larger functions, such as parish dances. In 1986, a new parish centre was built, which was officially opened by Bishop Sherlock on 16 November.

Sources: "Church of St. John the Divine Tenth Anniversary 1975" [London: 1975]; Jim O'Neail, "The Parish of St. John the Divine 1965-1990: The First Twenty-five Years" [London: 1990].

St. Joseph

With substantial growth of the Catholic population in the western part of the cathedral parish, arrangements were made with the London Separate School Board to use St. Joseph's school on Wilson Avenue in London West, as a temporary centre for the celebration of Mass. This area became a new parish, and Father Roy B. Cassin (1951-58) was appointed pastor, effective 1 July 1951. In September, the school board agreed to sell a parcel of newly acquired land on the west side of Charles Street and along Mount Pleasant Avenue to the diocese as a site for a church and rectory. On 4 November 1951, the first sod was turned. Initially, there was considerable resistance from many people within the new parish boundaries to being detached from St. Peter's cathedral, which had been the parish for many of their parents and grandparents. Built as a prefabricated church by the Gerry Supply & Lumber Company of London, St Joseph's was dedicated on 4 May 1952 with a Mass in the church basement. Mitchell & Sons continued construction and, on 9 July 1952, Monsignor Mahoney formally dedicated the church. The structure was blessed by Bishop Cody on 9 September 1952. During its first year, 190 families were registered as parishioners. A new St. Joseph's school was built to the immediate north of the church in 1954.

St. Joseph

At the time of the arrival of Father Paul D. Milne (1961-66), in June 1961, the parish had increased to 524 families. This number was reduced to 262, in 1965, with the formation of St. Pius X parish. St. Joseph's assessed dowry of $25,000, as a contribution to the establishment of its daughter parish, was paid in full by the end of April 1966. Father Milne continued as administrator of St. Joseph's after his appointment to St. Pius X parish, until Father William C. Cooney (1966-69) returned in October from the diocesan mission in Peru. Within two years of the arrival of Father John W.P. Graham (1969-71), sufficient funds were raised to renovate the church's exterior. In 1974, during the pastorship of Father Donald J. McMaster (1974-86), the church was completely renovated and the Blessed Sacrament and baptistry chapels were added. Further redecorating followed two years later, and again in 1978 and 1979. With the help of Sister Ann Wilson, Father McMaster established a ministry to shut-ins and the elderly at Chelsey Park. By the late 1970s and early 1980s, the number of parishioners was declining and the congregation consisted mainly of seniors. St. Joseph's school closed in 1983. When Father Jim Williams (1986-96) celebrated his first Mass as pastor of St. Joseph's, in May 1986, there was not a child present among the 160 parishioners in attendance. St. Joseph's became known as "the smallest parish in London."

In large part, through the engaging personality, preaching and leadership of Father Williams, the trend began to shift during the late 1980s and early 1990s, and there was a significant increase in the parish population. Father Williams would stand outside and greet the parishioners before each Mass, regardless of the weather, and St. Joseph's became known as a welcoming parish. A significant pastoral staff was formed to meet the needs of the community, with special attention placed on seniors, the sick, shut-ins and the youth. Once a month, Father Williams celebrated Mass at Chelsey Park and Meadowcroft senior residences. By 1992, over 200 parishioners were actively involved in various aspects of parish life. A door-to-door parish census in 1989 raised the number of registered parishioners and brought in some non-practicing Catholics. That same year also saw major structural renovations to the church. During this time, young families were once again settling in the parish as they sought affordable starter homes. At the time of Father Williams' departure, in June 1996, the number of registered households was in excess of 600.

The parish celebrated its twenty-fifth anniversary in 1977, and its fortieth in 1992. It marked its fiftieth anniversary, when Father Robert J. Remark was pastor, on the weekend of 7-8 September 2002. The parish was clustered with St. Pius X parish and in 2006 was closed with its last Mass on Sunday, 9 July.

Sources: DLA, Parish Files; *50th Anniversary 1952-2002 St. Joseph Parish London, Ontario* [2002]; Adrian Eys, "St. Joseph Parish, London, Celebrates 50 years," *Newsletter of the Diocese of London*, no. 105 (Advent/Christmas 2002), 4.

St. Justin

On 10 June 1977, Bishop Carter instructed Father Patrick J. Mellon (1977-89), a teacher residing at Regina Mundi College, that, effective 15 September, he would be entrusted with the formation of a new parish in the White Oaks-Southdale area. The rapid expansion of this area had already obliged Father M. Francis White, pastor of Holy Rosary (1969-81), to celebrate two extra

Masses in the area each weekend, one at St. Francis school in Westminster Park and the other in St. Anthony's school in White Oaks. By the time Father Mellon assumed responsibility as pastor of the newly formed St. Justin's parish, three Masses were required. In order to bring his parishioners together close to where the church would be built, he rented St. Stephen's Memorial Anglican church, east of the intersection of Southdale and Wellington roads, at fifty dollars per service. He celebrated two Masses at St. Stephen's on Saturday evening and Sunday morning, and a third Mass in the gymnasium of St.

St. Justin

Anthony's school. Meanwhile, that summer 2.3 acres (.9 ha) were purchased, on the southwest corner of Ernest Avenue and Jalna Boulevard, at a cost of $80,000 per acre, from Matthews Development Co.

In 1978, Mykola Wasylko was engaged as architect and Henry Komarek, a parishioner, built a model of the proposed church, rectory, offices and hall. Because of the estimated cost of the project it was decided to build the complex in two phases. The first phase would consist of the rectory, with housekeeper's quarters, the offices and the hall. This phase was given a substantial boost when Mary Merrill, a parishioner, offered to donate $360,000 to cover the cost of the hall in memory of her late husband. The groundbreaking ceremony for this first phase was held on 29 April 1979. By October, it was necessary to add a fourth Mass. In November, the contract for the construction of the first phase was awarded to Northside Construction of London. The hall, rectory and offices were completed in September 1980, and the first Masses were celebrated in the hall on the weekend of 13-14 September. Bishop Sherlock conducted the official opening of the Fred W. Merrill Hall on 19 October 1980. Two years later, the number of Catholic families within the parish had risen to more than

3,000, of which 1,400 attended weekend Mass regularly.

The spring of 1984 saw $400,000 on deposit towards the construction of a church proper, including a $100,000 bequest from the estate of the late Mary Merrill. Mykola Wasylko was again hired as architect, and, in May, the construction contract was awarded to Frank Van Bussel and Sons of Lucan. Mass was first celebrated in the new church on 1 September 1985, and Bishop Sherlock blessed the structure on 19 October 1985.

In 1989, Father Mellon, the founding pastor of St. Justin's, was succeeded by Father Gary N. Goyeau (1989-96), who was succeeded as pastor by Fathers James F. Roche (1996-98), Nelson M.M. Cabral (1998-2000) and Vincentius H. Gulikers (2000-05). Father Richard A. Hurdle arrived in late December 2005, first as administrator and then as pastor. Being one of the largest parishes in the diocese, St. Justin's has had the benefit of at least one assistant priest since 1979. One of the most enduring was Father Charles Fedy, CR, who from 1979 regularly assisted on weekends, and, when transferred by his order to Waterloo, continued to serve St. Justin parish's one weekend a month until 1989. In June 2002, Father Pio D'Oria became the first parishioner to be ordained a priest.

Sources: *History of St. Justin's Parish 1977-1985* [London: 1985?]; *St. Justin's Parish Celebrating 25 Years 1977-2003* [London: 2003]. Additional information supplied by Greg Nash.

St. Leopold Mandic

The origins of St. Leopold Mandic parish may have begun in 1966-67, when Father M. Vitomir Bobetic, then teaching at Regina Mundi College, offered to care for the Croatians in London and St. Thomas. After Father Bobetic left London, Father Ante Matacin arrived and celebrated Mass for the Croatian community in the Lady chapel at St. Peter's cathedral. When Father Matacin left Canada in 1971, Father Ivan Mihalic replaced him and took up residence in Holy Cross rectory. In 1975, Father Mihalic and the Croatian community hosted the visit of Bishop Mijo Škvorc, SJ, auxiliary bishop of

St. Leopold Mandic

Zagreb, Croatia. Father Mihalic left for the United States, in September 1976.

Bishop Carter then approached the Franciscan Friars of the Croatian Custody in Chicago, asking their superior to send one of their priests to provide pastoral services to the Croatians of London and St. Thomas. In November 1976, the Custodial Board of the Holy Family presented the name of Father Ante Cuvalo, OFM CC, and he was accepted by the bishop. His youthful and enthusiastic approach won the hearts of nearly everyone. Also in November, a small schoolhouse along Wellington Road, between London and St. Thomas, was acquired and services were held there. In December the building was named Blessed Leopold Mandic Croatian church in honour of a Croatian Capuchin friar, Father Leopold Bogdan Mandic. who lived from 1866 to 1942. He was declared blessed, on 2 May 1976, by Pope Paul VI. Three years later, in 1979, the London-St. Thomas Croatian community sponsored the Canadian-Croatian Folklore Festival. It did so again in 1985, 1992 and 2003.

As the congregation increased in size new quarters were needed. Land was purchased on the south side of Westminster Drive, north of Regina Mundi College, and, in the spring of 1980, the grounds were blessed. On 30 November 1980, the new Blessed Leopold Mandic Croatian church was officially opened, blessed and established as a parish.

Father Ilija Pulijic, OFM CC (1980-82), succeeded Father Cuvalo as pastor. On 16 October 1983, Pope John Paul II canonized Blessed Leopold Mandic. Subsequently, during the first term of Father Jozo Grubisic, OFM CC (1982-89), the parish's name was changed to St. Leopold Mandic. During

Father Pulijic's second term as pastor (1989-94), Cardinal Franjo Kuharic, archbishop of Zagreb, visited St. Leopold's. After the pastorship of Father Miro Grubisic, OFM CC (1994-2001), Father Jozo Grubisic (2001-04) returned a second time. Father Zvonimir Kutlesa, OFM CC, was appointed pastor of St. Leopold's in 2004.

Sources: DLA, London Croatian Mission File; St. Leopold Mandic Parish Files.

St. Maria Goretti

The beginnings of a permanent Italian community in London date from 1874 with the arrival of three families from the island of Lipari, but it may not have been until 1888 that the community had a regular priest who spoke the language. Between 1888 and 1891 and again between 1916 and 1919, the Italian community was served at St. Mary's church by Father Joseph Kennedy who, having been educated in Italy, was fluent in the language. Father West T. Flannery played a similar role from 1924 to 1956. Ironically, from its beginnings the Italian community had gravitated towards St. Peter's cathedral and worked hard at learning the English language and the ways of their adopted city.

A new and larger wave of Italian immigrants arrived in London after the Second World War and, by August 1956, St. Maria Goretti was established as a national Italian parish with Father Giuseppe M. Mariani as pastor (1956-65). St. Barnabas Anglican church, on the southwest corner of Dundas Street and Avondale Road, was purchased and renamed St. Maria Goretti.

Although Father Mariani expressed the hope, in November 1963, that a new church would be built within ten years, he realized at the same time that immigrant Italians were not very good financial supporters of the church. In October 1964, the parish debt stood at $30,000, while the annual revenue was about $8,000. Father Joseph Bagatto (1965-68) replaced Father Mariani as administrator, in June 1965. The parish was so impoverished that, for a time, he had to forgo his salary and pay out of his own savings for furniture and appliances to equip his residence situated immediately south of the church.

Lack of sufficient income was not the only burden Father Bagatto faced. Ninety percent of his parishioners were "from the deep south part of Italy" and, they showed some hostility towards their priest who had come from the northeast part in his late

St. Maria Goretti

teens. Moreover, both the Jehovah's Witnesses and the "Assemblea Cristiana," an Italian Pentecostal Church, were making inroads among the Italian immigrants as these Protestant denominations appeared to be doing more for them than the Catholic Church.

Father Bagatto sent out a questionnaire to over 850 post-war Italian immigrant families. From the 192 who replied, he learned that the majority wanted a territorial parish, in which the liturgy and sacraments would be celebrated in Italian, but would not exclude non-Italians. A more central location was needed as the majority of the Italian population was moving to the south part of the city, particularly into the Glen Cairn and Fairmount subdivisions. A meeting of Father Bagatto, the parish council, and the chancellor of the diocese, on 27 June 1966, appeared to show all in agreement with Father Bagatto, who for some months had promoted the idea of a territorial church in one of the established parishes. At the time, St. Maria Goretti had 300 active families, but the church had a leaky roof and was so cramped that on one Good Friday an elderly woman fainted and remained upright. There was no room for her to fall!

While serious consideration was given in February 1967 to purchase land on the corner of Deveron Crescent and Pond Mills Road as a parish site, the diocese realized that a national parish would not be self-sustaining in the foreseeable future. As a result, on 4 August 1968, St. Mary's parish became the spiritual and cultural centre for the Italian community. St. Maria Goretti parish ceased to exist and all its assets and liabilities were transferred to St. Mary's. To ease the transition, Father Bagatto was transferred to St. Mary's as associate pastor. With St. Mary's now the national Italian parish of London and area, many of the traditions, brought over from

Italy and continued at St. Maria Goretti, were, in turn, carried to it.

Sources: DLA, St. Maria Goretti Parish Files; Father John Comiskey, "Meet Father Joseph Bagatto," *Newsletter of the Diocese of London*, no. 32 (Lent/Easter 1988), 6.

St. Martin of Tours

Owing to the growth of population south of the Thames River in the late nineteen century, and the fact that people were less inclined to walk long distances to attend church regularly, Catholics in this area of London petitioned Bishop O'Connor and then Bishop McEvay to establish a parish in what is now Old South London. Finally, in 1899, Bishop McEvay authorized the purchase of a parcel of land on the northeast corner of Cathcart Street and Duchess Avenue for $3,000. The first order of business was to erect a school on this site. On 4 September 1901, Bishop McEvay blessed and opened St. Martin's separate school, which was named for Martin O'Sullivan, one of the leading Catholics in the area and a separate school trustee at the time.

The parish, however, was not founded until 15 January 1911. Its first pastor, Father François X. Laurendeau (1911-17), marked the occasion by celebrating Mass in the school. As soon as the ground thawed, volunteers excavated the basement, and on 20 August 1911, Bishop Fallon blessed and laid the cornerstone of the new church. Moore & Munro of London were the architects. J.G. Dodd & Son, also of London, appear to have been the builders but did not complete the work. As was the custom of the day, the church was usually given the same name as the adjoining school. Thus, on 5 May 1912, Bishop Fallon officially opened and dedicated St. Martin of Tours church.

Father John V. Tobin (1917-18) succeeded Father Laurendeau, but owing to ill health, he was forced to retire the following year. The third pastor was Father Daniel Forster (1918-24) whose sister, Sister Zita Forster, CSJ, had taught the first class at St. Martin's school in 1901-02. Although beloved by most of his parishioners, Father Forster managed to incur the enmity of a small faction of parishioners known as the "contentious families" and of Bishop Fallon himself. Longstanding feuds

St. Martin of Tours

over matters as diverse as an addition to the school and the suitability of candidates for confirmation led to the public humiliation of the pastor by the bishop on at least two occasions and Father Forster's formal suspension in July 1924.

The daunting task of healing a divided and bewildered parish fell to Monsignor Peter J. McKeon (1924-38), whose heroic practice of Christian charity during his long tenure was in large measure successful. On 6 March 1937, fire destroyed the altar and most of the sanctuary. Following Monsignor McKeon's death on 23 September 1938, Father William J. Phelan (1938-50) served as administrator and in September 1940 was appointed pastor. During his pastorate the present Stations of the Cross were acquired. Monsignor West T. Flannery (1950-68), the founder and host of the "School For Christ," succeeded Father Phelan. His successor, Father Albert P. Spencer (1968-78), oversaw the removal of the pulpit and communion rail, the carpeting of the sanctuary floor, the repainting of the dome and the welcoming of the Korean community.

Father Spencer was succeeded by Father R. Brian Hunter (1978-84). The seventy-fifth anniversary of the parish was celebrated in November 1986 during the pastorate of Father Clare J. Coleman (1984-90). Father Coleman's successors were Fathers John F. Sharp (1990-93), Thomas P. Mooney (1994-2001) and David Rankin, SJ (2001-03). Since 2003, Father Fred Howard-Smith has been administrator of the parish.

In recent years, social justice issues have played an important part in the parish. A monthly breakfast and dinner program have been established to serve the needs of the hungry within the community. In addition to the Korean community, the Hispanic and Slovenian communities and the parishioners of Holy Rosary, which closed in 2005, have found a home at St. Martin's.

Sources: John K. A. Farrell, with revisions by Father W.J. Phelan, "The History of St. Martin's Parish London — Ontario" (typescript: 1950); John R. McMahon, "Homecoming Day Highlights 75th Anniversary," *Newsletter of the Diocese of London*, no. 29 (Summer 1987), 20. Additional information supplied by Robert Adams.

St. Mary, Hill Street

In order to help the Irish immigrants in south London be near their work at the Great Western Railway roundhouse, a parcel of land near the southwest corner of Hill and Maitland streets was purchased on 21 May 1872 for $600. The local firm of Robinson & Tracy was selected as architects and David A. Denham as the contractor for the construction of the mission church. However, a gale on the morning of 4 December 1873 blew the structure down, causing about $400 damage and destroying the project. On 10 May 1874, the Gothic-like white frame structure was dedicated to St. Mary by Bishop Walsh, and a collection, amounting to about $400, was taken up to go towards the cost of the building, which amounted to nearly $4,000.

The church, with a small belfry over the front entrance, topped with a cross, was 80 feet by 35 feet (24.4 m by 10.7 m) and seated about 400 people. According to *The London Free Press*, it had stained-glass windows. The building was heated by two large coal stoves, which stood near the entrance, and two long rows of black stovepipes suspended by iron rods 10 feet (3 m) apart and extending the full length of the church. Illumination was provided by coal oil lamps with mirrored reflectors. The church floor consisted of plain planks. Immediately inside the front entrance was a massive stone baptismal font. The main altar was very plain, backed by a large oil painting of the Crucifixion, a gift of Bishop Walsh. When incense was required for High Masses, benediction and funerals, an altar boy would go across the street to the home of Michael Gray, who carefully drew burning coals from his stove and placed them in the censer.

Over the years, this mission church was served

by priests residing at the bishop's palace next to the cathedral. The first priest was Father Patrick Corcoran. The church was open from three o'clock, Saturday afternoon until Sunday evening. Confessions were heard on Saturday afternoons and evenings. The confessional, with its bright red curtains,

Old St. Mary's Church, Hill Street
Property Purchased May 21, 1872

St. Mary, Hill Street

was to the left at the front, near the altar dedicated to the Blessed Virgin. The priests enjoyed supper at various homes in the area. In inclement weather, or if the roads were impassable, they stayed the night at the home of Michael Durkin on Hill Street. On Sundays, Low Mass was celebrated at 8:30 a.m. and High Mass was sung at 10:30 a.m. Breakfast for the priests was often in the home of William Fitzhenry or William Kelly, also on Hill Street. Vespers and benediction were at 4:00 p.m.

To help with finances, a gala garden party was held on the church grounds each summer. These parties drew large crowds from throughout the city. Illumination was provided, in the evening, by powerful engine headlights, borrowed for the occasion by the railway workers.

Extensive renovations took place in the summer of 1889, under the direction of Father Joseph Kennedy. The roof was reshingled and the coal oil lamps were replaced by gas fixtures. A substantial wooden fence was erected around the perimeter of the property. One of Bishop Walsh's last acts as overseer of the diocese was to preside at vespers and benediction at St. Mary's on 6 September 1889.

In early December 1899, St. Mary's became the second Catholic parish in the city of London, with Father Hubert G. Traher as its first pastor. He chose the house that had been owned by Martin Durkin on Hill Street as his residence. On 10 December 1899, Bishop McEvay indicated that a new church would be built in the near future. In the early morning hours of 13 April 1901, a fire broke out in the church, causing damage that was largely confined to the main altar. Services continued in the old church until

the opening of the new St. Mary's in east London. The last Mass in the old church was celebrated on Sunday, 25 May 1902.

Sources: "Consecration of St. Mary's Church," *Daily Advertiser* (London), 11 May 1874, 3; "Dedication Yesterday," *London Free Press*, 11 May 1874, 4; Mary Turner, *St. Mary's Parish London, Ontario 1872-1942* [London: 1942].

St. Mary, Lyle Street

On 10 December 1899, Bishop McEvay announced to the congregation of St. Mary's on Hill Street that a new church was planned for the recently established parish. Plans for this building, to be erected on the northwest corner of York and Lyle streets, next to Holy Angels school, were made public on 22 May 1901. The local architectural firm of Moore and Henry drew up the plans, and the cornerstone was laid by Bishop McEvay, on 28 July 1901. The church was dedicated by Archbishop O'Connor of Toronto on 25 May 1902. Just two days earlier, the parish's founding pastor, Father Hubert G. Traher, died without seeing the completion of his work. His successor, Father Peter J. McKeon (1902-14), worked tirelessly on behalf of the parish. He reduced the parish debt, built St. John's school in 1903 and a new rectory in 1908 and installed the two side altars in 1914 – dedicated to the Blessed Virgin and St. Joseph – to replace those from the original church. The first diocesan Eucharistic Congress, which was also the first Eucharistic Congress in Canada, was held at St. Mary's on 11 October 1911.

The parish debt was retired during the pastorate of Monsignor Michael J. Brady (1919-36), who also oversaw the installation of the Casavant pipe organ in 1921 and the redecoration of the church in 1926 by Ilario Panzironi of New York, the same mural artist who decorated St. Peter's cathedral. St. Mary's was the official church in the city for Catholic chaplains and soldiers during the Second World War. Under the guidance of Father John T. Maloney (1936-49), the parish celebrated the fortieth anniversary of the church in 1942. It was from St. Mary's, in April 1948, that the worldwide Family Rosary Crusade was launched by Father Patrick Peyton, CSC, of the United States.

Father Wilfred T. O'Rourke (1950-65) oversaw

the celebration of the church's golden jubilee in 1952, and, on 17 February, with special dispensation from the Vatican, he celebrated Mass at a new altar that faced the people, possibly the first such Catholic altar in Canada.

St. Mary, Lyle Street

St. Mary's has had a tradition of ministering to ethnic groups, particularly the Italians, Poles, Ukrainians and Portuguese. In August 1968, St. Mary's also became the parish for the former members of St. Maria Goretti, the first Italian parish in London, and was to change its name to Our Lady of Good Counsel parish. The name change, however, never happened. Father Joseph N. Bagatto came to St. Mary's with his Italian congregation and was made associate pastor. In 1970, he became pastor of St. Mary's (1970-74). The centenary of the establishment of the mission was celebrated in September 1972, with the return of Father Patrick Peyton as guest speaker at the concluding banquet.

Missionaries of the Precious Blood, an Italian order, were placed in charge of the parish in 1979. Father Oreste Cerbara, CPPS (1979-83), oversaw considerable renovation to the church's interior and the restoration of its original design. Father Luciano Baiocchi, CPPS (1983-90), continued the restoration work, concentrating his efforts on the steeple and the installation of a new slate roof. The elevator was installed in 1996 during the pastorate of Father Mario Bufalini, CPPS (1993-96).

The parish was once again placed in the hands of a diocesan priest with the appointment of Father Joseph F. Hardy as pastor (1997-98). His assistant, Father Joseph A. Dabrowski, CSMA, was appointed pastor in 1998. For the first time in the parish's history, and as a sign of the times, there was no assistant priest at St. Mary's. Fathers Hardy and Dabrowski oversaw major renovations to the church. The newly renovated Chapel of the Perpetual

Eucharistic Adoration was completed in time for the new millennium. The bell tower and spire were once again made safe. The interior received a new carpet, a new marble floor for the sanctuary and four new stained-glass windows that were installed in time for the centenary celebrations of the present structure on the weekend of 10-12 May 2002.

Sources: Mary Turner, *St. Mary's Parish London, Ontario 1872-1942* [London: 1942]. Additional information supplied by Father Joseph A. Dabrowski, CSMA.

St. Michael

Prior to October 1911, Catholics in the northern part of London and the southern part of London Township attended services at St. Peter's cathedral. St. Michael's became London's fourth parish. After being appointed the parish's first pastor, Father James A. Hanlon (1911-21) immediately took up residence in north London and began to organize the parish. St. Nicholas school, on the south side of Cheapside Street, between Waterloo and Colborne streets, which had served the children of the area since 1892, became the interim site for services. The parish's first Mass was celebrated there on 12 November 1911.

Having already built two churches elsewhere, Father Hanlon set to work to oversee the construction of a church, rectory and school on property previously acquired at the southeast corner of Maitland and Cheapside streets. The local firm of Moore & Munro, which had designed St. Martin's church the previous year, was hired as the architect. Bishop Fallon laid the cornerstone for the church on 7 July 1912. He returned on 29 June 1913 to dedicate St. Michael's church. The red pressed brick and white stone used in the construction of the church was also employed in the building of both the adjacent rectory and four-room school. Like the church, the rectory faced Maitland Street. The school was dedicated by Bishop Fallon on 6 January 1914. In its early years, St. Michael's was the garrison church for the soldiers of the Royal Canadian Regiment stationed at Wolseley Barracks. During the First World War, hundreds of soldiers attended a special Mass at St. Michael's, celebrated by their chaplain, Father William T. Corcoran, every Sunday morning.

St. Michael

Father Hanlon was succeeded by Father Edward L. Tierney (1921-41). Other pastors were Monsignor William S. Morrison (1942-44), Father Thomas J. Ford (1944-51), Father Peter E. McKeon (1951-62) and Father Leo J. Flynn (1962-67).

Despite the fact that two new parishes, Blessed Sacrament (1951) and St. Andrew's (1964), had been formed from St. Michael's, the number of families had grown from 92 in 1911 to over 900 by the late 1960s. Consequently, during the pastorate of Monsignor Joseph A. Feeney (1967-77), a new church, rectory and hall were built. Tillman & Lamb of London was the architectural firm for the $560,000 complex, and Ellis-Don Limited, also of London, was the general contractor. The sod-turning ceremony for the new rectory and parish hall was held on 19 November 1969, and they were completed in June 1970. The following month, the old church to the immediate west of the hall was torn down. The cornerstone-laying ceremony for the new St. Michael's was held on 1 November 1970. The ultra-modern church seats 860, as compared to 375 in the first church. Another feature of the church-hall complex, joined via the narthex, was a colourful modern kitchen, complete with heating ovens, two gas stoves and six stainless steel sinks. Bishop Carter was the celebrant of the first Mass in the new church, on 12 February 1971. The official opening and blessing of the complex was held on Sunday, 2 May 1971, with Bishop Carter again officiating. On 23 May the new, two-manual Casavant Frères organ, which cost $36,000, was blessed and dedicated.

Monsignor Feeney was succeeded by Father John B. O'Donnell (1977-82), who was followed by

Fathers J. John McCormick (1982-92) and James E. Mockler (1992-2004). In 1993, receipts were $395,000 and expenditures $307, 991 for a surplus of $87,008. A four-day parish retreat was conducted in December of the same year by Father Michael Sullivan, OSA, of the Augustinian Preaching Apostolate at Villanova University in Pennsylvania. Father Murray W. Sample succeeded as pastor of St. Michael's in June 2005.

Sources: DLA, St. Michael Parish Files; London Public Library, Ivey Room, clipping files, St. Michael church.

St. Patrick

In August 1912, the Redemptorists of the Baltimore Province expressed an interest in establishing a parish in the diocese of London. Bishop Fallon consented but signified a preference for their locating in London rather than in Windsor. An agreement was concluded with Father Joseph Schneider, CSSR, provincial of the Baltimore Province, on 26 September 1912, and property for a church, school and monastery was acquired on 17 February 1913. Father John McPhail, CSSR was sent to London on 8 April to begin the building process. Benjamin Blonde was hired to build the church. St. Patrick's church was dedicated by Bishop Fallon on 29 June 1913, the same day he dedicated St. Michael's church in London. Father Peter N. Doyle, CSSR, was the first superior of the Redemptorist community in London and the first rector of St. Patrick's (1913-21).

By 1922, the congregation of St. Patrick's had outgrown the little church. As it was beyond the parish's finances to build a new church, the original building was enlarged. Also, under the new rector, Father John Barry, CSSR (1921- 24), a permanent monastery was built and completed in January 1924. St. Patrick's school was opened on 14 September 1927, under the rectorship of Father Anthony McBriarty, CSSR (1924-30). Father William McCullough, CSSR (1930-33), the next rector, fostered devotion to Our Mother of Perpetual Help. During the time of Father Archibald McDonald, CSSR (1933-36), two native sons, James Fallon and Ronald W. Reeves, were ordained priests, Father Fallon for the Jesuits and Father Reeves for the Scarboro Foreign Missionaries. The interior of the

St. Patrick

rectory was revamped during the rectorship of Father Francis Lawless, CSSR (1945-47).

Excavation began for the new church on 16 April 1951, and the building was ready for use for midnight Mass that year. Designed by Barry Byrne and built by Fassel & Baglier Construction, the church was consecrated by Bishop Cody on 16 March 1952.

On 22 May 1975, the Redemptorist Fathers departed St. Patrick's, owing to a lack of vocations, and Father Richard W. Tremblay became the parish's first diocesan pastor (1975-93). Understanding the great attachment that the parishioners had to the Redemptorists, he continued many of their traditional devotions, such as the Tuesday Novena, celebrated daily Mass and retained the schedule for confession. Mass was also celebrated each Sunday in the Chapel of Hope at the London Psychiatric Hospital. Father Tremblay oversaw the construction of a new rectory and offices over the parish hall. Built at a cost of $350,000, they were opened on 29 June 1979. The former Redemptorist monastery was then torn down and replaced with a parking lot.

The church furnace was replaced at a cost of $97,000 during the pastorate of Father Christopher S. Beausoleil (1993-95). According to the 1995 parish directory, issued during the pastorate of Father Robert G. Couture (1995-2002), the congregation consisted of 1,000 families, sixty percent of which lived outside the parish boundaries. On 30 May 1996, the sixty-seven stained-glass windows executed by Toronto glass artist Josef Aigner, at a cost of $80,000, were dedicated. The handmade panels, all rendered in a representational style using techniques virtually unchanged over the centuries,

depict the story of Joseph and Mary, the fifteen mysteries of the Rosary, the four evangelists, the Last Supper, St. Bridget — one of the patron saints of Ireland, second only to St. Patrick — and St. Alphonsus Liguori, the founder of the Redemptorist Order.

Since August 2002, Father David P. Furlonger, CSSR, has been in charge of St. Patrick's. A former parishioner of St. Patrick's, he was entrusted with the decommissioning of Blessed Sacrament, which had been clustered with St. Patrick's, in June 2006.

Sources: *St. Patrick's Parish London Ontario 1995* [London: 1995]; "Solemn Opening and Blessing The New St. Patrick's Church, London, Ont." [London: 1952].

St. Pius X

In 1956, the diocese purchased land in Oakridge Acres for $20,250 as a site for a new church. A portion was sold to the separate school board for $1 and became the site of Notre Dame school, opened by Bishop Cody in 1957. During 1963-64, two Masses were said each Sunday in the school until the large room used for Mass was divided into two classrooms.

Believing that the spiritual welfare of the faithful in the western portion of St. Joseph's parish could be promoted more effectively as a distinct parish, Bishop Carter established Notre Dame parish, Oakridge Acres, on 28 May 1965, and inaugurated Masses at St. Paul and Oakridge Secondary schools. Father Paul D. Milne (1965-70) was named pastor.

On 15 June 1965, the western portion of St. Joseph's parish, together with territory taken from the parishes of St. Peter and St. George, was decreed a new parish and named St. Pius X. On June 26, the first Mass was celebrated in the auditorium of Oakridge secondary school, and the collection that day amounted to $588. St. Joseph's and St. Peter's parishes were assessed $25,000 and $10,000 respectively as a dowry towards the foundation of the new parish. The northeast corner of Valetta Street and Deer Park Circle, part of the 1956 purchase, was selected as the site for the new church and rectory. By the end of January 1967, Father Milne had taken up temporary residence in a house on the south side of Valetta Street at Cramston Crescent. In early June 1966, Philip Carter Johnson was selected as

St. Pius X

architect. By December, however, the preliminary sketches for a church to accommodate 600 people had to be revised to seat 800. In the end, the original design had to be scrapped. In the autumn of 1967, the tender of Ellis-Don Limited to build the church at a cost of $392,700 was accepted and work began on 6 December 1967. The first Sunday Masses were celebrated in the new church on 27 October 1968, and the episcopal visitation and solemn blessing took place on 15 December 1968.

A council of the Catholic Women's League of Canada was officially established at St. Pius X on 27 September 1965. The parish conference of the St. Vincent de Paul Society was founded on 2 November 1969.

Father Aloysius L. Nolan (1970-73) recorded that receipts were $93,381.22 and expenditures $93,001.07 for the parish in 1971. Two years later, he was instrumental in establishing the parish's first Beaver Colony. The 42nd London Scout Group was granted its charter by the Boy Scouts of Canada in October 1966. The annual September golf tournament was inaugurated during the pastorate of Father John B. O'Donnell (1973-77). Father Joseph G. Snyder (1977-87) introduced wireless microphones, computers, air conditioning and electronic church bells. A new organ was installed and the parking lot expanded. On 24 June 1986, the mortgage on the church was burned. A month earlier, on 28 May, the parishioners joined with Father Snyder in celebrating his twentieth anniversary as a priest. Father Murray W. Sample arrived as pastor in 1987 and supervised the refurbishment of the church and the construction of a new meeting room

and much-needed handicap-accessible washrooms and ramps to accommodate an aging congregation. Everything was completed in time for the celebration of the parish's twenty-fifth anniversary in 1990. On 1 May 1993, a native son of the parish, Father Graham R. Keep, was ordained a priest of the diocese.

In 2002, St. Pius X was clustered with St. Joseph's under Father Robert J. Remark. On Saturday, 8 July 2006, the closing Mass at St. Pius X was celebrated with Bishop Fabbro as presider. The next day, at 6:30 p.m., on the same site, Bishop Fabbro celebrated the opening Mass of the new Holy Family parish, the amalgamation of the former clustered parishes of St. Pius X and St. Joseph's.

Sources: DLA, St. Joseph Parish Files; *50th Anniversary 1952-2002 St. Joseph Parish London, Ontario* [2002]; *St. Pius X Parish 25th Anniversary 1965-1990* [1990].

St. Stephen of Hungary

In 1960, Bishop Cody established a Hungarian mission for London and area to be served by Father Jenö Boday, SJ (1960-70). At first, there was no permanent place to worship and Mass was celebrated in various locations. As chaplain at Fontbonne Hall, Father Boday lived at 534 Queens Avenue. Under his leadership, the Hungarian community purchased a piece of land on the west side of Webster Street and a portable army barracks. With $7,000 raised by the Hungarian community through various fund-raising activities, a $13,000 loan from the diocese and hours of volunteer work, the barracks was transformed into a church. Mass was first celebrated there on 17 May 1964. The church, named in honour of St. Stephen of Hungary, was blessed by Monsignor J. Austin Roney, the chancellor, and the community was elevated to parish status.

Father Béla W. Ugrin, SJ (1970-71), Father Boday's successor, lived in an apartment at 525 Queens Avenue. He was succeeded by Fathers Csongor Rajmond (1971-72) and Tibor Furák, OSM (1972-74). This rapid turnover of priests had a negative impact on the parish. Community functions ceased, and Sunday Mass attendance decreased.

Over the next few years, however, positive changes took place under the guidance of Father Miklos Molnár, SJ (1974-90), assisted by Father

Tamás Beöthy. Realizing that a more centralized location was needed, the congregation moved to 375-379 Horton Street on 26 September 1976. This second St. Stephen's church was blessed by Bishop Attila Miklosházy, SJ, bishop of Hungarian emigrants worldwide. The next step was to select a building that actually looked like a church.

St. Stephen of Hungary

In 1981, the former Methodist church on the southeast corner of Bruce Street and Wortley Road was purchased as the third site of St. Stephen's church. One hundred thousand dollars was raised to help with the restoration and renovations. On 2 May 1982, the new St. Stephen's was blessed by Bishop Gervais. The 100th anniversary of the structure itself was celebrated with an open house on 6 March 1983. Opened as Knox Presbyterian church in 1883, additions were made to it in 1923. With Church Union in 1925, the Gothic-style church became Knox United church and so remained until 1972 when the congregation joined Wesley United church. It then became the London Wesleyan church and remained so until 1981.

With the recall of Father Molnár by the Jesuit community in the spring of 1990, Father Stephen Bodnár of St. George's Hungarian Byzantine Rite Catholic parish in Courtland came to celebrate Mass every Saturday and Wednesday afternoon at St. Stephen's. Since the church was too much for the Hungarian community to keep up on its own, it became an administrative centre for the London diocese and some additional offices were built. The church, hall and kitchen remained with the Hungarian community, and space was shared with the Hispanic and French communities. The re-named St. Stephen Centre was blessed by Bishop Sherlock on 10 February 1991. In addition to Father Stephen Bodnár, the Hungarian community in London has been served by three other Greek

Catholic priests: Father Lajos Angyal of Windsor, Father Nicholas Deák of Welland and, since 2005, Father Ferenc Mák, pastor of St. George's Hungarian Byzantine Rite Catholic parish in Courtland. Since 1990, the congregation has been governed by a seven-member advisory board and a three-member financial committee, with Margit Hattayer as parish administrator.

In January 2002, it was found that structural problems with St. Stephen's made the building unsafe for occupancy. The groups using the building were dispersed throughout the city, with the Hungarian-speaking congregation going to St. Patrick's church. St. Stephen Centre was then demolished.

St. Stephen of Hungary parish, centred at St. Patrick's church, was canonically suppressed effective 30 June 2007, and was established as St. Stephen of Hungary Hungarian Catholic Community, with Father Mák as priest-chaplain.

Sources: DLA, Parish Files. Additional information supplied by Margit Hattayer.

Vietnamese Catholic Community

In July 1986, Father Thomas De Nguyen-Dang, then stationed in Windsor, started coming to London to celebrate Mass with the area's Catholic Vietnamese community. At first there were approximately fifteen families and Masses were celebrated either in London or in St. Thomas. Permission was granted, the following year, to have a Mass once a month in the Lady chapel at St. Peter's cathedral. Through the efforts of Father De Nguyen-Dang and Dinh Nguyen, the first president of the Vietnamese Catholic community (1986-92), the congregation swelled to as many as sixty to seventy families. In July 1992, Father De Nguyen-Dang left for further studies in Rome and was replaced by Father T. Francis Tran, CSJB, as pastor of the Vietnamese communities of the diocese. He was stationed in Windsor.

In 1995, the local community moved to Blessed Sacrament church where Mass was celebrated twice a month. Of late, Mass has been celebrated only once a month on Saturday afternoon. Blessed Sacrament's connection with the Vietnamese community dates to 28 August 1979, when a Vietnamese refugee fund was established in the parish. Among the fifteen refugees sponsored by the parish in 1980, three were Catholic.

It was customary during the Easter season for Vietnamese priests from other jurisdictions to celebrate Mass with the London community and conduct a special retreat. In addition to the specific liturgical celebrations of the Church during the year, the community gives particular place to its Vietnamese New Year's Mass, towards the end of January or the beginning of February, and to the Masses on 1 October in honour of St. Theresa of the Child Jesus, on 7 October to venerate Our Lady of the Rosary and on 24 November in memory of the 117 Vietnamese martyrs. This latter feast day commemorates St. André Dung Lac and Companions, who represent the hundreds of thousands of Christians who died for the faith in what is now Vietnam, during the eighteenth and nineteenth centuries, and who were canonized by Pope John Paul II on 19 June 1988. Until the closing of Blessed Sacrament Church, the statues of St. André and Our Lady of Vietnam stood just inside the main entrance door.

The community's choir is named after St. Theresa of the Child Jesus. This group, comprised of both adults and young people, was founded in October 1994 and also performs flower dances in May, in honour of Our Blessed Lady, and in October in honour of St. Theresa. It also performs traditional dances and conducts children's fashion shows and skits on Christmas and New Year's Day. Each June, London's congregation joins with other Vietnamese communities in southern Ontario and from the United States to take part in a pilgrimage to the Shrine of the Canadians Martyrs in Midland and, in September to Our Lady of Fatima Shrine in Buffalo, New York. Each summer, in either July or August, the London congregation gathers for a communal picnic, which sometimes takes place in St. Thomas or Chatham.

When Father Tran is unavailable, Bishop Sherlock celebrates Mass with the Vietnamese community. As in the early years in this diocese, when the visits of a priest were both irregular and infrequent, the Catholic Vietnamese congregation holds a prayer session at the home of one of its members on alternate Saturday afternoons. Families are contacted when it is known that a priest will be available for Saturday afternoon Mass. The last Mass at Blessed Sacrament was celebrated on 3 June 2006 and was attended by approximately fifteen families. With the closure of that church in July, St. Patrick's church on Dundas Street became the spiritual home of the Vietnamese Catholic community.

Presently, the congregation has some twenty to thirty families. Several reasons are given for this. The time of Mass is inconvenient for those who work Saturday afternoons; often the Saturday on which Mass is scheduled to be celebrated gets changed; and many families are now involved in their local churches. It is hoped, however, that the re-organization at St. Patrick's will increase the numbers.

Sources: Information provided by Hoa Tran, Father John Van Damme and Peter Khong.

Adelaide: St. Patrick

Father Lawrence Dempsey of St. Thomas (1831-33) inaugurated annual visits to Adelaide Township in 1831. Following Father Dempsey, priests from St. Thomas and London continued to minister periodically to the needs of Catholics in and near the hamlet of Adelaide. So too did the missionary priest from Sandwich and later Dean Thadeus Kirwan from Sarnia (1856-64). There is evidence that a log church had been erected in Adelaide Township prior to 1849 and was still standing near the hamlet forty years later.

Patrick Mee, a leading Catholic in the township, petitioned Bishop Power in 1844 for a church, cemetery and rectory, and attached a list of the names of fifty Catholic families, comprising 122 individuals in the area. In September 1849, 4 acres (1.6 ha), which appear to have been the block bounded by Yonge, Henry, King and Kent streets, were granted to the Catholic Church. A white frame structure was built, with a cemetery adjoining it. As late as the summer of 1853, however, the church still did not have an altar. It also served Catholic families in Metcalfe and Warwick townships. Father J.A. Strain was pastor of Adelaide when he abandoned his post in 1862. With the construction of the Great Western Railway between London and Port Sarnia, through Strathroy, however, the population of Strathroy began to increase rapidly while that of the hamlet of Adelaide declined. As a result, it was

Strathroy that was erected into a parish in 1868, and St. Patrick's in Adelaide became its mission. Father John Scanlan, the assistant at Strathroy between 1869 and 1872, took a special interest in the Adelaide mission.

During the pastorate of Father Peter H. Feron (1881-84), a census of the Strathroy parish was taken. It showed that there were twenty-nine Catholic families for a total of 154 persons in Strathroy and area and twenty-eight Catholic families or 161 persons in and around the hamlet of Adelaide. Having discovered during his visitations that through mixed marriages many Catholics had fallen away from the Faith, Father Feron strongly warned the faithful in both communities to avoid such unions at all costs.

Apparently, the frame church was destroyed by fire. In any case, Patrick Murphy, a member of the mission obtained the deed to the church property in October 1903, and the cornerstone for the mission's third church was laid and blessed, in the presence of 500 persons, by Bishop McEvay on 26 June 1904. The white brick structure, when completed on the corner of Kent and Egremont (later Highway 22) streets southwest of the former church, featured a small, square tower at its southwest corner. Its thirteen stained-glass windows were the work of the London artist Henry E. St. George, proprietor of The Western Glass Decorative Works. Largely financed by the Langan family, the church accommodated some 100 worshippers and its choir loft contained a small compact organ. For many years, a priest came out from Strathroy to celebrate Sunday Mass once a month, first by horse and buggy and later by automobile.

St. Patrick's was suppressed as a mission of Strathroy in 1982. In grave disrepair, the church was demolished in May 1984. Four of the stained-glass windows were salvaged and, in 1995-96, they were placed as interior windows in the choir of the newly-renovated All Saints church in Strathroy. They were rededicated, on 25 July 1999, by James A. Cardinal Hickey, archbishop of Washington, DC, a descendant of the original Irish settlers whose names appear on the windows. In the village of Adelaide, however, only a few old gravestones near the original church site bear silent witness to this largely forgotten Catholic mission community.

Sources: DLA, Pierre-Adolphe Pinsoneault Papers, Box 1, Correspondence Book 5, 1861-65, 33-5,36a-37a. Additional information supplied by Helen Green.

Biddulph: St. Peter

From the early 1830s the Catholics of McGillivray and the neighbouring townships of Stephen, Usborne and Biddulph were served by the priests of St. Thomas and London. In 1843, John Glavin's four-year-old son, Patrick, died. On travelling to London to inform the priest, the father was directed by Father Patrick O'Dwyer of that town (1842-43) to bury the child on a little hill near a certain tree on what appears to have been the northwest corner of lot 10, concession 1, Biddulph Township, along the London-Goderich

Biddulph: St. Peter

Road, now Highway 4, and the priest would bless the grave the next time he came out. This site became St. Peter's cemetery, and a small stone still marks the final resting place of Patrick Glavin. One of the last burials in this cemetery was that of Father E. Raphael Glavin, who was interred here on 25 January 1991. Some time thereafter, the cemetery was officially closed.

In June 1850, Father James Flyn (O'Flyn) was appointed pastor for the townships of Biddulph and McGillivray and took up residence in the former where a church had just been built. Father Flyn left in November, however, and the church in Biddulph once again became a mission of London.

In the summer of 1853, Dean Thadeus Kirwan, pastor at London (1848-56), described the frame mission church in the northern part of Biddulph as newly built. Prior to this, a committee of twelve men, including Patrick Cowley, was appointed to build a church in Biddulph Township, on the Cowley farm, lot 10, concession 1, beside the cemetery. With the re-establishment of St. Patrick's as a parish in 1854, the mission, known as McGillivray, was detached from London and attached to Biddulph, with Father Peter F. Crinnon (1854-59) as pastor.

In early1860, the McGillivray mission was dedicated to St. Peter, the pastor at the time being Father James Murphy of Biddulph (1859-63). In January 1869, Father Philip J. Brennan was appointed the first pastor of Our Lady of Mount Carmel, at what was then the village of Limerick, and is now Mount Carmel. It was about this time that St. Peter's was detached from St. Patrick's and became a mission of Our Lady of Mount Carmel. In 1871, the second St. Peter's church, a brick, Gothic-like structure, with a steeple over the front entrance, was opened. It was noted, in 1886, during the pastorate of Father Martin Kelly (1878-89), that the church property comprised 2.5 acres (1 ha) in what was then the postal village of Adaire.

Like most rural congregations, the one at St. Peter's declined in numbers over the years, from 250 in 1886 to 160 in 1902 and 117 in 1924. Expenditures also tended to exceed revenues. In the period from 1 June 1904 to 1 January 1905, receipts were $339.65, but expenditures were $448.82.

St. Peter's remained a mission of Mount Carmel until about 1971 when it became a mission of Sacred Heart in Parkhill and was called St. Peter's, Biddulph. The pastor of Sacred Heart at the time was Father J. Charles Caruana (1970-80), and it was during his term that St. Peter's was closed in 1977.

It was slated for demolition in 1987 when a recently founded group calling themselves the Franciscan Friars of Mary Immaculate, under the leadership of Father David L. Przedwiecki, received permission from Bishop Sherlock to renovate St. Peter's and erect an adjoining monastery, the latter to be named the St. Maximilian Kolbe Friary. But the group refused to sign a legal document giving it status as an Association of the Faithful, the first step towards becoming a full-fledged religious order, and Bishop Sherlock ordered them to leave the diocese. They left in May 1990. Three years later, St. Peter's and the addition were demolished. Today, only the cemetery marks the location of the former mission of St. Peter.

Sources: DLA: Our Lady of Mount Carmel, Mount Carmel and St. Patrick, Adelaide Parish Files; Mathew Ingram, "Robed residents saving St. Peter's," *London Free Press*, 28 July 1987, A6; Kelly Teahen, "London diocese won't demolish friars' church," *London Free Press*, 25 January 1990,

B6; *McGillivray Township Remembers 1842-1992* (Ailsa Craig: 1992).

Bornish: St. Columba

In the autumn of 1849, some 125 evicted Catholic families from North and South Uist and Benbecula in the Outer Hebrides, off the northwest coast of Scotland, made their way to Nairn, in what was then Williams Township, where they were cared for over

St. Columba

the winter by their Presbyterian hosts. A few families, including that of Lachlan McDonald, chose to settle on the land, in what became West Williams Township. During their first winter, McDonald's wife died and was interred on top of a hill on lot 8, concession 12. This became Old Hilltop Cemetery and, on 3 July 1977, a monument was dedicated to the fifteen Scottish pioneers buried there between 1850 and 1860.

Donald McDonald donated a parcel of land on the northwest corner of the crossroads of the present settlement of Bornish, named after Bornish in South Uist, for the erection of a church, school and rectory. That summer, Dean Thadeus Kirwan (1848-56), who ministered to these Highlanders from London, noted that his mission church, a log structure, at Williamstown was newly-built. Bishop Pinsoneault's first visit to Bornish is said to have occurred in 1862.

The second church, a frame building, was opened in 1864. The first resident priest was Father Patrick J. O'Shea (1871-72). He wrote that on 4 October 1871 Bishop Walsh had placed the church of West Williams under the protection of

St. Columbkill (Columba), the same saint to which the church at Bornish in South Uist was dedicated. Father James Lamont (1872-74), a Gaelic-speaking priest, succeeded Father O'Shea in January 1872, and resided at the home of Lachlan C. McIntyre, until he had the vestry fitted up as a temporary residence for himself, but soon after moved to Parkhill. For a brief period in the late 1880s, Bornish was again a parish with Father Donald A. McRae as pastor. In the absence of a rectory, he lived with his brother John. With Father McRae's appointment as pastor at Parkhill (1889-1903), Bornish reverted to a mission. Father McRae dismantled the old vestry at St. Columba's, renovated the interior of the main body of the church and added a new vestry on one side of the sanctuary and a confessional on the other.

On the advice of Bishop McEvay, Father McRae oversaw the building of a new church at Bornish. The Gothic-style brick structure was erected at a cost of under $6,000, had a seating capacity of 160 to 180 and was debt-free when consecrated, on 1 January 1903, by Bishop McEvay. During the pastorship of Father John P. Dunn (1903-10), the church was redecorated. On 4 July 1949, when Father Joseph L. Paquette (1946-54) was pastor, the centennial of the Catholic faith in West Williams was celebrated with an outdoor High Mass offered by Bishop Cody at St. Columba's. During Father J. Charles Caruana's pastorship (1970-80), a memorial to the pioneers of Bornish and Parkhill was dedicated, on 5 July 1970, in the adjacent St. Columba Cemetery. The Bornish church was completely redecorated in the spring of 1980. After several severe winters, when a trench had to be dug through the snowdrifts to reach the church from Parkhill, it was decided that Masses would be discontinued at Bornish from the first Sunday of Lent until Easter Sunday. Father Richard D. Charrette (1980-83) limited the celebration of Mass at St. Columba's to the summer months of July and August.

The weekend of 1-4 July 1999 saw the gathering of many descendants of immigrants at Bornish to mark both the 150th anniversary of the arrival of the first Scottish Catholics and the fiftieth anniversary of the post-war influx of Dutch and Belgium settlers.

No services have been held in the church since 2005.

Sources: Alice Gibb, *Outline History of St. Patrick's Parish, Lucan, Ontario* (London: 1985);

Sacred Heart - St. Columba Parish Since 1849 [1985]. Additional information supplied by Andrew Bartley and Alice Facchina.

Churchville: St. Henry the Emperor

The Church in Aldborough dates back to the 1850s with the arrival two German Catholic families by the name of Schnekenburger. They were followed by other German Catholics and, in 1858, by some Irish Catholics. Priests came from Chatham about once a year to minister to their spiritual needs, first on horseback and later by train to Newbury. By 1860, priests from St. Thomas were also visiting the area. Mass was celebrated in various homes, one being that of Henry Schnekenburger on Middle Street. Before Henry died in 1867, he expressed a wish that a church be built on the farm in order that a priest might have a house of worship in which to celebrate Mass and that the faithful would have a place to meet each Sunday between the visits of a priest. Henry Schekenburger's remains were interred in Wardsville, then the location of the nearest Catholic cemetery.

When soliciting subscriptions in the area in the autumn of 1870, the pastor of St. Thomas, Father William Flannery (1870-98), contacted both Catholics and non-Catholics and, to everyone's surprise, received more from the latter. The following Sunday, at Mass in one of the area homes, he read the amounts of the Catholic contributions and then those of the Protestants, and concluded by asking, "What am I to build – a Protestant or a Catholic church?" The question had the desired effect and Catholic subscriptions immediately increased.

The grounds for a church and cemetery were donated, in 1871, by Henry Schnekenburger's widow, Regina, who also procured the altar, pictures and vestments from Buffalo. Regina and her brother-in-law, Wendelin Schnekenburger, borrowed $250 from Findley MacDairmid of New Glasgow to complete the church in 1872. Xavier Pfeifer, his sons Francis and John and other members of the faithful had erected a frame building 22 feet by 30.5 feet (6.7 m by 9.3 m). There was no formal opening, but it became St. Henry's church in honour of Henry Schnekenburger. The church may have had

St. Henry the Emperor

a shingled exterior that was replaced by clapboard siding by 1905. In keeping with their European traditions, the men and women sat on opposite sides in the church. Adolph Musaile, a local Protestant furniture and coffin maker, hewed an oak cross and carried it a mile to St. Henry's cemetery. By 1963 the lower portion of the cross had rotted. This was sawn off and Jerry Coleman encased the upper portion in a cement base with metal supports and placed it further back in the cemetery.

In 1876, Father Flannery was making monthly visits to St. Henry's and each family was making an annual contribution of four dollars. With some $350 provided by Robert Schnekenburger of Buffalo, William Schnekenburger built the gateway into the church and cemetery property in 1922. In part, through money left by Laban Schnekenburger, in 1931, Robert Schnekenburger and John Cowan dug out the church basement and a bee was held to put in the foundation. The front porch was built by Richard B. Dewsnap, during the pastorship of Father Jeremiah P. Gleeson (1928-33). A new roof was installed in 1944, and in 1953, Joseph Pfeifer, John's son, covered the exterior with insul-brick siding at a total cost of $447. During the pastorate of Father John B. O'Donnell (1955-59), Mass was celebrated in the mission church once a year on 13 July, the feast of St. Henry. In 1978, Father Jozef G. Denys and a group of volunteers put a new cedar shingle roof on the church and covered the old insul-brick siding with one-inch by six-inch (2.5 cm by 15.2 cm) clear tongue-and-groove cedar shingles in keeping with the building's architectural heritage. After insulating the roof and walls the people redecorated the interior in pale cream, the original colour.

Over the years, the community came to be called Churchville as it had three churches: Evangelical, Lutheran and Catholic. By 1978, only the Catholic

one survived. Within a few years, however, the mission was suppressed. The church, which still stands on the Thomson Line, was subsequently boarded up to prevent vandalism, and on 30 June 2007, was officially closed.

Sources: DLA, St. Mary Parish Files, West Lorne; Ralph Hubert Dignan and Joseph P. Finn, "A History of the Diocese of London," ed. by Guy Alden (unpublished manuscript, 2002); Wilfred C. Johnston, "Catholic Churches of West Elgin" [1979]. Additional information provided by Andrew Bartley, Jack Boyde, Evie McCaffery, Duncan C. McKillop and Linda Van Raay.

Delaware: Sacred Heart

Prior to 1950, few Catholics lived in the Delaware area. Those who did, such as the tobacco families of Cletus Kelleher and Frank Brennan of Caradoc Township, attended Mass either in Strathroy or in London. Early in 1950, the Sacred Heart priests from the Netherlands purchased the Belvoir estate of the late Senator Edgar S. Little with its large mansion. The drawing room was converted into a chapel and the few Catholics in the area, some twenty in all, such as the Verhallens from Lobo Township and the Rastins from Caradoc, were invited to attend services here.

As early as April 1950 plans were being implemented to detach a portion of All Saints, Strathroy and establish it as a separate parish under the care of the Sacred Heart priests at Delaware. That summer, more Catholic immigrants, mainly from the Netherlands, arrived in the area, and regular attendance at the Sacred Heart chapel swelled to between fifty and one hundred. The Roks family was among the first to arrive, followed by the Duynisveld, Gubbels, Buren and Vanoosterhout families. In September, the Sacred Heart Fathers opened a junior seminary with seventeen students. In July 1951, the parish boundaries for Delaware were established and Father John R. Van Buuren, SCJ, the superior of Sacred Heart Junior Seminary, appears to have been appointed the first pastor. In the following years, more students arrived and more area residents attended services at the chapel. Consequently, an annex to the mansion was built in 1952, and services were held there to accommodate some 150 people. This new chapel or church was blessed on 14

Sacred Heart

December 1952.

By August 1953, the pastor was Father Alphonse Vander Vorst, SCJ. He later reported that receipts were $1,981.09 and expenditures $2,045.76, for a deficit of $64.67 for the last six months of 1953.

In 1954, the Roks families donated land for a separate school in Delaware. Our Lady of Lourdes, a two-room school, was built on the site and opened with fifty-two pupils. The Roks also donated land for a church, and in September 1957, building commenced. Blackwell & Hagerty of London was the architectural firm and Ellis-Don Construction, also of London, was the general contractor. The church, which cost $75,000, was first used for Sunday Mass on 2 March 1958. On 16 March, Bishop Cody consecrated the church to the Sacred Heart of Jesus. Father John Van Wezel, SCJ, succeeded Father Vandervorst as pastor in June 1959, and Father Van Wezel was succeeded by Father Jacobus (James) A. De Jong, SCJ, in August 1961. By December 1968, Father Vandervorst was again pastor of Sacred Heart. Father John Van Rut, SCJ, succeeded Father Vandervorst on 15 September 1971. After Father Van Rut came Father Joseph A. Eliëns, SCJ, in July 1973, and Father Joseph Coppens, SCJ, on 9 February 1977.

The Sacred Heart pastors continued to reside at Sacred Heart Seminary until the Priests of the Sacred Heart departed from Delaware in September 1986. At that time, Father Geoffrey J. Raymakers, SCJ, was pastor and continued to minister to the needs of the parish for the next eight years. The house next to the school was purchased and became the parish rectory.

Father Raymakers was the last of the Sacred Heart Fathers to serve as pastor of Sacred Heart

parish. Since 1994, the parish has been served by diocesan priests. The first was Father J. Douglas Mercer, followed by Fathers Richard A. Hurdle and Peter W. Poel, the latter a son of Dutch immigrants. Sacred Heart is presently clustered with St. Charles Garnier parish in Glencoe. Father Francis L. Murphy became pastor on 30 June 2005. The parish covers the former Delaware Township, the southern part of Caradoc, including Mount Brydges, and the southern part of Lobo township, including Komoka, and consists of more than 600 families. Our Lady of Lourdes school has more than 400 pupils.

Sources: DLA, Parish Files.

Dunwich: St. Columkill/St. Columba

The origins of the Church in Dunwich Township can be traced back to 1827, when Bishop McDonell accepted Colonel Thomas Talbot's invitation to visit the area. Bishop McDonell was accompanied by Father James W. Campion, the pastor of St. Vincent de Paul, Niagara (Niagara-on-the-Lake) and all the missions and stations in the Niagara Peninsula, Dundas, Hamilton, Guelph and the Talbot Settlement. They spent several days under Colonel Talbot's roof. Mass, baptisms and one marriage were celebrated during 27-30 July. The first baptisms performed in Dunwich Township, and indeed in all of present-day Elgin County, were performed by Father Campion on 27 July 1827: James and Mary Ann, children of James and Ellen (Cannon) Taff. The next day, Bishop McDonell married the children's godmother, Bridget Taff, to Edward Brady. A few years later, priests from St. Thomas or London would periodically visit Dunwich and celebrate Mass in various homes, one of these being that of the Hooley family.

In January 1869, Michael Hooley donated one acre (0.4 ha) on the northeast corner of lot 17, concession 9, Dunwich, for the purpose of erecting a Catholic church. With a Mr. McFarlane as contractor, a frame building, 24 feet by 30 feet (7.3 m by 9.1 m), was built at a cost of about $500. It is said that a pew was reserved for the Hooley family. The first priest to celebrate Mass at the church was Father Charles Zucker of St. George's (Holy Angels) in St. Thomas (1861-70). On 28 July 1884, Bishop

Walsh blessed the apse and vestry that had been added to the church under Father Donald A. McCrae, a curate at St. Thomas and dedicated the church to the sixth-century St. Columkill or St. Columba, Scotland's most revered saint and one of Ireland's patron saints. It was St. Columba who went to Iona, off the coast of Scotland, with twelve relatives in 563, and built a monastery that grew into the greatest in Christendom.

On 1 October 1887, Timothy Crowley donated 1.1 acres (0.5 ha) on the northwest corner of lot 7, concession 6, in Dunwich, for a cemetery. The Crowley family then fenced it in with chestnut boards, 6 inches by 16 feet (0.2 m by 6.5 m), and tamarack posts. Patrick Crowley was assisted by Thomas Cahill of West Lorne and Hugh McDonnell of Wallacetown in planning the measurements and shaping the plots and driveway in the cemetery. The first interment was that of the remains of Timothy Crowley's daughter, Maggie, in 1894. Commonly referred to as the Crowley Cemetery, this was intended as a burial ground for St. Mary's in West Lorne as well as St. Columkill's, and it is still in use by the members of St. Helen's in Wallacetown.

As for Patrick Crowley, he studied for the priesthood, but ill-health caused him to withdraw from the Grand Seminary in Montreal after one year of study. He continued in poor health until his death at the age of thirty. Meanwhile, in 1887, Dunwich and Bismark (West Lorne) were detached from St. Thomas and, together with Wardsville, formed one parish for a brief period. Soon after, however, St. Columkill's and St. Mary's again became missions of Holy Angels in St. Thomas. In April 1894, St. Mary's was elevated to the level of a parish, and the Dunwich church became one of its missions. By the end of the century, Mass was celebrated every Sunday and Holy Day at St. Columba's, except for two months in the winter when it was celebrated every second Sunday.

In 1902, the faithful of Dunwich agreed to build a new church in the more centrally located Wallacetown. After the opening of St. Helen's later that year, the former St. Columba's, also known as the little "White Church," was then sold to Michael Delaney and used as an implement shed.

Sources: Ralph Hubert Dignan and Joseph P. Finn, "A History of the Diocese of London," ed. by Guy Alden (unpublished manuscript, 2002); Wilfred

C. Johnston, "Catholic Churches of West Elgin," [1979]. Addition information provided by Duncan C. McKillop and Linda Van Raay.

St. Paul

Fingal: St. Paul

In Southwold Township some 7 miles (11.2 km) to the southwest of St. Thomas lies the village of Fingal, the oldest in the township. Surveyed into lots in 1830, it was named by Colonel Thomas Talbot and harks back to his Irish roots, the prefix "fin" or "finn" being the old Gaelic word for "saint." St. Gall was born in Ireland in the sixth century, was believed to have accompanied St. Columba to Scotland and was thought to have bestowed his name to Fingal's Cave on the Isle of Staffa, one of the islands of the Inner Hebrides off the west coast of Scotland. In fact, it was another sixth-century Irish monk, St. Columban or Columbanus, whom St. Gall accompanied, and to Gaul not Scotland. St. Gall died in Switzerland and is considered the apostle of that country.

On Sunday, 28 July 1884, Bishop Walsh celebrated Mass at the home of P. Kildea in Fingal. After Mass, the Bishop was accompanied by Father William Flannery to Dunwich where Father Donald McCrea had enlarged the church by the addition of an apse and vestry. After Mass, the Bishop blessed the church under the patronage of St. Colomkill or St. Columbkille.

By 1886, Fingal had been a station within Holy Angels parish, St. Thomas, but by 1900, it was no longer one. In 1904, however, it was again established as a station with a monthly Mass. By 1905, there were eleven families within this station, increasing to fourteen by 1907.

Some years later, Richard McCahill of Southwold Township donated a spacious corner lot, adorned with large trees, in Fingal, for the building of a church – a white brick structure, 36 feet by 60 feet (11 m by 18.3 m), with a basement. The church, which seated 250, was furnished by the Fingal congregation. The altar and its graceful reredos were of Gothic design, the colour scheme being pure white with gold enrichments. Occupying the two great panels above the altar were mural paintings by Mrs. John Butler. One was of St. Peter, the chief of the Apostles, holding two massive keys, and the other was of St. Paul lightly resting his hands upon a sword, the weapon of martyrdom. The front portal of the church was connected with the street by means of a broad pavement of artificial stone and a good drive shed was also erected.

Sunday, 27 September 1914, the day of the dedication of the church to St. Paul, began with High Mass celebrated by Father W. Thomas West, pastor of St. Thomas (1903-33), assisted by the Holy Angels choir. Bishop Fallon arrived by automobile from London, at 3:30 p.m., accompanied by his brother, Father Charles Fallon, OMI, and the assistant at St. Thomas, Father Arthur E. Goodwin. Half of the people assembled for the dedication were non-Catholic. Benediction of the Blessed Sacrament followed Bishop Fallon's sermon. The faithful of this mission then comprised fifty-six individuals. By 1925, however, the number of families in this mission had dropped to nine and Mass was celebrated only "at intervals."

Sources: DLA, Holy Angels Parish Files; "St. Paul's, Fingal, Dedicated," *Catholic Record*, 10 October 1914, 8.

Lambeth: St. Dominic

As the village of Lambeth expanded in the 1950s, so too did the desire for a Catholic elementary school. The Minhinnick family donated a large plot of land, situated between Howard Avenue and the present Colonel Talbot Road, for a church and school. In 1957, plans were drawn up for the construction of a three-room school. The sod-turning ceremony took place on 2 June 1958, and in November, Bishop Cody blessed the new school, which was dedicated to St. Dominic. Within a few years, an addition to the school was built, consisting of four classrooms, a small staff room, office, two sets of washrooms and extra storage space.

As of 8 September 1965, Father J. Brian Fitzmaurice, assistant pastor of St. Martin's parish, was given exclusive charge of the people of Lambeth. It was Bishop Carter's intention that Mass should be celebrated in Lambeth as soon as a suitable place was found. When the gymnasium at St. Dominic's school was completed, the Catholic community attended Mass there for the next four years.

It was probably in 1968 that Monsignor West T. Flannery, then retired, went to live at 75 Sunray Crescent in Lambeth, and St. Dominic mission was formally established under his charge. By 25 September 1969, the mission had not yet completed a full fiscal year. Mass was celebrated in Trinity Anglican church on the southwest corner of Highways 4 and 2 in Lambeth. Built in 1863, this church was consecrated on 10 January 1864 by Benjamin Cronyn, first bishop of the Anglican diocese of Huron. On 24 June 1973, Monsignor Flannery, who was still in charge of St. Dominic's, represented Bishop Carter at the ecumenical rededication ceremony for the newly-restored Lambeth cemetery.

With the establishment of St. Justin's parish, in 1977, St. Dominic's was left as a mission of St. Martin's, although it was separated from that parish by St. Justin and St. John the Divine parish boundaries. By early 1978, there were some 105 Catholic families in the Lambeth area, of which about eighty were practising Catholics. Sunday Mass was still celebrated at the Anglican church. After the pastorate of Father Albert P. Spencer, however, Mass in Lambeth had to be discontinued in February 1978. One of the last acts of the mission was to host the World Day of Prayer, attended by the various Christian denominations in Lambeth. Meanwhile, St. Justin's already had more than 1,000 families exclusive of those of Lambeth and area.

As a result of a meeting held on 25 February 1978, it was decided that Lambeth and area be included in St. Justin's parish. But announcement of this change was deferred until the end of the school year, so that the religious instruction of pupils at St. Dominic school, particularly those preparing for their First Communion, would not be disturbed. St. Dominic mission council then wrote to Bishop Carter the following month, stating that the long-term needs of the Lambeth and area Catholic community could best be met by association with Sacred Heart parish in Delaware. The arguments of the council were as follows: the two communities were similar in makeup; family and church ties between them already existed; the parish and school territories had common boundaries; this tie would strengthen the spiritual life of the community by keeping it intact; the Catholic community was growing in Lambeth; long-range municipal planning then included four new subdivisions and a senior citizens home; and St. Dominic's school should receive regular visits from the clergy.

Despite these arguments, Lambeth and area was placed under the care of Father Patrick J. Mellon, pastor of St. Justin's. Five years later, on 30 June 1983, St. Dominic's school was closed, a victim of dwindling enrolment.

Source: DLA, St. Martin Parish Files.

Lucan (Biddulph): St. Patrick

In 1829, the Canada Company surveyed the London-to-Goderich road as part of its campaign to open up the Huron Tract for permanent settlement. Six years later, James Hodgins, a native of Tipperary, Ireland, became a Canada Company agent and succeeded in enticing Irish immigrants to settle in what became Biddulph Township in 1842. Another great impetus to settlement was the successful completion of the Toronto-to-Sarnia portion of the Grand Trunk Railway in the 1850s. The line would run through Lucan, which was incorporated as a village in 1872.

Father Patrick O'Dwyer, pastor of London, is said to have celebrated Mass, in 1847, in Robert Collison's barn, lot 11, on the north side of the London Road, Biddulph Township. Father O'Dwyer started but did not complete a log church on the farm, immediately north of Collison's, owned by Patrick Nangle.

Father Thadeus Kirwan came to London in 1848, and was appointed rural dean in 1850. Dean Kirwan oversaw the erection of a church in Biddulph, on a 5-acre (2 ha) parcel of land donated by James Kelly from his farm on lot 10, immediately west of Collison's farm and on the west side of what became the Roman Line. This simple frame church was finished in 1850, and a contractor, Thomas

St. Patrick

Howard, installed an altar and altar railing the next year. Meanwhile, in June 1850, Father James Flyn (O'Flyn) was appointed Biddulph's first pastor and resided with the Patrick Nangle family, across the road from the church. When Father Flyn left towards the end of the year, the church became a mission of London. On his first visit to St. Patrick's, 9 February 1853, Bishop Charbonnel confirmed 114 adults, including forty-four from McGillivray Township. There were 150 Catholic families in both townships at the time. The following year, they subscribed £250 ($800 US) towards the erection of a rectory.

Prodded by Dean Kirwan, who had missions in St. Thomas, Adelaide, Wardsville and Williamstown (Bornish), as well as Biddulph and McGillivray, Bishop Charbonnel appointed Father Peter F. Crinnon (1854-58) as Biddulph's second resident pastor. He started work on the second and current St. Patrick's church, but left its completion to his successor, Father James Murphy (1858-65). Constructed of stone quarried at St. Mary's and white brick from nearby Elginfield, St. Patrick's is a good example of early Ontario Gothic, featuring a square brick tower and a tall slender spire, rising to 110 feet (32.8 m), and tall, slender Gothic windows. It resembles a smaller, less imposing version of the second St. Lawrence/first St. Peter's church, completed in London in 1852. Bishop Pinsoneault blessed the bell on 4 October 1863. The Italianate-style rectory was built in 1869, under the pastorship of Father Joseph Gérard (1865-76). Father John Connolly (1879-95), better known for his role in the Donnelly murders on 4 February 1880, and the subsequent coverup, oversaw the church's facelift. Bishop Walsh performed the re-blessing in 1882. Father Connolly also provided funds for the one-room brick schoolhouse that remained in use as a school until 1962.

The arrival of Dutch immigrants after the Second World War did much to reinvigorate parish life. Father Joseph P. Finn (1979-86) supervised extensive renovations in 1984-85. The work included removal of the two side balconies and extending and tiering the rear balcony, reinforcing the floor, redecorating the interior, repointing the tower brickwork, repairing the spire and replacing the framework supporting the bell, and building a chapel at the side of the church. Bishop Sherlock rededicated the church on 16 June 1985. A fire, started by lightning, destroyed the wood-supported spire in May 1996. A new spire, built on a steel frame, was hoisted into position on 12 December 1996.

One of the oldest and best preserved churches in the diocese, historic St. Patrick's has functioned continuously as a house of worship since its opening in 1860. As a parish, it celebrated its 150th anniversary on 25-26 June 2005.

Sources: Alice Gibb, *Outline History of St. Patrick's Parish, Lucan, Ontario* (London: 1985); Orlo Miller, *The Donnellys Must Die* (Toronto: [1963]); Ray Fazakas, *In Search of the Donnellys* (Hamilton: 2001).

Parkhill: Sacred Heart

After the construction of the Grand Trunk Railway line between Stratford and Sarnia, a number of Irish labourers and their families remained in the vicinity of what became the town of Parkhill, which was on the railway line. In 1864, Charles McKinnon, almost singlehandedly, built a small, white frame Catholic church on Broadway Street. With the erection of Bornish into a parish in 1871, Parkhill became its mission. The rapid growth of the village, and its incorporation in 1871, however, convinced St. Columba's second pastor, the Gaelic-speaking Father James Lamont (1872-74), to transfer his residence to a rented house in Parkhill, thereby elevating it to parish status.

Parkhill's second pastor, Father Patrick Corcoran (1874-89), oversaw the construction of the present brick church, on a 4-acre (1.6 ha) parcel of land donated by the same Charles McKinnon who had built the first church. Constructed at a cost of $4,000, the new church was dedicated by Bishop Walsh, on 7 November 1875, to the Sacred Heart of Jesus. A rectory was also built. During the pastorate of Father John P. Dunn (1903-10), the church was extended 16 feet (4.9 m) for a new sanctuary and vestry, the tower was erected and electric lights and stained-glass windows were installed. Father Michael D. O'Neill (1910-25) oversaw the addition of a veranda to the front and east side of the rectory and the installation of two side altars in the church. A highlight of the parish at this time was the hosting of the fourteenth diocesan Eucharistic Congress on 19 June 1924. Bishop Fallon celebrated the open-air Pontifical Mass, followed by a procession through the town and closing benediction.

Over the next few decades, however, attendance and the accompanying financial support for both Sacred Heart and its mission church at Bornish declined owing to a combination of factors: the Great Depression, the Second World War and the migration of the young people to work in the cities. When Father Joseph L. Paquette was pastor (1946-54), the decline of the parish was reversed somewhat with the arrival of Dutch and Belgian immigrants, beginning in the spring of 1949. Six years later, some seventy-five new Catholic families had settled within the parish. By January 1954, Don Gooding Construction had completed an addition to the church that housed the priest's residence and parish hall. The former rectory became a convent for the Ursuline Sisters, who had come from Chatham in September 1952.

During the pastorship of Father J. William Farrell (1969-70), the high altar was replaced with an altar facing the people. A curtain backdrop and large wooden cross were installed on the back sanctuary wall. The parish debt was completely eliminated during the first three years of Father J. Charles Caruana's stay (1970-80). The centennial of the church was celebrated on 6 July 1975. In 1977-78, both the church and convent were renovated. During Father Richard D. Charrette's pastorate (1980-83), a large crucifix was installed in the Parkhill Cemetery, the southern part of the public cemetery having been blessed as a Catholic burial ground in the mid-1950s. The early 1980s also saw the addition of new concrete steps and pad in front of the church

Sacred Heart

and trees planted around the property. The former convent was stripped to the brick, completely renovated by volunteer labour and once more transformed into a rectory during Father James F. Roche's pastorate (1987-91). The doors inside the entrance of the church were redone with glass panel inserts, the interior painted, the pews refurbished, a new heating system installed and the choir loft floor raised, levelled and carpeted. Further extensive changes were undertaken during the pastorates of Fathers William F. Kornacker (1991-94) and Joseph A. Kannath (1994-2003).

Sources: Janis McCahill et al., *The History of St. Christopher's Parish St. Christopher's Church 1893-1993* [c. 1993]; *Sacred Heart – St. Columba Parish Since 1849* [1985]. Additional information provided by Alice Facchina.

Port Stanley: St. Joseph

Beginning in 1852, Father James D. Ryan, the assistant priest at London, is said to have celebrated Mass in the house formerly occupied by Colonel John Bostwick, Port Stanley's first settler. After that structure was destroyed by fire in 1854, various other homes were used. In 1860, the former Sons of Temperance Hall, a frame building, was purchased. This was used as a mission church until 1912. The pastoral report of 1886 appears to indicate that the church was dedicated to the seventh-century saint Winifred of Wales. By 1904, however, the church was rededicated to St. Joseph, and Mass was

celebrated on the third Sunday of the month. Three years later, Mass was celebrated about once every two months and by 1910, every month and every Sunday in the summer.

Monsignor W. Thomas West of St. Thomas (1903-33) saw the need for a more centrally located church in the growing summer resort of Port Stanley. Consequently, land was purchased from the Gerster family for $1,000 and a brick-faced structure, capable of seating 300, was built on George Street at a cost of $3,000. Much of the church's furnishings,

St. Joseph

including pews, altars, Stations of the Cross, stained-glass windows, and even the bell for the belfry, came from the second Holy Angels church in St. Thomas, in use between 1872 and 1911. The Stations of the Cross were produced in Germany and originally framed in black walnut with gold slip by Z. Darby of St. Thomas. The new St. Joseph church was blessed by Bishop Fallon on 8 September 1912. Built on a slight rise, it could be seen from the lake. The mission consisted of fifteen year-round families in 1886, but that number had dropped to six by 1925.

In order to produce a more respectful atmosphere for the altar, occasionally used beneath the church, the basement was dug out and painted by Father A. Joseph Schwemler (1944-51), one of the curates at Holy Angels, and a group of altar boys during the 1940s.

Up to 1963, the priests from Holy Angels took turns celebrating Sunday Mass at St. Joseph's. After that year, Father Ernest F. Deslippe, chaplain of the Ontario Mental (St. Thomas Psychiatric) Hospital, had responsibility for the mission. Monsignor William S. Morrison of Holy Angels parish (1944-68) had the interior of St. Joseph's repainted in a soft green that covered a battleship grey colour. During the 1980s, parish volunteers renovated and redecorated the church, producing a warm, homey atmosphere for the resident faithful who are joined by many seasonal visitors during the year.

In 2006, Holy Angels parish provided a preliminary building condition report for St. Joseph mission. The future of the church is under review.

Source: DLA, Holy Angels Parish Files. Addition information provided by Andrew Bartley, Jean Burnham and Steve Peters.

St. Thomas: Holy Angels

Bishop McDonell and Father James W. Campion, missionary of Niagara and Dundas, were the first Catholic clergy to visit St. Thomas, in late July 1827. In 1831, McDonell severed much of what became the eastern part of the London diocese from St. Augustine's parish in Dundas and sent Father Laurence Dempsey (1831-33), in September 1831, as resident priest of St. Thomas.

Archibald McNeal donated 3 acres (1.2 ha) of land for church purposes in May 1831, a year after a chapel had been built on it. The first Mass was celebrated in St. George the Martyr church on Christmas Day 1831, making St. George's the first parish east of Sandwich and Amherstburg in the present diocese of London. In the autumn of 1833, a rectory was built. For much of the period between 1843 and 1854, St. Thomas was without a resident priest and was ministered to from London and Brantford. It was not until Bishop Charbonnel appointed the assistant priest at London, Father James D. Ryan, to St. George's in January 1854 that St. Thomas would begin an uninterrupted life as a parish. Father Ryan (1854-57) had a brick rectory built that lasted until 1906. On Sunday, 21 June 1857, Bishop Pinsoneault first visited St. Thomas and administered the sacrament of confirmation.

Upon being transferred to St. Thomas, Father William Flannery (1870-98) soon realized that the small frame church, 40 feet by 26 feet (12.2 m by 7.9 m), was inadequate for the 160 families in the area and convinced the parishioners that a larger structure was needed. Langley & Co. of Toronto was selected as the architect. The cornerstone was laid on 2 July 1871, and Bishop Walsh returned on 10 November 1872 to bless the new brick church. Dedicated to the Holy Angels, the church cost $14,000 to build. The former church was removed to the rear of the property and served as a separate school for the next

Holy Angels

six years until it was replaced by a four-room brick building with living quarters for the three teaching Sisters of St. Joseph. In May 1874, 10 acres (4 ha) were purchased for a cemetery on the west side of the road leading into Port Stanley (now Highway 4) from Samuel Day, at a cost of $2,300. It was blessed on 14 June 1874 by Bishop Walsh. By 1886, the parish of Holy Angels also included the missions of Port Stanley, Dunwich, Bismark (West Lorne) and Alvinston, and the stations of Fingal, Glanworth and Aylmer. On 6 October 1895, the congregation staged a lavish celebration to commemorate the twenty-fifth anniversary of Father Flannery as its pastor.

The pastorship of Father W. Thomas West (1903-33) saw the building of a new rectory in 1906. This was followed by the construction of the present church. Bishop Fallon laid the cornerstone, on 4 June 1911, and he returned to dedicate the church on 25 February 1912. The total cost of the white stone structure with its twin towers, Munich windows and furnishings, was $94,640. Of particular interest to visitors is the window depicting Christ raising the daughter of Jairus. This work of art captured first prize at the 1904 World's Fair in St. Louis. In 1912, the parish hosted the Diocesan Eucharistic Congress, and was so honoured again in 1945, the same year in which the shrine to Our Lady of Perpetual Help was erected. The first Holy Name rally in the diocese was held at Holy Angels on 13 June 1921.

As Holy Angels entered the twenty-first century, the church was beginning to show its age. Consequently, a major restoration project was begun in 2001, with Patrick Coles as architect and Empire Restoration as contractor.

Included among the many vocations from this parish is that of Archbishop Philip Pocock of Toronto.

Sources: DLA, Parish Files. "The Church in St. Thomas," *Catholic Record*, 29 Dec. 1882, 1. Additional information provided by Jean Burnham and Steve Peters.

St. Thomas: St. Anne

St. Thomas began to develop and expand to the east and the south after the Second World War. Consequently, in the early 1950s, Monsignor William S. Morrison, pastor of Holy Angels (1944-68), purchased 9 acres (3.6 ha) in the east end of St. Thomas as a site for a future parish. St. Raphael's school was constructed in the middle of this site in 1957. On 25 July 1967, Bishop Carter formally named Father Patrick J. Costello as pastor (1967-92) of the city's second parish. St. Anne's, named in honor of Father Costello's mother, who had died the previous year, was built on land adjacent to the south of the school, which was purchased in a trade-off with the Catholic school board.

The first parish Mass was celebrated in the Central Elgin high school auditorium on 10 September 1967. In the spring of 1968, Sunday Mass was transferred to Parkside collegiate, while weekday Masses were celebrated in St. Raphael's school. There, the first parish council meeting was held on 5 November 1967.

The sod-turning ceremony for the new church was held on 29 September 1968. Carlos Ventin of Smale-Dickson Architects, Simcoe, designed the structure, which cost $300,000, and Evans-Kennedy Construction of London was the general contractor. The church and altar was blessed by Monsignor Andrew P. Mahoney on 27 May 1969. Four days later, Bishop Carter officially opened the building, which has seating for 600 people, followed in the evening by a dinner at the Stork Club in Port Stanley. Jane Street, on which St. Anne's is located, was renamed Morrison Drive, in honour of Monsignor Morrison.

In 1972, Father Costello announced the establishment of a community festival. Its aims were to develop and promote community spirit within the parish and to take this spirit to the community at large, to display Christian love and concern by

St. Anne

donating money for the needs of the community and to raise funds to build a parish centre. St. Anne's first Community Festival was held in June 1972. The parish centre was opened on 6 May 1977, at a cost of $375,000 (assisted by a Wintario grant of $125,000). It is the "centre" of parish activities and celebrations, and the host of many community events during the year. The Community Festival continues to this day and has generated some $750,000 for the community over the years.

In September 1977, a special relationship began between the parishioners of St. Anne's and the future bishop of the diocese of Mbala, Zambia, Telesphore Mpundu. Also in 1977, St. Anne's and James J. Komba, the first African bishop of the diocese of Songea, Tanzania, developed a special connection, which continued with his elevation, in 1986, as the first archbishop of a new archdiocese in southern Tanzania, and lasted until his death in 1992. Over the years, the parishioners generously responded to numerous charitable projects in the dioceses of these two bishops. The parish's Apostolic committee carries on this special African work.

A board of directors was formed in 1983 for the purpose of building a seniors apartment complex directly across from St. Anne's on land granted by the city. Under the auspices of the Canada Mortgage and Housing Corporation, a forty-unit apartment building was constructed and solemnly blessed as Festival Gardens Homes by Bishop Sherlock on 14 December 1985.

It fell to Father Richard G. Dales (1996-2007) to oversee major renovations to the church in excess of $1 million. Always generous and willing to sacrifice, the parishioners managed to pay off this debt. Beginning with 300 families, St. Anne's is now a faith community of 975 families.

Sources: Parish Files; Martel Clarke and Pat Maxwell, eds., *St. Anne's Parish St. Thomas, Ontario A History 1967-1992* [1992].

Strathroy: All Saints

The completion of the Great Western Railway line, in 1858, between London and Port Sarnia, via Strathroy, led to a rapid increase of population in Strathroy at the expense of Adelaide. Therefore, Strathroy was erected into a parish in December 1868, with Father Philip J. Brennan as its first pastor (1868-69), and St. Patrick's in Adelaide as its mission. Father Patrick Egan (1869-70) succeeded Father Brennan, on 4 January 1870, and, on 26 June he signed the contract with Fawcett & Bro. to build a church at Strathroy for $5,475. Named All Saints, it was blessed by Bishop Walsh on 7 November 1869.

In June 1876, both the church and rectory were consumed by flames. A new church and rectory were quickly built by William F. Fawcett of Strathroy and dedicated by Bishop Crinnon of Hamilton on 29 October 1876. Tragedy befell the parish for a second time when Father Thomas Cornyn (1884-89) accidently shot and killed himself on 31 January 1889 while cleaning his gun. During the pastorate of Father Albert J. McKeon (1889-1901), All Saints was again destroyed by fire, this time on 2 August 1892, when sparks from a fire at a knitting factory on the north side of Front Street landed on the church. Bishop O'Connor officially opened the third All Saints church on 13 December 1892. By the end of Father McKeon's pastorate, the parish was free of debt.

When the newly ordained Father E. Raphael Glavin (1927-28) was curate, he had young Ed Healy chauffeur him to the Watford and Adelaide mission churches. During the pastorship of Father John J. Young (1925-32), a new rectory was built at a cost of $10,000. Following the Second World War, many new immigrants, especially from the Netherlands, arrived in the parish while Father E. Raymond Moynahan (1944-1961) was pastor. The result was the construction of Our Lady Immaculate school, which opened in 1955.

The mid-1950s witnessed the first arrival of Portuguese from the Azores. By 1971, there were enough of them in the parish to have the 10:15 am Sunday Mass celebrated in their language. Even before 1971, it was obvious that a larger church was required. The municipality closed Mill Lane, east of All Saints, and the parish purchased and demolished the house situated beyond it and work on the new church began. For nearly two years, Mass was celebrated in the local arena and later in the gymnasium at Strathroy District Collegiate Institute. Bishop Carter officially opened and dedicated the new church on 13 December 1971. The following Sunday, an open house was held for the people of Strathroy and area.

Renovations to the church began with a groundbreaking ceremony on 31 May 1995. The first phase concerned the church, the washrooms and two multi-purpose meeting rooms. The second phase was the construction of the parish centre with a full kitchen, offices and meeting/teaching rooms on both levels. Bishop Sherlock presided over the rededication of the church on 18 May 1996. The parish centre was blessed and opened October 2002. The church now seats 600 people. The baptismal font is reminiscent of the baptismal pools used in the early Church and offers both traditional and full immersion baptisms, while the Chapel of Reservation offers a quiet place to be in the presence of the Blessed Sacrament and to pray.

Currently, the parish consists of some 1,700 families, representing many cultures, the most dominant being the Dutch and Portuguese. One of the Sunday Masses is still celebrated in Portuguese.

Sources: *London Advertiser*, 2 June 1876 and 19 July 1876; Information supplied by Helen Green.

Strathroy: Middlesex (West of London) and Lambton: Portuguese Mission

Father Manuel A. Louro, a native of Portugal, had been appointed to the newly established Portuguese mission in London, in September 1965. Periodically, he ministered to the Portuguese community in the Strathroy area. With his sudden departure, about September 1967, Father James F. Summers, pastor of All Saints (1965-68), had a Portuguese-speaking priest from Detroit visit the Strathroy parish, but he was from Bolivia and spoke with a different accent. This may have been Father Luis Amado, who was then a student at the University of Detroit, and was ministering to the Portuguese community in London on weekends. By March 1967, Father Joseph F. Hardy, an assistant at All Saints, expressed concern to Bishop Carter about the lack of a Portuguese-speaking priest in the parish. By May, Protestants were sponsoring a Sunday-morning Portuguese radio program over CHLO in St. Thomas. As it was the only Portuguese program in the area, Father Hardy feared it would draw away some of the Portuguese Catholics.

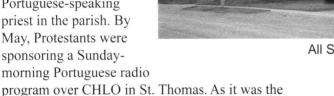

All Saints

By the latter part of 1967, Father Joseph Silvera dos Anjos, SJ, had arrived from Brazil, and undertook a visitation of the Portuguese families throughout the diocese. He met with most of the 150 Portuguese families in All Saints parish. In January 1968, Father Summers proposed to Bishop Carter that the Jesuit superior in Toronto be petitioned for a Jesuit from Portugal who had worked in the Azores, and who would come for a period of two years. Father Summers also wanted to have two of the diocese's senior seminarians sent to university in the Azores or the mainland, for a six-week summer course in Portuguese literature or history. He suggested that Father William C. Cooney be released for such a course, if he were so inclined.

Prior to being assigned to the Portuguese mission in London, in July 1972, Father Orlando Fazzenaro, a native of Brazil and formerly a friar of the Capuchin Order, had assisted in the Strathroy parish. Bishop Carter then wrote to Bishop António dos Reis Rodriques, president of the Portuguese Episcopal Migration Commission, requesting a Portuguese priest for Strathroy or Leamington. By the end of 1975, Sarnia and Strathroy each had a Portuguese-speaking priest. In the former case it was an Italian priest. By October 1976, Bishop Carter had entrusted Bishop Sherlock, his auxiliary bishop, with the responsibility of assuring the Portuguese people in the counties of Kent and Lambton that they would receive "whatever assistance may presently be available."

Meanwhile, Father António Seara, O de M, formerly of Madrid, Spain, who had been appointed to the London Portuguese mission in October 1974, also ministered periodically to the needs of the Portuguese communities throughout the diocese. Father Henry G. Kea, CSSR, a native of the Netherlands, succeeded Father Seara to the London Portuguese mission in April 1977, and, like Father Seara, he felt responsible for all the Portuguese in the diocese.

With his transfer to Our Lady of Mercy church, Sarnia, effective 16 November 1978, Father Kea was placed in charge of the recently formed Kent, Lambton and Middlesex (West of London) Portuguese mission. He served this Portuguese mission from All Saints, Strathroy, from 1980 to 6 June 1986, when he was succeeded by Father Nelson M. Cabral, a native of San Miguel, Azores. As associate pastor of St. Joseph's, Chatham (1982-86), Father Cabral had also been responsible for the Portuguese in Kent County. Restructuring of the Portuguese missions in the diocese took place about 1987, and Father Nelson's mission was called the Middlesex (West of London) and Lambton Portuguese mission. Father Cabral was succeeded by his predecessor, Father Kea, in 1990, and his charge was known as the Middlesex (West of London), Elgin, Kent and Lambton counties: Portuguese mission. Father Kea continued to serve this mission until his death in 1994.

Sources: DLA, London: Portuguese Mission Files and Gerald Emmett Carter papers, Box 23; "Rev. H.G. Kea," *Newsletter of the Diocese of London*, no. 63 (Fall 1994), 5. Additional information supplied by Father Nelson Cabral.

Wallacetown: St. Helen

By 1902, the congregation of St. Columba or St. Columkill in Dunwich Township, agreed to relocate to a more central location. Land was purchased, for $125, in Wallacetown, through Father

Patrick J. Quinlan, pastor of St. Mary's in Bismark (West Lorne). John Doyle was engaged as the contractor for the building project, and the cornerstone

St. Helen

was laid on 21 September 1902. The 150-seat, red-brick church was erected and furnished at a cost of $4,096.46. As was the custom in Ireland, the women sat on one side and the men on the other. Later in 1902, Bishop McEvay officially blessed and dedicated the church to St. Helen. The first baptism is said to have been that of James Frederick, son of James and Catherine Lynch, on 19 April 1903. The first marriage was that of Terrence Lynch and Mary McCaffrey, on 28 June 1904. The bell was blessed in October 1910, by Bishop Fallon, and the sheds with fourteen stalls were built eight years later during the pastorship of Father Augustine Fuerth (1910-21). In August 1933, the church, its furnishings, the sheds and the land were valued at $13,688. The church was re-roofed and a new furnace was installed during the Second World War, under the guidance of Father J. Henry Chisholm (1933-46).

The 1950s saw an influx of Dutch immigrants into the area, thereby infusing new blood and additional financial resources into the mission. In 1953, the parish sold the sheds that had been built in 1918 and used the money to gravel the lane and the parking lot at the rear of the church. In 1962, the church interior was completely gutted and renovated with new plaster, woodwork and flooring and the altar was remodelled. Renovations in the church basement took place in 1960 and again in 1962. Water services were installed in the basement in April 1964. In 1978, the exterior trim of the church was repainted, new eavestroughs installed, and the interior redecorated. New sidewalks were also laid.

In May 1961, Bishop Cody honoured Clara

Casey, the church's sacristan, with the Mother of the Year award. She had donated 2.5 acres (1 ha) of land in Wallacetown for a separate school. As the opening of a school in the village proved to be unfeasible, the diocese sold this property, in December 1967, to William H. and Anna K. Dietrich, for $1,500. Meanwhile, the first Mass at St. Helen's in which the priest faced the congregation, was celebrated on 8 November 1964, and the first Mass in the vernacular was offered on 14 February 1965. The centennial of St. Helen's church was observed with a special Mass celebrated by Bishop Sherlock on 11 August 2002.

On 15 August 1954, a large oak cross, painted white, was erected in St. Helen's cemetery (the former St. Colomkill cemetery). John Kairns and the Keogh family re-surveyed the burial ground, in May 1957, and staked corner posts for 200 plots. By 16 August 1958, the Keogh family had mapped out burial locations, purchased unmarked graves, placed twenty-nine grave markers on them and encased thirty-two old markers in concrete. On 28 September, the fourteen oak and concrete Stations of the Cross, designed and completed by the Keogh family and prepared by Milner-Rigsby Co. of West Lorne, were dedicated by Monsignor Vito H. Grespan, the chancellor. The present cemetery gates and fence are the result of the bequest of the late John Kairns who, together with Timothy Crowley, Jr., had been caretaker of the cemetery for many years without remuneration.

Over the years, three vocations to religious orders have come from St. Helen's, namely, Mary Kairns (Sister Barbara, CSJ), Kathryn Pauline McGuire (Sister Pauline, CSJ) and Nellie Hooley (Sister Raphael, RPB).

Sources: Ralph Hubert Dignan and Joseph P. Finn, "A History of the Diocese of London," ed. by Guy Alden (unpublished manuscript, 2002); Wilfred C. Johnston, "Catholic Churches of West Elgin," [1979]. Additional information provided by Evie McCaffery, Duncan C. McKillop and Linda Van Raay.

West Lorne: St. Mary

Before the incorporation of the police village of West Lorne in 1904, the portion of the village north of the tracks was known as Bismark and that to the south as Lorne. By the early 1880s, an increasing number of Catholic families lived in the vicinity of

Lorne-Bismark. St. Henry's church in Churchville was considered too small and too distant, being four miles (6.4 km) southwest of Bismark Station. In April 1883, the diocese purchased four village lots in Bismark from Archibald Leith for $100. In April 1885, work was begun by the contractor, Thomas E. Montague, under the supervision of Father Philip J. Gnam, the curate at St. Thomas, to erect a frame church with a seating capacity of 250. The main altar was built by Francis Pfeifer of Rodney, whose son, Charles H., was the first person to be baptised at the church, on 18 May 1885. St. Mary's was opened and blessed on 18 December by Bishop Walsh. The total cost, including furnishings, was $1,422. In 1892, four village lots on William Street were purchased for a cemetery. A new section opened in the spring of 1944, and St. Mary's cemetery was enlarged by two town lots in 1965.

Meanwhile, in April 1894, the missions of West Lorne and Dunwich were detached from St. Thomas, and St. Mary's was elevated to parish status with Father Patrick J. Quinlan (1892-1906) as the first pastor. A rectory was built the same year at a cost of $1,588.63. William and Thomas Daley of West Lorne were contracted, in 1904, to raise the church and put in a new foundation and to brick the exterior. John Brady of Lake Road, Port Stanley, donated a bell in memory of his brother James. Cast by the Mannely firm in West Troy, New York, it weighed 1,050 pounds (476.3 kg) and cost $483. The church was re-opened and rededicated by Bishop McEvay on 12 September 1904.

During the pastorship of Father Augustine Fuerth (1910-21), the church was redecorated and re-roofed, an addition to the rectory was built, and natural gas, electricity and bathroom facilities were installed, all at a cost of $4,220.73. In 1944, during the tenure of Father J. Henry Chisholm (1933-46), St. Mary's was redecorated and a new bathroom and hot water heating system were installed, at a cost of $7,500, which was paid in full by the parish's sixty-five families. Father John B. O'Donnell (1955-59) oversaw renovations to the rectory in 1955 and to the church in 1957. The basement for the church hall was excavated in 1958, and a new furnace and modern kitchen were installed.

With the influx of Portuguese families during the 1960s and 1970s, the custom of carrying the statue of Our Lady of Fatima through the streets of West Lorne on the second Sunday of May was initiated.

St. Mary

During the pastorate of Father William G. Smith (1965-77), the second St. Mary's was built. The sod was turned on 4 June 1972, and, on 5 March 1973, Bishop Carter blessed the new church. A parish retirement party was held for Father Smith on 28 December 1977. Tragically, he was killed two days later in a head-on bus-car crash near Watford. At his retirement dinner, he had jokingly asked Father Stanley E. McGuire to give the same homily at his funeral, little realizing that he would be doing so in less than a week.

During the pastorate of Father Josef Denys (1978-81), the mortgage on the new church was burned on 8 October 1978. The following year, a very fine history of St. Mary's and its two missions was published as a result of Father Denys' desire to begin reclamation projects at St. Helen's and St. Henry's. The present rectory and parish hall were constructed in 1993, when Father Ronald G. Paquette (1988-97) was pastor.

Sources: Ralph Hubert Dignan and Joseph P. Finn, "A History of the Diocese of London," ed. by Guy Alden (unpublished manuscript, 2002); *St. Mary's West Lorne, Ontario St. Helen's Wallacetown, Ontario 2003* [2003]; Wilfred C. Johnston, "Catholic Churches of West Elgin" [1979]. Additional information supplied by Evie McCaffery and Linda Van Raay.

7. Huron-Perth Deanery

Ashfield (Kingsbridge): St. Joseph

As early as 1842, Father Thomas Gibney of Guelph (1836-43) celebrated Mass and conducted baptisms at McGlades' cabin, located south of Port Albert. Mass continued to be celebrated there periodically over the succeeding years. About 1844, William O'Neil granted ten acres (4 ha) of land to the diocese of Toronto, and the present church is located on part of this land. Catholics tended to gravitate to that area in anticipation of a future church. The population of this missionary station, which was visited once or more annually, was described in 1853 as consisting of Irish in the interior and French Canadians along the lakeshore. A schoolhouse was used temporarily as a church while preparations were made for building a proper church.

The first church at Ashfield was opened and dedicated to St. Ignatius by Bishop John Farrell of Hamilton, in 1858. Father Louis A. Wassereau, Father Peter Schneider's assistant at Goderich (1857-61), celebrated Mass once a month at St. Ignatius' and made the occasional sick call. Meanwhile, the Catholic population in the area continued to increase, necessitating building an addition to the church in 1860. In 1861, St. Ignatius' was detached from Goderich and elevated to parish status, under the patronage of St. Joseph, with Father Wassereau as its first pastor (1861-75). In order to accommodate the ever-growing numbers, the church was enlarged in 1865 and again in 1872. At this time the parish included the mission at Wawanosh (St. Augustine) and stations in Morris and Turnberry (Windham).

During the pastorate of Father Francis Xavier Darragh (1875-76), an addition was made to the small rectory, built during Father Wassereau's time, and the entire building was placed on a stone foundation. By the end of 1879, while Father Richard Beausang was pastor (1876-84), the parish consisted of 175 families. By that time, the two-acre (0.8 ha) cemetery, situated near the frame church, was enclosed with a neat fence. In 1842, on the site of this cemetery, settlers in Ashfield Township came upon the remains of an old building believed to have been that of a former Indian mission.

During Father Bartholomew Boubat's time

St. Joseph

(1884-90), the rectory was renovated, the church was enlarged and a belfry was erected. Both the church and the bell, which weighed 2,000 pounds (907.2 kg) and was christened "Leo," were blessed by Bishop Walsh in 1887.

Father Michael J. McCormack (1900-18) oversaw the construction of the present church. The cornerstone was laid and blessed on 13 September 1903, by Bishop McEvay, who returned on 15 October 1905, to open the new church. Built at a cost of over $20,000, it was 130 feet by 53 feet (39.6 m by 16.1 m) and seated about 700 people. Both the altar and the bell from the old church were retained. On 15 December 1915, the parish hall in the basement of the church was opened. It was renovated during the pastorate of Father John R. Quigley (1935-46).

Plans to build a spacious and comfortable red-brick rectory were made by Father Francis A. McCardle (1926-35), who also improved the church grounds and the cemetery. The late 1950s marked the end of an era when the large church shed, used since the nineteenth century to shelter the horses while the parishioners were at Mass, was sold, dismantled, and moved.

In 1963, the Missionary Society of St. Paul, a Maltese order, was placed in charge of the parish, followed, in June 1972, by the Congregation of the Resurrection. In 2003, St. Joseph's was once again administered by diocesan priests. The parish was canonically suppressed effective June 2007, but the church remains open as a non-parochial worship site of St. Peter's, Goderich.

Sources: "Parish of Ashfield," *Catholic Record*, 19 September 1903, 5; *Our Historical Heritage Par-*

ish of St. Joseph's, Kingsbridge 1905-1980 [Kingsbridge: 1905]; Sister Teresita Kennedy, CSJ, "History of London Diocese Part Two," *Newsletter of the Diocese of London*, no. 56 (Easter 1993), 14-15.

Bayfield: English Martyrs

As a result of the union of several Protestant denominations in 1925, to form the United Church of Canada, the Methodist church in Bayfield closed. On 20 November 1929, Bill Jenkins purchased this twenty-three-year-old structure, located on Isabella Street, and donated it to the diocese of London. This became the English Martyrs mission and was attached to St. Peter's in St. Joseph. After many renovations, and donations of pews, chairs, kneelers, Holy Water fonts, statues, altar vestments and sanctuary furniture, the church was ready for Catholic worship. St. Peter's pastor Father Leo H. Marchand (1929-38) celebrated the first Mass in the mission church on 13 July 1930. In August 1933, the replacement value of the church was set at $7,509 and the land was valued at $100.

English Martyrs

Father Marchand was succeeded by Father Oscar Martin (1938-45). Fathers Joseph A. Cook and Edgar H. Robert ministered to the needs of the mission until the appointment of Father (later Monsignor) William Bourdeau (1946-54). During the pastorate of Father Isidore J. Poisson (1954-61), all the children in the parish started attending the same elementary school — École Ste Marie. With Father Poisson's death, in July 1961, Monsignor Bourdeau returned as pastor of St. Peter's (1961-70). To him fell the task of implementing the changes brought about by the Second Vatican Council. After his retirement, Mon-

signor Bourdeau took up residence near Bayfield and served the English Martyrs mission during the summer months. With his death in March 1986, English Martyrs was once again served directly by the pastor at St. Peter's, Father John J. Bensette (1973-88). His successors were Fathers Elwin A. Morris (1988-99) and Andrew Sipek (1999-2001).

In 2001, with the arrival of Father Francis Thekkumkattil, CST (2001-06), St. Peter's and its mission, English Martyrs, Bayfield, were clustered with St. Boniface parish in Zurich. Two years later, in 2003, Immaculate Heart of Mary, Grand Bend, was added to the cluster. English Martyrs mission closed in September 2006.

This little church had seating for 158 people and was normally filled to capacity at the 8 a.m. Mass on Sundays between mid-June and mid-September. It never had running water or bathroom facilities. The caretaker would take the sacred vessels, cloths and anything else to his home for cleaning or washing when needed. During its seventy-six years of existence, English Martyrs witnessed but one baptism, one marriage, and one funeral service within its walls.

Sources: St. Peter's Parish (St. Joseph) File; DLA, Parish Files.

Blyth: St. Michael

Irish Catholics, mainly from County Tipperary, commenced arriving in Morris Township in 1852. The first Mass is claimed to have been celebrated, about 1858, by Father Louis A. Wassereau, in the log cabin of John Kelly in Blyth. In 1858, Kelly set aside some land for both a church and a cemetery. A large frame church was erected and, in the years that followed, Mass was celebrated once a month other than in winter and always at Christmas and Easter. Blyth was detached from Goderich and attached to the newly formed Ashfield parish in 1861. At the mission church in Blyth, on 25 September 1863, Bishop Pinsoneault confirmed sixty-two individuals. Father Wassereau, Ashfield's first pastor (1861-75), made the trip on horseback from Ashfield until 1873, when the mission of Blyth was detached from St. Joseph's parish and attached to St. Columban's in Irishtown. About this time, there were more than 180 Catholics in Morris Township.

Mass continued to be celebrated once a month.

Within a few years, however, the Blyth congregation had outgrown the tiny church and Father James Murphy of Irishtown (1865-1900) decided that a new church was needed. It was built in 1878 and dedicated to St. Michael the Archangel. The church measured 93 feet by 36 feet (28.3 m by 11 m), with a 78-foot (23.8 m) tower, and it was built at a cost of $4,000. The altar was donated by Patrick Kelly, son of John Kelly, Sr., and cost $1,000. Although the old church had been replaced, the adjacent cemetery continued in use, the first burial being that of Sarah Bradley in 1854.

St. Michael

Blyth, however, was still a remote mission for the priests at St. Columban's, and, in 1880, St. Michael's was attached to the newly-formed parish of St. Augustine in St. Augustine. Father John G. O'Connor (1880-84) served the spiritual needs of the faithful of the Blyth mission until 1884, and was succeeded by Fathers W. Thomas West (1884-88), Charles E. McGee (1889-92), Thomas Quigley (1892-96), Peter J. McKeon (1896-99) and Daniel P. McMenamin (1899-1901).

At the beginning of the twentieth century, rumours were spreading that Blyth and Clinton were to be detached from St. Augustine and Goderich, respectively, and joined together to form a new parish. The big question was: would the priest reside in Blyth or in Clinton? Soon, a holy horse-and-buggy race ensued along the roads in Hullett and Morris townships to obtain subscriptions, supporting either Blyth or Clinton as the location where the rectory would be built. In the end, largely through the efforts of Father West, then pastor of St. Peter's in Goderich (1888-1901), Clinton got the nod, and in January 1901, Ashfield's Father McMenamin was appointed first pastor of the newly established parish of St. Joseph's in Clinton and the mission of St. Michael's in Blyth.

After Father McMenamin, St. Michael's was served from Clinton by Fathers Joseph D. Pinson-

neault (1903-05), James A. Hanlon (1905-10), John P. Dunn (1910-13), John J. Hogan (1913-21) and Bartholomew G. Gaffney (1921-28). Until the automobile made it possible to cover the distance between the two churches handily and celebrate Mass at both on the same Sunday, the priests celebrated Mass at St. Joseph's and St. Michael's on alternate Sundays. Father Gaffney's successors were Fathers Maurice N. Sullivan (1928-39), Simon J. McDonald (1939-51), Joseph L. O'Rourke (1951-53), John W.P. Graham (1953-58), Leo E. Reed-Lewis (1958-62), Marcel A. Gervais (1962), Stanley E. McGuire (1962-65), J. James Kelly (1965-72), Donald J. McMaster (1972-74), Joseph F. Hardy (1974-80), John G. Pluta (1980-88), Raymond R. Renaud (1988-94), Mark P. Poulin (1994-97) and Dino Salvador (1997-2001). On 27 June 1997, St. James's in Seaforth was clustered with St. Michael's in Blyth and St. Joseph's in Clinton. The 100th anniversary of the union of St. Michael's with St. Joseph's in Clinton was celebrated on 28 October 2001, under the guidance of Father Lance W. Magdziak (2001-05).

Sources: DLA, Parish Files, St. Joseph, Clinton; Agnes Carbet, "St. Joseph's Catholic Church," in *History of Clinton 1875-1975* [Clinton: 1975], 38; "Parishes celebrate 100 years," *Newsletter of the Diocese of London*, no. 101 (Lent 2002), 16.

Brussels: St. Ambrose

Before there was a church at Brussels, a Father C. Cochrane is said to have travelled from Seaforth every third Sunday and celebrated Mass in a house on lot 5, Grey Township, near the intersection of the sideroad and the road between concessions 12 and 13, south of Brussels.

On 20 July 1876, while Dean James Murphy was pastor at Irishtown (1865-1900), one and a half acres (0.6 ha) of land was purchased from Hugh and Charles R. Cooper in Brussels. A substantial church of fieldstone was built on this site and dedicated to St. Ambrose of Milan.

The first baptism in the new church was that of James J. Ryan, who was born on 17 August 1879. James later studied for the priesthood at Assumption College, Sandwich, the Grand Seminary, Montréal and St. Mary's Seminary, Cincinnati, Ohio. In 1908, he was ordained a priest in Kansas City, Kansas, for the diocese of Leavenworth. His priestly ministry, however, was relatively short. He died on 20 March 1918, in St. Joseph's Hospital in Chatham after a two-year illness.

Meanwhile, in 1880, the Brussels mission was detached from Irishtown and attached to St. Augustine's. With the establishment of Wingham as a parish in 1911, St. Ambrose's was attached to Sacred Heart, where it has remained as a mission ever since. Father John J. Blair, Wingham's first pastor (1911-14), travelled by train every second Sunday and on alternate holy days to minister to the needs of the faithful in Brussels. In 1912, the mission comprised thirty-two families of 121 individuals.

Before land for a cemetery was purchased in the north half of lot 1, concession 12, Grey Township, on 20 February 1915, burials from the mission of Brussels took place in either Seaforth or Blyth. Consequently, some of the remains were later exhumed and transferred from Blyth to Brussels. The first interment in the new cemetery was that of the daughter of Dan Cooper and his wife, Anna Christine, who died on 31 October 1915. In 1964, the cemetery was landscaped and a large cross was erected, which was replaced by a new one in 1981. A new fence was placed around the cemetery in 1979.

Under the pastorate of Father Remi J. Durand (1950-59), the congregation of twenty-five families raised approximately $3,000 to cover the exterior of the church with grey imitation-block siding and to install a new furnace. Previously, the church was heated by two stoves, one in the vestry and the other at the entrance of the church. It was common for members of the congregation to gather around the stove at the door before and after Mass to get warm.

Father Gerald J. Freker (1959-64) was instrumental in introducing a more active congregational participation in the liturgy. During the pastorate of Father John G. Mooney (1964-70), a kitchen and parish hall were added to the church and the grounds were beautified. In 1964, the cemetery grounds were improved, a perpetual care fund was established and the records were updated. In a move to save on fuel

St. Ambrose

costs, Father Aloysius L.J. Nolan (1973-77) insulated the church in 1976. It was repainted the following year, in preparation for its centennial. Bishop Carter celebrated Mass in the church on Sunday, 22 May 1977, and a centennial Mass was celebrated on 19 June 1977. At this time, there were some 200 families in this mission. One hundred and fifty people attended Mass regularly, and 125 supported St. Ambrose's both spiritually and materially.

By the early 1990s, however, a more modern and larger church was required. Thanks in large measure to the generosity of the Terpstra family, the present 8,000-square-foot (743.1 m²) structure was built in 1993, during the pastorate of Father Joseph J. Nevett (1991-97), and the old church was dismantled. A mortgage-repayment party was held at the church on 7 June 1998, to celebrate the repayment of the diocesan loan incurred to complete the building of the new structure.

Sources: DLA, Sacred Heart, Wingham; Ralph Hubert Dignan and Joseph P. Finn, "A History of the Diocese of London," edited by Guy Alden (unpublished manuscript, 2002). Additional information supplied by Father John B. Johnson and Father John Van Damme.

Clinton: St. Joseph

St. Joseph's owes its existence to Father W. Thomas West, pastor of St. Peter's in Goderich (1888-1901), who decided to transfer his mission on concession 5, in Hullett Township, to the town of Clinton. Originally known as Rattenbury Corners, after William Rattenbury of Devon, England, Clinton was incorporated as a village in 1858 and as a town in 1875. While it had a population of 2,600 by 1887, it is said to have had but two Catholics in 1890, James Flynn and his wife, when Father West purchased the former Presbyterian church, a white frame building, and converted it for use as a Catholic church. Worship at the church in Hullett township was discontinued when this new mission church in Clinton was formally opened, blessed and dedicated to St. Joseph, by Bishop O'Connor on 1 July 1891. When it was rumored that a new parish would be carved out of St. Augus-

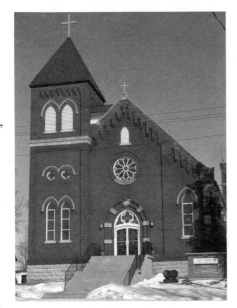

St. Joseph

tine's in St. Augustine, and St Peter's in Goderich, and established in either Blyth or Clinton, Father West successfully campaigned for Clinton.

Consequently, St. Joseph's was elevated to parish status in January 1901, and Father Daniel P. McMenamin was appointed its first pastor (1901-03). A rectory was opened next to the church in 1902. Father Joseph D. Pinsonneault (1903-05) succeeded Father McMenamin and was in turn succeeded by Father James A. Hanlon (1905-10). By this time, the old church, with six Gothic-style windows along each side and a bell tower over the entrance, was badly in need of repair. Rather than pour money into an already worn-out structure, the parish built a new church. Monsignor Joseph E. Meunier of Windsor, vicar general and administrator of the diocese, laid the cornerstone on 31 May 1908, in the presence of some 2,000 people, and he returned, on 17 December 1908, for the formal opening. W.J. Ireland of Stratford was the architect and Thomas MacKenzie was the general contractor. The Gothic-style church, complete with a tower, was built of red pressed brick from Milton. The stone trimming was the work of the Canadian Art Stone Co. of Toronto; the stone for the foundation was supplied by the Thomas Quarry Co. of St. Marys; and the interior walls were plastered and finished with black ash and cherry trimmings. The pews were furnished by Valley City Seating Co. of Dundas and a new Doherty organ was installed. The electrical fixtures were specially made in Toronto, and the furnace for the hot air heating

was supplied by the Western Foundry Co. of Wingham. The carpets and linens were furnished by Tozer & Brown of Clinton. All the memorial windows were donated and installed by early April 1909. On 27 February 1909, the former St. Joseph's church was disposed of by public auction.

Father Hanlon was succeeded, in October 1910, by Father John P. Dunn (1910-13), who was remembered for his wit and eloquent preaching. He was followed by Father John J. Hogan (1913-21) and Father Bartholomew G. Gaffney (1921-28). During the pastorate of Father Maurice N. Sullivan (1928-39), extensive repairs and renovations were made to both the church and the rectory, including the installation of a central heating plant to serve both. While Father Simon J. McDonald was administrator and then pastor (1939-51), No. 31 Radio School, as part of the British Commonwealth Air Training Plan was opened at Clinton in September 1941. Mass was celebrated at the station, each Sunday, by Father Herbert T. Fallon, the assistant priest at St. Peter's in Goderich.

St. Joseph's parish was canonically suppressed, effective 8 July 2007, and its territory was absorbed into St. Peter's in Goderich.

Sources: DLA, Parish Files; Agnes Carbet, "St. Joseph's Catholic Church," in *History of Clinton 1875-1975* [Clinton: 1975], 33, 38.

Dublin: St. Patrick

In early June 1837, Father Joseph L. Wiriath, of Wilmot (later St. Agatha), in what became Waterloo County, enumerated nine Catholic families in Hibbert Township. Thereafter, the Catholics of the area were served periodically from Guelph by Father Thomas Gibney (1838-43) and from Goderich by Father Peter Schneider (1844-52). By 1850, the faithful of Hibbert Township were ministered to by priests from the newly formed parish of St. Columban in Irishtown (now St. Columban), two miles (3.2 km) to the west. This continued for the next half-century.

In 1899, however, the mainly Irish and German families in the area petitioned Bishop McEvay for the establishment of a new parish. Permission was granted, on condition that a Catholic school also be established. Property for a church, along with a residence to be used as a rectory, was purchased in

St. Patrick

Dublin from J.J. McKenna. The residence had been built earlier by Joseph Kidd, the founder of the village in Hibbert Township, and uncle of the diocese's sixth bishop, Bishop John T. Kidd. Father William Fogarty was put in charge. During the winter of 1900, the congregation drew fieldstone from St. Marys and dug the foundation. Moore & Henry of London was selected as the architect; Davis and Eizerman of Mitchell was the contractor; and John Whyte, a Scot from Cromarty, was appointed clerk of works.

On 27 May 1900, Bishop McEvay blessed the cornerstone. The church was built of white brick on a fieldstone foundation and sat about 550 people. The square bell tower rose to a height of 115 feet (35.1 m) and a basement hall seated 300 comfortably. The building was consecrated by Archbishop O'Connor of Toronto, on 25 November 1900, and placed under the patronage of St. Patrick. The total cost of the land, church and rectory was about $18,000. On 1 January 1901, St. Patrick's was elevated to parish status. Land was donated, adjacent to the church, for a Catholic cemetery; this was blessed by Bishop McEvay in the summer of 1902. He returned, on 10 December 1902, to bless the new 2,100-pound (952.5 kg) bell, dedicated to St. Joseph. The bell tolled for the first time at the funeral of the church's first pastor, Father Fogarty, who had developed pneumonia and died on 21 December 1902.

During the pastorate of Father Thomas Noonan (1903-23), the parish debt was liquidated and stained-glass windows and a pipe organ were donated. A Catholic school and a convent for the Ursuline Sisters were built in 1902. Then, in 1914, a Catholic high school – a rarity for the period – was opened. The building still stands and now serves as offices for the school board.

Father Noonan was succeeded by Father J. Brian Ffoulkes (1934-59), who holds the distinction of being St. Patrick's longest-serving pastor. Father Remi Durand (1959-71) implemented many of the changes in church liturgy and the interior of the church, as directed by the Second Vatican Council and the 1966 diocesan synod. The next pastor was a native son, Father T. Gordon Dill (1971-81), who oversaw the replacement of the original rectory with a modern, one-storey building that cost $40,000. The redecoration of the church's interior and the construction of a new side entrance, which included an elevator and wheelchair-accessible washrooms, was commenced in Father James J. Carrigan's time (1981-90) and completed during the pastorate of Father Thomas W. Janisse (1990-94).

St. Vincent de Paul mission, Mitchell, was attached to St. Patrick's parish, on 1 July 1994, and, on 27 June 1997, St. Columban's, the mother parish, was also added to this cluster. The centennial celebrations of St. Patrick's were held in 2000, when Father Maurice O. Charbonneau was pastor (1999-2004).

This rural parish, centred in Dublin, began with some 140 families in the closing years of the nineteenth century, and it has continued to remain spiritually and financially stable over the years. Its modest growth during the last several decades to a little more than 200 families, is largely owing to the arrival of Dutch, Belgian and Swiss immigrants in the 1950s and 1960s.

In June 2007, St. Patrick's was clustered with St. James parish in Seaforth.

Sources: "Death of Rev. Wm. Fogarty, P.P. of Dublin, Ont.," *Catholic Record*, 3 January 1903, 8; Helen (Flanagan) Krauskopf and Margaret (O'Rourke) Rowland, *St. Patrick's Parish: Heart of Faith and Learning* (1996). Additional information provided by Margaret Rowland.

Exeter: Precious Blood

According to Father John G. Mooney, pastor of Our Lady of Mount Carmel (1970-76), a mission dedicated to the Most Precious Blood of Jesus was established, in 1880, in Exeter, but it "quickly disintegrated" owing to Protestant opposition. Again, in 1945, the Roman Catholic chaplain from the Royal Canadian Air Force Base at Centralia undertook to celebrate Mass in the Royal Canadian Legion Hall in town but was asked to stop doing so by some of the local citizenry.

With an increase in the number of Catholic families in the Exeter area, however, Father J. James E. Kelly of Mount Carmel (1956-65) began celebrating Mass in Precious Blood school, Exeter, in 1956. By the time of Father Mooney's arrival, there were some seventy families. This had grown to 100 families by 1973, and a new location for the Catholic Mass Centre was required. After discussions with the Anglican community and its rector, Rev. George Anderson, arrangements were made for the Precious Blood mission to use Trivitt Memorial Anglican church, which had seating for about 600 people. The first Mass was celebrated there on 2 June 1974. Father Mooney had wanted to name the Catholic Mass Centre "St. Peter's mission," after the name of the pre-Reformation cathedral in Exeter, England, but this suggestion was squashed. In early October 1975, an ecumenical service to mark one year of the joint use of Trivitt Memorial church was celebrated by Bishop Carter and Bishop T. David Ragg of the Anglican diocese of Huron. Although the idea of a Catholic parish in Exeter was suggested in Father Mooney's time, the first serious work was not undertaken until the pastorate of Father Gary Goyeau (1986-89). He established an account for a new Precious Blood church with the Diocesan Loan Fund and initiated the first campaign to solicit pledges to build a church. Efforts at fund-raising continued under the brief pastorate of Father Francis Murphy, but for a variety of reasons — all beyond the control of the Catholic community — the project ground to a halt in the early 1990s. Nevertheless, even at this time, it was the opinion of the diocese that something should be done to accommodate the needs of the Catholics in Exeter. Beginning in 1996, the accounts for the Precious Blood mission were maintained separately from Our Lady of Mount Carmel parish.

Precious Blood

A task force was assembled in February 1998 to refine the perceived needs of the mission, and it recommended the construction of a new church. At the same time, a fund-raising committee was established. Robert Ritz of Stratford was selected as architect, and Father Murray Kroetsch of the diocese of Hamilton was the liturgical consultant. Plans were completed by September 1999, with the projected cost of the new church complex of more than $1.9 million. The plans were unveiled at a gala evening held at the South Huron Recreational Centre, on 22 October 1999, and the pledge campaign was launched. The site for the new building was a 3.4-acre (1.4 ha) parcel of land at what became 200 Sanders Street East. On 21 November 1999, the Roman Catholic community of the Precious Blood mission and the Anglican community of Trivitt Memorial church celebrated the twenty-fifth anniversary of sharing a church. Among those present were Bishop Sherlock and Bishop C. Robert Townshend of the Anglican diocese of Huron. The sod-turning ceremony for the new church was performed on 26 March 2000, by Bishop Sherlock, Father Paul E, Baillargeon, the pastor of Mount Carmel (1997-2003), and two-year-old Kira Westelaken.

Although raised to parish status by Bishop Sherlock, on 6 October 2000, Precious Blood remained clustered with Our Lady of Mount Carmel, under the pastorate of Father Baillargeon. On 16 June 2002, Bishop Sherlock dedicated the complex, which consists of a 450-seat church, a hall for 160 people, a meeting room and ample office space.

Sources: DLA, Parish Files.

Goderich: St. Peter

Father Lawrence Dempsey of St. Thomas (1831-33) inaugurated annual visits to Goderich, beginning in 1831. In November 1835, Father Joseph L. Wiriath of St. Agatha (1834-37) travelled to Goderich on foot. Father Thomas Gibney of Guelph (1836-43) oversaw the building of the first church in Goderich. Dedicated to St. Isidore the Farmer of Madrid, Spain, the frame structure on North Street was built by Hugh Chisholm.

In 1838, the northern mission was divided, and Father Peter Schneider (1838-52) was transferred from Sandwich to minister to the faithful in Waterloo, Wilmot and Goderich. In 1844, he left for Goderich and became its first resident priest. By the time of Fathers John J. Ryan (1852-53) and Robert Keleher, Sr. (1853-54), the mission comprised Goderich, Ashfield, Irishtown (St. Columban) and Stratford. Father Schneider, known as the Apostle of Huron County, returned in 1854. The following year Stratford was removed from Goderich, leaving the missions of Irishtown, Ashfield and Bayfield with the latter parish. Father Schneider (1854-68) travelled to his missions on foot or on horseback. With the completion of the Buffalo and Lake Huron Railway in 1857, he took the train to some of his charges. That same year, Father Louis A. Wassereau became his assistant (1857-61) and cared for Ashfield, Wawanosh, Hay, St. Joseph and St. Columban. Father Bartholomew Boubat (1869-74) oversaw the building of a new rectory in 1869 and convent in 1873, and the former rectory became a school. He also enlarged and remodelled the frame church built by Father Wiriath in 1834. It was rededicated by Bishop Walsh, on 29 June 1870, and renamed St. Peter's in honour of the prince of the Apostles. In 1871, there were 104 Catholic families in Goderich and area.

During the pastorate of Father W. Thomas West (1888-1903), work was begun on a more permanent church structure in 1886. Father West supervised the hauling of the building stones from the nearby quarries. Built in the English Gothic style, at a cost of $17,000, the church was dedicated by Bishop O'Connor, on 8 November 1896.

On 12 March 1910, the interior of the church was seriously damaged by fire, and the main altar was completely destroyed. Restoration work was undertaken by Father Donald A. McRae (1904-21), and the result was even more impressive than before. In 1921, the CWL was founded in the parish as a charter member of the League in Canada. Devotion to Our Lady of Guadalupe was introduced in the parish by Father Jeremiah P. Gleeson (1947-59). A base-

St. Peter

ment under the church was excavated for a parish hall, which was opened in 1964 during the pastorate of Father E. Raymond M. Moynahan (1959-77). He also refurbished the interior of the church to its present appearance.

Father Arnold F. Loebach (1977-84) established the St. Vincent de Paul Society in the parish and, beginning in December 1980, he was instrumental in bringing dispossessed Cambodian families into the community. The 150th anniversary of the parish was celebrated, on 24 June 1984, with a Mass and banquet. Father Joseph F. Hardy (1984-87) is remembered for his revitalization of the parish through his work with the youth and the introduction of the RCIA program. The roof and steeples of the church were renovated; wood carvings were added to the interior of the church; and the old St. Joseph convent and school were demolished, making the church more visible. All this took place when Father Terrence R. McNamara was pastor (1987-93). During Father John G. Pluta's tenure (1993-2004), the present rectory, built in 1914, underwent major repairs and updating in 1995, and the Marian Chapel was renovated and refurbished. The most ambitious project, however, was the restoration of the church itself, at a cost of some $750,000. St. Peter's was rededicated by Bishop Fabbro, on 3 November 2002, and, by the time of Father Pluta's retirement, in October 2004, the debt was completely repaid.

Sources: Francis G. Carter, *History of St. Peter's Parish Goderich, Ontario 1834-1984* [Goderich: 1984]; Ralph Hubert Dignan and Joseph P. Finn, "A History of the Diocese of London," edited by Guy Alden (unpublished manuscript, 2002); *St. Peter's Roman Catholic Church Goderich, Ontario 1996* (Norwich: 1996). Additional information supplied by Adolfo Spaleta.

Grand Bend: Immaculate Heart of Mary

In the spring of 1939, a delegation of Grand Bend residents and summer vacationers petitioned Bishop Kidd for a priest to come and celebrate Mass for them. Interestingly, the delegation's request had been the idea of the developer Peter Eisenbach, a non-Catholic. When Bishop Kidd appointed Farther Leo J. Kelly as first pastor (1939-45) of St. Christopher's in Forest, he thought that the Grand Bend project would add considerably to parish revenues. But it also meant more Masses on Sundays with a 25-mile (40.3 km) drive for the pastor before breakfast. Nonetheless, Father Kelly acceded to the request. The first Mass was celebrated in a home. This was followed by Masses in a public school and then in the "The Hub," a dance hall, from 1940 until 1949, when the owner withdrew his permission. Mass was then celebrated in an open-air pavilion near the water's edge but was often interrupted by activities on the beach.

Immaculate Heart of Mary

A group of the faithful approached Father Herbert T. Fallon, the third pastor at Forest (1949-56), with a proposal to build a church in Grand Bend. A committee was formed to meet with Bishop Kidd, who gave permission to purchase a suitable site for the erection of a permanent place of worship. As the site purchased proved to be too small, and adjacent land was not available for future expansion, the lot was sold and the proceeds used to purchase two 80-foot (24.4 m lots) at a cost of $1,900, from Peter Eisenbach, who then donated a third lot. The site, with its 240-foot (72.2 m) frontage along Highway 21, was about one mile (1.6 km) south of the village's main intersection.

Harold Weber Construction was awarded the contract for a 70-foot by 40-foot (21.3 m by 12.2 m) frame building, but before the work began, it was decided to increase the dimensions of the building to 120 feet by 40 feet (36.6 m by12.2 m) to handle the annual influx of summer visitors. Construction on the $17,000 structure, the first of the prefabricated "Cody's Cabins" in the diocese, commenced in 1950. In August 1951, Monsignor Mahoney blessed the church and dedicated it to the Immaculate Heart of Mary. At one time there had been only four year-round Catholic families in the area, but their numbers, as elsewhere in the diocese, were augmented

in the 1950s with the influx of Dutch and Belgian immigrants. By 1955, two Masses were celebrated in Grand Bend each Sunday, from May through October. Father Jozef N.A. De Neef, a Belgian immigrant, settled on the property now known as the Pinery Fleamarket and celebrated Mass every Sunday in Grand Bend until his tragic death on 8 April 1958, when a wall he was building for a barn collapsed on him.

Grand Bend was detached from Forest and elevated to parish status on 21 May 1982, with Father Robert J. Morrissey (1982-86) as its first pastor. Father Paul J. Beck (1986-2003) succeeded as pastor in June 1986. But the very close relationship between Grand Bend and its mother parish continued with the children of Bosanquet Township attending St. John Fisher school in Forest, once St. Damien's school in Grand Bend closed. Father Beck, who was school chaplain, died at the altar at the end of Mass, on 17 May 2003. On 26 June 2003, the parish was clustered with St. Peter's in St. Joseph, English Martyrs in Bayfield and St. Boniface's in Zurich, under the pastorate of Father Francis Thekkumkattil, CST.

With the closure of Holy Rosary church in London, late in 2004, some of the pews were purchased and installed in Immaculate Heart of Mary church by Exeter Furniture in July 2005. At one time, the church had a seating capacity of 470, but now it is 350, plus thirty additional seats for the choir. Some forty years ago, the Grand Bend parish was very family-oriented with many young families in attendance. Today, it is considered a seniors' parish.

Sources: Janis McCahill et al., *The History of St. Christopher's Parish St. Christopher's Church 1893-1993* [Forest: 1993]. Additional information supplied by Jim Dalton and Father John Van Damme.

Hesson (Mornington): St. Mary of Perpetual Help

In the opening decades of the nineteenth century, the Catholics of Mornington Township occasionally trekked to Hamilton to attend Mass and receive the sacraments. Gradually, churches were established closer to the township, first in Berlin (Kitchener), then Galt, and finally in St. Agatha. In 1848, Father Lucas Caveng, SJ, of St. Agatha became the first priest to visit Mornington. In 1849 and again in 1853, Father Rupert F. Ebner, SJ, walked from St. Agatha and celebrated Mass in the log dwelling of John Nauer.

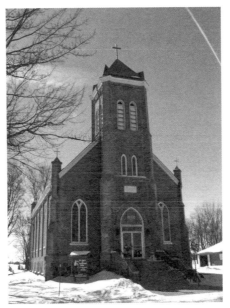

St. Mary of Perpetual Help

With the establishment of a resident priest at St. Clement's in Waterloo County, in November 1852, the faithful of Mornington Township made it their religious centre and attended Mass there every second Sunday. In 1867, during the pastorate of Father Edward Glowacki, CR (1866-70), a log house, together with one acre (0.4 ha) of land on lot 15, concession 13, in the northeast corner of the township, was purchased from Michael Kuhn for fifty dollars and converted into a separate school. A small sanctuary was built onto it where the attending priest from St. Clement's could celebrate Mass. At the time the mission consisted of some twenty families.

The rapid influx of settlers during the pastorate of Father Francis Breitkopf, CR (1871-81), led to the replacement of the schoolhouse. Father John J. Gehl, a diocesan priest, succeeded Father Breitkopf as pastor (1881-97) and visited the North Mornington mission about every seventh Sunday and occasionally on weekdays. His charge over this mission, however, ended abruptly in 1883 when Bishop Walsh appointed Father John Heitman as pastor at Listowel and directed him to assume charge of the North Mornington mission. The arrival of Father Heitman on the same Sunday as Father Gehl was the first indication to the congregation that the mission was actually part of the diocese of London and not Hamilton. Moreover, the Irish families in the area had made Macton, in nearby Peel Township, Wellington County, also in the diocese of Hamilton, their centre of religious worship. After three months, Father Heitman transferred his residence to Bethlehem, where the post office of Hesson had recently been estab-

lished, thereby elevating the mission to parish status. With the death of Father Heitman, on 27 May 1890, Father Gehl again ministered to Bethlehem, which was soon renamed Bethune, as a mission of St. Clement's. With his visit, in the autumn of 1891, Bishop O'Connor became the first bishop to set foot in the township. Plans for the building of the present church followed his visit, and, in the autumn of the following year, he returned to solemnly bless the church.

Father John J. Gnam (1894-1904) became St. Mary's second pastor, and during this time the hamlet was renamed Hesson. After Father Gnam's departure, St. Mary's became a mission of St. Joseph's parish, Macton, for a few months. During the pastorship of Father M. Daniel Monaghan at Hesson (1944-50) renovations and upgrades were made to the rectory and church grounds. Major renovations to the church were undertaken during the pastorate of Father J. Hugh Fleming (1950-58) and, on 13 July 1952, the parish celebrated the church's diamond jubilee. In 1961, Father John W.P. Graham (1958-65) undertook a door-to-door census of Catholics in Mornington, Wallace and Elma townships and the town of Listowel. The liturgy in the English language was celebrated at the new altar for the first time on 1 March 1965. The church's seventy-fifth anniversary was commemorated in 1967, and, in 1968, Father Leo A. Lariviere (1965-70) oversaw major renovations to the church. The church's interior was completely renovated in 1973 during the pastorship of Father Carl A. Pettit (1970-75). Father John G. Pluta (1975-80) is remembered for beginning "Coffee Sundays," both in Hesson and in Listowel, and for the positive interaction he had with the youth of the parish. Over several months in 1983, during the pastorship of Father J. Henry Cassano (1980-84), the centenary of St. Mary's, Hesson and St. Joseph's, Listowel were celebrated.

St. Mary's was canonically suppressed, effective June 2007, and its territory absorbed into the new parish of St. Joseph, Listowel.

Sources: Theobald Spetz, *Diamond Jubilee History of the Diocese of Hamilton* (1916); *St. Mary's*

— St. Joseph's Hesson — Listowel 1883 1983 Our Religious Heritage [1983].

Hullett: Mission Church

Hullett Township in Huron County was named after John Hullett, a member of the firm of Hullett Brothers, one of the leading financial supporters of John Galt's scheme for the establishment of the Canada Land Company. By 1844, the township contained a population of 195 people. Hullett was settled predominantly by immigrants from England, with the Scots being the next largest group. In time there would be a small sprinkling of Irish Catholics.

The first Irish Catholics arrived in 1848. They were Dominick and John Reynolds from County Sligo. Dominick settled on lots 21 and 22, concession 5 in Hullett Township. The brothers were soon joined by other Irish Catholics, such as the Blakes, Flynns, Gallaghers, McDonalds, McIntoshes, O'Haras, Quigleys, Scanlons, Shanahans, Tahoneys, Taylors and Tighes. The neighbourhood became known as "Paddy's Settlement." Father Peter Schneider of Goderich is credited with celebrating the first Mass in one of the log cabins there "not later than 1855." Bridget Tahoney, daughter of Patrick Tahoney and Bridget Flynn, was baptized on 8 September 1850, and she is said to have been the first Catholic child born in the area. Dominick Reynolds and Mary Walshe were the first Catholics to be married, on 22 November 1850, following three publications of their banns.

Dominic Reynolds donated the land on the southeast corner of lot 21, concession 5, on which the first Catholic church, a log structure, was built in 1857. Father Louis A. Wassereau, Father Schneider's assistant at Goderich (1857-61), celebrated Mass once a month in this church. Like Father Schneider, he was a native of the Alsace-Lorraine region of France. After Father Wassereau's departure in 1861, Father Schneider again ministered to the Catholics of Hullett. He was succeeded for a short time by a distant relative, Father Louis Schneider (1868-69), who in turn was succeeded by Father Bartholomew Boubat (1869-74), another native of France. In 1871, the Hullett mission consisted of forty-five families.

Meanwhile, a Catholic school was opened in 1863, with Thomas Blake as the teacher and fifteen pupils in attendance. Between 1870 and 1874, however, the church was used as the school until a new one was erected, in 1874, during the pastorate of Father Patrick J. O'Shea of Goderich (1874-80). This school was built on concession 4 and was still standing in 1975. While Father Bernard J. Watters was pastor at Goderich (1880-88), he was assisted, first by his uncle, Father B. McGauran of the archdiocese of Québec, then by Fathers Donald A. McRae (1883-84), a native of Ross-shire, Scotland and Henry B. Lotz (1884-88) from Alsace-Lorraine. Bishop Walsh conducted confirmations in Hullett in February 1881.

Father Watters' successor was Father W. Thomas West (1888-91), a native of Sheffield Township, Addington County in what is now eastern Ontario. He decided to transfer the Hullett mission to the town of Clinton, which was in the southwest corner of the township, spilling over into the townships of Goderich and Tuckersmith. In 1890, he purchased the former Presbyterian church, a white frame structure. James Flynn and his wife were said to have been the only Catholics in the town at the time, although Felix Hanlon, who ran a boot and shoe business, is said to have been the only Catholic in 1885. The mission church in Clinton was formally opened, blessed and dedicated to St. Joseph, by Bishop O'Connor, on 1 July 1891, and worship in the church on the fifth concession was discontinued. The cemetery on this site continues to serve St. Joseph's parish in Clinton.

Sources: DLA, St. Peter's Parish, Goderich, "Parish Register, 1843-1926"; St. Joseph's, Clinton, Parish Files; Agnes Carbet, "St. Joseph's Catholic Church," in *History of Clinton 1875-1975* [1975], 38; Francis G. Carter, *History of St. Peter's Parish Goderich, Ontario 1834-1984* [1984]; James Scott, *The Settlement of Huron County* (Toronto: 1966).

Kinkora: St. Patrick

Father Peter Schneider of St. Agatha (1838-44) probably celebrated the first Mass in Ellice Township, in 1842, in the Hennesseys' log house on lot 31, concession 4. In the mid-1840s, the intersection of today's Line 42 and County Road 145, in Logan and Ellice townships, was known as Saint Patrick's Settlement. Several years later, the name was changed to Kinkora Corners, and then to Kinkora, with the establishment of the Kinkora post office in 1857.

Tenders for a frame church, 80 feet by 45 feet

(24.4 m by 13.7 m), were called in late June 1857, with a deadline of 1 December. The land for the church was purchased from John Cavanagh for £50. St. Patrick's was elevated to parish status in 1869, with the arrival of Father John O'Neill (1869-1904). Uncompromising and unmerciful in his anti-liquor campaign, he succeeded in ridding the parish of every saloon.

In 1879, Father O'Neill laid before his congregation the idea of building a new church to replace the small old one. John McGlen of Toronto was clerk of works on the project. The cornerstone was blessed on 11 June 1882 by Bishop Walsh, who returned to dedicate the church on 28 October 1883. Built at a cost of $30,000, the church, both in its exterior and interior, is symmetrical in design. Its spacious and lofty nave and chancel and altars, arches, windows, turrets, tower and spire all draw the eye towards heaven in true Gothic style. The 157-foot (47.9 m) spire is topped by a seven-foot (2.1 m) high Celtic cross and is visible from the farthest points of the parish. Joseph Connolly was the architect. He was responsible for St. Peter's cathedral in London, St. Joseph's in Chatham, the Church of Our Lady in Guelph and St. Paul's basilica in Toronto. His church in Kinkora has rightly been called the "Cathedral of the North."

Father Alfred D. Emery took over the parish as administrator in March 1904 and, on the death of Father O'Neil in June, he was appointed pastor. During his mandate, the present, ten-room, red brick rectory was built and the old box stoves in the church were replaced with a steam heating system. In January 1911, Father Emery was succeeded by Father Thomas P. Hussey (1912-17; 1919-33), who had a parish hall erected, in 1914, at a cost of $1,000. T.M. Kelly built the foundation, and, until September 2003, the building was the scene of numerous meetings, potluck suppers, concerts, dances, bazaars, showers and fund-raisers. In 1916, Father Hussey arranged for the Sisters of St. Joseph to take charge of the school, and he supervised the building of a convent.

In 1936, under the pastorate of Father Edward

St. Patrick

P. Weber (1933-50), the church was redecorated by Alliston & McDougal. Father Weber was also responsible for bringing electricity to Kinkora. His successor, Father Thomas P.C. Donnellan (1950-64), oversaw the restoration of the church's interior in 1962. Two Italian painters, Gaetano Valerio and his brother Joseph, both from London, hand-painted the ceilings and walls and repainted the two existing murals on either side of the altar. Oil heating replaced coal in the church, rectory and hall. In 1964, a fully equipped kitchen was added to the parish hall. The side altars were painted white to harmonize with the main altar, during the pastorate of Father Donald J. McMaster (1967-72). Both he, and his successor, Father Lawrence J. Coughlin (1972-77), a former parishioner, implemented the changes in the church in accordance with the directives of the Second Vatican Council.

Additional major church renovations were undertaken during the pastorates of Fathers Aloysius L.J. Nolan (1977-85) and Peter H. Keller, who arrived in 1999. Some $26,000 was raised through Father Nolan's "Golden Egg" fund-raising campaign. The last project, costing $1.5 million, was completed in time for the rededication of the church by Bishop Fabbro on 17 June 2005.

Since 1994, St. Patrick's was clustered with St. Brigid's, Logan. With the suppression of St. Brigid's in 2007, St. Patrick's was clustered with St. Vincent de Paul parish in Mitchell.

Sources: DLA, John Walsh papers, Box 1, "The Status Animarum for the Diocese of Sandwich"; "Diocese of London — Dedication of a Splendid Church in Kinkora," *Catholic Record*, 3 November 1883, 5. Additional information supplied by Josephine Schoonderwoerd.

Listowel: St. Joseph

It is believed that the first Mass in Listowel was celebrated in April 1878, most probably by Father Edmund B. Kilroy of St. Joseph's in Stratford (1874-1904), who had charge of the mission at Listowel until 1883. It was then through some misunderstanding that Bishop Walsh sent Father John Heitman to

Listowel, in 1883, as its first and only pastor. The impression was that Listowel had a fair-sized congregation, and together with the mission at Mornington, it could provide a decent living. Alas, there were only about thirty families attached to the parish, and Father Heitman was

St. Joseph

met with indifference and poverty. Unable to pay even his house rent, after only three months Father Heitman moved to the relatively more populous and prosperous Mornington mission. Listowel was reduced to a station with the priest from Mornington/Hesson renting quarters to celebrate Mass in Listowel or its Catholics trekking to Hesson. In 1903, there was but one practising Catholic family in Listowel. Father Jeremiah Dantzer of St. Mary's in Hesson (1904-23) began celebrating Mass once a month for about fifteen persons at the Graham residence in Listowel. Age and ill health, however, forced Father Anthony M. Stroeder (1933-44) to discontinue this practice. By this time there were only three or four Catholics attending.

The Catholic population of Listowel increased during the Second World War, and Father Joseph F. Paquette, pastor at Windham (1933-46) and chaplain to the Listowel Regiment, began celebrating Mass for the Catholics at Listowel once again, in both the Armouries and the Capitol Theatre. When Father Edward Weber succeeded Father Paquette as chaplain, he procured a little room over the Dominion store, later Miller's shoe store, for the small congregation, and celebrated Mass there.

Father M. Daniel Monaghan, pastor of Hesson (1944-50), commenced to celebrate Mass every Sunday and on Holy Days for about ten families in Listowel. He also organized religious instruction classes for the children after Sunday Mass, and helped to organize and direct the Holy Name Society for the men and St. Martha's Circle for the women. Under Father Monaghan's guidance and leadership, plans were made for a church in the community in the near future. This was realized, however, under the pastorship of his successor, Father J. Hugh Fleming (1950-58). Blocked by the town council from building within Lindsey, construction of a modified Georgian-style church began beyond the town's northern limits in January 1954. Captain Fred Green, RCAF, of St. Thomas, was the architect and Charles Medcraft, of nearby Aylmer, the construction foreman. Eighty-two men from Hesson and twelve from Listowel worked around their day jobs and farm chores to assist in building the church. Among them, Father Fleming was often the busiest. On 4 July 1958, St. Joseph's church, which had a seating capacity of 250, was solemnly blessed by Bishop Cody. During the pastorship of Father John W.P. Graham (1958-65), many alterations and additions were made. Elwood O'Grady, a former member of St. Joseph's, left a very substantial bequest in 1960, which helped in large measure to retire the church debt. Further renovations occurred during the pastorship of Father Leo A. Lariviere (1965-70), and in 1966, the church debt on the original building and the addition to the church property was liquidated.

By 1985 the church was beginning to show its age and was proving too small for the congregation. The sod-turning ceremony for a new church was conducted by Bishop Sherlock on 15 May 1990, and Jim Gregus of Lucan was engaged as the general contractor. Under Father Adam Gabriel's leadership (1986-92), with the exception of some finishing touches, the building was completed by December 1990.

St. Joseph's was established as a parish, effective 24 June 2007, and clustered with Sacred Heart parish in Wingham.

Sources: *St. Mary's — St. Joseph's Hesson — Listowel 1883-1983 Our Religious Heritage* [1983]; Father A. Gabriel, CSMA, "St. Joseph's Church, Listowel," *Newsletter of the Diocese of London*, no. 44 (Advent/Christmas: 1990), 16. Additional information supplied by Father John Van Damme.

Logan: St. Brigid

In the late spring of 1837, Father Joseph L. Wiriath of St. Agatha reported two Catholic families in Logan Township. Beginning in 1852, Father Peter Schneider, stationed in Goderich (1844-52; 1854-

68), came to Kennicott in Logan on horseback, every third Sunday, and celebrated Mass in what became the S.S. No. 5 schoolhouse. He also visited Mitchell.

St. Brigid

The first church in Logan, a log building, was erected in 1860. At the time, the mission consisted of some sixty families. In 1869, the Logan mission was detached from Goderich and attached to the newly established parish of St. Patrick's, Kinkora. A frame church was erected to replace the log structure during Father John O'Neill's time as Kinkora's first pastor (1869-1904). It was formally on 9 January 1875, by Bishop Walsh and dedicated to St. Brigid.

Logan was elevated to parish status in 1897. There were eighty families. The first order of business for Father Denis J. Downey, its first pastor (1897-1900), was to build a rectory beside the church. On 6 January 1899, less than two years after his arrival, fire destroyed the frame church. The cornerstone for the present Gothic-style, red-brick building, designed by H.W. Powell of Stratford, was laid on 28 May 1899. The church, which cost about $7,000 and seated about 500 people, was formally dedicated by Bishop McEvay on 17 December 1899. The parish hall, excavated beneath the church, was completed in May 1930, while Father Bartholomew Gaffney, a former parishioner, was pastor (1928-33). Steam heating was installed in the rectory, the garage was enlarged, and church suppers were instituted during the pastorate of Father John M. Moran (1933-38). Father John T. Gibbons (1938-43) organized the Catholic Youth Organization (CYO) and the Old Boy's Reunion held on 3-5 July 1942. Father Gaffney is remembered for keeping bees and using the proceeds from the sale of the honey for the good of the parish, and Father Gibbons raised chickens and turkeys for the same purpose.

Even after the Second World War, a few families still came to church by horse and buggy. Consequently, when the large shed was taken down, in 1946, a smaller one to shelter the horses was built. In

the same year, while Father Edgar E. Veitenheimer was pastor (1943-49), a new oil heating system was installed in the church. As in other rural parishes, the influx of immigrants, particularly from the Netherlands, between 1950 and 1965, swelled the ranks of the parishioners.

Following the Second Vatican Council, major renovations were made to the sanctuary and the parish council was established, under the direction of Monsignor Clement G. Adams (1971-84). The Knights of Columbus Council 9252 was formed in 1982, under the guidance of Father A. Francis Loebach (1984-90). Since its beginnings, the CWL has been a leader in parish activity, from quilting bees during the Second World War to card parties, bingos, community bazaars, funeral receptions and other ongoing functions of the parish community.

In 1994, St. Brigid's was clustered with St. Patrick's in Kinkora, with Father Wieslaw Gutowski as pastor (1994-97). St. Vincent de Paul mission in Mitchell was henceforth served by the parish of St. Patrick in Dublin. Father Gutowski continued the updating and redecorating of St. Brigid's. On 4 May 1997, Father Paul K. Nicholson, a native son, celebrated his first Mass at St. Brigid's. Father Peter H. Keller, who arrived in 1999, oversaw the removal of the tall tapering spire, in 2003, and its partial replacement. The bell, cast by the Meneely Manufacturing Co. of West Troy, New York, has been in use since 1899.

The parish was canonically suppressed, effective June 2007, and its territory was absorbed into St. Patrick's parish in Kinkora.

Sources: *London Advertiser,* 10 January 1875 *St. Brigid's Church, Logan 1899-1979 80th Anniversary* [Logan: 1979]. Additional information supplied by Father John P. Comiskey and Tim and Susan Nicholson.

Lucknow: St. Mary

Prior to 1890, there was but a sprinkling of Catholics in the Lucknow area. Occasionally Mass was celebrated in people's homes and later in the upper floor of the old town hall, probably by priests from St. Joseph's, Kingsbridge. The Cains, Corrigans, Carrolls, Floods, Gaynors, O'Loughlins, McGarrys, McDevitts, MacKinnons and Macmillans were among the early Catholic families of the area. Some living north of Ashfield Township, such as the Hogans and Gilmores, also attended Mass in Lucknow, although they lived in Bruce County and belonged to the diocese of Hamilton.

In 1890, these families petitioned Bishop O'Connor for permission to purchase the little stone church recently used by the Lucknow Baptist congregation. The Baptists had purchased the church, in 1884, from the Presbyterians who had built St. Andrew's Presbyterian church in 1873. Membership in the Presbyterian church had flourished so well that a larger building was needed just ten years later, while membership in the Baptist church, after some six years, had so declined that the Baptists discontinued services in Lucknow.

Bishop O'Connor granted permission for the purchase of the church, which was refurnished and renovated. Officially opened as St. Mary's, on 27 February 1891, it was established as a mission of St. Joseph's in Ashfield. The pastor, Father Nicholas J. Dixon (1890-1900), celebrated the first Mass at St. Mary's. He and his successor, Father Michael J. McCormick (1900-18), journeyed to Lucknow once a month. In 1906, six stained-glass windows were installed in the church.

St. Mary's became a mission of St. Augustine's in St. Augustine, in 1911. The pastor at the time was Father William A. Dean (1911-18). In the 1920s and early 1930s, the pastors of St. Augustine's made the trip to Lucknow every third Sunday. During the winter this was sometimes a challenge and necessitated the use of a horse and cutter. Father Oscar A. Martin (1936-38) began celebrating Mass every Sunday at St. Mary's, when possible. For many years, it was the custom of the priest to partake of a sumptuous meal after Mass at the home of J.L. MacMillan. A pleasant chat over cigars followed dinner. Both the

St. Mary

MacMillan and William Schmid families were stalwart supporters of St. Mary's for many years.

In 1964, St. Augustine's ceased to be a parish and once more became a mission of St. Joseph's in Ashfield. As for St. Mary's, it was closed between June 1964 and September 1965. When it reopened, it too became a mission of St. Joseph's and was placed in charge of the priests of the Missionary Society of St. Paul, Malta. The Paulist Fathers who had charge of the parish and its missions were Fathers J. Charles Caruana (1963-67), Albert Zammit (1967-68), Horatio Galea (1968-69), and J. Henry Cassano (1969-72). The Resurrectionists from Ashfield ministered to St. Mary's between 1972 and 2003. The pastors were Fathers Edward J. Dentinger (1972-89) and Harry Reitzel (1989-2003), along with Brother Carl Voll (1972-92). In 2003, St. Joseph's and its mission were once again assigned to a diocesan priest. The first was Father Zbigniew Sawicki (2003-05). He was followed in 2005 by Father John P. Jasica, who is also pastor of St. Peter's in Goderich.

St. Mary's was canonically suppressed, effective June 2007.

Source: "St. Augustine Church 75th Anniversary 1903-1978."

Mitchell: St. Vincent de Paul

A church is said to have been built in Mitchell on today's Blanshard Street, south of Highway 8, about 1858, and to have been served by Father Peter Schneider of Goderich. This mission included the present parishes of St. Patrick's in Dublin, St. Brigid's in Logan and St. Patrick's in Kinkora.

The present site of St. Vincent de Paul church was conveyed to the diocese on 27 June 1862, but it was not until 1882 that Dean James Murphy, pastor of St. Columban's, oversaw the building of the present church at a cost of $8,000. Simple in design, the brick structure measured 80 feet by 40 feet (24.4 m by 12.2 m) and had a seating capacity of 200.

With the elevation of St. Brigid's to parish status, in 1897, St. Vincent de Paul mission was detached from Irishtown and attached to Logan. Father Dennis J. Downey, St. Brigid's first pastor (1897-1900), thought that the rectory should be built in Mitchell, but his parishioners pressured him

St. Vincent de Paul

to build it in Logan instead. St. Brigid's third pastor, Father William J. Kelly (1910-28), celebrated the first midnight Mass in Mitchell, in 1918. When snow ruined Father Kelly's car, following another midnight Mass, the men of the parish responded by taking up a collection and presenting him with a new Ford coupe.

For many years the congregation at Mitchell was small. Gradually the numbers began to increase, and, as they did, so did the renovations and beautification of the little church. In 1962, while Father Stephen W. Toth was pastor of St. Brigid's (1955-71), the interior of St. Vincent de Paul was painted and carpeted and the overhead furnace pipes were removed. During the pastorate of Monsignor Clement G. Adams (1971-84), structural repairs were completed; additional lighting was installed; and, in 1974, the exterior was painted. A new heating system was installed two years later. In 1979, stained-glass windows replaced the original plain ones and a new organ was installed. By the early 1980s, the need for a church hall became apparent. One was built on the north end of the church, in 1984.

St. Vincent de Paul mission really seemed to come into its own during Monsignor Adams' mandate. In addition to the regular Sunday Mass, special liturgies were held during Holy Week and at Thanksgiving and Christmas. It was also decided that baptisms, confirmations, marriages and funerals could be conducted at the mission rather than at the mother church. Hence, 210 baptisms, 53 marriages and 53 funerals took place at St. Vincent de Paul between 1980 and 2005.

With the restructuring of parishes by the diocese in 1994, St. Vincent de Paul mission was detached from St. Brigid's and attached to St. Patrick's in

Dublin, the pastor being Father Antonio G. Del Ciancio (1994-99). By this time, however, there was a movement underway to have St. Vincent de Paul elevated to parish status. In 1997, Bishop Sherlock declared Mitchell a parish, clustered with Logan and under Father Del Ciancio's pastorate. St. Columban's joined this cluster on 27 June 1997. With the closure of St. Columban's and St. Brigid's parishes, however, St. Vincent de Paul parish was clustered with St. Patrick's parish in Kinkora.

Changes to both the interior and exterior of the church were undertaken in 1997, with the interior decorating being contracted to John Vallerio and Son. On the outside, new steps and a railing were added, and the church was made wheelchair-accessible. Also, improvements were made to the grounds. In 2004, the heating system was converted to natural gas from oil, and both the furnace room and vestry were painted. The vestry and hallway were also carpeted, all owing to the generosity of the parishioners with both their finances and time. A vibrant mix of both young families and retirees, St. Vincent de Paul's parishioners are actively involved in a number of ministries and organizations.

Sources: *St. Brigid's Church, Logan 1899-1979 80th Anniversary* [Logan: 1979]; *St. Vincent de Paul Church Anniversary Celebration* [Mitchell: 1982]. Additional information supplied by Agnes Gaffney.

Mount Carmel:
Our Lady of Mt. Carmel

It was probably in late 1859 that a frame church was completed on a hill one and a quarter miles (2 km) west of the church at Mud Creek. Although it may have been known as Our Lady of Mount Carmel, as late as May 1864, the former pastor of Biddulph, Father James Murphy (1858-64), still referred to it as the mission of Mud Creek. In 1867, the Cranford post office was opened at this crossroads on the line between Stephen and McGillivray townships. It was renamed Offa, in 1868, but the settlement itself was called Limerick.

A frame rectory was built, in 1869, for Mount

Carmel's first resident priest, Father Philip J. Brennan (1869-78), who noted that his charge consisted of two churches, one station and about 220 families.

During the pastorate of Father Martin Kelly (1878-89), the present church was built. Monsignor Jean-Marie Bruyère, the vicar general, blessed the cornerstone on 24 July 1887. The brick was drawn from nearby Crediton. The structure was completed in the summer of 1888 at a cost of $35,000, and dedicated by Bishop Walsh on 26 November 1888. The church quickly became a landmark for travellers in the area. The common reference to that part of the country was "over near Our Lady of Mount Carmel church." In 1889, both the post office and community were renamed Mount Carmel.

Father Daniel Forster was pastor (1904-18) when the rectory beside the church was demolished in 1909 and a new rectory was erected in its place, the red bricks coming from Preston. The imposing white pillars for the lower and upper porches were the work of Alexander McIntosh. An innovative feature of the rectory was running water, pumped by a windmill to a large tank on the upper floor. This tank also supplied water to the barn.

Meanwhile, in the early 1860s, a log schoolhouse had been built one and a half miles (2.4 km) north of Mount Carmel. Later, a school was built closer to the present community, and in 1872, a one-room frame structure was built on the southwest corner of the present school property. It gave way to a two-room yellow brick school in 1906. In 1924, the Ursuline Sisters from Chatham arrived to take over the teaching duties. A third classroom was opened in the parish hall in 1934, making it possible for students to finish their junior matriculation (grade 12) in what was known as a continuation school. On Friday nights, all the furniture was cleared and put away on the stage in readiness for the popular dances that were held in the hall.

Father William T. Corcoran (1921-35) encouraged his parishioners to put on plays and pursue

Our Lady of Mt. Carmel

other cultural activities. The first diocesan Eucharistic Congress held outside London was hosted at Mount Carmel on 6 May 1921. It was also in 1921 that the parish CWL was founded. Nine years later, the church was redecorated.

A new three-room school was built, in 1965, just south of the old one, and it evolved into a central school for all Catholic children in the area. By 1968, buses were bringing in pupils from Crediton, Dashwood, Shipka and Grand Bend.

Garden parties were held almost every year on the church lawn, featuring a ham supper, games of chance and other activities. A chicken barbecue has become an annual event in recent years.

In 1983, during Father Joseph P. Nelligan's time (1980-86), the Father J.M. Fogarty Council 8480 of the Knights of Columbus was formed. During the pastorate of Father Gary N. Goyeau (1987-89), the church was extensively renovated and redecorated in time for the centennial celebration of Mass by Bishop Sherlock on 5 July 1987. By this time, twelve native sons had been ordained priests for the diocese or the Basilian Fathers and about three times that number of women had entered the sisterhood.

There were 232 registered families in the parish in 1999. With the elevation of Precious Blood, Exeter, to parish status, on 6 October 2000, the two parishes remained clustered with Father Paul E. Baillargeon as the pastor (1997-2003).

Sources: DLA, Pierre Adolphe Pinsoneault Papers, Box 2, "Rev. James Murphy file"; John Walsh papers, Box 1, "The Status Animarum of the Diocese of Sandwich"; Fr. Gary Goyeau, "Mount Carmel Church 100 Years Old," *Newsletter of the Diocese of London*, no. 29 (Summer 1987), 12; *McGillivray Township Remembers 1842-1992* (Ailsa Craig: 1992), 68-69; *Our Lady of Mt. Carmel Church Mt. Carmel, Ontario 1887-1987 Diocese of London, Ontario* [Mount Carmel: 1987]; Susan Muriel Mack, *The History of Stephen Township* (Crediton: 1992), 238-39, 271-73.

Mud Creek: Mission Church

Tradition has it that the first settlers to this area came about 1835 and were mostly Irish immigrants who had previously settled in Pickering, east of Toronto. An advertisement in the *Kingston Mirror* offering land at £12 per 100 acres (40 ha) enticed them to the Huron Tract. Six pounds was to be a down payment and transportation would be included. By 1840, Stephen Township had 213 settlers. In 1842, it was organized as a township and annexed to Usborne and Hay townships for municipal purposes. Between 1845 and 1850, it operated as a separate municipality, but was united to Usborne from 1850 to 1852.

Dean Thadeus Kirwan of London (1848-56) visited the area on horseback, carrying his vestments and sacred vessels in a carpet satchel. He is known to have celebrated Mass at the home of Ro(d)ger Carroll, in Stephen Township, two and a half miles (4 km) northeast of the present site of Mount Carmel church. Carroll was the father of James Carroll, the alleged leader of the murderers of five members of the Donnelly family on 4 February 1880. Mass was also celebrated in the home of Michael Hall at Mud Creek, just one and a quarter miles (2 km) west of what became Mount Carmel. Michael Hall was married to Ellen Glavin, by Father James Flyn (O'Flyn) of Biddulph, on 1 October 1850. The first Irish Catholic to settle in this area, however, is said to have been T. Coughlin, who arrived in 1848.

Early reports suggest that the largely Irish-Catholic population had built a small log church on the Hall farm as early as 1850, but the general view is that the structure was erected in 1854 under the direction of Father Peter F. Crinnon, pastor of St. Patrick's, Biddulph (1854-58). Some sources claim that it was located in the northwest corner, but it seems more likely that the church was in the southeast corner of lot 20, along the road dividing the present Huron and Middlesex counties. Father Crinnon's successor, Father Michael Prendergast, visited the area for most of 1858. In December, he was succeeded by Father James Murphy (1858-64), who moved the site of the church from Mud Creek, probably in late 1859, to the hill, one and a quarter miles (2k m) to the west. It became known as Our Lady of Mount Carmel at Limerick. The first entry in the new register bears the inscription "Registry of Births and Deaths of R.C. Church of Mount Carmel"

and is dated 6 January 1860.

Sources: DLA, Parish Files, Mount Carmel; Biddulph Parish Register; Mount Carmel Parish Register; "History of Holy Name of Mary Parish 1865-1990" (unpublished manuscript, 1991); James C. Reaney, ed., *The Donnelly Documents: An Ontario Vendetta* (Toronto: 2004), 34, n. 395; Susan Muriel Mack, *The History of Stephen Township* (Crediton: 1992), 236.

Seaforth: St. James

Tradition has it that Dr. William Chalk's log cabin in Harpurhey, Tuckersmith Township, had been used, from 1834, by missionaries on their way to the Indian missions on Lake Huron. Be that as it may, the diocese acquired a piece of land in Harpurhey from James Dickson, the local member of the Upper Canada legislature, but whether it was the site of Chalk's log cabin is not clear. In any case, it was sold about nine years after St. James's church was built, less than a half mile (.8 km) to the southeast, in Seaforth.

Father Peter Schneider of Goderich is known to have celebrated Mass in the log house of Michael Donovan, about one mile (1.6 km) south of Egmondville and, therefore, within the boundaries of what became St. James's parish. As pastor at Irishtown, Father James Murphy (1865-1900) initiated the building of the mission church at Seaforth in 1869, and a site was purchased from Dr. T.T. Coleman. The white-brick church, built at a cost of about $20,000, was officially dedicated by Bishop Walsh on 17 July 1870.

St. James's continued as a mission of St. Columban's in Irishtown, until the appointment of Father Patrick J. O'Shea as pastor of Seaforth (1880-90) on 29 January 1880. Father O'Shea boarded in a local hotel until a spacious frame house was purchased for use as a rectory. Later, Father Peter McCabe built a rectory. Father O'Shea's successor, also an earlier assistant at St. Columban's, was Father John L. Cook (1890-92). Father Joseph Kennedy (1893-97) was able to reduce the parish debt considerably, and in 1893, he established a parish cemetery just outside the town limits. In the late spring of 1901, St. James's fourth pastor, Father Peter McCabe (1897-1901), exchanged parishes with Father Patrick Corcoran of LaSalette. While at Seaforth, from 1901

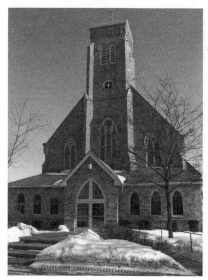

St. James

to 1918, Father Corcoran established a separate school and invited the Sisters of St. Joseph to take charge of it in January 1913. He also contributed personally towards the new Karn pipe organ installed in July 1915.

During the pastorate of Father Edward F. Goetz (1918-33), the original high altar and side altars were refinished in white and gold leaf, and the memorial stained-glass windows were installed. Father Thomas P. Hussey, a former chaplain during the First World War, arrived in June 1933. Twenty parishioners had also served in that war and another fifty-four would serve in the Second World War. Two were killed in action in each war. A bequest by Frank O'Hara financed the decoration of the church's interior during Father Hussey's incumbency (1933-50). Scotty McDougall, the artist, painted the four murals on the sanctuary walls. The vestry was also furnished with pews for winter use. Father Hussey was succeeded by a native parishioner, Father Edward P. Weber (1950-58), who undertook several improvements in the church, including a new floor covering and new pews. In implementing the liturgical changes required by the Second Vatican Council, Father Harry J. Laragh (1965-79) sought the advice of Murray McCance.

On 1 July 1994, in keeping with the anticipated policy that a priest would serve a minimum of 500 families, four clusters occurred in the Huron-Perth Deanery. One of those clusters brought together St. James's in Seaforth and St. Columban's with Father Joseph F. Hardy as the pastor (1994-97). On 27 June 1997, St. James's was clustered with St. Joseph's in Clinton and St. Michael's mission in Blyth, under the pastorate of Father Dino Salvador (1997-2001). As for St. Columban's, it was clustered with its daughter parishes: St. Brigid's in Logan and St. Vincent de Paul in Mitchell. In June 2001, with the

appointment of Father Lance W. Magdziak as pastor (2001-05), St. Columban's was again clustered with St. James's, as well as with St. Brigid's parish. The suppression of St. Columban's in June 2005 left the previous clustering of the Seaforth and Clinton parishes.

Sources: DLA, Parish Files; Ralph Hubert Dignan and Joseph P. Finn, "A History of the Diocese of London," edited by Guy Alden (unpublished manuscript, 2002); *St. James' Church Seaforth, Ontario 105th Anniversary 1870-1975* [Seaforth: 1975]; "'Clustering' of Parishes," *Newsletter of the Diocese of London*, no. 63 (Fall 1994), 2. Additional information supplied by Father John Van Damme.

South Easthope Township: St. Anthony Mission

While Father Peter Schneider of St. Agatha (1838-44) is credited with having a log church erected on the southwest corner of lot 14, concession 2, in 1839, it may very well be that his predecessor at St. Agatha, Father Joseph L. Wiriath, served the Catholics of South Easthope Township as early as 1835. In any case, on his departure to his native Alsace in 1837, Father Wiriath reported that the Catholic population of South Easthope consisted of twelve families, totaling fifty-four persons. Between 1844 and 1847, Father Simon Sanderl, a Bavarian Redemptorist from Baltimore, served the largely German-speaking congregation while he was stationed at St. Agatha, and he kept a separate register for the mission. From the late 1840s until at least the mid-1850s, the church doubled as a school. It is said that a male teacher, hired in 1855 without close scrutiny of his credentials, made himself useful in the absence of a priest by occasionally preaching and hearing the confessions of the congregation! He only left because his chickens, which he kept in the attic of the church/school, disrupted both churchgoers and scholars.

In 1863, Father Eugene Funcken, CR, of St. Agatha (1857-88), erected the present stone church, with its small sanctuary, three altars and small tower. The original list of subscribers totaled forty-six names. Mass continued to be celebrated at St. Anthony's no more than once a month, until 1866. The mission was then transferred to Berlin (Kitchener), but it was discontinued in 1871 or 1872.

With the establishment of a church at New Hamburg in the diocese of Hamilton, the settlers in the vicinity of St. Anthony's petitioned the bishop of London to permit them to be permanently attached to this church in Waterloo County. The bishop agreed to this request. The main factor appeared to be that the settlers would be served in the German language at New Hamburg. About 1890, Bishop O'Connor instructed Father John Heitman (1883-90) to include the Catholics of South Easthope in Mornington (Hesson) parish. They, however, complained about the distance and the primitive roads to St. Mary's church, and the bishop rescinded his directive. Bishop Michael F. Fallon announced that the Catholics of the South Easthope mission would henceforth be attached to Immaculate Conception parish in Stratford. Again, there were complaints. After some time had passed, Bishop Fallon compromised by permitting the families in question to choose; some opted to attend Mass in New Hamburg and others went to Stratford.

During the pastorship of Monsignor William T. Corcoran at Immaculate Conception (1935-56), the neglected cemetery surrounding St. Anthony's church was refurbished. A few of the families in the South Easthope area then became interested in re-opening the church, which had been closed for more than sixty years. The building was replastered and cleaned up, and permission was granted for Mass to be celebrated once a year in the reconditioned church. The first such Mass was celebrated on 12 November 1939. Because the heating system has been inadequate for that time of the year, annual Masses of Thanksgiving have been held in September.

During the pastorship of Monsignor Vincent W. Walsh (1960-71), many improvements were made to the exterior and interior of the church, and children from the surrounding countryside were transported to the church by bus every Friday. The Ursuline nuns would give them an hour of religious instruction. Also, the churchyard monuments were repaired and the property fenced. By this time, however, the

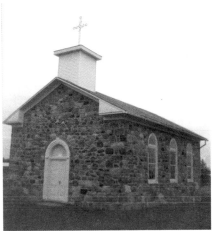

St. Anthony

church, while still part of Immaculate Conception parish, was no longer regarded as a mission.

A twin to the church in St. Agatha, St. Anthony's holds the distinction of being the oldest Roman Catholic church in Perth County and also one of the county's smallest and most attractive, built in the early nineteenth century rural classical style. Lastly, St. Anthony's and Hesson are the only two churches in the diocese of London that were truly German in origin, like their neighbours to the east in the diocese of Hamilton.

Sources: Theobald Spetz, *Diamond Jubilee History of the Diocese of Hamilton* ([Toronto]: 1916); [Msgr. W.T. Corcoran et al.], *Immaculate Conception Church 100th Anniversary 1905-2005*, [2005]; Jana Miller, "Oldest Catholic church in Perth, Angels have S. Anthony's to themselves," *New Hamburg Independent*, New Hamburg, 14 February 1996, H30. Additional information supplied by Mary Bannon.

St. Augustine: St. Augustine

Father Peter Schneider of Goderich is said to have been the first priest to minister to the faithful in this area, beginning in 1850, in the log house of Michael McCabe, which was located on lot 23, concession 6, in what became West Wawanosh Township in 1866. Later, Mass was celebrated in George Brophy's log house. In 1857, a log church, with an adjoining cemetery, was erected on the Brophy farm. Prior to this, interments were in Goderich.

Wawanosh became part of the newly formed Ashfield parish in 1861 and was served by Father Louis A. Wassereau (1861-75). In 1864, a little log school was built and opened near the site of the later one in St. Augustine. A new larger frame church, without a basement, was erected in 1872, a few metres west of the present church and possibly nearer to the road. Patrick Kelly of Blyth was the contractor. A wooden platform at the edge of the road allowance permitted horse-drawn vehicles to stop beside it so that the women and children could dismount, walk down the steps onto the wooden walkway and enter the church without tracking in mud. The present cemetery lands were also acquired at this time. Shortly thereafter a new frame schoolhouse was erected, which served the Catholic children of the area until its closure in June 1966.

St. Augustine's was detached from St. Joseph's in Ashfield and elevated to parish status in 1880. The first pastor, Father John O'Connor (1880-84), also had charge of the missions of Blyth and Wingham. During the pastorate of Father James A. Hanlon (1900-04), the present church was constructed. A limestone quarry was opened on the south bank of the Maitland River, on the west half of lot 28, concession 6, East Wawanosh. A Protestant family named Wallace owned the land and donated the stone in a spirit of good will. The contractor for the church was Sam Cooper of Clinton, and Stothers Bros. of Nile constructed the stone foundation. The cornerstone was laid in 1903, and the church, built at a cost of $18,000, was officially opened in 1904. The stained-glass windows were made and donated by A.H. Moore, and all but one are still in place. A storm in 1920 blew out one of the original windows.

In 1964, St. Augustine's ceased to be a parish and once again became a mission of St. Joseph's in Ashfield, which was now under the administration of the Paulist Fathers from Malta. The Maltese priests left in July 1972 and were succeeded at Ashfield by the Resurrectionist Fathers. In 1974, a new steel pre-painted roof was installed. The following year the interior of the church was repainted, better light fixtures installed and a new carpet laid. The seventy-fifth anniversary of the present church was commemorated in 1978 with the publication of a booklet outlining the history of the Catholic Church in the area.

Several priests sought out the serenity and tranquility of St. Augustine's after they had retired from active ministry. Monsignor Louis J. Phelan arrived in June 1970 and stayed until his death in December 1976. His fortieth anniversary as a priest was celebrated on 6 June 1976. In May 1977, Father Lawrence J. Coughlin took up residence (1977-82)

St. Augustine

in the former rectory, followed by Father Frank A. Dentinger, CR (1982-92). Father Joseph Lupo was administrator for a short time prior to his retirement in June 1993. With the appointment, in 1996, of the recently retired Father Patrick Sheridan, CR, as administrator, the church was opened in warm-weather seasons only.

St. Augustine's closed on 3 September 2003. Bishop Fabbro celebrated the final Mass on 24 September 2006. Over the years, St. Augustine's had nurtured the vocations of at least four priests — one of whom became a bishop — two brothers, and twenty-five sisters. Of the latter, twenty were members of the Congregation of St. Joseph in London and, of these, six were the daughters of Patrick and Johanna Troy.

Source: "St. Augustine Church 75th Anniversary 1903-1978"; "St. Augustine's Church, St. Augustine, Ontario, Sunday, September 24, 2006, Final Mass & Celebration."

St. Columban (Irishtown): St. Columban

The origins of St. Columban's may be traced to the arrival, in the early 1830s, of Irish immigrants who came mainly from Tipperary and Clare counties and who settled in McKillop and Hibbert townships. The accepted leader of these Irish Catholics was Dennis Downey, grandfather of Father Denis J. Downey. The settlement, along the present Highway 8 and between Dublin and Seaforth, became known as Downey's and was later renamed Irishtown.

Father Joseph L. Wiriath of St. Agatha visited the settlement on foot in November 1835. His successor, Father Thomas Gibney of Guelph (1838-43), oversaw the building of a log church in 1840. By 1853, Irishtown was a large and populous Irish settlement, but the church was in a dilapidated state and inadequate for the needs of its congregation. The faithful decided to erect a new stone church. During the pastorate of Father Peter Schneider of Goderich, the mission's church bell "was baptized and consecrated under the glorious name of MARY" on 1 September 1858. On 17 October 1858, Bishop Farrell of Hamilton blessed the small white-brick church dedicated to St. Columban.

While Father (later Dean) James Murphy was the pastor of Irishtown (1865-1900), the 1858 church was enlarged in 1877, making it one of the largest churches in the diocese at the time. It was not until 1911, however, that the parish was debt free and the church was consecrated, on 15 May 1911. Father Albert McKeon was pastor (1901-11) at the time. It was also during Dean Murphy's pastorate that the cemetery next to the church was closed and a new one was opened in a more desirable location about a half mile (0.8 km) away.

During the early years of his pastorate, Dean Murphy was in charge of the far-flung missions of Seaforth, Clinton, French Settlement, Zurich, Clinton, Blyth, Wingham, Brussels, Mitchell and Dublin. As the years passed, however, the area of his jurisdiction slowly shrank until his last mission, Dublin, was erected into a parish and given to his curate, Father William Fogarty. Dean Murphy showed his displeasure by declining an invitation to a dinner held in Father Fogarty's honour at Dublin's only hotel. Not even the presence of Bishop McEvay persuaded him to attend. Instead, while the celebration was in full swing, Dean Murphy, wearing a long black frock coat and tall black silk hat, and walking with cane in hand, strode into the hotel and had his dinner alone.

Irishtown became St. Columban in 1898, with the opening of the community's first post office. The "splendid parochial residence" was erected in 1882 and remodelled from attic to basement in 1939, during the pastorate of Father Francis J. Odrowski (1939-51). It was demolished and replaced by a modern structure, blessed on 8 January 1978, while Father Peter A. Oostveen was pastor (1969-84).

While pastor of St. Columban's, Father Joseph F. Hardy was also administrator of St. Patrick's in Dublin until 1994. On 1 July 1994, he became pastor of the parishes of St. Columban and St. James in Seaforth (1994-97). On 27 June 1997, St. Columban's

St. Columban

was detached from St. James's and clustered with two other daughter parishes — St. Brigid's in Logan and St. Vincent de Paul in Mitchell — under the pastorate of Father Antonio G. Del Ciancio (1997-99). Then, in June 2001, with the appointment of Father Lance W. Magdziak as pastor (2001-05), St. Columban's was clustered with St. James's and St. Brigid's.

Faced with a church that was in a very dilapidated condition, a small congregation and a shortage of priests, the diocese suppressed St. Columban's, "the mother church of the Huron Tract." The final Mass was celebrated on 26 June 2005. St. James's in Seaforth absorbed St. Columban's boundaries and became the repository of its sacramental records. In 2006, St. Columban's church, an historic landmark on Highway 8, was torn down.

Sources: DLA, Parish Files; Ralph Hubert Dignan and Joseph P. Finn, "A History of the Diocese of London," ed. by Guy Alden (unpublished manuscript, 2002); *St. James' Church Seaforth, Ontario 105th Anniversary 1870-1975* [Seaforth: 1975]; "'Clustering' of Parishes," *Newsletter of the Diocese of London*, no. 63 (Fall 1994), 2; "St. Columban Parish 1832-2005: 173 Years of Faith and Community." Additional information supplied by Father John Van Damme.

St. Joseph (French Settlement): St. Peter

In 1849, Father Peter Schneider of Goderich celebrated Mass in the homes of French-Canadian families living along the shore of Lake Huron in what was known as French Settlement. In 1854, this area was part of the vast territory that Bishop Charbonnel of Toronto entrusted to Father Michael Moncoq (1854-56). Father Moncoq visited French Settlement on 8-9 February 1855, and baptised three children. Later that year, a combination log school and church, dedicated to "Saint Pierre aux Bouleaux," was built near the present church. This served the German settlers in the Zurich area. With the tragic death of Father Moncoq on 1 January 1856, the settlement was again served from Goderich by Father Schneider (1854-64) and his assistant, Father Louis A. Wassereau (1857-61). It would appear that Father Wassereau had commenced building a frame church, but just as it was nearing completion, it was destroyed by

St. Peter

fire on 15 December 1859. The poverty of the people necessitated the continued use of the log building for more than another decade. Bishop Pinsoneault made the first episcopal visit to the settlement on 8 October 1860.

When Irishtown was elevated to parish status in 1865, French Settlement was detached from Goderich and placed under the charge of Father James Murphy (1865-1900). The cornerstone of the yellow-brick church, erected on a stone foundation and surmounted with a steeple, was laid on 6 July 1873.

With the building of a rectory in 1875, St. Peter's became a parish in 1876. Father Louis Schneider, a distant relative of Father Peter Schneider, was its first pastor (1876-79). His successor, the Polish-born Father Joseph J. Moran (1879-1883), bought and installed the parish's first bell, which was christened "Philomena" by Monsignor Jean-Marie Bruyère on 25 January 1882. Father Moran also set the pastoral dues on a basis of ten cents an acre. This made him very unpopular. With his departure, in the spring of 1883, St. Peter's reverted once again to mission status and was served from Irishtown.

Father J.A. Kealy (1884-89) was appointed pastor of St. Peter's in October 1884, but being rather extravagant, he left the parish with a $900 debt. Father Joseph-G-E Courtois (1889-1901) reintroduced the pew rent system, and also with additional subscriptions, he was able to pay off the parish debt in four years. Moreover, he established a separate school, repaired the church and rectory, fenced in the grounds, cleaned up the cemetery and erected a wooden cross therein. The rectory was badly damaged by fire, on 18 March 1894, but within four months, a new one was completed. On 22 October

1899, Bishop McEvay blessed the church, enlarged to 95 feet by 53 feet (29 m by 16.2 m). Father Remy Prud'homme (1901-04) founded the Blessed Virgin Sodality, the Ste. Anne Society and the Association of the Stations of the Cross. His successor, Father Joseph A. Loiselle (1904-09), is credited with being the first priest in Ontario to own a car. Father Achille A.E. Rondot (1913-24) oversaw the decoration of the church's interior, the renovation of the rectory, the installation of a new heating system in the house and church and the erection of a monument to the Sacred Heart. During the pastorate of Father Oscar Martin (1938-45), the parish hall was built where the horse shed had stood. The hall was extended by 25 feet (7.6 m) when Father William Bourdeau was pastor (1946-54). Monsignor Bourdeau is also credited with finally abolishing the practice of renting pews, in 1953.

With the arrival of the present pastor, Father Francis Thekkumkattil, CST, in June 2001, St. Peter's and its mission, English Martyrs in Bayfield, were clustered with St. Boniface's in Zurich. Two years later, on 26 June 2003, Immaculate Heart of Mary in Grand Bend, was added to this cluster.

Sources: DLA, St. Peter Mission Register, 1854-1861, French Settlement; Parish Files; Ralph Hubert Dignan and Joseph P. Finn, "A History of the Diocese of London," edited by Guy Alden (unpublished manuscript, 2002); [Leo H. Marchand], *30th Anniversary of Dedication of St. Peter's Church, French Settlement, Ont.* [French Settlement: 1929].

St. Marys: Holy Name of Mary

The earliest known visit of a priest to St. Marys in Blanchard Township is said to have occurred in 1849, when Father Thadeus Kirwan (1848-56) came from London to minister to the dying George Horner. Father Kirwan is also said to have returned, in 1854, to celebrate the first Mass in the town, but this event may very well have occurred four years earlier, as Father Kirwan performed three baptisms in "Blanchard Town" on 5 January 1850, and another three on 29 January. In 1854, a lot is said to have been purchased on Church Street, and a small log church was erected. As it was being completed, the people realized that it was too small for the growing Catholic population. Alex Harrison's harness shop was next used for church services, but it also proved to be too small.

St. Marys was detached from London and became a mission of Stratford, in 1856. A new frame church was built, in 1858, on Widder Street East. One Sunday morning it was discovered that the four large wooden blocks on which it was standing and securing the building on the hillside had been sawed through by "evil-doers," so that the building would tumble down the hill. The result was the construction of the town's first stone church high on another hilltop. This church faced Peel Street and was opened by Bishop Pinsoneault in 1861.

Holy Name of Mary mission was elevated to parish status, in 1865, with the appointment of Father William B. Hannett. He was succeeded, in June 1866, by Father Bartholomew Boubat (1866-1868), who built the present rectory, in 1867, and opened the first Catholic school in the town in two rooms in the rectory. Father Boubat also purchased the plot for the present cemetery. During the pastorate of Father Edmund B. Kilroy (1869-72), who was renowned for both his learning and public speaking, a Catholic school was built adjacent to the church.

The cornerstone of the present church, built during the pastorship of Father Philip J. Brennan (1878-1909), was blessed by Bishop O'Connor on 11 September 1892. Surprisingly, for the time, the church was lit by electricity. In 1913, Father John J. Ronan (1910-33) had a convent built and petitioned the Sisters of St. Joseph to take charge of the school. He is also remembered as an excellent speaker and for his keen interest in lawn bowling. In the mid-1940s, during the pastorate of Father Patrick J. Harrigan (1945-66), the church was decorated, and in 1965, the exterior of the church received a "face-lifting" and changes were made to the interior to accommodate the recommendations of the Second Vatican Council. Some Italian immigrants had settled in the

Holy Name of Mary

parish after the First and Second World Wars, but the main source of new settlers in the area after the Second World War came from the Netherlands. By 1962, of the 420 parishioners, ninety-four were of Dutch or Flemish origin.

Many changes to the church were undertaken by Monsignor Harrigan's successors. A major renovation to the interior occurred during the pastorate of Monsignor Vito H. Grespan (1980-87). Bishop Sherlock attended the rededication, on 21 September 1986, and returned to celebrate the parish's 125th anniversary on 6 October 1991. Father Charles C. Campbell (1987-93) was the pastor at the time, and he also built the hall linking the church and the rectory.

Three memorable links with the early history of the Church in St. Marys are contained in the present structure. The solid wooden cross, which adorns the present confessional, is the original one used by the faithful at the time of the establishment of the first mission church. The bell was obtained by Father Kilroy for the first stone church. And the sanctuary lamp, which Monsignor Grespan had discovered in the attic rectory, and which later accidentally struck him on the head, badly injuring him, was the same sanctuary lamp that had fallen on Monsignor Harrigan when it crashed to the marble floor of the sanctuary.

Sources: Bill Eckert "History of Holy Name of Mary Parish 1865-1990" (unpublished manuscript, 1991); Bill Eckert, "Holy Name of Mary Parish to Celebrate 125 Years of History," *Newsletter of the Diocese of London*, no. 48 (Fall 1991), 8. Additional information supplied by Father John Van Damme.

Stratford:
Immaculate Conception

An increase in the Catholic population in the east end of Stratford, where the CNR railway yards had been located in the early years of the twentieth century, prompted the establishment of a new parish in Stratford. Following the death of Dean Edmund B. Kilroy (1874-1904), Father John V. Tobin, the administrator of St. Joseph's in Stratford, purchased a house that would serve as a rectory and a suitable site for a church on Well Street. Work on the foundation for the church began during Father Tobin's time, but he suffered a nervous breakdown and the project was delayed until the arrival of Father Charles E. McGee (1904-20). The cornerstone of Immaculate Conception church was laid, on 9

Immaculate Conception

July 1905, by Bishop McEvay, who returned to bless the completed church on 25 March 1906. The structure had been designed by the local architectural firm of Orr and Russell. That June, Father Daniel J. Egan (1906-28) was appointed the first pastor.

One of Father Egan's initial tasks was to complete the interior furnishings of the church and then oversee the excavation of a basement parish hall. The hall was opened on 17 November 1909. Next, a vestry was built and opened on 8 December 1910. It served as a schoolroom for beginning classes, there being no separate school in the parish. In 1914, a lot was purchased on the north side of the church property, and the first rectory, which was built of brick, was moved to that site, and a new rectory was built in its place next to the church. It was completed on 17 October 1915. Immaculate Conception school was opened in 1922, and the former Kennedy home, at 36 Well Street, was acquired as a convent for the Ursuline nuns who took charge of the school in September 1923. Father Egan's silver jubilee was celebrated on 21 December 1924. During the administration of Father William T. Corcoran (1935-60), the church's interior was redecorated and upgraded. Monsignor Corcoran is also remembered for his cultivation and development of various kinds of irises. Many major improvements were made to the parish property and buildings during the pastorship of Monsignor Vincent W. Walsh (1960-71). Several alterations and structural changes to the church were undertaken while Father Vincent J. Gleeson was pastor (1971-78), and, in 1976, major repairs were carried out in the convent. In 1981, during Father Bernard R. Laverty's tenure (1978-82), the seventy-fifth anniversary of the parish was celebrated. Father

John F. Sharp (1982-89) oversaw the installation of an elevator and the construction of a new side entrance, in 1985. In 1986, a courtyard was laid out between the rectory and the church and the church was redecorated. Father Wilfred J. Bourque (1989-99) is remembered for his success in integrating L'Arche residents into parish life and for overseeing the most costly renovations and upgrades in the parish's history. Costing $700,000, they included the replacement of the church's boiler, furnace and pipes, a new front entrance, wheelchair-accessible washrooms and alterations to the parish hall.

Since the mid-1990s, both Immaculate Conception and St. Joseph parishes have been working to form a cluster. A "Cluster Mission" was held with celebrations alternating each night between the two churches. Later, a joint Sunday bulletin for the Stratford Catholic Parish Community of St. Joseph's and Immaculate Conception Church was published. A joint pastoral advisory board for the two parishes was formed in 2003, and both parishes participated in a parish mission in 2004.

On Sunday, 29 May 2005, the 100th anniversary of Immaculate Conception as a faith community was celebrated with Bishop Fabbro present, and on 1 September 2005, Immaculate Conception was fully clustered with St. Joseph's, with Father Richard P. Bester as pastor of both parishes.

Sources: [Msgr. W.T. Corcoran et al.], *Immaculate Conception Church 100th Anniversary 1905-2005*, [2005]; Judy Purcell, "Immaculate Conception, Stratford Marking 100 years," *Newsletter of the Diocese of London*, no. 117 (Easter 2005), 10. Additional information supplied by Mary Bannon.

Stratford: St. Joseph

Father Lawrence Dempsey of St. Thomas (1831-33) inaugurated annual visits to Stratford, beginning in the autumn of 1832, and he was there again on 4 June 1833. The following year, his successor, Father Daniel Downie (1833-36), visited the settlement. In 1834, the northern district of what later became the diocese of London was detached from

St. Thomas and assigned, together with the German settlements in what later became Waterloo County, to Father Joseph L. Wiriath of St. Agatha (1834-37). He paid his first visit to Stratford, on foot, in November 1835, staying at the Widow Cashin's log dwelling. In early June 1837, he reported forty-three families, consisting of 187 persons in the area. His successor, Father Thomas Gibney (1837-43) of Guelph, oversaw the building of the first church in Stratford, in 1838. The frame building, dedicated to St. Simon, was 40 feet by 40 feet (12.2 m by 12.2 m) and remained unfinished for many years. Bishop Power administered confirmation in Stratford in 1843. With the division of the northern mission, in 1838, Father Gibney retained Guelph and Stratford. In 1844, Stratford was detached from Guelph and added to the mission of Goderich. It was subsequently served by Fathers Peter Schneider (1844-52), John J. Ryan (1852-53) and Robert Keleher, Sr. (1853-54). Father Schneider returned to Goderich in 1854.

Although 1856 is traditionally given as the year that St. Simon's was elevated to parish status, with Father Peter J. Canney as pastor, he was, in fact, in charge by 1 July 1855. During the pastorate of his successor, Father Peter F. Crinnon (1858-74), the cornerstone of the present church was laid by Monsignor Jean-Marie Bruyère on 27 September 1867. The Gothic-like structure was built of Guelph cut stone and Brantford white brick. John Turner of Brantford was the architect. Bishop Walsh blessed the church and dedicated it to St. Joseph on 8 November 1868, but it was not until 6 June 1886, when the heavy debt was fully discharged, that Bishop James Joseph Carberry of Hamilton consecrated the church. Meanwhile, on 1 January 1870, the church bell, named Michael, was blessed by Bishop Walsh. Cast in Troy, New York, it weighed over 2,500 pounds (1134 kg) and cost $1,186.14. It was, at the time, the largest church bell in the province west of Toronto. During the pastorate of Father Edmund B. Kilroy (1874-1904), St. Joseph's school was built, Loretto Academy was founded in 1875 and the present Catholic cemetery, now part of Avondale Cemetery, was established in 1882.

While Father Charles E. McGee was pastor (1904-20), a new heating plant was installed in 1908

St. Joseph

and renovations were made to the church in 1909. In 1956, under the direction of Father Joseph L. O'Rourke (1955-68), the parish renovated the church, rebuilt the rectory and constructed a new parish hall. Both the rectory and hall, built by Curran & Herridge of Sarnia, were blessed by Bishop Cody on 30 November 1956. The main altar, of Carrara marble, was installed in 1958 at a cost of $4,600. It was reconfigured, in 1966, to conform with the demands of the new liturgy. All the artwork in the church's interior was executed by Valerio Brothers of London, the senior members of the firm – Gaetano and Joseph – having studied at the Michael Angelo studio in Rome. The American red oak pews were manufactured in L'Isletville, Québec. The crowning feature of the church's exterior came, in 1961, with the construction on the existing bell tower of a 44-foot (13.4 m), copper-sheathed spire, topped by a 10-foot (3 m) cross.

On 1 September 2005, Immaculate Conception parish was clustered with St. Joseph's under the pastorate of Father Richard P. Bester. The process had begun in 2003. St. Joseph's continues to be a vibrant parish, in particular its music ministry, which consists of three adult choirs, two children's choirs and a praise-and-worship team. A bereavement ministry was established in 1999.

Sources: Parish Files; "The New Catholic Church," *Stratford* Beacon, 4 October 1867, 2; *True Witness* (Montréal), 6 Nov. 1868, 4; "Opening of the New Catholic Church," *Stratford Beacon*, 20 November 1868, 1; [T.J. Dolan,] *St. Joseph's Church, Stratford, Ontario, 1867 Centennial 1967* [Stratford: 1967].

Wingham: Sacred Heart

It is doubtful that the few Catholic families in Turnberry Township had the services of a priest prior to Father Louis A. Wassereau's call to a sick man early in January 1862. Father Wassereau had discovered that the township was in the diocese of London and that it contained six Catholic families. Meanwhile, the settlers instructed their children in the faith, recited the rosary and gathered in one another's log cabins on Sundays to read the Epistle and Gospel and to sing hymns. Supposedly, baptisms and marriages were conducted by laypersons.

After Father Wassereau, the area was visited by Father Joseph Bayard, the first pastor in Ashfield (1861-75), and he celebrated Mass in the King William Hotel in Wingham and later at the home of a Mr. King in Lower Wingham. In 1867, Father James Murphy, pastor of Irishtown (1865-1900), was assured that there was a sufficient number of Catholics in the Wingham area to erect a church. A site was selected far from the main thoroughfare, owing to the fear of violence from the far more numerous Orangemen in the area. Patrick Kelly of Blyth, who had been the contractor for the church in St. Augustine, was engaged to superintend the building of this church, which was completed in June 1877. Bishop Walsh was scheduled to bless the new brick structure, dedicated to the Sacred Heart, but Father Murphy officiated in the bishop's absence.

In 1880, Wingham mission was detached from Irishtown and attached to St. Augustine. During the pastorate of Father James A. Hanlon of St. Augustine's (1900-04), a new Catholic church at Wingham was built. Then, in 1911, Sacred Heart was elevated to parish status with Brussels as its mission. Until a residence on Shuter Street was purchased, Father John J. Blair, the first pastor (1911-14), boarded at the Brunswick Hotel. He took an active part in civic affairs and was much in demand as a public speaker at various civic gatherings. The concerts and plays he produced were fondly remembered by both Catholics and Protestants years after he had left the parish.

The second pastor, Father M. Joseph Fallon (1914-23), possessed an outstanding physique. Seeing the need of a parish hall, he excavated a basement by hand and put down a floor. His priestly solicitude for the sick, especially during the great

Sacred Heart

influenza epidemic of 1918, was legendary. In 1923, he himself became ill, and Father Arthur M. McHugh (1923-33) was sent as his relief. Father McHugh exchanged the residence on Shuter Street for the later rectory. Despite the Great Depression, Father Joseph F. Paquette (1933-46) succeeded in having a new roof placed on the church, the church itself redecorated and rewired, the basement remodelled and finished, and new furnaces installed in both the church and rectory.

In 1961, during the pastorate of Father Gerald J. Freker (1959-64), Sacred Heart school was established, the first classes being conducted in the church basement. Later, in the summer of 1974 and 1975, the school was made available to the parish for catechism classes. As many as 200 children, from Brussels, Ethel, Blyth and Clinton, as well as Wingham, attended these very successful summer schools.

Under Father Aloysius L.J. Nolan (1973-77), the parking lot was constructed in 1975 and the church was insulated in 1976 to reduce heating costs and was repainted in 1977, all in anticipation of the centennial of the first Catholic church in Wingham. Various centennial celebrations were held in May-June 1977.

With an expanding parish of 200 families, a new church was needed. During the pastorate of Father Stanislaw Soltysik (1984-91), a new church building, with a basement hall, rectory and offices, was built. The altar and stained-glass windows of the 1877 structure were incorporated into the new 300-seat church, which Bishop Sherlock officially blessed on 14 October 1990.

Sources: Parish Files; Ralph Hubert Dignan and Joseph P. Finn, "A History of the Diocese of London," edited by Guy Alden (unpublished manuscript: 2002); "New church for Sacred Heart, Wingham," *Newsletter of the Diocese of London*, no. 37 (Pentecost 1989), 8; "New church for parishioners of Sacred Heart, Wingham," *Newsletter of the Diocese of London*, no. 45 (Lent 1991), 5. Additional information supplied by Father John Van Damme.

Zurich: St. Boniface

Beginning in 1849, Father Peter Schneider of Goderich celebrated Mass in the homes of various French- and German-speaking families in Stanley and Hay townships. In 1855, a log schoolhouse/church, near the present St. Peter's, was built in French Settlement on land given to the diocese of Toronto by the Canada Land Company. For more than a dozen years, both groups worshipped here. By 1869, however, the congregation had grown sufficiently to be financially able to build a larger church. The first plan was to build a church in a more central location to accommodate both ethnic groups. After somewhat animated discussions, however, it was decided to have a separate church in each township. In 1870, a church site was obtained in Zurich. Father James Murphy, pastor of Irishtown and its missions (1865-1900), blessed the small brick church, dedicated to St. Boniface, the patron and apostle of Germany, on 5 January 1871.

With the decision of Bishop Walsh to place the Zurich and French Settlement missions under one priest, who would reside at French Settlement, the St. Boniface congregation showed its displeasure by refusing to contribute its share to the construction of the rectory. The first pastor of St. Peter's parish and St. Boniface mission was Father Louis Schneider (1876-79). Fluent in French and German, he celebrated Sunday Mass weekly at both locations. This soon affected his health, however, and, in 1879, he was transferred to Stoney Point. During the next several years, Mass was celebrated every third Sunday at St. Boniface's. On the other Sundays, the parents taught their children the faith at home, and when possible, they drove the long distance to the French Settlement church to attend services.

Then, in 1896, Bishop O'Connor informed the St. Boniface congregation that, if it could raise $400 for the priest's salary, Zurich would be made a parish. The amount was raised quickly by the mission's approximately forty families, and on 5 May 1896, Father Theophile J. Valentin, a nephew of Dean James T. Wagner of Windsor, was appointed as St. Boniface's first pastor (1896-1902). A brick rectory was completed, on 23 November 1898, at a cost of $1,300. Also, the church was enlarged, stained-glass windows were added, and Bishop McEvay rededicated the church on 21 November 1901.

Between 1902 and 1905, St. Boniface was

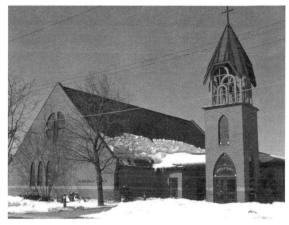

St. Boniface

placed under the charge of the German-speaking Franciscan Fathers from Cincinnati, Ohio. Diocesan priests returned in January 1905, in the person of Father Anthony M. Stroeder (1905-1928).

In 1987, under the direction of Father Paul F. Mooney (1978-88), a building committee decided that, owing to the deteriorating condition of the church, a new church and rectory were needed. On 22 April 1990, during the pastorship of Father Peter J. Hayes (1988-93), the final Mass was celebrated in the old church, and until the opening of the new St. Boniface, services were held in the school. The groundbreaking ceremony took place on 5 June 1990, and the new church was blessed by Bishop Sherlock on 2 December 1990. The remaining original stained-glass windows were placed in the north and south walls of the new church and the bell was installed, in 1996. A round stained-glass window was designed for the sanctuary wall behind the altar. The total cost of the church, narthex, basement hall, meeting room, offices and rectory was $1,119,364.20. The Knights of Columbus financed the construction of the bell tower.

With the arrival of Father Francis Thekkumkattil, CST, in June 2001, St. Boniface was clustered with St. Peter's in St. Joseph and the mission of English Martyrs, Bayfield. Two years later, on 26 June 2003, Immaculate Heart of Mary, Grand Bend, was added to the cluster.

Sources: Parish Files; [Father Paul F. Mooney], *The History of St. Boniface Parish, London Diocese, Zurich. Ontario, 1849-1980*, [Zurich: 1980]; Father P.J. Hayes, "St. Boniface Church, Zurich," *Newsletter of the Diocese of London*, no. 44 (Advent/Christmas: 1990), 16.

8. Ingersoll Deanery

Aylmer: Our Lady of Sorrows

Although Father Joseph Bayard, of St. Thomas, is said to have celebrated the first Sunday Mass in Aylmer on 18 January 1901, the town is listed as one of the stations of Holy Angels by 1866. By 1904, a Mass was held in Aylmer about once every two months, sometimes on Sundays. The curate of St. Thomas, Father John Hogan (1909-11), set up a more permanent place of worship by renting and equipping a hall in the second storey of a building that later became the Foodland Grocery Store. The first Mass in St. John's church was celebrated on 7 July 1911. A frame residence was purchased on St. George Street in August 1912. A part of the building was fitted as a temporary chapel dedicated to St. John. Mass was celebrated every third Sunday. While curate at Holy Angels in St. Thomas, Father William T. Corcoran would take the Wabash train for Aylmer early Saturday afternoon and stay at the Brown House, the most modern hotel of the day. He would visit all the parishioners to remind them of the time of Mass the next day. By 1933, the congregation consisted of about seventeen persons.

In the autumn of 1937, the church was relocated above Miller's Hardware Store and the old residence on St. George Street was sold. Early in 1939, Monsignor Stanley inaugurated the new policy of "Pay and pray." He said, "These people in Aylmer must be taught that if ever they intend to have a parish church, they will not only have to pray, but also make great financial sacrifices for their faith." That summer, the Catholic population was greatly augmented when fourteen Belgian and Hungarian families from Delhi, Tillsonburg and Langton settled south of Aylmer in the new tobacco belt.

On 12 July 1939, Bishop Kidd appointed Father Simon E. White as pastor of the new parish of Our Lady of Sorrows (1939-58). In the interim, Mass was still celebrated above the hardware store. On 4 September 1939, a lot was purchased from a Mrs. McConnell, and the house on the lot became the rectory. The first sod for the church was turned, on 14 November 1939, and Bishop Kidd laid the cornerstone on 10 December 1939. The first Mass in

Our Lady of Sorrows

the new basement church, another of "Kidd's caves," was celebrated on 14 January 1940. The official opening was held on 21 July 1940.

Forty-three families had attended the first Mass in January 1940, and ten years later the number of families in the parish had swelled to 350. In January 1951, Father White announced a campaign to build a church on the foundations of the basement church. Work began about 1 May 1951, with J. Fred Green of St. Thomas as the architect, Don Rawlings the contractor and Howard Sykes the foreman. Built in the New England Colonial style, the structure measured 130 feet by 40 feet (39.6 m by 12.2 m) and had a seating capacity of 450. Its 38-foot (11.6 m) steeple was surmounted by a six-foot (1.8 m) "Irish" cross. The 1,600-pound (725.7 kg) bell, donated by four Hungarian families of the parish, was purchased from the Stoermer Bell and Foundry Company of Kitchener. Bishop Cody blessed the church, which cost $65,000, on 8 December 1951. Murray McCance, a liturgical consultant, oversaw some $35,000 in renovations to the church interior in 1977. Wytze Hiemstra, a local woodworking artist, constructed three Byzantine-style screens made of oak: one for the Tabernacle, one for the lectern and one for the chair of the presider. The Greek inscription in gold leaf frieze that translates as "Glory to God in the highest and peace to men who seek His favour," on the front of the main altar, was suggested by Father Charles T. McManus, the pastor (1972-81). The brass chandelier was made in the Netherlands, and the Crucifixion scene behind the altar was carved near Milan, Italy.

Our Lady of Sorrows parish again became part of the London deanery in June 2006.

Sources: DLA, Parish Files of Holy Angels parish in St. Thomas; *Our Lady of Sorrows Parish, Golden Jubilee Year Book, 1901-1951* [Aylmer: 1951]; "Greek Doric Architecture Effectively Applied Building New Aylmer Catholic Church," *St. Thomas Times-Journal*, 6 December 1951, 13; "Interior decoration of Catholic church cost $35,000 in 1977," *St. Thomas Times-Journal*, 31 January 1978, 8A. Additional information supplied by Father Gilbert Simard.

Beachville: St. Augustine

Before Ingersoll and Woodstock became sizeable communities Beachville was the most populous settlement along the south branch of the Thames River in Oxford County. The first Mass

St. Augustine

in Oxford County was probably celebrated, in the spring of 1835, by Father Daniel Downie of St. Thomas (1833-36). There were eight in attendance on that occasion: James Henderson, his wife, their two young children, John and Andrew, Mary Kenny (James' sister in law), James O'Neil and John and Nicholas Dunn. The Mass was celebrated in O'Neil's blacksmith shop, with a dry goods box serving as an altar and covered with linen lovingly donated probably by the Henderson household. (In 1967, the site of the blacksmith shop, on the north side of Main Street, three lots east of the Town Hall, was occupied by William Bannister.)

Meanwhile, in November 1835, Father Joseph L. Wiriath of St. Agatha (1834-37) walked to Beachville from Stratford to conduct services. The previous year, he met the Dunns and John Shehan in Ingersoll and had promised to return the following year if a suitable place for celebrating Mass were provided. In 1837, Father Wiriath listed but one family, presumably the Hendersons, consisting of five people, in the Beachville mission.

Father Joseph Maria Burke, OFM of London

(1836-38), was at the Beachville station in 1837, and on 16 July 1837, he obtained a half-acre (0.2 ha) of land from R. Martin for a church and burial ground on what became the south side of Church Street. On 20 September 1837, Father Burke celebrated the first Mass in the new church, dedicated to St. Augustine. All this was in the same village where, just two and a half years earlier, Father Downie "could not procure a bed... because he was a popish Priest."

By 1856, Father Robert Keleher, Sr., of Ingersoll (1854-57) was celebrating Mass at 8:00 a.m., every other Sunday at St. Augustine's, situated about midway between what were later Water and Zorra streets. The average attendance was sixty-eight. Yet, in 1857, he lists the number of families in the Beachville mission as only four. This is in keeping with his predecessor's, Father Augustine Carayon's, reference, in 1853, to the Beachville congregation as being small and static.

The chapel was still in use in 1876, but later burned. Its site was occupied by the home of J. Smith in 1967.

Sources: *Beachville the Birth Place of Oxford* [1967]; "Chapter III — Religious Organizations," Ontario Genealogical Society, Oxford County Branch, *The Tracer* (February 2006): 8. Additional information supplied by Daniel V. Walker.

Courtland: St. Ladislaus

Hungarians migrated to the three-county tobacco belt of Norfolk, Oxford and Elgin in three waves: after the First Word War, the Second World War and the 1956 Hungarian Revolution. In June 1938, Stephen W. Toth, a Hungarian, was ordained a deacon by Bishop Kidd and immediately appointed to St. Mary's in Tillsonburg to visit all the Catholic Hungarians in the entire district. He was also given faculties to preach in Hungarian. Ordained the following year, Father Toth returned to St. Mary's. He was instructed to visit the Hungarians in the surrounding parishes and to celebrate Mass and preach in Hungarian. In June 1940, he was appointed assistant at Delhi and continued to work principally among the Hungarians until his appointment as administrator at Port Burwell.

Father Stephen Bekesi, a Hungarian Jesuit priest, came to the tobacco district in 1948, visiting and organizing his fellow Catholic countrymen.

Soon after, he was joined by Sister Mary Schwartz of the Sisters of Social Service in Hamilton. Five hundred Catholic Hungarian families were found to be living in the district, and Sister Mary claimed to have the addresses of 860 individuals. Father Bekesi was succeeded by Father László Cser, SJ, who conducted two very successful missions in November and December 1949 in Langton and Tillsonburg, respectively.

St. Ladislaus

Sister Mary and the priests were successful in convincing Bishop Kidd that a national parish for Hungarians was imperative. On 1 January 1950, just before the 11:00 a.m. Mass in Delhi, and after having already celebrated Mass for the Hungarians in Langton and in Tillsonburg, Father Cser was informed that a Hungarian national parish would be established in the area immediately. A 147-acre (59.5 ha) farm was purchased near Courtland and twenty-five acres (10.1 ha) were retained by the diocese. In February 1950, it was decided to name the parish St. Ladislaus, after the king of Hungary who reigned from 1077 to 1093. On 27 June 1950, the feast of St. Ladislaus, the first Mass was celebrated under a tent on the site of the proposed church. Approximately 4,000 Hungarians, some from as far away as Detroit, were in attendance. Sunday Masses continued to be celebrated under the tent during the summer.

The $135,000 church was built by Cochran Construction Co. of Hamilton, and was blessed by Bishop Cody, on 29 June 1952. In 1956, a section of the church property was opened as a cemetery. A shrine to Our Lady of Fatima was erected in front of it in 1958. Later, a new 16-room rectory was built beside the church. Stained-glass windows were installed in the church in 1961. In 1962, George Bakos, a leading parishioner, obtained salesman-rights for ten fertilizer companies. The commission from sales were turned over to the parish, and within three years, $50,000 had been accrued and applied against the parish debt. On 5 April 1966,

St. Ladislaus was established as a territorial parish, encompassing portions of the parishes of Tillsonburg, Langton, LaSalette and Delhi.

The Sisters of Service, who had ministered to the Hungarians in the district since the time of Sister Mary, left in the summer of 1968. Meanwhile, George Bakos donated fifty-seven acres (23.1 ha) of land, adjoining the church property, for what became Sacred Heart Villa. Owned and operated by the Sisters of the Sacred Heart from Hungary, it was opened and blessed on 15 May 1969. The sisters left in 2003, however, having sold the villa, now known as Caressant Care, to a private company.

The Jesuits left St. Ladislaus in 1998, and Father Steven Bodnár, pastor of St. George's Byzantine Rite church in Courtland, became administrator until the parish was clustered with Sacred Heart in Langton, and Father Michael T. Ryan, pastor of Sacred Heart (1992-2000), became pastor of St. Ladislaus.

The parish was canonically suppressed effective 30 June 2007 and established as St. Ladislaus Hungarian Catholic Community, with Father Maurice O. Charbonneau as priest-chaplain.

Sources: Parish Files; J.H. O'Neil, *Diary of a Priest* [1970]; *20th Anniversary of St. Ladislaus' Church, Courtland, Ont. and Millennium of Hungarian Christianity 1972* [Courtland: 1972].

Delhi: St. Casimir

People were emigrating from Lithuania and settling in Canada by the late nineteenth century. Most settled in large cities or mining communities. The Great Depression, however, forced many to turn to agriculture in the tobacco counties of Norfolk, Oxford and Elgin. Most began as labourers on the tobacco farms. Later, they became sharecroppers, and in time many were able to purchase their own farms.

The conclusion of the Second World War saw a mass migration of Lithuanians and other Eastern Europeans to Canada to escape the oppression of the Soviet Union and life in its Eastern Bloc countries. Several hundred Lithuanian immigrants came to work on the tobacco farms and, like the generation before them, eventually were able to purchase farms.

At first, pastoral care in their own language was not available. But by the early 1950s, they were ministered to by Fathers Vincent Rudzinskas and Father Francis Jokubaitis. These Lithuanian priests were succeeded by Father Kazimir Rickus-Rickevecius for some six years.

By the late 1950s, the Lithuanian community was large enough to have its own religious, social and political centre. A delegation approached Bishop Cody about the possibility of establishing a Lithuanian national parish. As in the case of other ethnic groups within the diocese, the Bishop agreed, and on 9 December 1959, Father Jonas J. Gutauskas (1959-76) was appointed pastor of "St. Casimir's National Parish for Lithuanians, Delhi." The parish derived its name from the patron saint of Lithuania, whose remains lie in the cathedral of Vilnius, the capital city. There were nearly 200 families (and more than 500 individuals) in the parish. As the boundaries of this national parish encompassed an area within an approximate radius of 25 miles (40 km), with Delhi as its centre, that town was selected as the site for the parish church.

The former St. John Brebeuf and Companions church and hall on Talbot Road was purchased for $13,000. By early 1960, $2,200 had been spent to buy twenty-four pews and $400 for 100 chairs. The church itself sat about 150 people. Before the end of June 1960, another $1,200 was spent on church repairs, $500 on parish hall repairs and some $1,600 on an organ and liturgical furnishings. Moreover, $4,000 from the parish account, plus $2,000 as a donation to the parish from the Catholic Church Extension Society, was paid directly against the loan that had been obtained from the chancery office. During the last half of the year, another $3,151 was paid against the debt owed to the diocese. In April 1962, Father Gutauskas requested permission to purchase the old St. John's rectory. Although its market value was between $5,500 and $6,000, the chancellor, Monsignor J. Austin Roney, insisted that

St. Casimir

St. John's parish be paid $9,550. Father Gutauskas was able to move into his new quarters on 17 April 1963. In January 1964, permission was granted to spend $2,000 to redecorate the church, provide a main altar and two side altars and a new entrance door. In 1966, a new furnace, costing $1,500, was installed. At the time, about ninety-six percent or 500 Lithuanians of the tobacco district counties were parishioners of St. Casimir's. During the summer of 1966, Father Gutauskas planned to erect an 18-foot (5.5 m) oak cross beside the church. The cross, dedicated to those who died for God and country, was fashioned according to traditional Lithuanian craftsmanship.

Owing to his age, Father Gutauskas retired in 1976, and Father Jonas Staškevićius (1976-79) was appointed administrator on 10 September 1976, and Father Laurynas Kemėšis (1979-97) was appointed administrator on 27 February 1979. By the mid-1990s, his health was declining and there were also fewer parishioners. Bishop Sherlock considered closing the parish. Monsignor Staškevićius, however, then pastor of Lithuanian Martyrs parish in Mississauga, offered to administer St. Casimir's on a temporary basis and to provide Sunday vigil and funeral Masses. Monsignor Staškevićius was still ministering to some forty families in St. Casimir parish in 2007.

Sources: DLA, Parish Files; "Population Up 10-Fold Since 1935," *Catholic Register*, 23 April 23 1966. Additional information supplied by Tony Murphy.

Delhi: St. John Brebeuf and Companions

A station of LaSalette by the end of the nineteenth century, Delhi became a mission in 1932 with the closing of the Vienna mission. Father John F. Mahoney (1919-49) directed the building of a church on Talbot Road, on land purchased from Charles Hickling. This mission was served by Father Mahoney and his assistant, Father Henry Van Vyncht, until Delhi was elevated to parish status in

1935.

In March 1935, Father John Uyen was appointed pastor of St. John Brebeuf and Companions (1935-58). During the summer of 1938, a new rectory

St. John Brebeuf and Companions

was built adjacent to the church, also on property purchased from Charles Hickling. At the same time, the house next to the rectory was bought from the Burgess family. This house was subsequently sold and moved to Main Street, and on the now-empty site a four-room school was built — Delhi's first Catholic school. Next, the house and property abutting the school were purchased by the parish to provide a convent for the Sisters of St. Joseph.

With the great influx of Catholic farmers after the Second World War into "the heart of Canada's tobacco belt," the church was bursting at the seams and preliminary plans were initiated to build a new structure. The separate school was also overcrowded. Although there was no immediate construction of either a new church or school, it became increasingly obvious with each succeeding year that both were needed.

At last, in the summer of 1956, five acres (2 ha) of land was purchased in the W.E. Adams subdivision and plans were finalized for a new church. The first sod was turned on 30 September 1956 by Monsignor Augustine Fuerth, dean of Ingersoll. In planning the new church, the designers kept in mind the Canadian Martyrs and the colourful ethnic background of the parish, which then comprised twenty-four different nationalities. The new church, an example of modern simplicity, with traces of the grandeur of the traditional Gothic

design, was built by John Gilvesy Construction Company of Tillsonburg. The cornerstone was blessed by Monsignor J. Austin Roney, chancellor of the diocese, on Easter Sunday 1957, and the completed church was blessed by Bishop Cody on 16 December 1957. On the same occasion, he blessed the new four-room school built adjacent to the church. The name St. Frances Cabrini was selected for the school. This native of Italy, who had immigrated to North America, was a school teacher and in 1950 was named patroness of immigrants by Pope Pius XII. The parish celebrated Father Uyen's twenty-fifth anniversary as a priest in June 1958, a few days before he left for Blessed Sacrament parish in Chatham. In the summer of 1959, while Father John Halter was pastor (1958-71), four rooms were added to the school. Another four were added in the summer of 1963.

During the autumn of 1960, work began on converting the church basement into the parish hall. Construction of a new rectory began in October 1962 and was blessed by Bishop Cody on 19 May 1963. By the spring of 1966, the number of families in the parish had increased tenfold from the original eighty in 1935, and the number of individuals was about 3,000. The parishioners celebrated Father Halter's silver jubilee in the priesthood on April 20, 1966.

On 29 November 1987, during the pastorate of Father Francis X. Paul (1984-93), the CWL celebrated its fiftieth anniversary, having received its charter on 30 November 1937. A statue of St. Isidore, patron of farmers, was placed at the wall over the southeast door when the church was built, and on 17 May 1993, special honour was paid to this saint.

In 2002, St. John Brebeuf and Companions was clustered with its mother parish, Our Lady of LaSalette. Both were canonically suppressed on 30 June 2007 and re-established as Our Lady, Queen of Martyrs parish, Delhi-LaSalette.

Sources: "Population Up 10-Fold Since 1935," *Catholic Register*, 23 April 1966; "St. John Brebeuf Parish, Delhi, honors St. Isidore, patron of farmers," *Newsletter of the Diocese of London*, no. 58 (Fall 1993), 16; Victoria Luki, "What's New from Ingersoll Deanery," *Newsletter of the Diocese of London*, no. 31 (Advent/Christmas 1987), 3. Additional information supplied by Denise Dalton.

East Oxford: Mission Church

By the late 1840s, a strong Irish Catholic settlement had developed in East Oxford Township, in an area south of the present hamlet of Eastwood. It became one of the stations of the Ingersoll mission, by 1848. Labourers, working on the Great Western Railway at Eastwood swelled the numbers of Catholics in the area. In 1854, during the pastorship at Ingersoll of Father Augustine Carayon (1852-54), a church was erected on lot 5, concession 3, on the northeast corner of Pat Kearney's farm. By 1856, East Oxford had a congregation of 180, and the interior of the church had been plastered and furnished with an altar by Father Robert Keleher, Sr. (1854-57). Two years later, this mission, together with the station of Woodstock, was detached from Ingersoll and given to the newly established parish of Norwich. Norwich ceased to be a parish in 1864, and the Catholics of Norwich and those in East Oxford and Woodstock were again a part of Sacred Heart parish and continued so until the establishment of Woodstock as a parish in May 1874.

The mission of East Oxford continued to flourish until the late 1880s, when a mission church was built some six miles (9.6 km) to the northeast in Princeton. After it opened in 1888, the church in East Oxford closed. The building was then sold and became a private residence. It still stands today on the same site and is now the home of the Kenny family.

East Oxford had a Catholic population of 236 in 1861, but it was reported in 1934 that "with the passing of the present generation, and those who are comprised under this term are now over fifty years of age, the East Oxford settlement will have completely disappeared."

Sources: DLA, St. Mary Parish Files, Woodstock; *A History of East Oxford Township* [1967]; *History of Princeton 1795-1967* [1967]; J.H. O'Neil, *Diary of a Priest* [1970].

Ingersoll: Sacred Heart of Jesus

The first priest to visit Ingersoll was Father Joseph L. Wiriath of Guelph. In 1834 he met three Irishmen: John Shehan and John and Nicholas Dunn. In 1837, Father Wiriath reported that there were ten families at the Ingersoll station, consisting of thirty-four people, and one family of three individuals at the Embro station.

Sacred Heart of Jesus

By 1847, a piece of land was given by a Mr. Carnegie, a non-Catholic, on which was built the first Catholic church in Ingersoll. The 30-foot by 50-foot (9.1 m by 15.2 m) frame structure was completed on John Street in 1848. Two years later, Father Michael Monaghan was named Ingersoll's first pastor (1850-52).

By 1853, during the pastorship of Father Robert Keleher, Sr. (1852-57), the Ingersoll mission included Ingersoll, Beachville, Norwich, Windham, Vienna and Port Burwell. His congregation at Ingersoll numbered 320, in 1856, the same year in which a rectory, 24 feet by 34 feet (7.3 m by 10.4 m), was built on John Street. The first Catholic school in Ingersoll, a frame building, was established in 1858 on Carnegie Street, when Father Michael J. Lynch was pastor (1858-61). He also oversaw the erection of a steeple on the church and an addition to the rectory. Father Gabriel Volkert (1866-68) oversaw the extension of the church by 30 feet (9.1 m). Finding no record of the dedication and blessing of the church, however, Bishop Walsh authorized Father Joseph Bayard (1866-77) to adopt the Most Sacred Heart of Jesus as the church's patronal feast.

The first sod for the present Sacred Heart of Jesus church was turned on 18 March 1878 when Father Bartholomew Boubat (1877-84) was pastor. Bishop Walsh laid the cornerstone, on 19 May 1878, and he dedicated the church on 22 August 1880.

The architect was George F. Durand of London. He designed a church that was Early English Gothic in style and used white pressed bricks in its construction. On 26 September 1886, during Father Joseph P. Molphy's time as pastor (1884-94), Bishop Walsh returned to bless the organ, which was manufactured by S.R. Warran & Son of Toronto for $2,000.

During the long pastorate of Father Augustine Fuerth (1921-61) many renovations were undertaken to the rectory and church, and the church and school grounds were landscaped. The 433-foot-long (132 m) natural stone fence, which included two archways, was built along Thames Street and was referred to as the "great wall of Ingersoll." The four electrically operated bells, imported from the Netherlands and installed in the tower, were the personal gift of Monsignor Fuerth.

Father Joseph E. Brisson (1961-70) supervised a second landscaping of the church property and the construction of a badly needed parking lot. When he felt he had won the confidence of the parishioners, he introduced the system of weekly tithing. He then oversaw renovations to the church interior, the construction of a new rectory, the demolition of the church hall and its replacement with the new Henderson Hall, formally opened in 1969. During the pastorship of Monsignor Vito Grespan (1970-80), the debt on the new parish hall was liquidated, and more renovations to the interior and exterior of the church took place. In 1972, eight stained-glass windows, designed and crafted by Christopher Wallis of London, replaced the older windows in the nave of the church.

By 1979, twenty-eight women from the parish, including five daughters of Michael Shannon and his wife, had become members of religious orders, and by 1982, sixteen men had been ordained priests.

The 100th anniversary of the arrival of the Roman Catholic faith in Oxford County was celebrated in Ingersoll, on 8 October 1933, albeit a year prematurely. The highlight of the 150th anniversary celebrations was a Mass, on 18 June 1988, with Bishop Sherlock as chief celebrant. He had also been the principal celebrant at the Mass, on 9 September 1979, commemorating the centennial of the present church building.

By 1990, the parish consisted of some 825 families.

Sources: Parish Files. "Bishop Walsh at Ingersoll," *Catholic Record*, 2 October 1886, 1; [Carman Mott, ed.], *Ingersoll, Ontario Sacred Heart Church 1880-1980 Retrospect* [1980]; "Chapter III - Religious Organizations," Ontario Genealogical Society, Oxford County Branch, *The Tracer* (February 2006), 8.

Langton: Sacred Heart

Patrick Murphy is credited with being the first to bring the Catholic faith to the area when he settled on the Tenth Concession of Walsingham (later North Walsingham) Township, near Silver Hill, in 1842. A Father Dillon from Scotland is said to have celebrated Mass in the township hall in Langton and in Walsingham Centre, in the late 1840s. Some French-Canadians, who worked in the timber trade and had settled along the shores of Lake Erie, purchased land and started to build a church at Walsingham Centre. Although they succeeded in setting up the framework and rafters, the church was never finished because so many Catholics suddenly moved away with the depletion of the forests and the end of the lumbering. The building was sold after the First World War. Starting around 1875, a priest supposedly came from Simcoe two or three times a year and celebrated Mass, at Silver Hill in the home of John Murphy, brother of Patrick.

By 1926, the Langton area had been detached from Simcoe and was a part of St. Mary's parish in Tillsonburg. During that year, the first Belgian family, that of Constant Vuylsteke, arrived. Over the succeeding years, the Vuylsteke family was joined by other Belgian families, and by Hungarians and people of other nationalities who were engaged in tobacco farming. Father Leon M. Blondell, a Belgian, arrived in the diocese in 1933 and was sent to St. Mary's in Tillsonburg to assist Father Joseph H. O'Neil, particularly in the Langton area.

A five-acre (2 ha) site was purchased for a church in Langton and on 18 November 1935, Father O'Neil turned the first sod. Bishop Kidd celebrated the first Mass in the church basement, on 3 March 1936, and, at the same time, he appointed Father Blondell as the first pastor (1936-41). The small brick church was completed on 16 August 1936. During Father Blondell's pastorship, the Flemish heritage of the people was kept very much alive. The annual "Chicken Supper" was initiated to

Sacred Heart

celebrate the end of the tobacco harvest and to give the parishioners an opportunity to get together for an evening of fun and merriment.

When Father Henry Van Vyncht was pastor (1941-52), the area farmers erected a grotto to Our Lady of Lourdes, in thanksgiving for a providential rain in 1946. The grotto was blessed by Bishop Cody in October 1947. The Sacred Heart CWL was established in 1953, and a new rectory was built in 1955 while Father Cameron F. McMartin was pastor (1952-56).

Under the initiation and guidance of Father R. Jerome Langan (1959-67), plans for a new church were put into action. Warren M. Smale of Simcoe was selected as architect, and the church was completed in March 1964 at a cost of $175,000. The church's blessing was delayed until 15 June 1965, when some 10,000 people came to the village of Langton to celebrate the 750th anniversary of the signing of the Magna Carta. Bishop Carter, who blessed the new Sacred Heart church, paid tribute to Stephen Langton, archbishop of Canterbury, and described the cardinal as the architect and real author of the Magna Carta. The stained-glass window in the vestibule, a gift of Monsignor O'Neil, depicts Langton receiving the charter from King John of England. The stained-glass windows above the sanctuary came from the earlier church building. The old church was used as a parish hall until it was pulled down in the early summer of 1969 to become the site for Sacred Heart school gymnasium.

Under Father James T. Hollerhead (1968-73), the sanctuary was redesigned in 1972 to accommodate the revised liturgy of the Second Vatican Council and a new carpet was laid. The fiftieth anniversary of the parish was commemorated on 11 May 1986, with

a Mass celebrated by Bishop Sherlock. Later that day, the parish celebrated the fortieth anniversary of the ordination of its pastor, Father Albert P. Spencer (1978-92), with a banquet held at the Belgian Hall in Delhi.

Sacred Heart was clustered with St. Ladislaus in Courtland in June 2000, when Father Michael T. Ryan (1992-2000) retired as pastor.

Sources: Parish Files. "Bishop Carter Blesses New Church in Langton," *Catholic Register*, 26 June 1965; J.H. O'Neil, *Diary of a Priest* [1970]; Victoria Luki, "Anniversary Celebrations for Sacred Heart, Langton, and its Pastor, Fr. Spencer," *Newsletter of the Diocese of London*, no. 25 (Summer 1986), 11; *Sacred Heart Parish Langton, Ontario, 50th Anniversary 1936 to 1986* [n.d.]

LaSalette:
Our Lady of LaSalette

About 1876, Father Henry Japes of St. Anthony's in Windham (1873-80) purchased thirty-seven acres (15 ha) at the proposed junction of the Canada Southern and Port Dover and Lake Huron railways in Windham Township, and he began to clear the land. In 1877, he petitioned for a post office at the junction, to be named LaSalette in honour of the Blessed Virgin Mary who appeared in 1846 to Melanie Mathieu and Maximin Girand, in LaSalette-Fallavaux, France. Father Japes' request was granted and he transferred his parish seat to LaSalette.

On 20 May 1879, Bishop Walsh consecrated the new cemetery at LaSalette and laid the cornerstone for the new church to be called Our Lady, Help of Christians. The Gothic-style edifice was dedicated on 4 September 1881, when Father William Dillon was pastor (1880-89), by Monsignor Jean-Marie Bruyère, the vicar general. By 1900, the church was known as Our Lady of LaSalette.

Father Patrick Corcoran (1889-1901) paid off the parish debt in 1896 and made major renovations to both the interior and exterior of the church. The rectory was destroyed by fire, on 13 May 1899, and a new brick residence was built and ready for occupancy in November 1899. Father Peter McCabe (1901-04) and George Longstreet, a Plymouth Brethren adherent, were able to close down the hotels in LaSalette and nearby Hawtrey.

During Father John P. Brennan's pastorate (1910-19) Our Lady of LaSalette church was destroyed by fire during the night of 22-23 April 1913. The present church was built in the Gothic style on the foundations of the former, with C. Dietrich of Detroit the architect and G. Blonde of Chatham the general contractor. The new church was opened and blessed on 23 April 1914 by Bishop Fallon. The statue of Our Lady, Help of Christians, which had been designed

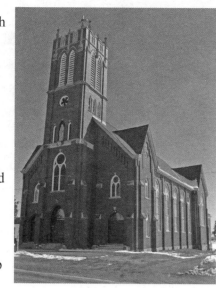

Our Lady of LaSalette

by Father Japes and executed by T.R. Atkinson of Simcoe, had adorned the tower in the old church. It had survived the fire and was placed in the tower of the new church. In 1933, owing to water leakage, the steeple and part of the church tower were removed. This was done by Piggott Brothers of Hamilton, at a cost of $8,100. Father John F. Mahoney (1919-49) spearheaded the establishment of a Knights of Columbus Council at LaSalette in 1919. This fraternity replaced the Catholic Mutual Benefit Association and the Catholic Order of Foresters, both of which had provided fraternity and life insurance for its members but had ceased activity in the parish a few years earlier. The LaSalette Subdivision (Council) of the CWL was established about 1921. Father Mahoney is well remembered for his hour-long sermons from the pulpit in the centre aisle.

Father John J. McCowell (1961-63) organized a brush-clearing bee to clear up the old St. Anthony's cemetery, and Father Frederick M. Doll (1964-66) appointed the parish's first cemetery board on 1 April 1965. Also under Father Doll's direction, in the autumn of 1964, negotiations began which ultimately led to the union of the parish's four separate schools, on 1 January 1966, to form The Combined Roman Catholic Separate School

Norwich, South Windham. The new Our Lady of LaSalette school was blessed and officially opened by Bishop Carter on 15 June 1966. The new rectory, attached to the church, was built by Ken Martin, a parishioner. It was completed in 1968 at a cost of some $60,000, during the pastorate of Father George F. Childs (1966-84). The Holy Cross Brothers, who were teaching at Our Lady of LaSalette school, then moved into the old rectory. After the departure of the Brothers, in 1971, the old rectory was sold, together with a couple of acres behind it, to the regional school board for $20,000. Father John W.P. Graham (1984-2001), like Father Childs, was another long-term pastor.

In February 2002, Our Lady of LaSalette and St. John Brebeuf and Companions in Delhi were clustered. Both were suppressed on 30 June 2007, and re-established as Our Lady, Queen of Martyrs parish, Delhi-LaSalette.

Sources: "LaSalette," *Catholic Record*, 6 June 1879, 5; "Windham Mission," *Catholic Record*, 16 April 1880, 5; "Grand Opening of the New Church at LaSalette," *Catholic Record*, 9 September 1881, 5; "Church Burned," *Catholic Record*, 29 March 1913, 1; *Catholic Record*, 25 April 1914, 8; *Our Lady of LaSalette Parish: History 1836-1979* [LaSalette: 1979]. Additional information supplied by Denise Dalton, Tony Murphy and Daniel V. Walker.

Long Point: St. Peter's by the Lake

It is believed that a mission called St. Peter's was started at Long Point in 1953, by a vacationing priest from Hamilton. While residing at Long Point, he celebrated Sunday Mass in a car garage for the resident and vacationing Catholics during the summer. After his departure, Sacred Heart parish in Langton assumed this responsibility, and by 1960 Port Rowan, Long Point, was listed as a mission of Langton. In 1961, the Anglican Diocese of Huron paid $676 to the Ministry of Lands and Forests for the lot at 144 Erie Boulevard. It is believed that about 1964 the Anglican church that had been built on this lot was used in the summertime for Sunday Mass by the priests from Langton and was described as the mission of Long Point Beach (Highlands). Some time after 1977, the mission was discontinued.

In 1983, during the pastorship of Father Albert P. Spencer (1978-92), the Anglican church on Long Point came up for sale, and summer residents at Long Point requested that the London diocese purchase it. The people raised the necessary funds, and the church was purchased from the Anglican diocese of Huron for $23,000. It was named St. Peter's by the Lake.

When Father Michael T. Ryan was pastor (1992-2000), the Saturday Vigil Mass was celebrated weekly from the Canada Day weekend until mid-September and the Sunday Mass from Victoria Day weekend until Thanksgiving weekend. Numbers at both Masses totalled 250 to 300 during Father John P. Kuilboer's pastorate (2000-03).

Plans were underway in 2003 to mark the fiftieth anniversary of the celebration of Mass at Long Point. But the anniversary celebration never took place. Father Kuilboer was offering a total of four Sunday Masses in Walsh and Long Point from May through October, while, at the same time, the diocese had a shortage of priests. In a move to prevent priest fatigue and stress, the deanery cluster committee recommended that St. Peter's be closed. The pastor was duly instructed by Bishop Fabbro that, effective 24 May 2002, St. Peter's would cease as a mission. This announcement was made after the second Mass of the summer season and many of the residents and cottagers at Long Point were very displeased.

After his arrival in June 2003, Father Richard D. Charrette, under pressure from members of the former congregation at St. Peter's, investigated whether the closure was reversible. He was informed that the decision was indeed final.

On 22 June 2004, the church was sold, for $101,000 to Dana and Dayle Reibling of Bright.

Sources: DLA, Sacred Heart, Langton, Parish Files; *Sacred Heart Parish Langton, Ontario, 50th Anniversary 1936 to 1986* [1986]; Monte Sonnenberg, "Closure stuns church-goers," *Simcoe Reformer*, 18 September 2002, 1; Ibid., "Bitterness remains over closure of church," *Simcoe Reformer*, 24 March 2005, 3. Additional information supplied through Sacred Heart, Langton, Parish Files and Frank Brock.

St. Peter

Norwich: St. Peter

Norwich station had fourteen families and forty-five persons in 1837, and accounted for more than half of the Catholic population of Oxford County at that time. One of the homes in which Mass had been celebrated during these early years was that of Thomas Carlin, located one mile (1.6 km) north of the town of Norwich. Also, about 1841, a log church was built on the south side of lot 25, concession 5 in North Norwich Township. This was the property of Peter McNally, who had come from Ireland and settled in the township in 1820. This church was apparently used for about ten years.

In 1853, Norwich was listed as having no church, but land had been purchased for one, on 18 May 1853, from Michael Stroud, consisting of lot 25, on the east side of Washington Street in the town of Norwich. But nothing further appears to have been done and in 1865, the land was sold to John Williams. Meanwhile, in 1854, Peter McNally deeded a part of his land to the diocese of Toronto for a church. Bishop Charbonnel directed McNally to supervise the building of what became a hand-hewed frame church. Norwich continued to be a mission of Ingersoll until 1863.

In that year, Norwich was elevated to parish status with the missions of Woodstock and East Oxford. Its first, and only pastor, was Father Denis O'Donovan (1863-64). A rectory was built across the road and a little to the west of the church. Unfortunately, the faithful of Norwich were unable or unwilling to support a pastor, and Father O'Donovan returned to Ingersoll as an assistant to Father Lewis Griffa (1861-64). Thus ended Norwich's brief existence as a parish. The rectory was sold to the Segner family, and the house was moved to concession 7, near Otterville. It was still used as a residence in 1967.

When Woodstock was elevated to parish status in 1874, the Norwich mission was transferred from Ingersoll to Woodstock. In 1894, during the pastorship of Father Michael J. Brady (1883-97), a new brick church was erected in Norwich. The cornerstone was blessed by Father Brady, on 15 August 1894, and the church was formally opened in October. The architect was Fred Henry of London. A new heating system was installed in the church basement during the pastorate of Father John F. Stanley (1906-24).

From 1908 until he was appointed pastor of Tillsonburg in October 1910, Father Edward F. Goetz, Father Stanley's assistant, had charge of the Norwich mission. When Father Goetz went to Tillsonburg, the mission of Norwich went with him. In 1912, as pastor of Tillsonburg, Father Goetz (1910-18) oversaw the decoration of the interior of the church at Norwich. Between Easter Monday and August of 1926, both Tillsonburg and Norwich were served by priests from St. Peter's Seminary and St. Peter's cathedral in London.

Father Joseph H. O'Neil became pastor of Tillsonburg in August 1926. From 1926 to 1968, he accomplished many things. Mass was celebrated every Sunday and Holy Day in Norwich, the census was taken, missions and Forty Hours were held regularly, and the cemetery grounds were levelled and gravestones straightened. The parish census of 1926 revealed fewer than twenty-five families and about five single persons in the mission. Father Joseph L. O'Rourke, Father O'Neil's assistant (1938-45), had the entire interior and exterior of the church at Norwich decorated and saw to the upgrading of the cemetery. The fiftieth anniversary of the church was celebrated with a Solemn High Mass. Father Goetz, the first pastor of Tillsonburg and its mission of Norwich, was the celebrant. It was probably in the 1960s that the church was stuccoed. It was closed as a mission, about 1970, and sold to the Christian Reformed Church.

Sources: Theobald Spetz, *Diamond Jubilee History of the Diocese of Hamilton* (1916), 4; *Catholic Record*, 25 August 1894, 1; J.H. O'Neil, *Diary of a Priest*, [1970]; Stella Mott, ed., *North Norwich and Norwich 1810-1960*, [1960]; *Times* (St. Thomas), 17 August 1894.

Port Bruce: St. Birgitta

Mass was first celebrated in Port Bruce on 8 October 1921, the feast of St. Birgitta, in the McGuigan home. The celebrant was Monsignor W. Thomas West, pastor of Holy Angels in St. Thomas. In addition to Abraham McGuigan and his wife, the other persons present were Eva and Orlin B. Franklin and Walter Franklin Shingler and his wife.

By 1922, Mass at this station within Holy Angels parish was celebrated monthly. Two years later, this station comprised four families, consisting of ten persons. In 1925, a church was built on the northeast corner of Rolph and Walnut streets, the gift of C.A. Smith of Aylmer. It was officially opened by Monsignor Denis O'Connor, the vicar general, and dedicated to the fourteenth-century Saint Birgitta or Bridget of the royal house of Sweden, the most celebrated saint of Sweden and the northern kingdoms. Apparently the church did not function for long.

Father Joseph H. O'Neil, pastor of St. Mary's in Tillsonburg, had been an assistant to Monsignor John F. Stanley at St. Mary's in Woodstock. About 1937, while visiting Monsignor Stanley, by now pastor of Holy Angels in St. Thomas, Father O'Neil mentioned that he was starting a mission in Port Burwell. Monsignor Stanley offered him the small church at Port Bruce, which was no longer in use. Father O'Neil did not act on the offer, however, because he had no property in Port Burwell where he could relocate the church. In the spring of 1938, however, the parish of Tillsonburg had purchased sufficient land in Port Burwell for the church. In the winter of 1941, Father O'Neil, while visiting Father Simon E. White, pastor of Our Lady of Sorrows in Aylmer, mentioned that the unused church in Port Bruce had been given to him some four years earlier. Half-serious and half in jest, Father White said: "You can have it since I don't want to have a mission in Pt. Bruce."

The following spring, without saying a word to Father White, in case he should have changed his mind, Father O'Neil engaged a mover to convey the Port Bruce church to Port Burwell, at the agreed price of $75. Father O'Neil was at the site to help the mover and his men lift the church onto moving wheels. He then informed the mover that, as the bridges to the east were too narrow, he would have to haul the building west first and then by way of

Tillsonburg. No mention was made of compensation. No sooner had Father O'Neil returned home, having assisted the mover and his men in getting the church on the wheels, when the telephone rang. It was Father White.

"What do you mean by stealing my church?" he growled.

"I didn't steal your church. I told you that Monsignor Stanley gave it to me some years ago and you told me last winter that I could have it," explained Father O'Neil.

"Well, I was only fooling. This afternoon after a siesta, I went south and lo and behold, I saw my church going down the road on wheels. I immediately called the provincials and we overtook it. The truck driver told me that you had instructed him to take it to Pt. Burwell," blurted out Father White.

"Sure I did," replied Father O'Neil.

In time both pastors could laugh about it. The priests of the diocese, however, would often needle Father White with, "While Simon slept, Joe stole his church." Even Bishop Kidd himself could not resist getting in a jab. When Father O'Neil, together with Fathers Joseph L. O'Rourke and J. Arthur Finn, met about June 1945 to propose joining Port Dover mission with the parish in Walsh, Bishop Kidd started pointing out other places west of Port Dover where Catholic churches were located. After Port Burwell was mentioned by Father O'Neil, Bishop Kidd said, "Yes, and then?" Father O'Neil replied, "Port Stanley."

"No, no," said the bishop, "that little place from where you stole the Cathedral."

Sources: Hugh Joffre Sims, *Sims' History of Elgin County*, vol. 2 (St. Thomas: 1986); J.H. O'Neil, *Diary of a Priest* [1970]; Thomas West, *History of the St. Thomas Parish 1803-1921* (1921).

Port Burwell: St. Joseph

Dean Thadeus Kirwan of London (1848-56) visited Port Burwell about 1851. In 1853, Father Augustine Carayon of Ingersoll (1852-54) noted that there were few resident Catholics at Port Burwell but their number was augmented by the presence of French-Canadian lumbermen. Later, the Catholics of the area would be part of the mission of Vienna.

St. Joseph

After making a thorough census of the Catholics in and around Port Burwell, in the spring of 1937, Father Joseph H. O'Neil of Tillsonburg enumerated thirty-five families, some of whom had to drive twenty-five miles (40.2 km) or more to attend Mass at St. Mary's. They agreed to support a church in Port Burwell if Father O'Neil opened a mission there. The first Mass was celebrated, on 20 June 1937, in the large concrete block home of Michael Thomas. Thereafter, Mass was celebrated in Port Burwell on the first and third Sundays of the month. Mass was celebrated, beginning on 8 November 1937, in the Sampson house on Pitt Street. This property was purchased, on 9 May 1938, for $2,200. Then, with the help of an assistant, and other priests, Father O'Neil was able to have Mass celebrated in Port Burwell every Sunday. In 1941, Father O'Neil "stole" St. Birgitta's church in Port Bruce and had it moved to the Sampson property. The first Mass in the relocated church was celebrated on 3 August 1941, and Father O'Neil named the church in honour of St. Joseph.

In the spring of 1945, Father O'Neil found that there were 100 Catholic families south of Straffordville within seven miles (11.3 km) of Port Burwell. On his recommendation, Port Burwell ceased to be a mission of Tillsonburg and became a parish on 8 June 1947. Bishop Kidd appointed Father O'Neil's assistant, Father Stephen W. Toth, as its first pastor (1947-51). He celebrated Mass in the Sampson house. Father William G. Smith (1951-56) oversaw the transformation of this building into a more suitable place of worship, seating 125 people, and remaking the second storey into a residence. Shortly after Father J.T. Hollerhead became pastor (1959-68), the debt incurred for the conversion of this house into a church was paid off.

On administering the sacrament of confirmation at St. Joseph's, in April 1964, Bishop Carter immediately saw that a new church was badly needed. That spring the diocese had set up the Diocesan Loan Fund, whereby parishes were to put their excess money into the fund for the benefit of parishes in need of a loan. Port Burwell was possibly the first parish to benefit by this new program. Warren M. Smale of Simcoe, who had already designed St. Bernard's in Waterford, was hired as the architect, and Hendricks Construction Company of Dorchester was the general contractor. The first sod for the new church was turned by Monsignor O'Neil on 1 August 1965; the cornerstone was laid by Monsignor Mahoney on 31 October 1965; the first Mass was celebrated on 30 March 1966; and the church was blessed by Bishop Carter in November 1966.

On 6 November 1987, during the pastorate of Father John G. Mooney (1981-2003), an anniversary banquet and dance were held at the Straffordville Community Centre to celebrate the fiftieth anniversary of St. Joseph's and the fortieth anniversary of Father Mooney's ordination. In the early 1990s, a Mass in Spanish for migrant workers was provided weekly, usually by Father Francis E. Brown of London. The peak period was from mid-August to mid-October when more than 100 workers attended Mass. Following the death of Father Mooney, on 29 April 2003, the parish was suppressed, effective 23 June 2003, and its boundaries were once again absorbed into the mother parish of St. Mary's in Tillsonburg. The sacramental records were likewise deposited there.

Sources: John Mooney and G. Byer, "Catholic parishes welcome migrant workers," *Newsletter of the Diocese of London*, no. 55 (Lent 1987), 7; Victoria Luki, "What's New from Ingersoll Deanery," *Newsletter of the Diocese of London*, no. 31 (Advent/Christmas 1987), 3.

Port Dover: St. Cecilia

The precise location of encampments by seventeenth-century French missionaries, within St. Cecilia's parish boundaries, have been determined and marked. The 1669-70 wintering site of Father François Dollier de Casson and Deacon René de Bréhant de Galinée, two Sulpicians, is marked by a cairn at the junction of the Lynn River and Black Creek near Port Dover. The cairn was unveiled on 16 September 1924. Their

encampment of 26 March 1670 at Turkey Point, was commemorated by a plaque erected by the Historic Sites and Monuments Board of Canada in 1928.

Father Joseph L. Wiriath of Guelph travelled on

St. Cecilia

foot from Oxford County to Port Dover in December 1835. Two years later, he reported that there were four families consisting of fifteen individuals in the Port Dover area. In March 1858, Father Louis Schnyder, Simcoe's first pastor (1857-58), reported that there were thirteen Catholic families and a number of servant girls in Port Dover, plus three very poor German-Catholic families in Port Ryerse.

During the nineteenth century, many homes in Port Dover were used for church services, but the home of Bernard McNally, dubbed "Pope" McNally, at the present 124 St. Andrew Street, was made available for the visiting priest for "over thirty years." It was probably in late August 1842, while staying overnight with the McNallys, that the mane and tail of the horse of Father Michael R. Mills of Brantford were cut off. Tradition has it that the two or three Orangemen who perpetrated the dastardly deed had a curse put on them, and soon met with misfortune.

During the latter part of the 1870s and the early 1880s, the saintly Rose Lummis resided off and on in Simcoe. In the absence of a full-time priest in the area — Simcoe and Port Dover still being within LaSalette parish — she instructed the youth for miles around in their faith. As she prayed the rosary with them, one decade was offered that some day Port Dover would have a church. Among the children who walked from Doan's Hollow, on the Second

Concession of Woodhouse Township, to attend these religion classes, was Dan Forster. In later years, he credited his vocation to the priesthood to Madame Lummis, and as pastor at Simcoe (1897-1900), he fulfilled another of her hopes and aspirations by building a church in Port Dover. The site on Drayton Street was purchased in August 1890, during the pastorate of Father Hubert G. Trayer of Simcoe (1887-92). Bishop O'Connor laid the cornerstone, on 15 July 1898, and returned to open St. Cecilia's on 8 January 1899. The church cost between $2,000 and $3,000 and seated about 200 persons. R.F. Powell of Stratford was the architect, and George Hussey and Charles Walsh of Port Dover were the general contractors.

Since 1887, Port Dover was part of St. Mary's parish in Simcoe. Effective 1 July 1945, Father Joseph L. O'Rourke (1945-51) was appointed the first "administrator of Walsh & Port Dover," and soon after Port Dover's first pastor. Later that month, he bought from Dr. Berry of Caledonia a completely furnished cottage located directly behind the church for his residence.

Father Elwyn A. Morris was pastor (1951-63) when Port Dover's first Catholic school was situated in St. Cecilia's choir loft. The new St. Cecilia school opened in Lynn Park, along Highway 6, on land previously purchased by Father O'Rourke. In October 1954, the parish purchased three acres (1.2 ha) of land adjoining the school property for a new church, but it was not built until 1976. In July 1976, during the pastorate of Father John W.P. Graham (1971-81), the new St. Cecilia's, which cost $350,000, was dedicated by Bishop Carter. The holy water fonts and windows from the former church were set in the new one. A new roof and lighting system were installed in 1994.

In 1995, Bishop Sherlock dedicated a memorial to the unborn children of the world on the church grounds. St. Cecilia's was slated to be clustered with its mother parish, St. Mary's in Simcoe, by 30 June 2008.

Sources: DLA, Parish Files; St. Cecilia Parish Files; Ralph Hubert Dignan and Joseph P. Finn, "A History of the Diocese of London," edited by Guy Alden (unpublished manuscript, 2002); *Catholic Record*, 3 March 1894, 8; 21 January 1899, 8; Elsie M. Murphy, *The Parish Experience: St. Cecilia, Port Dover — St. Michael, Walsh* [n.d.]; Margaret

F. Margetan, *History of Wintering Site 1669-1670 Dollier Galinée* [Port Dover: 1994]. Additional information supplied by Denise Dalton.

Princeton: Most Sacred Heart of Jesus

Through the generosity of Victoria Larmour, the wife of the local station agent in Princeton, and her sister, Elizabeth Markham, a white-brick Catholic church seating 400 was built and completely furnished in the village at a cost of about $7,000. Father Joseph P. Molphy, the pastor at Ingersoll, blessed the cornerstone on 9 October 1888, and Bishop Walsh dedicated

Most Sacred Heart of Jesus

the church to the Most Sacred Heart of Jesus on 27 January 1889. Before this church was built, the closest church to Princeton was the mission church of East Oxford, some six miles (9.1 km) to the southwest. Sacred Heart church was built by William Reath of St. Thomas and measured 96 feet by 37 feet (29.3 m by 11.3 m), with a bell weighing 441 pounds (200 kg) in its tower. Sacred Heart continued as a mission of St. Mary's parish in Woodstock until it was closed in 1929. Meanwhile, on 8 October 1891, Bishop O'Connor conducted the first confirmations in this church. Between 1925 and 1929 Mass was celebrated in Princeton once a month.

Although the Catholic population of Princeton had "dwindled to two families" by 1934, just seven years later, in 1941, Bishop Kidd re-opened Sacred Heart as a parish and placed it under the care of the Capuchin Fathers from Blenheim. The first pastor was Father Damas Van Dycke, OFM, Cap. (1941-46), who had his rectory at 19 Railway Street East.

He was succeeded by Father Masseo Bogaert, OFM, Cap. (1947-51), who lived at 47 Main Street North. During Father Masseo's tenure, some $15,000 were spent on embellishments and additions to the church. The interior walls of the church were plastered, a new floor was laid and the basement was dug out by hand. In 1947, the windows were restored by Edwards Brothers Glass Co. of London at a cost of $243. To accommodate the growing number of parishioners with cars, Father Masseo had a parking lot constructed beside the church. As a consequence of the work of Fathers Damas and Masseo, membership exceeded 100 people by the end of the 1940s. Then, in 1950, Bishop Ryan of Hamilton opened a chapel in Burford to the east. As a result, the congregation at Princeton declined by two-thirds because those living on the south side of Princeton were now obligated to attend church in Burford. Father Damas returned in 1951 and was joined by Father V. Aubain, OFM, Cap. (1952-54), the following year. On 24 January 1952, the CWL was formed, and in July 1952 the parish hall was redecorated.

In 1954, the parish was transferred to the Franciscan Fathers. Father Otger Devent, OFM (1954-60), was the first of these priests to serve at Sacred Heart. Father Oderick Schmidt, OFM (1960), was pastor for but a few months and was succeeded by Father Isidoor Risse, OFM (1960-63). In August 1963, the parish was again placed in the hands of diocesan priests. Monsignor Fergus J. Laverty (1963-64) was pastor for a few months, and he was followed by Father Jan A. Achtabowski (1964-70). During Father Achtabowski's time, there were two Sunday Masses celebrated each week.

With Father Achtbowski's departure, in May 1970, Princeton was declared a mission of St. Rita's parish in Woodstock, on 5 June 1970, and was henceforth ministered to by the Holy Ghost Fathers. Under the direction of Father Nicholas McCormack, CSSp, the first parish council was established in 1970. The Dart League began in 1974 as a men's social evening. New stained-glass windows were installed in 1985. The old stained-glass windows, although beyond restoration, were converted into chandeliers by John DeKoning, Sr.

In 1988, the front doors were replaced by new doors of solid oak, and the interior of the church was redecorated. Also in 1988, the 100th anniversary of a church in Princeton was commemorated with the celebration of the Eucharist on 16 October 1988 by Bishop Sherlock and the publication of a booklet on its history.

The mission was suppressed, effective June 2006, and its boundaries were absorbed into the newly formed Holy Trinity parish in Woodstock.

Sources: St. Mary, Woodstock, Parish Files; "Laying the Corner-Stone of Princeton Church," *Catholic Record*, 20 October 1888, 8; "Dedication of Princeton Church," *Catholic Record*, 2 February 1889, 5; *History of Princeton 1795 -1967* [1967]; *100th Anniversary — Sacred Heart Roman Catholic Church Princeton, Ontario 1888-1988* [1988]. Additional information supplied by Ray Galloway, Mary VanVeen and Daniel V. Walker.

Simcoe: St. Mary

As late as 1837 no Catholics were listed as residing in Simcoe, but Father Joseph L. Wiriath of Guelph reported three families in Townsend Township and one in Woodhouse Township. Between 1842 and 1856, the area was periodically served by priests from St. Basil's parish, Brantford, beginning on 27-28 August 1842 with Father Michael R. Mills (1842-43). Windham was established as a parish about November 1856 with Simcoe and area as part of its mission. Then, about September 1857, Simcoe was elevated to parish status with Father Louis Schnyder as its first pastor (1857-58). When he suddenly departed in March 1858, Simcoe became a mission, first of Ingersoll and then of Windham.

Land for Simcoe's first church was purchased on 18 June 1858, and the completed structure was blessed and dedicated to the Nativity of the Blessed Virgin on 4 April 1859 by Father Bartholomew Boubat of Windham (1859). On 5 March 1862, Father James T. Wagner (1860-64) was given approval to reside in Simcoe rather than in Windham. A rectory was eventually built in Simcoe. His successor, Father Gabriel Volkert (1865-66), who took up residence in Windham, established a short-lived separate school in Simcoe in early 1866.

Much of the work that preceded the re-establishment of Simcoe as a parish was done by Rose Lummis. In the latter part of the 1870s and early 1880s, prior to becoming a member of the Religious of the Sacred Heart, she devoted her time and talents to catechizing the youth. Although a decision was made in April 1883 to erect a new church in Simcoe, work on the actual structure did not begin until 1886, when Father William Dillon of LaSalette (1880-89)

St. Mary, Simcoe

initiated the construction of a brick church on the northeast corner of Union and Queen streets in Simcoe, to the west of the old frame church. The cornerstone was blessed by Bishop Walsh, on 30 May 1886, and the church itself was dedicated to Mary, Help of Christians, on 4 October 1886. The following year, St. Mary's was elevated to parish status, and Father Hubert G. Traher was appointed pastor (1887-92).

In 1954, when Father Simon J. McDonald was pastor (1951-75), a new main altar with canopy was erected. With the church "bulging at the seams" at this time, the parish faced the question whether a new church should be built or the old one expanded. In the end, St. Mary's was enlarged into a cruciform shape, with its seating capacity increased from 232 to 532. Warren M. Smale of the architectural firm of D.N. McIntosh was in charge of the design, and Gilvesy Construction of Tillsonburg was the general contractor. Work had begun in mid-October 1958, and the church was dedicated by Bishop Cody on 12 June 1959. In 1962, an addition was made to the rectory that was originally erected in 1911 during Father Charles F. Nagle's first stint in Simcoe (1911-24).

The reredos, designed by Karl Rothammer of Kitchener at a cost of about $3,500, was blessed on 26 May 1963 by Bishop Cody. Preserved in the east transept, and incorporated within the expansion of the late 1950s and the liturgical changes of the 1960s, are two of the three statues ordered from

Paris, France, in the mid-1880s, and donated by Madame Loomis, namely Our Blessed Lady and St. Joseph. The statue of Our Divine Saviour disappeared, however, during the reconstruction and changes of the 1950s and 1960s.

Father John D. Marentette (1975-79) oversaw the opening of the parish centre in November 1978. The 100th anniversary of the parish was celebrated in 1986-87, during the pastorates of Fathers Melvin J. MacIsaac (1979-86) and Francis E. La Prairie (1986-96). Father Brian J. Klooster (1996-2002) oversaw repairs to the foundation, floor, walls, tower and roof, completed in 2002.

In June 1998, St. Mary's was clustered with St. Bernard of Clairvaux, Waterford.

Sources: "From Simcoe," *Catholic Record*, 16 April 1887, 1; Delia Gleeson, *Madame Rose Lummis* (London: 1907); *A History of Simcoe Parish, A.D. 1930* [Simcoe: 1930]; Ron Kowalsky, *The History of St. Mary's* (Simcoe: 1986); Vincent Taylor, "Blessings in return — campaign a financial/spiritual success and will maintain our churches for future generations," *Newsletter of the Diocese of London*, no. 103 (Pentecost 2002), 15. Additional information supplied by Frank Brock.

Tillsonburg: St. Mary

The first Mass was celebrated in Tillsonburg in 1861. By the early 1870s, preparations were made to erect a church in the community, on the south corner of Venison and Rolph streets.

Construction began on 19 August 1874 under the direction of Father Joseph Bayard, of Ingersoll, Tillsonburg then being in Sacred Heart parish. The frame Gothic-style structure was 48 feet by 29 feet (14.6 m by 8.8 m). It seated eighty-five people, cost $1,500 and was dedicated to St. Paul the Apostle by Bishop Walsh on 4 July 1875. Prior to 1877, Tillsonburg was a mission of Ingersoll. In that year it was attached to Windham (later replaced by LaSalette). In 1895, two-and-one-half acres (1 ha) of land were purchased adjoining the public cemetery on Goshen Street, for a Catholic burial ground. It was later consecrated by Bishop O'Connor. In 1899, during the pastorate of Father Patrick Corcoran (1889-1901), the church roof was reshingled, a new foundation constructed and the interior painted, all at a cost of $300. Sometime between 1901 and 1906,

St. Paul's had transformed into St. Mary's church.

Tillsonburg was elevated to parish status in 1910 and given the mission of Norwich. On 19 October 1910, Father Edward F. Goetz was appointed its first pastor (1910-18). A brick rectory was built in 1911, at a cost of $3,882, and blessed by Father W. Thomas West of St. Thomas.

On 4 August 1926, Father Joseph H. O'Neil was appointed pastor (1926-68). Before he came to take up residence, however, a fire broke out in the rectory on the night of 19 August 1926. During the first year, the outlook for the parish was rather bleak. Sometimes the Sunday collection was as low as $2.85. Only seven persons attended the New Year's Day Mass in 1927. Beginning in December 1927, however, with the arrival of several Belgian families, who started to grow tobacco, a new agricultural crop in the district, the congregation began to swell. Two of the newly arrived Capuchin Fathers at St. Mary's in Blenheim spoke Flemish and were invited to visit these Belgian families.

By the late 1920s, even with two Sunday Masses, the congregation had outgrown the small church. The first sod for enlarging the church was turned, on 17 March 1930, by Mrs. Sydney Johnston, a lifelong resident of the area. The architect soon discovered that the old church had developed serious structural defects and an entirely new church would have to be built. The cornerstone was laid by Bishop Kidd on 5 June 1932. The architect was Arthur Holmes of Toronto and the contractor was Roy Pigott Construction Company of Hamilton. Although Roy Pigott's tender was only $24,140, he spared no personal expense to give St. Mary's the very best. As an example, the white plaster mouldings on the arched ceiling of the sanctuary and baptistry were actually made by workmen in the basement of Christ the King cathedral in Hamilton, then under construction, at no expense to the Tillsonburg parishioners. Bishop Kidd opened the new church on 23 October 1932, and the parish debt was paid off a

St. Mary, Tillsonburg

dozen years later. A $9,000-Casavant pipe organ was installed in the church, in January 1952, and on 4 April 1952, St. Mary's Credit Union was formed.

By 1955, four Masses were required each Sunday. Consequently, the church was enlarged. Rawlins Construction of Aylmer was the contractor. On 5 June 1957, Gerald V. Livingston, chairman of the building committee, turned the first sod, and on 16 October 1958, Bishop Cody blessed the expanded structure. He returned on 16 June 1963 to bless the new rectory, designed by the architectural firm of Blackwell, Hagerty and Buist of London. Since then renovations to the church and parish hall have taken place, and the parking lot has been expanded and paved.

Sources: DLA, Our Lady of LaSalette, LaSalette, Parish Files; "Bishop Walsh at Ingersoll," *Catholic Record*, 2 October 1886, 1; J.H. O'Neil, *Diary of a Priest* [1970]. Additional information in Parish Files.

Turkey Point: Chapel

Little is known about this chapel in Turkey Point. From about 1969 until 1974, during the pastorates of Fathers Arnold F. Loebach (1968-1971) and John W.P. Graham (1971-81), Sunday Mass was celebrated in this lakeside community during the summer months.

The chapel was probably a converted cottage or house purchased by St. Cecilia's parish in Port Dover, which in 1977 was "lying idle and useless." The CWL of St. Michael's mission in Walsh believed the property could be used for some worthy community purposes such as a senior citizens home, as it was in a quiet location and close to shopping facilities. Moreover, there was also a need for a community centre in Turkey Point where people could meet and attend Mass. Thus, on 28 November 1977, the president of the CWL wrote a letter to Monsignor Fergus J. Laverty, the chancellor, pointing this out. It is not known what, if any, action, was taken in this regard, as no information is available.

Sources: DLA,. St. Cecilia, Port Dover, Parish Files; *Ontario Catholic Directory* (Toronto), for the years 1969-75.

Vienna: Mission Church

Although a quiet village today, Vienna was once a booming lumber town on Otter Creek that was navigable from Vienna to Lake Erie. The number of resident Catholics was small in the 1850s

Vienna Mission Church

but was augmented by the presence of French-Canadian lumbermen. One source puts the number of Catholic families, in the early 1850s, at twelve, at which time Vienna was part of the Ingersoll parish. A great setback to Vienna occurred in the spring of 1855 when a fire destroyed the business section. It was never completely rebuilt.

On 9 September 1857, the stations of Vienna and Port Burwell were transferred to Windham and its first pastor, Father L. Andrew Schweiger (1856-58). In November 1857, Father Schweiger wrote that he was going to Vienna to prepare a new chapel, even though the town had only two Catholic families in early 1858.

Father Schweiger left for Buffalo, New York, in January 1858 and was succeeded by Father Louis Schnyder, who was given the Windham parish, in addition to that of Simcoe. In February 1858, he reported that he had been in Vienna and Port Burwell for three days and received only $2.80 from the faithful in the area. After Father Schnyder's own sudden departure in March 1858, the parishes of Simcoe and Windham, together with their stations, were again attached to Ingersoll. Between October 1857 and December 1858, Mass was celebrated in Vienna about once every two months. Father Michael J. Lynch of Ingersoll (1858-61) arrived every Tuesday evening and celebrated Mass the next morning. His authoritarian approach and caustic language, however, did not endear him to the faithful of Vienna and Port Burwell, and a letter of complaint was lodged with Bishop Pinsoneault.

It was reported that there were nearly thirty Catholics in Vienna by the end of 1858. With the appointment of Father Bartholomew Boubat as pastor of Windham and Simcoe (1859-60), Vienna became one of his stations about March 1859. Henry Vogt, whom Father Schnyder had described in early 1858 as "a very good catholic and responsible man," donated land for a church in the village. Both Catholics and Protestants worked together, building a beautiful little frame church that was dedicated on 25 August 1861 by Father Lynch. After Mass, the congregation contributed sixty dollars in the collection. At the time, Father James T. Wagner of Simcoe (1860-64) was pastor of this mission. In 1864, Bishop Farrell of Hamilton was in Vienna to confirm twenty-two persons.

Disaster again hit the village in 1867. Fires, deliberately set, burned the village and Vienna never really recovered. Services in the Catholic mission church appear to have ceased about 1883, "there being no Catholics in the village or neighbourhood." In 1901, the church and property were sold to Alexander Stilwell for $100. As late as 1968, the building was still in good condition and owned by the local Masonic Lodge.

In 1911, the pastor of Tillsonburg, Father Edward F. Goetz, found some Catholics in Vienna and celebrated Mass and administered the sacraments in the home of Charles Graves, but the village continued to be a mission of LaSalette. With the establishment of Delhi as a mission in 1932, Vienna ceased to have mission status. A little better than a decade later, in 1937, nearby Port Burwell was established as a mission for the Catholics of the area.

Sources: DLA, Pierre-Adolphe Pinsoneault Papers, Box 1, Letterbooks vol. 3, 7; Our Lady of LaSalette Parish Files; True Witness (Montréal) 6 September 1861, 5. J.H. O'Neil, *Diary of a Priest* [1970].

Walsh: St. Michael the Archangel

In 1943, John Dertinger purchased five acres (2 ha) in Walsh for a church and school. By 1944, Father John Uyen of Delhi (1935-58), the beloved "Depression Priest," was celebrating Mass in a

St. Michael the Archangel

house on this site. It became a temporary chapel under the patronage of St. Michael the Archangel, and Mass was celebrated every Sunday and Holy Day. In 1946, ash pews, costing $92 each, were purchased for the church from the Globe Furniture Company of Waterloo.

Meanwhile, Bishop Kidd elevated Walsh to parish status, in June 1945, and he transferred, to St. Michael's, the territory from the Ninth Concession of Charlotteville Township down to Lake Erie. Father Joseph L. O'Rourke, who since June 1938 was assistant to Father Joseph H. O'Neil of Tillsonburg, was appointed pastor but to reside in Delhi. Father O'Rourke, however, was clearly not pleased with this appointment to a hamlet with an old house for a church. Father O'Neil located Walsh on a map and saw that Port Dover was nearby. If only the Bishop would join that village with Walsh and allow the priest to live in Port Dover, "it would be a decent set-up." The morning after the announcement of the appointment, the two priests undertook an on-site investigation of the situation and found that Port Dover was exactly eleven miles (17.7 km) from Walsh. The next step was to persuade Father J. Arthur Finn, pastor of St. Mary's in Simcoe, to give up the Port Dover mission. Father Finn graciously agreed, and the three priests met with Bishop Kidd, who assented to their proposal. Consequently, Port Dover was detached from Simcoe and ultimately elevated to parish status, while Walsh, the shortest-lived parish in the history of the London diocese, once again assumed mission status and was attached to the new St. Cecilia's parish.

At the urging of Father O'Rourke, Port Dover's first pastor (1945-50), volunteers began work in the summer of 1947 on a permanent church in Walsh. The new St. Michael's was dedicated by Bishop Kidd on 25 October 1947. This church was not only the community's focus of worship, but also its entertainment centre and school. The furniture in the church basement was rearranged by the Frank Handsome family for each new activity. St. Michael's school was opened in the church basement with eighteen pupils. Although the school trustees paid $2,500 for a parcel of church land for a school site in April 1952, classes continued to be taught in the church basement until 1961, when the new St. Michael's school was opened beside the church for kindergarten through grade eight. In 1969, the school consisted of five classrooms. It has been enlarged a good deal since then.

St. Michael's church was completely refurbished in 1994. The pews were refinished and two stained-glass windows were installed behind the altar. While there is a good attendance during the year, numbers increase in the summer months, owing to the proximity of both Turkey Point beach and Turkey Point provincial park. The congregation maintains a high level of involvement in church clubs and organizations, which has helped to build a strong sense of fellowship and community. St. Michael's was slated to be detached from St. Cecilia's, Port Dover, closed as a mission, and become a second (non-parochial) church within the parish of Sacred Heart, Langton, by 30 June 2008.

Sources: DLA, St. Cecilia, Port Dover, Parish Files; St. Cecilia's Parish Files; *Canadian Register*, 23 April 1966; J.H. O'Neil, *Diary of a Priest* [1970]; Elsie M. Murphy, *The Parish Experience: St. Cecilia, Port Dover — St. Michael, Walsh* [n.d.]; Margaret F. Margetan, *History of Wintering Site 1669-1670 Dollier Galinée* [Port Dover: 1994]. Additional information supplied by Denise Dalton.

Waterford: St. Bernard of Clairvaux

About 1939, St. Mary's in Simcoe established a mission in Waterford for some thirty-five families in Sacred Heart Ukrainian Greek Catholic church, located on the corner of St. James and Nichol streets. With the expansion of tobacco farming in the area, however, the number of Roman

St. Bernard of Clairvaux

Catholics increased, and Father Douglas F. Boyer, who had been the curate at St. Mary's in Simcoe since 1950, initiated the process for establishing a parish in Waterford. On 13 May 1951, Father Boyer celebrated Mass in the Sacred Heart parish hall, formerly the Knox Presbyterian church building. In June 1951, he was appointed administrator of the Waterford mission. The hall was purchased from the Ukrainian Catholics on 15 August 1951, and Bishop Cody dedicated the church to St. Bernard of Clairvaux on 16 December 1951.

In June 1952, St. Bernard's was elevated to parish status; on 23 June 1952, Father Boyer was appointed its first pastor (1952-57); and in 1953, a rectory was built behind the church. Owing to a growing congregation and the poor accommodation provided by St. Bernard's, Father Joseph V. McGraw (1957-64) started a financial campaign in the autumn of 1959 for a new church. In September 1958, a five-room school was opened. On 27 November 1963, property for the new church was purchased at a cost of $4,500 on Concession (now Thompson) Road adjacent to the school. Father Percy V. Drouillard (1964-68), Waterford's third pastor, was directed by Bishop Carter to proceed with the construction of a new church. Warren M. Smale of Simcoe was selected as architect and instructed to design a building that would be the first church in the diocese to "carry out the new liturgical spirit of the Church." The contract was awarded to W.G. Ross Building Corporation of Galt at a cost of $146,209.05, and the first sod was turned on 18 February 1965. Construction began on 1 April 1965, and the "First Stone" was cemented into place by Monsignor

Fergus J. Laverty, chancellor of the diocese, on 4 July 1965. Mass was celebrated in the new church on 27 November 1965. About 1,000 persons toured the building at an "Open House," held on 1 December 1965, and about 100 members of the clergy toured the "liturgically correct" church early in January 1966. Bishop Carter officially dedicated and blessed the new St. Bernard's on 23 January 1966. The church seated about 400 persons, and the parish hall accommodated about 250.

During the pastorate of Father Elwin A. Morris (1968-81), the parish debt was eliminated, the school was expanded to nine classrooms and the parish increased to 375 families. Father Michael J. Hughes (1981-89) is remembered for introducing the Saturday evening Mass, a children's Mass and an early Mass on Christmas Eve. In the case of the children's Masses, the young people took an active part and Father Hughes would use props to draw attention to the homily and to add a touch of humour. The parish advisory board was re-activated, and the Men's Service Club was formed. The first parish family album was prepared, and a parish census was carried out in the 1980s. In 1990, when Monsignor Patrick E. Cavanagh was pastor (1989-95), a long-planned renovation and decoration of the church interior was undertaken.

On 25 June 1998, St. Bernard's was clustered with its mother church, St. Mary's in Simcoe, and Father Brian J. Klooster (1998-2002) became pastor of both parishes. In 1999, it was determined that the church needed a new heating system and an elevator to provide access to the parish hall in the basement for the physically challenged and the elderly. This work was completed in 2002.

St. Bernard's was slated to be clustered with the new Our Lady, Queen of Martyrs, Delhi-LaSalette parish, effective 30 June 2008.

Sources: "The 'First Stone' Is Blessed for New Church in Waterford," *Catholic Register*, 17 July 1965; *Saint Bernard of Clairvaux Parish Family Album, Waterford, 1994* (Concord: [1994]); Vincent Taylor, "Blessings in return — campaign a financial/spiritual success and will maintain our churches for future generations," *Newsletter of the Diocese of London*, no. 103 (Pentecost 2002), 15. Additional information supplied by Denise Dalton.

Windham: St. Anthony

The earliest presence of the Church in what became Norfolk County dates to the time of Father François Dollier de Casson and Deacon René de Bréhant de Galinée, French missionaries in the latter part of the seventeenth century. It was more than a century later that Father James W. Campion, another missionary, appeared. He baptized two children of Delamir and Martha Minon in Middleton Township, on 19 July 1830, on his return journey to Dundas or Niagara-on-the-Lake.

German and Irish immigrants started settling in Windham Township in the mid-1830s. In the late spring of 1837, Father Joseph L. Wiriath of St. Agatha reported a total of seventeen Catholic families in Windham and Norwich townships. Late in 1840, Father Michael Mills was appointed to the mission of Dundas, which included Brantford. By 1842, he had moved to Brantford, and in late August he made what appears to have been his first visit to Windham and other parts of Norfolk County. He returned in January 1843 before being succeeded at Brantford by Fathers Stephen Fergus (1843-44) and William Mackintosh (1844-45).

It was probably in 1846, when Father James Quinlan was stationed at St. Basil's in Brantford (1845-49), that a frame church was erected on the southeast corner of lot 22, concession 9 in Windham Township. Built on one acre (0.4 ha) of land, donated by George Joseph and Margaret Dertinger, the church was about 50 feet by 30 feet (15.2 m by 9.1 m). It seated 300 people. The church was dedicated to St. Anthony. By January 1852, when Father Patrick O'Dwyer was pastor at Brantford (1850-52), it served thirty-five families in Windham, Norwich and Middleton townships.

After his appointment to St. Basil's, Father Jeremiah Ryan (1853-59) kept a separate register for the Windham mission. The first bishop to visit and administer the sacrament of confirmation was Bishop Charbonnel of Toronto in 1855.

With the formation of the diocese of London in 1856, St. Anthony's was elevated to parish status. Father L. Andrew Schweiger was appointed pastor about October 1856. One of his first projects was to build a Catholic school next to the church. Father

St. Anthony

Schweiger suddenly left the area in January 1858, and was succeeded by Father Louis Schnyder, who was also pastor at Simcoe. Father Schnyder reported thirty-one Irish and twenty-one German families in the Windham parish before he too suddenly departed for Buffalo, New York.

Both Windham and Simcoe reverted to mission status and were served by Father Michael J. Lynch of Windham (1858-61) until March 1859, when Father Bartholomew Boubat was appointed pastor at Windham. Father James T. Wagner (1860-64) had a rectory built near the church in 1860, but he took up permanent residence in Simcoe in 1862. In 1871, St. Anthony's parish also included the Simcoe and Vienna missions and three stations. There were about 250 families in all.

A succession of pastors followed at St. Anthony's. In July 1873, Father Henry Japes (1873-80) arrived, but he decided to transfer his parish seat to the junction of the Canada Southern and Lake Huron and Port Dover railways, now the site of Our Lady of LaSalette church. By April 1880, the rectory built by Father Wagner had been removed to the new site, and St. Anthony's church was also removed to LaSalette once the new church was completed. St. Anthony's last pastor became the first pastor of Our Lady, Help of Christians (later Our Lady of LaSalette). He was Father William Dillon (1880-89). The old Windham church probably closed with the opening of the LaSalette church in 1881.

Today, a Canada Centennial project cairn marks the site of the first Catholic church and cemetery in Windham Township.

Sources: DLA, Pierre-Adolphe Pinsoneault Papers, Box 1, Letter books Vol. 3, 55, 55a, 66-66a, 67-68; Ibid., John Walsh Papers, Box 1, The Status of Animarum for the Diocese of Sandwich; *Our Lady of LaSalette Parish History 1836-1979* [LaSalette: 1979]; Janis McCahill et al., *The History of St. Christopher's Parish St. Christopher's Church 1893-1993* [Forest: 1993]; Vincent Dertinger, "Letter to the editor," *Newsletter of the Diocese of London*, no. 61 (Easter 1994), 16.

Woodstock: Holy Cross

Holy Cross

In March 1958, the Poles of the Woodstock area petitioned Bishop Cody to have a Polish-speaking priest celebrate Sunday Mass and preach in Polish, in one of Woodstock's existing parish churches. Little action, however, seems to have been taken.

Then, in the early summer of 1965, Bishop Carter received a deputation representing some 150 families from the Polish Catholic community. Little was done in the intervening months, and three representatives wrote to the Bishop in early March 1966. The result was the establishment of a committee composed of Woodstock's two pastors and Monsignor Vito H. Grespan, the spiritual chancellor of the diocese. By early April, it was agreed that there would be an 8:00 a.m. Mass on Sundays, celebrated by Father Mitchell S. Kaminski, at St. Mary's church. He would also spend one full day each week at the service of the Polish community. This was to be on a six-month trial basis. In October, representatives of the Polish community requested a full-time priest and parish status. While Bishop Carter was reluctant to establish a national parish at the time, he did announce in December 1966 that a full-time priest would be assigned to the Polish community and would reside at St. Mary's rectory.

Within the month, Bishop Carter established Holy Cross mission and placed Father Edwin J. Malak (1967-68) in charge. The Poles were responsible for his room and board at St. Mary's and the payment of $150 per month for the rental of the church for services. As this proved difficult, St. Mary's pastor, Father Wilfrid T. O'Rourke (1965-81), suggested some months later that the Holy Ghost Fathers of St. Rita's parish in Woodstock might be able to find a Polish priest in their order who would live with them, minister to the Polish people and do other parish work.

In the meantime Father Rafal I. Grzondziel (1968-82), who succeeded Father Malak in June 1968, learned that four and one-half acres (1.8 ha) of farm land along Ingersoll Road, which included the original farm house, were for sale. The owner, an 82-year-old Protestant woman, insisted that the price be paid in cash and at once, owing to her advanced age. Father Grzondziel was able to do this, with the full support of the parish committee. Later, Bishop Carter congratulated him on his decisiveness and encouraged him by quoting Shakespeare: "Although poor, but on your own, move quickly as possible to be independent." Father Grzondziel, and not the Episcopal Corporation, however, was the legal owner of the property. While this matter was being ironed out, the congregation of 135 families was busy transforming and expanding the frame structure into a church, a priest's residence and a place for parish activities. By early March 1969, with all the work being done gratis by the congregation, all costs had been paid for and there was just the installation of the heating system remaining to be done. On 31 October 1971, the church, now valued at $125,000 and seating 312, was officially opened by Bishop Carter. Mounted inside were several pieces of stainless-steel art by Marian Owczarski, a native of Warsaw who lived in Woodstock.

In 1982, Holy Cross mission was placed under the care of the Michaelite Fathers in the person of Father Wladyslaw Krukar, CSMA (1982-85). On 28 January 1986, Holy Cross was elevated to parish status, with Father Edwin P. Mucha, CSMA, as pastor (1986-2006). He also celebrated a Polish-language Mass in Waterford once a month. Following his death, on 9 April 2006, Father Matthias Wronski, a diocesan priest, became pastor on 31 July 2006.

Holy Cross parish was canonically suppressed, effective June 2007, and established as Holy Cross Polish Catholic Community, with Father Wronski as priest-chaplain.

Sources: DLA, Parish Files; Gerald Emmett Carter Papers, Box 23, Holy Cross, Woodstock.

Woodstock: St. Mary

In late November 1835, Father Joseph L. Wiriath of Guelph travelled on foot from Beachville to Sergeant Egan's home and celebrated the first Mass in Woodstock. Between 1852 and 1867, Mass was celebrated in the Woodstock town hall. By 1861, the Catholic population had reached 242, but still the congregation had no church of its own. In 1863, the station was detached from Ingersoll and given to the parish of Norwich. In 1864, Norwich reverted to mission status, and Woodstock again became an Ingersoll station.

Father Gabriel Volkert of Ingersoll (1866-68) oversaw the erection of the first church at Woodstock, made possible by a generous donation of $500 from a benefactor in Brantford. The cornerstone was laid and blessed on 31 March 1867 by Bishop Farrell of Hamilton. On 8 December 1867, Bishop Walsh dedicated the church under the patronage of the Immaculate Conception of the Blessed Virgin Mary.

With the appointment of Father Nicholas Gahan as pastor (1874-77), on 21 May 1874, St. Mary's was elevated to parish status, with Norwich and East Oxford as its missions. The rectory was built early in Father John Carlin's pastorship (1877-83).

While Father Michael J. Brady was pastor (1883-1897), an attempt was made to change the location of the church to a more central part of Woodstock, but Bishop Walsh opposed this plan. He laid the cornerstone of the present church, on 5 September 1886, and returned to bless the new St. Mary's on 8 December 1886. Designed by George Durand of London, it faced the street, whereas the previous church faced the cemetery.

Father John L. Cook, a former pastor of St. Mary's (1900-06), died in 1909 and left his entire estate as a trust fund for the poor of the parish. Under the leadership of his successor, Father John F. Stanley (1907-24), the church and surrounding properties were extended and improved. Bishop Fallon re-opened the church in September 1919.

Father Stanley organized the Holy Name Society in the diocese and was its first diocesan director.

In 1925, during the pastorate of Father Michael

St. Mary

D. O'Neill (1925-28), the interior of the church was badly damaged by fire. On 15 September 1939, during the term of St. Mary's longest-serving pastor, Father E. Ambrose O'Donnell (1928-50), the twenty-seventh diocesan Eucharistic Congress was conducted in Woodstock.

In 1946, land for a new cemetery was purchased on County Road 9. In 1951, when Father W.J. Phelan was pastor (1950-61), renovations to the church were undertaken and St. Mary's hall was built. In 1970, during the pastorship of Father Wilfrid T. O'Rourke (1965-81), the parish assumed responsibility for the Oxford Mental Health Centre. Father Jozef G. Denys, while pastor (1981-1987), assisted in the extensive renovations to the rectory and in the building of parish meeting rooms.

The 125th anniversary of St. Mary's as a parish was commemorated on the weekend of 30-31 October 1999, with Bishop Grecco as celebrant at all Masses.

Owing to structural problems, the church was closed in July 2005. The two priests assigned to Woodstock and Princeton, Father Andrew Kowalczyk, CSMA, and Father Chris Gevaert, took up residence at St. Mary's rectory and established a parish office at St. Rita's.

St. Mary's parish closed, effective June 2006. It and St. Rita's and Sacred Heart, Princeton were absorbed by Holy Trinity parish. A six-acre (2.4 ha) site for the new church has been selected on Devonshire Avenue, between Landsdowne Avenue and County Road 4.

Sources: "Bishop Walsh at Ingersoll," *Catholic Record*, 2 October 1886, 1; "Catholicity in Woodstock," *Catholic Record*, 1 January 1887, 1; J.H. O'Neil, *Diary of a Priest* [1970]; *True Witness* (Montréal), 19 April 1867; 5:1. F. Michael McMahon, "Holy Trinity Catholic Parish, Woodstock," *Newsletter of the Diocese of London*, no. 122 (Summer 2006), 18. Additional information supplied by Father John Van Damme and Holy Trinity parish members.

Woodstock: St. Rita of Cascia

In 1950, Father William J. Phelan was appointed pastor of St. Mary's in Woodstock (1950-61). He quickly foresaw that, owing to post-war immigration and the increase in the birthrate, the parish needed another school and that it made sense to build a new one in the eastern end of the city where the population increase was occurring. He persuaded the separate school board to find a site for a new school. It purchased part of Tom Dent's farm at the east end of Dundas Street. A school was officially opened by Bishop Cody on 27 September 1953 and dedicated to St. Rita of Cascia. (A wife, mother, widow and nun, St. Rita lived in Italy during the last part of the fourteenth century and the early years of the fifteenth century.)

In 1953, Father William L. Brolly of the Congregation of the Holy Spirit was sent by the congregation's Irish province to seek a foundation in English-speaking Canada. Father Demers, CSSP, of St. Joachim's in Detroit, introduced Father Brolly to Bishop Cody, who, had been educated by the Holy Ghost Fathers at St. Alexander College, in Hull, Québec. Bishop Cody welcomed the opportunity of having the Spiritans in his diocese and suggested that the congregation accept a new parish in Woodstock. An agreement between Father Francis Griffin, CSSP, the superior general of the Holy Ghost Fathers, and Bishop Cody, was signed in 1954 and that October, St. Rita of Cascia parish, consisting of some 135 families, was established. The congregation purchased property adjacent to St. Rita of Cascia school for $18,000. The four families living in the house at 904 Dundas Street when the purchase was made soon vacated the premises. Father Brolly then spent several weeks renovating and preparing the building for the arrival, on 18 October 1954, of the first group of Holy Ghost Fathers from Ireland. Father Nicholas C. McCormack, CSSP, one of the five members of this "Mission Band," was appointed the first pastor (1954-72).

A former army barracks from the Second World War, subsequently used for rearing mink and later turned into a motel, was converted into a temporary church, and the first Masses were celebrated on 19 December 1954. The building was heated by two gas space heaters which, having no thermostatic control, had to be turned off at night.

By early 1956, plans for a permanent church

St. Rita of Cascia

were implemented. George Schnieder of Hamilton was engaged as architect, and Arnold Construction Co. of Hamilton was hired as the contracting firm. The first Mass was celebrated in the unfinished structure on 14 April 1957, and Bishop Cody officially opened and blessed the new St. Rita's on 21 May 1957. The old church then became the Knights of Columbus hall.

Father Hubert Roche, CSSP, was St. Rita's second pastor (1972-75). The house on Dundas Street had proved impractical as a place of work. In 1978, during the pastorate of Father Michael Wasser (1975-77), a new rectory designed by Thor Stecura, was built next to the church. Father Kiernan Kenna, CSSP, was the fourth pastor (1977-84), and Father James Dunne, CSSP (1984-98) was the parish's fifth and last Holy Ghost pastor. In 1998, St. Rita's was placed in the hands of the diocesan priests, with Father Alan M. Dufraimont (1998-2005) becoming its pastor on 26 June 1998.

On 30 June 2005, St. Rita's and its mission, Sacred Heart in Princeton, were clustered with St. Mary's in Woodstock under the pastorate of Father Andrzej Kowalczyk, CSMA. All three were suppressed, effective June 2006, and their territorial boundaries were absorbed into the newly-established Holy Trinity parish.

Sources: G.A. McCarthy, ed., *St. Rita of Cascia Church, Woodstock, Ontario: 1954 ... 25th Anniversary ... 1979, Looking Back*, [Woodstock: 1979].

Part V
Diocesan Life

1. St. Peter's Seminary

In 1912, Bishop Fallon made the monumental decision to found St. Peter's Seminary, largely prompted by his own unhappiness with the Grand Séminaire in Montréal and by a misunderstanding over the status of the recently opened St. Augustine's Seminary in Toronto. Fallon assembled a faculty of five priests, appointed Father John V. Tobin as the first rector and installed them in the cathedral rectory. Fallon insisted on using diocesan priests as instructors to assure a pastoral orientation for his students. In 1923, he withdrew his philosophy students from Assumption College in Sandwich (Windsor) and placed them in St. Peter's School of Philosophy on Queens Avenue in London. Two years later, he successfully negotiated the affiliation of the school of philosophy with the University of Western Ontario, through Ursuline (later Brescia) College. In 1939, St. Peter's Seminary obtained its own affiliation with the university, enabling the seminary to grant an Honours BA in philosophy to its arts students in preparation for theology. In 1964, an Ontario government restructuring of the province's confessional colleges bestowed upon the seminary a charter, which gave it the legal authority to grant its own degrees and allowed it to offer a Bachelor of Theology (B.Th.) program.

On 29 September 1926, Bishop Fallon's grand dream took physical shape with the opening of the present seminary, although it lacked a chapel, cloister and finished fourth floor. It was designed by John R. Boyde and built in the imposing collegiate Gothic style, in "Sunshine Park" in north London, for the grand sum of $500,000. Forty-five students and six faculty members moved in. Fallon opened the jewel of his crown, the seminary's St. Thomas Aquinas chapel, on 30 June 1930. It was also designed by Boyde and cost $200,000. Sick with diabetes, Fallon died on 22 February 1931, his mission accomplished, and he was buried in the crypt beneath the sanctuary floor of his beloved chapel.

Father Tobin was seminary rector for only one year. He resigned in 1913 owing to ill health. Succeeding him was Monsignor Denis O'Connor, who ran the seminary, always in Fallon's shadow, until 1930, when he became bishop of Peterborough. Monsignor Andrew P. Mahoney, the third rector, enjoyed an epic term of thirty-six years, and

Monsignor Leonard Forristal was house spiritual director from 1924 to 1968. Other long serving faculty included Fathers Maxime A. Brisson, Francis J. Brennan, J. Herman Pocock, Lester A. Wemple, West T. Flannery, Anthony J. Durand, Leo J. Flynn, Philip F. Pocock and Thomas J. McCarthy.

The seminary enrolment expanded to approximately 130 students in the 1940s. An "Honour System" prevailed at St. Peter's. At its centre was a tiny, brown "Rule Book." Composed in pithy prose, it carefully guided every student, and each year the rector publicly commented upon its importance to the seminarians. Students from dioceses such as Scranton, Pennsylvania and Toledo, Ohio internationalized the roster. Also, the Congregation of the Resurrection built St. Thomas Scholasticate next door to the seminary in 1930, beginning an association that lasted until 1981, when the community moved to Toronto. In 1958, under the guidance of Monsignor Fergus J. Laverty, a new wing was added to the seminary that provided a much-needed auditorium, student lounge and a library reading room in the former cloister.

The hallmarks of this era were consistent teaching, a consolidated and loyal seminary spirit, an alumni association founded in 1939 that published an annual *Alumni Bulletin* and hosted triennial reunions, and an internationally recognized theological and pastoral program that produced well-formed and competent pastors. And the seminary bulged with students.

The close of the Second Vatican Council introduced another era, which lasted until about 1985. Most of the first generation of faculty had concluded their teaching and administrative careers in the 1960s, paving the way for Father James J.Carrigan, the new rector, and new faculty members, such as Fathers Patrick E. Cavanagh, Michael R. Prieur and Michael T. Ryan, to guide the seminary through the tumultuous period immediately following the Council. In 1968, the student body was divided into groups, which allowed for greater intimacy of staff and students and a more team-oriented ministry model. The monastic model of seminary life, which had prevailed since the seminary opened in 1912, shifted to individual self-reliance and more personal creativity. Friendships were now formed more often within one's group than within one's entrance year.

This era also saw the emergence of a new affiliation agreement between the seminary's affiliate, Christ the King College, and the University of Western Ontario. As King's outgrew the seminary, it sought and achieved its own affiliation with Western in 1972. At the same time, lay students began to take theology courses at St. Peter's. In 1969, a B.Th. degree was awarded to a lay student, and in 1975, another lay student earned a Master of Divinity (M.Div.) degree. The 1970s welcomed St. Peter's first women professors: Sister St. John McCauley, CSJ, and Joan Lenardon. In 1985, the seminary instituted a formation program for lay people. At its head was Sister Margaret Ferris, CSJ. St. Peter's Seminary now officially recognized its dual role of preparing both seminarians and lay people for ministry in the Church.

The years from 1985 to the present involved much restructuring. It began with the unnerving experience of an accreditation process conducted by the Association of Theological Schools (ATS). The oral tradition of the seminary's life needed to be articulated and put on paper. The compilation of

policies, practices and rationales became the order of the day. A second accreditation in 1990, along with an Apostolic Visitation in 1995, deepened this new drive for "hard copy." Much good came from all this writing. It brought about the separation of the roles of formation adviser and spiritual director, curriculum changes and a wider consulting process with alumni and the Catholic community. Under the direction of the rector, Father Frederick B. Henry, and the head librarian, Lois Côté, the library was expanded in 1985 with the generous assistance of the Knights of Columbus. A computerized catalogue was introduced in the 1990s, enabling even a closer relationship with King's College and the University of Western Ontario.

Subsequent rectors, Father Patrick W. Fuerth and Father Thomas C. Collins, helped to expand the training of seminarians beyond the walls of the seminary. A biennial Mission Awareness program, spearheaded by the seminary's Father T. Francis O'Connor, enabled seminarians from St. Peter's and other Catholic seminaries to visit Mexico, Brazil, India and northern Canada. Additional links were made with community-related assignments in London. Among staff and students, there was an increase in the knowledge and appreciation of the roles of women. As for the seminary itself, its role as a spiritual and academic centre grew in prominence with frequent prayer days, retreats, symposia, extended liturgical sessions and theological events. In addition, the alumni association promoted more reunions in regional venues.

Other changes helped to define this era. The seminary purchased St. Thomas Scholasticate from the Congregation of the Resurrection in 1987 and updated the interior in 1991. Father John J. O'Flaherty and the transitional deacons used it for seven years. Also, a massive refurbishing of the building's stone exterior began. In 1990, significant financial assistance for St. Peter's Seminary was provided by Pentecost 2000, a campaign that was inaugurated by Bishop Sherlock.

During the rectorship of Father William T. McGrattan, many advances have taken place. A Mission Statement, drafted by the faculty in 1999, sheds a great deal of light on the spirit of the seminary in this period. A Master of Theology (M.T.S.) for lay people, a purely academic degree with no formation component, and another ATS accreditation in 2001, breathed new life into the seminary.

At the beginning of the new millennium, Father McGrattan instituted a broader-based seminary board to work in collaboration with a new Seminary Foundation. In-depth feasibility studies were conducted on the buildings and grounds, staffing and the prospects for future student enrolment. New avenues for the training of lay people are in progress under the direction of Carole Murphy. In 2000, Bishop Sherlock approved the inauguration of a four-year Permanent Deacon Formation Program to be managed by the seminary. Fourteen deacons were ordained in 2005, and twelve in 2007. A new propaedeutic program (similar to a novitiate) was added to better prepare seminarians for their formation. In 2007, plans were announced for an Institute for Catholic Formation, aimed at providing formation for all who provide ministry in the diocese.

St. Peter's Seminary has always had a strong pastoral orientation. It has been true to authentic Catholic teaching in the light of the Second Vatican Council. The seminary has maintained strong ties with current academic, medical and social justice movements, with its faculty involved in national and international issues of justice, bioethics, catechetics, ecumenism, liturgy, the charismatic renewal, Ignatian spirituality and multi-media teaching opportunities.

For over 1,000 priests (of whom twenty-one have become bishops), 100 lay graduates and countless other individuals, St. Peter's Seminary has lived up to its motto: *"Dabo vobis pastores iuxta cor meum, et pascent vos scientia et doctrina"* — "I will give you shepherds according to my own heart, and they will feed you with wisdom and understanding" (*Jeremiah* 3:15).

Submitted by Father Michael Prieur. See also Michael Prieur, "St. Peter's Seminary: A Brief History in Four Phases," St. Peter's Seminary, *The Alumni Bulletin* **(2000-2001):** 30-35.

2. King's University College

On 14 September 1955, Christ the King College welcomed some fifty first-year students and a faculty of eight professors, six of whom were priests. The small group of guests present shared the conviction that this was indeed a "happy occasion" for the diocese of London, and especially for young Catholic men seeking a higher education in a religious setting. Monsignor Lester A. Wemple was appointed dean of the college by Bishop Cody and served as chief administrator and academic dean. The central focus of Wemple's vision of the college was that "Christ is the King of Education." A graduate of King's would not only be a highly educated and cultured gentleman, but also be strongly committed to the Catholic faith.

Given its small size and limited numbers, the college soon became a "happy place" that early graduates remember fondly. In the early 1960s, however, Wemple's vision became increasingly difficult to sustain. Student recruitment became more difficult in an increasingly secularized society. Declining enrolments compounded the dean's difficulties in financing a college that received only half the government grants provided to secular institutions. Unable to control the yearly deficits, Monsignor Wemple resigned, ten years after he began.

Bishop Carter chose Monsignor Eugène LaRocque as the new dean. The difficult task of trying to right the situation led Monsignor LaRocque to introduce changes that might bring more students to King's. The name of the institution was changed to King's College and student discipline was relaxed, but these and other departures from the "Wemple years" were to no avail. Students and faculty began to leave the college. In response to this developing crisis, Bishop Carter dismissed Monsignor LaRocque and, in November 1967, directed that the college should be closed and its property sold to the University of Western Ontario (UWO). Anger and frustration followed, as students and professors faced the bleak prospect of becoming "academic orphans." By the summer of 1968, the crisis had abated. A recently appointed board of directors took matters in hand and guaranteed that King's would remain open for at least one more year. During that same period, the board also completed its search for a new principal.

The new appointee was Dr. Owen Carrigan, professor of history at Wilfrid Laurier University. Over the next three years, Carrigan was able to complete a program of reforms that addressed the college's problems in a coherent and systematic manner. Central to his approach was the stabilization of the financial situation, which required a sustained increase in enrolment. To that end, the Social Welfare (later Social Work) program was established. This meant that King's would have to admit women students. An aggressive recruitment campaign produced immediate results: registration rose from 300 in 1968 to 700 in 1971, half of the students being women. Attracting students required an equally aggressive campaign to recruit additional faculty, and some twelve new professors, most of whom had their doctorate, were added.

The need for classroom, office and "living space" was pressing, since the increase in the number of students and professors overwhelmed the limited capacity of the Wemple building. This pressing problem was partly solved with the addition of a library wing, the townhouse residence for men and an administration wing. In three short years, Carrigan succeeded in implementing his plans, supported by the diocese and the board of directors. It was said by many that Carrigan had saved King's College, but it would be more accurate to say that he created a new, forward-looking institution and set in motion a program of gradual expansion that produced the King's College we know today.

Dr. Arnold McKee, Carrigan's successor as principal, had to confront the absence of administrative structures usually found in a university setting. Resolving this thorny problem took a great deal of time and often-acrimonious negotiations. Eventually, the constituent bodies of the college developed proper mandates and procedures that clearly defined their respective responsibilities. Also, the appointment of Dr. John Morgan as academic dean helped to lighten the principal's heavy workload.

One of McKee's continuing concerns, shared by Bishop Carter, was that King's was drifting away from its Catholicity. This prompted the bishop to appoint a Commission of Inquiry, which issued a report in early 1975 that offered many suggestions for the restoration of the Catholic character of the college. Two of those suggestions were the return of the chapel to a more proper location and the enhancement of the role of the chaplaincy team. While the college was waiting for the release of the commission's report, there erupted another financial crisis. The core problem was no government funds for the Social Work program. Fortunately, the minister for universities and colleges provided timely relief, announcing in December 1973 that denominational colleges would receive full operating grants for all programs in the coming years. This windfall made possible the realization of another of McKee's major projects: the purchase of the Silverwood property from UWO. When the purchase was completed in 1978, "The Mansion" provided much-needed additional space for the growing college.

McKee's tenure as principal witnessed the sustained growth of both student and faculty numbers. A Continuing Education program was launched in 1975, under the leadership of Professor John Campbell, in an effort to reach out to those in the London community unable to pursue a university education. Although initially successful, this program fell victim to competition from other institutions. Also that same year, the Alumni Association was reorganized under the stewardship of Professor Paul Webb. A systematic census of the alumni (5,000 by 1975) was used to invite alumni to contribute to various fund-raising schemes. A new women's residence was named Alumni Court in recognition of the alumni's generosity. Meanwhile, students founded or revived a number of student clubs, such as the King's Players, a drama club that staged its productions in the small theatre located in the lower level of the Silverwood house. By the end of McKee's term, King's had "turned the corner," having solved many of the problems that at times had threatened its very existence.

The promotion of Dr. John Morgan as principal was the beginning of a period of stability and sustained growth that has lasted to the present. Financial uncertainties remained a source of anxiety, primarily because of the annual "battle of the budget" at Queen's Park and at King's College itself. Such things as tuition freezes and nearly annual cutbacks in government appropriations for higher education averaging five percent a year made long-range financial planning a difficult undertaking. The college, however, managed its affairs with sound budgeting practices and the considerable input of its board of directors, which together helped to keep annual deficits to a minimum.

Morgan's primary concern was the further development of King's as an academic institution. The college introduced new courses and programs and added to the faculty highly qualified professors, who kept pace with the needs of the steadily increasing student population. Morgan himself offered courses in the new field of death and bereavement studies, which grew into an annual summer conference that attracted participants and distinguished scholars from Canada, the United States and occasionally from Europe. Finally, Morgan gave the King's community frequent opportunities for self-examination in the light of its special mission as a Catholic college. More specifically, philosophy and mission statements helped to create a bridge between the academic and religious sides of the campus community.

Dr. Philip Mueller, who had served as academic dean during Morgan's tenure, was appointed as his successor. He too would serve a ten-year term, during which his calm and deliberate approach to his many tasks served the college well. Mueller continued the academic development of what was becoming one of the best Catholic colleges in Canada. His time in office, however, was not without its occasional difficulties, such as those that arose from the imposition of a "social contract" by Premier Bob Rae and his NDP government. Salaries and all special grants were frozen, and all employees paid from public funds were required to take twelve days off without pay, known as "Rae days." To those institutions that could show significant "economies," the government offered an inducement in the form of a reduction in the number of "Rae days." In the spirit of Christian community, King's made every effort to mitigate the impact of these policies, succeeding in reducing the number of unpaid days to two.

One of Mueller's accomplishments was the construction of the Cardinal Carter Library. He was deeply involved in the fund-raising campaign and the detailed planning of every part of the new structure, so that it would meet the needs of the college for the coming decades. Since its opening, the Cardinal Carter Library has undergone a series of upgrades in keeping with the ever-changing developments in digital communication.

With the end of Mueller's tenure, Dr. Gerald Killan became the new (and present) principal. His great ambition is to make King's College the best middle-size liberal arts university in Canada. He is also committed to the active retention of the college's Catholic mandate, which is central to its identity.

An examination of the recent course calendars showed that almost all disciplines offer an Honours program. At the same time, specialized courses of study highlighted the college's contributions to peace studies and social justice issues. These and other new programs necessitated more space. Opened in 2003, the Elizabeth "Bessie" Labatt Hall is another attractive building on an expanding campus. Construction was greatly facilitated by a one-million-dollar gift from the Labatt family. Much of the fund-raising for various other projects is now in the hands of the King's College Foundation, the Alumni Association and kindred support groups. Their work has enabled King's to take advantage of matching grants from the government and different foundations.

While its many academic programs have produced graduates who have contributed to the diocese and the London community, during the past ten years, King's has become part of the process of "globalization." Some 300 international students are expected to enroll at King's in the autumn of 2007. A number of faculty and students have benefited from exchange programs with universities from as far away as China and Korea.

It is difficult at this time to anticipate what the future holds for King's University College. Killan's principalship comes to an end in 2009. Over a span of twelve years, he has "re-invented" King's and made it truly worthy of its name. And over the course of fifty years, more than 12,000 young women and men are proof that it is possible to reconcile higher learning with religious faith.

Submitted by Jacques R. Goutor.

3. Catholic Women's League

The London Diocesan Council is a constituent member of the Catholic Women's League of Canada (CWL). The diocesan council's origins are best understood within the context of the early history of the national organization. The CWL was officially organized on 17 June 1920, at a meeting in Montréal, in response to the call of Bishop Emile-Joseph Légal of Edmonton and the federal government for a greater participation of Catholic women assisting with the settlement of immigrants. The delegates chose "For God and Canada" as their motto and placed the league under the patronage of Our Lady of Good Counsel.

Attending the CWL's inaugural national meeting was Bishop Fallon of London. As soon as he returned home, he encouraged the formation of councils throughout the diocese. Mrs. B.C. McCann organized the first diocesan subdivision or council at St. Peter's cathedral in 1920. Other councils quickly followed until there were fifty-eight represented at the diocesan convention of 25-26 October 1921. Bishop Fallon used the occasion to speak on Catholic education, as part of his province-wide campaign on behalf of separate schools. He found a receptive audience among the CWL members. The London Council was the third diocesan council to receive its charter from the Catholic Women's League of Canada.

Chosen to serve on the 1921 diocesan executive were the following:

President: Mrs. B.C. (Evelyn) McCann, London
First Vice-President: Mrs. J.P. Dunn, Chatham
Second Vice-President: Mrs. Patrick Meehan, St. Thomas
Third Vice-President: Mrs. A.H.C. Trotter, Belle River
Secretary-Treasurer: Mrs. Joseph Leech, London
Councilors: Mrs. Francis Cleary, Windsor; Mrs. John Bohan, Logan; Mrs. George Dawson, Sarnia; Mrs. A. Lebo, Tilbury; Mrs. M.J. Trophy, Woodstock; Mrs. John McDonald, Brussels; Mrs. M. Fleming, St. Mary's

Over the years, four presidents of the London Diocesan Council have served as president of the National Catholic Women's League: Evelyn McCann (1925-26); T.E. Durocher (1949); Mrs. James Freeman (1955); and Catherine Toal (1976). Eight other presidents have served in various capacities on the executive of the Ontario provincial council: Sheila Howard, Lillian Mousseau, Fran Vrooman, Angela Debryn, Eva Mitchell, Muriel Murphy and Shirley George, who is the current president for 2005-07.

There are no membership statistics available for 1921. From 1925 to 1986, the number of dues-paying members grew from 4,616 in 49 councils to 17,128 in 115 councils. As of 2004, there were 13,575 members in 116 councils in the London Diocesan Council, which is divided into seven regions. Each region corresponds to a deanery and is represented on the executive of the diocesan council. In terms of membership, the London Diocesan Council is the largest in Canada. Indeed, it is larger than any provincial or territorial council, except for Ontario. It is also unique for having a council — St. Peter's in Norwich — without a parish, the church having been closed for some forty years. And it is one of the few diocesan councils that has a Catholic girls club for girls from twelve to sixteen years of age — at St. Mary's parish, Tillsonburg.

In the CWL prayer, one finds these words: "help us to share with others at home and abroad the good things that you have given us." London CWL members have consistently put these words into action during their eighty-five-year history. At the parish level, members have financed equipment purchases, renovations to parish facilities and gifts to clergy and staff. They are also involved in the preparation of children for First Holy Communion and of adults for the Rite of Christian Initiation of Adults (RCIA), serve as ministers of Holy Communion and as lay readers, and prepare funeral lunches, among many activities.

Outside the boundaries of their individual

parishes, members support missions in Canada and the Third World, community organizations such as the Red Cross, the Cancer Society, food banks and shelters for the homeless; they participate in refugee appeals and the work of Development and Peace; they are involved in Guides, Scouts, Christ in Others Retreat (COR), other outreach for youth and foster homes; they finance local scholarships; and they work with seniors and shut-ins. Many people mean many gifts, and the numerous members of the diocesan CWL have been generous in sharing their gifts with a wide cross-section of people inside and outside the Church.

On the political front, the CWL of the diocese of London supported the national organization when it condemned the atheistic persecution of Catholics in Mexico (1935); asked for stricter divorce laws (1939); encouraged Canadians to participate more actively in civic programs (1945); supported a national flag for Canada (1954); petitioned the Ontario government to maintain centres for developmentally handicapped people and to provide better care for discharged mental patients (1983

and 1985); demanded informed consent in respect to abortion (1993); proposed an appeal process for refugees whose claims for status had been denied and defended the traditional definition of marriage (2005).

Father Joseph J.L. Hennessy, diocesan spiritual advisor to the CWL under Bishop Cody, summed up the practical and spiritual dynamism of the CWL when he wrote on the diocesan council's fortieth anniversary in 1960: "I am sure that you will be able to read between the lines the corporal works of mercy that abounded and continue to do so until the present. You will also realize that the written record cannot convey the spiritual growth of many souls through the labors and kindness of League members. From the beginning to the present hour, thousands of dedicated and devoted women in the League family of London have given unselfishly of their time and talents to carry out, to the very letter, the motto "For God and Canada." These words are still true today.

Submitted by Maria S. Odumodu.

4. Knights of Columbus

Father Michael J. McGivney chartered the Knights of Columbus, a society of Catholic men, on 29 March 1882. "Dedicated to the principles of charity, unity, brotherly love, and patriotism," according to the *New Catholic Encyclopedia* (vol. 8: 215), "the society provides a system of fraternal insurance benefits to its members, promotes social and cultural intercourse among them and engages in educational, charitable, and religious activities, and social welfare, war relief, and public relief." These principles of purpose have remained constant since the inception of the Knights of Columbus 125 years ago. At the same time, the Knights have brought these principles to practical fruition by means tailored to the prevailing social and cultural climate.

J.P. Kavanaugh, Charles F. Smith and Dr. J.J. Guerin founded Montréal Council No. 284, on 22 November 1897, the first council in Canada, with the hard-won support of Archbishop Paul Bruchési. He was disinclined to sanction the formation of yet another society in Montréal, and two years later he would have condemned the Knights as a secret society if not for the intervention of James Cardinal Gibbons of Baltimore. In 1899, J.P. Kavanaugh, district deputy for Canada, established Québec Council No. 446 and a second council in Montréal,

Dominion Council No. 465. Between 1900 and 1909, nineteen councils were formed in Ontario, including ones in London, Chatham, Sarnia and Stratford. The charter for London Council No. 1410 is dated 15 March 1909, which marks the beginning of the work of the Knights in the diocese of London. Claude Brown was Grand Knight, and John M. Doyle was financial secretary. By 2005, there were eighty-seven councils in the diocese.

Newspaper stories record two important early activities of the Knights in the diocese: the opening of the new Knights of Columbus hall and club rooms in Chatham, on 13 February 1911; and, the formal presentation of a purse of gold worth $210 to Monsignor John T. Aylward, the rector of St. Peter's cathedral, on 24 February 1911, in recognition of his important priestly service. Chatham Council No. 1412, which had spent $20,000 on its building, used the occasion to bestow degrees on seventy-five candidates in the presence of 500 fellow Knights from across Canada and the United States. It was a spectacular display of Catholic fraternity in what was a small city.

The First World War, from 1914 to 1918, provided the first significant test for the Knights in terms of their charity and patriotism. Aided by Bishop Fallon, who became state (Province of Ontario) chaplain in 1911 — a post he would retain for the next sixteen years — the Knights of the diocese of London in 1917 participated in a million dollar drive on behalf of the Knights' Catholic Army Huts Association in Great Britain. In co-operation with the Catholic chaplaincy attached to the Canadian Expeditionary Force, the huts provided recreational, educational and spiritual opportunities to soldiers, either in camp or in hospital. Their motto was simple and very clever: "Everyone Welcome and Everything Free." The huts continued to operate until 1922.

Dr. Claude Brown, who became Grand Knight of London Council in 1909, and a lieutenant colonel during the First World War, was one soldier who did not forget the good work of the Catholic Army Huts. Dr. Brown, a dentist, had risen to District Deputy, Master of the Fourth Degree and State Deputy of Ontario prior to his appointment as Supreme Director in 1926. As Supreme Director, he personally contacted each state deputy in Canada, on 13 September 1939, less than two weeks after the commencement of the Second World War, to organize welfare services for members of the Canadian armed services. Dr. Brown spent his own money on a cross-Canada tour, galvanizing Knights in every district, and in 1940 he went to England to direct the revitalization of the huts program.

Dr. Brown's term as Supreme Director ended in 1941. Other supreme directors from the diocese include Al DeWitte (1986-91), Grant Ertel (1991-2000), Philip Zakoor (2000-03) and Robert Cayea (2003-06). There has been one Vice Supreme Master from the diocese: Mr. Justice J. Maurice King

(1958-67). Moreover, the Knights of the diocese of London have provided eight state deputies: J.O. Dromgole (London, 1911-13); George Hanrahan (London, 1921-23); Mr. Justice J. Maurice King (Stratford, 1947-49); Frank Hyde (Wallaceburg, 1949-51); Paul Cecile (Belle River, 1968-70); Al DeWitte (Chatham, 1984-86); Philip Zakoor (Windsor, 1986-88); and Robert Cayea (Windsor, 2002-04). The diocese of London has hosted Ontario state conventions thirteen times, from 1912 to 1993. Diocesan councils have won the Best Council Award on eighteen occasions.

In addition to their participation in the general charitable work of the Ontario State Council, such as the Council's permanent principal charity, the Canadian Arthritis and Rheumatism Society, the Knights of the diocese of London have made substantial donations to hospitals, police departments, the "Keep Christ in Christmas" billboard campaign, adopt-a-street program, the Children's Aid Society, church restoration, St. Peter's Seminary and Right to Life Associations.

In 1967, the Ontario State Council chose Dieppe Park in Windsor as the site for its centennial peace memorial. The monument is entirely in granite and consists of a forty-foot (12 m) fluted pillar as a backdrop, a half-globe (northern hemisphere) that is situated on its own platform at the base of the pillar, on which are carved the words "Pray for Peace," and the figures of a man and a woman who are contemplating the words in prayerful repose. The monument was dedicated on 22 October 1967.

Different councils from the diocese of London have also sponsored Right to Life monuments. Powerful and eloquent reminders of the sanctity of human life, they can be found in cemeteries and in front of churches.

Submitted by Robert Cayea. **Sources:** *Catholic Record*, 4 March 1911, 1; Christopher J. Kauffman, *Faith and Fraternalism: The History of the Knights of Columbus 1882-1992* (New York: 1982); "Knights of Columbus," *New Catholic Encyclopedia*, vol. 8 (New York: 1967), 215-17; *Knights of Columbus, War Services of Canadian Knights of Columbus 1939-1947: A History of the Work of the Knights of Columbus Canadian Army Huts* (1948); Arthur Peters, "Ontario State Council — Historical Notes," [n.d.]; W.J. Sheedy and Vincent Kelly, *Knights of Columbus in Ontario 1900-1975* (1975).

5. Peru: Our Mission in the Diocese of Chiclayo

In 1959, Bishop Cody of London and Archbishop Patrick J. Skinner of St. John's, Newfoundland inaugurated a joint mission in Peru, in response to Pope John XXIII's urgent call to the bishops of North America to assist the Church in the Third World. Father Richard L. Morse from London and Father Charles Conroy from St. John's were chosen for the mission. They arrived in Lima in December 1960 and traveled 750 kilometers north to their new home, the parish of Monsefu in the diocese of Chiclayo.

In the summer of 1961, London sent Father Paul F. Mooney and Father William C. Cooney. The following July, the London priests left Monsefu for the rural parishes of Zaňa, Cayalti and Mocupe, forty kilometers south of the city of Chiclayo in the Zaňa Valley. Cayalti, the largest parish, was a sugar-producing hacienda of 20,000 people. The pastoral area stretched from the Pacific coast to the foothills of the Andes Mountains.

In March 1962, Mother Julia Moore, CSJ, and Mother St. David, OSU, visited Peru at the request of Bishop Cody and the missionary priests. The result of their trip was a decision to send members from their communities to Peru. In November, four St. Joseph Sisters — Eugenie Bond, Cyril Reynolds, Jean (Oliva) Dochstader and Joan (Julianna) Kerrigan — arrived in Peru and were quickly established in Cayalti. Around the same time, four Ursuline Sisters — Virgina Laporte, Angela Theresa Hoffman, Mary Teresa Antaya and Alice Meuller — arrived in Chiclayo and at the request of the local bishop founded the College of Saint Angela, an elementary school for girls.

The diocesan priests who ministered in the northern coastal diocese of Chiclayo from 1960 to 1992 were Fathers Robert L. Cartwright, Clare J. Coleman, William Cooney, Vincent J. Gleeson, F. John (Jack) Hurley, William F. Kornacker, Thomas J. Lever, Melvin G. MacIsaac, John D. (Jack) Marentette, Paul Mooney, Thomas P. Mooney, Richard Morse, Daniel A.J. Morand, Francis Murphy, Francis O'Connor, Gerard G. Prince, Eugène Roy and Paul A. Roy. From 1960 to 1985, the mission was located in the rural Zaňa Valley, and from 1985 to 1992, it was in the Urrunaga district of the city of Chiclayo.

The Zaña Valley ministry experienced various stages of growth and development as the territory expanded to include Oyotun and Nueva Arica, and later the mountain area of the neighbouring diocese of Cajamarca. Changes to national economic policies turned the traditional family hacienda into a government co-operative and then into a state corporation, which shaped the direction of pastoral work. It was essentially threefold: priests preached the word of God, celebrated the sacraments and participated in the building up of parish community.

In light of the Second Vatican Council, these were exciting times of pastoral change as the Peruvian Church encouraged the training of lay leaders within the Church and in society. Base ecclesial communities, charismatic prayer groups, family and marriage preparation courses and youth and worker apostolates were some of the ministries that emerged. The construction and renovation of churches accompanied the more crucial and urgent need to alleviate conditions of extreme poverty among the people, by establishing credit and mining co-operatives, providing essential medical services and educating the people in consciousness raising and leadership formation.

The following Sisters of St. Joseph served in the Zaña Valley from 1962 to 1994: Eugenie Bond, Eileen Campbell, Joanne Campbell, Suzanne Chevalier, Veronica Cooke, Wendy Cotter, Helen Diesbourg, Connie Dignan, Jean Dochstader, Loretta Hagen, Marie Celine Janisse, Toni Joris, Joan Kerrigan, Ann Knotek, Janet Menard, Cyril Reynolds, Nora Reynolds, Teresa Ryan, Kitty Stafford, Mabel St. Louis, Cathy Van Herk, Sue Wilson and Janet Zadorsky.

During the early years, they taught catechetics in the state schools and with the local women set up sewing and cooking programs, an ocean side summer camp for children and youth, charismatic renewal sessions, marriage encounter and sacramental preparation. These activities eventually expanded into working with the people to strengthen their church communities. Human development, health committees and women's circles for reflection and action were always a part of the Sisters' involvement.

The arrival of two nurses, Sisters Connie Dignan and Joanne Campbell, in 1968, and the opening of a medical clinic in Zaña, provided the Sisters with an opportunity to practice community health care. They operated the clinic for several years. After it closed, their concern for the health of the people carried on with the formation of women's health groups. The floods, droughts and depressed economy led to the organization of common kitchens. These provided not only food but also a community setting where both social and faith formation took place.

The Sisters shared their gifts of art, music and crafts with Peruvians in order to promote Peruvian art and culture and, in the exchange, they learned to appreciate and foster the remarkable artistic, musical and cultural talents of the people.

The Ursuline Sisters have served in the city of Chiclayo from 1962 to the present are: Noreen Allossery-Walsh, Mary Teresa Antaya, Claudette Cecile, Loretta Ducharme, Margot Fish, Karen Gleeson, Angela Teresa Hoffman, Eleanor Kuntz, Virginia Laporte, Pauline Maheux, Elizabeth Anne Miller, Alice Mueller, Patricia Pride, Mary Jane Racz, Irene Schnell and Dolores Senay.

The Ursulines began their Peruvian ministry in 1963, teaching in an elementary and secondary school for girls in an upper middle class area of the city, at the request of the bishop of Chiclayo. They turned the school over to Peruvian parents in 1975. The Ursulines then moved into a poor and neglected district of the city called Urrunaga, where they continue to minister today in the person of Sister Loretta Ducharme, who works and lives alongside the many Peruvians that were educated by the Ursulines.

Answering the call to incarnate more deeply God's love for the poor, the Ursulines moved into Immaculate Conception parish in Urrunaga, where they work with the laity and priests to build up Christian community. From 1985 to 1992, priests from the diocese, who had moved to Chiclayo, joined the Ursulines. Pioneering parishioners in Urrunaga, who were devoted to reflection and service, founded the Centre St. Angela, which

still thrives today. It provides a permanent home for health services, children's programs, literacy programs for women and adult faith training.

In Chiclayo, religious, priests and laity from our diocese joined with many Peruvians and foreign missionaries to encourage and support base ecclesial communities in parishes and districts. This has resulted in several permanent institutions that continue to serve the people today through the leadership of many competent and committed Peruvians.

In the Zaña Valley, Our Lady of the Magnificat Women's Centre, established by the Sisters of St. Joseph, provides education for children with special needs and faith formation for families, and it preserves and promotes cultural traditions and values. The women's centre also supports rural libraries, particularly in the mountain communities of the neighbouring diocese of Cajamarca. A missionary exchange organization, called Heart-Links, was started in 1995 as a means to provide support of these efforts and an opportunity for lay people in Canada to visit Peru and to participate in a work/awareness program.

In the city of Chiclayo, the "Centro Esperanza" (Hope Centre) was set up by Peruvian women, supported by the Ursuline Sisters, to provide education, human promotion and civic action on behalf of the poor, especially women and children. In Canada, the Ursuline Sisters have also established "Seeds of Hope," an international program that seeks to facilitate connections between women in Canada and Peru through study, exchange visits and common actions.

Fathers Eugène Roy and Frank Murphy officially closed the mission on 12 December 1992. Sisters Theresa Ryan, Janet Zadorsky and Loretta Hogan departed Peru on 1 May 1994. Sister Marie Celine Janisse stayed for an additional six months.

The consensus of those members of the diocese of London who have been privileged to minister in Peru is that they have received a remarkable education and have been more deeply formed in their own faith and brought to a more universal vision of the Church and the world, by the life, faith and love of the Peruvian people who have so graciously welcomed them.

Submitted by Father Frank O'Connor.

6. Liturgy Office

In the wake of the Second Vatican Council, the diocese of London established a liturgical commission to regulate pastoral-liturgical changes as called for by *Sacrosanctum Concilium*. Father Joseph A. Feeney, Father John B. O'Donnell, Father Michael J. O'Brien (member, 1968-79; chairperson, 1973-79) and Father John J. O'Flaherty provided the early leadership. The diocese established an office in the chancery for the chairperson of the liturgical commission, which produced numerous publications to assist the clergy and faithful in understanding the liturgical reforms.

The diocese was a major leader in (and an experimental centre for) the introduction of the renewed liturgy not only in Canada but also around the world. Bishop Carter of London was chairman of the Episcopal Board of the International Commission on English in the Liturgy (ICEL) from 1972 to 1975, and Father Marcel Gervais of the diocese was chairperson of the ICEL advisory committee that was responsible for translations of the ritual books, from 1975 to 1978. At the diocesan level, and preceding the above two appointments, Father O'Donnell and a committee organized two liturgical conventions. The first and most important one was called "Christ Builds Community" and was held in 1970 at the Cleary Auditorium in Windsor. In addition to talks from members of the diocesan clergy, there were presentations by Father Aidan Kavanagh, OSB ("Eucharist and Community"); Cardinal Michele Pellegrino, archbishop of Torino, Italy ("The 'New Mass' in the Christian Life and in the Pastoral Life"); and George B. Cardinal Flahiff, archbishop of Winnipeg ("Penance in the Life of the Church"). Liturgical musician C. Alexander Peloquin was responsible for the music.

The reputation of the diocese of London as a leader in the liturgical renewal is also evident in its participation in the development of all three editions of the *Catholic Book of Worship*, the national Catholic hymnal of Canada. Father O'Donnell came up with the idea for the hymnal. He took it to Bishop Carter, who gave him an office in the chancery building and allowed him to work on the project full time. Along with Father O'Donnell, Margaret Pierce, who wrote the notation for the music, Father O'Flaherty, and David Young belonged to the twelve-member committee that compiled the first *Catholic Book of Worship* (1972). Kelly McCloskey, Father O'Donnell and David Young

were members of the fifteen-member committee that produced *Catholic Book of Worship II* (1980). And three members of the diocese were involved in the publication of *Catholic Book of Worship III* (1994). Lorraine King of Windsor and Father Eugène Roy served on the committee, and Sister Loretta Manzara, CSJ, was the executive secretary of the hymnal committee.

Working in collaboration with the liturgical commission, the diocesan music committee has promoted the liturgical and musical formation of parish musicians through regional workshops, times of reflection and renewal and the provision of music for the major liturgical seasons of Advent, Christmas, Lent and Easter. In 1990, the "Future Organists" program was established to "ensure a strong future for sacred music by developing and fostering a new generation of liturgical musicians." In 1995, the Council of Priests approved an expansion of the program to include cantors, guitarists, and keyboard players and gave the program a new name: "Liturgical Music Bursary Program." The bursary has provided formation in liturgical music to over ninety diocesan musicians. In 2003, the diocese hosted the annual Ontario Liturgical Conference Summer School for Liturgical Musicians. Nearly a hundred people from across the province and other parts of Canada participated in this week-long session at St. Peter's Seminary.

When the Rite of Christian Initiation of Adults (RCIA) was promulgated for use in 1974, the education and formation of priests, pastoral ministers and other lay leaders in RCIA was necessary before it could be introduced into the diocese of London. The diocesan RCIA committee began in the late 1970s. Members were drawn from the liturgical commission and from the staff at the London Christian Renewal Centre. Over the years, the committee conducted numerous workshops and conferences to introduce initiation teams to the spirit and vision of the program and to give direction on the proper implementation of the rites. Leading scholars and presenters on Christian initiation, including Father James Lopresti (1983), Father Robert Duggan and Maureen Kelly (1986) and Father James Dunning and Catherine Ecker (2002-04), have helped in the development of initiation teams within the diocese. In 1996, as a tool for the ongoing formation of initiation team members, the committee undertook the publication of a newsletter, *Journey into Mystery*. Elaine Damphouse, at that time the director of the John XXIII Centre in Windsor, agreed to serve as editor and remained in that position until 2001.

Sister Loretta Manzara, CSJ, was the director of the liturgy office from 1990 to 1999. During her time, the office produced a variety of liturgical publications and resources and offered workshops. The work of liturgical formation continued with Liturgy in a Formative Environment (LIFE), a two-week program that was held annually in August at St. Peter's Seminary until 2001. It was facilitated by Sister Joyce Ann Zimmerman, CPPS, and Sister Kathleen Harmon, SNDN. Over eighty people,

including sixty-two from the diocese, took the LIFE program.

Christina Ronzio was appointed director of the liturgy office in February 2001 and served until September 2007. Over 130 workshops have been offered on various topics relating to liturgical formation and education, at parish, deanery and diocesan gatherings. The office also provided training courses, written guidelines, articles and consultation. The office served in a consultative and research capacity for the bishop of the diocese and co-operated with the work of the Ontario Liturgical Conference and the National Liturgy Office. The director of the liturgy office oversaw the diocesan RCIA committee and the music committee, and served on the diocesan liturgical commission and the diocesan building commission.

With diocesan reorganization, announced in the autumn of 2007, the Office of Liturgy was discontinued, with the understanding that all formation in liturgical matters would be the responsibility of the newly-established Institute for Catholic Formation.

Information provided by Christina Ronzio and others.

7. Save A Family Plan

Save A Family Plan (SAFP) was the dream of Father (later Monsignor) Augustine J. Kandathil, a priest of the Syro-Malabar Rite in the diocese of Cochin in Kerala, India. A Fulbright Scholar, he obtained a Ph.D. in chemistry at the University of Notre Dame and later did post-doctoral work there on a grant from the National Science Foundation. At Notre Dame he became friends with Father Michael Ryan of the diocese of London, who was working on a Ph.D. in philosophy.

In 1963, Father Kandathil joined the faculty at the University of St. Thomas in Fredericton, New Brunswick. The following year, while attending the International Eucharistic Congress in Bombay (now Mumbai), India, he heard Pope Paul VI's urgent plea for the world to join in the struggle against hunger and poverty. Returning to Fredericton, Father Kandathil enlisted the support of Father (later Archbishop) James MacDonald, CSC, and Dr. Leo Ferrari, fellow professors at St. Thomas University, and in 1965 they started SAFP.

From the beginning, SAFP had several basic principles. One, it sought to establish a personal connection between a family in India and a family in North America by means of regular correspondence between them. Two, the overall aim of SAFP was to provide the financial means for a poor family to become self-sustaining. Assistance would allow a family to buy a goat and sell some of its milk for income, for example, or make it possible for a family member to obtain some schooling and then assist the others. The selection of families and the ongoing monitoring of their progress are carried out by means of a well-established network of priests, Sisters, and lay leaders in India. Finally, by encouraging donors to send financial support in a single sum for an entire year, and then by giving the money to the family on a monthly basis, SAFP was able to invest the donations as they came in and to use the interest to meet office expenses, prior to the transfer of funds to India. It became the proud boast of SAFP that "100% of the money donated actually goes to the poor."

In 1972, Father Kandathil suffered a heart attack. He shared with Father Ryan his fear that his plan to help the poor would die with him. Father Ryan, who was teaching at St. Peter's Seminary in London, spoke with the rector, Father James Carrigan, about the possibility of locating SAFP at the seminary. Father Carrigan obtained Bishop Carter's permission to invite Father Kandathil to live at the seminary for free.

In 1973, Father Kandathil arrived in London. He was given a room in which to live and a small office. At the time, SAFP was assisting approximately 4,000 families in India. He often said that his moving to the seminary was the best thing that could have happened to SAFP because the seminary gave it the sort of visibility and volunteer assistance that enabled it to grow very quickly. Seminary students became volunteers, along with many generous people from the London area, and when SAFP outgrew its one-room office, the seminary provided more space.

SAFP subsequently became incorporated and established a board of directors. Over the years, many dedicated and talented people from the diocese have served on the board, guiding SAFP through its growing pains and helping it to develop into the large organization it is today. Its annual budget has grown to more than six million dollars.

As SAFP grew, it branched out into other community development programs in India oftentimes in co-operation with the Canadian International Development Agency (CIDA). Today, SAFP operates in seven states in India, in partnership with forty-two Catholic diocesan social service societies, twenty-six homes of healing and 10,500 sanghams (grass roots community-based organizations). More than 15,000 families benefit from the family-to-family program.

SAFP has assisted in the construction of many hundreds of homes, launched income-generating projects, in particular for women, and set up a number of training schools. Water and sanitation programs, natural resource management and conservation initiatives and renewal energy projects are just some of the areas in which SAFP has worked with families and the communities in which they live. SAFP families include farmers and agricultural labourers, fishers, construction and plantation workers, casual labourers, factory employees and street vendors. Many are Dalits (casteless people), indigenous tribal people and members of ethnic religions. After the terrible earthquake in the state of Gujarat in 2001, SAFP, relying on special donations, undertook the project of rebuilding an entire village.

SAFP always sought to be primarily a development organization, not a band-aid or welfare solution. Since true development is the development of persons, SAFP, along with CIDA, has in recent years offered programs to raise the level of people's awareness and to provide leadership training and also the means to take greater control of their own lives. Not surprisingly, the Coady Institute at Antigonish, Nova Scotia, has been a useful resource for SAFP on many occasions, especially in the establishment of micro-credit co-operatives. Needs assessments are done and programs are developed in association with everyone involved. Also, environmental and gender impact assessments and program evaluations are regularly carried out, in co-operation with all the partners.

Monsignor Kandathil returned to India in 1989 to supervise the SAFP operations there. He died on 18 July 2001, possessing little more than the cassock in which he was buried. On his tombstone are the words: "The Poor Deserve the Best."

After the founder's return to India, the position of executive director in Canada was taken over by Father (later Bishop) Sebastian Adayanthrath, a much-loved young priest who became involved in the seminary and the wider community while overseeing SAFP.

In 2004, Save A Family Plan entered a new era when Mrs. Leslie Porter, who had worked for SAFP in the London office and also in India, was appointed the first lay executive director.

Submitted by Father Michael Ryan.

8. Ministry to The Deaf

Interest in the spiritual welfare of the Catholic deaf in the diocese of London began with Father Dan Higgins, CSSR, who spoke to the students at St. Peter's Seminary about the apostolate to the deaf, in the late 1930s. After his visit, several students began to take lessons in sign language. Father Edgar Robert was the first diocesan priest to work directly with the deaf. Following his ordination in 1940, he formed a group of the deaf in Windsor, which met regularly at St. Alphonsus church.

On the recommendation of the deaf communities from Ontario, Buffalo and Detroit, and with the support of Cardinal James C. McGuigan, archbishop of Toronto, the International Catholic Deaf Congress met for the first time, on 7 July 1949, at the King Edward Hotel in Toronto. Approximately one hundred people were in attendance. Father James Carrigan of the diocese was one of three Canadian moderators at the conference (there were seven moderators from the United States). In 1954, Bishop Cody appointed Father Carrigan the diocesan director in charge of the Catholic deaf, with Father Robert and Father James F. Summers as his associates. Ordained in 1953, Father Summers was the son of deaf parents. Beginning in 1955, there was a special Mass for the deaf every second Sunday in Windsor with a sermon in sign language. There was also confession before Mass. Three times a year, there was a luncheon after the Mass and an evening social.

The diocese of London actively supported the International Catholic Deaf Association (ICDA), and a charter was granted to the Windsor-Chatham Deaf Communities on 28 January 1960. The moderators over the years have included Father Carrigan, Father Summers, and Father Thomas C. Ashton. Ordained in 1979, Father Ashton succeeded Father Carrigan as the diocesan director of the deaf. In 1995, Mary Mousseau became director, and Father Ashton remained active in the ministry as the chaplain.

Owing to a measles outbreak in the mid 1960s, there was an increase in the number of deaf students in the 1970s and 1980s. A religion teacher was hired at the Robarts School for the Deaf in London, but provincial funding for that position ended in the early 1980s. In response, the diocesan office of ministry to the deaf began to provide catechesis and sacramental preparation for the Robarts students.

Logistics for interpreting in Catholic settings is always a challenge. Two of the most demanding experiences for the ministry to the deaf were working out the logistics for the nuptials of two deaf-blind sisters, Maricar and Marissa Marquez, who had been Robarts students. Father Ashton was the celebrant at both weddings. Each deaf-blind person requires an individual intervener with specialized training by the Canadian National Institute for the Blind. Moreover, American sign-language interpreters must be in place for the deaf community.

The work of the Holy Spirit is clearly evident during such joyous faith-filled liturgies, as the ministry to the deaf continues to provide sacramental preparation and educational services for the deaf community and a presence at all diocesan celebrations in St. Peter's cathedral. In late 2006, Father Graham R.J. Keep, as chaplain, and Colleen Pickering assumed the leadership to the deaf ministry.

Sources: Archives, Ministry to the Deaf, Windsor, Ontario; Michael and Frances Preston, *The Journey of the ICDA from 1949 to 1989* (Silver Springs, Md.: 1989); "Transitions in deaf ministry," *Newsletter of the Diocese of London*, no. 124 (Advent/Christmas 2006), 11.

9. Madonna House

"Servant of God" Catherine de Hueck Doherty (1896-1985), a Russian refugee and immigrant to Canada, founded the Madonna House Apostolate, in Toronto, on 15 October 1930. It is a community of lay persons and priests, who are are dedicated to loving and serving Christ in one another and in all men and women. Since May 1947, Combermere, Ontario has been the Apostolate's headquarters and training centre. There are missions in Canada, the United States, England, France, Belgium, Africa, Brazil, Russia and the West Indies.

Madonna House on Benjamin Avenue in Windsor was founded on 17 June 1983. The first director was Beverly Maciag, who was accompanied by Irene Toupin. The current director is Mary Beth Mitchell, who is assisted by Renate Zanker. Bishop Sherlock asked that Madonna House be a prayerful presence in Windsor, the main mandate being for members to pray for bishops, priests, religious and all people in the diocese. It is essentially a prayer-listening house that is dedicated to the spiritual works of mercy. Each visitor is greeted on a personal basis, and his or her concerns are taken to the Lord in intercessory prayer.

The Apostolate serves those who are lonely and desperate in mind and spirit. Help and prayer are offered to families and single people to strengthen their Catholic and Christian lives, and support for priestly vocations is made through prayer and fasting.

It is the hope of Madonna House staff to make the lives of others more meaningful by offering a loving heart to listen to the worries and difficulties of everyone, be they young people, parents or the elderly. Some people want to talk about God and ask for help in maintaining a personal relationship with Him. Others come for "Poustinia" — to spend time with the Lord in prayer, fasting and quiet. For this, a small room is provided with a desk and chair, a bed, a large cross, a Bible, and bread and tea. This Byzantine tradition of prayer presents a wonderful opportunity to regain one's perspective and to nurture one's spiritual hunger. Madonna House does not charge for these services, but it accepts donations.

For several years, Madonna House in Windsor was instrumental in aiding Sudanese refugees as they settled in the city, by finding apartments, appliances and household items, locating tutors and helping the refugees get acquainted with service organizations. As the number of refugees grew, however, Madonna House staff had to withdraw from direct assistance. Leaders of the Sudanese community took over the work, and today contact between the Sudanese and Madonna House is maintained in a personal way of friendship and spiritual help, with some organizational guidance.

Each staff member of Madonna House makes a promise of poverty, chastity and obedience, and a lifetime commitment. There are always bills to pay, and no one receives a salary. The Providence of God, through generous donations, takes care of the needs and wants.

Madonna House is dedicated to Mary, the Mother of God. She brings each member into the Apostolate, to receive peace, hope, joy, encouragement, consolation and a more profound relationship with her Son. Having been called by God, each member gives the gift of their presence and so enriches the lives of all.

Catherine Doherty had a vision for living the Gospel in every situation and aspect of life. "No part of the Gospel is abstract. The ordinariness of the routine of daily life is the warp and woof of living the Gospel without compromise, of restoring the world to Christ…. We live the Gospel with our hands, our minds, and our hearts, as we go about the tasks of our daily lives. We discover the holiness of the little things done well over and over again for the love of God … and this is truly the vocation of anyone who would follow Christ."

Submitted by Mary Beth Mitchell.
Sources:"Catherine: A Newsletter to Promote the Cause for Canonization of the Servant of God, Catherine de Hueck Doherty," 1 (Summer 2001); "Madonna House" (official brochure).

10. Institute of Secular Missionaries

Members of the Institute of Secular Missionaries (ISM) arrived in the diocese of London from Spain in the autumn of 1959, at the invitation of Bishop Cody, to staff Holy Family Retreat House in Oxley. Bishop Cody offered this vocational opportunity to young women, and the ISM was eager to serve in a new frontier, making it the first secular institute in the diocese.

The Institute originated in the north of Spain in 1939, born of the prophetic vision of Father Rufino Aldabalde, who dedicated himself to the spiritual renewal of the Church after the Spanish Civil War. Father Rufino believed that women should take a leadership role in this work and in spreading the Gospel in society. With the help of Maria Camino Gorostiza, a young war widow, and several other women, a small group began to take shape.

One of the first tasks undertaken by the women was the promotion of the human and spiritual development of the laity, and of women in particular, through their presence at retreat houses, which were centres of spirituality for the laity. ISM members sought to embody a theology of the laity and of human work that promoted the values of the reign of God in the workplace and in the midst of society.

When Father Rufino died in 1945, only six years after the foundation of the ISM, the group came under the directorship of Maria Camino Gorostiza. It continued to flourish: formation houses were opened in Vitoria and Salamanca, where women undertook scriptural and theological studies, practised a life of prayer and developed a solid formation in human values such as joyfulness, integrity, responsibility and personal maturity. In 1955, the pious union of Diocesan Evangelical Missionaries became a secular institute of diocesan right under the name Institute of Secular Missionaries, which refers to the vocation or mission of each Christian to the world.

Members make a lifetime commitment to celibacy and live the Gospel values of poverty and obedience according to their lay vocation. Some choose to live alone; others share living quarters with family, friends, or fellow members, gathering regularly for spiritual and theological dialogue and for celebration. All members participate in an ongoing program centered on common themes, which are adapted to the particular country in which they live.

By the early 1950s, the Institute was present in most dioceses in Spain, working in various fields and moving from predominantly Church ministries to a wider involvement in the secular world. Some members moved to working class "barrios." Others joined different occupations and professions, such as public education teachers, university professors, health care workers and social service workers.

Thirty members undertook a variety of works in Ecuador in 1949, and soon after others went to the Belgian Congo. Missions to Chile, Mexico and Peru followed. When economic problems in Spain led to the migration of Spanish workers to other countries in Europe, ISM members were sent to France, Germany, Switzerland, Belgium and Italy, to minister to the material and spiritual needs of these immigrants and also to the needs of the people in the host countries. By the 1960s, there were over 770 members in twelve different countries.

Father Rufino had insisted on the need to discern and respond to the movements of the Holy Spirit manifested in the "signs of the times," and the ISM has sought to be faithful to this directive. The ISM embraced the liturgical renewal movement in the 1950s and then the theology of the Second Vatican Council as it affirmed and challenged the laity in its responsibility to work with the Spirit in the modern world. Later, the ISM felt a strong call to respond to the preferential option for the poor as proclaimed in the Latin American episcopal conferences of Puebla and Medellin, a call that continues to challenge all Christians today.

Subsequent waves of renewal have left their mark on the members' understanding of their mission: liberation movements that have defended the dignity and rights of the poor and of women; scripture renewal, including feminist insights; the call to care for the earth; and ecumenical and interfaith dialogue.

Maria Teresa Bianchi, a co-founder of ISM, was

the leader of the first ISM members who came to London in 1959: Angela Aisa, Araceli Echebarria, Margarita Irigoyen and Julia Bellord. A second group followed in July 1961 to supplement the staff at Holy Family Retreat House and to work at the chancery office in London. They were Aurelia Hernandez, Natalie Monforte, Beth Tellaeche, Rosario Echaniz and Julia Zalbidea.

In subsequent years, other ISM members arrived and entered into a variety of new works. These included Nuria Aragones, Ruth Beitia, Carmen Guenaga, Ana Maria Gonzales, Maria Lopez de Heredia, Pilar Sanchez Orus and Carmen Serrano. In time, several young Canadian women began a formation program with the group. Of these, two remain: Lois Côté and Paula Marcotte.

There was an ISM presence at the Holy Family Retreat House from 1959 to 1989, the year that Ruth Beitia left. ISM members worked at the chancery office from 1962 to 1996, when Aurelia Hernandez retired. She was the first woman to serve as director of the Marriage Tribunal, assistant chancellor and chancellor of the diocese of London. Angela Aisa was secretary for Bishop Carter from 1962 to 1978. Natalie Monforte was one of the founding staff members of the Christian Renewal Centre in 1969. Beth Tellaeche worked at the Cross Cultural Learner Centre in London from 1976 to 1993, where she developed the Settlement Program for Refugees and Immigrants. Lois Côté was director of the library at St. Peter's Seminary for thirty-five years, twenty as a faculty member. Very involved in Save A Family Plan in Canada and in India, she was named SAFP president for Canada in 2005. Paula Marcotte taught for the Catholic school board in London from 1969 to 2003, and during the last twenty of those years she was seconded to the faculty of education at the University of Western Ontario (UWO), as instructor of religious education and social studies.

ISM members have served in the following institutions and fields of work in the diocese: librarians at Divine Word Centre, Regina Mundi College, St. Peter's Seminary and the London Public Library; pastoral ministers at St. Mary's parish in London and at St. John Vianney and Christ the King parishes in Windsor; social workers with Catholic Family Services in Windsor; jail ministry in London; teachers for the Catholic school board in London and the UWO faculty of education; staff of the Christian Renewal Centre in London; housekeepers for Bishop Carter, Bishop Marcel Gervais and Bishop Sherlock; university chaplains at UWO; nursing care providers at various nursing homes; refugee service workers in Windsor; ministry to immigrants and refugees at the Cross Cultural Learner Centre in London; Spanish teachers at Fanshawe College in London; and participants in the development of St. Joseph Hospital Foundation in London.

Members worked or continue to work with the following: COR movement; Project Moosonee; Canada-El Salvador Education Development Association; Development and Peace; Project Ploughshares; Save A Family Plan; St. Peter's Coffee House; Bethany Centre; Rite of Christian Initiation of Adults; peace, justice and solidarity organizations; human rights groups; ecumenical and inter-faith gatherings; women's groups; and youth ministry.

At present, there are only five ISM members in London. Several have returned to Spain, and some have died. Members are enriched by their close links with the 400 other members, who live and work in the United States, Chile, Ecuador, Colombia, Peru, Brazil, France, Germany and Spain. The ISM is open to associate members who are called ISM Companions.

Submitted by Paula Marcotte.

SELECT BIBLIOGRAPHY

ARCHIVES

Archives of the Edmonton-Toronto Redemptorists
Archives of the Society of Jesus of Upper Canada (ASJUC)
Archives of Ontario (AO)
Archives of the Roman Catholic Archdiocese of Toronto (ARCAT)
Archivio Secreto Vaticano Delegazione Apostolica Canadese (ASV DAC)
Diocese of Calgary Archives (DCA)
Diocese of London Archives (DLA)
General Archives of the Basilian Fathers (GABF)

UNPUBLISHED MANUSCRIPTS

Dignan, Ralph Hubert. "History of the Diocese of London." Unpublished manuscript, ca. 1919-1932.
Dignan, Ralph Hubert and Joseph P. Finn. "A History of the Diocese of London." Edited by Guy Alden. Unpublished manuscript, 2002.
Point, Pierre. "Histoire de Sandwich." Unpublished manuscript, ca. 1860.

NEWSPAPERS

Amherstburg Echo
Buffalo Express
Canadian Freeman
Catholic Record (London)
Catholic Register (*Canadian Register* and *Register*)
Catholic Union and Times (Buffalo)
Daily Times (Hamilton)
Detroit Free Press
Evening Record (Windsor)
Globe (Toronto)
London Advertiser
London Free Press, The (*Daily Free Press* and *Evening Free Press*)
Newsletter of the Diocese of London
Ottawa Citizen
Ottawa Free Press
Sarnia Canadian
Toronto Mirror
True Witness, (Montréal)
Windsor Star (Border Cities Star)

THESES AND DISSERTATIONS

Comiskey, John P. *The Foundation of the Diocese of London in Canada 1760-1856.* Licentiate diss., Pontifical Gregorian University, 1997.
_____. *John Walsh: Second Bishop of London in Ontario 1867-1889.* Ph.D. diss., Pontifical Gregorian University, 1999.
Farrell (O'Farrell), John K.A. *The History of the Roman Catholic Church in London, Ontario 1826-1931.* M.A. thesis, University of Western Ontario, 1949.
Fiorino, Pasquale. *The Second Synod of London.* M.A. thesis, Gregorian University, Rome, 1989.
Fitzpatrick, Michael Joseph. *The Role of Bishop Michael Francis Fallon and the Conflict Between the French Catholics and Irish Catholics in the Ontario Bilingual Schools Question 1910-1920.* M.A. thesis, University of Western Ontario, 1969.
Flynn, Jerome Terence. *The London Episcopacy, 1867-1889, of the Most Reverend John Walsh, D.D., Second Bishop of London.* M.A. thesis, Catholic University of America, 1966.
McMahon, John R. *The Episcopate of Pierre-Adolphe Pinsoneault: First Bishop of London, Upper Canada, 1856-1866.* M.A. thesis, University of Western Ontario, 1982.
Meehan, Peter M. *From College to University: The Basilian Fathers and Assumption, 1950-1963.* M.A. thesis, University of Windsor, 1991.
Somers, Hugh Joseph. *The Life and Times of the Hon. and Rt. Rev. Alexander Macdonell, D.D. First Bishop of Upper Canada 1762-1840.* Ph.D. diss., Catholic University of America, 1931.

BOOKS AND ARTICLES

Allaire, J.B.A. *Dictionnaire biographique du clergé canadienne-français.* Vol. 1. Montréal: 1910.

Baillargeon, Paul. "Bishop Michael Francis Fallon: Founder of St. Peter's Seminary." St. Peter's Seminary, *The Alumni Bulletin* (December 1996): 28-51.

Barber, Marilyn. "The Ontario Bilingual Schools Issue: Sources of Conflict." *Canadian Historical Review* 47, no. 3 (September 1966): 227-48.

Boland, Edgar J. *From the Pioneers to the Seventies: A History of the Diocese of Peterborough 1882-1975.* Peterborough: 1976.

Campeau, Lucien. *The Jesuit Mission to the Hurons 1634-1650.* Translated by William Lonc and George Topp. 2nd ed., rev. Midland, Ontario: 2004.

The Canadian Annual Review of Public Affairs (*CAR*), various years.

Cecillon, Jack. "Turbulent Times in the Diocese of London: Bishop Fallon and the French-Language Controversy, 1910-1918." *Ontario History,* 87, no. 4 (December 1995): 381-87.

Choquette, Robert. *Language and Religion: A History of English-French Conflict in Ontario.* Ottawa: 1975.

Coffey, John F. *The City and Diocese of London, Ontario, Canada: An Historical Sketch.* London: 1885.

Daly, Bernard M. *Beyond Secrecy: The Untold Story of Canada and the Second Vatican Council.* Ottawa: 2003.

_____. *Remembering for Tomorrow: A History of the Canadian Conference of Catholic Bishops 1943-1993.* Ottawa: 1995.

Daniels, Tony. "An Occasion to Remember: London's Bishop Celebrates Double Anniversaries." St. Peter's Seminary, *Alumni Bulletin 1999-2000* (2000): 1-4.

Dictionary of Canadian Biography. 15 vols. (Toronto: 1967-2005).

Dictionary of Jesuit Biography: Ministry to English Canada. Edited by Angus J. Macdougall et. al. Toronto: 1991.

Farrell (O'Farrell), John K.A. "Michael Francis Fallon, Bishop of London, Ontario, Canada: The Man and His Controversies." Canadian Catholic Historical Association (CCHA) *Study Sessions* (1968): 73-90.

Fiorino, Pasquale. "The Nomination of Michael Fallon as Bishop of London. CCHA *Historical Studies* 62 (1996): 33-46.

Flynn, L.J. *Built on a Rock: The Story of the Roman Catholic Church in Kingston 1826-1976.* Kingston: 1976.

Grant, John Webster. *A Profusion of Spires: Religion in the Nineteenth Century.* Toronto: 1988.

Gwynne-Timothy, John R.W. *Western's First Century.* London: 1978.

Higgins, Michael W. and Douglas R. Letson. *My Father's Business: A Biography of His Eminence G. Emmett Cardinal Carter.* Toronto: 1990.

Jubilee Magazine: John Christopher Cody, D.D., Bishop of London. April 1962.

Journal des Visites Pastorales de 1815 et 1816 par Monseigneur Joseph-Octave Plessis Èvêque de Québec. Québec: 1903.

Kelly, Edward. *The Story of St. Paul's Parish Toronto.* Toronto: 1922.

Lajeunesse, Ernest J., ed. *The Windsor Border Region Canada's Southernmost Frontier: A Collection of Documents.* Toronto: 1960.

Lambert, James. "The Face of Upper Canadian Catholicism, Culture and Metropolitanism in the Establishment of the Roman Catholic Church in Upper Canada, 1800-1825," CCHA *Historical Studies,* 54 (1987): 5-25.

Leblanc, Jean. *Dictionnaire Biographique des Évêques Catholiques du Canada.* Ottawa: 2002.

McGowan, Mark G. *Michael Power: The Struggle to Build the Catholic Church on the Canadian Frontier.* Montreal and Kingston: 2005.

Merchant, F.W. *Report on the Condition of English-French Schools in the Province of Ontario.* Toronto: 1912.

Miller, Orlo. *The Donnellys Must Die.* Toronto: 1962.

Morgan, Henry James. *Canadian Men and Women of the Time.* Toronto: 1898.

_____. *The Canadian Men and Women of the Time: A Handbook of Canadian Biography of Living Canadians.* 2nd ed. Toronto: 1912.

Muggeridge, Anne Roche. *The Desolate City: The Catholic Church in Ruins.* Toronto: 1986.

New Catholic Encyclopedia. 15 vols. New York: 1967. *Supplement,* Vol. 16, 1974. *Supplement,* Vol. 17, 1978.

Nicholson, Murray W. "Michael Power: First Bishop of Toronto." CCHA *Historical Studies,* 54 (1987): 27-38.

The Ontario Catholic Year Book and Directory, various years.

Paré, George. *The Catholic Church in Detroit 1701-*

1888. Detroit: 1951.

Perin, Roberto. *Rome in Canada*. Toronto: 1990.

Power, Michael. *Assumption College: The O'Connor Years 1870-1890*. Windsor: 1986.

_____. *Assumption College: The Road to Independence 1940-1953*. Windsor: 2003.

_____. *Assumption College: The Struggle to Survive 1920-1940*. Windsor: 2000.

_____. *Assumption College: Years of Uncertainty 1855-1870*. Windsor: 1987.

_____. *Bishop Fallon and the Riot at Ford City 8 September 1917*. Essex County Historical Association *Occasional Paper*, no.3 (1986).

_____. "Fallon Versus Forster: The Struggle Over Assumption College 1919-1925." CCHA *Historical Studies*, 56 (1989): 49-66.

_____. "Father Edmund Burke: Along the Detroit River Frontier 1794-1797." CCHA *Historical Studies*, 51 (1984): 29-46.

_____. *A History of the Roman Catholic Church in the Niagara Peninsula 1615-1815*. St. Catharines: 1983.

_____. *A Promise Fulfilled: Highlights in the Political History of Catholic Separate Schools in Ontario*. Toronto: 2002.

Prang, Margaret. "Clerics, Politicians, and the Bilingual Schools Issue in Ontario, 1910-1917." *Canadian Historical Review* 41, no. 4 (December 1960): 281-307.

Rea, J.E. *Bishop Alexander Macdonell and the Politics of Upper Canada*. Toronto: 1974.

Roberts, Charles G.D. and Arthur L. Tunnell. *A Standard Dictionary of Canadian Biography: The Canadian Who Was Who*. Vol. 1. Toronto: 1934.

Roche, Anne. *The Gates of Hell: The Struggle for the Catholic Church*. Toronto: 1975.

Sissons, C.B. *Bi-lingual Schools in Canada*. Toronto: 1917.

Skidmore, Patricia. *Brescia College 1919-1979*. [London]: 1980.

Souvenir Book Centenary of the Diocese of Victoria British Columbia. [Victoria: 1946].

Teefy, J.R., ed. *Jubilee Volume, The Archdiocese of Toronto and Archbishop John Walsh*. Toronto: 1892.

Thwaites, Reuben Gold, ed. *The Jesuit Relations and Allied Documents: Travels and Explorations of the Jesuit Missionaries in New France*. 73 vols. Cleveland: 1896-1911.

Trigger, Bruce. *The Children of Aataentsic: A History of the Huron People to 1660*. 2 vols. Montreal: 1976.

_____. *Natives and Newcomers: Canada's "Heroic Age" Reconsidered*. Kingston and Montreal: 1985.

Walker, Franklin A. *Catholic Education and Politics in Ontario*. Vol. 2. Toronto: 1964.

Zucchi, John, trans. *The View From Rome: Archbishop Stagni's 1915 Report on the Ontario Bilingual Schools Question*. Montreal and Kingston: 2002.

INDEX

INDEX

INDEX

INDEX

INDEX

INDEX

INDEX

INDEX

INDEX

INDEX

INDEX

INDEX

INDEX

INDEX

INDEX